TL;DR

The Best of
ODD THINGS CONSIDERED

Anita Dalton

NINE-BANDED
BOOKS

TL;DR: The Best of Odd Things Considered

Copyright © 2018
Anita Dalton

ISBN 10: 0-9907335-7-2
ISBN 13: 978-0-9907335-7-7

Published by

Nine-Banded Books
PO Box 1862
Charleston, WV 25327
NineBandedBooks.com

Cover illustration by Josh Latta
LattaLand.com

Cover design by Kevin I. Slaughter
UnderworldAmusements.com

TL;DR: The Best of Odd Things Considered

For Mr. OTC,
who always understands why I
need just one more book…

~ CONTENTS ~

For if the modern mind is whimsical and discursive, the classical mind is narrow, unhesitating, relentless. It is not a quality of intelligence that one encounters frequently these days. But though I can digress with the best of them, I am nothing in my soul if not obsessive.

—Donna Tartt, *The Secret History*

PUBLISHER'S FOREWORD
Chip Smith

There are rules. Book culture is governed by rules.

If you've read more than a few high-end book reviews in your life, you may already know what I'm talking about. If you're not sure, I bet you at least sense it. Whether you peruse the pages of the *New York Review of Books* or *The New York Times Book Review* or *The London Review of Books* or *Bookforum* or any number of lower-rung metro-branded repositories of editorially vetted literary review and commentary, I'd wager a paycheck that you have cultivated some gut-level familiarity with the informal strictures and injunctions that are generally (with some deviation) observed by prestige critics. These are the rules in force, or what I shall refer to as **The Rules of VIP Book Salon**.

If the rules aren't always obvious, that's by design. Because the First Rule of **VIP Book Salon** is, of course, *Don't Talk About VIP Book Salon*. Which means you don't talk about the rules, as I am doing now. I can talk about the rules freely because I am excluded from the inner circle. But bankrolled critics, along with aspirants to higher Club status, are obliged to observe them in a state of solemn humility, lest the trance be broken.

Too cryptic? Yeah, I'm bad about that. In TL;DR fashion, let me try being *circuitous* instead. Stay with me. I'll bring it around.

Let's say your eye catches the boldface pitch for a review of a "major" new work by some literary or intellectual dynamo. Maybe it's something new by someone old,* like DeLillo or Auster. Or maybe it's another doorstop installment by that scraggly Scandinavian diarist who writes about his bowel movements. It might be a confessional memoir by a sex-addicted feminist fashion editor who claims to have invented clickbait. It doesn't really matter. It could be a new Churchill biography, or even a certain species of cookbook.

The important thing is that you're drawn in. But why? Is it the *byline*? Has an elder statesman been summoned to weigh in on some new kink in the culture wars? Are the editors tempting your nostalgia for literary cage matches of yore, from the days when Vidal and Mailer engaged in literary—and

---

* It surely won't be anything new by anyone *young*. Trendy feminist polemicists notwithstanding, I challenge you to name four writers under the age of 30 whose names have currency in contemporary book culture. No? Make it three names and up the age to 35. I'll wait.

literal—fisticuffs? Is the review penned by Kurt Anderson? Mary Gaitskill? Simon Winchester? Leon Wieseltier? Clive James? Harold Bloom? If any of these particulars have played on your peepers, then you have been exposed to **The Second Rule of VIP Book Salon,** which I call *The Rule of Tastemaker's Choice.* This one is relatively innocuous, but it's also insidious. It simply refers to one aspect of the editorial *framing* that infects much of book culture, subtly nudging your sensibilities toward a common glorified trough. Literary celebrity looms large in this domain, along with credentialist upmanship.

Or is it the *subject* that hooks you? Do you feel compelled to read about another insider's posthumous account of Watergate? Is your interest piqued by a long-suppressed story of a Romani cobbler who escaped Auschwitz? Are you lured by the lyrically limned memoir of a childless stockbroker's wife who left the suffocating bonds of marriage to discover the joys of beekeeping in a Tuscan lesbian commune? (I hear there's an important environmental subtext in that one.) If so, then you are *au fait* with **The Third Rule of VIP Book Salon,** to wit, *The Rule of Culture-Bound Curation.* This one is tricky because at first glance it seems a lot like the Second Rule. The salient distinction is that the priming is less oriented toward literary taste and more toward prevailing social sensibility. The steering committee insists that you understand what's important, and by implication, what's not.

But let's say it's neither the promise of a high-profile endorsement (or veto) nor a socially relevant subject-line that grabs your attention. Let's say, just this once, it's because you've actually *read* the book being reviewed. It's fresh in your memory, this one—a book that you hated or loved or regarded with qualified interest. So you decide to read the review out of informed curiosity, to see how your armchair opinion sides up with that of a professional book critic. This is the best vantage, really, if you want to understand the rules that follow.

The first thing you may notice is how the review starts off with an anecdote that bears no obvious or direct relation to the book's content. If the book is about Cold War espionage, the review might kick off with an obscure commentary about *L'affaire Dreyfus.* If the book is *about* the Dreyfus Affair, it might open with a passage from a Slavoj Žižek lecture. And if the book was published in 2017 or 2018—even if it's about topiary gardening—there's a 93.2% chance the rocket will be lit with some gloomy rumination over the spiraling horrors of the Trump presidency.

Now, do you feel slightly off your footing? Do you fidget as you wait for the topical segue? Then you have brushed up against **The Fourth Rule of VIP Book Salon,** namely *The Rule of the Oblique Hook.* This one is more of a stylistic fixation, and it's violated at turns. It means simply that credentialed book reviewers generally avoid cutting to the chase. To begin a review with the words "This book"—as so many earnest Amazon reviews do—is *infra dig.* Dig?

Once you've made the transition from the contrived framing to the substantive core of the review, the next thing you may notice—having already read the book, remember—is that many of the things you took note of during your bedside hours spent engaged with the text at issue *will not be discussed* by the critic on hire. Maybe you thought the dialogue was stilted, or that the characters were poorly developed, or, if it's nonfiction, that important counterarguments were scarcely addressed. Maybe you discerned plot holes, or you had a problem with the ending. If you are momentarily flummoxed by the reviewer's apparent disdain to discuss such commonplace readerly notes that seemed immediately relevant to you, then you are in propinquity with **The Fifth Rule of VIP Book Salon**, which I pronounce *The Rule of Generalized Critique*. I'm uncertain as to why this one has entrenched in the minds of book critics, but I see it all the time. Rather than grapple closely with the text under consideration, the reviewer will rely on a kind of strained vocabulary to situate the book within some broader theme or tradition, with critical or analytical discussion following in broad sweeps and at careful remove. Dwelling over loose threads and turgid prose is for hoi polloi, Roy.

The Sixth Rule of VIP Book Salon is endemic. Sticking with that hypothetical book you've already read (assuming it's a certain *kind* of book, i.e., one that arouses an emotional response), I'm confident you will notice as your surrogate critic tacitly observes what I call *The Rule of Affective Denial*. More specifically, this refers to the *denial of the human experience of reading*. To be clear, I'm not saying that a modicum of critical distance can't help us arrive at a sharper analytical understanding of the books we read. That wouldn't be true. What I am saying is that the subjective or *felt* experience of reading, something immediately familiar to those of us who devote our lives to books, is, according to the ineffable rules of the embedded culturati, a kind of taboo.

If we ultimately engage with a *text* on more cerebral terms, our first encounter with a *book* is tactile, emotive, personal, even visceral. Everyone who reads (even, I suspect, the critics who avoid mentioning it) knows this. A book makes you laugh or cry, or it arouses feelings of revulsion or pity or palpable distress. Or it stirs feelings of kinship with the author—like you want to chat it all up over drinks. Some novels may leave you pining restlessly because you feel invested in the plight of the characters, or of a particular character. And some nonfiction books may leave you feeling weirdly preoccupied, perhaps over the implications of a provocative argument or an engrossing historical narrative. This is reading in the key of *I and Thou*— exposing yourself to words that resonate, that meld with your precious life experience, sometimes in the form of a long psychic afterburn.

But this lived-in experience, however universal and privately cherished among human beings who nourish on literature, is not to be broached. Oh, a savvy critic might *hint* at the whole sordid business, perhaps with a shopworn shorthand vocabulary—terms like "revelatory" or "elegiac" or "*tristesse*"—but it won't go much further. There'll be no dwelling, no wallowing, no introspection. Certainly no *confession*. The cult of the text is not to be sullied by the intrusion of so much grubby gut-level psycho-baggage. Keep that shit to yourself, elf.

Thus we have laid bare the rudiments, the basic **Rules of VIP Book Salon** that have been insinuated and enjoined from on high since the arrival of modernity. At this point, you may think it's all so much innocuous parlor culture, or you may have mentally dog-eared some exceptions that prove I'm full of shit. Fair enough. For what it's worth, I may as well admit that I actually *enjoy* reading smartypants book reviews. I'll even go so far as to say that I get a kick out of the very tropes and pretenses that I am clearly exaggerating for emphasis here. It's like being a horror movie fan. You look for what works and forgive the clichés. I like Mary Gaitskill and Karl Ove Knausgård. Even Clive James in measured doses. I also like the word "elegiac." It's fun to say.

This doesn't mean I don't recognize a highfalutin' bag of tricks when I see one. And it doesn't mean I'll play nice as I turn your attention the remaining rule—the prickliest woolybooger in the nest.

Yes, there is one **Final Rule**—the meta-Rule, perhaps—under which the others operate in diffident quiescence. Allow me to state it bluntly in ALL CAPS, because **The Governing Rule of VIP Book Salon** is this:

MOST BOOKS DO NOT EXIST.

Establishment book mavens may pay lip service to "independent publishing" from time to time. Don't be fooled. Such obligatory gestures of acknowledgment almost invariably distill to abstraction upon scrutiny. The clubhouse critics seldom wade into the murkier waters where brightly-colored stingy things lurk and evolve in wait of discovery. No, the major channels of contemporary highbrow (or exalted middlebrow) book criticism want nothing to do with the bleeding edges of booklife, no matter how many sell-sheets they receive from down-market imprints. It's easier—and safer—to take cues from the Big Houses and select university presses, thus ensuring that genuinely radical and challenging press ventures remain cordoned off in relative or resolute obscurity.

And the gatekeeping ethos is pervasive. It applies equally to the avant garde and the garden variety. Committee-approved deviations will be obliged with strategic discretion, but the tacit decree of literary nonexistence proscribes discussion of most genre fiction, true crime, experimental writing, dodgy smut, and pretty much any pulp product that advances a point of view a shade out-of-step with wine-and-cheese orthodoxy. With scant exception, that means no Christian lit, no occultism, no paranormal studies, no extreme horror, no Forteana, no fringe science, no (truly) heterodox political theory, no self-published *anything*, and a resounding self-satisfied "Fuck, no!" to pretty much any book that trades in what can reflexively (typically without first cracking the spine) be dismissed as "conspiracy theory" or "hate speech."

If VIP Book Salon still seems like a harmless safe space, I am compelled to remind you that shit runs downhill. I don't know when you're reading these words, but I am writing them as the year 2018 peeks from the womb. It's a very strange cultural moment. As the chattering classes ratiocinate over the moral vicissitudes of punching "Nazis," few seem to notice an ominous sea change in the spirit of public discourse. I am referring to nothing less than the "normalization" (to use a ruined word) of censorship.

We may look askance as *Kirkus* retracts an anodyne book review, caving to the hair-trigger reaction of a hyperventilating hive of self-appointed "sensitivity readers"; or as a steady queue of ostensibly "problematic" speakers are driven by violence or threats of violence from public forums; or as dissident speech is deplatformed or demonetized or otherwise decontaminated by Internet powerbrokers just because they can; or as the world's largest online book retailers (you know the ones) quietly *prohibit the sale of dozens of books* that are deemed, by someone other than you, to offend ecumenical sensibilities. And indeed such events, all of recent vintage, have beeen met with little protest among our anointed culture czars. If the same smart set can be relied on to clap politely when Banned Books Week rolls around next year, they're just as eager to insist that none of *this* amounts to *real* censorship.

Which is exactly the point, isn't it? As the seeds of "soft" thought control root and sprawl like kudzu, inveigling into every nook and fiber of a once open society, we can expect to be lulled. The echo chamber resounds ... with echoes. Under the right spell, we might not notice what comes next. *You say you like "odd" books? Very well. Let me direct you to our Pynchon collection.*

Well, fuck that noise.

Why do I consider this book odd?
Anita Dalton has been writing about odd books—including the ones that don't exist—for at least as long as I've been publishing them.** She's not the only book blogger who flouts convention,*** but she's my favorite. Loath as I am to taint the festivities on offer with a whiff of sanctimony,**** I sincerely believe Anita's self-styled approach to the discussion of literary and cultural

---

**   I suppose I would be remiss not to acknowledge that this anthology includes Anita's generally positive commentary on several texts published under my own imprint, Nine-Banded Books. If you think this is bad form, or that it constitutes a crime of literary incest, you are welcome to suckle at your precious opinion. I really don't care. I'm happy that she reads and writes about these books.

***   Ben Arzate and Grady Hendrix get honorable mentions here.

****   Assuming an implicit defense of Millian free speech principles can be understood as such! If you need a primer, Google "Why Is Freedom of Speech Important" and "The View from Hell."

forms must, in light of the insidiously censorious shitshow to which we are currently in thrall, be viewed as a liberating corrective.

To be clear, I don't think Anita sets out to *break* The Rules of VIP Book Salon. That would imply a degree of guile that seems incompatible with her character. It's just that her writing breezily contravenes every unspoken stipulation in the stylebook. Credentialism is laughable in the parallel universe of *Odd Things Considered*. There's no pretense of tastemaking, just modestly expressed taste—however idiosyncratic. And if Anita snares you with a hook, you can bet your trifocals she'll bring it into crystal-clear focus in the next beat. Without spoiling a twist, she serves up dead-earnest reader-surrogated review-essays that unapologetically embrace and explore the immersive, gut-level, down-in-the-dirt, lived-in, messy, psychodramatic, frustrating, boring, hilarious, disturbing, and at times confounding experience of reading and grappling with culture more generally. The inner life of the bookworm isn't merely intimated from some safe distance—it's embedded and interwoven thematically and biographically throughout her obsessive and personally wrought studies of books and sundry curiosities. *TL;DR* is punctuated with so many confessional detours and conversational asides (subsuming, curiously, lots of information about pharmaceuticals and obscure medical conditions, as well as a poignant love story, and a few dead cats) that it often feels like you've picked up a memoir. One of the good ones.

In Anita's unsafe space, what matters is *sincerity*.

Of course, there are other things that matter. Intrepid curiosity. Fairness. Critical independence. Measured skepticism. A good one-liner. And homework. Yes, *homework*. I've worked with writers who play somewhat fast and loose with facts. Not Anita Dalton. She knows more about crime and conspiracy theory than I could ever hope to forget, and it seems that no matter what subject catches her studious gaze she approaches it with a steely determination to set things straight. A good example is her nearly exhaustive survey of alleged and verified specimens of anthropodermic bibliopegy (books bound in human skin—see pages 577–600). As an editor, I almost dread the prospect that one or more of the purportedly genuine examples cited in "A Flay on Words" should prove to be fake, or vice versa. We'll have to print a new edition!

What else matters in Anita's free-range salon? I'm hesitant to define it precisely, but I think there's a kind of relaxed interpersonal intimacy in her writing—a *cosiness*, perhaps—that carries the show. I've told Anita, probably too often, that her writing reminds me of Pauline Kael. I'm not referring to style necessarily. When popular movie reviews consisted of so much proto-snark and word-counted tease, Kael's personally inflected reinvention of the form was a revelation. Her approach was full-contact, where the all-in subjective experience of watching and assimilating projected images seemed to matter as much as the synopses and analyses that she supplied in dutiful, conversationally pitched stride. Reading Pauline Kael, or Anita Dalton (who also writes about movies˙˙˙˙˙), you feel like an observer to an intense discussion, where everything is on the table. There's a resonance of goodwill. It feels like something is at stake. It absolutely doesn't matter if you disagree, as humans often do.

I think the brick-dense anthology you're currently holding is good. I think it's smart and brimming with insight. I think it's a hoot. Above all, I think *TL;DR: The Best of Odd Things Considered* provides a spirited introduction to a unique and mostly overlooked body of book-centered journalism that stands athwart an ugly tide of intellectual police work. It's also an outpost for kindred spirits who have little use for such fetters and constraints that threaten the pure buzz of discovery, literary and otherwise. If I have felt compelled to stage the preliminaries with a digressive account of trends that I, as a publisher and freethinker, regard with frankly hostile suspicion, it should be noted that Anita's bookblogging habit was initiated long before nascent trends coalesced into something more sinister than a joke. Don't blame her for my fatuous spin.

Despite its heft, the present volume is by no means comprehensive. It is instead a showcase, or a curio cabinet, arranged to provide a more relaxed reading experience than you get with a hyperlink-enabled trawl. Feel free to take it in bite-size pieces. But if you go in for the deep dive, I think you'll come away with a better appreciation not only for an unassuming Pflugervillian book-blogger's counter-conventional literary nous, but for the dizzying range of subjects that she considers, in glorious long-form, under the rubric of "Odd Things."

To the extent that Anita's laser-instinct for provocative subject matter has occasionally stirred controversy—or contretemps—among a rotating cast of Web-addicted trolls and prudes, you may rest assured that such excursions are well represented in the pages that follow. If you missed her withering vivisection of Tao Lin's alt-lit hucksterism the first time around, buckle up for a bumpy ride. Her pin-prick study of kid-slayer *cum* word-slinger Ian Brady is also on full display, having been substantially revised and supplemented for deadwood posterity. Likewise revisited is her incisive analysis of Franklin Scandal conspiracy theory and its curious pizza-scented penumbras. And since Anita has caught plenty of flak over her nuanced discussions of Peter Sotos' writing, we ended up devoting an entire section to that problematic terrain.

As for high-voltage material that was withheld from the current program, well, we have a good explanation for *one* conspicuous omission; if you're

---

˙˙˙˙˙   See pages 555–568, and especially her Kael-esque contrarian take on Adam Rehmeier's *The Bunny Game.*

wondering why Anita's in-depth examination of Anders Breivik's interminable manifesto, *2083 – A European Declaration of Independence*, isn't in the mix, the surprising explanation is nested in a footnote.******

If you are a longtime reader of Anita's various blogging excursions, I think you will still find value in this collection. In addition to the new material mentioned above, every essay has been substantially revised and rebuffed for prime-time presentation. Anita has also amended her older texts with footnotes and postscripts as suggested by whim or by subsequent events, and most of the book discussions now come appended with "Further Reading" lists.******* If a few niggling typographical errors have slipped through the net (inevitable, since we are not Jim Goad), the fault is mine, not Anita's.

Anyway. I've gone on far too long. I suppose I felt I had license to bloviate a bit, since most of you will have wisely skipped over this part anyway. A publisher's foreword is like ice water served before you get in line for a grand buffet; you may take a sip, then it's time to fill your pie-hole. In any case, it doesn't matter. What matters is that you, lucky reader, are in for a feast. So scrape the residual gunk of high culture off your plate and get ready to fill up on something deliciously odd. You're in good hands.

****** This book has lots of footnotes. Footnotes, not endnotes. Footnotes, when they don't involve dead cats, are fun. Footnotes are like a party that moves to the kitchen after everyone's sufficiently buzzed and the people with kids have checked out for the night. You just step right in and help yourself to another beer and a handful of those guacamole-flavored tortilla chips that Sarah keeps raving about. See where the conversation leads. Endnotes are a different matter. When you come across an endnote marker in the main text of a book, it's like being assigned a tedious chore. Or it's like getting one of those slips in your mailbox informing you that a package is being held at the local office. As much as you may want to try out that Mezzaluna salad chopper thing that you ordered after you saw the guy at Subway chop-chop-chopping so efficiently, you'll get to it when you get to it.

******* I should note that Anita graciously allowed me to supply a few of my own precious book recommendations, so ... *caveat lector*. Don't rush to blame her if you feel you've been steered wrong.

INTRODUCTION

I've written four different introductions and none of them have sounded right. For some reason, my words have been stiff, forced and lacking resonance. I sent the last version to Chip Smith last night and about an hour later was overcome with nausea. Literal nausea. Not ennui or some sort of metaphysical manifestation of misery. I straight up felt *sick*.

I woke up this morning and the first thing I did was throw up. True story. And when I was finished being sick, I immediately knew what to write. It became so clear to me what I needed to say to prepare people for this compendium, this enormous brick of a book.

Fay Weldon might say that I was throwing up all my fear and doubt that I am worthy of a book. Or maybe she wouldn't—she's sort of mercurial. But it's hard not to assign a psychological motive to the nausea that followed emailing my intro and immediately knowing what to write after throwing up. People like symbolism, and I am definitely a person.

Though I have yet to discuss in depth any of her works, Fay Weldon is my favorite writer. I began reading her when I was a junior in college, devouring her books instead of reading *Candide* or *As You Like It*. Her books have been a staple in my life as I have aged. I began reading her when I felt like I knew all there was to know and I continue to read her now that I'm older and know how little I really know. I certainly am sure of less now than I was in my twenties. I think that's how it goes for a lot of people. Fay Weldon captures that confusion. Her writing captures the moral complexity, the human frailty and strength, the cruelty and kindness, the sexual relationships that fail and the friendships that endure. All of that pathos is distilled through her own experiences.

Yet it was only after I read her memoir, *Auto de Fay*, that I began to see her body of work as thinly veiled autobiography. Fay Weldon has lived a life that almost defies the belief that people are expected to suspend when reading some types of fiction. And she tells us her life story in all of her books, sometimes in little flecks, sometimes in huge chunks. An example of a fleck: in her novel *Praxis*, the heroine is permitted into college because her name sounds masculine. Fay, whose real name is Franklin, was accepted into a traditionally-male subject major in college because she was assumed to be male. Her novels are littered with moments like this.

But the larger chunks are the the price of admission, as I am fond of saying. Imagine my delight (and horror) when I discovered that a subplot of *Down Among the Women* wasn't just a literary cribbing of the emotional disasters Sylvia Plath and Assia Wevill wrought all for the love of Ted Hughes. Fay was friends with Assia, and if you read closely you realize that she may feel some guilt over how it all played out. She certainly felt anger at the community that shunned Assia while embracing Ted, an opinion certainly out of place among the literati of the time.

Most stunning was her novel *Affliction*, which tells the story of a marriage disintegrating due to the influence of an unethical therapist who seduces the husband and encourages him to leave his wife and take up with her instead. A version of this happened in Fay's own life, when her husband Ron left her for some dippy astrological therapist (who knew such a thing existed?), who told him the reason he and Fay had problems was that their stars were not aligned (one presumes the astro-therapist felt she and Ron had more orderly stars).[*] Fay, who had gained the courage to write after undergoing psychotherapy, found herself questioning the whole of the psychiatric community. She saw the power therapists wielded over the lives of those they treated and how much damage a wicked person with the right credentials can cause.

Fay Weldon's characters embody the notion of Walt Whitman's multitudes in oneself. They are contradictory. They change their minds. They are one thing then they are another. They are very human, displaying all the aspects of an author's humanity and the humanity of those she observes.

I don't know why it didn't hit me until after I threw up this morning that I write book reviews like Fay Weldon writes fiction. But I do. Confessional book discussions. Autobiographical essays disguised as book reviews.

It started slowly. I began my book blogs, *I Read Odd Books* and *I Read Everything*, with the intention of being a traditional, though certainly dogpatch, book critic. Looking back over my blogs, I noticed that I was inserting some of my personal experiences into my reviews. I didn't realize it at the time, but I was doing it, telling parts of my own story as I dissected the stories of others. It's no accident that my discussions became longer as I found catharsis in writing about why a book really mattered to me.

Have details of your life have been made clearer after reading a book that spoke to you? Has a novel ever revealed to you the different ways characters have dealt with the dramatic struggles that punctuate your life? It often happens to me, as you can see in my book discussions. When I read Roddy Doyle's *The Woman Who Walked into Doors*, I found myself replaying the tiring grossness of waking up in the body of an adult while still a child. In Tama Janowitz's *Slaves of New York*, I saw so much of myself in Cora, a young

---

[*] Ron Weldon died the day his divorce from Fay became final, another twist of Fay-te that seems better placed in fiction.

graduate school dropout whose experiences in academia mirrored my own. In college I embodied the pretense and pomposity of Richard Papen, the narrator of Donna Tartt's *The Secret History*. His desire to escape his humble upbringing, to fit in among the eccentric and monied elite at an expensive private college in New England rang a bit too true for me to have seen it when first read the book. But I see it now, all too clearly.

When I engage closely with stories, I discover bits and pieces of myself, of my life, my thoughts, my hopes and desires. And it is this commonality of experience—this revelation—that fuels my wordy and emotional response to books. Fay Weldon has produced a body of work that spans fifty years, with over forty novels (as well as some television scripts) to her credit. It can take a lot of words, a lot of time and a lot of work to tell your story in your own words. When you tell your story through someone else's work the words multiply, as this collection demonstrates.

Not every book I read inpires me to write at such length, and I don't always reveal my soul when I write about literature or movies or anthropodermic bibliopegy. I have some brief book discussions here and there and some snarky ones, including in the pages that follow. But when you write about what affects you, it is often necessary to go long and look inward. Some people really dislike this confessional approach to cultural criticism. Such people have offered earnest critiques, not realizing that the length and emotion are features, not bugs.

The two finest pieces of writing I have ever done are reproduced in this book. Jason Hrivnak's *The Plight House* provoked in me a deep soul-sorrow that showed me what my husband must have experienced when I suffered a psychotic break and nearly killed myself. I never saw through his eyes the landscape of misery my illness created until I read that devastating book. The knowledge wrecked me for a while, then humbled me. My resulting essay is, among other things, an account of this revelation.

Then there is my reaction to Sarah Perry's work of antinatalist philosophy, *Every Cradle Is a Grave*. Perry's book reexamines the belief that life is always a moral good, questioning prohibitions against suicide and exhortations to have children. Of course my own suicide attempt is prominent in my discussion, but I also write about another family suicide and how our refusal to let the terminally ill die without suffering devastates survivors and forces us into bizarre platitudes and incomprehensible cruelty. I read *Every Cradle* as my mother was dying and it utterly changed how I processed what was happening. Writing about this book—and my experience reading it—was intensely personal, necessitating a candid look at my own life and family.

Like the other texts and cultural artifacts discussed in this anthology, these books are what I describe as "odd." While my criteria for literary and aethetic oddity are somewhat fluid, my abiding interest in outré subjects is also part of my story. I had the decided advantage of growing up in a nice suburb of Dallas. The public library was less than a mile from my home and if my parents didn't want to drive me I could bike there. I quickly read my way out of the kids' section and because it was the seventies and early eighties, the librarians didn't think it necessary to ask my mother if it was okay for me, a ten-year-old, to read books about the Kennedy assassination, fusty occult tomes or true crime novels complete with pictures of death and gore.

Some kids in my position become readers of great literature. I became an avid reader of what lots of cultural gatekeepers would describe as low-brow dreck. That's okay with me. One of the benefits of having received the kind education my grandparents could only have dreamed of is that I have the capacity to read and discuss the great books if I choose to. I recall checking out Dostoevsky novels in the fifth grade because he was mentioned so often in Charles Schultz's *Peanuts* comics, but I can assure you I didn't get around to reading *Crime and Punishment* until college, and I didn't really enjoy it when I did. I preferred my odd books—and my Fay Weldons—because I had the freedom to explore, to choose my own path. Though I did eventually develop more mainstream literary tastes, my obsessive interest in eccentric and fringe topics has proven resilient. It's a reflection of who I am. It's also my niche.

For a long time I could not find a niche, a place where I could coherently share my obsessive love of books based on my own very subjective tastes and opinions. But in the Internet Age, when you find it difficult to find your place, you simply build one of your own. You create a digital stomping ground where kindred spirits can find you and perhaps even find value in your work. It still takes me by surprise to realize I began *I Read Odd Books*, the site that became *Odd Things Considered*, almost ten years ago. But the calendar doesn't lie. For nearly a decade, I've managed to channel my genre-blind reading habits into this curious project. It has allowed me to indulge and share my obsessions in my own way, without word limits, and with no restriction as to what books or subjects I prefer to discuss. And it has allowed me to tell my story as I react to the stories of others.

I am very grateful that I am not the only person obsessively interested in a variety of peculiar topics. Obsession can often be an alienating experience and it's almost miraculous to discover that people share and engage with my interests. I will never stop feeling grateful to all the people who read *Odd Things Considered* and leave me comments, even the ones who chastise me for being verbose or hyperanalytical, or for making it personal. Thank you for reading.

Anita Dalton
December 8, 2017

PART ONE

Odd Books

(Mostly Nonfiction)

We've all heard that truth is stranger than fiction. I don't know about that, but the interesting thing about *odd* nonfiction is the commingling of subjective truth and inventive storytelling. Interpreting facts quite often leads to better stories than you'll find in the horror and science fiction shelves, and enjoying the way facts and interpretation come together to form something nonfictionish is key to reading and discussing the sorts of "nonfiction" that I have obsessively explored on *Odd Things Considered*.

CRIME & CONSPIRACY

It's funny, in a way, how many of the books I read about crime involve a conspiracy and most of the books on conspiracy involve the commission of terrible crimes. Sometimes it's hard to tell which came first—the conspiracy or the crime, the crime or the conspiracy, the chicken or the egg. And did the chicken cross the road willingly, or was she forced, at gunpoint, after witnessing an assassination? Don't be surprised if you never get the answers to these questions.

THE ADDERAL DIARIES
By Stephen Elliott
Graywolf Press (2009)
Original post: 09/16/2011

Why do I consider this book odd?
I don't even know anymore. I finished it months ago and put it in
the "Odd To Be Discussed" pile. It may not be odd but I don't recom-
mend a normal person with normal interests and a normal constitu-
tion read it—not because it is outré, but because I suspect the typical
reader would give up after the first few chapters.

You know, I'm gonna go ahead and cop to the fact that this isn't going to be a favorable discussion of Elliott's book. But I also want to make it clear that this is not going to be the full-bore assault I think *The Adderal Diaries* likely deserves. I'm pulling my punches because I'm still reeling from the mental ordeal of digesting and discussing Anders Behring Breivik's sprawling manifesto.[1] After reading 1500 pages of undiluted bigotry and murder blueprints, I'm pretty sure I would be kindly disposed toward even the biggest pile of crap ever to be released in trade paperback.

So just remember my perspective may be favorably skewed, even as I skewer.

I bought *The Adderal Diaries* when it caught my eye in the True Crime section at BookPeople, an independent bookstore in Austin. The memoir part didn't seem out of place, especially since I had recently read James St. James' *Party Monster*, which is a drug memoir interwoven with a first-rate true crime narrative. I think that's what I expected when I picked up this memoir about a man with a drug problem who was writing about what the back cover described as a "notorious San Francisco murder trial" and expressing an "electric exploration of the self."

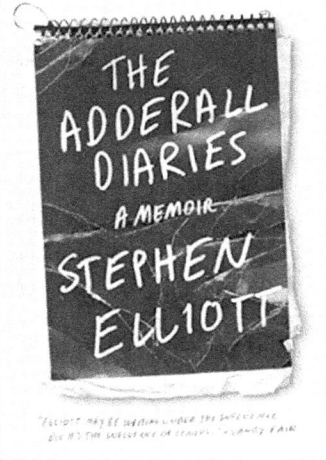

---

1   If you have the stomach for it, my four-part discussion of Breivik's *2083* is posted on the *Odd Things Considered* website. Just Google it. Masochist that I am, I will be revisiting Breivik's text (along with the polemical writings of other violent and desperate humans) in a forthcoming book tentatively titled *Manifesto!*, which will be published—hopefully before the *year* 2083—by Nine-Banded Books.

But the back cover gets it very wrong when it asserts that Elliott "seamlessly weaves them together." Alas, Elliott is no St. James. The murder trial barely registers as a side story in *The Adderall Diaries*. Though I read this book very closely, I have to flip through it again to jog even the most basic details about the murder. But I can tell you a whole lot about Elliott and, frankly, most of it is devoid of emotional meaning and context.

I don't intend to demean the power of the addiction or sexual discovery memoir, and I don't want to demean those who may have found something relevant in Elliott's narrative. I fully admit that I may have missed something because I have not read any of Elliott's other works (I wonder if I would have cared more if I had read his other books). But the fact remains that I did not care much about this book. The narrative was flat and uninvolved. The addiction barely registered as being damaging. The bondage and S&M details were tossed out with no emotion, with no attempt to lure the reader into a deeper sense of understanding. It may seem bizarre to say that a memoir is self-absorbed, but that was the problem.

How can a memoir be self-absorbed? Actually, it's easy. When someone you find interesting goes on and on about him or herself, your interest trumps the self-absorption. It's subjective, to be sure, but a memoir has to make the reader care that they are reading the words of a stranger going on and on about their life. Given its proliferation, this flat, disengaged writing style must appeal to someone. But I am not that person. (Which is odd, in a way, because I am quite aware that my book discussions are utterly self-indulgent, written to please myself as much as to entertain and inform.)

The subject matter of this book—addiction, sexual taboos, a murder trial—should all be interesting. But conveyed through Elliott's numb prose, it's all unexciting. It's the literary equivalent of tapioca with a dash of tequila. Or white bread with a dab of mold on it. It's a boring man telling boring stories to a barely interested audience. I contrast the content of this book with much more taboo writing, like the works of Peter Sotos, and it becomes clear why Elliott's writing did not appeal to me. Sotos, in his extremity, forces the reader to think, or to react at the very least. Elliott's numb tale was more like watching a Warhol movie. As I read his book, a quote from Charles Bukowski came to mind: "Boring damned people. All over the earth."

How can I convey how little it interested me? Discussing the plot is hard. Elliott does drugs, has extreme sex, comes to terms with some of his feelings about his family and muses about the murder. In a way, this is no different than many other memoirs, but when I consider the emotionally numb and at times alienating manner in which Elliott writes, any structure would be lost to the ennui his words provoke. At times the "meta" irritated me, but perhaps some will find it delightful. Perhaps some will also report back on what it feels like to snort ketamine and take an icepick to their frontal lobes.

Perhaps some will find this book so utterly transcendent they will be forced to send me half-assed, unintelligible emails to show their indie cred. Perhaps some think I should stop typing entirely until I am in a better mood. Perhaps those people are right, but fuck it, I'm sitting here, computer in my lap. Let's get this over with.

Let me give my examples of why this book was terrible so I can move on to something else.

The meta. I swear, if I never again have to read a book about a person who writes about how they are writing the book as they write it, I will die happy (or at least, happier). Take this scene where Elliott is listening to a lawyer give a terrible argument in court:

> "If the platypus doesn't fit, you must acquit," I whisper to the producer seated next to me.
>
> "You should use that in your book," she says.

More problematic for me was the jarring way in which Elliott writes. His idea flow is not what I consider logical, even for a man under the influence. For example:

> In the morning I take ten milligrams of Adderall and then ten more of the extended release. I sit down in the coffee shop then go into the bathroom and snort a few more lines. I thought I had stopped snorting Adderall, but I keep coming back to it. In the 1950s when Dexadrine and Dexamyl and other amphetamine combinations were being mass consumed as diet pills, research started coming out about tolerance and the return of lost weight. When the National Academy of Science advised the FDA that amphetamine weight loss products were not very effective, the pharmaceutical companies suppressed the information for years. Now Lindsay Lohan and Nicole Richie are taking Adderall for weight loss like fifties housewives, because it's the same thing. The amphetamine hasn't changed. They are all forms of beta-phenyl-isopropylamine: synthetic adrenaline.
>
> The closing arguments are over and I bicycle through the city. All the pot clubs are open at night, their unlocked doors throwing green light onto the streets. I pass the line of bike messengers waiting to get into the Zeitgeist for a cold beer. I bike Valencia, Guererro, Dolores. These streets are noisy, crowded. This is where I live, in the city I arrived at accidentally. It's good to have a home, to know I am going to be here for a while. That I'll stay where I am, sharing a one-bedroom apartment close to the park and the coffee shop I like, in the middle of everything, with my young roommate, for as long as I can.
>
> "Little kids need their mother," Paul Hora said in his summation. "Little kids miss their mother."

Just for the record, this cited portion is a new section that followed directly after the platypus part I quoted above. There are a couple of reasons I cite this chunk of text to show why this book wore so very, very thin for me. Elliott is evidently seamlessly weaving together his story and the story of the murder trial (if we are to believe the blurbs on the back cover), but this passage shows that no—oh, no—he is not. In fact, one could argue the seams he weaves are not even on the same garment. He snorts Adderall in a public john, he muses on the history of amphetamines and their current use amongst third tier starlets, he bikes and vomits up locations as if they mean anything to anyone who doesn't live there and then he segues into the trial. I see the seams.

And again, the details that mean nothing are tiring. Why did we need that information about amphetamines following an explanation of why he can't stop snorting Adderall? What sense did this make? Why include pop culture references that were dated when Elliott threw them out? You tell me.

I get that Elliott was writing a memoir that just happened to feature a murder trial but there are contrived moments like this:

> I tell her what Hans said, his last words before he was led away, "He said, 'I've been the best father that I know how.'"
>
> "By killing their mother?" she asks.
>
> "It was as if he was talking to me," I say.
>
> "Does he know you're writing a book?"
>
> "I doubt it."

I don't know. As an aficionado of the true crime genre, I find moments like this hackneyed. I didn't think I would ever long for the engagement and focus of a pulp true crime writer but those are infinitely preferable to scenes like this where Elliott somehow creates such a strange and irrelevant connection with the killer. Worse, he follows that up with an observation about Hillary Clinton's stance on Israeli politics and his own fear of holding babies. Stream of consciousness has its place but generally I can do without it when a person is relating to me details of a crime, even if it's wrapped up in a memoir.

And perhaps that is part of the reason I find this so self-absorbed and self-indulgent. There is a fine line between exploring the self through empathic projection and exhibiting a shocking level of egoism as you insert your emotions where they don't belong.

Here's an example that would have made Truman Capote blush:

> Nietzsche said there are no facts, only interpretations. Nina Reiser was five feet five inches tall and weighed 114 pounds. She was the mother of Cori and Lila. She met Hans through a bride service in St. Petersburg, Russia. These are facts. There are things that can be known.
>
> I know I entered the mental hospital August 31, 1986, and was released three months later into the McCormick House, where I shared a room with Cateyes, a member of an all-black gang called the Vice Lords. These are facts. He tattooed a dagger on my left shoulder, which I later covered up

with a larger, more colorful tattoo. He called himself Cateyes because of his large green eyes that pinched slightly at the corner toward his ears.

These may be facts and they may be known, but they don't flow in anything approaching a coherent or relevant narrative. One thing that can be known is that if Elliott had decided to simply write about his life without this half-assed juxtaposition with a murder trial, I may have been more kindly disposed. It's not necessarily a bad thing to be self-absorbed. It's just best to be clear about it.

I also wonder what it is that I was supposed to take away from Elliott's descriptions of his sexual predilections. The next scene begins descriptively enough, as he is in thrall to a woman whom he describes thusly: "European and Asian and looked like Jessica Rabbit if Jessica Rabbit had starred in *Venus in Furs*." He describes his interactions with her:

> "I don't like giving people pleasure," she said. Then she sat on the sofa and I kneeled in front of her and she slapped me several times. She held her cigarette near my face and I could feel its heat about to burn my eyelids. She laughed loudly. Then she pressed the cigarette into the back of both my hands. "Those are going to blister."

I left passages like this feeling empty because I don't think I ever understood what motivates Elliott. The pain? The thrill of enthrallment? The danger? The deep pleasure that comes from submission? I have no idea. He tells me the details but he never lets me into his brain. This is why I invoked Sotos earlier. Sotos disturbs me to my very core, yet he explains himself so thoroughly. There is no sense in giving the details of the wallow without giving us the feelings in it. I focus on this passage because I am a person who suffered a terrible burn and I remember the white hot searing pain that left the taste of lemons and chalk in my mouth during debridement treatment and because I scar with every bump it seems. I feel like a walking autobiography in a language few others can read. Elliott and I have some similar damages beyond that—drugs, unsettling personal histories. I wanted to understand him and should have been able to understand him but he kept too much to himself. He was an interesting study in how it is one can be utterly honest without laying oneself bare.

Take another scene of intense sexual experience that reads like pure fucking nihilism:

> The house madam leaves and I take my clothes off and the woman from Culver City fastens leather cuffs around my ankles, latching a spreader bar to them to keep my legs forced apart. She fastens nipple clamps with weights on the ends, pushes me over the bed and slides inside me with her strap-on. I'm wearing a rubber mask and a blindfold so I can't see her boyfriend moving behind us with the camera. She leans over me, one hand gripping my throat and the other pressing down my back. This is fine, I think. I'll

just stay like this. When the filming is over and I'm getting dressed, the boyfriend offers me a can of energy cola. "You were great," he says. "We couldn't ask for a better victim."

Why did he do this? Compulsion? Maybe, but it seems too remote for compulsion. He has no affection for the woman from Culver City, so it was not passion. It was not a test of his limits. It was not a financial transaction. I have no idea why he engaged in this interesting extremity. Much of the book is exactly like this—a recitation of interesting facts that reaches no conclusions, emotional or otherwise.

This was all the more infuriating to me because there were moments when he described so perfectly the problems I often have in my brain:

> Sometimes I think of this depression setting its hooks in me as a failure of my file system. I call up files I shouldn't be thinking of. I mislabel documents and store them in a folder I'd rather bury.

> Modern file systems don't just catalog data; they move it into the best available space. This information is continually shuffled into equal-sized digital blocks. It's the most human part of a computer. We remember events in our lives in specific order and importance relative to our identity.

Later in the same musings, he discusses how he more than doubled his prescribed Adderall dosage.

> The speed lets me lock into my own thoughts, build and rebuild my framework for understanding the world.

> "You have to be careful about not sleeping," Roger tells me. "You can do permanent damage to your memory."

Don't I fucking know it. It annoys me that this was as close to an understanding and a kinship I had with Elliott's words.

There were moments where I think Elliott was conveying that he had no idea how to express feelings, only facts:

> Katie sprawls across me, crying. She's been seeing someone else since a little before we met. She likes him and she likes me too.

> "Last night," she says. "I was going to break up with you. But I was enjoying your company too much."

> I keep my arms around her. I feel my stomach harden and try to look behind us into that little room where she keeps her washer-dryer. I was with her when she picked that thing up. We'd gone to the Best Buy below the highway. The store was full of bright plastics, shelves covered in gadgets nobody needed. We found help from a salesman in a blue polo. *This is what couples do*, I thought.

And that's it. A sobbing woman sprawled across him and he has a tightening of the stomach and that sort of consumerist familiarity that often gets mistaken for real memories and kinship. He concludes with this, told after he goes off on a tangent about meeting a woman to whom he confessed his love for Katie:

> I run my finger along Katie's cheek. I tell Katie I'm not trying to audition to be her boyfriend. She'll have to make up her own mind and fuck whoever she wants.

He thought he was falling in love with this woman. Selecting an appliance with her created in him the notion of being a couple. And this is what he says—make up your mind and fuck who you want. As much as I may have in common with those whose minds have been affected by chemicals, whose psyches are bent and scratched, I cannot tolerate this level of nihilism. I am constitutionally unsuited for it, and to read this nihilism wherein Elliott is pumped full of drugs, burned, tied up, fucked, loved and abandoned and saved, and to see it summed up in a sort of "whatevs" shrug is more than I can bear.

This scene actually illustrates my lack of tolerance for emotional nihilism pretty well:

> It's a quiet evening with fifty students and faculty sitting patiently while I read an essay about Lissette carving "possession" in my side. She spelled it wrong, leaving out one *s*. The metaphor was too obvious. It was like Jim Morrison dying or Ronald Reagan's tax cuts. It meant exactly what you thought it meant.

And what I think it meant was nothing because he does not long for Lissette, he does not belong to her, and she does not possess him. What is the point of enduring this prose that describes damage with no revelation?

Hilariously, to me at least, that is followed with this paragraph:

> In Los Angeles, Bearman had told me I needed to find a new story. I had written four novels based loosely on my life and multiple essays. "Listen," he said. "Stick to Hans and Sean and keep yourself out of it. My friend Kay encourages me to write something accessible, and to keep a journal for the rest. "Write something that people want to read," she says. "Think of Dave Eggers. He wrote a book about himself and moved on to other things." Twelve years ago, when I was hospitalized following my overdose, my friend Louie came to visit me. He said, "You better never write about this." He was trying to distinguish between being a real human being and someone who only lives on the page.

Is this what Louie was warning about? Is this book the end result of living one's life on the page? Having written four books about himself and then producing a fifth that is so remote, so wordy yet so insistent that the reader cannot get close to him, I have to wonder if Elliott is, in fact, living his life on the page. Thoughts and conversations and actions reproduced faithfully but to what real end? Few readers, even those with similar damage, can find much truth in this true crime/memoir hybrid. I ask again, what is the point of sharing the scars if you don't explain what they mean and how they haunt you?

So I read the scars, I read the horror, I read the words of a man who was struggling to be human outside the page and it failed because Elliott's writing does not show enough emotional depth for me to give a crap about the scars, the horror, or the struggle.

FURTHER READING

In Heaven Everything Is Fine: The Unsolved Life of Peter Ivers and the Lost History of the New Wave Theater
Josh Frank and Charlie Buckholtz

Blood Will Out
Walter Kirn

Most Outrageous: The Trials and Trespasses of Dwaine Tinsley and Chester the Molester
Bob Levin

Party Monster: A Fabulous But True Tale of Murder in Clubland
James St. James

The Covert War Against Rock
By Alex Constantine
Feral House (2001)
Original post: 10/06/2010

Why do I consider this book odd?
It posits unusual theories about the deaths of famous rock stars.

I am highly skeptical of conspiracy theory even though I can't ever read enough about it. Yet even as a skeptic I have a conspiratorial bias, depending on how much my belief is beggared. I think there was a covert CIA plot to kill JFK. And the more I read about the death of RFK, the more uncertain I am about whether Sirhan Sirhan acted alone (and whether his current mental state is due to organic schizophrenia).

Embracing such ideas means that a little part of me believes that elements of the American government could want specific celebrities dead. And while some of the claims in Alex Constantine's *The Covert War Against Rock* seem unlikely to me, others hit my belief-o-meter. I would need to read and research more before I could completely buy into some of Constantine's claims, but there's a lot of information in this book that has the ring of truth.

I was already familiar with a lot of the territory that Constantine covers, yet I am surprised by my reactions to the parts that were new to me. I mean, I always suspected there was much more behind the deaths of Bob Marley and Peter Tosh than just cancer and a gunshot, respectively. When the CIA decides to destabilize an entire country, it isn't too much to believe that they would also take steps to assassinate reggae musicians who, through their charisma and music, were overt opponents of American political control. Did Bob Marley really get cancer when the son of the director of the CIA gave him a pair of boots containing a copper wire that may have been dipped in some sort of cancer-causing chemical? I tend to think maybe not, but then again I also live in a world where dissidents get killed with umbrella guns containing ricin "bullets."[2]

The part that was the newest to me was the section about Tupac Shakur. I recall clearly when he died but I thought little of it. He had seemed like a

---

2   From Wikipedia (https://en.wikipedia.org/wiki/Georgi_Markov): Georgi Markov was a Bulgarian dissident novelist and poet who was also a harsh critic of the Bulgarian government. In 1978, he "was assassinated on a London street via a micro-engineered pellet containing ricin, fired into his leg from an umbrella wielded by someone associated with the Bulgarian secret police. It has been speculated that they asked the KGB for help."

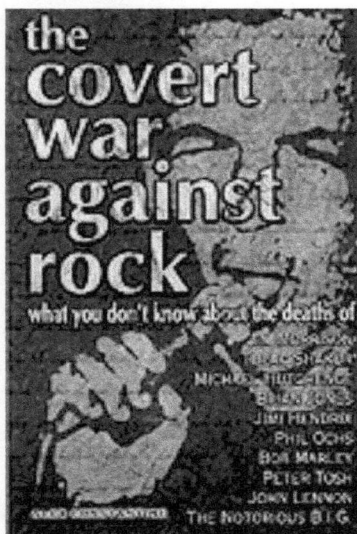

gangsta to me and gangstas sometimes get shot. I didn't (and mostly still don't) listen to rap and knew little about Tupac Shakur that was substantive. But if the media portrayal of Tupac Shakur painted a picture that substituted itself for real information, Constantine's research into his death reveals a completely different picture that suggests very sound reasons why there might have been a conspiracy to kill him. The fact that Shakur was the heir apparent to an activist family (one of whom, notorious cop-killer Assata Shakur, escaped from prison and defected to Cuba) is one possible reason, and Constantine's account of the way the shooting occurred and the seeming lack of police attempts to solve the murder make it seem as if there may have been some sort of conspiracy to kill Tupac and obfuscate the investigation. But even as I type this, I also think that it's just far more likely that Shakur had some shady people in his life and that police investigations are all too often flawed.

Aside from the claim that Mama Cass Elliot may have been the victim of a government-sponsored assassination, there was not a single case in this book that I could completely dismiss (Cass Elliot died of an undetected heart defect, nothing more, nothing less). Whether or not you're inclined to believe that the government killed John Lennon, Phil Ochs, Jimi Hendrix or Jim Morrison, Constantine raises interesting questions about time-lines and the government's interest in these performers. He brings up details that were blurry then and are blurrier now.[3]

Of all the deaths presented in *The Covert War Against Rock*, it was Michael Hutchence's that affected me the most. Born in 1970 (neatly sandwiched between the deaths of Jimi Hendrix and Janis Joplin), I was too young to be much interested when most of the stars profiled by Constantine died. In some cases, I was not alive yet. But INXS was a band I adored as an adolescent and young adult. I recall seeing INXS perform on their tour for *Listen Like Thieves*. Terence Trent D'Arby opened and despite being in nosebleed seats, my friends and I danced and danced, thrilled to be there. *Shabooh*

---

3   Actually, I did sneer a bit when Constantine referred to Donald Bains' *The CIA's Control of Candy Jones*. I found that book so lacking in anything approaching proof that I didn't even want to keep the book once I discussed it (see: http://www.oddthingsconsidered.com/the-cias-control-of-candy-jones-by-donald-bain/). Candy Jones was a victim of her own sad mind and the utter incredulity of Long John Nebel, not the MK-Ultra program.

Shoobah and *The Swing* are two of my favorite pop albums. Hutchence's death just seemed so unlikely—death by auto-erotic asphyxiation? Really? The information Constantine presents about elements of Hutchence's death, important details that never made the public airways, genuinely make me wonder.

This was an interesting book. It took itself seriously, so I took it seriously.[4] Constantine certainly knows his conspiracy theory, and he can write a tight sentence. I think the chapter on Tupac Shakur and Biggie Smalls is worth the price of admission, and the chapter on Marley and Tosh is a welcome double feature. I don't buy all of Constantine's arguments, but he raises provocative questions, not only about the deaths of celebrated rock stars, but also about the government's role in policing popular culture. When dealing with content of this sort, that's often the best you can ask for. I still think Mark David Chapman acted alone, but just because he beat the government to John Lennon doesn't mean the feds didn't want him dead. This the OTC corollary to "just because you're paranoid doesn't mean they aren't out to get you."

FURTHER READING

Psychic Dictatorship in the U.S.A.
Alex Constantine

Secret and Suppressed: Banned Ideas and Hidden History
Edited by Jim Keith

---

4   Upon reflection, aside from Mama Cass and Candy Jones, other aspects of Constantine's investigation did strike a major discordant note with me. Maybe rock conspirators can help me out. Constantine asserts that Joan Baez claims she is a survivor of ritual abuse due to being a part of the Monarch Project. However, the sources he uses combined with his specific verbiage do not support the conclusion that Baez ever *said* she was a victim of ritual abuse. Though he says Joan makes this claim, his actual sources never verify anything other than that she is a vocal opponent of torture and that she has been in intensive therapy. So I fired up the ol' Internet to see what I could find out.

After several hours online reading lots of assertions that Baez survived the Monarch Project (and cringing as the sites pinged my anti-virus software), all I could find were people saying that because her father worked for Cornell, the supposed site of many government mind control experiments in Ithaca, and because she wrote a song called "Play Me Backwards," which has lyrics that can be interpreted as the words of an abuse survivor, Baez was a victim of mind control. I could not find a single source with a direct quote from Baez indicating she was a victim of the Monarch Project. Those sites that claim she says such a thing use her song lyrics as a *de facto* admission, which is hardly the same thing.

More troubling is that the longer I read, the more familiar the phraseology the sites used became. In fact, I began to think there was a single source that asserted Baez was a victim of the Monarch Project, likely based on the fact that she once lived in Ithaca and wrote a disturbing song, and endless others cited that first source. See for yourself what I mean. Google "joan baez ritual abuse." Soon the phrase *self-described victim of ritual child abuse* will become very familiar, as all the sources for this information seem to be revisiting one original source that I cannot run to ground. If Baez outright stated somewhere that she was a victim of ritual abuse, I could not find it. That she has been through therapy and speaks out against torture is not enough proof in my books. Interpretation of song lyrics is not enough proof either. Baez has worn her beliefs on her sleeves for years, and seldom hesitates to speak out about what she considers to be injustice. If she was a victim of the Monarch Project, I would expect there to be a direct quote from her saying so, not innuendo about song lyrics.

THE PRANKSTER AND THE CONSPIRACY
By Adam Gorightly
Paraview Press (2003)
Original post: 04/29/2010

Why do I consider this book odd?
Well, Robert Anton Wilson wrote the foreword. That's sort of a clue right there. This book covers a whole lot of oddness: Kennedy assassination conspiracy, Jim Garrison, the 60s in general, Discordianism, CIA spooks, and, Jesus help us all, Sondra London.

You know, I still sort of love the Discordians, even though the whole riff often wears thin for me now. Twenty years ago I was an avid member of a Discordian offshoot, The Church of the SubGenius. But as I got older I just didn't see the point. I still see some value in that sort of social satire, but I'm pretty earnest these days, and cloaking oneself behind so many layers of sarcasm and inside jokes in order to make a point is more work than I am willing to do in order to prove I am not *one of them*.

But when Kerry Thornley (Lord Omar Khayyam Ravenhurst) and Greg Hill (Malaclypse the Younger) created Discordianism and co-wrote the *Principia Discordia*, it was a natural rebellion against the postwar rage for order that permeated life in the 1950s, and the tricksterism had a profound point—a point that has become diluted over time, especially now that the Internet makes being a trickster almost mandatory. But 50 years ago, before 1960s rebellion embraced chaos and dissent, Discordianism was a precursor and perhaps a catalyst for serious social change.

Kerry Thornley, as described in Adam Gorightly's *The Prankster and the Conspiracy*, was a man who inspired and in many senses created the counterculture in the United States. While Gorightly's estimation of Thornley's influence seems overstated to me, his role in creating the counterculture has been overlooked in many quarters, and one has to wonder

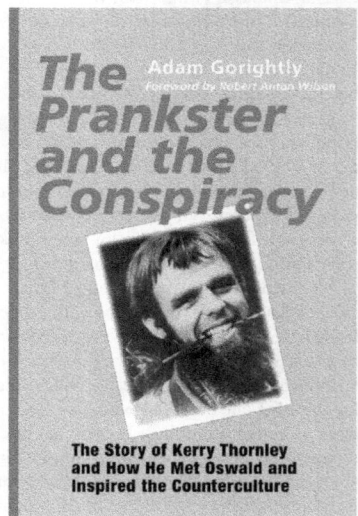

The
Prankster
and the
Conspiracy

Adam Gorightly
Foreword by Robert Anton Wilson

The Story of Kerry Thornley and How He Met Oswald and Inspired the Counterculture

how much Thornley's unwitting and unwilling role in the assassination of John F. Kennedy contributed to his name being forgotten more than it is remembered.

The Prankster and the Conspiracy is both Thornley's biography and an examination of conspiracy theory. Where conspiracy theory is concerned, Gorightly's refusal to settle on a specific opinion—preferring instead to lay out and analyze the facts—gives his book far more impact than would have registered had he just put on a tinfoil hat and delivered the standard "Warren report bad, Garrison good, Oswald patsy" line that has tarred those who truly worry that there was a CIA conspiracy to kill John F. Kennedy (hi, I am one of them).

One fact alone is strange enough: Thornley served in the Marines with Lee Harvey Oswald and wrote a book about Oswald *before* the JFK assassination.[5] According to Gorightly, he may also have been manipulated by the CIA during his time in New Orleans. Then again, Gorightly also considers evidence that he may *not* have manipulated by the CIA. Given how insane and paranoid Thornley became later in his life, it is hard to tell what really happened.

For example, Thornley claimed to know a very creepy man, Gary Kirstein, to whom he gave the nickname "Brother-in-law." Unfortunately, the only person who could have proved that Brother-in-law really existed died before anyone could question him on the subject. Others who lived in New Orleans at the time and knew Thornley could not verify that Brother-in-law existed. Whether he really existed or not, Kirstein was an unsettling influence in Thornley's life, planting ideas that made him think that perhaps he was subject to mind manipulation by the CIA. Specifically, Thornley believed this because he somehow or another (if at all) picked up rogue radio waves with his mind—a phenomenon that Brother-in-law, if he existed, seemed to know all about. Thornley later came to believe that Kirstein was actually the notorious CIA officer E. Howard Hunt. Gorightly is of the opinion that Brother-in-law could have been Hunt but does not stake his reputation on it.

And with the mention of E. Howard Hunt, the creepiest of the creepiest of spooks, you can tell that this is one helluva fun conspiracy tome. It's also one of the better ones because Gorightly, while clearly subject to interesting beliefs (aren't we all), maintains an air of interested speculation without ever confirming or denying anything. I was left with the feeling that Thornley was very likely on to something, that perhaps he was an unwitting participant in one of the darkest moments of U.S. history.

It's just that his subsequent mental illness makes it impossible to know the truth. One of Thornley's friends at the time, then Grace Caplinger, now better

---

5   The infamous picture of Oswald holding a rifle and a copy of a Communist rag, supposedly taken in his backyard, is very likely Oswald's head grafted onto Thornley's body.

known to some as character actress Grace Zabriskie, adds to the idea that Thornley's memory, or at least his interpretation of memory, is to be held in doubt. Thornley described himself as having a long affair with Grace. Grace recalls one incident of not-very-interesting sex. Thornley's ex-wife Cara likewise says she never experienced some of the things Thornley claimed, like three black helicopters flying over their home. As Thornley drifted further and further into psychosis, it is impossible to know what happened and Thornley's life does not make it any easier to parse out.

Peripatetic, even when he remained in one city for a while, Thornley never seemed to live in the same place for long. He was a man who both brought about change and was subject to it. Like a Whitman poem, his mind contained inconsistent multitudes. He initially believed the Lone Gunman theory of the JFK assassination and wrote a book, *Oswald*, explaining this theory. He later recanted this theory, becoming convinced Oswald was a CIA plant who was assigned the job to ferret out Communist sympathizers in the military and was later a part of a fringe CIA conspiracy to assassinate JFK. Jim Garrison, no small loon himself, called Thornley to a grand jury in order to recount the testimony he gave to the Warren Commission, and was so angered with Thornley's about face that he charged Thornley with perjury, though the charges were later dropped.

Though *The Prankster and the Conspiracy* does speak of a mentally healthy Thornley (relatively speaking), much of the book documents his decline into mental states that even I find unnerving. After his divorce from his wife Cara, Thornley went through an exhibitionist sexual phase. This seems normal enough in some quarters; people experiment with all forms of freedom when long-term relationships end. But in the manner of many recent biographies that find terrible skeletons hidden in long-forgotten closets, it is suggested that Thornley may have had pedophilic tendencies (though if he had them, they were of a short duration and he regained his sense of restraint and decency). One can see this man becoming so mentally adrift that the sexual freedom he helped herald in could, in a drug haze, cause him to misapply his sexual freedom to children. If it seems like I am using too many words and dancing around the topic, that's exactly what I am doing. I hate the idea that even unhinged Thornley could wander so far afield that he could not see the lack of morality in sexual interaction with children. Though this is a very small part of the book, it stuck with me.

Thornley died in 1998 of complications from a rare disease called Wegener's Granulomatosis, and though his madness cleared enough at times to permit him moments of humor and clarity, one of the ways I know he was probably deeply entrenched in psychosis is that in his last days, he evidently had a friendship, if not a romantic relationship, with Sondra London. My distaste for London runs hard and deep. She has become such a scourge in her by now routine attempts to cozy up to violent murderers for a chance at love, fame and potential book fodder that actual death row inmates call her a skeeve. She pissed on the memories of the brutally murdered as a self-admitted serial killer lovingly serenaded her in court while she beamed like a teen girl being courted for the first time. I never really saw her as a person much interested in telling the stories of the insane, the broken or the criminally violent as much as someone who would do anything for money, publicity or to satisfy her admitted hybristophilia (or, to paraphrase her, she likes bad boys).

London is a loathsome human being who has made a career out of manipulating deeply mentally ill or psychopathic, if not psychotic, killers into collaborating with her on books (her collaboration with the disturbed and completely ill Nicolas Claux is truly disturbing—asking that man to illustrate a book on vampire killers is in no way subversive or in the spirit of Discordianism; it's just exploitative and completely callous).

That Brother-in-law set off Thornley's creepometer while London did not speaks of deep psychological pathology on his part. Gorightly had her number though, stating that even though London possessed recordings of Thornley that would be important for any biographer, she claimed her status as his one true love prevented her from sharing them. Until she was offered money. And poor Thornley, to be on that woman's list of "true loves," right there with Gerard Schaeffer, Danny Rolling and Keith Jesperson, vile killers who now revile her.

But back to Thornley. No matter what your opinion is of the JFK assassination (or even Thornley's role in it), it's safe to assert that the madness and paranoia that plagued him in his later life was sparked by those who were either involved in the assassination or who used the assassination to push their personal agenda. He started off as a sparkling trickster and died sick and paranoid, a very sad ending to be sure. *The Prankster and the Conspiracy* is an excellent biography and conspiracy synthesis. It is complex, interesting, mildly skeptical and interested in the truth but willing to admit it may never be known. It's evenhanded, open, scrutinizing, yet ultimately kind. I highly recommend it.

FURTHER READING

Historia Discordia
Adam Gorightly

The Illuminatus! Trilogy
Robert Shea and Robert Anton Wilson

The Franklin Cover-Up: Child Abuse, Satanism, and Murder in Nebraska

By John W. DeCamp
AWT, Inc. (1996)
Original post: 03/15/2010

Why do I consider this book odd?
The explanation is unavoidably circuitous, but here goes. *The Franklin Cover-Up* first crossed my radar shortly after Jeff Gannon—porn star and male escort *cum* White House reporter and Bush apologist—was outed. I simply wanted to know how such a man manged to secure high-clearance press credentials, but as I began reading up on him I stumbled upon a website devoted to a kidnapped child from Iowa. That's where I discovered that there are those who think Jeff Gannon is actually the grown-up incarnation of this cold-case kidnapping victim, named Johnny Gosch. Gosch's mother Noreen maintains that after her son was kidnapped in 1982 (when he was 12), he was forced into child porn and prostitution. The case of Johnny Gosch is as fascinating as it is sad, and reading about it means trawling through the bowels of many low-rent conspiracy websites. It was on one such site that I found a thread accusing Hunter S. Thompson of being linked to the Gosch kidnapping. Why? Because a supposed-ly "reputable" source claimed that Thompson produced kiddie porn snuff films. And that "reputable source," as you've probably guessed, was this book—*The Franklin Cover-Up*. So, Yeah. When a book has you yelling, "Oh my god!" before you even crack the spine, you know you're in for a walk on the odd side.

John DeCamp's *The Franklin Cover-Up* is catnip conspiracy theory. It's amaz-ingly insane and involved, with just enough grains of truth here and there that you can't help but get sucked in. I probably buy about one eighth of what DeCamp is selling. The rest is just so whacked and beyond the realm of reason that it'll make your eyes itch.

Conspiracy theories about ritual and Satanic sexual abuse are cyclical in nature. It can be tempting to trace them back to resurgent conservative cur-rents, but it's not that easy to pin down why we get clusters of these sorts of stories in the United States. The so-called "Franklin Scandal" (or Franklin "Cover-Up," as DeCamp would have it) is especially confounding in this regard. The scandal got its legs during the Reagan administration, and the conspiratorial speculation that followed targeted conservatives and liberals alike (notably George H. W. Bush). At its core, the Franklin Scandal is a homosexual panic. Once you move past the hard evidence of financial wrongdoing and outright treason involved in the Franklin Savings and Loan and its links to the Iran-Contra scandal, the salacious rumors of sexual deviancy revolve around adult men preying mainly on younger men and adolescent boys. Not all of the claimed victims in the Franklin Scandal are boys—Alisha Owen plays a large role as a victim in the narrative—but when you read the evidence DeCamp provides in his book, you'll see a trend. He can't help but casually equate homosexuality with deviance, even as he proclaims love and respect for his deceased homosexual brother.

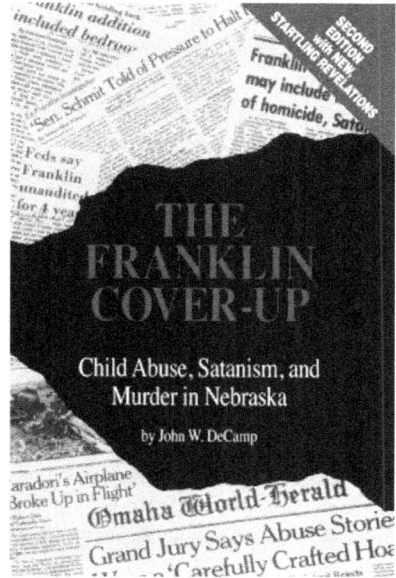

The recent Pizzagate conspiracy theory has revived interest in the Franklin Scandal among a new generation of online conspiracy enthusiasts. While Franklin-centered speculation has long been engaged (and expanded) in the chambers of a surprising number of fringe web communities, and while people have never really stopped discussing the details and arguing over whether or not Jeff Gannon is really Johnny Gosch (and over exactly what happened at those Bohemian Grove gatherings), it was Pizzagate that broke the dam. It was Pizzagate that brought the sordid details of this Reagan-era conspiracy theory back to the first page of Google hits. If you're not familiar with Pizzagate, then you might want to pause for a moment and go Google it. It's a sprawling conspiracy theory, but somewhere near its core is the assertion—or speculation, if we're being careful—that Democratic campaign weasel John Podesta used coded verbiage that pedophiles use to communicate with each other in emails and online forums. While I am still digging around in the various communities that discuss Pizzagate, I can say that the emails *are* strange. "Cheese pizza" is evidently commonly used as a byword for "child pornography" among pedophiles, and the ways that references to "pizza" come up in Podesta's emails are, to an outsider like me, inexplicable. Then again, people have advanced persuasive counter-arguments and provided innocuous explanations as to what Podesta and those he was emailing were trying to communicate, so who knows?

Regardless of whether or not there is a tendril of truth in the Pizzagate conspiracy theorizing, it neatly fits in alongside the Franklin abuse conspiracy theory. Both theories presuppose that political and financial elites use their power and money to prey upon children, and both theories implicate political power-brokers at the highest levels of government (though Pizzagate is more conspicuously partisan in that respect).

The sprawling nature of Pizzagate and the whole Franklin-descended pervert-elite narrative comes into sharper focus as we broaden the cultural lens. Consider Anthony Weiner's conviction for sexting a fifteen-year-old girl, or the recent revelations of sexual harassment and rape in the entertainment industry. And as I write these words there are alarming roilings among the "former child actor" community regarding predation and rape by Hollywood elites. All of this has surfaced alongside Pizzagate, or shortly after the Wikileaks-enabled analysis of those curious emails came to light. Whatever your assessment of Pizzagate or the Franklin scandal that preceded it, we are left to contend with credible evidence that there is indeed a coterie of elites who do what they want to whom they want with very little interference, at least until their behaviors become too outrageous to ignore.

The sense that elites prey upon the common man (or his children, in the current narrative) fuels much modern conspiracy theory. To Franklin Scandal True Believers, the narrative rests on the assertion that politicians and financiers during the 1980s shipped children from Nebraska to be sexually assaulted at GOP gatherings. The names and places have changed, but it all fits in extremely well with the assertions made among Pizzagate True Believers. That's the backdrop for any relevant analysis of conspiracy theory that follows, even if it's complicated by credible—and verifiable—revelations of sexual abuse involving political snakes and Hollywood casting couch creeps.

So I'm going to tread carefully. It's important to note, after all, that issues of proof with reference to the set of lurid claims in DeCamp's *The Franklin Cover-Up* are not resolved just because we are now being shown the underbelly of the entertainment industry. People do terrible things to the weak, and that has always been the case. Acknowledging this is important. It can even help us understand why the Franklin sex abuse theories—and similar theories surrounding Pizzagate—continue to enthrall and appall those who are suspicious of people who wield power. It is not, however, enough to redeem the whole of a narrative that ultimately rests on hearsay and innuendo rather than hard evidence.

First, let's dispense with the whole Hunter S. Thompson thing. There are two sentences in *The Franklin Cover-Up* that refer to Thompson as someone who filmed kiddie snuff porn. The person making the central accusation is a man who evidently suffered from Dissociative Identity Disorder (or Multiple Personality Disorder as it was called when this book was initially written). I have no idea what DeCamp really knows of Thompson, but he quotes another source who describes him as a "well known sleaze-culture figure," whatever that means. In any case, it does not appear that Thompson was ever visually identified by Paul Bonacci, the man making the claim, and no greater research went into proving it. Evidently another young woman claimed that Thompson tried to make her watch a snuff film but she didn't watch whatever it was. Was it the horror film *Snuff*? Was it *Cannibal Holocaust*, which some still believe qualifies as a snuff film because of the live animal deaths included in it? Was she making it up? Did she misunderstand? We don't know. All we have is an unverified statement from some woman and two lines in a nutty book attributed to a young man whose origins no one has been able to trace and whose lies or delusions have fueled a bizarre conspiracy theory.

The Franklin Cover-Up was initially released in 1992, when Thompson was alive and active. If anyone had any evidence that the famed Gonzo journalist filmed children being killed during sex, he would have been investigated thoroughly. By no other account was Thompson a man who showed such vile proclivities. Yet he was a thorn in the side of authority, and if there were any credible reason to suspect he had been involved in something so reprehensible, the police would have been only too glad to bring the hammer down. The libel against Hunter S. Thompson is based on a couple of dubiously sourced lines in a dubiously conceived book.

So let there be no more said on this topic. On your head be it if you decide to smear the name of a man whose career completely belied any association with such deviance without any proof other than hearsay from a fragile man who makes all sorts of extraordinary claims because one suspects he may be too mentally ill *not* to make such claims. Case closed.

Now, let's get back to the heart of the book. Because even for the seasoned conspiratologist, it's a humdinger. We get a full dose of Satanic Panic, with cabals of Satanists killing children, burning their bodies and grinding up their bones and teeth. We get pedophile rings, with well-stationed VIP members ranking all the way up to the White House flying kids out from Nebraska for sexual purposes. We get the full panoply of Bush era fusion paranoia, with references to militias, Oklahoma City, the Montana Seven, the Monarch Project, Bohemian Grove and the Gosch kidnapping (but no Jeff Gannon, alas—perhaps DeCamp will issue a new edition?). Along the way DeCamp reminds us of the utter shittiness of Bob Kerrey (a subject on which I whole-heartedly agree[6]) and he weaves in links to Iran-Contra, Lyndon LaRouche and the obligatory conspiracy to murder witnesses. We

---

6   I can easily see a man who lied about being a war criminal for so many years lying about all the other things DeCamp claims.

also find a ready chorus of True Believers in the background, insisting that a default judgment in a civil court case means proof of wrongdoing, that it is impossible that anyone involved in the scandal could possibly have died in a commuter plane crash that was wholly unrelated to the alleged cover-up (so it had to be a murder), that using candles is "Satanic," and that there can be no possible reason anyone would want to lie about such terrible things.

When you consider the sheer *density* of conspiratorial content on display, it's sort of an amazing achievement. And I'm leaving out a lot. Honestly, there's too much to go into, even given my verbose nature.

For all this madness, on the most basic level, I think there is still a *kernel* of truth in *The Franklin Cover-Up* that needs to be acknowledged. If seven eighths (if not more) of DeCamp's feverish speculation can be readily dismissed, we are left with the fact that the Franklin Credit Union in Omaha was run by a man named Larry King (not *that* Larry King), who embezzled approximately $40 million and almost undoubtedly molested children. The credit union was probably involved in the Iran-Contra scandal. Although the stolen money was never reliably traced, it appears that most of the embezzled funds went into parties, stretch limos and access to private planes. King probably did have the sex parties described in the book, though I think the truth of the situation is exaggerated. But yeah, I can see that happening. Most of DeCamp's stories are at least implausible, but this much seems to be backed by evidence.

Not all the kids were in complicit foster homes, nor were they "of the street" (didn't the orphanages or parents notice when the kids, some youngsters, went missing for days on end as they were carted from one locale to the other for sex). And some of the things that the chief witnesses described could have caused grave harm, certainly permanent scars or physical damage, so it seems important to note that there is no mention of a physical examination being given to any of the witnesses. Moreover, one of the witnesses claims she gave birth to a police chief's child. A paternity demand to this day could prove her side of the story, and since she is serving hard time for perjury, it's baffling that this obvious step hasn't been taken.[7]

You have to keep in mind that DeCamp, while clearly holding some wacky beliefs, also fell down the rabbit hole in the 1980s. Do you remember the 1980s? That was when *Michelle Remembers* was still believed to be a factual account of ritual abuse and recovered memory. That was when not even accredited psychologists knew how to question abused children without leading them to say all sorts of fanciful things. DeCamp is a True Believer. As

---

7   Alisha Owen's child has since been definitively proven not to be the result of any sort of sexual activity between Alisha Owen and police chief Robert Wadman. That's is a huge problem for anyone who wants to believe Owen's tales of institutionalized and systemic child rape condoned and committed by Omaha police.

such, he dismisses any lack of evidence as evidence of a greater conspiracy. The conspiracy is easily expanded to involve law enforcement, and any reticence among the media is just as easily explained in terms of institutionalized stonewalling. As for any evidence that should weigh against the panic narrative, well that can be discounted as the handiwork of shadowy figures who will concoct lies to cover up and covertly encourage the abuse of children. I don't know exactly why men like DeCamp fall down this rabbit hole, but I understand how it happens. So while I find his wild-eyed speculation to be a little icky, his intent belief in the unbelievable does not surprise me.

Nor was I surprised to find the unpleasant, sticky presence of Ted Gunderson, former FBI agent, in this book. Gunderson believes in Satanic Panic mythology to this day. He also believes all kinds of bizarre things, as I will discuss. He's either a loon or crazy like a fox. Either way, he is dangerous. Gunderson is also lawsuit-happy, suing people whom he claims have slandered him, including people who have clear screws loose and are more deserving of pity than a litigious smackdown.[8] I can say without any hesitation that Gunderson's investigative presence in the Johnny Gosch kidnapping (and sadly, as most believe, murder) has kept the vulnerable Noreen Gosch in a realm of desperate credulity, where she will believe anything as long as it provides some vestige of hope that her son is alive. It has made her prey to con men and trolling tormentors. I dream of seeing Gunderson in a whacked-theory cage match with someone—I just can't think of whom I would inflict Ted on. Art Bell already won an out of court settlement against him,[9] so he's out of the running. To this day, Gunderson believes the McMartin preschool molestation/Satanic ritual abuse case happened as initially reported, and he has fought to send falsely accused people to prison. He is a wicked and nasty man who preys on vulnerable souls. Perhaps it's not entirely logical for me to assert that I automatically believe the opposite of anything he has to say, but that's actually close to the truth.[10]

The Franklin case is riddled with the same issues that plague every other Satanic Panic case. For starters, there are no bodies. DeCamp reports that the murdered children and babies were killed and subsequently burned, their bones and teeth crushed into meal. What happened to that meal remains, conveniently, a mystery. If a sample could be produced, it would still be laden

---

8   Google Ted Gunderson and the name Barbara Hartwell and just marvel at the sadness of it all.

9   The former host of *Coast to Coast AM* won an out of court settlement against Gunderson, who accused Bell of being a child molester. Since the settlement came with a gag order, there are no firm facts available for public consumption, and such information that is available comes from sources that I would rather not mention, lest I become overrun with avid True Believers from the whole rainbow spectrum of conspiracy-land—and if you think *I'm* verbose...

10   A moot point, since Gunderson has been dead since 2011. I should also note that John DeCamp died on July 27, 2017, around the time I was revising this discussion for the *TL;DR* anthology.

with forensic evidence that would back these lurid claims. Sites where bone grinding occurred could to this day be excavated and tested for evidence of human remains. It's also worth noting that the allegedly murdered kids were not the children of presumed cult members, so where did they come from? The insertion of Johnny Gosch's sad story is likely a cynical attempt to persuade readers to believe that missing children were used in cult rituals, but was any attempt made to match the descriptions of those the witnesses say they saw killed with contemporaneous case files of abducted children? In a book about such an investigation, there is no mention of such due diligence.

The Satanic Panic was the Salem Witch Trials with a newer face. These trends of mass delusion and hysteria have always happened and will continue to happen. I certainly do not believe that Paul Bonacci watched as a baby was sacrificed, nor do I think he was raped with a cattle prod-like instrument (how he could survive that without immediate emergency surgery is beyond belief). I don't think he was forced into necrophilia with a murdered child. I think he was molested, and I think the experience left him damaged beyond belief. I think a bunch of adults led him to conclusions he knew they wanted him to reach.

Unlike the skeevy psychologist involved in the whole *Michelle Remembers* hoax, I don't get the feeling that DeCamp operates from a place of jaded cynicism. I will, however, note that with the publication of the second edition of *The Franklin Cover-Up*, it seems that DeCamp is now working more with militias than purported SRA survivors. I find that interesting. But to reiterate, DeCamp does come off as sincere. He also makes some points that resonate, even with a skeptic like me.

But there are elements of the book that are...off putting—not the least being that DeCamp was willing to defame Hunter S. Thompson based on the testimony of a very fragile witness. While I can't go into every single problem I have with this very dense book, I will touch on a few egregious examples to provide a better sense of where and why DeCamp goes astray. I am well aware that I can't debunk a conspiracy. The minds of True Believers will simply widen the lens to account for anything that doesn't fit. What I can do to my own satisfaction is discuss a few WTF moments in *The Franklin Cover-Up*, moments when I felt kind of annoyed with DeCamp's credulous narration, or disgust at the presence of Ted Gunderson.

One big problem, as touched on above, is DeCamp's heavy reliance on witness testimony without corroborative physical evidence, or even common sense. DeCamp believes Bonacci because Bonacci can describe in very sound detail an event that DeCamp himself attended, and that goes to the core of the issue of proof. On its face, this seems like a reasonable baseline. If the kid had access to the same event that DeCamp attended, he would have the same details. But how could children have attended national fundraisers for the GOP to serve as sex slaves, yet no one else has any memory of such doings? It defies reason to suggest that every single person in attendance was a pedophile or a pedophile sympathizer and would therefore keep silent about their peers committing child rape. So if those kids were there, how were they explained? Some people brought their children, but how is it that the victims have memories of these events but no one remembers the presence of random children?

Could it be because they were fed information, perhaps unwittingly, perhaps even by DeCamp? Analysis of recordings of questioning tactics used in famously discredited Satanic Panic cases show how even people who think they are scrupulous interviewers pass leading information to their subjects. The main questioner in this case is dead so all we see is DeCamp's account, and he seldom shows the back and forth between Gary Caradori and the witnesses. Moreover, the stilted dialogue DeCamp uses to further his conspiratorial narrative should cause any reasonable reader to question his recall, as hopefully some of the passages I quote will show. He seems to be only too willing to fill in blanks. I will admit this is a judgment call on my part, but it's based on my familiarity with the shameful history of similar investigations.

At the risk of courting reprisal, I will once again assert that DeCamp, a religious family man, has issues with homosexuals. He is quick to protest this assertion, noting that his own brother died from AIDS and that he considered him a fine human being. I don't doubt that this much is true and I don't for a moment want to minimize a family tragedy, but in light of what comes next, DeCamp's preemptive rejoinder has the familiar ring of the old "some of my best friends" line that people use to deflect accusations of racism. Thus in a case where a man may have been sexually harassed by another man at work, the situation, as DeCamp frames it, quickly comes to entail a homosexual cabal that pressures men into deviancy. The way DeCamp discusses homosexuality, even keeping in mind the context in which he is discussing it, it's difficult to shake the impression that he sees homosexuality as something inherently sinister.

> "So tell me," I said, "just what is at the bottom of it? If it is not laundered money involved in the Iran-Contra scandal, what the blazes is it? How could Larry King get away with this, without you or somebody else knowing what was going on? Looks to me as if he had to have one heck of a lot of powerful political protection at the highest levels."

> "Homosexuals," Fenner said. "Franklin finances the biggest group of homosexuals any state has ever seen…"

> "Are you telling me that the Franklin theft and scandal was just one big queer party, with a bunch of rich people who don't want their involvement known?" I asked.

> "Yes," replied Fenner…

I can't even be sarcastic here. *Queer party*. Even in the pre-PC language age, this is a dick statement, especially for a man with a gay brother.

There's more.

> Gray's own sexual proclivities were the subject of an article in the July-August 1982 issue of *The Deep Backgrounder*,[11] entitled "Reagan Inaugural Co-Chairman Powerful 'Closet Homosexual'?" The Deep Backgrounder tabloid featured exposes of homosexual networks in Washington, DC…

Homosexual networks, eh? How very nefarious. My god, will no one do anything about the Log Cabin Republicans? If DeCamp really has no issue with gay people, the way he uses words and the way he portrays purported "homosexual networks" are tough to explain.

DeCamp's puritanism and his willingness to discredit people on the basis of hearsay about their sexual habits runs deep. This next passage refers to an Assistant US Attorney who felt Alisha Owen was lying and was over the top in his attempts to get to her recant:

> Long before Thalken's behavior in dealing with Owen, his name had surfaced in Gary Caradori's investigation, as an alleged pedophile who frequented adult book stores in Council Bluffs, Iowa.

Oh man, *I've* been in an adult book store. Several. In Dallas. Which is way seedier than Council Bluffs, Iowa. What, I wonder, could DeCamp find me guilty of? Also, hearsay, hearsay, hearsay. But then, all the pedophilia allegations in this book rely on hearsay. The only proven fact is that Larry King embezzled money.

But worse than the implicit gay bashing, consider how DeCamp justifies some of his other information. For the record, Larry King is a black man.

> If King was involved with CIA money laundering, that jibes with a report from a member of Concerned Parents: "I heard from two different black people in North Omaha that King used to send limousines down to Offutt Air Force Base [home of the Strategic Air Command] to pick up CIA personnel for parties."

Well that seals the deal, doesn't it? Not only is this some topnotch investigation (hearsay of hearsay from unidentified people), but of course, because every black person must know every other black person in Omaha, how can this solid proof be impeached? Bleah.

Then there are moments so bizarre that I had to read them several times to make sure the text was saying what I thought it was saying. In the midst of describing what she considered to be Satanic behavior, one witness (who later died and I have no desire to sully her name further) says:

> There are certain things that are in common with the children's stories

---

11   AND LOL AT THAT PARTICULAR TITLE!

when we talk about devil worship... There are things that come up in every single story, such as candles. They all talk about sex."

Candles? Really? Is that really a marker for Satanism? Even the vanilla scented ones they sell at Target?

There are unintentionally revealing moments in the same woman's testimony.

> We were real sure, we knew he had not been around these other children and heard anything, but we began to question ourselves, "Are we asking strange questions. Is there something odd about us which makes children come and dump these things on us?"

Yes, I'd wager there is something odd about the people who manage to get this sort of information out of children consistently, children who do not know each other, children who did not even have, according to some of this woman's earlier words, the power of speech until they came to live with you. Every Satanic Panic can be traced to an epicenter. At that epicenter you will find people who get on a hobby horse and ride it until they get the information out of suggestible witnesses, mostly children, that feeds their particular conspiracy.

This same woman died in a car crash that "former FBI abuse specialist Ted Gunderson" deemed "a satanic contract suicide."

> The other driver didn't die, but well could have; in satanic lore, a person who loses his life in such a contract murder/suicide will be reincarnated with more power, granted by Satan.

What lore, one wonders. A basic Google search for "satanic contract suicide" leads me nowhere but back to Gunderson and this book. And how did *reincarnation* get mixed in with Satanism anyway? Seeing as how Satanism is a pretty concretely wedded to Christianity, where one gets one life and one life only, isn't that the basis for why offering that life to a force of evil has such power? If you get multiple lives, you can be a wicked Satanist in this life, accept Jesus in the next, and keep playing until you're ahead of the game, right? How did we get to such bizarre ideas? Could it be because Ted Gunderson made them up?

Finally, it should come as no surprise that DeCamp refuses to name many of his sources. I'm sure you can imagine the excuses.

The fact of the matter is that most people know by now that the world can be a terrible place. We are exposed to atrocity daily. In this Information Age, we have come to expect the worst and we have no trouble believing it when it is presented to us believably. Thus it is not too much to expect there to be more proof than hearsay in these matters. If missing children are killed in Satanic rings, produce forensic evidence. How about a name? Anything more than someone's word?

Despite any good intentions DeCamp had in writing this book, he really did more harm than good. Lacking evidence other than problematic victim testimony, no abuse victim was believed. None of those kids saw justice, aside from the mild justice Bonacci received when Larry King failed to respond to a civil case and Bonacci was awarded a million dollars (which he will never receive). No one went to prison for child abuse. If the goal was justice, DeCamp did not deliver. And I wonder how many children were disbelieved after this mess?

It's entertaining conspiracy theory, to be sure. If that's your drug, I say read it with a highlighter and a cocktail at hand. Just be aware that there is no justice, and little truth, down the rabbit hole. And Ted Gunderson is there. That, more than any of the content in this book, should keep you up at night.

Further Reading

We Believe the Children: A Moral Panic in the 1980s
Richard Beck

The Myth of Repressed Memory: False Memories and Allegations of Sexual Abuse
Dr. Elizabeth Loftus

Rumour in Orléans
Edgar Morin

Meta-#Pizzagate: On the 'Unspeakable Rites' of Those Who Rule Our Demon-ocracy
Andy Nowicki

The United States of Paranoia: A Conspiracy Theory
Jesse Walker

1996
By Gloria Naylor (yes, *that* Gloria Naylor)
Third World Press (2007)
Original post: 08/27/2010

Why do I consider this book odd?
Just bear with me for a moment. Back when I stumbled across information about Johnny Gosch and the Franklin Scandal,[12] I somehow ended up on the site of a woman called Eleanor White. Eleanor is a person who believes in "gang stalking," meaning that organized groups of government entities and private citizens are stalking her, breaking into her home, wearing out her clothes, destroying her furniture, leaving mounds of dirt on her kitchen floor, tapping her phone calls, harassing her at work, following her every move and using advanced technology to read her mind. The site had some unintentionally hilarious moments, like when White or someone else posted pictures of some very ratty long johns worn through at the crotch as proof that someone was breaking into their home and wearing out their clothes.

But ultimately there was nothing funny about any of it. Whether or not you believe these people's claims, the fact remains that they think this is happening to them and some are terrified. White had a substantial list of links to sites that explored gang stalking, and the first link in that list was to a review of Gloria Naylor's *1996*. So I had to get a copy. It took me a while to make myself read it. And I don't even really want to discuss it because I know that the end result will be a lot of emails and comments from people who genuinely think they are victims of gang stalking, who will accuse me of being part of the vast conspiracy of people loosening the buttons on their coats, replacing their new tires with bald radials or beaming thought rays into their brains to inspire suicide.

But I read it. And by my own messed up, self-imposed rules, discuss it I must.

I am a grad school dropout. I finished one semester and realized I just wasn't cut out for it. I was 26 and didn't want anybody telling me what to read anymore because I just wanted to be left alone with my true crime novels,

---

12   See my discussion of John W. DeCamp's *The Franklin Cover-Up* above.

my conspiracy theories, my Loch Ness monster photo analyses and my Fay Weldons. I flat out didn't have the mental discipline to get my Master's, which was no surprise really because as an undergrad I would stay up until the wee hours after studying to read the books I wanted to read, sometimes faking my way through classes because I couldn't bring myself to read *Beowulf* or *Mrs. Dalloway*. But in that one semester of grad school, I took an African-American women's writers class and studied Zora Neale Hurston, Alice Walker, Toni Morrison and Gloria Naylor. We read *The Women of Brewster Place* and *Mama Day*. *Mama Day* was not a great novel, but not a bad one either. *The Women of Brewster Place* won the National Book Award in 1983. It was also a favorite of Oprah Winfrey, who starred as one of the characters in the TV mini-series based on the book.

Gloria Naylor purchased a dream home on St. Helena Island in South Carolina. She set out to spend her summers gardening there, relaxing away from New York. All was idyllic except for Eunice Simon's cats. Her neighbor's cats routinely dug up and defecated in her garden. Visiting with Simon did Naylor no good and relations between the two degenerated. Things came to a head when Naylor put out poison to kill tree rats and ended up killing one of Simon's cats instead. (Yes, as in every book I read these days, there is a dead cat in *1996*.) Things spiral completely out of control when Naylor loses it in a supermarket and snipes at Eunice, "You bitch." Simon hears, "Jew Bitch," and it's Katy bar the door.

At this point, the book slides completely into speculation. We get a retelling of what Naylor thinks must have happened (and bear in mind, Eunice Simon is a pseudonym, as are most of the names in this book, so trying to research what happened is impossible). According to Naylor, Simon's brother is highly placed in the National Security Agency. Though he evidently tires of his sister's histrionic behaviors, he investigates Naylor for his sister and finds that Naylor has tenuous social ties to Black Muslims and begins to make her life hell on those grounds. Using the anti-Jew sentiment that Eunice misheard in the supermarket combined with antisemitism perceived as the aim behind Black Muslim groups, Dick Simon from the NSA not only launches an investigative campaign against Naylor, but he also calls in the local Anti-Defamation League to assist.

Naylor's garden is killed off by stalkers. Her home is broken into. She is followed everywhere she goes. Her computer is hacked. Three students recruited by the NSA to torment her—she calls them "The Boys"—terrorize her at all hours. A friend who visits her is threatened. She returns to New York and the organized stalking continues. Every few minutes, cars stop and open and slam their doors outside her apartment. Neighbors let the NSA set up a computer and satellite in their home so that thought rays can be beamed into Naylor's brain. The thoughts they transmit are meant to cause her to try to kill herself. When Naylor resists the thought rays, the NSA ups the ante and begins to read her thoughts and respond to them in real time via typed words on a computer, a sort of inter-cranial instant message conversation. Untold amounts of money and man hours are spent on tailing and antagonizing Naylor, who accidentally killed a cat and spoke admiringly of Farrakhan's Million Man March.

Sigh.

I am not going to dither here as others have, refusing to comment on the factual truth of the events as Naylor perceives them. Outside of sites dedicated to gang stalking, you will find scholars weasel out of dealing with the horror of the content by stating what is largely irrelevant: that whether or not you believe Naylor was a victim of organized citizen and government stalking, isn't this an interesting look at race relations in America, a sober reminder of the potential for a tyrannical police state or a fascinating combination of narrative fiction and speculation?

That's some bullshit right there, folks.

I won't waffle because it's a condescending move. It's condescending not to state facts plainly because I don't want to look like I am calling a renowned writer crazy. Yes, race relations are still terrible in this country. Yes, the government is intrusive. And maybe Naylor set off a Jewish neighbor with some ties to the NSA and Naylor was investigated a bit rigorously as a result. But nothing else here that Naylor describes as a fictional narrative of true events is even plausible. There are those who think that the fallout of her dispute with her neighbor caused Naylor to become mentally ill. I have no idea about that, but I can agree that this book is full of delusions.

When a person says they are stalked, I can believe them. When a person says they were investigated rigorously by the government, I can believe it. Believe me, I can believe it. We all have stories to tell in this post *1984*, post 9/11 age. But when a person tells me that the government has been reading their mind with a computer and a satellite, typing in responses to their thoughts in an abusive argument, not only can I not believe it, but it brings into doubt even the rational, reasonable accusations the person made. Given the paranoiac belief that Jews are fueling the attacks against her, believing that Naylor has

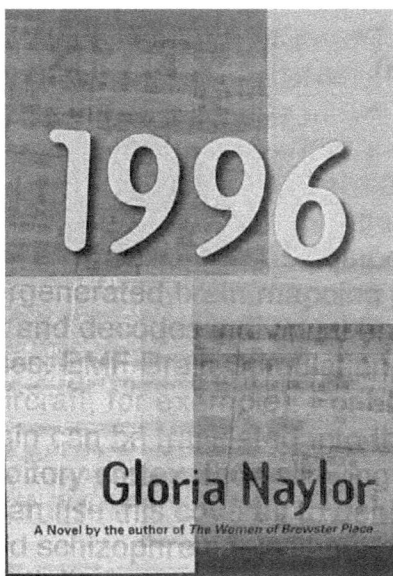

genuine understanding of what happened to her is crucial to being able to tolerate this book as much more than an anti-Jewish polemic in which a misunderstood insult in a grocery store can motivate the entire force of the Anti-Defamation League to wage a campaign of terror against a hapless author. But then again, I also think only a True Believer in the utter corruption and complete, almost God-like competence of our government will be able to believe the whole of *1996*.

Our government does terrible things and can never keep it a secret. The government tapped phones and monitored online usage of citizens after the invasion of Iraq and could not keep it secret. If our government had the power to read minds and implant thoughts, it would not be a classified secret for long and they would not invest the incredible man hours to use this technology on the handful of desperate people who think they are being abused in this manner. It took a team of people, if Naylor is to be believed, to organize the campaign against her, using private citizens in the ADL and members of the NSA, as well as students recruited and sent to the remote South Carolina island where she lived. Expensive and esoteric technology was installed in the homes of private citizens, agents were flown all over the country, homes were rented and countless man hours spent harassing Naylor, and not, say, the mafia, or suspected child molesters, or drug traffickers or groups the government thinks are subversive, like the actual Nation of Islam. Naylor, because she killed a cat and was suspected of uttering a Jewish slur, trumped all of the true criminals and counter-culture groups the NSA could have trailed.

Even if I am unable to believe much of what Naylor says, it also seems she was often her own worst enemy. She initially approached her neighbor with cookies to discuss the cats. The second time she went over, she was not particularly polite.

> She was doing what she could, she told me, but her babies needed exercise. I suggested she put them on a leash and walk them up and down the Avenue of the Oaks.

So, this little town has a New York writer who comes only for the summer and her closest neighbor is expected to keep her cats in when they are accustomed to having outside access. As an outsider in a small, insular town, Naylor's reaction to the situation with people who lived there full-time and for much longer than she had would have rankled everyone, even folk like me who think pet cats are safest indoors.

Oh yeah, this is where we also discover the cat Naylor dislikes the most is named Orwell. I am not making this up. Then she puts out poison for tree rats and accidentally fells the mighty Orwell. Had I been Eunice Simon, I too would have been terribly angry at Naylor for "accidentally" killing my cat.

As an outsider and a woman of color, Naylor's time in the South in a small town may have triggered some latent paranoia. And who's to say some paranoia was not warranted? Small towns in the South can suck mightily even for those who have lived in them for generations. The late Steve Gilliard discussed the complete culture shock he experienced when he, a man of color and a native New Yorker, visited South Carolina to see family.[13] As a woman who has lived in the South my entire life, I can tell you that despite the fact that we have a black President, entrenched and at times violent racism is still all too real. If Naylor got her neighbor's hackles up, I can understand why she may have had hers up as well. In the beginning, it seems easy to explain what is happening to Naylor, but later nothing is simple.

The death of Orwell the Cat triggers a series of suspicious events. There are break-ins. Naylor's garden gets ruined. And her computer is hacked. To someone not in the grips of paranoia, her computer compromise sounds more like hack-kiddies than a government probe.

> I booted up again, went back to into my WordPerfect program, and after a short while there was another spoof box that was labeled "Trouble." And the text in this window read, "Big Trouble. We're Gonna Die."

Naylor begins to wonder if the government was in fact responsible for the hack on her computer because the whole thing was very unprofessional. But instead of assuming that she was hacked because some hacker somewhere wanted to see if he or she could do it, she decides that perhaps private citizens working with the government are responsible, civilians she thinks have "the power to disrupt my life."

For the first fifty pages or so, I clung to the idea that maybe this was not going to be as bad as I anticipated but the next passage of Naylor's imaginings killed any hope that I was going to be able to finish this book without a heavy heart. This next passage comes from what Naylor imagines are the thoughts of an NSA agent.

> Looking around at the group gathered in Eunice Simon's living room, he realizes it isn't going to be easy. The room is packed with operatives from the ADL and NSA, and each is arguing for a piece of the action.

Yes. A room full of NSA agents and private citizens have assembled to argue over who gets to stalk, harass and terrorize a woman who killed a cat and has a tenuous connection with the Nation of Islam. If that seems reasonable to you, you may want to stop reading now.

It goes on:

> Things will be a lot more efficient now. First of all, they now have the manpower for blanket surveillance. There is no place she can go or plan to go without their knowledge. There is no one she can talk to, fax, or e-mail

---

13   I'd love to refer you to the post in question, but it seems that a lot of his work was lost in the ether after his death. Try the Wayback Machine, I guess.

without them knowing about it. They can follow her on trains, on planes and definitely in that red truck. She is a woman alone, for God's sake. She has no organization behind her, has few friends and no help. If she tries to get help, they'll know about it in plenty of time to divert it, or at least to plan their next strategy.

This passage is a litmus test. If you see how this could happen, chances are all of my discussion is an affront to you. If you wonder why it is that the US government and citizen groups would stalk one woman with this degree of manpower and organization when there are anti-government, overtly anti-Semitic and openly violent groups that pose a far greater threat to the fabric of this country than Naylor, then chances are you understand why this book gave me stomach cramps.

Once she returns to New York, Naylor seals the deal for anyone who was still on the fence as to whether or not she was completely delusional. After installing a tiny computer and satellite in Naylor's neighbors' home—her neighbors, in Naylor's mind, are complicit in the campaign of terror—a man Naylor calls Agent Browne demonstrates how the whole setup works.

> "Now," Agent Browne says, "aim the dish toward my head and type any word into the computer."
>
> Paulo types in "hello."
>
> "You typed 'hello,'" Agent Browne says. "Now, type in a whole sentence." Paulo types. Agent Browne still has his back to Paulo. "You typed 'Bring me the keys to the kingdom,'" Browne says. "And how do I know? I heard it." He taps his forehead. "I know what you're probably thinking, and believe me, this is no magic trick. You have in your hands some of the most advanced technology in the world. We've known for a couple of decades that sound can be produced in someone's head by radiating it with microwaves. It's now been refined to work with this computer program. This program translates key strokes into bursts of microwaves that bypass the ears and hit the auditory section of the brain. You are, in effect, speaking directly to the brain. And the brain 'hears' you. For all the target knows, she's just had a fleeting thought that originated within her."

Naylor then goes on to say that the satellite has a 50-foot range and the vocabulary of the computer is 72,000 words. This is mad science. None of this science is now or has ever been a threat. The government may be working on it, but aside from the research of paranoiacs who believe every patent filed equals a complete project, there is no proof. This is science fiction and it gets more fantastic as more science fiction is added to the equation. When simply beaming thoughts into Naylor's head does not work, Dick Simon shows up with a newer infernal device.

> "This is vastly different from what you've been using because it gives you feedback. You know what an EEG is—a machine that reads brain waves.

Well, this is the mother of all EEGs because it translates the brain waves that make up thought. Every time you think a word or a sentence, you hear it inside your head, don't you. This machine hears it as well as prints it out onto this screen."

[…]

"It's a world without secrets," Paulo says.

"No more secrets," Simon says. "We've unlocked the last frontier where secrets can be kept—within the human mind."

"What's the vocabulary range?" Paulo asks.

"One hundred thousand words in English. But we've programmed in many more languages than that. The best part of this for you is that once you've read her mind, you can respond with the microwave hearing device, and she'll hear you the same way she's been hearing you for weeks."

"So, it's like she's holding a conversation with herself," Hallum says.

This mindreading, thought-implanting device drives Naylor to a psychiatrist, who ends up being bullied by the stalking crew and comes to believe Naylor's tale of persecution. I wish he had come forward to back up her story, but perhaps the psychiatrist is as speculative as the idea that Eunice Simon has a brother in the NSA willing to do all of this.

And from there, Naylor sets about gathering highly questionable evidence to prove that her mind is being read. She cites the case of John St. Clair Akwei, a former NSA employee who claims that in 1990-1991 he was harassed electronically with the same devices Naylor claims were used on her. He sued and his claims were entered into court record, and this "evidence" has been used by those who need it to prove a vast conspiracy on the part of the government to stalk its citizens and read their minds.

As Naylor continues with her evidence, she cites Barbara Hartwell as a source. That's when I almost quit reading in despair. But of course, Eleanor White—she of the site I mention above—is also given as a source that there is such a thing as synthetic telepathy. And Cheryl Welsh is mentioned. I can't even go into detail here about why these sources are so questionable. It's just too sad. Google their names if it helps to put all of this into perspective.

Naylor herself recognizes the terrible problem involved in all of this "proof."

Their problem was the same as mine and other victims of mind control technology: how do you get people to believe? Unfortunately, information on mind control is sandwiched between reports of underground tunnels where gray aliens work for the U.S. government and sightings of UFOs. Quack stuff… Most people who love their country don't trust their government. Even if you got them to concede that the government has such technology, their next question would be, "How do you know that it's happening to you?" Your only response would be, "I know it's happening to me because it's happening to me."

And that's a whole lot of problem, isn't it? Because given that believers in mind control think this technology is being kept in neighbors' homes, being used by arrogant college students recruited to stalk them, and is so available that it can be dredged up to be used against the innocuous likes of Gloria Naylor, Eleanor White and Cheryl Welsh, is it too much to ask for someone somewhere to get one of these machines and demonstrate how it works? You could take it to sympathetic authorities—like the psychiatrist that Naylor says believes her—and show the world, instead of relying on speculation.

Let me pose a hard question for those who believe they are victims of excessive government probes that include stalking, mindreading and the like: what makes you so special that the government or any person in the government wants you dead or wants to spend millions of dollars tormenting you? There is a damnably sad level of narcissism that permits a person to think they are the focus of such negative energy, expense and pointless aggravation. There is an even more damnable randomness to this—Eleanor White and Gloria Naylor have been subject to mind control but John Gotti and my third grade teacher have not. Why Naylor and not J.D. Salinger, Ingrid Newkirk, Spike Lee or, frankly, me? The randomness to which citizens get selected for this sort of abuse is baffling.

Naylor herself knows that discussing this is almost futile. Her pleas for understanding and her almost bitter reconstructions of how she thinks people will react are heartbreaking. In the following passage she is talking through Dick Simon. He speculates about how they will be doing Naylor a favor if they finally drive her to suicide rather than let her face the humiliation that will come from publishing a book about her ordeal:

> They will be saving her from the public humiliation of having this book trashed in every review medium in the country. That is, if she even finds a publisher. They'll shake their heads sadly over the fact that a writer of her caliber has gone bonkers. She's seeing Jews coming out of the woodwork, government agents tapping her phone and hacking into her computer, cars mysteriously driving past her when she's out in the street. Was she planning on fiction or science-fiction? Either way it would be doomed. In the best-case scenario for her, she would find a publisher to print her nonsense and it sells more than fifty copies, but there she would be the queen of the weir-does [sic], crowned by the same people who brought you UFOs at Roswell, time travel and invisible CIA agents.

It is a mistake to think that because Naylor is an intelligent woman whose writing shows integrity that she cannot also experience moments of deep instability. She has the self-awareness to understand how unbelievable her story is, but this it does not mean that she is not suffering from paranoid delusions. Many think that such delusions would render her a gibbering mess who could no longer write or have a normal life outside of the scope of her delusions. That is not the case. This happens to people. While it absorbs most of their lives, it does not mean they cannot pay rent or buy groceries. We just don't expect it to happen to a woman whose first attempt at writing garnered her such high accolades. We don't expect it to happen to a woman who has achieved great literary fame because Oprah liked her book. As Naylor says herself in *1996*:

> Paranoia is a slow poison, and a lethal one. It usually starts with small things and then grows to color almost everything in your life.

She is right. Yet I hope she is wrong in the long run because Naylor is a talented novelist whose place in literary history does not need to be tainted because she had a break with reality and wrote a book about it. I hope one day she leaves behind these delusions—she may have and we don't know. But in a way, Dick Simon was also right. The best case scenario has played out. Few people know about this book and hopefully this cancerous paranoia will not be a part of Naylor's legacy.

Postscript (2017)

I am still not entirely convinced that gang stalking is the reality many think it is but my stance on the issue is not as firm as it was when I initially wrote this entry. Interestingly, the FBI files that were released about Ernest Hemingway caused me to change my mind.[14] People dismissed Hemingway's insistence that his phones were bugged, that his mail was being intercepted and that someone was stalking him, but it turns out all of that was indeed happening. He was being investigated aggressively because of his pro-Cuban stance. Stranger things have happened since, and while I see no proof that there are microwaves that can read our minds, I can no longer dismiss the idea that large entities can organize against a single individual for very trivial reasons.

FURTHER READING

Dangerous Dossiers: Exposing the Secret War Against America's Greatest Authors
Herbert Mitgang

---

14   You can read the report online at https://vault.fbi.gov/ernest-miller-hemingway/ernest-hemingway-part-01-of-01/view (accessed 10/01/2017). The Feds' interest in Hemingway really began in earnest after he started his own strange anti-fascist resistance/spy organization in Cuba. The FBI also encouraged the notion that Hemingway was deeply mentally ill—which he *was*, but he was still grounded in reality. His complaints of being followed and monitored were ignored by his friends, who thought he was delusional. One such friend was his biographer A.E. Hotchner, who deeply regrets brushing aside Hemingway's seemingly paranoid reports.

ECCENTRICS

Douglas Coupland, one of the bards of my generation, asserts that people will pretend to be eccentric because they fear becoming just another cog in the machine. I don't think that applies to the eccentrics discussed in these books. I think we can tell real eccentricity from feigned wackiness because the former tends to leave the reader feeling uneasy or full of awe; the latter just produces annoyance. And thankfully there are enough genuine eccentrics out there because my site would be nothing without them.

STRANGE CREATIONS: ABERRANT IDEAS OF HUMAN ORIGINS FROM ANCIENT ASTRONAUTS TO AQUATIC APES

By Donna Kossy
Feral House (2001)
Original post: 05/26/2011

Why do I consider this book odd?
AQUATIC APES!

Donna Kossy clearly revels in bizarre ideas and she knows more about strange people and "crackpotology" than I can safely absorb in one sitting. Just reading the bibliography for *Strange Creations* was vaguely exhausting. I have extraordinary respect for anyone who has read Helena Blavatsky from cover to cover, even if it was abridged. (I have similar respect for anyone who manages to make it through *Atlas Shrugged* in one go; such people are made of sturdier stuff than I.)

I initially wanted to read Kossy's book because it discusses one of my all-time favorite whacked theories, that of the Aquatic Ape. But as I read, I discovered an entire world of bizarre, unique, unnerving and even upsetting theories. Kossy is an intrepid fellow-traveler in the weird and she possesses not only the skills to make some very dense and lunatic theories accessible, but also to reveal the humanity and humor that can be easy to overlook. While I never want to read the phrase "root race" again, I found Kossy's survey of strange beliefs fascinating and engaging—so much so that I was disappointed to discover that she has only written two books (and I already own the other, entitled *Kooks*), but I comfort myself that Kossy led me to some superb and truly outlandish books (I will totally discuss *Behold!!! the Protong* here at some point).

Strange Creations opens with a discussion of a subject that utterly thwarted me when I set out on my own to explore weird ideas: alien invaders shaping the

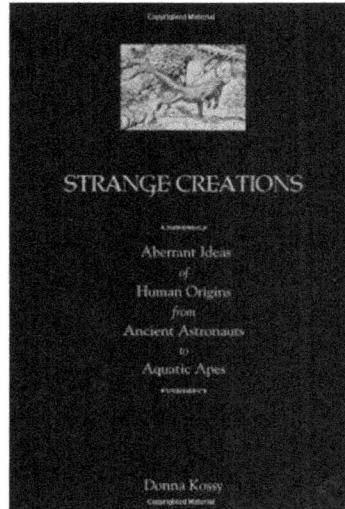

Earth. Here Kossy's distillation is incredibly dense, yet it comes very close to making sense. Because he was the most unknown to me, I was especially interested in her treatment of Zecharia Sitchin's ideas. His theories are intriguing but after slogging through Paul Von Ward's[1] similar work I'm not sure I can stomach Sitchin in long form. Fortunately, Kossy cut his strange interpretations down into small, chewable bites.

> Since the first specimens of Homo sapiens were created as hybrids—like mules—they were infertile. It was only through genetic engineering that our ancestors were given two sets of sex cells so that they could reproduce. This is what the story of Adam and Eve is about. In the story, eating the fruit of the tree of knowledge is a symbol for the primeval pair's newfound ability to reproduce.

I love stuff like this and I generally adore alternate history (to a point), but Kossy has no problem calling a spade a spade and is less amused by Sitchin and writers like him than I am.

> Obviously, Sitchin's popularity comes not from the strength of his arguments. He's more concerned with "proving" his alternative history by bending the available evidence than altering his theory to fit the facts. Like von Däniken, he has tapped into the imagination of the popular mind which is disillusioned and distrustful of hard science, even while embracing many of its accomplishments.

> Ironically, Sitchin's interpretations of myth are embedded in a stubborn materialism usually identified with science. To Sitchin, myths don't depict anything spiritual or intangible at all; they depict only hard, historic events. Ea wasn't the god of wisdom, he was the god of mining. Though Sitchin's conclusions seem imaginative, they stem from a lack of imagination shared with some fundamentalists, an inability to connect with the cosmos and its mysteries in any but the most literal way.

This was not a perspective I would likely have considered without Kossy pointing out the obvious. Because even as I am charmed by its strangeness, Sitchin's origin story very definitely mirrors some of the more detestable elements of fundamentalist religious interpretation. In that regard it is actually very common. I still find it exotic and interesting, but I didn't really see the complete lack of intellectual subtlety until Kossy pointed it out.

The next chapter covers de-evolution and was fun, fun, fun to read for this former SubGenius:

> Broadly speaking, de-evolution—the idea that humanity is in a decline, be it spiritual or physical—is a universal concept, common throughout history and among diverse culture. According to historian J.B. Bury, the modern notion of "progress," from which sprouted the theory of evolution, is a historical anomaly. Diverse peoples through the ages more often viewed life

---

[1]   See my review of *Gods, Genes, and Consciousness* on page 91.

and history cyclically, with humanity sliding down the declining arc of the cycle.

[…]

With the veneration of antiquity goes the denigration of the present.

Simple enough.

But never fear, Kossy takes a look at those who have made the theory of man's degeneration their life's work. Then again, maybe you should be afraid because part of her effort involves Madame Blavatsky's *The Secret Doctrine*. I cannot even begin to tell you how tiresome I find HPB and theosophy in general but Kossy explains it well and in a manner that doesn't necessitate clawing out my eyes:

> In Blavatsky's cyclic version of Earth history, humanity proceeded through seven "Root-Races" on seven primeval continents, each Root-Race representing a step down—spiritually—from that which preceded it. In the process, matter attempted to triumph over spirit, but failed, and humanity both "evolved" and de-evolved.

> During the first epoch, lasting millions of years, a race of immortal giants with ethereal bodies lived in the Imperishable Sacred Land at the North Pole. The second race—giant androgynous semi-humans—resulted from the first attempt at material nature; they lived on a continent called Hyperborea, south of the North Pole. The third race represented the "fall of man" because they were divided into two sexes; they lived during the Golden Age, 18 million years ago, when the "gods walked on Earth and mixed freely with mortals" on the continent of Lemuria. The fourth race lived on Atlantis, and the fifth, called "Aryans," lived in Europe. Two more races are supposed to follow before the end of this cycle or "Round."

So yeah, this makes *perfect sense* on every level and there's nothing to discuss, really. Except you know that when you read the word "Aryan," in nine contexts out of ten, it's not gonna be good. Since it's been at least two decades since I was foolhardy enough to try to read Blavatsky, I don't recall how overtly racist she was. It doesn't matter because the watchwords are there. Where there are references to degenerate men and the North (or in some cases South) Pole, it's a hop, skip and jump to repellent racist theories:

> Friedrich von Schlegel (1772-1829) first used the term "Aryan" to denote an aristocratic race of ancient Indians, purportedly the ancestors of the Germans. Thus some of the early freethinkers who rejected the biblical Eden replaced it with an Asian one, populated by Aryans. The Aryan myth, which developed during the first half of the nineteenth century, was first embraced by the German Romantics, then by Theosophists and occultists, and later, by the Nazis.

It goes on:

Jorg Lanz von Liebenfels (1874-1954), founder of "Ariosophy," was among many in pre-Nazi Germany who adhered to more esoteric versions of the Aryan myth. Calling the Aryan homeland Arktogaa, which is Greek for "nothern earth," von Liebenfels taught that non-Aryans were the result of bestiality between the ancient Aryans and beasts. One of his disciples lectured that humanity was the result of a forbidden mixture of angels and animals and used the Bible to back it up. Each race, he said, represented a different percentage of angel and beast, the Aryans coming out on top, with one percent angel.

Nothing says de-evolution like angel-animal hybrids. And we sink further down into the sewer:

The Nazis adopted their Aryan myth from Alfred Rosenberg, author of the 1930 best-seller *Myth of the 20th Century*, and through the revisionist science of Herman Wirth. In his 1928 book, *The Rise of Mankind*, Wirth wrote that humanity began at the North Pole, having split from the apes millions of years ago. After shifting continents and poles made the nether regions uninhabitable, the Arctic Aryan wandered South. The remnants of Aryan high culture survive to this day only in the blind, bearded Eskimos found by the Danish "Thule Expedition" of Knud Rasmussen. Implicit in all of these stories is the idea that much of present humanity has degenerated (for various reasons such as mixing with Jewish blood) from its former superiority and purity. Only Aryans retained the former glory.

Kossy goes on to discuss the works of the man who, after Nietzsche, is most quoted by "racialists" and those who attempt to give their racism a tinge of intellectualism. That man is Julius Evola. I can't even bring myself to discuss him at length. I've spent far too much time in my life talking to people who use Evola to present their race hate in esoteric terms, as a means rarefying their motives. I tire of such things these days, all the more so because I actually find a lot of inspiration in some of Evola's work. I find myself wanting to be the sort of woman who rides the tiger and who maintains my moral worth and mental strength even during the darkest of days. Don't worry, I'm not deceived by my motives—finding truth in Evola is not particularly different from finding truth in the words of Marcus Aurelius or the Bible. But in a sense this brings me full circle because it explains why even as I love strange theory, "origin" theories can set my teeth on edge. Sometimes it seems like even the kindest mind is able to take an origin story and twist it into evidence of his or her superiority. We are all looking to become the Chosen Ones in some respect.

With that much out of the way, let's just skip chapter three, wherein the Bible, the Koran and elements of evolution are used to prove that blacks and Jews are the devil, or that Caucasians are the devil, or that people from Asia and Africa are closely linked to simians, which means they are not godly and are therefore the devil. Yeah…

MOSTLY NONFICTION: ECCENTRICS

I almost don't want to discuss the next chapter on eugenics but there were elements of this chapter that were new to me. For example, I had always attributed "survival of the fittest" to Darwin, when it was really Herbert Spencer, a Darwinist philosopher, who introduced the phrase. I wonder how Christian libertarians would respond if they realized that their core beliefs were shared by a proponent of evolution (politics, strange bedfellows, etc.):

> To Spencer, biological evolution implied moral progress. "Progress," he wrote, "is not an accident, but a necessity. Instead of civilization being arti-ficial, it is a part of nature; all of a piece with the development of the embryo or the unfolding of a flower." Thus, the state was foolish in supporting wel-fare for the poor and diseased, tampering with the natural process of evo-lution. Instead, the unfit should be eliminated: "The whole effort of nature is to get rid of such, to clear the world of them, and make room for better."

It goes in a similar but uncomfortable vein. Then Kossy discusses the Oneida Community, and this was utterly fascinating. The brainchild of John Humphrey Noyes, the Oneida Community was a commune of sorts in New York. Based on bits and pieces of the Bible, the commune practiced "complex marriage" (which reads to me like a strange way for the middle-aged and older to prey sexually on the young but perhaps there is more to it than that) and "Stirpiculture," which was a form of selective breeding. In the mid-1800s, the commune produced 58 children, all of whom presumably were scien-tifically superior to kids whose parents didn't practice eugenics. Of course, the purportedly superior children (called "stirps") the Oneida Community claimed to have produced were likely better off because of the child-cen-tric mindset under which they were conceived. The community disbanded before any real scientific measure could be made of the children produced with "barnyard ethics."

The chapter on eugenics takes a dark turn when we move from positive eugenics, wherein people breed with an eye to excellent offspring, to negative eugenics, wherein those considered inferior are prevented from reproduc-ing or, in extreme cases, are killed off entirely. The usual "academic" studies are mentioned, including those concerning the Jukes and Kallikak families, which led "to the public crusade against what became known as the 'Menace of the Feebleminded.'" Somewhere along the way, this exploded into the belief that things adults engaged in, beyond the obvious ringers like drinking while pregnant, could make them a potential threat not merely to the moral fiber of the country but to the overall genetic health of the nation. After urging the youth of 1920s America to avoid victims of VD and the mentally deficient as potential spouses, the advice of Eugenicists just got ickier and ickier, as psychiatrists confidently advised that masturbation was "one of the great causes of insanity." So you'd have to be sure to avoid masturbators, too. Good luck with that.

At first I had a hard time understanding how eugenics could be considered an origin theory. Kossy cleared that up for me:

> Indeed, many scientists, educators and authors believed in eugenics with a religious faith: they replaced Jesus Christ with Charles Darwin, brotherly love with better breeding, and the Second Coming of Christ with the prospect of a perfect race. Though many mainstream clergymen—especially Catholics—bristled at this new religion, some accepted, and some even embraced it. In 1926 the American Eugenics Society sponsored a eugenics sermon contest. Three hundred sermons of various denominations were inspired by the contest, and 60 were submitted for judging. Protestants reinterpreted the Bible as a eugenics book, claiming that Jesus was born into a family resulting from "a long process of religious and moral selection." Jews accepted eugenics as just another commandment of God: as one Rabbi put it, "May we do nothing to permit our blood to be adulterated by infusion of inferior grade."

Of course, as it does with all origin theories, it breaks down into an us versus them situation wherein various people decided they were the best exemplars of genetic purity, aligning themselves with ideals of racial superiority, often with interesting and borderline humorous results. Kossy quotes from the 1937 book *Apes, Men & Morons* by Ernest Hooton, who attended a genetics conference to hear speak a man whom he had never met but who was evidently one of the best examples of the Nordic race:

> From my obscure and remote table of uncelebrities, I peered myopically to catch a glimpse of this dolichocephalic, blond Viking who was to embody the physical, intellectual, and scientific ideals of the "Great Race." At first I got the elevation of my sight too high and saw no one standing at the speaker's table except the blandly smiling president who had made the eloquent introduction. Then I heard sounds of broken English, and, lowering my gaze a foot or two, I was able to discern its source. It was a sawed-off, rotund person with a head round as a bullet, black hair, a blobby nose and a face reminiscent of the full moon—in short, the complete Alpine. I thereupon decided that every man is his own Nordic, and I am afraid that I leaped to the conclusion that eugenics is a lay form of ancestor worship...

Inevitably we slide into Hitler, Mengele, Nazis, Nazis, Nazis... Yep, almost all origin myths seem to result in genocide. And that's why I so love the Aquatic Ape theory because as of this writing, it has only resulted in anti-Aquatic Ape smuggery and nary an instance of race hate (though the body positivity movement has begun mentioning the theory to explain why some people evolved to have a ton of subcutaneous body fat and it's anyone's ballgame as to how that argument will play out). We'll get to the ape, but for now, let's have a look at Kossy's treatment of Creationism.

Sigh. Yeah, yeah, dinosaurs and man walked together. The Earth is 6,000 years old. I have little sympathy or affinity for those who espouse this utter bullshit. Yet Kossy explains them in a manner I would find impossible:

> Today's fundamentalists seek to convince themselves and others that their conception of natural history which relies entirely on a literalistic reading of one sacred text—is consistent with current observations of the world—and they'll do anything to defend it. Rather than endure a soul-testing crisis of faith, fundamentalists prefer to think that their creation myth is somehow different from all the other creation myths in the world. It's unique, it's literally true, and what's more, it's scientific.

Kossy then goes on to discuss the science that these creationists, mainly Christian, have to ignore (or warp) in order to ensure their version of events remains intact.

There wasn't a lot that was new for me here, but Kossy does raise some issues that should be of concern to those of us who have been standing on the sidelines as pseudoscience has been taking more and more ground in public discourse and education:

> The scientists slowly noticed that science education was under attack, and have been actively combating the creationists ever since. While the Tennessee law challenged by Scopes forbidding the teaching of evolution was obviously a draconian measure, the legislation introduced by creationists in the '80s looks much more benign. All they want, they say, is "equal time." If you teach evolution, they argue, then to be fair, the public schools should also teach creation. By this argument, the Aquatic Ape theory, various alien intervention theories, de-evolution, and countless creation myths and alternative theories of evolution should also be given "equal time" in the classroom. "Equal time," in fact, is just a device creationists use to ensure their own voices are heard over the threatening sounds of secularism they hear in the schools, on television, and at the movies.

I would go further to say that equal time is a ploy. Creationists hope to replace all other theories with their own—that's why the Aquatic Ape theory is not taught because it's not about equal time; it's about wriggling into the system and eliminating all other educational options. And it has worked. In the face of all reason, it has worked. Even as evolutionists and scientists work hard to dissuade the public from adopting methods of pseudoscience, their efforts seem to be falling on deaf ears.

> Explaining the subtleties of current evolutionary theory to people who get their history from docudramas and their science from the Discovery Channel isn't easy; evolutionists might do better if they simply accused creationists of molesting children.

It rankles people to read this, to realize that this is all boiling down to a lowest common denominator argument. But people who don't see creationism as dim should realize that creationists do, in fact, appeal to emotion and poor analytical skills.

The creationists want to have it both ways: when defending creationism, it's just a matter of philosophy, but when attacking evolution or demanding "equal time" in science education, it's a matter of scientific evidence. The authors are chained to Scripture, but refuse to admit it.

It gets far worse than just engaging in spurious reasoning. Some creationists take it to that next, repellent level.

But fossils that turn out to be genuine after all are not allowed as evidence for evolution, but instead "might well represent disease or degeneracy." And if that argument doesn't convince you to abandon evolution, try this one: evolution causes racism. "It is important to recognize," say the authors, "that racism in its virulent forms is mainly a product of evolutionary thinking," because even recent history can be shaped to fit the creationist mold...

Then the name Hitler is invoked and it goes downhill from there.

Finally we reach chapter six and can discuss AQUATIC APES. I have no idea why I love this theory so much but there you go. Life is strange. One day I hope to discuss the book, *The Aquatic Ape*. Until then Kossy's take will have to suffice. Anyway, Elaine Morgan, a feminist writer, came up with the Aquatic Ape theory and perhaps one of the reasons I love her theory so much (other than just how awesome it feels to say AQUATIC APE over and over again) is that, at first glance, it seems so reasonable. As Kossy puts it:

Its ideas were irresistible. The Aquatic Ape turned out to be one of those books—one of those theories—that fits everything together so well you feel it just has to be true. For weeks after reading, I pondered the theory. Soon I found myself preaching the gospel of the Aquatic Ape to my friends.

That was more or less my experience. Of course, after a while reality sets in and holes in the theory become apparent, but there are holes in all theories so I didn't get as hung up on them as I perhaps should have. Regardless, AQUATIC APES is the most charming, inoffensive origin theory I've been exposed to thus far.

So here's the Aquatic Ape theory (AAT) in a nutshell:

The Aquatic Ape theory observes that various human traits, such as bipedality, speech, lack of body hair, subcutaneous (under the skin) fat, weeping, face-to-face copulation and sweating are unique among primates and therefore hard to account for by conventional theories of human evolution. But if humanity was at one time aquatic or semi-aquatic, these traits could be easily explained. The AAT tells us that we share many traits with aquatic mammals which we don't share with our closer relatives, the primates. Therefore, says the AAT, we acquired those traits in an aquatic environment. The beauty of this theory is that is seems to solve, in one fell swoop, all the mysteries of human uniqueness. It's also championed by a skilled writer, unencumbered by the stringent guidelines of scientific research.

Yep, Elaine Morgan was no scientist. She was not an anthropologist. She was a feminist writer, and I think the whole AAT was basically a feminist reaction to a lot of rather masculine evolutionary theory that didn't have a whole lot to back it up. Kossy's on the same page as me:

> The Aquatic Ape began as an essentially female version of human evolution, an antidote to what Elaine Morgan then called "The Mighty Hunter"—a brutish ape-man who used to dominate popular stories of human evolution. The Aquatic Ape, by contrast, emerges from the sea, like Venus or an aquatic Madonna-and-child. Some of the appeal of the AAT might stem from Morgan's depictions of what is essentially a mother goddess.

Before Morgan presented her take on the AAT, a British marine biologist called Alister Hardy introduced the idea and it even gets a mention in Desmond Morris' *The Naked Ape*. But it wasn't until Morgan infused the theory with her feminist challenge to male-dominated theories of evolution that the AAT really got its controversial legs.

Riffing off Hardy's ideas and adding her own interpretations, Morgan postulated that resource scarcity forced early hominids from the forest out into the savannah. These hairy apes found life hard and were often felled by predators. Then one day, a former tree-climbing ape carrying her child fled into water to escape a quadruped predator and thus became the progenitor to aquatic apes. Fleeing into the water when in danger caused these hairy apes to undergo the same evolutionary changes that oceanic mammals underwent—becoming more hairless, developing subcutaneous fat, among other traits. Standing in the water aided walking in erect posture. Having to spend long periods of time in the water caused the apes' fingers to become more dexterous, facilitating more effective use of tools. One of the reasons I found this theory so compelling was how Morgan took Hardy's assumptions and added her own in her book, *The Descent of Woman*:

> Hardy had explained hair on the aquatic ape's head as protection from the sun while wading, but Morgan explained it as a way for the aquatic ape baby to cling to its otherwise naked mother... This also explained male baldness because "in communities where the males took no part in the bringing up of the offspring, there would be nothing to prevent their heads going bald as their bodies..."

She later refined these ideas in *The Aquatic Ape* and *The Scars of Evolution*. The media and the general public rather liked the AAT but the academic and scientific communities were not impressed, almost universally dismissing it.

Much of the chapter deals with scientists' efforts to prove that AAT is false. So we have scientists claiming that the fossil record does not support AAT, and Morgan insisting that the fossil record does, in fact, support her theory. I'm not a scientist but I tend to think the fossil record does not support the AAT. Most examples of hominids walking erect were found in dry places, whereas if Morgan were correct, we would expect to find them near water. But Kossy, who clearly has more discipline than I do, found the theory as embraceable as I did when I first read about it. This makes me want to get all of Morgan's books and read them in sequential order to see what I think once I am finished.

Chapter seven is sort of a trashcan chapter covering odd origin theories that didn't fit elsewhere. Kossy calls these "aberrant anthropologies" and begins with the strange anthropology found in *The Urantia Book*. The Urantia believers, whom I have to give due respect for slogging through that brick of a book (over 2,000 pages), believed that William Sadler, a surgeon, protégé of John Kellogg and key figure in *The Urantia Book*, witnessed Wilfred Kellogg channeling space aliens in his sleep and played a role in using those dream visions to create a new religious philosophy. There's a whole lot more to it but it's worth noting that Urantia theory was a strange Seventh-Day Adventist offshoot that attracted some members of the Kellogg family and espoused theories of eugenics as appalling as all the others discussed in this book. It seems that Wilfred Kellogg's sleep trances were a conduit for alien intervention urging humankind to achieve perfection through reproductive eugenics, and it's bleah all over again. As Kossy notes, followers of this weird cult were puritanical in their work ethic and their approach to life, and nothing in their lives seems to have been the least bit enjoyable. It's hard to see the appeal for even the most penitent among us.

In the same chapter, Kossy discusses Heaven's Gate, a group of mild and meek cultists who believed the cosmic mother-ship was coming for them behind the Hale-Bopp comet. They committed suicide en masse in California in 1997 and an appalled nation got all kinds of unseemly details as we learned most of the men had castrated themselves.

The most fascinating part of the "aberrant anthropologies" chapter comes when Kossy turns her attention to the work of Stanislav Szukalski. Oh good lord, this small section of a very involved book just revved up the part of my brain that loves the strange but has no desire to engage in dogma. Szukalski, I suspect, is perfect for my undisciplined mind because he is made less of strange religion than of rogue ideas filtered through the brain of a genius or a madman. Szukalski was a Polish artist who immigrated to America in the early 20th century and became friends with people like Clarence Darrow and Sherwood Anderson. His return to Poland to create art for the government was cut short when Poland was invaded during World War II, forcing Szukalski to return to the United States, where he would refine his theory, researching languages and archaeology.

Szukalski's origin theory involves humans, apes and de-evolution, but it's somehow wholly unique in its own bizarre right:

> According to Szukalski, our blood has already been mixed; not with inferior

human blood but with that of apes—human history is the story of the struggle between the true humans and the a-human Yetinsyny, who even now live among us in human society. They speak our language and they sometimes even take over our nations, but a few of their physical features give them away as the gluttonous anthropoids they are.

During his studies of language in California, Szukalski made a major discovery:

> His studies of pictographs and illustrations of archaeological finds culminated in the discovery of what he called "Protong," or the "proto-tongue." Protong, claimed Szukalski, is the mother of all languages, a pictographic language common to all cultures before the Tower of Babel.

He died not long after he wrote up his theories and his works were discovered by underground artists who exhibited his art and published his treatise on "Zermatism," the science that evidently explains all of his theorizing.

Szukalski's belief that humans had been sexually mixed with violent, rapacious apes, can be seen illustrated throughout history. To him, the Greek god Pan was an ape variant that raped women. Some of the ape women were seductive enough to attract men and the offspring of these interspecies unions have since ruined the world, creating a de-evolving race that is overwhelmed by war and strife.

> Szukalski enthusiastically identifies the descendants of these couplings by such traits as an "undercut nose," long upper lip, long torso, short upper arm, wart nose, pot belly, and sometimes even a tail. These bastards typically end up as dictators, political subversives, and communist agents in all nations. Their compulsive opposition to human decency is the cause of all our troubles, past, present and future…
>
> […]
>
> According to Szukalski, these Yetinsyny, once identified, should never be allowed to enter politics or the military service, for they are "devoid of all the genteel traits of [humanity] but retained all the avaricious, vengeful, ferocious traits." They only enter public service "for the purpose of attaining positions that allow them to gloat in Vengeance for their obsessive psychosis of Inferiority." And there they bide their time until they get a chance to "exterminate Handsome mankind by the millions." Politically dangerous Yeti have lately included such historically influential characters as Karl Marx, Mao Tse Tung, Nietzsche, Bakunin and Kropotkin.

Behold!!! The Protong contains many of Szukalski's drawings along with his writings on Zermatism. I ordered a copy after reading Kossy's book and I hope to read and discuss it sooner than later.

Aside from simply being an entertaining read, Donna Kossy's *Strange Creations* was important for me because it ultimately showed me why my innate atheism is the only rational choice I have. I have often wondered why it is that, given my predilection for lunacy, I have never been able to embrace for long any of the ideas that so enthrall me. I can dip my toe in the water but I can never go for a swim. In my attempts to find some truth, I have tried to open my mind to ideas uplifting and despicable, but none ever stuck. I had always been able to see the common threads that run in all the major religions, but I couldn't see the same tapestry in the more crackpot ideas that I, by all rights, should have adopted by now.

Perhaps I knew it subconsciously, but Kossy lines up clearly for me. All the commonalities. Alien intervention, eugenics, race hate, rampaging apes, bizarre castes of human existence—it seems that with the exception of the Aquatic Ape Theory, all of these origin stories weave at least two of the above threads into tapestries that ultimately do not look that much different from each other. With so many common elements, it's clearer to me why I, a borderline lunatic, have never completely descended into the swamp of belief. I find all the offerings at the crackpot buffet to have come from the same cookbook.

While I cannot personally embrace the bizarre, the ideas that Kossy examines put into perspective the less strange creations on the landscape. Crafted with precision and affection, yet with a distance that enables her to dissect and analyze dispassionately, Kossy's book is a masterful guide to crackpot origin theories. I highly recommend *Strange Creations* and I hope that when you read it, you love Kossy's style as much as I do.

FURTHER READING

Kooks: A Guide to the Outer Limits of Human Belief
Donna Kossy

The Aquatic Ape
Elaine Morgan

Behold!!! The Protong
Stanislav Szukalski

THE ECCENTROPEDIA: THE MOST UNUSUAL PEOPLE WHO HAVE EVER LIVED
By Chris Mikul
Headpress (2012)
Original post: 05/13/2015

Why do I consider this book odd?
Because it's wholly devoted to weird people.

It should come as no surprise that I'm a Chris Mikul fan,[2] and I think this is great book. Anyone with a love for strange ideas or eccentrics will need to add this book to their collection. *The Eccentropedia* discusses some of the usual suspects in the weirdo game—Helena Blavatsky, Charles Fort, Aleister Crowley, Michael Jackson—but it seems for every person whose name comes up all the time in compendiums devoted to self-styled mavericks and odd-balls, there were ten more I had never heard of.

Because this is quite literally an encyclopedia, the only way to discuss it is to outline a few of the more outlandish people featured in Mikul's gallery. This may not be the most exciting way to proceed, but hopefully the lunacy of the people I select will make up for it. So here's a short selection of some of the weird people I had not heard of prior to opening *The Eccentropedia*. Hopefully some of them will be new to you, too.

BARONESS ELOISE WAGNER DE BOSQUET was a horse-faced woman with buck teeth whose force of charm made her very attractive to people, if only for a short period of time. After four divorces, in the early 1930s she per-suaded two of her lovers to accompany her to Floreana Island, part of the Galapagos Islands chain, to join in with the settlers on the island. She wanted to establish a hotel there, and while visitors to the island found her delight-ful, the two families who lived there permanently were less impressed. After the lover's triad became abusive for one of the men, the Baroness and her other lover disappeared, never to be seen again. In the wake of that disap-pearance, there were two more mysterious deaths associated with Floreana, which is quite remarkable for an island with fewer than a dozen permanent inhabitants.

I read Mikul's entry about The Baroness and then immediately discovered a Netflix documentary called *The Galapagos Affair*. The film is an histori-cal account of the Baroness's antics along with the scandals and murders on

---

2   My discussion of Mikul's own "odd books" journal, *Biblio-Curiosa*, begins on page 601.

Floreana Island. I recommend it not only because it's a pretty good movie, but because it also helps viewers understand how the Baroness could possibly have had any sex appeal to the many men she attracted. In photos and a silent movie, she comes across as surprisingly attractive. Still, if you are going to be a part of a cuckold-trio, it seems better to be in thrall to a really beautiful (or rich) woman. That way when your body is discovered on a desert island with no fresh water source, at least people will see your sorry end as the inevitable result of more relatable human passion gone wrong.

Next, let's discuss **PERCY GRAINGER**, an Australian musician and composer. I was drawn to his entry in *The Eccentropedia* because he just seems so unlikely. Had he been a fictional character he would have seemed completely unbelievable. As a boy, Grainger's mother told him he was destined for greatness and encouraged him to practice piano for hours. She whipped him if she felt he was not working hard enough and those whippings became a part of his creative impulse as an adult. He eventually married a Swedish woman who both understood and did not mind that beating Grainger often was going to be an important part of their marriage. Grainger liked whipping others but his masochism, as well as sex in general, took up a lot of room in his psyche.

The childhood whippings must have worked because Grainger became a prodigy. And his marriage to a Swedish woman was more or less inevitable because, after a trip to pre-war Germany, Grainger became convinced of the superiority of the Nordic people. Despite his borderline-racist admiration for the Nordic people, he counted Jews in the number of his friends. He was also interested in and influenced by the Maori, and he was a fan of Duke Ellington. Grainger also invented a weird language he called "blue-eyed English" wherein he eliminated all words that did not have an Anglo-Saxon origin and replaced them with his own creations. This was an especially interesting thing for a composer to do, given all the Italian words used in music.

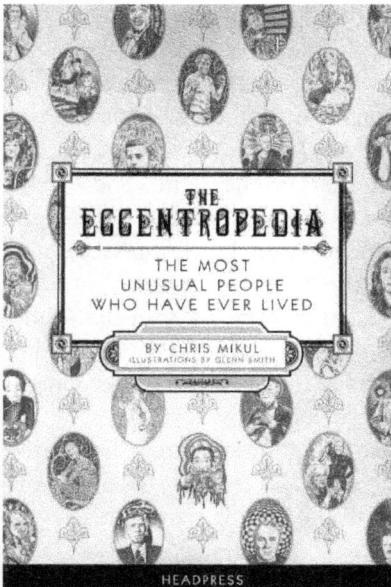

THE
ECCENTROPEDIA

THE MOST
UNUSUAL PEOPLE
WHO HAVE EVER LIVED

BY CHRIS MIKUL
ILLUSTRATIONS BY GLENN SMITH

HEADPRESS

I am not sure if I really consider **BENJAMIN LAY** to be a true eccentric. He seems more like an excessively devoted moralist. Regardless, the picture Mikul paints of his activities is pretty memorable. Born in England, Lay first encountered slavery in 1730s

Barbados, which made him become a staunch abolitionist. He and his wife, both Quakers, later emigrated to Philadelphia, where he found that some of his fellow Quakers were slave-owners. Lay was not one to be subtle in his advocacy. When he got tossed out of a Quaker meeting for being disruptive, he stretched out in front of the entrance so that everyone who left had to step over him. On other occasions, he engaged in some one-man theater that is both funny and dramatic:

> He invaded another meeting wearing a military uniform with a sword, and carrying a hollowed out book (to represent the Bible) in which was concealed a bladder containing pokeberry juice. Declaring that enslaving a man was no better than stabbing him through the heart, he drew the sword and plunged it into his 'Bible', spattering those nearest him with the red juice. He once sat outside a meeting in the middle of the winter with one bare leg deep in the snow. When passersby expressed concern, he said, 'You pretend compassion for me, but you do not feel for the poor slaves in your fields who go all winter half clad.' He was not afraid of taking direct action, and once went so far as to kidnap a slave owner's three-year-old child, so he would know how it felt to lose a loved one.

It also bears mentioning that Lay was a hunchback, rendering him 4'6" tall. He died happy because on his deathbed, just before his last breath, he learned that the Quaker church had voted to reject slavery. I wonder how much his activism influenced them to adopt their moral stance.

My favorite entry was **ELIZA DONNITHORNE**, the woman who was likely the inspiration for Dickens' Miss Havisham in *Great Expectations*. Eliza was born in India, where her father was a judge. Her mother and two sisters died during a cholera outbreak and her heartbroken father decided to relocate to Australia, moving there with the young Eliza in 1836. When it came time for Eliza to entertain suitors, she rejected all of her father's favorites, falling for a shipping clerk named George Cuthbertson. When George proposed to Eliza, her father, known for having a very bad temper, informed George that if he ever caused Eliza any anguish after the marriage, he would be severely punished.

We all sort of know what happened next. George jilted Eliza on the day of their wedding. Eliza believed he would eventually arrive to marry her and remained in her wedding dress the entire day. She came unhinged when she saw guests consuming food meant for the nuptial banquet. Concerned friends took her to her room, where she remained for a month, but honored her request that the wedding banquet be left alone and the dining room door locked. Unfortunately Eliza was pregnant by George, and when she gave birth the baby was given to a servant to raise, to preserve Eliza's reputation. (Perhaps that was why George ran away—the prospect of a baby born seven months after the wedding, given Mr. Donnithorne's threats regarding bad behavior, probably gave him pause.)

Eventually Eliza's father died and she inherited his estate, but that did not encourage her to resume normal life. She had spent years waiting for George to return to her, and had descended completely into madness.

> After his death, she had all the shutters on the windows of the house nailed up, and dismissed all but two of her servants... relying on them to conduct all her business with the outside world. She continued to wear her wedding dress, and the dining room with its uneaten feast remained locked.

It was never wholly proven that she was Dickens' inspiration, but it seems very likely that at some point he heard her story—the descriptions of the two women seem just too similar for coincidence.

I could go on but I won't because I don't want to ruin the book. Encyclopedias don't lend themselves well to my typical in-depth approach, and that's especially true given that *The Eccentropedia* is over 500 pages, with 266 entries covering almost all forms of human perversity, insanity, determination and genius. I should also mention the excellent illustrations by Glenn Smith. While I got through it in a couple of sittings, the book can easily be read in fits and starts, and it's a great one to have on hand when you suspect you may face interruptions, like if you're waiting in line at the DMV. Mikul, who can also write fiction well,[3] here combines journalism with clear affection for his subjects, and the result is both readable and engrossing. I love this book and highly recommend it!

FURTHER READING

Eccentric and Bizarre Behaviors
Louis R. Franzini and John M. Grossberg

Extraordinary Popular Delusions and the Madness of Crowds
John Mackay, LL.D.

Eccentric Lives and Peculiar Notions
John Michell

Subversive: Interviews with Radicals
Brian Whitney

---

3   Check out Mikul's short story collection, *Tales of the Macabre and Ordinary*, reviewed on the OTC blog at: http://www.oddthingsconsidered.com/tales-of-the-macabre-and-ordinary-by-chris-mikul/

Aliens!

Many years ago I watched the film Fire in the Sky, *a depiction of the alleged alien abduction of Travis Walton. I never really recovered from the examination scene, and I think that colored much of my outlook toward discussions about alien life and intervention. So when I forced myself to read books about alien life from beyond our solar system, I wasn't expecting what I found. What I found was a new attempt to explain human origins, with as much dogma and exotic myth as any mainstream deity-based belief system.*

THE CRYPTOTERRESTRIALS
By Mac Tonnies
Anomalist Books (2010)
Original post: 01/24/2012

Why do I consider this book odd?
Because it posits a theory that the little green men—er, I mean *grays*—are not from outer space but really live on—or *in*—Earth and have been deceiving us for years.

Most of alien-interventionist literature comes from a mindset that challenges my love of the odd, steeped as it is in strange science and spurious proofs that if challenged would result in months of unsettling emails from people whose sense of reality would make it hard to respond, even if their earnestness would demand a response. So I'm going to spread these books out, though it may take me years to discuss the handful I read. That way I can distribute the agony in such a manner that I don't get emotional cramps every time I check my inbox.

Plus I'm not really "into" aliens. Discussing aliens has become not unlike discussing religion for me, a tiresome argument that no one can win. Yet I'm still drawn to the topic periodically, and I find myself reading about alien intervention even as every bit of my common sense tells me to leave the topic alone. It's maddening.

You know how it is.

As far as odd theories of aliens meddling with humans beings go, *The Cryptoterrestrials* is actually a breath of fresh air. Mac Tonnies' study manages to be reasonable, even as it entertains highly speculative and fascinating ideas. So it was disheartening, to say the least, to learn that his interesting book was published posthumously, as Tonnies passed away in 2009 at the age of 34. If you have some time, comb through Tonnies' blog.[1] His ideas on transhumanism are engrossing.

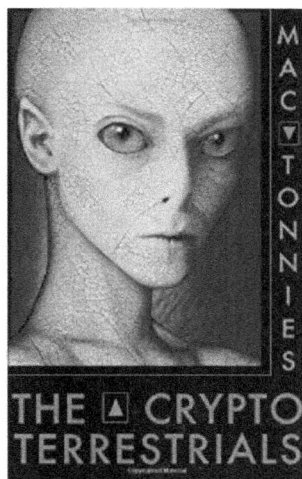

---

1   Mac Tonnies' blog is at http://posthumanblues.blogspot.com/

In a way, Tonnies' book is a perfect example of the sort of reading that made me a fan of the odd. When I was a kid, books on Forteana were not so insistent. They described what happened (fish falling from the sky), posited a few potential answers (waterspouts drawing water and fish from streams, or an angry god), and left the reader to come to his or her own conclusions. Nowadays if a book on fish falling from the sky uses dubious science to prove a particular conclusion, all other points are dismissed by skeptics, and the discussion becomes entrenched and adversarial. Tonnies' book made the fun of Forteana real again.

Tonnies puts forth the idea that aliens are not from other planets but may be "cryptoterrestrials," near-humans or humanoid-like creatures that live among us. Those who see little green men—or little gray men—are not seeing creatures from other planets but instead are seeing creatures that have lived among us on Earth. These cryptoterrestrials are hidden creatures that may or may not be our genetic brethren, but have nevertheless been with us for millennia.

This is an interesting idea and Tonnies goes about discussing it using a calm erudition that was thrilling (and also appalling in a way because he is gone and there will be no more from him). His prose is very crisp and delivers complex ideas in manageable bites so that readers like me don't choke. But I think the best way to show you this book is to give you snippets that resonated with me, examples of an excellent mind at work in the pages of an excellent book. When you know a book is encouraging you to think—that it's not an example of someone making a case for strange beliefs that are antithetical to science and history—it becomes a lot easier to just let your brain go with the "what-if."

The Cryptoterrestrials is more or less an attempt to reconcile the recurring appearance of "little people" in myth and folklore—fairies, elves, etc.—with the idea of a hidden species of humanoids on Earth. The book does not state, in that irritating manner that makes me despair of most books on this topic, that Tonnies had found the one and only true "faith." Instead, it seems that he was trying to get us to think about what the experiences of those who have "seen" little people or grays could mean if one was not actively trying to dismiss such experiences using current standards of rationality. Here's the premise of the book:

> I propose that at least some accounts of alien visitation can be attributed to a humanoid species indigenous to the Earth, a sister race that has adapted to our numerical superiority by developing a surprisingly robust technology. The explicitly reproductive overtones that color many encounters suggest that these "indigenous aliens" are imperiled by a malady that has gone uncured throughout the eons we have coexisted. Driven by a puzzling mixture of hubris and existential desperation, they seek to perpetuate themselves by infusing their gene-pool with human DNA. While existing

at the very margins of ordinary human perception, they have succeeded in realms practically unexplored by known terrestrial science, reinventing themselves at will and helping to orchestrate a misinformation campaign of awe-inspiring scope.

Though Tonnies does not try to invoke "science" and "history" (the oft-repeated insistence that aliens had to have built the pyramids because no human could have done it never fails to make me sad), he does use reason. Looking at some of the experiences people claim to have had, he offers psychological explanations that could lie behind the way "aliens" may present themselves.

For one, they pass themselves off as aliens because they know that claims involving alien interaction will be dismissed, and that people who state they saw aliens will likewise be dismissed as lunatics.

> By utilizing our innate fascination with interplanetary visitors, the crypto-terrestrials have ensured that any accidental sightings of their craft will be ascribed to the ETH [extraterrestrial hypothesis]. The mainstream media, quick to "debunk" for fear of inciting ridicule, thus ignores credible sightings and inadvertently assists the cryptoterrestrial agenda. And if by some chance the sighting is undeniable, its cultural connotations will almost certainly relegate it to our collective fortean attic.

While I am certainly not a True Believer in aliens on Earth, I can sort of see the logic in this, but only insofar as we are encouraging discussion and not an advocacy. Most interesting to me was Tonnies' discussion of the pageantry behind UFO sightings.

> In a related vein, I don't think it's accidental that so many UFOs are adorned with mesmerizing flashing lights. While one can always argue that conspicuous lights indicate the presence of some truly unearthly propulsion system, it's just as possible that they're a deliberate (and relatively low-tech) attempt to make a rather ordinary conveyance look unearthly, thereby eliciting the excitement of the very ET enthusiasts whose sightings are certain to be ignored… or, at best, published in some obscure journal or website.

The antagonist in me says, *of course it would be relegated to the unimportant or ignored because most UFO sightings are nonsense.* But Tonnies had a point. Several, in fact. The spectacle of the ships makes the mundane seem fantastic, and that which is fantastic is often dismissed.

Tonnies also offers an interesting explanation for why the SETI Institute has yet to confirm a message from ETs:

> Maybe one of the reasons we have yet to make irrefutable contact with extraterrestrials is because ET civilizations tend to reach a point of terminal decadence, an erotic cul-de-sac that precludes exploration. (Compare and contrast such an implosion to the "Singularity" many of us are waiting for with bated breath.) Sufficiently advanced ETs may while away the millennia

in a hedonistic stupor, brains (or their equivalent) melded to pleasure-generating devices.

When statements like this are made outside of a need to "prove" them, they are delightful to a person like me. Just speculating that the aliens are in their version of some Orgasmatron having no desire to answer our call or to call out to us is fun to think about. It's only unsettling when the things ancient peoples painted on jars are used as evidence of the theory.

Then again, one can wonder if SETI really wants us to know if they have had contact with aliens:

> In paranoid moments—and there can never be enough of them—I have to wonder if SETI has any real plans to disseminate the discovery of an ET message. After all, acknowledgment of the signal, while certainly hard-won vindication for many scientists, could conceivably trigger the end of the search—and with it the end of the SETI Institute as we know it.

This is the ET version of "they have a cure for the common cold, man, but the doctors won't let them share it!"

I think I liked how Tonnies dealt with skeptics who want to debunk the experiences of those who claim to have had contact with aliens (for the record, the only story I have read that ever struck me as true was the Travis Walton story, and I was pretty young when I first learned of it, so...). In this passage he is addressing the notion some hold that the "UFO mystery" is wholly unrelated to the claims of those who think they have encountered aliens:

> For the most part, the ufological landscape remains a sparring ground for entrenched notions of dispassionate ET visitors and equally tenacious claims of popular delusion. Consequently, we've gone about attempting to "debunk" a phenomenon that continues to defy definition. While many—if not most—well-known abduction narratives are indeed fallible, disquieting findings from emerging (or suppressed) disciplines promise to reframe the debate.

> I suspect the truth, if we can find it, will be considerably weirder than "mere" extraterrestrial visitors or sociologically induced fantasy.

I think this is important, the notion that things that have yet to be credibly defined as a unified phenomenon cannot really be debunked as a whole.[2]

I also enjoyed Tonnies' explanation of why it is that the aliens don't just show themselves already.

> There are a multitude of reasons a visiting civilization would refrain from "landing on the White House lawn," foremost among them the potentially

---

2   And if it matters, Tonnies tends to believe as I do that many people who report alien interaction may well have been suffering from sleep issues, hypnogogia and other organic brain altering situations. Not all, but some. He also addresses the common forms these interactions take, from the infamous anal probes to the wide belief that aliens are using us for DNA, involving all kinds of sexual interaction and hybrid babies.

debilitating effect open contact might wreak on terrestrials. History shows that relatively advanced sea-faring cultures topple less developed cultures, in part by collapsing defining assumptions and rendering cultural self-hood obsolete. If we're of any research value to a visiting civilization then interfering at the macro-sociological level might threaten to destroy years of patient work.

Interesting, but there's more:

> It's possible that UFOs would like to initiate something like formal contact but are restrained from doing so by the physics of perception, as Whitley Strieber has suggested. So the pageant in our skies might be an ongoing indoctrination, an attempt to become more substantial (in our universe, at least) so that a more meaningful dialogue can be reached at some indeterminate point in the future.

This next part was just awesome. Why? Because quantum physics gets invoked. Say hello to Schroedinger's Alien:

> If UFOs are attempting to breach our universe, our ingrained sense of disbelief might be preventing them in some arcane quantum mechanical sense. Strieber has argued that official denial of the phenomenon is designed to thwart a potential invasion of non-human intelligence, in which case it seems an enduring stalemate has been reached (with occasional power-plays made by both the UFOs and earthly officialdom). This idea is similar to the citizens of the Planck Brane in Rudy Rucker's science fiction epic *Frek and the Elixir*. In Rucker's novel, the inhabitants of a parallel universe must accumulate a critical level of prestige and notoriety or else cease to exist. The ruling class consists of six individuals who are so well-known and casually accepted by the other Planck Braners that they persist with their individuality intact while their fellows vanish during periodic "renormalization storms"; only when the main characters deride and purposefully ignore them to [sic] they fade into the quantum background.

You need to be really smart or really stoned to groove on a passage like that. I'm only moderately smart (and utterly sober), but there was a time when I found this sort of thing more likely than, say, Jesus rising from the dead. Rather than invoking quantum mechanics, I just think of it as the "Tinkerbell Syndrome." Wish really hard or she'll die. Believe really hard and the aliens can finally show themselves.

The only really new thing I picked up from this book was the idea that abduction experiences could be the result of excessive exposure to electromagnetic waves.

> If we're evolving faster to meet the demands of an increasingly compromised planet, I suppose it's not out of the realm of possibility that our brains are being forced to adapt to the ubiquitous electromagnetic fog spawned by the telecommunications industry. Maybe some UFOs are a way our minds have developed to make sense of the onslaught of radio and microwave

radiation that permeates modern culture. Radio inundation might be ripping holes in the collective unconscious, leaving conspicuous voids to be filled.

This is all very "woo," to be sure, but there's more:

> Albert Budden has speculated along similar lines; he describes "abductions" as the psyche's way of maintaining identity when faced with acute allergic distress. I'm actually quite interested in the esoteric neurological effects of EM exposure.

Of course anyone who has watched one of those ghost hunter shows knows that electromagnetic waves can cause paranormal-like activity, but I had never heard of the idea that abduction tales can be explained via fugue states brought on by allergic responses to electromagnetic waves. This is all very speculative and, in a way, silly; but in a way, it's not. Even the silliest idea in this book is no more than an invitation to think.

You may notice that I paid very little attention to the idea of cryptoterrestrialism in this discussion. In fact, it makes up only a small part of the book, as Tonnies explored the way we interact with and interpret the idea of aliens of all kinds. I may be wrong as my sole knowledge of Tonnies comes from this book and parts of his blog, but I get the impression that advancing a cryptoterrestrial hypothesis was not the real purpose of this book. I think the purpose of Tonnies' book was to lay forth a new interpretation of what we see in the skies and what we see in our nightmares, with ideas being posited so that we continue the discussion of what is out there and what could be happening. This book, full of strange and interesting ideas that if asserted as truth I would snert at, is an exhortation to join the conversation.

It's been a long while since a book on UFOs or Forteana did not insult my intelligence or try to force me to believe that which is unbelievable. *The Cryptoterrestrials* does not violate science or history to make a spurious assertion. It does not ask the reader to take sides. It just asks us not to close our minds, and it does so with eloquence, humor and intelligence. It is a fine book and a slightly melancholy read knowing it was the last book Tonnies would write.

FURTHER READING

Hollow Earth: The Long and Curious History of Imagining Strange Lands, Fantastical Creatures, Advanced Civilizations, and Marvelous Machines Below the Earth's Surface
David Standish

GOD, GENES, AND CONSCIOUSNESS: NONHUMAN INTERVENTION IN HUMAN HISTORY

By Paul Von Ward
Hampton Roads (2004)
Original post: 04/28/2011

Why do I consider this book odd?
Because the book attempts to explain how modern man and culture
have been shaped by the intervention of space aliens.

I decided to read this book after enjoying Mac Tonnies' erudite and accessible book, *The Cryptoterrestrials*. That slim but idea-laden volume caused my interest in alien theories to wax again and I picked up Paul Von Ward's *God, Genes, and Consciousness* ready to encounter new and interesting ideas. That didn't really happen. I read a chapter and felt restless. I played the Ramones at full volume and read another chapter. After the second chapter I wandered downstairs to find the cache of gummi bears I keep on hand as a reward for doing foul tasks, like weeding the front yard or cleaning up cat vomit. I bribed myself with little treats, rewarding myself when I finished a new chapter. I was tempted to quit but persevered because unless a book is really just an egregious pile of dishonest crap, I simply have to finish it. It's a compulsivity issue that's hard to overcome.

But I don't think this an Egregious Pile of Dishonest Crap sort of book. It is more of a Not Relevant to My Interests sort of book. I wasted copious amounts of time between each chapter. I watched black metal fan videos on YouTube because it seemed a better use of time. I cleaned an already spotless toilet. I ate lots of snacks. I hated almost every second I spent reading this book.

But I read the thing and I'm gonna discuss it. Because this is a level of weird that never really interested me that deeply (just one of those things—I can't read enough about Satanic Panic but aliens don't do it for me, odd book-wise), I was forced to read carefully to prevent my mind from wandering. Who knows, as I write this I may have some sort of epiphany, but for the moment all I know as I am typing is that I sort of dread the Zecharia Sitchin tome that's sitting on my bedside table.

I have to mention, because it always bears repeating, that when I slip into snark, it's not necessarily the fault of the author. Paul Von Ward sets out his thesis and uses all sorts of religious texts to draw what to some readers may seem like reasonable conclusions. In the eternal argument of "made" versus "just happened" I sit firmly in the camp of "just happened." I don't think God, gods or aliens shaped the earth in any manner and am still amused at people who look at the world of 4,000 years ago and marvel that our ancient ancestors could, you know, build stuff like pyramids (as if being human, brain-wise, was really that radically different from being a human now). Humans are marvelous and remarkable. Don't discount them when it comes to measuring, cutting, hauling and assembling things.

Anyway, Von Ward has a radically different worldview than mine. I respect that as far as it goes, but I must discuss *God, Genes, and Consciousness* as it filters through my worldview, and I will excerpt copious amounts of text as I proceed. Please understand that when metaphysical texts are used to verify a supposition that aliens came from space to do that which humans were certainly able to do on their own, I do not accept such texts as wholly historical documents. The *Epic of Gilgamesh* was not written to be a literal interpretation of historical events. Nor, in my opinion, was the Bible. This is not to say that religious texts do not reflect historical truths to some degree; it's just too much of a leap for me to believe that which was clearly written or related as parable somehow provides unassailable proof of alien overlords influencing mankind. The argument is a dead end to me because my mind is not colonized that way. This doesn't mean I don't enjoy reading about such topics or even discussing them with polite True Believers (though I'd rather discuss them with the late Mac Tonnies, or people who think like he did—that would be a marvelous conversation to have).

The essential premise advanced by Von Ward is that ABs (Advanced Beings), came to Earth and in many ways shaped the way things are now. He claims that religious texts from across the spectrum bear out the idea of ABs visiting Earth for various reasons and he further claims that human evolution could not have happened without alien intervention. While I think this is a highly questionable premise in a book that's full of borderline-ridiculous ideas, let me also note that Von Ward has clearly done exhaustive research and some of his borderline-ridiculous ideas could just as easily be described as audacious.

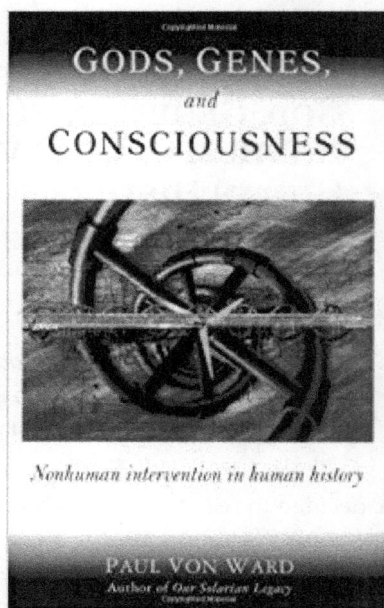

Audacious ideas get my respect. People can sit around and talk the same crap for years and then laugh at the guy who comes up with a new way of thinking about things. All disagreement aside, I have to respect the way that Von Ward looks at source materials and reaches his own conclusions. And he's careful in how he states what he believes is the truth, making it clear that he often interprets certain texts—and the ideas within—in a different way. Unlike some True Believers, he does not try to imply that his interpretation is the only correct one that all the sheeple have somehow missed. He just reinterprets things in the manner of how his own mind works. I respect him for outright owning this. Even if I think he's wackily wrong, he's honest and far more humble than many of his fellow-travelers.

One of the first examples of Von Ward totally reinterpreting the conclusions others have reached comes in the second chapter, "Who Were the First Gods?":

> A leading scholar of ancient civilizations, Arthur Cotterell, perhaps unwittingly, supports the case made in this book for considering the basis of myths as actual experience with ABs. He believes the work of psychologist Carl Jung suggested that images in "the collective unconscious stem from the actual experiences of our remote ancestors." Cotterell wrote, "The civilizations of the first planters—the cities of the Nile, the Euphrates-Tigris Valley, and the Indus—involved mythologies connected with a priesthood. The Sumerians even looked upon themselves as the property of their gods; they were workers on the divine estate." He quoted anthropologist Bronislaw Malinowski: "The myth in a primitive society. . .is not mere tale but reality lived."

> This chapter starts with the assumption that mythic and sacred material should be treated as at least a partial reflection of human experience and studied for its historicity.

If you can dig that myth is going to be used as historical text, then Von Ward's reading may seem okay to you. But again, I rebel against this idea. I worry about this concept, actually—just as I worry about kids being taught that the Bible proves the world is only 6,000 years old. Von Ward's approach is in the same camp, using text of questionable historical value to prove points of history.

I've learned all kinds of interesting things from the whacked-theory camps. I've learned, for example, that most people who believe that Atlantis existed claim a cataclysmic pole shift covered the islands in water. (Good luck with that because those stuffy, narrow-minded, establishment scientists are gonna disagree, seeing as how NASA says the last pole reversal happened 800,000 years ago.) However, when I came across the pole shift argument in Von Ward's book, I had one of those moments that I suspect only happens to me—a moment where I struggled for understanding but felt as if I must

TL;DR: THE BEST OF ODD THINGS CONSIDERED

have forgotten how the English language worked because the words just didn't form lucid ideas. In the following excerpt, note that "Andrews" refers to Shirley Andrews, "one of the preeminent modern researchers on Atlantis." And "B.P." means "before the present.":

> As a result of a planetary pole shift around 50,000 B.P., Andrews says Atlantis was left with only five islands. With another pole shift around 30,000 B.P. and the beginning of a new Ice Age, more land was lost, and only one island and an archipelago remained of the once mighty Atlantis. About 14,000 B.P., a bird-serpent war occurs, and about 12,000 B.P. the final destruction of Atlantis takes place, with the death of most inhabitants. Andrews believes a few remnants of that culture survived on various islands and shorelines. Around 4000 B.C.E., she believes another cataclysm destroyed a final outpost on Bimini Island off the coast of Florida, mostly underwater at the time. (Geological research findings support the pole shifts and cataclysms she describes.)

Wait...Geological research agrees with this? Admittedly, I was a liberal arts major from a state school but...seriously? A new Ice Age began less than 30,000 years ago? Does she mean a really bad cold front? Or is she using the term to mean what it really means—that there were sheets of ice in the northern and southern hemispheres? I sense that cannot be what she means because the last real Ice Age began 2.58 million years ago, and Andrews' usage implies something more catastrophic than just the presence of ice sheets near the poles. What am I missing? Atlantean artifacts were off the coast of Florida 4,000 years ago? I desperately want to know how Andrews came to these conclusions yet I suspect that if I find out I will end up with steam coming out of my ears.

Really, I shouldn't question any of this, but part of the problem is that Von Ward writes so earnestly and with such an outward appearance of scholarship. It's like I want to believe him, and I can sort of see getting sucked in. Then suddenly we've got a pole shift every few thousand years, several Ice Ages that come out of nowhere, remnants of Atlantis off the coast of Florida and the Great Bird-Serpent War to contend with.

In the midst of all of this questionable science and bizarre theorizing, I may have been a bit taken aback, but I still recognized something important. At the core of all of it, Van Ward really is trying to answer a question that many others have tried before to answer: *how did humans evolve?*

> Early humans, capable of conscious interaction with their environment, would have exercised a high degree of self-consciousness. While progressing slowly (by our modern standards) with tools, fire, foods and habitats, they could have developed more complex communication and social systems. They would have likely learned how to wisely relate to their environment, taking what they needed, storing seeds and roots for the winter, but leaving the plants and animals capable of replenishing themselves.

Something extraordinary happened. After hundreds of thousands of years, the gradual process of unfolding exploded in what is known as the "big bang" of human culture. Less than 50,000 years ago, social inventions began happening with increasing rapidity, and in the last 10,000 years full-blown civilizations burst upon the scene. Conventional theories simply cannot explain such a phenomenon. Other chapters deal with the problem by offering the AB-intervention hypothesis.

While I am pretty cool with the idea that Von Ward is trying to explain that which he thinks has not been explained, I'm also reminded of why this entire book required the overconsumption of sour candy to finish. Even as Von Ward dismisses some pretty interesting "conventional theories" that could explain the cultural explosion he describes, later in the book he dances with the very ideas that he dismisses. For instance, if one follows the way of thinking of Steven Pinker,[3] one might think that Darwinian selection for language skills caused this evolutionary explosion, and in a much later chapter, this very idea is discussed (though Pinker is never mentioned in this book and Noam Chomsky, whose ideas Pinker riffed on, has only one reference in this book's index). If one were looking to account for an evolutionary explosion, I think Pinker and Chomsky would offer a far better and simpler explanation than aliens interfering with mankind. And alien-free evolution is frankly a far more empowering idea.

Humans are capable of a lot, even primitive humans were, and that is an essential argument I have with Von Ward's thesis, so much of which rests on the notion that ancient man was somehow incapable of doing extraordinary things unless a greater power intervened. Hell, Terence McKenna's theory[4] that hallucinogenics and psychedelics changed the way ancient man's mind worked is far less complicated and far more plausible than the one Von Ward puts forth, and it's strange how easily Von Ward dismisses the very existence of such counter-explanatory ideas as he discusses his own bizarre theory. Then again, if he discussed competing explanations in depth, it would make it hard to continue with his own seriously flawed argument.

When I was able to suspend my disbelief, I saw Von Ward's imagination as a wondrous thing. Seriously. The man has created a human backstory that rivals that of any conspiratologist; he just traces it back a lot further. Think of those who focus on the Masons, the Knights Templar, the Jews, etc. They carve a backstory in stone so it becomes utterly believable to them as the only manner in which events could have happened. Von Ward similarly creates his own version of events, using a mishmash of myth to prove his suppositions. This is all the more loony when he uses his own unique interpretation

---

3   See especially *The Language Instinct*. My copy is a Perennial Reprint (1994). It stays in print.

4   See especially *Food of the Gods: The Search for the Original Tree of Knowledge – A Radical History of Plants, Drugs, and Human Evolution*. New York: Bantam. 1992.

of known texts and histories to support his even more unique theories:

> ...the Anunnaki leaders had different policies about helping humans. Some
> wanted only slaves, and others desired to help their human progeny real-
> ize their own potential. Because of the conflict among the ABs, groups of
> independent human thinkers apparently had to draw together in Mystery
> schools, dedicated to maintaining the secret teachings of the past. They, ap-
> parently helped by some Egyptian priests and other patrons, maintained a
> body of natural science from fields including cosmology, medicine, math-
> ematics and astronomy.

If we follow Von Ward and others who believe in alien intervention, mankind could not have possibly come up with advanced ideas without extra-
terrestrial assistance. The knowledge the Egyptians had was not theirs but
what they gleaned from otherworldly visitors. I find it sort of interesting that
even as Von Ward creates a new way of looking at human evolution and our
current state in this world, he posits the same duality that is part and parcel
with most religious beliefs. Bad Anunnaki who wanted to enslave men and
good Anunnaki who wanted to help men. Von Ward would say that the religious texts recreate the original good versus evil paradigm that the aliens
brought about. I suspect a different explanation. I think the tendency to see
the world in black and white terms is common among those who wonder
so much about human origins that they crave a specific answer. I think that
sometimes they crave this answer so badly that they will create a new dogma
to explain it all. Black and white, good and evil. I think that Von Ward is creating a system of duality just like all the other men before him have created
systems of duality. Mileage, as always, varies.

Still, I think it was the religious text documentation that really got me. It
was like the religious texts and Von Ward's theories were the loony bread on
a loony sandwich, with my brain being the meat in the middle. For example:

> Various Judaic sources provide details describing the progeny of inter-
> course between angels and humans which may offer further insight into
> some of the AB characteristics added to the human DNA pool. A fragment
> of the Book of Noah discovered with the oldest known Book of Enoch (an
> Ethiopian text) tells about a son (Noah) born to the wife of Lamech (son of
> Methuselah) who was thought to be fathered by an AB. In this version of
> the story, Enoch, who was Methuselah's father, was asked his opinion about
> whether Noah had an AB parent. Lamech had suspicions that his wife had
> been impregnated by one of the "watchers" and wanted his father to check
> with Enoch, who was now living among the ABs.

> The exchange between the two gives prima facie evidence that Noah was a
> hybrid. Methuselah told Enoch that Lamech had said his son was "unlike
> man, and resembling the sons of the God of heaven." Enoch responded by
> saying that in the time of his father Jared "some of the angels of heaven . . .
> united themselves with women . . . [and] have begotten children by them."

The implication was that this family line carried with it the DNA of those angels. So, even if Lamech was the immediate biological father, he would have passed on genes of the angels.

The Bible said it, I believe it, that settles it. Or it would if the Old Testament was a strict and accurate record of history and life was a bumper sticker. But god help me, Von Ward is so earnest. *Prima facie* evidence? One really has to be a True Believer in order to think the above is proof enough that the matter is, by all evidence, proven. This? This is why I read books like this even as I groan as I read them. I find minds like this exotic and interesting, wholly foreign to all of my first impulses.

The sheer speculation that Von Ward engages in is amazing and at times left me incredulous. Seriously, his spin on the Bible is a work of art, and I do not mean that with an ounce of sarcasm.

> Around 4,025 years ago, the time some believe the AB nuclear destruction of Sumer and Akkad (including Babylon) occurred, Abram became Abraham. He submitted to the circumcision ritual of the Semites to be accepted under the command of a different AB. Abraham's entanglement in the regional conflicts reflected the AB struggle for control of the spaceport in Sinai. Serving an unidentified AB, Abraham's body of troops and supporters headed to the Negev area to serve a defensive role. Afterwards he went into Egypt (where infighting pitted the sons of Enlil and Enki against one another) in an apparent diplomatic role (see Book of Jubilees). After perhaps five years there, he and his wife Sarai returned to Beth-el (a key AB stronghold) in Palestine.

Wait. If the ABs have nukes and a space station, what did Abraham think he was gonna accomplish? "Oh no, an ancient Jew and his followers are assembling a defense against an atomic power with space exploration capacity. RUN! RUN FOR THE HILLS!" That must have been one helluva circumcision!

I marked dozens of lines from the sections that examine the Old Testament God, or YHVH as the deity is called in the book, so many that I don't dare reproduce them here. I recommend that devout Christians give that a big old miss. I sense most Christians will find it hard to believe that Moses and others were selected by "YHVH—one of the now invisible gods—to serve as instruments for reestablishing an AB-oriented hegemony in the midst of the desolation wrought by the gods' wars." But non-Christians and atheists alike will have a difficult time as well because *God, Genes, and Consciousness* demands that the Bible and other religious and mythological texts be taken as a strict, though interestingly interpreted, historical record. Either way, Von Ward's approach is gonna test readers.

So let's stroll into the part of the book that purports to prove that ABs indeed came to Earth and mankind learned things we could never have possibly have figured out were it not for the superior Anunnaki. Let's begin at the beginning, which seems to be the best place to start:

> The scientifically dated evidence in this section leaves us with a forced choice between two fascinating conclusions. Either a very high level of human civilization has existed much longer than currently accepted theories permit, or beings more advanced than humans left evidence of their presence on Earth hundreds of thousands of years ago. The myths and legends of early humans do not claim human credit for this technology; they present the AB option.

Or—and I know I'm taking the easy way out—contemporary mainstream anthropology is correct and mankind has had plenty of time to advance to the point to where we could create fire, wheels, levers, houses, banks, antibiotics and suburban shopping malls, and myth and parable are not meant to be taken as a word-for-word recitation of fact. So there is a third option available to us.

Let's continue:

> Humans today have a strong tendency to identify new ideas and inventions with the individuals or groups responsible for their introduction. When somebody does something important and unique, they want to get credit for it. It is likely that our human ancestors were similar, and if they had been responsible for the discoveries and inventions described in these myths, would not humans have claimed the credit? Instead they gave Advanced Beings the credit.

I guess because we call tissues "Kleenex" and everyone knows who Bill Gates is, that settles it; human beings have always correctly assigned credit for inventions, and myth is again to be taken as a literal interpretation of events. Clearly that's why we call fire "The Sky Lizard's Angry Semen" and the wheel's official name is "The Space Demon's Roly-Thing."

That was sarcasm. But here are some of Von Ward's examples:

> Often, when researchers attempt to identify the oldest memories in current culture, they find that its traditions point to earlier peoples and their receipt of knowledge from ABs. For instance, an Inca shaman/teacher in Peru once told me the megalithic ruins in the Andes attributed to the Incas were traditionally known to be constructed by the ancients who preceded them. Further, he said those ancients were reportedly taught the construction techniques by the Apus (light beings). Similarly, in the Amazon, the AB Abe Mango reportedly taught the Tukano tribe building technologies, pottery making, weaving and cookery.

You'll forgive me if this is not enough proof to, you know, completely dismiss all the anthropology and evolutionary psychology that refutes all of this. It just goes on…

At the end of the last ice age, the Chippewa's Manaboshu (a Noah-like personage) received instructions from an AB on how to make a good bow and arrow and how to work with copper. These technologies defined their early culture.

Von Ward fascinates me because my first and only impulse is to think that the tale of this Chippewa leader's discoveries were passed along in a lore cloaked in superstition and ideas particular to the tribe. In other words, myths are composed of memes that make sense to the people who create them. Isn't this an infinitely easier explanation than the one that has ABs coming from space and interacting with humans for untold millennia before finally coughing up the recipe for smelting copper?

There are many more examples from different faiths:

The Bible's Old Testament is replete with stories of ABs communicating higher knowledge to early leaders. Enoch reportedly walked with the gods and was instructed by them. In another reference, he was taken into the heavens and taught "wisdom." Noah learned of the impending flood from one of the gods sympathetic to the human plight. Ezekiel received plans from the gods for the Temple at Jerusalem, walked with them and even left the Earth with them in a "fiery chariot."

Also:

On other continents, only space limitations here preclude me from presenting scores of legends like that of the ancient Frisians of Northern Europe. An AB seer and philosopher named Minno helped start their civilization. Their Earth-Mother Frya also gave them—as YHVH gave the Israelites— laws that would result in a good society.

And also:

An Azerbaijani legend credits an antediluvian personality, a wise Enoch known as a demigod in other texts, with being the first teacher of the Kiyumars and the first ruler of Iran.

We're not finished yet:

The Serpent God… gave knowledge from the Tree of Life to Eve and Adam. Prometheus gave fire (wisdom?) to prehistoric Greeks after stealing it from the heaven inaccessible to humans. A "water spider" who swam to the burning island no human could reach presented the "gift of fire" to the ancestors of the Cherokees and other Southeast U.S. tribes.

Not by a long shot:

The Sumerians admitted that the ABs they knew as the Anunnaki gave them all the sophisticated knowledge (described in their clay-tablet libraries) that current historians call "human firsts": mathematics, astronomy, medicine, agriculture, business, engineering, law, and music, among others. Gods common to Mesopotamia/Egypt and India have been identified with teaching humans advanced information: Sarasvati, the teacher of science and writing (like Ninki and Venus); and Ganesa, the giver of learning (like Thoth). Other gods are described who fit the Anunnaki pantheon: Kali of thunder and destruction, Vishnu the preserver (like Enki), and Shiva the destroyer and regenerator (like Enlil, who wanted the Cataclysm to destroy humans but was then convinced to give the survivors seeds and tools to revive civilization).

And it really does go on seemingly forever from here, with example after example of human endeavor explained by reference to religious texts and myths that invariably reveal the hand of Advanced Beings manipulating humans.

Von Ward's insistence that the similarities between all these texts and myths proves a common experience (outside of simply being human) and a common shared history with aliens is very similar to the insistence of those who believe that modern stories shared by purported alien abductees prove a common experience. The fact is, taken in their whole, most mythologies prior to the Greco-Roman period are quite different in detail. The commonalities are due to basic human personalities being turned into archetypes. The number of times Middle Eastern religions outright stole stories from older mythologies makes repetition and grafting inevitable, especially in the Old Testament. The similarities are easily explained.

I found the section on the development of language to be so annoying that I can't bring myself to discuss it in depth. How it is that humans began to speak is a difficult and contentious topic. The part of me that is still in recovery from being a Southern Baptist rebels and recoils at the very idea that anyone really thinks the story of the Tower of Babel, tarted up with aliens, holds water. It's interesting that this is the part of the book that was finally a bridge too far for me so I will share some of this section that I found so bizarre.

> Why would the Indo-European and Afro-Asiatic families split into so many branches in a small area with a concentrated population in such a short period of time? The circumstances surrounding the Tower of Babel story suggest an AB-based explanation. The word "Babel" has at least two possible origins. The Hebrew root "balal" means to "confound or mix." In Akkadian, "bab-ilu" means "gate of the gods." Both usages point to the same event.

> [...]

> Sumerian texts suggest that on two occasions ABs may have undermined human unity by forcing the adoption of different languages. But each Babel occasion actually arose as a result of conflicts among the gods. Sitchin believes one intervention (about 3450 B.C.E.) was to foil Marduk's attempt, using human labor, to achieve his own agenda... Another language-confusion event (about 2850 B.C.E.), he believes, reflected AB Ishtar and Enmerkar disputes over who would control kingdoms in Mesopotamia

and in the Indus Valley. If these interpretations are correct, then disputes among ABs (not humans) had significant language consequences for their human subjects.

Recent human history offers an unnerving parallel of dividing and controlling by the imposition of different languages. European colonists forced indigenous peoples to adopt French, English, Spanish, German, Dutch, or Portuguese in Africa, Asia and Latin America. Given the effectiveness of their manipulation in a period of a few generations, imagine what the Anunnaki could have done in a few hundred years.

Given that humans have in recent recorded history caused major shifts in spoken languages all over the world, I wonder why one needs to believe that we needed aliens thousands of years ago to achieve the same result?

As an atheist, the section that discusses the rise of "God-Cults" interested me about as much as erotica would interest a loaf of bread. Yet there was a small part in there that sort of hooked me. Discussing Jesus, Von Ward claims that Christianity is an "unintended cult."

> …Jesus believes the original light (life) was self-creating and that humans were direct manifestations of it.

> By stressing each individual's direct linkage to a self-manifesting creator, Jesus dethroned the idea that YHVH, any other AB, or their demigod and human lieutenants could be intermediaries between individuals and the ultimate source of consciousness (light). After his political execution, different groups felt empowered to establish communities of belief and lifestyle independent of the self-perpetuating priesthood that had served the AB rulers.

The last part of Von Ward's book discusses the current AB agenda where Earth is concerned. He's not wholly alarmed about the AB intentions but he warns that human beings, instead of cringing in fear and believing any story fed to them, must demand that governments share openly anything they know about ABs and their current activities. It's not surprising that Von Ward thinks there has been a cover-up. But why have governments and churches covered up such information?

> First, admission that ABs exist would cause a collapse of the entire "card house" of divine rights and powers. Second, institutional authorities do not wish to reveal that their predecessors wittingly or otherwise supported the Anunnaki who had opposed the natural development of humanity. To admit having been on the "wrong side" of that early choice between human freedom and further AB control (whether real or projected) could hardly be justified in the twenty-first century.

So, to prevent a "revolt of the masses," everyone stays quiet. Frankly, this makes the most sense out of all the cover-up explanations I have read. Too bad I have to buy into the rest of the backstory in order for it to work. *Gods,*

Genes, and Consciousness ends by suggesting that we humans (though I think, if the book is correct, some of us of us may be human-alien hybrids of some sort) are our own worst enemy and that an open discussion of our AB-influenced past will go a long way toward achieving a sustainable peace.

Okay, I snarked. I can't deny it. It's who I am. I can't help myself. At times I suspect that my complete lack of a soul where these matters are concerned works against me in ways I cannot yet understand.

Most people in this world want to know their origins. I just don't care. we're here and that's all that matters to me. To people with a more focused desire to know the origins of man, Von Ward's book is quite an astounding document. The rapid expansion of media has made new religion nearly extinct, almost ensuring that novel religions remain cults. New interpretations of old texts and myths are laughed at. So any person who looks at the breadth of human history and creates[5] a theory like this has my respect.

Though I think some of Von Ward's book is silly and some of it is outright annoying, such reactions don't really matter. In my anthropology class in college, I recall my professor talking about a debate between Richard Leakey and Donald Johanson. I don't remember the specifics but evidently the men were asked to explain gaps in the fossil record. Johanson stood up, wrote on a blackboard what, to the best of his knowledge, the gap would contain and why it was missing (and if I am incorrect in telling this story, I hope any anthropologist reading this corrects me). Leakey's response? To cross out what Johanson had written and to replace it with a huge question mark.

I have no idea if Johanson was correct. I do know that any contrarian asshole can stand in a place of intellectual safety and demean the work of those who are willing to put their ideas and egos on the line when presenting potentially erroneous or controversial information. Put up or shut up is the fairer response. And Von Ward certainly put up. But I'm kind of a contrarian asshole myself. I can see that. I simply will not accept a religious text as a factual account of anything except a human desire to tell stories, to explain that which currently lacks clear definition, to make life more interesting than it is. My deeply humanist worldview also tells me that mankind is capable of doing amazing and terrible things within the current, accepted evolutionary time frame. I look at the scope of history and religion and see the struggle of men. Von Ward looked at the same information and saw something vastly different. I'm happy that he shared it.

That is why this book is valuable. That is why this book is worth reading. Any asshole—like me—can tell you why a book is a load of nonsense. But it takes a brave and intellectually honest person to devour the necessary history,

---

5   "Creates" probably isn't the right word; it appears that Von Ward had help refining his theory, and he riffs heavily off the works of Zecharia Sitchin (not plagiarism, but rather as parallel points with differing interpretations).

religious thought and comparative literature and come up with a wholly new explanation of why we are the way we are. If I groan at times, the fact is that I have copped often to my own scattered nature. I lean toward softer forms of intellectualism. My mind is, at best, undisciplined, and a book like Von Ward's, whatever its faults, requires attention. As taxing as it was to read, I'm left with a strange affection.

FURTHER READING

Chariots of the Gods: Unsolved Mysteries of the Past
Erich von Däniken

Flim-Flam! Psychics, ESP, Unicorns, and Other Delusions
James Randi

There Were Giants Upon the Earth: Gods, Demigods, and Human Ancestry: The Evidence of Alien DNA
Zecharia Sitchin

Deviance & Death

Sexual deviance and death are topics already fraught with difficulties. Sex and death make people nervous. You definitely can't talk about necrophilia with your coworkers and you have to keep your voice down if you bring up death photography in a restaurant or the family at the table next to you may complain. Let my discussions tide you over until you find yourself in the right place with the right audience receptive to musings on eros *and/or* thanatos.

PERVERSITY THINK TANK
By Supervert
Supervert 32C Inc. (2010)
Original post: 10/19/2010

Why do I consider this book odd?
This tiny book's arrangement is in itself odd, with a scholarly discussion running across the top of the pages, a more personal narration running across the bottom, and large, black squares over all the pictures. Then there's the content...

I have a pretty serious book crush on Supervert. Every now and then you come across an author who seems very much like he or she is on your wavelength, whose words seem like they could have come out of your own brain. Supervert is one of those authors for me. I felt a great amount of kinship reading a few of the stories in *Necrophilia Variations* (and yeah, when you say that, when you admit a book with this particular title spoke to you directly, you are making a certain statement about yourself and now that I am officially a harmless, middle-aged woman, I feel I am safe making any sort of admission I want). Anyway, I found myself nodding a lot when reading *Perversity Think Tank* as Supervert tried to answer the question: "What is perversity?"

If I didn't know this before reading the book, I now understand that defining perversity can be very much akin to holding mercury, but Supervert manages to nail down some interesting perspectives on the topic. Mostly, I walked away knowing what perversity isn't, while marveling that there is another human being on the planet who had thought about the complete narcissism that is involved in reproductive incest. I will discuss this in a moment.

Supervert has a unique insight into perversion. He ran the site PervScan, wherein he scoured news for anything with a hint of sexual deviance. While this book was inspired by the musings that the PervScan articles inspired, it's not a compilation of the site's "greatest hits." Though a couple of

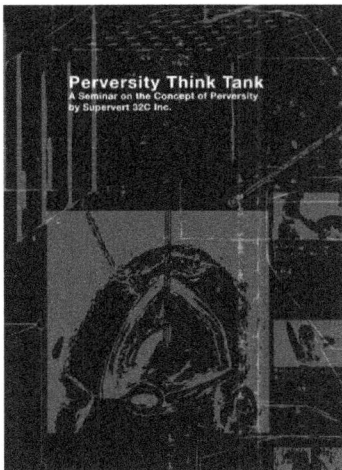

PervScan cases are referenced, *Perversity Think Tank* is more of an inquiry into the nature and meaning of perversion. Interestingly, compiling all those stories of strange sexual behavior convinced Supervert that most of the acts he cataloged were something other than true perversion.

> Many of the acts I covered on PervScan—like the three middle-aged brothers who sexually assaulted their bedridden mother while she lay suffering amid lice, roaches, and fecal matter—struck me less as perverse than as ignorant, heedless, cruel. There were days when I thought my compendium of deviant doings was nothing more than a catalogue of errors in judgement and lapses in common sense.

This is an important point. Despite my own sympathy for the devil (as well as my abiding interest in the bizarre and perverted), even I find myself defining any deviation from the erotic norm, up to and including the worst sexual crimes, as "perversion," when psychopathy or subnormal intelligence often provide a better explanation.

As Supervert studied more examples of sexual oddity, he found that behaviors that initially struck him as somewhat perverse began to seem somewhat tame.

> After you've read about a guy who wants to eat his own penis, you feel like you've pretty much heard it all. How could mere exhibitionism seem perverted in comparison to a man who wants to fry his genitalia in a pan?

Maybe this isn't the most profound of statements, but it struck me that I don't know another person in real life who speculates on such matters, who has, in fact, heard it all to the point that nothing is shocking and the outré seems positively normal and comforting. I often feel as if my interest in perversion is itself a perversion. I wish I knew more people who know the ins and outs of the Armin Meiwes[1] case or all the details about Sharon Lopatka.[2] It would make me happy to know that other suburbanites with gray hair, a

---

1   Armin Meiwes is a German vorerephile who posted a message in 2001 on a website called Cannibal Cafe looking for a young man who would be willing to let Meiwes kill him and eat him. Bernd Jürgen Armando Brandes answered the message, the two met up and Meiwes filmed the gory proceedings, wherein he indeed cut off parts of Brandes' body while he was still alive, and ate them. Meiwes was arrested after he shared details of the killing online, while asking for new victims. He received a life sentence in German prison. https://en.wikipedia.org/wiki/Armin_Meiwes

2   Sharon Lopatka in 1996 entered into a "consensual homicide" with a man named Robert "Bobby" Glass. She sold her used underwear on the Internet and engaged in sexual role play online that was violent enough that other users of the BDSM site found it upsetting. She met Glass through one of the violent sex sites she frequented and ended up driving from her home in Maryland to Glass' trailer in North Carolina, where she voluntarily permitted Glass to strangle her to death. After finding a note Lopatka left behind asking her husband not to look for her, her husband called the police and the crime was pieced together from emails on Lopatka's computer. Glass was convicted of voluntary manslaughter but died in 2002, two weeks before he was due to be released. The case was fodder for many media mills due to the sexual nature of the murder and because the case was one of the first wherein a murder investigation hinged on incriminating emails. https://en.wikipedia.org/wiki/Sharon_Lopatka_homicide

MOSTLY NONFICTION: DEVIANCE & DEATH

love for kittens and an interest in quilting wouldn't throw me out of their houses if they knew what goes into and on in my head.

Supervert discusses the various meanings of perversion, noting that one of the first philosophical interpretations held that sexual perversion refers to any act that thwarts reproduction. Easy enough, except this means that a married couple who continue to have sex after the wife has experienced menopause are therefore perverts. To further complicate this definition, Supervert brings up an episode from Sade's *The 120 Days of Sodom* in which a libertine expresses his desires to masturbate and ejaculate on the crowning head of an infant as it was born. That seems pretty perverted, but it can only happen because of human reproduction. In a sense, this shows the complete creativity involved in true perversion and how useless most definitions can be. Freud defined perversity as any sex act that diverted the focus of sex from the sex organs. By that restrictive definition, everyone who has ever been turned on by the way a patent leather corset hugs the waist is a pervert. The more the merrier, right? Maybe, but the point is that sweeping generalizations are of little value in an effort to understand the true nature of perversion.

In the course of his inquiry Supervert brings up all the usual suspects (like Sade) but he also discusses those whose opinions on sex are suspect at best (and therefore hilarious, at least to me). The sad, misogynistic, sexually inept Schopenhauer makes an appearance, to my delight. Evidently the dour philosopher had a foot in a pre-Freud camp, contending that perversion was anything not involving sex organs since this ensured that such genetically defective perverts would not reproduce. This makes my lack of children somewhat interesting. Then again, as Supervert reminds us, Sade had three children.

The groundwork is all very interesting, but it was Supervert's discussion of incest that confirmed my book crush. The first revelation was obvious, but not something that I had ever really considered. According to Supervert, the inbred yokel who has sex with his teenage daughter is likely not doing it in order to violate the taboo of inter-familial sex. Rather, he is doing it because she is likely the only female available to him when he wants sex. However repellent, the act might often be more about availability than perversion as such. It is a far different thing for a father to desire his daughter because she is his daughter (or a mother to desire her son because he is her son, etc.). And here we land upon a key component of perversion, by Supervert's reckoning—that it concerns consideration for the act itself, and not just the easy, sloppy depravity that leads a person to have sex with whomever or whatever is closest at hand.

Concerning incest, Supervert goes on to raise an issue that surprised me. It's something that I had considered, but that I didn't know anyone else had considered (and here I was secretly thrilled because when one entertains dark and perverted thoughts, one never thinks anyone else would ever in a million years think the same thing). The issue is the narcissism present in deliberate incest.

> A libertine doesn't molest his daughter because she just happens to be there. A libertine molests his daughter because he consciously wants to create a being who is both his child and his grandchild—and still a future sex object itself. Then he molests that daughter/granddaughter hybrid to obtain another new being who is child, grandchild, great grandchild—and still sex object.

Once you get to a certain point in this process, the end result is an appalling creation that is more or less masturbation by proxy.

> The incestuous libertine approaches ever closer to a reproductive act whose result is a child 100% himself, and yet that ultimate point is always deferred by increasingly small percentages. The libertine can never quite dispense with the shred of genetic material that belongs to the maternal line, and yet the fact remains that, by fucking the offspring of his own offspring, he is inevitably fucking more and more of himself.

It is this awareness of the act and the results that is important when considering perversion:

> And that, as Sade recognized, is one of the most striking characteristics of perversity: it is deliberate, self-conscious, pellucid. Its hallmark is… its intentionality… The libertine is able to reflect on his unwholesome activities. Self-awareness makes his pleasures all the greater.

I think this is an important insight. Too often people with dire sexual compulsions are labeled as perverts, when they are in fact people with little control over their acts, who are governed by needs that defy any sort of consciousness. Perversion, as a philosophical approach to depravity, requires far more than this.

The only part of this book that I found the least bit disagreeable was Supervert's passage about how rape could possibly be a part of the evolutionary process, though he is hardly alone in pondering whether or not rape is a part of natural selection.

> Evolutionary biologists have pointed out that natural selection provides an obvious impetus for it, insofar as rape improves the rapist's chances for reproductive success. That my friend was raped in Central Park was symbolic: in the greatest swath of grass and trees in New York, she was subject to the Darwinism of her attackers.

Back when I first heard this particular line of thinking many years ago in an anthropology class in college, I was skeptical. Even 10,000 years ago, didn't women understand the causality between sex and pregnancy, even if they didn't understand the precise mechanism? I think they did. I seem to recall that as early as 7th century BC in Greece that a specific plant was discovered to be an excellent contraceptive and abortificant and was so over-used it ended up extinct, accidentally eradicated.

The concept never made much sense to me, especially once mankind reached a place of reason, however primitive it may seem now. Women often don't look kindly on the offspring of rape. If they couldn't abort, those chil-dren would likely be abandoned or exposed, or they would be raised less kindly. And what about the men in primitive societies whose women were subject to rape? I think they would also have reacted poorly. The rapists would likely have been subject to physical violence that made them rethink their impulses, if they survived the violence. Or they would get kicked out of the tribe and would have had a far harder time surviving at all. If there was ever a genetic code for rape to ensure one's genetic material lived on, it likely got killed off when the offspring of such unions were subject to abor-tion, abandonment or resentful care, and when the rapists themselves were violently neutralized before they could spread very much seed at all. Even if women only became aware of how pregnancy happened during recorded history, I would think that societal reactions to rape would still be enough to wipe out any selective advantage for rape within a dozen or so generations.

Or that was my kneejerk reaction. My degree is in English literature so all my biological musings should be taken with a grain of salt. Yet it seems there are some who know quite a bit of evolutionary psychology who agree with me. Regardless of which side is correct, it's still interesting to analyze our dark and not-so-dark impulses, wondering what is innate, what is learned and what may be the result of sheer pathology.

Perversity Think Tank is full of enlight-ened philosophical inquiries into sex acts even I would describe as bizarre, or perverted. Some of the best parts might be located in Supervert's discourses on various blacked-out images. These images covered a lot of ground. Like men who like to ejaculate into a woman's eye. Like a pornographer who wanted to make a skin flick out of a woman giving birth. Like an almost touching picture of a couple on a bed, the man smoking, the woman lying on her side, staring at the man. Like the solipsistic nature of POV porn. Like his reaction to a simple painting and how this painting shows clearly how alone the pervert is in his or

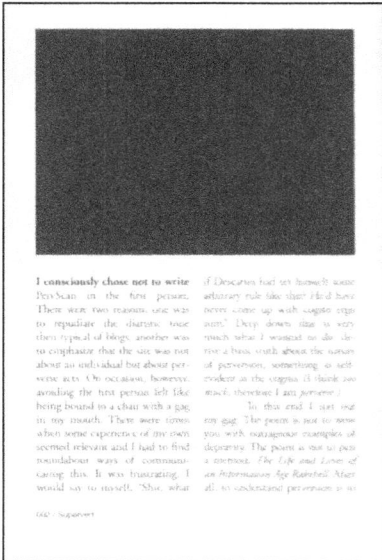

An example of a blacked-out image from *Perversity Think Tank*.

her own mind. Like a piece of art that provokes thoughts as to whether or not autoerotic asphyxiation is a "perveme" (Supervert discusses pervemes—perversion memes—in the book). Like a bestiality film clip that proved there is indeed a noise that can inspire disgust. I think I most enjoyed Supervert's reactions to the art he deliberately blocks out of the book.

This book isn't for everyone. But if you are a fellow traveler on certain roads, you will want to get a copy. It will be interesting to note how you read this book. I read the "top half" from beginning to end, then I read the "bottom half." I paused during the bottom half to read the descriptions that accompanied the blacked-out pictures. I read the book in this manner twice, then looked up the pictures (or as many as were available online), then I reread the descriptions. For a small, straightforward book, it requires a lot of attention. It's salacious enough to inspire prurient thoughts in those who are simply in this for the titillation, yet the book is not pornography. The goal is to inspire interaction and thought rather than arousal. It demands interaction and close attention. It's a book I expect to reread. I am unsure if the book available on Amazon has the same brown dust jacket as the copy I have, but it's quite lovely either way. Books as small works of art are rare these days.

Further Reading

Pure Filth
Jamie Gillis and Peter Sotos

Bob Flanagan: Supermasochist
Edited by Andrea Juno and V. Vale

Post-Depravity
Supervert

SLEEPING BEAUTY III, MEMORIAL PHOTOGRAPHY: THE CHILDREN

By Stanley R. Burns, M.D.
Burns Archive Press (2010)
Original post: 10/19/2010

Why do I consider this book odd?
Pictures of dead children.

I'd intended to discuss this book long ago but then I put it up on display with a piece of art that Mr. OTC bought for me. Once something is on a stand behind glass, I am loath to mess with it too much. After I installed software to analyze my website, however, I noticed a lot of traffic coming from searches about death photography. Then, shockingly, I noticed some hits coming from Pinterest. You know, the site where people share pictures of cake, high heels, knitting disasters and celebrities with cats. I never thought death photography would be a subject of interest on such a fluffy corner of the Web, and for some reason that discovery was enough to encourage me to get my book off the stand and discuss it. Actually, I have several Burns Archive books on creepy topics that I should discuss at some point.

For now, I'm going to discuss *Sleeping Beauty III*. This book is much smaller in size than *Sleeping Beauty I* and *Sleeping Beauty II*, almost appropriately small because this volume deals with children exclusively. *Sleeping Beauty III* has 125 pictures from the 1840s to present time. Though the book is definitely Western-centric—and truly most death photography is of white people—it contains some pictures from other cultures.

Some people find memorial photography morbid. If you stumble across a Facebook account where death photography is discussed or reproduced, the comments are always interesting. Some will express an appreciation for the history, while others will exclaim that parents long ago were insane or that the whole thing in general is somehow morally wrong or just gross. "Ewww! Why would anyone want to take a picture of a dead person?" As much as

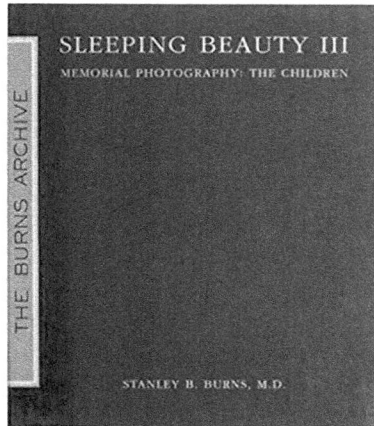

I dislike it when people react to these pictures from a strictly modern sensibility or out of some squeamish quasi-morality, I often have a hard time explaining why such images appeal to me. Burns does his best to explain why these images may seem so jarring:

> It is difficult for most of us today to understand the prior culture's need to take memorial photographs. We no longer live with personal death and dying as part of our everyday lives. By the 1930s, dealing with death had been left to professionals ranging from physicians to morticians. The advance of medicine, control of killer epidemics, the ability to treat disease, and the removal of the sick from the home made us unaccustomed to living with and seeing death. Children dying before parents, something so common in the nineteenth century, has become unusual in the twentieth century.

He goes on:

> Memorial postmortem photographs have deep meaning for mourners. These keepsakes become special icons that help survivors move through the bereavement process. Healthy grieving ultimately distances us from the dead. The human bond, our connection with others, is mankind's strongest guiding emotion and thus influences our fears and actions. These images represent confrontation with our loved one's mortality and our own.

I would like to think this fear of death that these images can provoke is behind the "Yuck!" reactions people sometimes express.

I often have a hard time discussing death photography because I relate to such images on an emotional level. While the appeal of the Burns Archive collection tends toward the visceral response, Burns offers useful information in the book to provide context and history. I find the best way to discuss this little book is to reproduce a few pictures and quote the information that Burns offers to help us put it all into an historical context.

> Reading postmortem photography comes with understanding the culture of death in a given era. Today it is traditional to close the eyes of the dead. But in the past, when a memorial photograph was taken, families frequently requested, especially for children, that the eyes be open. This was particularly the case for children who had never been photographed when they were alive. A second, eyes-closed photograph with changed pose would signal the memorial photograph. Photographs that depict the dead child in some sort of activity as if alive are considered "posthumous mourning portraits."

This picture is haunting. It looks to me like the child's eyes may have been painted on the print to make them look open. The symbolism of this little boy at death's door really isn't symbolism. He's dead and gone, and his eyes don't give this picture any ambiguity.

Photographing the dead with eyes closed is testimony to the acceptance of death. Keeping the eyes open seems to be an attempt to keep death at bay, to deny the undeniable. They reveal the heartbreaking pain of families fighting to keep the dead alive for one more image. In some cases the child is surrounded with toys or other objects to show his favorite possessions.

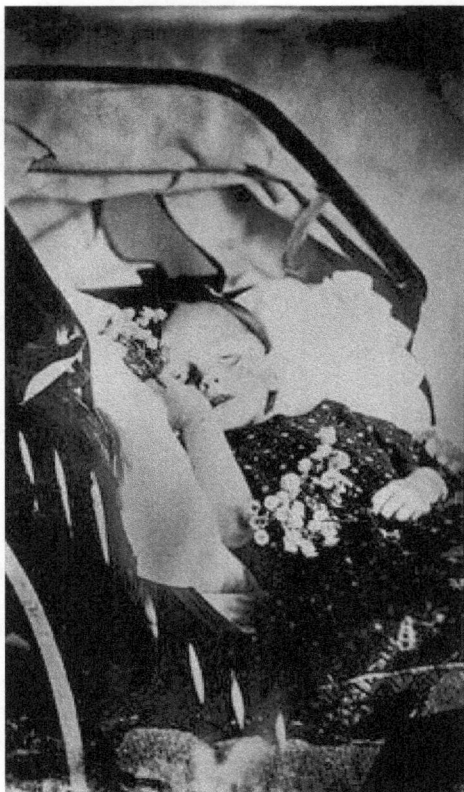

This little girl in her carriage had her eyes open but she's clearly dead. This is how so many of the children with their eyes open appear—even if the parents wanted pictures to show the child as if alive, the results to the modern eye seldom convey life.

We can observe something quite curious from this time: with the exception of children who died from dehydration or from viruses that left conspicuous skin rashes and adults who succumbed to extreme old age or deforming cancers, the dead would often appear to be quite healthy. Ironically, because of modern methods for sustaining life, contemporary corpses don't look nearly as robust as the remains of our ancestors.

This little boy does look very much like he is alive and is just unhappy at being photographed. His father's expression doesn't give us any real clue that this is a memorial photograph. In a sense, this makes the photo all the creepier.

This picture is a bit more ambiguous. There are signs that this is not a happy photograph—the mother's expression, who would have paid money back then for a professional photo of a sleeping baby? But the child, even with eyes closed, seems healthy.

The industrialization of the early nineteenth century drove the rural populace into cities and transformed them into overcrowded slums and factory towns: a fertile breeding ground for infectious disease. Along with epidemics of cholera, yellow fever, and small pox, childhood diseases devastated the country. Diphtheria, scarlet fever, measles and mumps spread rapidly and killed quickly. In a matter of days, a family and occasionally an entire village could lose all its children.

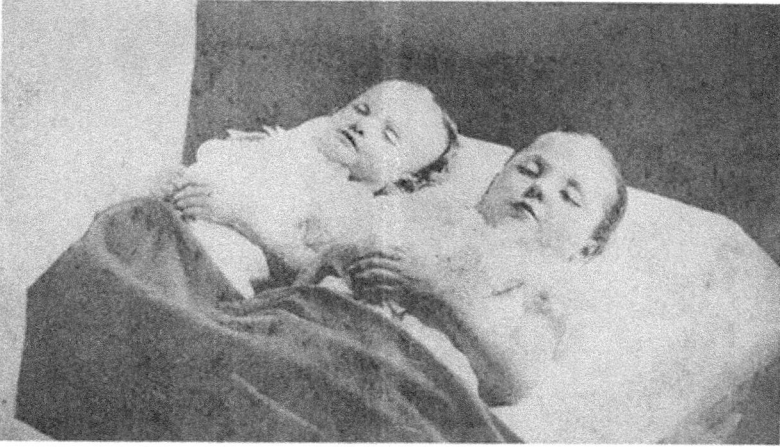

As observed above, these children don't show the horror of the illness that killed them on their bodies. They really do look like they are sleeping.

Of all the subjects in memorial photographs, images of children are the most common. Parents desperately wanted to preserve the lives and existence of their cherished loved ones. Often the memorial photograph was the only picture of the child. In contrast to memorial photographs of adults, memorial photos of children often emphasized the facial features, creating an increased feeling of intimacy.

This little girl looks like she may have suffered a while before she died but she is a perfect embodiment of the intimate look at the child in an attempt to record her features.

In the United States professional postmortem photography ended by the 1930s. In European, Latin American and other cultures it remained an active part of the bereavement process until the late 20th century. It was particularly popular in Eastern Europe...

For whatever reason, this is the one that haunts me the most. I think it's the somberness of the photo—the little casket laid upon a cloth on a table, the wreath, the siblings posing for the last time—with the obvious signs of everyday life in the background. Note the coats upon hooks hanging over their heads, the door with their apartment number. It's quite sobering to have death so close in the midst of everyday life.

This picture is notable not only because it is from the Philippines but also because of the expression on the face of the woman closest to the camera. We often see in these photographs a sort of solemn grace but it is not often we see a person clearly fighting back open sorrow. Several of the women have very sad demeanors. When I contrast them to most of the Caucasian adults featured in this book, their sorrow is almost refreshing. I am from stoic stock myself, for the most part, and there's something about a stoic face when a child has died that makes the observer feel like death was so common that perhaps parents were less affected than we would be now. That's untrue, of course, but it's just how I feel as I look at these pictures.

> During the past two decades memorial photography has had an increasingly significant place in children's hospitals and in grief and bereavement programs... Whatever the artistic or personal sensibilities of the bereaved, it is our hope that this series will help those who have lost a loved one to use photography to honor the lives of their children, however short, and to help overcome their grief.

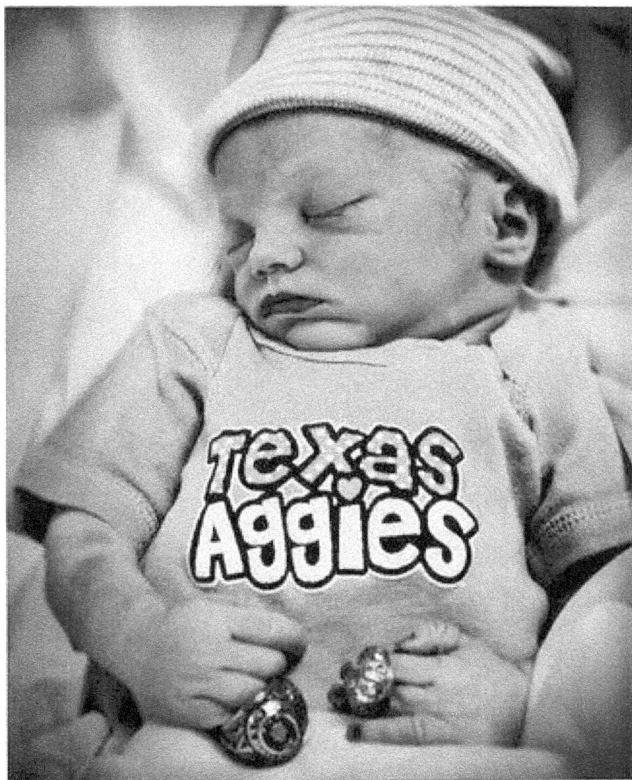

Most memorial photography, even as it varies, follows certain markers of decorum. This baby's death photograph almost has a lighthearted joviality to it that gives no quarter to ideas of gravitas. Her parents' college rings, the Aggie gear, painted nails... But death is so very personal, and humor can so often be married to affection and love. This is not one of my favorite photographs but it has a lot in common with the photographs that were so deeply personal that they needed no explanation. One cannot look at this picture and not see that it is deeply personal in spite of being so deeply affected, and that there is the same story behind it: all the plans the parents had for their little girl are gone.

That's what this collection is. That's the heart of this book. The loss of hope for a future even as parents tried to keep some memory of their lost child in the present. It's really quite something when a book of photographs conveys such a specific emotion. I highly recommend this book, but since I recommend every Burns Archive book published, that was probably a foregone conclusion.

Further Reading

Sleeping Beauty: Memorial Photography in America
Stanley B. Burns, M.D.

Sleeping Beauty II: Grief, Bereavement and the Family in Memorial Photography, American & European Traditions
Stanley B. Burns, M.D., with Elizabeth A. Burns

Wisconsin Death Trip
Michael Lesy

Death Scenes: A Homicide Detective's Scrapbook
Edited by Sean Tejaratchi; Text by Katherine Dunn

READING PETER SOTOS

With obsession often comes compulsion. I read Peter Sotos in the spirit of compulsion. Whether I want to do it or not, I do because the emotional laying-waste that happens when I read his books is perversely irresistible. The opinions I had about him changed when I read him carefully, and his work shows a truth about the extremity of the human experience that few others are brave enough to reveal. These are hard books to read, intellectually and viscerally, but they changed the way I look at the will to harm and the will to survive harm, the cruelty and the hope that haunt aggressors and victims alike.

TOOL.
By Peter Sotos
Nine-Banded Books (2011)
Original post: 09/09/2014

Why do I consider this book odd?
Because Peter Sotos is the sort of writer whose prose is so indescribable that I have to call it Sotos-esque.

I finished reading *Tool.*[1] at three in the morning and didn't really sleep that night. I read it in one sitting. It only took a few hours, but when I was finished I felt hollowed out. Sick. Queasy. Not unlike how it feels when you crash after a speed bender. Jittery and empty yet all too aware that sleep is not coming. Working through parts of this book I felt like I was being flayed. I think anyone who was ever victimized will find Sotos daunting, but of all his books that I have read thus far, this one was the most upsetting to me. The reason I was so upset? Because that which is wrong in this book is often wrong in me.

Of course we all know that I read upsetting books because I like being upset (or sickened or awakened or whatever happens to me when I confront difficult content). But even within that paradigm I take a beating when I read Sotos. Without engaging in too much self-analysis, I can only assume that it was a beating I needed or truly wanted in some way. I read Sotos because on some level we have similar thoughts—and a book like this could only be devastating to a person who has already been down this road. To the unaffected reader, it might just come off as vulgarity, or pointless obscenity.

Despite being trained to analyze literature in an academic manner, I prefer to observe my own emotional response when I read. I don't really care about the schools of thought and the tradition of aesthetic transgression that many attempt to apply to Sotos' work. When I read him I care only about my reaction, how he pokes at my own obsessions, how he knows so much more than anyone else about the will to harm and the will to survive harm.

I don't know how this fact had not jumped out at me before, but in every book, keeping in mind every little bit of genuine autobiographical data he gives, Peter Sotos is playing different roles and channeling different people. He is exploring humanity by speculating about the worst things that go through the minds of the worst people. Because he is taking on the roles of others, Sotos, in a very real sense, is engaging in psychodrama. That is why I

---

1   The period is part of the title.

am so wrung out at the end of each book he writes. His psychodrama speaks to my own worries, neuroses, experiences and fears.

This is purely incidental. Peter Sotos is not writing for you or for me. Never forget that. Any meaning you take from Sotos' words may have nothing to do with his intentions. He's not trying to relate to us. His psychodramas are his own, so deeply personal and so clearly not intended for the purgation of others. It is for this reason that I am interested in the extreme reactions his writing provokes, especially in those who find themselves angry at what they consider to be Sotos' wickedness.

But no matter how incidental my connection to Sotos' writing may be, reading *Tool.* was a great emotional purge for me. Even in the extremity of another person's psychodrama I found little pieces of my own experiences, most of them unpleasant. Something in me is perverse enough to enjoy being psychically poked. It's a useful kind of pain, I think.

This is the first time I have read the material in *Tool.*, though contents of this book have been published before, most notably by Jim Goad's old imprint, in a compendium of Sotos' early works entitled *Total Abuse*. Sotos' life took a beating in the mid-80s. He was charged with obscenity for publishing a 'zine called *Pure*, and was ultimately convicted of possession of child pornography.[2]

People interested in fringe culture often know there is a link between Peter Sotos and child pornography. Outside of hardcore fans, few know the details. Sotos did not have a pile of kiddie porn. He was not involved in the creation or sale of child pornography. He never violated a child. He indeed used an image of child pornography in his 'zine but it is important to note that the image was not why Sotos came to the authorities' attention. Rather, he was on the radar of the justice system because a copy of *Pure* was found in the possession of a suspected child abductor in Scotland. In the Internet Age, it seems almost impossible that the contents of *Pure*—a 'zine devoted to serial killer culture and the visceral, nasty details of murder—could be considered obscene. I tend to think the obscenity charges may have stemmed from the

---

2   Sotos was probably the first person charged under the revised Illinois Child Pornography Act. The act went into effect on November 18, 1985 and he was charged with possession of child pornography on December 5, 1985. He was indeed in possession of child porn, as he had used a photocopy from a kiddie porn mag in *Pure*, and he received a suspended sentence for using that image. A couple of years after his arrest, he began writing the content that makes up *Tool.*

fact that the legal system, like me, didn't immediately pick up on the fact that Sotos role-plays as he writes and was not personally advocating the murder or rape of children. In 1985, the American public was not subject to the relentless invasion of serial killer culture on television, in movies, books and video games. In 2014, there is nothing in any edition of *Pure* you can't find on, say, Best Gore, Documenting Reality and sites devoted to child abuse apologia. Now there are "creepypastas," short horror stories shared online, that dwarf Sotos in terms of repulsive and horrifying content. You don't even have to go to the much-touted and seldom-visited dark web to find content at least as upsetting as anything in *Pure*, if not far worse. Some of the content would be fodder for any of a number of police procedural programs on prime time television. But there you go. Times change.

The obscenity arrest and child pornography charge caused no small amount of chaos in Sotos' life, and *Tool.* is the document that the chaos inspired.

Part One is a slice of Ian Brady, as imagined by Sotos. This section was upsetting, to be sure. Sotos manages to channel the monster, the bully, the worm who thought he was a lion, yet who was also acutely aware of the real cruelty he was inflicting on a child and was unable to stop. And it's a thing to behold. I had a reaction that was wholly unexpected.

Take this small snippet, as Sotos portrays Brady tormenting a little girl, probably Lesley Ann Downey:

> No one but your mom cares, I guess. But you'll never see your mom again…
> so … I guess … no one cares for this poor fucking little cunt who sits in
> front of me, crying like a big fucking baby. Cry, cry. Crybaby. Fucking cunt
> crybaby.

Have you ever been at the mercy of someone bigger and stronger than you, someone who was intent on hurting you in some manner, who then went on to mock your reaction to being hurt? Someone who punches you or calls you the nastiest name possible and then laughs at you and calls you a crybaby when you recoil? I think most of us have. Maybe it was a demented parent, a cruel teacher or a callous bully. There is something so vicious in causing harm then mocking those whom you harm. This little snippet was like a punch in the gut in how evocative it was of my own memory.

I became aware of how much I knew of the murder of Lesley Ann Downey because, even though Sotos does not reveal anything Lesley would have said, he imbues Brady's brutal rants with elements of her pleading.

> Let me show you something. Let me show you … this.

I'll leave it to your imagination what it is that Brady via Sotos shows Lesley, but this passage was interesting to me because of something Lesley actually says on the tape recording that Myra Hindley and Ian Brady made

TL;DR: The Best of Odd Things Considered

of their assault on the little girl (the transcription is all over the Internet if you want to read the whole thing):

> Can I just tell you summat? I must tell you summat.

It's notable that Sotos channeled the cadence of Lesley's pleas into Ian Brady's menace. But more notable is that I, the reader, picked up on it. That's one of the major reasons a person should read Sotos' books—to see what it is you really know and how you react to finding out you know it. Despite having read Brady, and knowing about Sotos' obsession with Lesley Ann Downey, the Moors murders are not one of my own obsessions. Yet somehow I gleaned enough that I could recognize the mimicry of Lesley in those taunts. Down to the cadence of the words. I have no idea what this may mean other than that I spend a lot of time in very dark places. But it does explain to me why I keep reading Sotos. He's a dark mirror.

Part One also touches on the torment that Lesley's mother felt. Arguably, she was the most famous of the parents of the Moors murders victims. Her agony fueled a lot of media attention. Ann West's unending grief is previewed in this harangue:

> Think now – of how painful the rest of your mommy's life is going to be. How she'll hurt from the moment she notices you're gone 'til the day she dies. How she'll never be able to think of anything else. How nothing else will ever matter. How no other thoughts will be able to push the images of your pain and torture and desperate death out of her mind. You will always be there – like a Catholic's bleeding and crying christ on a cross – in the forefront of her mind. Everything she does from now on will be controlled by images of you laughing in your crib … turning into images of you silent in your casket.

And that is exactly what happened, though it's hard to see how it could have turned out any differently for Ann West.[3] Your little girl gets killed by two degenerate sacks of shit, and they make an audio recording of her torture, and one of the murderers sends you letters from prison, and you end up with very few emotional options. Ann West used her sorrow to court publicity whenever Myra Hindley sought release from prison, and her interactions with the press fueled some of Sotos' analysis of the role of the media in the continual re-rape and re-murder of famous child victims. I hadn't looked at Ian Brady this way, as much as I despise him, but it makes sense that Brady reveled in the potential pain caused to the parents of his victims before he ever killed them.

Sotos hammers this theme home later when he has his Brady proxy muse upon the state of American television and its enormous love for the victim,

---

3   I don't know a lot about Ann West but I do know she went to her death convinced that Myra Hindley was the person who strangled her daughter and swore to haunt Hindley from beyond the grave. I really love her for that.

with a dose of what caused so many people to think that the Satanic Panic could possibly be real—repressed memories.

> …children are so… innocent. And trusting. Kids' minds are so fragile. They can't handle abuse the way an adult might be able to. Kids' minds fall apart. I know all this is true because I saw it on TV.
>
> Do you watch GERALDO?
>
> OPRAH?
>
> 20/20? 60 MINUTES? FRONTLINE? HARD COPY? A CURRENT AFFAIR?
>
> christ – they've all done specials on child sexual abuse. They're fucking great shows, too. Kinda stupid – but great to watch. I've seen all sorts of weepy mothers on 'em. And they teach you all sorts of things. Healthy, moral sorts of things.

Sotos, via his Brady proxy, is laying out very neatly the dissonance in American discourse that existed in the 1980s and exists now. The precursors to the Nancy Grace-monsters made a lot of money off genuine victims and helped create new classes of victims—people who became convinced by lunatic therapists that they had repressed memories of horrific abuse. Another class of victims were those who were accused of the worst men can do because an eight-year-old told improbable tales after a True Believer worked on him for months until he said what he needed to say to make the badgering stop. In addition to the victim ouroboros that marks much of the 1980s and 1990s preoccupation with Satanism and ritual sexual abuse, it was during this time that the American public really got a chance to wallow in the victim mire.

All those abused people recovering memories, all those damaged people who were really abused and had the misfortune to cross paths with television producers, all those families trying to put themselves right again—they all became the side show that fed the American appetite for abuse. We first got a taste for it with some of the game shows a couple of decades earlier. (*Queen for a Day* was a hoot for people who wanted to see human misery alleviated with a brand new refrigerator.) But by the time the talk show circuit became a complete freak show, we no longer cared if the people who stood up and shared their grief, real or imagined, ended up with anything good at the end. Now we've decided that the worst men can do is great entertainment—many people know the names of exploited or murdered little girls (and a few boys here and there) because reliving their torture is evidently quite fun. Caylee Anthony, Elizabeth Smart, Jon-Benet Ramsey, Polly Klaas—B-movie actresses don't have that level of name recognition.

And what healthy, moral sorts of things have we learned? That some people are weak? That some people are easily led? That the depths of human depravity will never be plumbed? That we are superior because we haven't been easily led and haven't killed a child? You tell me.

Mostly, what we have learned is this, still coming from the mind of the Brady character as he speaks to his child victim:

> Your pain will make me want to keep you alive. I'll want to watch you die forever.
>
> Please stop crying.
>
> I'm sorry.

We are keeping these victims alive and watching them die forever. My jury is still out on whether or not this is a bad thing. In the case of a kidnapped child whose fate is unknown, relentless media attention is a good thing (for those who are afforded it). Mostly, however, it's just an orgy of salacious details. *Were you afraid? Did you miss your mother? What did the rapist say before he let you go? Do you feel lucky to be alive? Do you?* I'm as guilty as anyone else— as my at-times-encyclopedic knowledge of killers demonstrates.

But am I sorry? I hope I am. I sense Sotos is. I know Nancy Grace isn't.

What I am not speaking about from Part One is almost as important as what I did speak of, but this is a very hard chapter to read. Animal abuse, child porn, total abuse—all of it—spoken of without any mercy or even a chance for the reader to catch a breath. Sotos describes in nauseating detail the harm a man can do a little girl. He speaks of the mental torture such a man inflicts on the helpless—tears are as important as blood to the sadist.

Part Two comes from the mind of a john who is looking over the prostitute he paid to give him a blow job. It's far less horrifying than Part One, but still dark and obscene. The speaker discusses the prostitute's bad habits and how they directly cause her degradation:

> Her drinking – her drinking problem – her drunk existence is everything one sees. Her posture. Her gross sexual gestures. The shape of her mouth and nose and eyes. The veins on her neck and bony chest. Saggy tits, bruises, scars, nicks she doesn't feel, gaunt, stretched and hungry stomach, tooth-pick thighs and spindly legs, flat, flabby ass and gaping cunt. Her hairy, un-kempt... personality... everything is colored and modeled by the drunk she went to bed with. The drunk she put on first thing in the morning. The drunk that wets her brain and slacks her mouth and runs her life from one slow Sunday to the next.

So why does the speaker engage with such a woman? The wallow, ah the wallow.

> Filthy pigs. Beasts. Ten minutes and twenty bucks and the opportunity to wallow in their destruction. So cheap.

Really, hiring a low-end street prostitute is not much different than watching Satanic ritual abuse victims on Sally Jesse Raphael. We all engage in the wallow, to a person. All that differs is how we define the degradation.

Part Three contains the remembrances of a man in an old-style peep show establishment, the sort I associate with San Francisco and New York in the 1970s. The kind where a woman gyrates behind glass as masturbating patrons pay coins to watch. The speaker in Part Three is only too aware of his surroundings—floor sticky with semen, smeared glass, the smell of sweat— and cannot escape the foulness within and without as he engages in his own compulsions. The speaker here jumps in his reactions to what he sees and does, but unlike the killer in Part One, he seldom experiences guilt as he looks at the women, the often very young women, who provide a jaded exhibition. Still, there is in this section a sad understanding of the ways girls grow into women who have no other option but to sell their bodies and how too often the experience changes them forever.

> I should see that she feels pity, not contempt. I shouldn't see this as any big deal – it's not humiliating or desperate. I'm lonelier than she is whorish; I'm an animal, and she provides a service. And if she seems jaded, it's just because she's –
>
> –seen all types of men–
>
> –seen all types of cock–
>
> –heard all the moaning and filthy suggestions–
>
> –heard all the insults–
>
> –seen all kinds of orgasms and kinks.

Yet even as this man sees his own degeneracy, he can see how this girl, this young woman, is not just providing a service but is also falling down into a dark hole with each show.

> But she's a chickenshit actress. Her dance is crude ostentation. It's contrivance and artifice, and it belies much more than just a job. She can't pull it off, she's:
>
> –too naked–
>
> –too bare–
>
> –too alone–
>
> –too ugly–
>
> –too stupid.

This man shows his sadism when he goes on to say:

> It is a pleasure to see one so young and yet already used-up. It is heartening to know she'll raise more humans in her own image.

It's the truth for all too many women in sex industries. Experiences like this are what fuel the radical feminists who adopt a SWERF[4] attitude toward women who use their bodies to pay the bills. The speaker then goes on to speculate on the trauma that landed this young woman behind the smeared glass, the abuse, the lack of hope, the addictions, and the beatings. He does not, however, put energy into how he, the pig, came to be the person on the other side of the glass. He doesn't really need to—his dissection of this woman, his dark glee considering the brutality he speculates she has endured, tells us what we need to know. He's not going to directly victimize her with a bottle in an alley, or date her and molest her daughter. He's just going to watch the spectacle of her sinking down. He's made his choice in how he will express his id. He will not be an active Sadean, holding a whip. He really is just the pig, the worm, the man whose dick can only get hard as he thinks of damage, but damage done at a distance.

Part Four is a letter from a killer to the mother of one of his victims. This immediately caused me to think of the cowardly, despicable letter that self-proclaimed Super Man Ian Brady wrote to victim Keith Bennett's mother. Brady never mailed the letter but authorities and the Bennetts were aware of its existence. In the letter Brady supposedly revealed the location of Keith Bennett's body. I don't think Brady could have anticipated how this letter would haunt Winnie Bennett's life, but he could not have planned a better torment had he intended it. Keith's body still has not been found and Winnie died not having given her son a final resting place.

But there are elements in this section that make me think that perhaps Sotos was channeling Dennis Nilsen alongside Brady. I say this because Nilsen (whom I often think of as "The British Jeffrey Dahmer") preyed on young male runaways and prostitutes, and the man in this section is tormenting the mother of a young hustler. Nilsen, to my knowledge, also never taunted anyone with letters, though I may be wrong because it has been years since I read about him. Brady tended to concentrate on the very young, because they were easier to control but also because they were innocent. Nilsen wanted company—Brady wanted to kill innocence (among other things...).

Regardless of who did what and who was channeled in this section, Sotos returns to a similar theme—a killer's response to the media attention paid to a grieving mother:

> Nothing wrong with a little limelight, and I certainly don't mean to suggest that you're an empty, worthless media hog. In fact, I think the photo of you shrieking and crying at the courthouse when the caption below read "Danny's mother declined comment" was especially tactful.
>
> ...

---

4   Sex Worker Exclusionary Radical Feminist.

> You'll no longer be a piece of trailer-camp trash with a faggot junkie whore for a son; you're forever now a poor, blameless mother who has suffered unspeakable injustices. Inconceivable tragedies. Gross disadvantages.
>
> Violence is quite a purge, my dear woman, and when I think of the gleaming coincidences we share, it's mildly disturbing to me that we're not much closer. I'm sure you'll agree.

Violence is indeed a purgative. Reading about it certainly is, for those who like a good vomiting up of shame or sin. This is quite interesting to me, how Sotos looks at the mothers of the murdered in this manner, channeling the self-serving bullshit of men like Ian Brady, who would justify anything as long as he looked like the smartest man ever to live at the end of his explanation. Of course the murderer wants to know that once the victim is dead that those left behind are suffering and how can such a worm stop himself from mocking pain? Sotos' later works explore how it is that the murderer is abetted by an extremely tiresome media that needs a parade of sobbing victims as much as the killer. We've already visited this theme, and while we are reading the imagined thoughts of a killer or two, never forget that Sotos is the observer, and that there can often be several points he is making in one scenario. Once you've read him a few times, once the shock wears off, it becomes easier to see the point behind the onslaught.

Part Five may be the most autobiographical part of this book. In this section Sotos, or the speaker he channels, shows disgust for the police system that arrested him and even attempted to cause him dire harm by announcing to cell mates that he was in jail for possession of child porn. This section is hard to read because the speaker begins to discuss some of the confiscated child porn that he has seen the police looking at as they try to get a handle on his case. They wonder if he is a member of NAMBLA. They think he might be a Satanist. They ask him all kinds of questions completely irrelevant to the situation and completely misunderstand the 'zine that resulted in Sotos' obscenity charge. The speaker is tired of these cops, these stupid people who want the salacious details without ever trying to understand the victims or what has really happened to them. There is a lot I highlighted in this section but I don't want to reproduce it because even now I am still chewing over the content. But at the end, the point I largely came away with is that the speaker realizes that children abused in pornography need a hero to save them and none of these lummoxes measures up.

Part Six is a wallow wherein the speaker is thinking about the sorry, unattractive nature of hollow, unpleasant homosexual hook-ups in contrast to the crimes committed by serial killers who were also sexual sadists. The power of this chapter comes when the speaker muses on the pornography of reaction to sexual murders. The "money shot," as it were, comes when the parents of one of Randy Kraft's victims realize the torture their son endured, when Ann West identified her daughter in the morgue, when parents realized that their daughters fell victim to Peter Sutcliffe because they were prostitutes.

Then he shifts gears. The speaker, after all these dreadful musings, develops an almost metaphysical despair:

> My mind should be filled with these things. My brain should wash with images of Dean Corll fixing one of his young charges to his torture board and ramming home that big dildo. Of Ken Bianchi injecting ammonia into some dumb-titted coed's veins. Peter Kürten slashing some small child with a broken pair of scissors. Robin Gecht tying up the fat tits of a teenage nigger whore and then slicing 'em up and off. Of Dodd torturing a helpless five-year-old boy and recording all the baby's pain with his camera and tape recorder. Ted Bundy jamming a can of hair spray into a dying bleeder's discharging asshole.

> The pigs are wrong, stupid. Too much is made of the money shot. The humiliation, the desperation, the degradation, the weakness, the failure, the base stupidity – all givens. The cunts bring it with them. Nothing new. Nothing real. Hollow promises and lifeless stand-ins. Stunted onanism. Easy pantomimes designed for the sheepish magazine-and-video set.

I was once completely immersed in serial killer culture. Some of the people I knew from early serial killer websites got book deals out of their obsession, though I never really thought much about going down that path. Still, it was with no small amount of amusement that I found, more or less word-for-word, comments I had made about several fringe and obscure murderers reproduced in a book about serial killers published by a fellow traveler in the worst men can do. I am chaotic and sort of a nihilist. Nothing is new and everything is stolen so I didn't care. It was all the same thing, just an ocean of human tragedy and senseless impulse, bad decisions and degraded lives. When detailed accounts of the worst human cruelties cease to arouse any feeling other than boredom, you may soon find yourself unable to relate to anyone on any level. Best to shake it off and find your humanity again.

It all seems so fascinating in the beginning, trying to figure out what makes a killer and what makes a victim. In the end all you know is that people do despicable, nasty, bestial things to each other. That is the sole lesson. The only conclusion. You can make it a commodity, as all the crime and criminal procedural shows that exploded in the early naughts prove, but in entertainment you miss the sheer, random pointlessness of it all, how it is some people are born to kill and others are born to die and that's how it's always been.

This sort of aggressive ennui extends into Part Seven, but takes on a sadistic twist. The speaker is talking to a woman he wants to have sex with. I believe she is a prostitute. The speaker is making it clear that sex with this woman would hold little more appeal than masturbating to porn. The only reason this woman could possibly serve as a substitute to such solitary lust is if she shares the miserable life experiences that have caused her to come to this sorry end in her life. The speaker says nothing bad ever happened to him, and perhaps that is why he needs the eroticized, cruel details of the abused, the miserable, the degraded. He denies that he has a base interest in this woman's agony, but the next paragraph has him exhorting her to share her damage.

This is a theme in this book—the speakers' prurience is less oriented around the details of the murder, the torture, the rape, the blood. The real interest is the psychological damage. How did both of them—the victim and victimiz-er—wind up in this particular situation? These speakers want to know the worst people can do so they can see and perversely react to the reactions of those who have suffered.

The speaker says:

> I've seen some great kiddie porn – but never have I been attracted to the kids' bodies. It's the crime, you know. The damage. The situation. Not the body – I couldn't give a fuck if it's a girl or a boy or whatever. I just like the trauma and torture and general action. I like the mutilated innocence, the destruction of the naive and protected, the brutal reality and pain of knowledge.

It's praxis at its most fucked up, that moment when thought becomes action, that interests the speaker. How the bruised psyche picks up the knife or walks the streets.

Part Eight may seem like a relief to read. It's the last real section, so that alone is relief of sorts. You're almost to the end. This section is deceptive-ly pleasant. No visceral wallow, no profanity, no discussions of degrading sexuality. Yet this is the most perverse text in this little book. It's another epistolary chapter—a speaker has written another letter to another mother of another abducted and murdered child. If "Lisa Anderson" was real, I was unable to run her to ground—rather I think she is a composite of so many missing little children.

This letter is purportedly from someone who has been following the case of this missing child, wanting to connect to the grieving mother, give her hope for the future. This section is so obscene because it reads as a precursor to Nancy Grace, the vultures who pick the bones of the victimized for enter-tainment whilst patting themselves on the backs for being the moral sort of people who would never, ever do something so horrible to a child, even as they delight in the details of the horrors done. This section also shows the sick links people can develop with the families of the victimized. You see someone every day on television, pleading and crying, and you develop a sort of relationship with them, a one-sided emotional connection that for those with a very specific pathology can turn into something like the letter represented in this section.

> I've thought about you every day since Lisa went missing. I don't think you've ever left my thoughts. I've seen you weather through the search, her missed birthday, the terrible discovery of her body, her burial, and now, the adjustment and recovery. You, and your husband, have been very forth-coming with your pain. So many of your words have stayed with me. And I want to say thank you from deep within my heart for letting me really feel what you went through – your suffering and confusion and pain. It's an extraordinary feeling to share those intimate moments.

It's a terrible trade off, isn't it? Clever and constant use of the media is the only way to bring attention to a missing child case. But in order to use the media you have to be ready to strip yourself naked and permit every lunatic with a television or computer screen the right to gawk at you. The viewers will eat you alive. They will think you are the killer if you don't cry. They will think you are the killer if you do cry. Some will see you naked, crying and unprotected and will inveigle their way into your life because they will think your expressions on television mean you are directly sharing your misery with them as a form of entertainment. They will become as obsessed with you as some people are with fictional television characters, writing fan letters to parents of murdered children.

In this regard the media is meant to serve as a tool to help recover the lost but it really becomes a chance for the vultures to profit off pain and for the damaged to become enchanted with that pain. It is what it is but at the same time we lose nothing when we accept that what it is—is obscene.

A parent of a missing or murdered child does not want to know you think of them every day. That you appreciate how well they showed their pain. That you feel they shared an intimate moment with you. They do not want to serve as your misery-fix until the next Lifetime Movie of the Week. But they have no choice. The media and its control of victim narratives forces them to do this and if they choose not to do so they will be vilified and deemed suspicious.

There is another small section, an appendix of sorts. It's Sotos himself dis-cussing his work, his ideas. It's worth a read but in a selfish, egoistic way, I don't want to discuss it. I am mainly interested in my reaction to and my interpretations of the main part of the book.

While I love this book like a masochist loves her sadist, I can never tell other people to read Sotos. I have no idea if you should read *Tool*. It occurs to me that the sections I reproduced from *Tool.* are among some of the less pornographic, violent and upsetting passages in the book. If these passages upset you deeply you probably need to give this book a pass. Some men will want to read this book with their dicks in their hands, and that's nothing I care about, but for those with a decided love of the wallow, there are plenty of wallows in store.

But if you read my words often and like what it is that I seem to represent, you will want to read this book because you want that slap in the face. You may need the challenge of reading an unthinkable text and finding your own meaning in it. You may feel catharsis. I know I did. That hollow feeling I felt when I was finished was likely due to catharsis as some particular, closed off, frightening feelings came rushing out. I don't know if I will ever read this book again. It has served its immediate purpose. But I'm going to hang onto it because that need for a purge may come up again, and it may be a completely different purge. If you approach Sotos in this manner, using emotion to guide you, you may never have the same reaction twice. For the right person *Tool.* is therapy. I think I was the right kind of person.

Further Reading

Mercy
Andrea Dworkin

The Basement: Meditations on a Human Sacrifice
Kate Millett

Mountainhead
New Juche

Violence in Our Time
Sandy Lesberg

Only Words
Catherine A. MacKinnon

Apocalypse Culture
Edited by Adam Parfrey

Mine
Peter Sotos

*Child Pornography: An Investigation**
Tim Tate

Attorney General's Commission on Pornography: Final Report, July 1986
Issued by the U.S. Department of Justice, Attorney General Edwin Meese

Porn Row: An Inside Look at the Sex for Sale District of a Major American City
Jack McIver Weatherford

---

*   *Cum grano salis.*

Selfish, Little: The Annotated Lesley Ann Downey

By Peter Sotos
Void Books (2006)
Original post: 03/01/2010

Why do I consider this book odd?
Peter Sotos wrote it.

This is not going to be a coherent discussion. There is no way it can be.

The first thing that needs to be said about this book is that it is not an analysis of the murder of Lesley Ann Downey. It is not a biography about the ten-year-old child who died at the hands of Ian Brady and Myra Hindley, who committed what would come to be known as the Moors murders. They took pictures of the little girl, naked and bound, and they recorded her as she spoke, begging them to let her go. It was one of the most outrageous murders of the 20th century, the sheer horror of the media remnants of the crime surpassing even the pictures Harvey Glatman took of his victims. It took Manson to top the duo, in terms of shock and fetish value of the murder victim. It shocks me, the number of people online who picked up this book thinking it would be either a fictionalized account of the girl's life or her biography. Despite the title, there is remarkably little of Lesley in this book, in terms of cold, hard words. But as Sotos makes clear, she permeates every page. She is his muse.

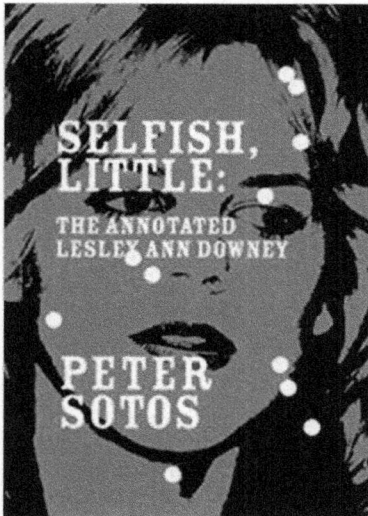

This book grew out of his epilogue to Ian Brady's load of horseshit, *The Gates of Janus: Serial Killing and Its Analysis* [see my extended discussion beginning at page 146]. Sotos was the only one, it seems, who had Brady's number. Somehow, knowing that enabled me to read this book a little easier. Just a little.

Sotos is hard for me to read. He is relentless. I have to put him down and come back to him. I can never read him in one go. He upsets me. He makes me sick. At times, I do not understand him and when I do, it bothers me because it makes me wonder about the sickness that lurks in my own soul. I comfort myself that what is happening to me is that Sotos is provoking a reaction, not a realization, which is why I think this book exists.

I expose myself to Peter Sotos for the same reasons I expose myself to any number of artistic darknesses: because I have to. It's a compulsion I gave up fighting years ago. Sotos leaves me bewildered, unsure about what I just read. Parts of the book are unclear. Was it truth, a remembrance of actual sexual couplings? Fantasy? Is he describing himself or is it a fiction? Would knowing the truth make any difference?

I don't know.

I flat out do not know.

Sotos is notorious for many reasons, but chief among them is that he once produced a 'zine called *Pure*. In the second issue, he reproduced an image copied from a magazine of actual child pornography and was arrested for obscenity and possession of child pornography. Only the second charge stuck and he received a suspended sentence. Is he a pedophile? There is a common misconception that he is. As in everything else in life, that is subject to definition. I know others violently disagree with this assessment, but in my head, until you behave inappropriately with a child, what exists in your brain is not enough to label you a pedophile. There are those who think that his use of certain images and his obsession with children like Lesley and Masha Allen make him a de facto pedophile. Regardless, because he was arrested for possessing kiddie porn and continues to produce such transgressive studies of crime and sexuality, Sotos has a huge target on his back for moralists to point at when they need a simple reason to dismiss him. But even though I say he is not a pedophile, his work exists in a mental realm that will disturb even the most ardent freak. If Sotos doesn't disturb you, that may be disturbing in itself.

Sotos is a transgressive writer, a real transgressive writer in a world where mainstream writers like Bret Easton Ellis are still considered transgressive. Being strange, being quirky, being sick is not enough. You have to horrify, or you have to provoke. People misunderstand what it really means to provoke. It isn't a cheap shot for short reaction. Genuine provocation is very different. You may have to hit the reader between the eyes with a sledgehammer and hope they see your words when they recover from the blow. In this, Sotos succeeds. The problem is that when I see his words, I filter it all as I see fit. Who the hell knows if my thoughts are correct.

In approaching Sotos, you must understand that you will read that which cannot be unread. You must have the stomach for it. It's not his fault if you don't. Morality is not needed here.

In my brain, even extreme literature has a middle road of experience. You experience the art at the edge of reason, then come to the center to see what it is you have experienced. Even mainstream fiction has a middle road, the place where meaning is clear, if banal.

For me, *Selfish, Little* falls into the same "cannot unsee" category where I file my memory of Throbbing Gristle's song "Hamburger Lady." I still recall the first time I listened to that song, on a loop, appalled, fascinated. Sotos fascinates me in the same sick vein. There is a horror to it all that enthralls me, makes me read, makes me endure even when I want to put the book down and never pick it up again.

But Throbbing Gristle's middle road—and indeed the middle road for Genesis Breyer P-Orridge—is far different than Sotos' middle road. After hearing "Hamburger Lady," I understood how very terrible it can be to be alive, that remaining alive is not always a blessing to the one who survives.[6] After all, Breyer P-Orridge became another sex, an entirely different person. However unsettling it may be seeing h/er with breasts and plumped lips, s/he shows us there are many ways of being human.

But when I look down Sotos' middle road, the place I must come to digest and make sense out of his words, all I see is Sotos. Sometimes there is a greater truth, but mostly it is just him. He isn't coming to terms with the world around him so much as he is coming to terms with himself, and it is an intensely personal process that has little universality. Sotos is not here to lead you to a transgressive epiphany, though he may. He is here to show himself. All you see at the end of the middle road of contemplation is Peter Sotos. This is neither a fault nor a condemnation. It just is what it is. You yourself have to decide if it's enough.

Sotos wrote this book to explain himself, in a way, to make clearer his obsessions:

> Every book I've ever written begins and ends with Lesley Ann Downey. Every single one. Every thing I've ever fucked has been a stab at the idea of her somehow in my pathetically happy hands. Not as flesh and hair and precisely examined childhood but as simple, personally degrading pornography.

Selfish, Little is also one of many places where Sotos examines the creation of victims and the media's role in stories of child abduction, rape and murder. The implication is that the media actually feeds the psyches of those who are aroused by such crimes, or who commit such crimes—or that media is often responsible for creating the monsters that feed the machine. He's probably correct on that point. But to get to that point, one has to consume a lot of vulgarity and sickness.

Is it worth understanding Sotos' mind and what makes him tick? I cannot answer that question but I suspect the real answer lies in the fact that I read him at all. This is not the first Sotos book I have read. It won't be the last.

---

6   Throbbing Gristle also performed a song about one of the Moors victims called "Very Friendly." Just mentioning it so we can come full circle in a way... "Ian Brady and Myra fucking Hindley, very very friendly..."

At times, Sotos arouses a visceral anger in me. I feel a need to find him and wrap my fingers around his throat and ask him point blank what was real and what was not. I want him to tell me what goes on in his head and what comes out of his hands, even though I think I already know the answer.

Take, for example, this:

> She's begging them now. Not to undress her. Her mother even heard it. But how vulnerable is a child then. How much more vulnerable. What degree was she cold and available and attempting to cover herself up. Who was fucking reaching for exactly what when. Cunt. She was begging the adults. She's begging for a chance to explain something she that she hasn't even figured out yet. Just a pause. A wait. So she can plot her innocent little personality into a convincing argument to fool the adults of her honest and purity. This simply must happen. She absolutely needs to go now. There is no time for this. She must be home or her mother will be mad at her. Which was the best excuse she could come up with. And correct. She knew it wasn't a total lie. And mum, ironically, bled safety into that mind then. She now just wants a little child's chance at pity. She wants a little child's chance to talk to them and tell them something that might – might – make them stop touching her. Please. She asks. She begs. She cajoles. She asks for just a minute. But wants more. Dirty liar. Dirty next step. Dirty little mind raging all her lessons into summations and bad guesses and pathetically lost chances. Dirty little bad sexy mistakes. Sweetheart. Sweetheart chances, Sweetheart naked chances with fingers all over her plans and mistakes and her open mouth and those little words on top of those fucking, fucking pictures. Where all she fucking does is fucking lay there. Alone. Though. She calls out for mummy. Or she calls out to her mummy. Or she may be calling fucking Myra Hindley mummy now. Anyone older must have her best protected safety in mind and should simply be her mummy right fucking now.

It's infuriating, and it is meant to be. But this nasty ramble goes somewhere, if you are willing to continue.

It continues…

> Her dirty filthy filled lowlife trash mouth. Calls Ian Brady dad as well. And she begs him to stop touching her skinny little body as if the little rat hadn't been touched ever before. Like it's the worst fucking thing in the world. As bad as the threats and yelling and worry about wherever could this go from here, darling. Little rat. All dolled-up naked as fuck. Like a little naked rat. Little fucking holed-out rat. They weren't shoving a cock in her mouth and rubbing her back and her chest like it was going to be a good blow-job and she had great little tits there someday soon. Like a child promises. Like you don't act like you want you filthy fucking fat pig. You fucking disease. You reactionary beast staring at her absence rather than her attributes.

You almost miss it. You almost don't see the shift, and it doesn't last long before he is back, thinking about naked Lesley, abused, the little rat who occupies his entire mind, but there it is, it happens. He spells it out, the realization that he is the filthy pig, the disease, the reactionary beast, and that all the eyes that looked upon this scene with relish in newspapers, that those ears that avidly listened to Lesley's cries on tape, are the beast too, looking with horror at what happened to this little girl and seeing their own depravity.

In all of this, after explaining how Lesley was a manipulative rat, he gives us this:

> She expected more of how she had grown up till then. She expected maybe pity. But concern, care and, at least, above all, help.

God, maybe I am so conflicted about reading Sotos because I resent this yanking around he does. Here is a revelation of the sickness blunted with a dose of humanity when I least expect it. Yet it's necessary in order for Sotos to show how Lesley is a canvas upon which are painted illegal sexual acts, a perverse interest in crime, hypocritical media examination and the genuine desire to help a child. She is what we have all made her, and she is what Sotos has made her. She is all things at once because the books and tabloids still poke at her corpse and because men like Sotos cannot get her out of their heads.

It is then that Sotos makes sense, complete sense, and you understand, for a moment at least, where he was going with this wallow:

> In fact, a danger arises in that one can easily see how the public's recalcitrant lust for the murder and rape and recording of Lesley Ann Downey could create the misunderstanding that a more specifically degenerate interest in her could be quietly acceptable or benign. Or that the responsive media fascination is a signpost for perverts to avoid help and instead find their ugly delusions more appropriate in light of the public's greater denials. That picky details are much bigger than petty... That there's more honesty than facts or proof... Nothing is as terrible as child pornography. Just like they said. I still absolutely believe that.

Sotos understands, as he says elsewhere in the book, that the media and those interested in Lesley have raped her over and over again without ever touching a hair on her head. Which makes it ironically hilarious that people get pissed off when they discover that this book is not a detailed look at Lesley's life. Sotos calls them out

Sotos also goes into excruciating detail about how he, or rather the narrator, has a collection of pictures of a specific little girl, a little girl he knows, a child he has watched grow up. Harmless pictures of a gawky child who wears swimsuits and sits awkwardly. All arms and legs, flat chested, long hair messy in that way that only a pre-teen's hair can be. I cannot recall now if he masturbates on her photos or if this is just the implication. He speaks of how many perverts masturbate onto innocuous photos of children, that pornography can simply be an innocent photo assigned sexual intent by the viewer. We know this, I think. Don't we? I think we do. Perhaps it is a revelation to some.

After reading that section, however, the cover of the book changed for me. All those little dots that look like the perfect round slivers left when you punch holes into paper suddenly became semen drops.

There are other wallows. Wallows that are not as clear to me as the wallow with Lesley. The wallow with the man with Down syndrome in the sling, the encounters with fat men in restrooms, the shit, the blood, the cum on the floor, the gaping wet holes in bodies, in walls. I became angry too because I don't think I wanted to get pulled down into that depth of self loathing. Sotos mocks himself sometimes with humor, and denies that he is as full of loathing as he comes off in print, but I don't buy it. There is some serious self hatred in these pages, in these almost stream-of-consciousness fantasies. Peter Sotos' writing borders on despicable and the subject matter, by its very nature, is going to sicken 99.9% of the people on this planet. It certainly sickened me.

So why did I read it? What does it say about me that I kept reading when it upsets me and even makes me ill at times? Why do I not declare this book a load of filthy trash and burn it and warn others to give it a wide berth?

I don't know. And that I don't know, that I wonder, that I have such an extreme emotional response during and after reading, makes *Selfish, Little* somehow worthwhile, I think. I respect Sotos for being willing to reveal his mind in order to prove the points he wants to prove.

Selfish, Little also forces readers—well, true readers and not just ideologues and pearl-clutchers—to examine what brought them to the book in the first place. There is no way for me to read Sotos and not wonder why I keep turning pages. There is no way for me to read him and not wonder why I know so much about serial killers. There is no way to read him and not wonder about your own motivations. This is an uncomfortable feeling.

In spite of all the wallow and internal contemplation, I still remember this passage best:

> I don't think I could bear it if anything happened to this child. She is worth protecting. I wouldn't be able to think of anything else.

I have always had a lot of sympathy for the devil, but if you read that line and still think Sotos is a pedophile, or some sort of apologist for evil, you have missed the point.

FURTHER READING

Comfort and Critique
Peter Sotos

The Gates of Janus: Serial Killing and its Analysis (First Edition)

By Ian Brady; Foreword by Dr. Alan Keightley; Introduction
by Colin Wilson; Afterword by Peter Sotos
Feral House (2001)
Original post: 03/08/2009

Why do I consider this book odd?
It was written by Ian Brady, who, along with his girlfriend Myra
Hindley, kidnapped, sexually assaulted and murdered children in
England from 1963–1965.

Had this book been a person approaching me outside the supermarket,
I would have crossed the street. *The
Gates of Janus* is a self-satisfied con man
who thinks he can pull the wool over everyone's eyes, assuming that his marks
are always far stupider than he is. It is
unwise to pay such people much attention, and it was difficult to care about
large chunks of Ian Brady's con.

Peter Sotos is the only person in this
book who doesn't come off like a rube
or a complete lunatic. If you are at all
familiar with Sotos' body of work, consider my statement and what it really
means. He is the only one who seems to
understand that in addition to being a
violent sexual predator, Ian Brady is also
a master manipulator whose word on any topic should be taken with a grain
of salt, if not completely disregarded.

I wanted to read *The Gates of Janus* because, based on just small snippets
of information, I thought in some sense it would provide an explanation of
what it was that made Ian Brady become a killer. I thought it would help
me to understand what it was about his personality that could have mes-
merized Myra Hindley, an otherwise unremarkable woman, into a *folie à
deux* murder streak that set the stage for similar fiendish duos like Fred and

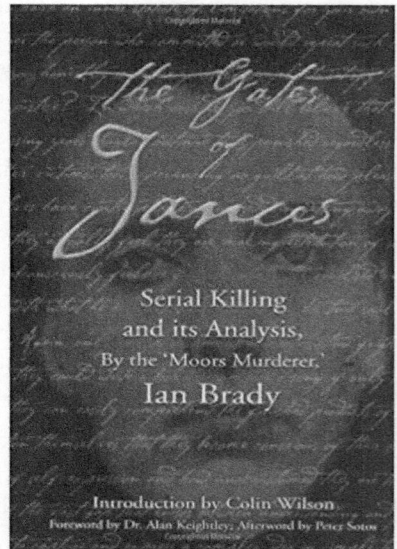

Rosemary West and Karla Homolka and Paul Bernardo. I had long heard that Brady's book was illuminating, a rare look into the mind of a serial killer. While it is, it also isn't.

All I learned reading this book is that I still have a sound psychopath-o-meter (though Brady fancies himself a psychotic rather than a psychopath because the former are interesting to him) and that the only real insight anyone would ever have into Ian Brady's mind is that he is a liar and a manipulator. He certainly conned Colin Wilson, who seems to think that the information that Brady provides about himself and fellow psychopathic killers somehow redeems the unrepentant murderer.

With a level of naïveté that he should not have possessed given his age and the range of his career, Wilson says:

> In a letter of a few days ago, [Brady] wrote to me bitterly, "My life is over so I can afford honesty of expression; those with a future cannot. If I had my time over again, I'd get a government job and live off the state… a pillar of society. As it is I am eager to die. I chose the wrong path and am finished."

> As this book shows, that, at all events, is untrue.

If you feel that sort of rush of saliva that makes you think you may puke, be aware you will feel it again and again as you read on. Part One consists of seven interminable chapters wherein Brady discusses psychopathy and psychotics while applying a really inappropriate interpretation of Nietzschean superman theories to killers. In doing this, he uses dense and at times overly intellectual (yet strangely specious) language to give himself some sort of authority on his topic. He formulates what he thinks are trenchant observations about the way the media and society handle crimes like the Moors murders, hilariously implying that we, the law-abiding people of the world, are really to blame for being interested and appalled when such crimes occur. At no time does Brady truly apply this analysis to himself, yet doesn't hesitate to share the love in Part Two, where he analyzes the true nature of other serial killers. Worse, what little Brady gives away about himself is contradictory, often without a hint of self-awareness.

Before I explain why this book is a sickening, masturbatory excursion into manipulative madness, let me share the sobering, sane words of Peter Sotos. His afterword should have been the preface because it could have saved readers from entering into this exercise of the damned with the expectation that they would be reading honest words.

A passage from Sotos reveals the only truth of the book:

> First off, you don't ask a child molester to write a book on serial killing. A child rapist. A child pornographer. A child murderer.

> Colin Wilson, from his introduction:

> "Therefore I advised him to do the thing I would have done: to think about

writing a book. Since he obviously knew about serial murder 'from the inside,' thus this suggested itself as the obvious subject.'"

You don't ask him to do the obvious. You especially don't ask him to do what you would do.

Because the child rapist and murderer and pornographer will obviously lie. And, because he wants to believe you need to hear more, he'll even start to enjoy telling you he's lying. Because it's the easiest thing to do. It is the obvious choice. He can adopt the dime-a-dozen serial killer front of puffed up superiority, all from his tiny cell and serve the typical cold dish of chest beating mental clarity over mental introspection…

Sotos is right, and the reader should know it before they even try to read this miasma of philosophical nothings. If you want to understand the impulse of true deviance, read Sotos or Sade. If you want to read the words of a man who has plenty of clarity but absolutely no desire to apply it to his own motivations—who is, in fact, probably lying to you—read *The Gates of Janus*.

It would be a lie if I said that I didn't hate this book. Reading Brady's tortured prose was difficult. Take the following sentence:

> On the other hand, it is mostly to the quiescent company of the atheist, the sceptic, the cynic, the nihilist, the existentialist, those self-absorbed who are content to propose and preach nothing, that we may sometimes escape the excessive demands of synthetic morality, and the jarring irritations of theological presumption.

Or, as those of us who have nothing to hide would say, association with outsiders provides relief in a repressive, priggish world. This sentence is more or less how this entire book reads. Pomposity without saying much.

After a careful study, what the reader can take from Part One is the following:

- Brady hates those of us who do not see how it is that he is a mentally and emotionally superior man because he gave into urges to do grave harm to innocent people, urges that he claims all humans have.

- Brady thinks the salacious media handling of sex and child murders feeds both those who want to commit such crimes and those who wish they could man up and commit such crimes (and here, I concede he has a point).

- Brady thinks that the man who lives for a lion as a day (raping and killing children is living as a lion for a day? Really?) rather than living as a lamb for a lifetime is a morally superior human being.

- Brady rails against the lack of humanity in the prison system, though one would think that a man who lived as a lion would understand brutality and not hypocritically bitch about it when such brutality is applied to him (more on this when I get to Brady's analysis of Carl Panzram).

- Brady has a complete lack of understanding of what institutionalized violence versus individual violence really entails, ascribing a sort of hypocrisy to the former.

- Brady thinks the reason he is in prison is because he did not channel his psychopathy in the correct way, that all politicians are psychopaths, as are captains of industry, etc., and he decries society as a mass of hypocrites for not seeing things in a similar manner.

Brady's book is the crazy man who thinks he is sane, yelling at you from a traffic island as you pray for the light to turn green. There may be some surface sanity to the statements (why yes, many politicians are sociopaths or psychopaths) but the rest is just weird and a little scary. There may have been more to take away from Part One, but my god, it took me two weeks to read the whole thing. It should have taken two days. I haven't slogged through a book so slowly since I was forced to read *Mrs. Dalloway* in college.

Part Two is superficially more interesting, as Brady turns his supposed powers of serial killer insight onto other killers. But after reading his first analysis, that of Henry Lee Lucas, it becomes clear that Brady doesn't seem to know what he's talking about. As a Texan and as a woman who at one point in her life knew almost every fact there was to know about American serial killers, I know a lot about Henry Lee Lucas. Brady gets too many facts wrong for his psychological profile to mean anything.

For example, Brady says:

> An abused Charlie Chaplin, Lucas' alcoholic father, abused him sadistically for years, unwittingly fashioning him into his mother's nemesis.

> An abused child usually does not focus hatred upon the parent who abuses but upon the parent who stood by and did nothing to stop the abuser. The hatred towards the abuser is effectively regarded as nothing compared to the betrayal of love and trust by the second parent...

> Lucas was twenty-three, his mother seventy, when he stabbed, strangled and raped her. Obviously, the viciousness of this act projected that the hatred for his mother would burgeon into a deep-seated distrust/hatred of the female species as a whole.

All of this sounds well and good to a point (women are not a separate species from men, just in case you were wondering), but many of his observations about Lucas are outright wrong. Lucas does not fit the bill of a killer who turns against the gender of the parent who was complicit but not active in their abuse (and I have a hard time thinking of such a killer, to be frank).

Lucas' mother was the instigator of most of the abuse Lucas suffered. She was the one who beat him into a coma, causing him to almost lose an eye (which he later did lose in an unrelated fight). She was the one who, upon learning Lucas' love for a family donkey, shot the donkey to death in front of Lucas. She was the one who was a prostitute, performing sex acts openly in front of her child. Lucas' father was no angel but he stood a far second to Viola Lucas as the parent who most abused young Henry. If Brady's interpretation of serial killer motivations is to be believed, then Lucas should have killed his father for permitting the abuse.

It is easy to see that in prison, and later a mental wing of a prison, Brady may not have had access to accurate information about Lucas. But Brady himself says that he was interested in Lucas because a noted author wanted his opinion and sent him information about the case. One wonders if he really was consulted at all, and if he was how the information he received was so inaccurate. Unless that information was really as bad as Brady presents it, it seems as if Brady just twisted facts around to fit his own pet psychological notion to give the appearance of being an important criminal psychologist.

Only in two of the criminal profiles and analyses does one get the sense that Brady knows what he is talking about. Examining Peter Sutcliffe, the "Yorkshire Ripper" who killed prostitutes, Brady's look into the delusions that led Sutcliffe to murder (God told me to kill hookers) to his current position (I was caught because it was Satan talking to me the whole time) rings true. But it should be noted that, aside from Graham Young (the poisoner with Nazi leanings), Sutcliffe is the only man he discusses with whom he spent any amount of time. One gets the impression that when Brady truly understands his subject, he does not have to hide his ignorance behind pompous verbosity.

Ironically, it is in his analysis of another killer that Brady utterly gives himself away. The American killer Carl Panzram is not a man many know much about today, but he was the textbook definition of a complete psychopath. Panzram killed for pleasure. He killed for money. He killed for sex. He was a born killer.

Panzram was in and out of prison all of his life, his jail tenure beginning with petty thefts. He was not an easy prisoner. He did not submit to rules, period. When he would disobey guards, they would lash out at him, often with punishments so bad that they almost killed him. But nothing could break Panzram, not even treatment that 80 years later would be considered torture worse than anything that happened at Guantanamo. Panzram escaped from prison twice and was a near unstoppable crime machine during both escapes. When he returned to prison in 1928, he swore he would kill the first man who gave him grief. And he did. It was the prison laundry foreman.

For this, Panzram received the death penalty and went to his death taunting the hangman. His final words were, "Hurry it up, you Hoosier bastard! I could hang ten men while you're fooling around!"

I am not trying to glorify Panzram when I say he was a complete badass. He was a vile human being. But if badassery can be divided into categories, honoring the daring criminal alongside the intrepid soldier or selfless rescuer, Panzram fits into the stone-cold killer category. He was a violent psychopath with no moral compass aside from an almost childlike need to be loyal to those who were loyal to him. When a warden gave him leave and he failed to return on time, he decided to stay out and escape rather than face the censure of the man who had believed in him enough to grant him privileges. In almost all other respects, he was a nihilistic monster.

But Brady recognizes Panzram's status as a badass, and in this recognition, one can see a longing in Brady's prose, almost a desire that he could be like Panzram. By Brady's own definition, Panzram was a man who did live as a lion, but instead of living like a lion for a day, he lived as a lion his entire life. Going to prison did not reduce Panzram to a lamb and he endured what came with, to use Brady's analogy, leonine ferocity. Brady's imprisonment has been much different. He complains about rules, he feigns insanity when it suits him, he taunts the parents of the children he killed.

Panzram, in his psychotic rage, would never have resorted to such passive-aggression and one can see how much Brady idolizes Panzram because Panzram was everything Brady is not. Panzram's very life makes Brady's pseudo-intellectual and moralistic railings against the modern treatment of prisoners seem weak, and Brady feels it acutely. Panzram walked what Brady talks.

Brady gives away his hero worship throughout the chapter on Panzram, but here are some examples:

> Panzram is another prime example of multi-motivational, multi-attributional reprisal. When dealing with authorities of any description, individually petty-minded tyrants, you must never wait for anyone to accept responsibility, for it is against their cowardly nature to do so. You must without hesitation or pointless consultation, confer responsibility on the obvious culprits, and decide the price you will make them pay, *one way or another*.
>
> In short, you must act as tyrannically as they do, but solely on your own authority.

Bear in mind, these are the words of a man who preyed on innocent children, who faked mental illness because he thought serving time in a mental ward would be easier than prison life and who tried to starve himself to death as a form of suicide. He has made no one pay for the harms he believes have been done to him. He just exercised his will against the weak until he was caught. Not his hero Panzram, whose actions Brady makes a small attempt to disavow even as his words convey praise.

> In Nietzsche's *Also Spake Zarathustra*, the pivotal factor is, in my opinion, the Great Contempt, or more precisely, the Great Self-Contempt. Once a

man has achieved, in a praise-worthy sense, contempt for himself, he simultaneously achieves contempt for all man-made laws and moralities and becomes truly free to do as he wills. Plunging into the very depths, he consequently rises above all.

Do you again feel that sort of nausea that comes right before you vomit? What is worse? Assigning such a philosophical identity to a psychopath like Panzram, or the slavering, Igor-like "yes master" admiration of and longing to be such a man? As I read the chapter on Panzram, my sole thought was that Brady loved him or wanted to be him, recognizing that there was a far better example of his own words than himself.

This book was trying, to say the least. I had planned next to review Peter Sotos' *Selfish, Little*, but I needed to step away from the Moors murders for a bit. This sort of thing wears on your soul if you engage in it without a break.

Let me leave you with the primary reason why I hated this book and feel great contempt for anyone who could find redemption in Ian Brady for writing it:

> It is rather significant to note that those members of the lower classes who assiduously adhere to law and prevailing morality usually display a smug self-righteousness, which appears to be based on the patent delusion that their virtuous qualities are inborn, rather than evidence of a servile constitution predisposed to the influence of social engineering.

That's right, dear reader. The only reason you have not kidnapped a little girl, recorded and filmed her torture and rape, killed her and dumped her body into a place where it might never be discovered is because you have a "servile constitution" and are overly influenced by social law, not because most human beings have a moral core that makes such actions despicable. This idea is a running theme in *The Gates of Janus* and it's one of the reasons I found the book so mentally tiresome. It wears thin, Brady's frantic attempt to persuade others that he isn't just a repellent worm who killed children because he got off on it. Your mileage may vary, but you have been warned.

Further Reading

Panzram: A Journal of Murder
Edited by Thomas E. Gaddis and James O. Long

Serial Violence: Analysis of Modus Operandi and Signature Characteristics of Killers
Robert D. Keppel

Beyond Belief: The Moors Murders
Emlyn Williams

SERIAL KILLING AND ITS ANALYSIS
BY THE MOORS MURDERER IAN BRADY
EXPANDED EDITION
INTRODUCTION AND NEW MATERIAL BY COLIN WILSON
EXPANDED AFTERWORD BY PETER SOTOS

THE GATES OF JANUS

THE GATES OF JANUS: SERIAL KILLING AND ITS ANALYSIS (EXPANDED EDITION)

By Ian Brady; Foreword by Dr. Alan Keightley; Introduction
by Colin Wilson; Afterword and supplemental text ("Bait")
by Peter Sotos
Feral House (2015)

Why do I consider this book odd?
Because it inspired me to write this goddamned much in response.

I was aware that there was an updated version of *The Gates of Janus*. I knew
about it for a while. I think. I mean, I may have been aware of it and then
promptly forgot about it. I really disliked the first edition and didn't feel the
need to read an update. Though the book itself was interesting to read, Ian
Brady made my teeth hurt. My jaw literally tightened reading the bullshit
Brady passed off as an enlightening look into the minds of killers. It was Ian
Brady being Ian Brady offering insight about what it's like to be Ian Brady,
and Ian Brady was a pitiful, gross, self-impressed and tiresome man. The
average DMV clerk can offer more insight into the minds of murderous psychopaths. So really I saw no reason to read an updated version of a book that
I have already outright pronounced a heap of horseshit.

But I was persuaded to read it when it was made clear to me that the updated version's new content came mainly from Colin Wilson, who apologized
for ever encouraging this farce in the first place, and Peter Sotos, who tore
Ian Brady limb from metaphorical limb in a way that was cruelly incisive
while being somehow being infinitely kinder than Ian Brady deserved. I have
now come to suspect that Adam Parfrey, the man behind Feral House, always
expected Brady to hang himself when given enough editorial rope. I should
have suspected that from the beginning. I hesitated because so many subversive minds really seemed to think that Brady was offering an amazing
opportunity to see the minds of killers through the mind of a killer. Now I
almost feel like I should offer Parfrey an apology for thinking he wasn't in on
the joke. That Peter Sotos was permitted to write the devastating afterword
to the first edition should have been a big clue. Mea culpa.

Writing about the updated edition gives me an interesting chance to look
into how my opinions about the first edition have changed, if they have
changed. I get to see my kneejerk revulsion to Brady, akin to finding insect
larva between seldom-used towels crammed at the back of a linen closet,
roiling tiny pale worms defiling that which should be clean, evolve into

something less reactive. I get to look at how Sotos distilled the case, how he appraised Brady and his bullshit, the victims and their suffering, the fans and their beliefs. It seems fitting to offer this very long example of my "tl;dr" tendencies at their most excessive to follow my far shorter initial discussion of the first edition of *The Gates of Janus*.

To be clear, all I am discussing here is the text called "Bait," consisting of a hundred and twenty some odd pages of new content that Peter Sotos wrote for the revised edition. Fewer pages to read, far more words to write on my end. Sounds about right.

Christ, Peter Sotos, when he writes directly to his reader without adopting roles and using different voices, can hone in on and explain difficult matters in a way that leaves me envious. Thus my ensuing discussion of his long coda to *The Gates of Janus* comes from a place of appreciation and great enthusiasm. I think I have finally come to understand what I truly feel and think about Ian Brady, and for those who earnestly promote him as a great thinker. Of course, I initially found Brady loathsome. That hasn't really changed much. But I now find his fans and acolytes at least as troubling. I've had some unsettling interactions with Ian Brady True Believers since I first grappled with *The Gates of Janus*. As regular readers will be aware, I cut most people with unusual ideas a lot of slack. My site wouldn't exist were this world not full of people with bizarre ideas and the will to share them. But some of Brady's ardent defenders tested my spirit of intellectual adventure, my ability to enjoy that which is odd, disturbing or frightening. I will explain in due course.

This essay assumes the reader has a certain amount of knowledge about both the Moors murders, Ian Brady, and the first edition of *The Gates of Janus*. It would likely be helpful to read my foregoing reaction to the first edition, but just to speed things along, I will provide a reasonably quick synopsis of the information readers new to this topic will need.

In 1963-1965, Ian Brady and his girlfriend, Myra Hindley, lured five young people—children and teens—to their deaths. They buried their victims in the Saddleworth Moor in Greater Manchester. Ian and Myra misjudged the nature of Myra's young brother-in-law, David Smith, and tried to include him in the murder of their last victim. Appalled, David went to the police and eventually both Ian and Myra were arrested for the murders they committed.

During the investigation, it was learned that Brady and Hindley had made an audio recording and had taken photographs documenting the abuse and rape of ten-year-old victim Lesley Ann Downey. The police were never able to locate one of the victims, Keith Bennett, and in the long aftermath Brady enjoyed toying with Keith's mother, relishing the pain she felt since her son's body was still lost out in the moors. After Brady had spent almost twenty years in general lock-up, he decided that doing the rest of his time in a psychiatric facility would be easier so he faked being a psychotic. The prison officials believed his act and sent him to Ashworth psychiatric facility. Brady claimed he was subject to terrible treatment in Ashworth and subsequently tried to convince his jailers that he had faked the diagnosis that got him sent to Ashworth, to no avail.

When it became clear Brady was not going to be transferred, he began a hunger strike and was outfitted with a nasal tube to prevent him from starving to death, though later the sincerity of his hunger strike was held in question. He spent years in prison cultivating relationships with fans and courting the press he claimed to despise. Myra Hindley died in 2002. Brady died in May of 2017.

While incarcerated, Brady wrote this book. Ostensibly *The Gates of Janus* is an intellectual and psychological study of the character and motives of other notorious killers, explaining why they acted out. That may sound intriguing, but, as I explain my preceding review, Brady didn't do a particularly good job of it. After the book was published with Peter Sotos' incisive afterword, Brady was so infuriated that he declared he was going to sue in order to have the afterword removed. That never happened but he disavowed the book entirely. The publisher asked Peter Sotos to expand on his initial afterword for the new edition and the result was "Bait," a penetrating look at Brady, the families he tortured, the nature of genuine madness, all couched in Sotos' trenchant observations. This text reveals exactly who Brady was.

When I heard Brady had died, I had two thoughts. The first was that I hoped he had revealed where Keith Bennett's body was buried. The second was to wonder if I would get a lot of unsettling emails from Brady's fans when they Googled his name and found my old article about *The Gates of Janus*. The former didn't happen but the latter did. Brady's fans disturb me more than any other group that I hear from as a result of my online writing. Reading their fervent defenses of Brady—because, you know, he was smart and totally into Nietzsche—is nauseating at times.

It would be nice if reading Sotos or my articles could demonstrate to Brady's fans that there may be a better way to react, but that's a dead letter. I'll discuss this in depth later. For now I will say that Brady's acolytes have an interesting take on Nietzsche and seem to reflexively regard any sort of nuance in thinking to be hypocrisy.

In so many ways, "Bait" is a better biography, of sorts, than any other attempt that has been made to tell Brady's story. Brady longed to be taken seriously and one of the best ways to show Brady contempt was to dismiss him or ignore him. Peter Sotos took him seriously enough to write about him honestly. Analyzing him as he did, Sotos did Brady a kindness even as he made a fool of him. So let's have a look at how Peter Sotos analyzed Ian Brady, and why it tore Brady up so much to be under Peter's microscope. Let's consider how it distressed him to finally be genuinely understood and exposed.

BRADY'S CAPACITY TO WRITE AND TELL THE TRUTH

One of the biggest stumbling blocks to discussing the Moors murders with the True Believers in Brady's higher philosophical self is that in order to have such a discussion one must allow that Brady was capable of telling the truth. The problem is, I don't think we could ever trust Brady to tell the truth, even about events that actually happened, physical events about which there was an objective record. Relying on him to discuss with any measure of honesty what any other murderer did was always a dicey gambit. He would filter all that data through his own personal mythology, projecting his own self-serving justifications for child murder, never understanding that few could care less about the moral relativism he tried to apply to his murders in order to prove that everyone but him was a hypocrite.

Sotos very ably whacks Brady on his literary nose with a rolled up newspaper:

> Brady starts off his book by "broadly" defining his use of the word "murder." Decides the word is a term that begs the personal slant only a murderer owns unless it sits down to explain it to the inexperienced by rapt. Announces his prejudices so that you'll understand, trust, his murder word, rather than his murder proof, as part of the conditions necessary to separate the intelligent, brave, personal from the conditioned, hesitant, political, fearful. He, not aware when transparent, even more broadly then, defines his audience. As excited but guilty. Jealous. He instead as jaded. And sadly, as bored. Sets up the gawkers while playing - not acting - to be the dirty line between irritated professor and cheery huckster. Seems to enjoy being called a criminal by those who aren't.

This is one of many reasons why I no longer reply to Brady's fans when they send me bloodless emails declaring that my disgust for Brady is evidence of my envy and hypocrisy. There is no way to explain to them that the vast majority of human beings do not envy any person who kills children. We don't look at the rape and murder of a little girl like Lesley and wish that we were so bold, so brave, so personally principled that we could also kill. Brady's fans really believe that fear and Christian morality and governmental hypocrisy are what prevent us from killing, raping, stealing, transgressing. Brady at times probably did enjoy being called a criminal by those who are not criminals because on some level he believed he was a higher man, looking down upon us rubes. But I also think, deep in his heart, Brady was too aware of who he was and what his genuine moral value was. And those beliefs correspond more with mine than any of his acolytes.

> Brady was a man capable of great self-deception but he also had moments of self-awareness. But that self-awareness was fleeting and as a result Brady's

definition of murder is pretty much only useful to him and those for whom the philosophy of murder is as important as murder itself.

Explains that he is going to tell everyone that bought his book about murder, and what happens within murder, from the rarified existence of real violence. Inviting life rather than the usual timid review of the subject lost to wide-eyed moral hypocrisy. Official sanctions masked as communities training that contradict man's, your, baser instinct. Desires. Murder becomes an act that challenges heaven when heaven doesn't exist, murder broadly becomes an act that stays broadly murder as long as you only broadly define your terms. Otherwise it's masturbating.

It's a tiresome endeavor, trying to discuss Nietzsche or existentialism in general with Brady's fans. There is an unmovable wall between those who are able to discuss Brady's crimes in the abstract, an exercise of will, and those who see such thinking as irrelevant when it moves from the abstract to the concrete. People who believe that child murder can be justified by invoking various philosophical tenets aren't going to be swayed by people like me who insist such thinking is indeed masturbatory excuse-making and a strange ego stroke for the person who feels murdering children is a sign of a strong, self-driven will.

The problem that plagues Brady's interpretation of Nietzsche's superman or higher man theory and applying it to murder is that the person who accepts this potential world of lions stalking lambs must be sanguine with the possibility of becoming a lamb. When does the will of the stronger outweigh the value of your own? If you are unwilling to consider the possibility that adopting Brady's explanations for killing children also means that you could be the one to die at the hands of a will stronger than your own, to be the person whose death proves someone else has evolved a morality beyond the sanctimonious admonitions of the herd, you're as full of shit as Brady was. Brady wasn't ever a victim of predation like that which he visited upon children, but his whining response to the consequences of encountering a will formed in a similar environment yet far different than his own—David Smith, who had no use for murder—shows his own hypocrisy. He wanted the consequences for defying conventional morality to be a soft berth and he felt terribly betrayed when reality didn't yield to his whim. You can define murder however you want to meet your ends but never forget that such analysis is useless at best and often clearly masturbatory if you aren't willing to live and die, however metaphorically, by those broad terms.

The punchline to this philosophical joke never changes—no one who thinks like Brady ever suspects there is a will stronger than their own.

Sotos shows us some more of Brady's masturbation:

In 2013, during a public hearing on Brady's continuing treatment and incarceration at a hospital rather than a prison, Brady answered that the murders he had been convicted of were an "existential experience." This was Brady repeating what he wrote in *Gates of Janus*. Unkindly, it was Brady repeating what he learned from writing it. As existential, murder exists as the act of killing that spurs - not settles - the forever broad terms that one can gaze through and reflect backward as long as a transgressive moment is suggested instead of digested. The spiritual answers to the unanswered will always be an exercise, always be appreciating nature as real while hoping to challenge it as fake. Sadly masturbating is as good as it's going to get.

I wish I had been this pithy and coherent when I first panned Brady's efforts. Because isn't it alarming to think of people who may genuinely apprehend child murder and rape as existential exercise? Their freedom, in this instance, requires you to give up your own in all respects—a surrender they would justify because their will was superior to your own if your blood was spilled before theirs. Would Brady's fans have the same resolve if *their* necks were on the other side of the existential knife? Of course they wouldn't. We have Brady's own example to demonstrate how that played out. More on that in a bit.

In "Bait," Sotos discusses one of the best ways we know Brady was absolutely full of shit and I'm frankly appalled this didn't occur to me when I first read *The Gates of Janus*. I sneered at how much Brady revealed about himself, especially in the course of his telling analysis of Carl Panzram. But what about the information that Brady failed to show us by refusing to analyze those who did what he did? Sotos notices that Brady assiduously avoided dissecting anyone like himself:

> Sidney Cooke and his pedophile gang are noticeably absent from Brady's review of serial killing analysis. Since he researched murder over raped child disposal.

Could Brady have discussed Sidney Cooke, a man led by virtually identical impulses as Brady? No, he couldn't have discussed Cooke, a carny who raped and murdered boys and teenagers, abetted by accomplices in the exercise of his sick will. Best to stick to Henry Lee Lucas, even if much of the information he conveyed about Lucas was factually wrong. Can't have people drawing certain conclusions about two men so similar in their drives and lusts and tempt us to wonder if Brady might have assembled his own pedophile gang had David Smith not been so recalcitrant.

But then again, maybe not, as Sotos notes:

> Pauline, proving a struggle that Brady didn't want to repeat, gives a good argument to his predilection in crime having more to do with murder or violence than the sexual, than any predisposition with even a young girl coming into her full adulthood before full adulthood ruined the perfect unavailable tease.

This may well be true. Brady may have focused on children merely because he was too weak to control mature bodies. But Sotos goes on to shows us what he really thinks, noting that Brady avoided another prime criminal to analyze:

> After Sidney Cooke, he didn't choose Robert Black, either. To discuss his understandings of murder and, significantly, parceling evidence. Crimes with still missing corpses, suspicious tastes and body counts, predisposition to a type, a sex, specific acts therein. What young meant, or too old, or too tiny.

Black abducted and raped girls ranging from six to sixteen, telling police he "always liked young girls since I was a young kid." I can barely bring myself to wonder what he meant by young girls in this context if he was young himself when his obsessions began. Brady's interactions with Lesley, recorded and photographed, show me, at least, that he was indeed a violent pedophile but the fact remains that that may not have been all he was. People bring up Pauline, an older teenager when Hindley lured her to her fate, as proof that Brady wasn't a pedophile because Pauline had the appearance of a young adult woman. So he killed a girl who looked like a young adult woman. That just means he was attracted to varying victim pools in similar age ranges: teen boys, young boys, teen girls, young girls. It's not like he couldn't be a man who had predilections for different victim pools. But that doesn't make it any less telling that Brady carefully avoided discussing killers whose crimes were very similar to his, and I assert he made these editorial choices because he absolutely did not want to apply his theory of murder as an existential exercise to like-minded killers. Brady, in his mind, was the sole higher man entitled to kill kids. The rest of those pedophile murderers were just scumbags, you know?

Peter Sotos also decimates those who would frame Brady as a sort of murderer as a fine artist, a man who channeled sixties rebellion into violent transgression. Brady liked to place his actions in a rebellious, artistic framework and that's utter bullshit:

> When explaining the public's obsession with the case, he [Brady] often refers to the gothic presentation of the time and cites the Rolling Stones' sixties as more suitably evocative of the culture he lived free amongst. But. David Smith recalls that Brady was no fan of the Stones or any of the pop songs that younger Myra and her sister preferred then. And. Keith Richards and Pete Townshend both start their recent biographies with the same gothic English grey of rough disinterest, poor social struggle and common drunkenness. These men looked around themselves and their lot and chose different expressive modes of frustration to creating jobbing pop songs before they discovered leaning on art as some form of violent or voiced sexual acceptance. Brady isn't talking about the times he was part of. Instead takes credit for living at the same time, as if he were part of a cultural shift. Artists recognizing the bright not bloody colors in heady upheaval and the shit

stayed the same. Brady bought a camera. And hid.

Sotos sees the dishonesty in the book and sums it up very neatly:

> All these years to think and the victims are not in the book.

The victims are why anyone knows who Ian Brady is. And he hated that. An honest killer would have been able to see his victims as important as he was, especially when he was writing a book analyzing why other men selected specific victims. His choice of Lesley showed a lot about him—his inability to control older children, his inability to lure in a child without a woman helping him, his need to document his existential experience because it was likely less an exercise of the will than a desire to relive a pornographic experience. Brady could never have written honestly about those like him because he refused to analyze himself honestly.

But his inability to tell the truth extends beyond his attempts to discuss other killers. There's no sense in believing that Brady told the truth about anything, especially his own motives for murder. I found myself appreciating the time Peter Sotos took looking at what I missed, the real reasons that may have fueled Brady's murder streak. I tend to sum up Brady as a vicious asshole who preyed on the weak, and while that explanation may stand beside some of the theories Sotos offers up, there are interesting potential motives at play.

Pornography

Sotos wonders if, through his murders, perhaps Brady was protesting too much. Comparing him to Black and Cooke:

> Cooke and most of his associates in crime were fixated on boys. It is another glance downward that Brady's interests did not choose an exclusive gender, Black, girls, small. Cooke, boys, preteen plus. However, the only ones Brady photographed his way were Lesley and Myra. For whom, possibly, there was a bigger market. Or rather, an easier, less contentious market. The photo of Keith isn't assumed to be more than a souvenir and an insult. The market for child pornography in the early unsophisticated years hadn't been parentally conflated with murder yet but the commercial viability for such rape shots would have, even if Brady had the dubious network, been very difficult to maintain after sale.

Of course if Brady did release photographs of Myra and Lesley to pornographic media outlets, no one has found them yet. That doesn't mean that he didn't have that potential goal in mind.

Homosexuality

So why did Brady have such a varied victim pool, consisting of children and teens of both sexes? Well, it could very well be because he was a self-loathing homosexual. From a history of gay life in Manchester, an elderly gay man remembered often seeing Brady at a gay club called the Rembrandt. Taking it further, a book called *50 True Tales of Terror* speculates that Brady lied about not knowing victim Edward Evans before luring him to his death:

> Could Brady have known him from his visits to the Rembrandt? It is possible they met at the Rembrandt on the night of the murder?

> Could Brady have lied about where he met Evans that night, rather than have it come out that he was a regular at the Rembrandt? Could Brady and Hindley have come up with that story before their arrest, perhaps to tell David Smith.

The same article later posits that perhaps Brady's appearances at the Rembrandt were not a sign that he was gay but rather clear evidence that he was a criminal. Of course homosexuals were not de facto criminals but because homosexuality was still a criminal offense in the UK, they were marginalized. Their clubs were in unsavory places, they had to meet in criminal-like secrecy. Worse, homosexuals were subject to the predatory schemes of criminals, especially in the form of blackmail. By associating with people at gay clubs, if Brady was not gay, he was most assuredly surrounding himself with people upon whom he could prey and on whose confidence he could rely, since they would be too fearful of police to seek legal help.

Does any of this seem to suggest the motive of a super man or a higher man? Either hiding his true sexuality due to shame, or deliberately associating with people with little social or legal recourse should he decide to prey upon them? Brady decided to attack smaller children after Pauline Reade put up a fight, but perhaps when he later wanted to exercise his will again against stronger adults, he selected a victim pool he knew would not seek help should they manage to escape his grasp before he could kill them.

And, as Peter notes, we'll never know the truth:

> We don't know if his trash at Ashworth are lying about his mental degeneration. And try as he might to convince everyone listening. And his paltry insulting disloyal or favor-counting pals. No one is helping him get what may well be his honest side out. Of him. Maybe the lawyers and health watchers who are forced to deal with him don't care. About the principles, even. Maybe they fill their lives being cruel to him for the very reasons he says exist in everybody else, unacknowledged.

On some level it might have been nice had anyone managed to get Brady to speak honestly, but criminal science and psychology have a pretty good idea of what it is that motivates men like Brady. I don't think the principles mattered to those who had to deal with Brady at his worst—they had his number even as he sneered that no one could possibly understand his philosophical complexity.

THE "REAL" TRUTH

Brady, throughout his time in prison, spoke of letters and documents that would tell where Keith Bennett was buried, that would tell the real truth about what he and Myra did. He claimed he was working on a book that would be released after his death, an autobiography:

> Various friends and confidants have publicly laid claim to possession of the book, originally reported to have been delivered to his lawyer, and a publishing deal had already been finalized as the book sat in a safe.

It sounds like it may be a humdinger—Sotos quotes a statement from a public tribunal to judge Brady's overall health and mental state:

> In another attempt to display his dominance, Brady had been collaborating on a book to be released on his death. According to co-author Alan Keightley, it will claim that there are nine victims of the Moors murders - and reveal where Keith Bennett is buried. I have seen sections of the book and it contains deeply disturbing graphic detail of the killings, along with directly implicating Hindley in the sexual abuse of victims.

Keightley has confirmed that the book exists, and that he assembled it from thousands of hours of conversations he taped with Brady. He says the 100,000-word book is up in his attic and that he will release it after Brady's death (and it appears that he did so—a book Keightley authored is up on Amazon, listed five days after Brady died. I have not read it but lurid British tabloids have indicated that Brady claims he did kill nine victims, and implicates Myra for being as violent and sexually deviant as he was).

I don't know which-book-discussed-where may represent the final words of Ian Brady but Sotos makes clear which documents reveal the correct portrait:

> Brady's complaints against his life at Ashworth some nearly fifteen years after the Fallon Inquiry [an investigation into the shortcomings in how Ashworth was run] resulted in a 116-page judgment on Brady's hopes, care, situation, and misunderstandings and are more his biography than any author's attempt at definitive.

BRADY'S SAD TIME AT ASHWORTH

So, what does that 116-page document contain? What did Brady say that Peter Sotos thinks tells his story better than any biography?

> Here was a legal document that pitted Brady against the lies he's made to further himself. The hospital's possible desire to further torture him being better understood as them taking him at his word, making him accountable for his lies, then attempting to explain the severe problems they'd have convincing others what lies they're supposed to fall back on as interested, compassionate providers.

Brady's situation was not helped by his refusal to speak to doctors once he was at Ashworth. And because they were responsible for the well-being of a man who insisted he was insane so he could be placed there, they took care of him. When he had a seizure and his heart stopped, they started it up again with a defibrillator, to his furious disappointment when he regained consciousness. When he said he was starving himself to death, they outfitted him with a nasal feeding tube. Brady, who talked so much shit, really regretted the lies he told about himself in the end.

But he kept talking shit:

> "Much of his behaviour stems from his legal battles with Ashworth Hospital. He is adamant that he is not mentally ill. He says he committed the murders at a time when, if he had been distracted by something else, they may not have happened. He talks about understanding the effects the killings had on the families of his victims. He does speak of remorse. He acknowledges he has taken from the families and knows what he did was heinous and wrong, but says, 'If you ask me to say 'sorry' that is a word I cannot use because it is meaningless."

He wasn't acting like a petulant child because he had the mentality of a petulant child. Nope, he acted the part because Ashworth wouldn't take the word of a self-professed psychotic that he was lying and send him back to prison.

He didn't kill five people because he is a killer asserting his will in a godless world. He did it because he lacked sufficient distraction.

He feels remorse at the misery he caused the families and refuses to say he is sorry because it is meaningless, but he still refused to reveal where Keith's body is though he knew this information would give his family, especially his mother Winnie, more comfort than a meaningless apology.

It absolutely beggars belief that anyone can look at what this man says about himself and believe him, let alone believe he has access to some greater truth about the human condition. He was a liar, and not even a particularly good one.

Malingering: Hoisted by His Own Petard

Brady wasn't insane when he went to prison. The worst anyone could say about the nature of his mental state came from a medical officer in 1970. He said he was free from mental illness but:

> "He is, however, a schizoid psychopath of utter untruthfulness who has the rather unusual ability in this type of personality of dissociating himself from the crimes of which he has been convicted.... Increasingly I feel that it is a symptom of the terrifying intensity of his psychopathy, and that he is not defending against recalling his offences but that, as far as he is concerned, they fail to rise above his mental horizons."

If you've read *The Gates of Janus*, perhaps you recall Brady discussing how much more interesting he feels psychotics are than psychopaths. Even after he wanted to get out of Ashworth and back into regular prison, he clung to that definition of himself that he felt portrayed him in the most interesting light. A psychotic is not grounded to reality. A psychopath is a person with an anti-social disregard for laws and the well-being of other people. One could say a psychopath is a person who could read Nietzsche and walk away with the idea that such philosophy encourages people to abduct, rape and murder children.

But Sotos, in the end, sums up this masquerade rather well:

> Brady eventually created himself psychotic. His "will" was destined to turn into madness.

Not the first time this has happened. You play a role long enough you can become what you pretend. Brady by his own account pretended to be psychotic for an eighteen month spurt. Sotos says:

> Within his book. Brady responding to the single salve monologue he re-writes from conversations. Uses quotes for silent support, backup, decontextualized lead he's finding agrees with him. Better that he's an old man thinking he's got something to say, even when talking to the air. Cites his rights. And doesn't recognize that his gorgeous violence and rarified sexual degradations have been reduced to talking about using cereal and honey. Instead of confronting God and the great God-given evils available to those who dare, pleasure or regret, his intensive understanding of evil writhing and painful pleas for absent sympathy and irritating hard-ons and universal recognition, his responses are to continually argue that he was "provoked."

This above refers to an incident where Brady became angry during a telephone call. Out of his sight, another patient was reading a magazine. When finished with his call, Brady marched up to the patient reading the magazine and began to scream abuse at him. The patient, confused about what was happening, asked Brady what was going on and Brady brandished a pen in his fist in some sort of gesture of threat. Staff corralled Brady into his room and Brady insisted that the patient had been throwing cereal around and smearing honey on chairs to annoy and upset him. This was manifestly untrue and such a sign of Brady's character—roiling rage with no cause but always willing to invent a reason for it.

Brady was a liar. Never forget that. Sotos sums up Brady's behavior so aptly:

> Brady wants to win but trusts he has rights he simply doesn't. More than win, he wants to sell. And may have gotten used to selling over winning. Customers seldom settle for a single purveyor. Middlemen have a hard time keeping customers happy and stupid. He believed that his book would be a best seller, checking the sales figures and top tens, and then said he knew the lists were rigged. It is a legitimate worry over whether or not all these trained healthy care professionals and his lousy legal and medical defenses

ever had an effect on his own thinking rather than his options.

In the end I think Brady did value selling over winning. He had fans. He had people seek him out and stroke his ego. He stayed in the psychiatric prison he lied to get into and then tried to tell the truth to leave. His will was thwarted by his own weakness. He had nothing left but the sell.

In a way, Sotos shared a strange sympathy for Brady, or it reads as sympathetic to me.

> The entirety of *Gates of Janus* is Brady interacting with the world as he wishes to see himself teaching... Cunning Brady working his Brady puppet, he tells you. Came up with the green face for Harrison. Later told Cowley it was spin. Tribunal got method acting. Once he was saying he had a sickness. Here's the list to prove it. Now he was saying he tied everything together as any old man looking back on his life would do. Who'd fall back on clean lists when finding a mess. And he wants to go back to where it was less shit than this has become.

Brady lost control of the narrative. He wanted to take control again. He was an old man living in a psychiatric prison, his entire life lost due to impulses he never really understood even as he tried to convince people he knew so much about criminal psychology. This book was an attempt to grasp his story back, and he failed miserably. The end was as shit as the time before it. In a way, that's sad. In another way, that's justice.

Brady insisted that he put on an act to persuade prison officials that he was a psychotic, and in the end he was believed enough to win a transfer from regular lock down to a psychiatric prison. When he gave testimony before a tribunal about his time in Ashworth, he was classic Brady—arrogant and superior. Sotos tells us about Brady's tribunal testimony through an article Helen Pidd wrote for *The Guardian*.

> Claiming to have feigned psychosis for 18 months in order to be transferred from prison to Ashworth, he said he practiced Stanislavksi system of acting, expressing contempt when asked by Dr. Cameron Boyd, a forensic psychiatrist sitting on the tribunal panel, to explain what he meant. "I would have thought any informed person would grasp the meaning immediately," Brady scoffed.

This would be funny if it were not so sad. All Brady had left in life were these moments wherein he could posture and behave in an arrogant and learned manner. Sneering at a forensic psychiatrist was the only way he could demonstrate intelligence and it likely gave him thrills to think he knew more about method acting than the man asking him questions.

Brady evidently spoke in the same affected manner that characterized his prose in *The Gates of Janus*. Still quoting Pidd:

> Still present is his superior attitude to everyone around him. Giving evidence on Tuesday, he was keen to demonstrate an advanced grasp of

language and learning. Explaining why he sometimes listened to "white noise" while taking his daily feeds through a nasal tube, he said it was simply to block out the racket his fellow patients were making. It was better than listening to "nattering disc jockeys." To do so was, he said, pragmatic—something which would be "axiomatic to anyone with sense."

Again, this pretense of superiority was all he had. He was too intelligent to listen to the radio, he felt such a declaration should be "axiomatic" to anyone as smart as he was. It had to have been infuriating listening to him, or perhaps those assembled had to stifle the need to laugh at him.

Time in that psychiatric prison Brady lied his way into was more brutal and unpleasant than he anticipated and he wanted to go back to regular lockdown. However, he couldn't persuade his way back into prison. It may be that Brady had pretended for so long that he became unhinged. Or it may be that the prison officials understood that he was not insane and felt keeping him at Ashworth was the best sort of punishment for him. But in Ashworth he stayed. Eventually, Brady claimed to have embarked on a hunger strike so he could starve himself to death. He was probably just acting then, too. Was the hunger strike really bullshit? His nurse says it was. Still quoting Helen Pidd in *The Guardian*:

> He remains slim, save for a slight double chin and paunch which were a mystery to those watching the video relay of the tribunal—until his nurse revealed that the "hunger strike" he claims to have been observing for the past 14 years involved him snacking daily on toast and soup, supplemented by the feeding tube hanging out of his right nostril.

So, he ate toast and soup as he was force fed through a nasal tube. No one should be surprised by this.

The Guardian asked Alan Bennett, brother of still missing Keith, for his reaction after watching Ian Brady give testimony to the Tribunal. This is what he had to say:

> I am happiest knowing Brady will be at his unhappiest. I know he hates Ashworth and I cannot be sure he would feel the same about any other place he may be sent to. Besides that, I do not think he should be allowed to move just because he wants to.
>
> It's a good feeling to know that the truth is out now and the public knows Brady's "hunger strike" is nothing more than another publicity stunt. He does eat normally and the nasal tube should now be seen for what it is really - an empty, meaningless symbol of his supposed protest at his "mistreatment" and also an empty symbol of his act of defiance at the system.

Remember how much Brady loved Carl Panzram? As I stated in my initial discussion of *The Gates of Janus*, Brady admired and probably was attracted to Panzram because Panzram was a far better exemplar of what Ian Brady claimed to be. Brady put so much store by his will but whined and cried and lied and engaged in low theater to escape the will of others. Panzram just asserted his will harder, continuing to be the same man in prison as he was in the course of his criminal life outside of prison. That Brady staged a largely faked hunger strike to protest the terrible conditions he felt he endured at Ashworth should tell anyone all they need to know about him and his will.

Sotos keenly notes how Brady would always be a day late and a dollar short because he was an outsider and because he continually deprived himself of a platform via his ridiculous decisions.

> No matter what he says, he won't be the one saying it. No final word. Arguments will be chaotic forever, go on, get angry. How's that working for you? You big passionate fella you. Hospital is working out well for him, better than he says, better than he knows, which says it all, really. Helping him quell the symptoms of his prevaricating alternating madness, then and now, attempting to get him to understand how deep it sits and how well he is doing as a result of them knowing more truth than them. The conclusions of the tribunal are double binds with impossible evidentiary catches that Brady did not consider were possible before he entered into the public well away from his hated Ashworth. Maybe that's all he wanted. For a little while. Now explain petty. Maybe the fight was a bigger deal to those he was irritating with paperwork than it was for him...

Did Brady lose steam at the end of his protest? Maybe, but all in all Sotos may be correct. Perhaps Ashworth was the best thing that could have happened to Brady because it forced him to consider whether or not he was indeed mentally ill. Even if he arrogantly evinced erudition and sanity, the refusal of those around him to believe him a second time had to have instilled some doubt in him. If Brady died wondering if he was really the man he claimed to be, then perhaps it was all worth it in the end. To us though. Not him. When it comes to the topic of Brady's redemption, I don't particularly care, but it feels nice to think he may well have realized, at the end, that he really, truly had lost, that all he did can be summed up by the fact that he was mentally ill and not a one-man philosophical juggernaut.

It's interesting, in a way, to wonder how much genuine insanity fueled all that Brady did. Sotos explores this in the following:

> Brady in Harrison's book tells the author that he can't talk about the details. The blocks will come down. The book Harrison released was finished during the years that Brady now says he was malingering. This was the time, repeated in the transcripts of the tribunal hearings, as sacrosanct. This is the period when Brady's madness had got the better of him and is the time that Ashworth uses against him to suggest he isn't in control of his health. That his insanity was clear then and may or may not be creeping somewhere lower without his or his doctors' ability to recognize that which definitely did happen then, might occur again. Whether or not Brady is lying now is a matter for language experts, not doctors, since the proof is labeled clearly

by the law that decided to move him from prison to hospital. He wants to return to prison but his choice, or his insanity, smears any further options as unreadable. Try as he might to say he was lying then, he only looks like a liar that no one has to trust or forgive. What has playing with was, yet fucking again, too big to weight future consequences against current want. Not spoiled, Not even demanding. Just confused. Officially.

I don't know if Brady was genuinely insane. I can't parse it out. He was a pompous, self-impressed asshole, but that doesn't exclude mental illness. But as I said before, I don't care. I'm glad he was hoisted by his own petard and I'm glad he died in a place he hated. If he wasn't insane, all the better. Wanting a good experience for Ian in prison is, in a way, an admission that he never had much of a will to be the superman he claimed he was. It is far kinder, in a perverse way, to think him better off suffering in the world of Christian morality that he condemned. Because if he had an ounce of honesty in him, he would have spurned all pleasant mercies.

An Indictment of Brady's Fans

Throughout this discussion of Peter Sotos' "Bait" I have mentioned that Brady's fan base appall me. I could spend several thousand more words discussing in depth some of the fans I have met, but for now I think I will let Sotos explain my reactions for me. I absolutely love this passage, as Sotos riffs further on the ridiculousness implicit in Brady defining murder:

> In kind, let me explain his audience. In kind, let me explain his critics and customers. In kind, let me explain what I bought instead of what he sold. Let me tell you about the purchase-only experience. Let me tell you why broadly doesn't fucking work, shyster. Easy fucking clearly faggot hack. Let me tell you how easy it is to listen and think elsewhere, see what you are. How you fucking hide like kids do. How one blowhard recognizes another.

Yeah, I may be a blowhard, but I like to think I refused to buy what Brady was selling and if that is why—that I recognize the obfuscation and slippery definitions because I am deceitful—I'm fine with admitting it. Never shit a shitter, isn't that what they say? I can't read all of this, react to it using more words than a Tao Lin novella, and not, at some point, acknowledge that personal experience in bullshit helps parse out bullshit.

But even as I admit this, it's not uncommon enough to be remarkable. We all lie, for different reasons, self-serving or self-sacrificing, white lies or cruel knife twists. What *is* remarkable is when people can look at Brady's words, feel the darkness, and see truth in what he says about the will and the virtue of axing away all externally imposed morality in order to show superiority.

> The interest in the Moors murders must come from a serious discussion of what happened as long as a side between good and evil is flat pity; it must have a purpose to accomplish something more than an elastic truth that wouldn't allow the sympathetic and sorrowful to abut the prurient and vicarious.

And this is such a big fucking problem I have with Brady's fans, those who think there is such truth in his approach to murder and how he considers what he did to be little more than a philosophical musing—children died. My heart bleeds for the parents and siblings left behind. My heart bleeds for those kids whose deaths were explained away as an existential exercise by the man who killed them. What does a Brady acolyte's heart bleed for? What does yours, as you read again about the little girl whose rape was recorded and photographed? Her mother, whose body gave out after years of rage? What do you think when you remember Keith's mother, hopeful to the end that this man, who is so base he faked a hunger strike in order to undo a lie he perpetrated against himself, would tell her what he did with her child's body?

There are moments in "Bait" where I wanted to scream, specifically when Sotos quoted Jean Rafferty, who wrote a speculative novel about the Moors murder case. A lot of Brady fans think as Rafferty does, engaging in seriously weak thinking regarding war, institutionalized violence and what rejecting contemporary morality means for the liberated philosopher and murder king.

> And yet when Brady said Bush and Blair bore the responsibility for more deaths than he did, I had to agree. When he said that powerful people were rarely held accountable as he had, I had to agree. The fact that he had killed those children and left their bodies on the moors did not alter the fact that he was right, that he was a thinking person with a moral perspective, even if few people would agree with him on the subject of murder.

Some of Brady's fans really resent that Brady was held accountable for murders he committed with his own hands, rapes he committed with his own penis, when Bush fomented chaos in the Middle East and caused the deaths of people as innocent of wrongdoing as Lesley. They absolutely refuse to acknowledge that deaths in the course of disastrous foreign policy endeavors are different in definition (broadly, even) and different in terms of morality and legal justice. In their minds every act, every belief, is comparable to What Brady Did. A soldier who shoots insurgents shooting at him is as guilty of murder as Brady or all is hypocrisy. They have no capacity for nuance.

I experienced this on my blog, when I examined how it was that Brady salivated over the corpse of Carl Panzram because Panzram embodied all that Brady wished that he was but wasn't. Carl Panzram lived up to Brady's lion versus lamb theory because he exercised his will without cringing in fear at the potential repercussions. Because I was able to see how Panzram lived up to Brady's own bizarre definitions of heroism while Brady fell short, Brady's fans accused me of hypocrisy. To them, pointing out that Panzram achieved what Brady wished he could was an admission that I must admire Panzram and that therefore I didn't dislike the concept of transcendent murder as much as I insist. For them it is impossible to compare two murderous psychopaths—one murderer is exactly the same as another because for them all results come from identical wills. In their minds, a man who kidnaps women and keeps them as sex slaves has the identical motive as a police officer who arrests such a man and sends him to prison—the will to deprive others of freedom.

But all of this begs the question: why it is that Brady would need to engage in such comparisons and equivocations? If Brady really believed that as a superman or higher man he had chosen a different moral path he would not be making the comparison in the first place. He would have accepted that as a moral trailblazer whose new created and self-defined morality allowed him to murder he would be misunderstood by the rabble. Why would Brady worry about the deaths caused by Western leaders and their Middle Eastern debacles if he genuinely had created a new morality for himself defined by what he thought was proper for him to do in the course of exercising his will? It seems his sole moral idea relies on equivalences, false or otherwise, in order to make it understandable to others.

And even if Bush and Blair are guilty of murder, what difference would that make? Is there an upper limit of victims that has to be achieved before society can declare a person a murderer? Did Brady need to kill thousands before the British penal system stepped in? And what if Bush and Blair were themselves Nietzschean supermen whose wills, like Brady's, required death? As always, the only will that matters is Brady's and we all needed to tamp down our own and permit him to run amok and kill young people because war happens.

Rafferty goes on:

> He wasn't some animal, blindly driven by his urges. He was a man enthralled by ideas, by the thought that in a godless world man has to make his own laws, his own decisions, has to have the courage to follow where his desires lead him.

I don't want to be unkind to Rafferty because she actually seems like a writer whose fiction I would enjoy, but in two sentences she contradicts herself. He wasn't blinded by urges but he had the courage to follow where his desires led him. An urge is a very strong desire. He was driven by his urges, but I guess that because he pushes his status as a superman the key word here is "blindly." But even if I grant Rafferty the benefit of the doubt, it's hard for me to understand why she doesn't understand that if Brady was making justifications—he wasn't as bad as Bush and Blair—then he wasn't engaged in the advancement of his own decisions, recreating morality in a godless world. Rather, he was making excuses for why what he did, the result of his courage to follow his desires, was not so bad in comparison. If he had any truth in him he would have owned what he did as the result of his decision to follow his own path and then would have continued to follow that path even in prison, as Panzram did. Instead he faked a mental illness diagnosis, tried to starve himself when that fakery blew up in his face, lied, cheated and sniveled because the strength of his conviction, of his path, ended the moment he had to own his decision.

> I think he had gifts which have been distorted and perverted... I'm kind to him because I hate the thought of anyone being in prison, whatever they've done. I'm not suggesting that either of them should have been let out, just that I would hate to be in their situation...

Rafferty is probably right—I have to think Brady had some talents and gifts that he decided were less important than following his desire to kill people. And yeah, Rafferty herself would not want to be in prison and I have to tell her that such fears, however low they may be in terms of philosophical reasons for avoiding criminal behavior, are a good thing—sometimes fear of life imprisonment among others who created similarly dark moral paths keeps people from raping and killing little girls.

Look, one of the ways Nietzsche was a genius was in how he showed that in all of us there is a lion, a wolf, a vicious animal poised for the kill. He was clear about that, yet if you look at his life, those he admired did not kill. He did not count as higher men those who killed or raped, even as he spoke of the chaos in his godless world. He made a larger philosophical point about how confining Christian morality is to atheists who hold no allegiance to such ideas and urged us to imagine a world where people made a morality that was not subject to the soul-confining nature of churchy urging regarding human behavior, making natural life sinful, crushing the individual in the quest for sanctified obedience.

Brady focused on the visceral, the "whoot, I can kill because Christianity blows" element that plagues teenage school shooters' intellects. And I'm rather certain that Brady's attention to Nietzsche was born of a puerile aversion to Christian morality. Note that I am not saying that aversion to Christian morality is inherently puerile, but that Brady's reaction was puerile. I feel confident in this assessment due to Brady's love of Sade, who alongside Nietzsche was one of the greatest visceral critics of Christian morality. I posit that Brady was rejecting Christian prudery through these two men and used them to create a fantasy role of himself as a vanguard in the new, post-god world. Really, he just liked the idea of killing and found ways to shoehorn his urges into a framework that made him a philosophical hero rather than a degenerate piece of shit. His inability to continue to exercise his will when a more organized will moved against him shows his actions for what they were.

I believe Brady appeals to people who feel they have a spark of greatness in them that they can release however they see fit, with no responsibility to others who may be harmed when they act out. The acting-out proves their superiority and those who cannot see their superiority are weak-willed shee-ple. They developed this sort of thinking through their own selective focus on Nietzsche or Brady's focus, but the end result is the same. Nietzsche's discussions regarding the hypocrisy of past and present Christian morality and master-slave morality get absorbed, but less so Nietzsche's discussion of the sorts of morality key to being a superman or higher man, and the positive ethics such men would demonstrate in action. Nietzsche's examples of men whom he thought were higher men—Beethoven, Goethe, and Nietzsche himself—bear no resemblance to a man who decided a proper exercise of his will was to rape and murder children. One of Nietzsche's chief complaints against Christian morality was the unnatural morality that forced men to act in ways that violated what Nietzsche considered natural life instincts. It is difficult to imagine actions possessing less natural life instinct than killing children.

Moreover, Brady's life prior to prison and while in prison was laughably lacking the elements that Nietzsche outlined as being the five characteristics of higher men:

- desire for solitude and separation from the rabble that may delay him from reaching his goals;
- possession of an instinctive drive that leads him to seek out and accept responsibility and burdens;
- mental resilience that rejects pessimism and depression;
- possession of a sort of affirmation of life that means they would willingly relive their lives over and over; and
- possessing carriage and a demeanor that shows others nobility and demonstrates mental and emotional certainty.

Let's compare this to the reality of Ian Brady's life:

- Brady persuaded a daft secretary to help him kill and ultimately was undone by his desire to pull others into his criminal pursuits;
- Brady can be said to have killed knowing he would be punished if caught, which is a burden of sorts, but part of the responsibility in taking the course of murder was accepting consequences, their own burden, if caught;
- Brady possessed nothing close to mental resilience as he faked mental illness, staged fake hunger strikes and whined his way through imprisonment;
- there is zero way Brady would relive this life if he left it bitterly complaining about what had been done to him, and however wavering or insincere his suicide attempts were, he still showed the idea that he

wanted to end this life sooner than natural death would allow; and

- while it's subjective whether or not Brady had noble carriage, his mental and emotional certainty were always in question outside of his desire to posture as a great man and torment the families of the kids he killed.

Yeah, even on paper Brady only demonstrates a very small, terribly selective portion of what Nietzsche discussed.

One doesn't have to be a scholar to read Nietzsche and see how he exhorted mankind to look critically at the moral standards of prior and contemporary civilization and to question if there is a better choice for individual freedom. It's simply beyond me, how some people end up thinking the way to achieve this new morality involves killing children. Yes, Nietzsche said that the upheaval entailed by such thinking may result in acts of destruction (but that the end result will be better than the tyranny of Christian tradition), but no one ever explains with any degree of clarity how recruiting a lonely secretary into helping you abduct, rape and murder kids results in a basis for a new moral order. Of course the premise that God is dead implies that there is a void, a chaos wherein all morality under the old Christian doctrines is gone. So maybe therein lies the trick for Brady's fans. The prospect of a godless void helps because in that absence what difference does a few dead kids make?

The problem of course is that God wasn't dead when Brady killed, and even if the forces that represent God were indeed dead, the new individual gods didn't smile on Brady's will to harm. There was no real chaos outside of Brady's head, and, in fact, the real chaos of societal upheaval with more permissive morality happened in a world that Brady did not occupy. God in the form of the old moral guard was not separate from permissive revolution because factions from both were poised and ready to deal with murderers of children. But that's the trap door, isn't it, in the way fans of Brady think—they believe the premise that in a moral chaos left by an absent moral authority that the man who creates a new authority is his own god. If Brady and his fans were correct philosophically Brady would never have seen a day in prison as the new world grappled with the formation of a new moral path forged by the will of individuals. Rather than Nietzsche's stars born from chaos, it would have been a sanctioned blood orgy with the strongest left standing. But the strongest left standing—the penal system, a society that embraced free love yet would have killed Brady and Hindley themselves if they had access to them—reveal the faultline in the crude interpretation preferred by Brady's acolytes. An inability to see the metaphor in philosophy is often problematic but thankfully it seldom leads to such terrible ends.

More on his love of Sade, from Myra Hindley, from a letter she wrote to John Kilbride's mother:

"Not only did I help procure the victims for him, I knew it was wrong, to put it mildly, that what we were doing was evil and depraved, whereas he subscribed to de Sade's philosophy, that murder was for pleasure.

"To him it has become a hobby, something one did to get absorbed into, interested and fascinated with, and it had become literally a deadly obsession."

I don't have a great opinion of Myra Hindley's capacity for contemplation yet one has to assume she knew Brady better than we do. If she describes Brady as a man who engaged in a deadly obsession, it calls into question how deliberate his actions were, how will-derived they were. As opposed to looking at him as a man who needed to kill due to various compulsions he could not control, we see how he shoe-horned them into philosophies that made him feel noble. Perhaps Brady was just clever enough to filter his desires through philosophy.

While I am not as upset by those looking for details about the murders as some may be, the fact remains that Brady's crimes have created an obsession in some people, mainly men, who are desperate to see Lesley's naked body abused and destroyed. That these men are looking for something so hard to find about a specific child says to me that they are not pedophiles in search of a fix. Such men can find the porn they want without revealing themselves to a book blogger during the search. Rather, they have within them a specific darkness that Lesley has come to represent and they must know what happened to her. Here's what Sotos says about these people:

> ...I figure it's got to be pretty bad. Because you have to keep fucking going on about it. And as a drunk friend, tell you that I listen to you, those of us who really care about you and your pain, as difficult as that is, as hideous as it is, and then remind you that all the books and, really, the forests of newspapers and hours of Internet scrolls, all do the same fucking thing. They're looking for answers about those two. And they're looking because the answers aren't there and closure doesn't exist, you twice-divorced rag, and, here's where I fuck up, again. The looking is getting in the way of what really happened. The intentions. Fuck the intentions. Fuck your level asking me for the intentions. And then the mistakes and the possibility of your good giving grace.

Lesley has ensured that the forest will always be lost for the trees. There is no answer. We will never know why Hindley and Brady (or Bernardo and Homolka or the Wests) did what they did because they did it because they wanted to do it and their reasons make no sense even to those of us desperate to understand. We can't understand it, we are not them. The men looking for Lesley may be doing so with their dicks in their hands but at the end they know what I know—they cannot understand themselves by looking at what Brady did. They are obsessed with a specific innocent child who came to a bad end. Brady's obsessions were with being that bad end. Even if the focus on Lesley is sexual or violent, the focus is still on the victim, not the person conveying the rape and murder. People who sanctify Brady will always be scarier to me than those who dig up Lesley.

Sotos goes on, obliquely addressing those who have been digging into the Moors cases in the hopes of understanding why:

> He's been telling you. It's all there and you're too fucking self-impressed with spotting his own ego that you won't fucking read it right. All of you cunts. It is all intensely about plans. And what you do with plans when they don't work is ask for help. Plans and help. Fucking been talking to Ashworth every fucking sentence. And there's been a crowd of hysterical child porn cocksuckers listening in like palsies. Myra, when she was lying, still thought this was what you wanted to hear. And you did...

This is why I like reading Peter Sotos. He knows his devoted audience needs to be told the truth and this is a truth-telling moment for me because I am one of those who is so interested in spotting Brady's ego. Did I miss him telling me why he killed? Did I lose sight of the forest for the trees? I certainly find myself appalled by the creation of pornography around Lesley, and most of us have our theories as to why Brady killed, but if Brady told us outright anything more than that he wanted to kill and that he cloaked his diseased will under high-minded existential experiments, I missed it. And if I missed it, I am among the self-impressed who just don't see.

I wish every person who insists that Brady was acting because Nietzsche wanted him to follow his will could read what Sotos has to say about Brady's reaction to the collective will of society:

> The existential experience had a wall it wasn't supposed to reach. The part where he learns that he made mistakes that forced the universe, if not his jailers, to act back at him and teach him that the plan wasn't just that, wasn't in his head. We can take what little you like and what more you think is rotten and unfair – how dare you ask someone to be fair – away from you, you powerless poor little confused thrashing mite.

Brady declared God dead and then asked for mercy. He couldn't have it both ways and neither can those who still cling to Brady's explanations.

The Visceral Delight in Watching Others Nail Brady

Throughout "Bait," Sotos praises Carol Ann Lee's work on the Moors murders. Through her book about David Smith, the man who turned Brady and Hindley in to the police (finally someone who knew Brady, who drank a pint with him and was related to Hindley through marriage), we get to see someone telling Brady the simple truth. Smith says to Brady:

> I'd like to know what you think you saw in me, Ian, and, even more than that, I'd like to know what made you think you had the right to kill? I've got no time for medical and psychiatric explanations. All that blaming your

illegitimacy and misspent youth is bullshit, pure and simple. Take it from someone who knows. Each person, as they grow up, is responsible for their own deeds, and no amount of Freudian analysis should be allowed to diminish that. You love the old ego massage and mind games, though, don't you, Ian? But you're nothing special and you never were, regardless of how the doctors fuss over finding the right label for your 'personality disorder.' You are a man who got his kicks from raping and murdering children. I still can't understand why anyone would want to make excuses for you.

I know you've spent countless hours wondering why you ended up in prison when you and she were so careful, so meticulous in planning your crimes and covering them up afterwards. But maybe I can help you with that, at least.

You're where you are now because you misjudged me.

Background matters. A person who is battered and molested as a child, who lived in poverty and had parents who were themselves unsound, finds it hard to rise above such a childhood. Yet there is truth in what Smith says— Brady may have grown up in poverty and endured the stigma of being illegitimate, but that has little bearing. Brady killed because he wanted to. Like Leopold and Loeb before him (mostly Loeb), he found a bit of philosophy that he was certain meant he was superior to all others. He killed to demonstrate his superior otherness. Or he killed and hid behind a ruse of superiority. Either way, he gave himself permission to do the worst because he felt he was entitled to do so.

Brady spoke of existentialist philosophy fueling his murder but the truth is that he killed because it got his dick hard to do it. He killed because he liked preying on young people, more boys than girls in the final tally, and because it sexually excited him. His kicks, as Smith put it. And as Smith said, there's nothing special about being a murderer who kills teens and children. Brady is not *sui generis* because he decided to kill people weaker than him—we see men who make similar choices in true crime books and cable television programs all the time. And every single person who tries to cloak Brady's sexual desire to fuck young people and kill them in some philosophical treatise on the will of the superman needs to know that they are rubes, taken in by a worm whose words about himself told them something they needed to hear about themselves, that their own nasty impulses made them special.

Smith knew Brady. He knew him far better than me, far better than anyone who leaves unsettling and outright stupid comments on my blog. David Smith conquered Brady's superman. Listen to him.

Frankly, even Myra, whom I consider to have possessed a middling intellect, had his number:

> "Ian Brady was quoted as allegedly saying he'll confess if he is given the means to kill himself afterwards. He no doubt regrets his ambition from as

long ago as 1970 to get out of Home Office clutches as he put it, and into a mental hospital. Had he not hoisted himself with his own petard, he'd be able to commit suicide in prison."

I worry that choosing to place this quote here may diminish it, but remember that: Brady's ruse about being psychotic deprived him of far more will than subjecting himself to contemporary morality and refusing to kill would have, in the long run.

Alan Bennett also went on to explain why anyone buys Brady's shit:

> The victims do not matter to Brady and neither do their families. The only people that matter to Brady are himself and the people he can manipulate, and there are too many people willing to be manipulated by him.

They want to be manipulated because Brady tells them that as they go through their lives, dealing with their dick of a boss, praying that they can pay all their bills each month, desperate for some meaning, that if they pick up a knife, a garrote, a gun, they can assert their will in a world designed to deprive them of basic dignity. I don't dismiss the tiresome and often degrading nature of modern life. We all limp. I just refuse to honor the notions of those who make Brady their cane.

BRADY'S FURY AT THE GATES OF JANUS

Hoo boy, was Brady ever pissed off when he read what Peter Sotos had to say about him in *The Gates of Janus*. Poor Colin Wilson, who had been taken in by Brady's charm, wrote a love letter to this despicable man in his introduction that was absolutely nauseating (before he died he was able to correct himself in the revised edition and I am glad he did—I always liked Colin Wilson and am happy he was able to clear up why he placed such faith in Brady's skills). But Sotos saw Brady for who he was, stated plainly that it was ridiculous of Wilson to encourage a liar to write a book meant to be full of truth, and it angered Brady (to an almost comical degree when one considers that he was still in Ashworth, still under the thumb of those he felt inferior to him).

It should surprise no one that Brady was full of excuses as to why *The Gates of Janus* was a bad book despite his best efforts to school us all on the nature of killers:

> Brady sees the decision to publish *Gates of Janus* with his name a mistake, done under duress from his forced feeding schedule. His author's note explains that it was his decision but this is no longer to be trusted. He now contends that his name made the book impossible to be read as he had intended. No readers, no reviewers or reporters who wanted to discuss the material vainly or objectively could now due to his infamy.
>
> Where I see the book as Brady's only argument against the dull simplicity of life as simple crimes, it is true that few of the reading public have approached

the book willing to be won over by his dispassionate perspicacity.

And honestly, the public refusal to be swayed is Brady's fault because his text was not particularly good. Compare *The Gates of Janus* to Ted Kaczynski's manifesto. Kaczynski was a terrorist who murdered people but there is truth in the manifesto that explains why he did what he did. Few would take it to Kaczynski's lengths, meaning few would murder in the name of anti-industrialism, but many saw the condition of the modern world as Kaczynski saw it. The technological machine, far from liberating the individual, was crushing the human spirit while destroying the sanctuary of genuine privacy. Few people would be inspired toward violence after reading *Industrial Society and Its Future*, but Kaczynski's arguments resonate.

Not so with Brady. Had his treatise been published pseudonymously, any reader with a rudimentary knowledge of certain crimes would have sized it up as a book written by a person only marginally familiar with his own subjective truth. Sequestered from the authorial punch-line, such a reader would scoff at the purportedly objective truths the author claimed to share about notorious criminals and their motives. And this reader would be quick to fact-check so much erroneous case information, all while questioning the author's digressions of overconfident speculation that bear no resemblance to any school of criminal analysis or profiling. The argument that serial murder represents a new individualist morality would be met with deserved ridicule regardless of who wrote the book.

If the reading public dismissed this book, it's because it's a bad book—with or without Brady's name on the cover. And apart from Brady's unmovable fan base, many readers did flag the outright errors Brady produced as facts in his crime analyses. The author's unsettling adoration of Carl Panzram would be evident without a murderer's byline. The specious word choice and tiresome, overwrought writing style would remain just as cloying, and just as revealing of a self-impressed pseudo-intellectual creep, anxious to be seen as far more intelligent than he was.

From the BBC:

> The American publisher Feral House, has already received hate mail. But the company argues that the book may help criminologists to understand the minds of killers like Ian Brady.

Did Adam Parfrey really think this? Probably not. He knows as well as I do that serial killers overall are people whom we can't really trust to tell us their motivations. They dance around and obfuscate, they lie, they create stories to aggrandize themselves. For every Jeffrey Dahmer and Edmund Kemper (killers who, if they were not self-aware, were at least as honest as they could be, once they were caught), we have dozens of Ian Bradys who just need to fuck with victims and their families, who need to paint themselves as heroes, who want to expand their victim pool from beyond the walls of the prisons that house them.

Sotos, in "Bait," captures so neatly all that I found tiresome with the first edition of *The Gates of Janus*:

> Possible that his whittling education requires him to convince himself of possibilities, present and past. Becoming reality. Frustrating theories and irritating the constant maddening lack of peaceful proof. The requirement coming from the outside definition of what the man looks like, sounds like what he's always doing to himself. Unconsciously but necessarily. He impresses himself with what he finds impressive. Dissolving into the forms of insanity rather than the forms of success he latches onto to display to his judges and mirrors. His plans to put to the theory denounce him as weak when he is desperate for bravery. When one shouldn't follow the other, an intelligent man wouldn't think of himself as intelligent. Intelligent means what, exactly? A bunch of morons willing to give you the benefit of the doubt a bit quicker than they've become accustomed to.

To Brady's credit, he did manage to hook people with what he found impressive. I wouldn't have dreaded opening my email in the days after his death had he failed in this regard. In the hopes of impressing people, Brady wrote an entire book that ultimately revealed him to be a weak, tiresome little man whose intelligence, while evident in some regards, ended up stretched thin as he engaged in strange and arrogant word choice and talked himself in circles. Feel free to also file this under "indictment of Brady's fans."

I really loved how angry Brady become at Peter Sotos. Here Sotos is quoting Brady's written complaint:

> Next, American and UK friends informed me of press attacks on an 'Afterword' by Peter Sotos inserted into Janus without my being consulted or informed by Parfrey or anyone else. I now see why Sotos was attacked as "appalling" [sic], etc. I wrote Janus deliberately avoiding the voyeuristic or sensational throughout and assumed Parfrey had published in similar good taste. When I read Sotos' "Afterword" it was like opening a toilet door of wall scribbles. So *Janus* has again been used as a vehicle, this time by an illiterate pornographic hack.

I find this so amusing. Brady's life was nothing if not "voyeuristic" and "pornographic," and he wasn't honest enough to confess this in his book. Had he been honest maybe he could have controlled the narrative. But it's absolutely fascinating that the man who ended Lesley Ann Downey's life gave himself the moral authority to dismiss anything anyone else says as being akin to obscenity written on a toilet stall. Surely if Bush's foreign policy resulting in unjust deaths means we are all hypocrites for wanting to send murderers to prison, Brady should allow that his own sexually grotesque murders may serve as a counterbalance against his inclination to dismiss Sotos as an "illiterate pornographic hack."

Sotos also brings home the ridiculousness of Brady's insistence that he was ill-used or treated unfairly:

> Brady's "spineless" hurl at Wilson and Parfrey missed his target. Brady at infant stage, sat living as the only one gathering attention. If he had known what was happening and, to be fair, he didn't. To be fair, I don't think any of it was any of Brady's concern. To be fair, Brady didn't or couldn't figure out what was going on. To be fair, I don't think he really understood why the book was being published at all. To be fair, he may have been confused on how a spotlight actually worked. Being fair here suggests that he might not have wanted to think - or act - otherwise. Fair enough. Looking for his situation to rob him of his accomplishments is desperate. Fair becomes paltry, frightened, gullible and jealous. Inclusive.

To be honest, Brady wasn't. To be honest, Brady wrote a dishonest book. To be honest, Brady was not as smart as he thought if he didn't see that a publisher might want to bracket his dishonesty with some home truths. To be honest, I laughed.

I laughed even more when Sotos quoted the following. This was Ashworth's reaction to his first afterword:

PETER SOTOS CHAPTER

> Somewhat ironically this seemed to be of more concern than practically everything else put together though much of this seemed to stem from the fact that it seems unclear to many as to what it's actually about.

Yep. This is a problem Peter Sotos has always faced. Few readers have anything close to a clear idea what he is talking about. I like to think I do but I put a lot of my own reactions and values into his words. At times I'm mostly analyzing myself as I interpret what Sotos writes. It's not surprising, yet it is vaguely funny that trained psychological professionals were uncertain what Peter was saying about Ian Brady.

Equally amusing is this concern delivered through Colin Wilson:

> Colin: Yes, I'd certainly be grateful if you would change the cover comment to "England's most notorious serial killer". The reason is simply that I am pretty sure that Ian really wants to publish this book to hand a copy to his mother, who is in her nineties, And you wouldn't want to hand your mother a book declaring that you are America's most hated man, would you?

Where to begin? Brady was worried about his elderly mother reading that he was "England's most hated man." For him, being called "England's most notorious serial killer" was a far better and less offensive description *for his mother to read* on his magnum opus. For the love of sanity, Brady's mother had been forced to live decades in the country that hated her son. None of this was new to her. But god forbid she read that her son was hated after he had spent decades in prison for killing five children.

I mentioned before that I am fond of Colin Wilson. I have dozens of his books on my shelves, dealing with true crime, mysterious phenomena, the occult, the supernatural, etc. His books, alongside those of Hans Holzer, were key texts in my adolescence, when I first began to develop my tastes in the unusual. So it was hard for me to see that Colin Wilson was so taken in by Brady. The revised edition of *The Gates of Janus* permitted him a chance to set things straight, to realize what a miserable little man Brady really was. Wilson later said that Brady's reaction to the publication of *The Gates of Janus* was "just a typical example of Brady's incredible spoiltness." Isn't that something? Brady, even as he complained of the brutality he faced in Ashworth, was still so cosseted and protected that Peter Sotos' negative reaction to him was an appalling affront.

But it's important to note that even though Colin Wilson and Ian Brady were initially upset with the way Peter Sotos described Brady, they were not the only ones to see the reality in the text.

> Perhaps Brady and Wilson should have given more thought to what Adam and Feral House do rather than appear to sell. The idea to treat *Gates of Janus* as a book of philosophical insight to an audience of suckers may well have been something that Ian didn't quite grasp or thought was bitter good fun. Maybe he's gotten used to that, too. The bulk of reviews the book received tend to mention Brady's intelligence as almost as often as a transparent desire to seem intelligent.

I was not alone by a long shot in my reaction to Brady's stilted attempts at erudition. That's comforting because, as anyone who shares content online can tell you, you are more likely to hear from people who disagree with you than from those who think your work hit the mark. After a while it felt like everyone understood and admired Brady and that was uncomfortable to experience.

The next passage from Sotos, explaining who it was that read this book, is another platinum example of how he knew Brady and his fans better than Brady himself.

> Only ostensibly did Brady intend the book to be a review of serial killers. Those he saw himself related to only by the common misunderstanding of law and green universalities. Assuming he could strip apart all others' hypocrisy as he refused to lower himself to the level of his audience - an audience that he chooses to imagine rather than understand. A necessary audience in his case. Arms folded around his chest, sunglasses fit to hide his piercing or cataract eyes, he pretended that he was talking to those interested in the subject rather than those whose interest was, if not in him, then already more learned than he wanted. Prick's truth is, Brady's audience is not made up of the serial killer fawns who write him letters and send him packages and save his signature. His fans are almost as entirely those who despise the choices he made.

The fans Sotos speaks of here are not fans I speak of. The fans in Sotos' context are those who picked up Brady's book and read it with an eye to truth, rather than hoping to have their already strange preconceptions of who Brady was and what he did reinforced. In this context, I would be a fan. I would be a fan because I knew enough about other killers and enough about Brady to realize I was being lied to. Sotos nails this. I actually had a Brady acolyte come to my review of *The Gates of Janus* and tell me I was wrong about Brady, then end her comment by letting me know she hadn't actually read the book yet. She didn't need to read it. She loved Brady. She knew he was brilliant so his analysis of other criminals simply had to be perfection. She believed he was a terribly intelligent man so she didn't need to see how he strung together words and ideas. The book itself was secondary to the fact that someone had maligned her personal superman, even if the basis for the perceived insult was the book itself.

I found this very interesting as well, because I don't think that Ian Brady ever really understood that when it came to him and the things he did, there was no dividing line between serious press and tabloids:

> Brady likes to think he's writing for the engaged, the intellectuals, the middle classes in the UK, the *Guardian* readers, rather than the tabloids, the quick garish headliners and pub talkers the good earth, the commoners. He should understand, in my opinion, that the articles in the quality press, his phrase, report on his doings and casing almost always as a review of the tabloids rather than him and his new complaints.

This is another realization that escaped me until I read Sotos' take on Brady. The fact is that Brady's crimes were so outrageous and terrible that simply discussing them at all brings to mind the worst excesses of the tabloid press, where the topic, so horrible and sordid, was journalistically consigned. His behavior and antics behind bars were unbelievably base, and just telling the truth about him resulted in seedy and lowbrow reportage. So did the high-brow press just crib stories about him from the tabloids, or was the content so low that discussions of Brady ended up in the gutter? Sotos thinks Brady was unworthy of quality press consideration. I wonder if there was any way to draw a distinction.

Brady's outrage over Sotos' afterword is in fact hilarious. These can stand alone, these various complaints Brady leveled against "an illiterate pornographic hack," so steeped are they in arrogance and petulance, coupled with a complete lack of personal insight.

> "You merely throw Sotos' rambling rubbish in as a sop to the rabble, ignoring the fact that the book was not about me but by me...

> "Further, you expect me to believe that it would've been "inappropriate" not to include Sotos' incomprehensible obscenity...

Wasn't Wilson's lengthy "Introduction" - to the "Moors Case" rather than me - negative enough, or, as I state in *Janus* did you wish to conform to the authority/rabble conditioning that not "nice" to say or ascribe anything positive to "criminals."

I wrote the whole book in a deliberately detached, clinical, unsensational – or prurient style...

...then at the end an "afterword" equivalent to "opening a lavatory door of wall scribbling." The fact that Sotos was lying throughout (or had been briefed to lie for the book) is reinforced by the totally opposite review he gave in other publications - or is he schizophrenic as well as exhibitionist?

Brady claimed to be taking legal action to get the afterword removed. One wonders how he could possibly have gone about it. Not even psychiatric professionals were entirely sure what Peter was talking about. It would have been very hard for Brady to convince a court that he had been illegally maligned, and Adam Parfrey committed no libel in printing a negative reaction to a serial killer's literary posturings. Colin Wilson, for all his error, was correct in the end—Brady was incredibly "spoilt."

Sotos in response:

He's directing attention to what I should know "factually" as I've gaudily, carefully researched every public inch of what's only theatrically and then facetiously available.

There's an uglier problem here. Locked to the desperate information that has Brady keeping his truth and lies and lessons and confessions and denotations and remorse and revenge and sights and smells and assholes and realizations and denials to whatever is now or ever has been left of himself. And me wanting to buy what he wants to sell. Wanting others to thrash around in lurid "facts" for him to let loose in price is the degenerate-cum-shylock merely repeating his press and fan letters and biographies.

Brady reacted to Sotos like a teenager reacts to negative comments on Instagram. He insisted Sotos was obsessed with him, implying such interest was the result of an unstable stalker digging up information. As if interest in Brady didn't fuel the purchase of his ill-advised serial killer analysis. As if he didn't court the press and hope people knew who he was. As if the obsession he created in others who deified his murders and dissected his victims was somehow not the other side of the same coin. Brady continually resorted to childish reactions more suited to flame wars on boy band message boards when people did not stroke his ego in the manner he demanded.

None of this should have been unexpected. Brady's anger toward those who control the funnel of information about him had been a constant in his life. No journalist is smart enough to understand him, no scholar is erudite enough to speak to him as an equal, and the press was somehow far worse, far more immoral than he was. A recurring theme in Brady's discussions about the murders he committed is that the press, in their desire to uncover all the sordid details and discuss the victims, was somehow complicit in his crimes because they kept discussing the children and upsetting their families. Brady genuinely believed press like *The Daily Mail* were far more morally bereft than he was. Peter lays out why Brady's view on the press was self-serving at best, hypocritical at worst.

> Not surprisingly, Brady seems to side with the derisive view, complaining in letters to his fan base about the parasites and scavengers in the media. What might be surprising, however, is that it's Brady who seems to try harder than most to keep the news - or the non-news - away from the families. Or at least away from where they might read what may bother them. More. To a point. *Gates of Janus* being the biggest example. His public concern changes when he's arguing against his treatment or sharing his writ-large cell thoughts on fair and unfair play in the treatment, nature and care of the working classes. Their degrading taste for, say, celebrity culture or trivia. He sweeps moral issues into pecuniary accounts, debates as demands, and is embarrassingly tied to the public domain he judges sensational and prurient. But. He's been telling the families they're being used for a while now. Some of his letters to his pen pals make it to the larger media outlets, many are shared online in personal blogs and serial killer forums. He most often sounds more like the tabloid format has taken too strong a hold, like someone who needs to give you some information you don't already have on something you don't care about. Likes to hear himself talk.

I absolutely understand why Brady wanted to make sure no one read *The Gates of Janus*. Peter Sotos called him out as a liar. But Brady, a man who spent so much time courting the press, trying to have his various cases covered by the press, who preened and acted and performed, always derided the press until he needed them, and even then he kept deriding them. The problem is this: raping and killing children ensures the public is going to want details and the media is going to oblige. No matter how much Brady insisted the press exploited victims of crime, had he not killed then none of this would be a problem.

It's also cowardly to resent press coverage of such murders. As irritating and amoral as the press may be sometimes, attention to murders like these help grease the wheels of justice. Brady knew that media attention ensured his imprisonment and that media attention would keep him locked up. The press showed him as the whining fool he was.

Brady had a lot to say about the media and the way that exploitation of murder victims in the media is hypocritical, but as Sotos notes he was himself a media creation.

> ...it might be tacky, though just as mawkish, to see Brady's reluctance to talk about what happened or talk about what he did as an old man looking back at extremity, faced with the emotionally delicate caterwauling from

the media but more directly owned by the victims' family members who are immutably intent on asking for more and more information. For whom? As if it was possible. As if they wanted to hear it. As if they didn't. Be brave, you. And as if Brady could say the body is over there, is that really all you want?

Not now.

Because the script becomes demographics.

Brady is a construction of the media, the only one readers like me have. A couch painting version created by the lowest forms of circulation-mad media.

And those circulation-mad media outlets needed a clever, Hannibal Lecter type, a man who rubbed his hands together over the location of Keith Bennett's body, plotting how to torment the families, how to remain in the public eye. This pitiful old man who couldn't undo his wolf-cry of psychosis, who desperately clung to the idea that he was a genius and superman, who had decades to think about what he did and relive the sordid details—the media needed him to be a powerful villain and not just some loathsome punk who had grown old and may have grown tired of thinking about his victims, even as the families and hungry media did not.

And Brady was right to a certain extent—the media often behaves in a repulsive manner. There are some talking heads I would cheerfully punch in the face if given a chance because they have done much harm. Their salaciously pitched ratings-driven obsession with the Moors murders is distressing at times. But perhaps the long gaze of tabloid reporters is, as Brady would understand it, a manifestation of existential will. Perhaps their experience of the objective reality Brady brought into existence has value. Perhaps Brady could have avoided a press he demeans by not killing little children. Brady was not a victim—he made the reality he felt proved his value as a higher man. If people want to discuss it, obsess over it, masturbate to it—that's their will. Brady, existentialist that he claimed to be, should have respected that.

God, the negative critical response his palaver received by men far more learned and accomplished infuriated Brady. When Theodore Dalrymple, a medical doctor and renowned writer and essayist, reviewed *The Gates of Janus* truthfully Brady lost his shit. He melted down and wrote a long letter in response, demeaning the profession of prison physician.

He proclaims me as unreformed after 37 years' imprisonment but fails to accept his concomitant responsibility and part in a penal system that does not work to reform, rather to exacerbate or create criminal behaviour by penal staff example.

While charging me with adopting a tone of moral superiority, he adopts it himself in referring to prisoners throughout his review.

For twenty years in maximum security prisons, I daily transcribed books into Braille on my own initiative for schools for the blind. I also offered to donate a kidney. What altruistic act has Dr. Dalrymple ever performed?

This made me laugh. How much did Brady know about Dalrymple before the good doctor had the effrontery to share his opinion about the load of horseshit he packed into *The Gates of Janus*? This is not to advocate for Dalrymple's ideas, but if Brady knew much about him before he condemned Dalrymple as the worst sort of morally superior asshole who never performed an altruistic act, he had to have been really stung on a soul level that Dalrymple panned him and his book. Dalrymple has written dozens of books analyzing crime and its causes. He has very little use for the sort of existential nihilism that fueled Brady and he gives no credence to the idea that Brady was shaped into a murderer because of poverty or abuse. That he invoked altruism makes me think he knew plenty about Dalrymple, who criticizes the sort of good works that are meant to make the do-gooder feel superior to those whom he helps, be it the West as a whole in regards to developing countries, or, perhaps, a man who raped and murdered children who patted himself on the back for transcribing books into Braille.

In response to all of Brady's tantrums, Sotos sets the record straight regarding how he came to know of *The Gates of Janus*, how little all of it meant in the end. I assert, like those genuinely haunted by Brady's crimes, Sotos was obsessed with Lesley far more than Brady really interested him:

> I'm not looking for proof of his paranoia to discount what he says. And he doesn't have to worry about me. I'm named in the book by Tate, obviously the reason it was included. Perhaps less obvious is that anyone who already knew my work and that particular book would understand that I was drawing a parallel in sensationally incorrect histrionics. As if anonymity was even possible. It confused a couple lawyers and self-important arbiters, Brady among them... Brady's record label pal asked to meet me because she was working on a film and wanted me to help her with it. The person who conveyed her introduction request first told me about the book. Met her because I wanted to know about the book, the film, and didn't want to be impolite. Colin wasn't shopping the book around much or maybe hadn't had much luck, I asked Adam to contact him. I give a fuck now.

SUFFERING AS UNDERSTANDING AND OBJECTIVE TRUTH

I am often torn when it comes to Brady's opinion of himself. There are moments when I am sure he thought he was one of the smartest men alive. There were other moments when I think he understood what a worm he was. Ultimately, I think Brady really did believe he was so much smarter than everyone around him.

One of the best aspects of Sotos' analysis is how he uses "Bait" as a palate cleanser. When reading Brady, even if you bristle at his affectations of superior intelligence, there are times when you feel the force of his charm. But when you step away from the psychobabble, when you decide that you don't care to hear a madman's interpretation of *Thus Spake Zarathustra*, you get to see, in simple language, why it was folly for anyone to expect a man like Brady to offer insight of any real value. The spell wears off and it's all self-referential monologue.

Take this from Danny Kilbride, the brother of Brady's victim John Kilbride:

> "To write a book about inside the mind of a murderer - he knows what he's done, and he knows how he felt, but he doesn't know about what anyone else was thinking, the other murderers he is writing about."

Winnie Johnson, mother of Keith Bennett, didn't dismiss the book out of hand. She hoped Brady might show his hand regarding where he buried Keith without realizing it:

> "I am convinced he will have put something in the book about it. They say it is not about the killings he did, but I think he will try to hide something in it. That's how his mind works. He likes to play games because he thinks he is cleverer than everyone else. But he won't pull the wool over my eyes."

People who adore Brady really don't like it when the families of his victims are brought into the conversation. But the only truth Brady had to offer was the suffering he caused them. He had no real insight into why others kill. But in looking at the loved ones of those he killed we find the truth of who Brady was, and the only real explanation for why he did what he did. In spite of that, or perhaps because of that, the fans dismiss what they consider mawkish emotional reactions to Brady's crimes. For them, Brady represents a hard reality with no shades of gray that might come filtered through a criminal's use of high-minded philosophical justifications. But without the families, we miss the blunt emotional reaction that shows us a different truth, and we miss a far more useful reality than one finds in such pedantic analysis that would instruct us as to why one killing is bad but another justified. The people whom Brady made suffer understand him. They understand him far better than those who need him to justify their own wishful superiority.

As you look at Brady, the things he did to victims, the way he led his life in prison, a genuine picture of who he is emerges. Sotos sees it and explains it so clearly that it's almost beautiful:

> And those who start to think that Brady represents anything other than the realist form of grief and inaction that caused unending filthy responsibilities and grotesque excuses need to be educated about what we're all talking about. All this noise, all this garbage and now to stop it save a mission to refocus assholes and offer chances of divinity to the bereft.

When people condemn Peter Sotos as a Very Bad Man in an attempt to tarnish his reaction to Ian Brady, it is likely because they resent being called out. Brady's words offer them a chance to see their own darkness and failure as a moral struggle against pointless ingrained and stultifying morality. This means they won't be able to understand. Which doesn't make it any less needful to say. Those who suffered at Brady's hands know him far better than those who read *The Gates of Janus* and binge with relish on what Brady brings to the table.

It's tempting to look at the families and think that on some level they eventually got used to it, the loss, the sadness, the rage. Sotos quotes an article about Winnie Johnson, whom the *The Guardian* interviewed just before she died, and whom *The Sun* published a photo of in her hospital bed:

> You wonder if she can bear to be asked again yet again about her missing murdered child. Does she mind being asked about Keith? With her characteristic, surprising flashes of good humor, she replies, "No! Do I heck! I'd rather people talked to me about Keith than look at me and stare at me - I can't stand that. It makes me feel better talking about him."

She felt better talking about him. Of course she did. Winnie was made of stern stuff. But don't be fooled. Time had not given her closure or distance from the horror of losing her son. She maintained her poise because she was desperate to get her son back. Brady fucked with her relentlessly. Her son is the one whose body was never recovered. He is still buried out in the moors somewhere and she died never being able to give her son the burial she wanted, a proper Christian burial.

Oh god, poor Keith's body. How many letters have there been that supposedly reveal where he is buried? Alan Keightley says Brady told him outright where Keith is buried but that the police never acted on this information. I cannot imagine that is the truth, but who knows. Perhaps the police are tired of following every lead to Keith Bennett's body because too many people close to Brady claimed he told them in some manner where the body was located. Notable among them, a certain Jackie Powell, who claimed to be a mental health advocate for Brady, who said Brady had left her a letter to give to Winnie Johnson upon his death, and that the letter might contain the location of Keith's body. Might. Maybe. This was reported to the press in the days before Winnie died from cancer, a lovely little knife in Winnie's heart because she knew Brady was going to outlive her, and she knew what he was and that he would never tell where her son lay buried. So many of the people like Jackie who cozied up to Brady ended up abetting his cruelty and Winnie kept hoping to the very end.

Sotos explains that willingness to be Brady's pawn as only he can:

> First. Some prayer, actually. Being hope, actually. Fucking exactly like Brady who has written an entire book talking about the nonexistence of God while shaking his fist at where he thinks a God should be since God doesn't answer and he can prove that. And these good God-fearing people who aren't thinking right at all, keep looking to the same bad God-fearing

person to ask him - politely to him whole angrily to the villagers - to help them. Restore hope over experience. When that fails. Again. They look to the creep and seek to understand him. So they can ignore everything he says so they don't feel hopeless. Maybe.

There is an appalling innocence that was shown over and over again as people asked Brady to do the right thing. He murdered their children and tortured them beforehand yet so many of the loved ones of those Brady had killed never gave up hope that this relentlessly terrible man would do the right thing. How could they have been so naïve? It wasn't naïveté. It was desperation. Brady was the only person with answers. When the worst person is the man with the answers, all you have is hope. And, as we all know, hope is never a plan.

I like to think that after it became clear that Brady had no intention of doing anything more than fuck with me mentally, I would have shut down contact, made his cleverly withheld information useless because I refused to pump his ego, court the press in his name, beg on my knees for him, King Brady, to tell me where my child was. Let him choke on it. If there is a God above then any burial is a Christian burial. But I'm a childless atheist and who knows what they would do in such a situation when a man steals your child and all you have left is faith. I'm sure Brady sneered at these people whom he reduced to faith when he refused them concrete evidence, but he was a creator of faith as much as any savior-based religion—an interesting turn of events for a man who so loved Nietzsche.

But there are many ways to express desperation. Winnie's good cheer was her choice, and a good one in a way because Brady loved knowing he tortured the families. But even if the madman enjoys your outburst, that doesn't mean you should hide your disgust. This is Lesley's stepfather:

> Asked how it felt to hear him describe the child murders as "recreational," he said: "That was a sickening jab... only a madman would say that. It was sickening, it really upset me.

"Keep that tube up his nose, fill it with gasoline."

Ann West, Lesley's mother, exhibited reactions that made the most sense to me, and interestingly, given Brady's explanation of himself as a man who bucked against Christian morality, Ann's reactions were the least Christian. She understood that she was dealing with human beings who were beyond redemption. She understood God had blinked when Brady found her daughter. She had no use for comforting platitudes. She stoked the furnace of her rage and refused to be an inspiring story of a mother finding a new purpose after her child was killed. Sotos quotes this interview Ann gave to Joan Bakewell:

> Joan: You don't feel that the hatred is making you ill?

Ann: Well, I don't think I could be any iller.

Joan: Everyone who knows this story wants nothing more than that you should find some peace of mind.

Ann: When she dies, when she dies. When she dies, I'll find some peace of mind.

Ann's suffering brought her to a place of certain knowledge—the only way peace comes is when the wicked are wiped from the face of the earth. But for those who follow the law and tenets of basic human decency it's difficult to see such rage through to its logical conclusion. There is no forgiveness for those who kill your child. There is only waiting it out until they die or you die. It's interesting, in a way, to compare her to Winnie. And Sotos himself compares them, Ann and Winnie, the two mothers given the closest analysis by the press. Ann's daughter brought her scrutiny because Brady and Hindley's audiotape and photographs of her torture gave the case a horrible rubbernecking quality. Winnie's son was never recovered from the moors and Winnie knew she would die without ever bringing her murdered son home. Each woman knew more about Brady than any true crime reader.

Peter Sotos brought both women into sharp focus for me, permitting me to understand that Brady's murders cannot be cordoned off in halls of philosophical action and questionable moral relativism. This is his reaction to the photo published of Winnie in her hospital bed:

> And that's the afterword to the afterword. There's the dispassionate updates and smarmy lack of self-control. Just the very old sad woman in care, dying. And, like the author Carol Ann Lee, who sought to get the facts right finally after all these decades of books and articles and scrolls and stares on Ian Brady and Myra Hindley, I can leave it up to the reader. Without saying where it all laid in morals and ethics and want and taste and tragedy. Just facts, displayed, in color, as the truth. The poor woman photographed in her final bed that not all couldn't read as hideous. Proof that Brady's inadequacy extends decades where this wretched dreary woman allowed herself to be photographed expiring for the world to watch and gray. Just so it got back to Brady.

Sotos wondered if just that picture of Winnie was enough and he decided the whole picture was incomplete unless you added Ann West into the visual.

> There would have to be two photos at the end of the afterword. First, Winnie. Second, Ann West. Stand-ins for the differences between two mothers. Their unique personal attempts to see the same thing through to the end.

Of the two, I would have ended up like Ann, promising to kill Myra Hindley if she were ever released from prison, promising to haunt her if I died first.

> Ann West and Winnie Johnson wrote to the murderers of their children. Requested information from them. Ann publicly dedicated herself to the

promotional campaign to make sure Myra spent the rest of her life in jail. Left a film of her last wishes for the media just before her death. Winnie left one, too. Good idea perhaps. Winnie asking Ian for an understanding of respect, to do the decent thing. Obviously, maybe, neither side had respect for the other. Decency doesn't exist between the two, it can't. Not when only one side is listening and the other side is demanding anything remotely like decency. Yet there were pleas. And side-stage remarks that Ian sadistically enjoyed those pleas. Good idea, perhaps.

The sadism toward the families is as much a crime as the murders. The suffering Brady inflicted came in waves, washing over decades. It was murder paid in installments.

And there's some deep love and deeper rejection and screaming sacrifice directly in the way of any less compassionate grasp. And prurient, and vicarious, and bent; the atavistic sickness in what Brady and his victims have suffered, The graspable exciting cutting ugliness of those smarmy, grandiose details is even more excruciating to miss when buying tragedy. And those bleating on revenge, the justified that stormed his police escort and gave interviews, will still be absent their children.

And they knew that. Had they torn Myra and Ian to pieces with their own bare hands, had they descended into the nihilistic stage play that Brady made out of killing their children, that vengeance would have paid no dividends. Their children would be still be gone and they would still be bereft, sick and feeling that absence.

Sotos goes on to express how it is that even though Keith Bennett met the same fate as Lesley, meaning he was raped and murdered, attention to his fate focused less on what was done to him than on where his remains lay. His role in this case was to be the body everyone wanted brought home for a decent burial. Not so with Lesley. And what happened to Lesley was so awful that Ann West needed the public to understand it so she permitted the terrifying audiotape of Lesley's attack as well as one picture of her to be used in a documentary. The audio tape was ultimately deemed too horrible to share in the film and the photo of Lesley, bound and gagged on a bed, had to be cropped so closely that little of the real horror seeped through. What happened to Lesley was too awful for the public to understand. But many remember it, and many seek it out. I wish I could tell you how many search strings looking for pictures of Lesley naked and violated, as well as searches for the audiotape or its transcript, hit my site. No condemnation toward those who looked for it—Brady's why those media exist and blame lies with him.

But those photos shift the focus, as do Bennett's unlocated remains. Never forget that what happened to Lesley happened to all of the victims, even Pauline Reade, the teenager who fought back so hard. I wonder if Winnie would have been able to maintain such a calm and cheerful demeanor at the end if a photo set existed of what happened to Keith. She knew it happened but the proof of it was not shoved in her face. The proof of what happened to her daughter destroyed Ann West. She couldn't sleep and when she could she had nightmares. There is some belief that the stress she felt after Lesley was murdered exacerbated the cancer that eventually killed her. But even as she was riddled with cancer she said she could die in peace as long as she knew Hindley would never be released from prison. Winnie wanted them to tell her the truth, knew they wouldn't, but kept her chin up. Ann knew the truth and resented all the effort spent trying to convince her the truth didn't matter.

It's very interesting how the search on the moors for two victims—Pauline Reade and Keith Bennett—eventually became the focus of the case. Once Pauline's body was found, the focus then remained on Keith. Prior to this, the focus had been mainly on Lesley Ann Downey, and when the focus was on her one could not lose track of how much suffering Brady caused.

> Replacing Lesley as the focus of what actually occurred in the crimes that sent Brady and Hindley to jail, the proof of evil was now psychological rather than sexual: only vaguely pornographic.

Later Sotos says this about the battle in the public mind in the Moors murders:

> Two more things, slurred and rambling: I was writing about the photo of Lesley. She's taken second place now. Keith fucking Bennett's fucking empty church-laid coffin has taken pride of place and I fucking miss her and that language riddled with sex rather than forgiveness.

He misses Lesley because Ann's rage is better then Winnie's hope and because Lesley showed the suffering better than poor also-dead Keith, whose lost corpse seemed more sanitized than the pornographic end visited upon Lesley. Rage is harder to manipulate. Missing Lesley is the same as missing the rage at what happened to her. Missing Lesley is the same as understanding the real suffering inflicted upon her. Missing her is a promise that we won't try to sanitize what Brady did.

Was there any way for Brady to know how the case would go, that among the people who knew of this case that the search for bodies would take the heat off the child porn Brady and Hindley created as they killed Lesley? The hell of it is, this shift in focus didn't happen with some of the devotees of this case. There was no Internet in the 1980s to prove my point, but there is now and you should see some of the tortured responses I receive from people, mostly adult men with families, who are obsessed with Lesley. She is in their mind to a degree that alarms them. In quiet moments they imagine the torture she endured, wondering what exactly was put into her mouth during the audiotaping, and they fear the reasons why they think of her so much.

These men are not pedophiles, or at least they say they aren't, but they show how it is that Lesley's story infects people's minds and emotions. When the search for bodies overtook outrage at what Hindley and Brady did to Lesley, the story, using Brady's broad definition of murder, became far less appalling. Brady, for many, stopped being the fiend who killed children and became the movie cliché of the super-intelligent criminal playing games with police and the public. He became a plot device in television crime procedurals.

The reason these men think of her is because they know the truth Ann knew. They have become obsessed with her suffering, because the suffering is the only truth left. Ann's suffering, the suffering the children experienced, the suffering thinking about the children causes those who try their best to understand the case today. There is no philosophical truth that can ever outweigh the truth that all the suffering tells us.

Ann West was criticized for her desire to make sure a specific story was told about Ian Brady and Myra Hindley. Sotos says this in response to Ann's pride that she managed to shut down three separate plays about the Moors murders:

> All reasons perfectly understood as long as her place in the crimes is owned. Which is to say that she had final word on Brady. As long as it stayed hard with her daughter. Which, she proves by her success with never wavering capitulants, is true. Her place is complex, never uttered without explanation that it is a wretched place and unfair and literally mind-numbingly cruel from every single side that by dint of inconsideration is yet another sadistic attack. Never answered by anyone listening that they are without extreme sympathy for her and the shared hatred of the buried evil that destroyed her and - it must be remembered - her child. That absence. Her life is greater than any Petri dish, asshole. That's what lies inside the words you fucking play with. Her drug-soaked requiem life and the horror of the past, the brutal emptiness of the missing always future.

Suffering gave Ann a hard-won truth that is more accurate than cold facts. Her suffering, the suffering of her child, are the truth.

Throughout "Bait" Sotos evinces an admiration for Carol Ann Lee's work on the Moors murders and reading this quote makes me want to read what she has written about the case because she clearly gets it. She knows that facts are filtered through third party sentiments, the desire to tell the story as if it is a mystery, searching for a cause that has always been apparent to people well-versed in serial killer facts, that was always apparent to Ann, always apparent to Sotos. Here's what Carol says about her refusal to write a biography of Ian Brady:

> ...a biography of Brady isn't for me. I agree that there is no definitive book about him at present, but he isn't someone I feel I could write about in any more depth than I have done in One of Your Own/Witness. There is no ambiguity about him to explore, and his motives for committing the crimes he did

are all too transparently terrible, plus I think in order to write about him with any sort of insight, a certain kind of contact would have to be begun and then seen through to the end, which I neither want to do, nor am I in a position to achieve with the kind of objectivity necessary to make it succeed. I know there are other people lining up to publish books about him after his death, but I have no faith in any of them being anything other than pseudo-intellectual rubbish along the lines of 'I Knew the Moors Killer Best.'

This is why it will likely take me a while to read Alan Keightley's book about Ian Brady. I too have little faith that anyone will approach him honestly. I worry the book will be a handwringing attempt to figure out how this bright, amazing, morally-centered man committed murder. I am afraid his take on Brady will sound like Rafferty's beliefs on Brady's nature. I am afraid it will be another attempt to engage in serial killer upmanship, in a manner similar to what is happening now around the increasingly frail Charles Manson. I am afraid the sole truth, the truth that Ann knew—that a loathsome man and a weak woman killed children, raped them and tortured and killed them because they wanted to do it and decided their desires meant more than the lives of five people—will be lost.

SOTOS BURYING BRADY

One of the reasons to read "Bait," especially if you are not a person who buys all the philosophical excuses and various fan-based attempts to categorize Brady as a man with a sense of morality, is that Sotos buries Brady by clearly and simply asking the most obvious questions about Brady's words.

Sotos says:

> An existential experience becomes reality. No longer an experiment after the results are issued to the next phase. You don't get to call it an experiment any longer. Unless you're saying sorry. Saying, then, I was ignorant. I know more now. What, you were hoping to find exactly what you already knew? Testing what for whom? What were you hoping for?

It ceased being an "existential experiment" after the first heart stopped beating. Yet he continued, knowing the results of his grand experience with one dead body in the moors. What was he hoping to find after that? What more was there to know?

Sotos says:

> Brady's mythic biography would be the part where he, possibly, says he made mistakes and apologizes and can't bring himself to let go of the single thing that helps him pass the time. Say, learning a way into pedophilia as a practice. Comes from fear. Existentialism is apt. Leaving something to tell everyone how stupid he's been. And he knew. Because he hated what happened. Hate being much bigger than the language allowed. And still swimming in it, learning to enjoy that, learning to tell idiots that learning anything made something.

Is there value in learning about this existential experience? Is one man's existential experience able to inform anyone else seeking their own? Or is it, in the end, that the knowledge that Brady claimed to have earned through murder, knowledge that is useless to anyone else because existentialism by its very fucking definition means that one must learn it for oneself alone, through direct experience?

Sotos says:

> The first time I ever saw child pornography, I knew that it wasn't sex. Knew it wasn't for cash, even. Knew that pain was being caused. And murder was less than that. Not more. And certainly a killer would understand that. And he could tell you. What was petty. What was existential. They had mouths and talking was the last thing you'd want from that. Literally. Proved. Ann West knew the effects and was done fucking telling you. You won't walk away from it. And, really, you can't imagine it.

If existential knowledge could be transferred from Brady to his fans, they would know what Ann knew and they would quail from this topic as their innate decency overtook them. Or they would stop talking and kill so as to have their own existential experience. That neither happens is a sign, a clue, that support for Brady is just a buttress for a weak, deluded will.

Sotos says:

> Brady's use of existential as a term for the murders shouldn't be confused with him also finding a godless world unworkable. He shouldn't be misread by those insisting he was a pedophile finding release in rape rather than riddance. Those creating his drive as sexual, as madness, as indifferent and base and morally subversive or bitter rage display all the worst aspects of what they want and miss rather than him. They, not him, have been humping and heaping and digging for nothing worth anything more than the filth in their own filth.

Brady made child pornography and became a form of pornography for those too dishonest to admit what they need to see and hear.

Sotos says:

> The fact is Ian Brady didn't become Mick Jagger, Harrison Marks, Albert J. Reiss, Boyd MacDonald, Pierre Molinier, Ole Ege or Francis Bacon not because he couldn't write "Cocksucker Blues." Not because he didn't. Not because he couldn't take care of business. But because he didn't know how to watch the antics of them. And his mistakes couldn't be helped because he wasn't special enough to repeat what Sade said. He was one of those idiots who did. There's too many examples of him telling Myra and David and Jackie and the Alans how to think and more examples of him proving an easy job. Any self-help asshole, talking to you like he knows something about you because he's always telling you how he came to realize it. The second sentence will always be loaded with contempt. And it's galling that it's so easy to see through. It's tiresome.

Talk to them, leave me alone. And, most likely, they can't leave you alone. It's going to go on and on.

This reminds me of Louis Theroux's interview with Jimmy Savile, where he boasted that Louis never got the measure of him but he got the measure of Louis within minutes of meeting him. These loathsome men who make a game out of preying on the weak will always think they are smarter than we are. They will always think their minds are impenetrable to us as they claim to see through us. An asshole is an asshole. A man who rapes and kills children is easy to figure out, even if we don't understand.

And at the end of Brady's life it would have been so nice had people looked at Brady and realized that he was unable to see the words of men smarter than he, and understand how truth can be conveyed through extremities of exaggeration and that no one expects you to reenact those words. That you are expected to understand the difference between instructions and deliberate philosophical overkill. That sometimes killers cloak themselves in philosophies that reduce great thinkers to coarse excuse makers.

But here we are. Brady's fans, those left standing after his death, if they read this essay, will likely send me appalling emails. And those who need a living philosopher king will find a new hero in some person in the future who does something abhorrent. And if there is a book about that abhorrence I will probably read it and discuss it using too many words.

But Brady is finally dead now, and that makes all the rest a little easier to bear.

Further Reading

Ian Brady: The Untold Story of the Moors Murders
Alan Keightly

Desistance
Peter Sotos

The Outsider
Colin Wilson

MEMOIR & BIOGRAPHY

A biography is an outfit of clothing that sits on the skin of the subject of the book. Sometimes it is a well-made suit that shows clearly the person wearing it; sometimes it's a trashbag with holes cut strategically so the subject doesn't suffocate entirely. This is a distinction made all the odder with memoirs because one would hope a person penning their own story would create something true and meaningful. But strangely plenty of memoirs are plastic garbage liners filled with trash. When you find a well-tailored memoir, it can be absurdly glorious.

THE STRANGE CASE OF EDWARD GOREY
By Alexander Theroux
Fantagraphics (2010)
Original post: 02/02/2012

Why do I consider this book odd?
Because it is a biography (ostensibly) about odd-icon, Edward Gorey.

As biographies go, I guess you could say *The Strange Case of Edward Gorey* is one. But if you love a *good* biography, you're not going to want to read this book. You may not even want to read this discussion.

If you're a Gorey fan like me, I'm sure you will buy and read Alexander Theroux's book even after I tell you it's largely a waste of time. Gorey fans, like all fanatics, want to read anything and everything about the man. I myself am a *moderate* Gorey fan. I have one of his drawings tattooed on my body, I have a little shrine set up to him, and I aspire to collect first editions of all of his books. Being just a moderate fan, I know that if I had I had read a review like the one I am writing before I put this book on my Amazon wish list, I would have purchased it and read it anyway.[1] Because that's what an ardent fan does. We collect things relating to the object of our adoration, even if those things are mediocre.

The Strange Case of Edward Gorey has some interesting moments, but they are few, and even the most interesting of the interesting moments won't be news to long-time Gorey obsessives. It was pleasant being reminded of how eccentric Gorey was, how he eventually stopped wearing fur because of his love of animals, how he sewed stuffed animals by hand as he watched television, how he would do work for anyone who asked, even those who could pay very little.

But after one admits that this book has some charm, one can only list its many problems. To begin with, in the first fifteen pages Theroux manages to write in a way that is so alienating that a casual reader might be tempted to give up. I am a reasonably intelligent woman who has devoted my adult life to reading. I fancy that if a reasonably well-educated person with a de-votion to books found Theroux's verbiage cumbersome, then it is safe to say it was, in fact, too much for a biography of a beloved pop-culture icon. But who knows? Perhaps the words *enchiridion, coloraturas*, the French phrase *le cercle lugubrieux*, and the German term *karfreutagian* have slipped into

---

1   Actually, my copy was a Yule gift from Mr. OTC.

the common lexicon without me noticing. If not, they were odd word choices in a biography such as this. Luckily Theroux stops showing off so egregiously around page 15. Still, not a good start.

Another problem is that this book has so little to say that it would have been far better as a long magazine article. The only reason the book reached 166 pages is due to sheer repetition. Theroux loves lists, enumerating all the things he found interesting about Gorey over and over and over again. The lists of his shock at the lowbrow media Gorey consumed grew quite uninteresting, especially since it would be hard to say this book follows any sort of real timeline—it's just Theroux's memories as he remembers them, and while that can be very charming, when it results in so many interminable and meandering paragraphs documenting Gorey's various likes and dislikes, it soon becomes annoying. Recitations of Gorey's tastes wear thin without a balanced study of what he accomplished.

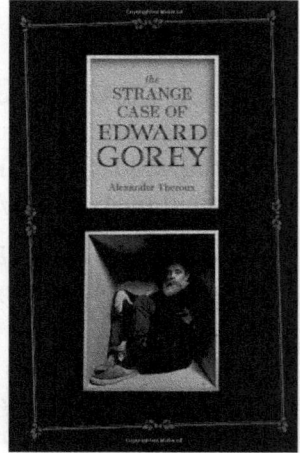

I am not kidding. The lists are all over the book and all over the map. Let me give you an example from the section about the things Gorey liked to collect:

> Gorey collected everything. Sad irons. Signs. Dolls. Telephone pole insulators. Masks. Puppets. The statue of an elephant. Big and little seashells. Eggs. Cape Cod candles. Paintings. Odd ashtrays. CDs. He deeply loved chunks of architecture—rare examples of Victorian gingerbread, entablature, cornices, dentil molding, dormer pieces, and so forth. Another strange collectible that excited him was decorative finials, for lamps, swifts, curtain rods, pots, Torah finials, newel caps, general blacksmithiana, and cobbling tools, etc. He had a mummy's hand in a case!

Would it surprise you to learn that this paragraph goes on for another 31 lines, and is followed by another page and half of Theroux's bloodless rendition of the things Gorey collected, with the occasional quote from Marianne Moore to break up the boredom? Does that seem a bit... heavy?

Oh, dear reader, you have no idea how long the lists in this book become and how repetitive they are after a while. Let me give you a few more small examples of Theroux's lists of what Gorey liked and did not like that clog this book like a wad of greasy hair in a bathroom sink. Here Theroux engages in a flat, lifeless recitation of what it was that made Gorey eccentric:

> Who are you acquainted with, for instance, who has read all of Trollope, all 17 novels, all 47 books, but would not miss a single episode of TV's

All My Children or Andy Griffith in reruns of *Matlock*? Read Lao-tse with understanding but collected true crime magazines and loved *Doctor Who*, that improbable science fiction TV series. Cherished *Oliver Onions*, but watched *The Mary Tyler Moore Show* episodes and collected current videos? Could speak with total authority on the novels of Theodore Dreiser or Yukio Mishima and yet was word-perfect in the films of English actress Pamela Franklin and could quote chapter and verse from the 1958 film, *Fiend Without a Face*, in which a scientist materializes thoughts in the form of invisible, brain-shaped creatures which kill people for food? Sat up dutifully by himself to watch movies virtually every night?

This list, this litany of things that Theroux recites as if it means anything at all about Gorey's eccentricity, comes close to rendering Gorey boring. I dare say almost everyone reading these words knows people with extraordinarily disparate tastes, people who are interesting but at the same time are not geniuses in the way Gorey was a genius. Yet Theroux is so out of touch with people and society that he thinks these renditions provide evidence of Gorey's eccentricity. More important, it shows us a certain snobbery in Theroux that he thinks watching *Matlock* while being conversant in Trollope means one is quirky. We'll see more of that snobbery later in this discussion.

Here's another list to make your eyes glaze over. Theroux is still discussing Gorey's eccentric tastes and interest in lowbrow culture.

> He loved *Fu Manchu* movies, *Charlie Chan* and the *Thin Man* series, and *The Perils of Pauline*. He was word-perfect about the silents and was widely familiar with early Hollywood and could cite the *eclat* of long out-of-date actors and actresses, people like Hugh Hubert, Veree Teasdale, Reginald Owen, Walter Catlett, Estelle Winwood, Rex Caldwell, Frank McHugh, Aubrey Smith, ZaSu Pitts, and "dahling" Tallulah Bankhead in her Wanda Myro phase, "the fake Serbian princess." He knew how early films were made and where and who on the sets was bonking whom. Small things were not lost on him, and he had opinions on everything from John Boles's mustache to Jane Darwell's dewlaps to Jerry Colonna's eyes.

Theroux's book is just so thick with these lists. Perhaps 75% of the book consists of little more than the recitation of lists, lists, lists. Part of the problem may be that Gorey led an inner life that doesn't lend itself well to biographical treatment, yet I have read discussions of Gorey that manage to draw life out of his interests.[2]

Theroux just can't seem to manage it without turning Gorey's peripatetic mind into some sort of book-length laundry list.

---

2   A better biography is actually an epistolary biography, *Floating Worlds: The Letters of Edward Gorey and Peter F. Neumayer*. In this collection of letters exchanged for just a year we get such an excellent look at Gorey, and Gorey gets to tell the tale in his own letters to Neumeyer rather than have his collection of interesting door knobs belabored in list after list.

Do you want to know what is worse than those lists? Lists that are just a dump of ideas and names, lists that don't even try to be sorted.

> Gorey also had lots of peeves. He hated brussels sprouts, false sentiment, minimal art, overcommitment to work, being solicited for blurbs, the music of Andrew Lloyd Webber, the works of the Marquis de Sade ("absolutely paralyzing prose"), churchgoing, Nixon and Agnew, right-wingers, discussions about his own work, prattling and didactic fools, and all Al Pacino movies.

This goes on and on, but I feel I should mention that it also describes me, my father-in-law and my third grade teacher (though she may have liked *Dog Day Afternoon*).

Don't even ask me about the tangent Theroux takes describing W.H. Auden's life as it compares to Gorey's. Having reread the section three times, it makes no sense to me. Theroux says they had a lot in common but I'll be damned if the text he writes would lead anyone to that conclusion. They were both men who liked cats and liked being alone. The rest of the comparisons seem quite forced, and what they had in common hardly warranted several pages of digressive exposition.

The best reason to detest this book is that it is not really about Edward Gorey. This book is about how Alexander Theroux interacted with and interpreted Edward Gorey. It is about Edward Gorey as he pertains to the mind of Alexander Theroux. If you picked up this book knowing nothing about Gorey or Theroux, you would walk away knowing about as much about Alexander as Edward. For example, I know much of Theroux's political leanings and his opinion about Columbine. Clearly, that's a problem. That problem is made worse when what one learns about Theroux is not particularly endearing. Discussing Gorey's natural introversion, he opines:

> Above all, he *enjoyed* being alone, something dim, unoriginal, lazy and uncreative people pathetically often have not a clue about.

Note that this not a quote from Gorey. It's Theroux sharing his uncharitable opinions of mankind. That's right, extroverts! You can suck it.

Discussing Gorey's enjoyment of doing domestic and crafty work like sewing and cooking:

> I believe he sought preoccupations in arts and crafts and such menial work as collecting objects and sewing things to take him away from other preoccupations, more serious things, knocking about in his head. Don't be fooled. No one with that matchless—and mad—imagination was simply Betty Crocker making buttermilk biscuits.

Oh dear… Would anyone but Theroux think cooking and sewing would somehow diminish Gorey unless they were explained away as a means of keeping deep thoughts at bay? Are there really people left in this world who, upon learning that Gorey sewed, would immediately think him a housemaid and dismiss all his work? Reading this gives you a very good idea of what Theroux thinks of work that is not borne from a place of deep intellectualism.

Goodness, Theroux really does not like the horror genre. Remember—this is him going on at length and not anything Gorey himself expressed:

> The cognitive quality of Edward Gorey's books, that strange dark art opulently, often contagiously assembled out of his searching mind—the seven-zephyred suavity of his impeccable drawings and exact text—rise in the matter of the macabre so much higher than all of those bulbous not-quites—hideously lacking all the conviction while full of passionate intensity—like Stephen King and Dean Koontz, Robin Cook and James Patterson, and their crapulous, hand-cranked, artless, throw-it-up-in-the-air-to-see-what-comes-down doorbuster books stuffed with high-school hoodoo and toy horror.

I don't know how this passage affects you, but it annoyed the crap out of me. It seems like Theroux is trying to defend his friendship with Gorey, a man known to have many low-brow tastes, by saying, "Well, at least he was better than all those other writers." Also note that this is a good example of Theroux's style when he is not showing off his erudite vocabulary.

And take this passage, as he is discussing how Gorey could best be described as asexual:

> Suffice it to say, Gorey saw no reasons to pretend, but he also saw no reason to proclaim either. Whatever anyone chooses to refer to one—a bent, a gay, an invert, a chap Irish by birth but Greek by injection, etc.—I never saw him with a foop, a joy-boy, a shirtlifter, a poof, a puff, or a tootle-merchant, no one, neither an older man—no "dad" or "afghan"—nor even a younger boy, a cupcake, a capon or a Ganymede.

There are two, far simpler ways to have said what Theroux tries to convey in this passage. 1) Though Gorey was likely a homosexual, Theroux never once saw him with anyone who seemed to be a male lover. 2) Alexander Theroux is an utter asshole who thinks he is very cute.

Oh dear lord, why did I need to know Theroux's opinions on Lucas films? Why?

> Once or twice I was truly amazed at Gorey's inexplicable taste—or lack of it! I remember him saying, "Star Wars is very important," a film (and its sequels) I myself considered not so much Hollywood trash as a fat, inconsequential farce or ersatz theology and simpleminded New Age bollocks all cobbled together out of a thousand filched sources, including ancient Greek Fable, Buck Rogers movies, naval jumpsuits, Japanese samurai swords, mempo masks, World War I German blaster guns, over-simplified "evil empire" fables, Nazi myths, fascist uniforms, quest literature, and, I'm convinced Xerxes of the Persian Wars marching down through Thessaly to Salamis! Except of course, those were interesting.

We can file this under pointless knowledge about Theroux, Theroux's intellectual snobbery, and interminable lists! It's a three-fer!

Given that Gorey was a fan of Agatha Christie, and one of his best works was an homage to her (*The Awdrey-Gore Legacy*), why on earth does Theroux need to let us know he personally dislikes Christie? Why would we care what he thinks? The answer is, we don't care, and this book is half-ruined with his nasty observations and pointless self-references.

To summarize, this book is not good. It is actually terrible. The few bits we get about Gorey that could mean something—like that he never spoke of his mother—are lost in a sea of irrelevant words. We are confronted by list after list, with Theroux's cultural snobbery and prejudices, and we get to know far too much about Theroux in a biography of another man.

If you are a Gorey fan, you're going to buy this book. You know you will. I know you will. You can't help yourself. We have to read and then keep all we read about him. My copy will go into my bookcase with my other Gorey books even though I know I will never read it again. If I were to give it away, there would be a strange itch in the back of my brain wherein I would know my Gorey collection was not complete. But just because you buy it doesn't mean you need to read it. Those of you who are Gorey fans, maybe read it from a John Waters-esque desire to see how bad it really is. Otherwise, let's all pretend this didn't happen. Let's go recite *The Doubtful Guest* until this terrible memory fades.

FURTHER READING

Floating Worlds: The Letters of Edward Gorey and Peter F. Neumeyer
Edited by Peter F. Neumeyer

Ascending Peculiarity: Edward Gorey on Edward Gorey
Edited by Karen Wilken

SWIMMING UNDERGROUND: MY YEARS AT THE WARHOL FACTORY

By Mary Woronov
Journey Editions (1995)
Original post: 02/29/2012

Why do I consider this book odd?
Most of the people who made up the Factory are very interesting
and quite strange, and Woronov is no exception. Plus her prose is
unusual (in a glorious way).

I read Ultra Violet's *Famous For 15 Minutes* just after finishing Woronov's *Swimming Underground*, and I think the comparison made me understand what makes Woronov's book odd. Ultra Violet was a conventional woman drawn to unusual people, and her memoir, while interesting, shows that her adopted scene was far more interesting than she was.[3] Woronov, however, outshines those around her in the Factory. She writes with an icy fire, a remarkable combination that seems to encapsulate who she was at the time (and who may well still be—aside from knowing her work as the principal in *Rock 'n' Roll High School* and the female lead in *Eating Raoul*, I know little about her beyond this book). Her tale is not just a perfect capture of a moment in history, it's the odd tale of an odd woman with an odd mind. Oh, I have such a crush on Mary Woronov now. I intend to read everything she has written and see every movie she has been in.

Before I begin, I have to admit that I'm not a Warhol fan. I don't condemn those who love him; it's just that I personally find him tiresome. He was an amazing parasite who convinced his hosts that it was to their benefit that he consume them. He gave little back, and when they finally objected to him

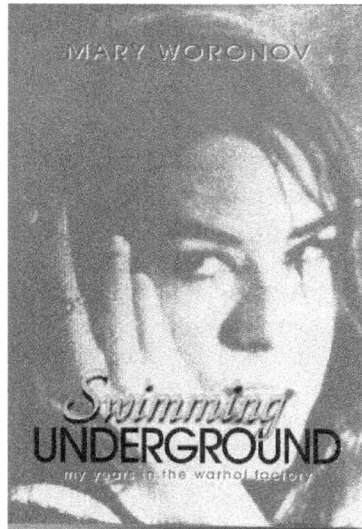

---

3   Though if I think about it, I shouldn't be too hard on her—better than anyone else I have read, she seems to understand why Valerie Solanas just needed to shoot Andy Warhol.

leeching them dry, he finished them off and moved on to fresher hosts. Even the ones who understood this seem to remember him fondly. He must have been very good at it because he was able to easily surround himself with such talented people. But that skill ultimately means that I find the people he surrounded himself with infinitely more interesting than Warhol himself.

Woronov's tale of her time in the Factory is a sharp slice of a tin-foil covered history. An intense woman, she seemed naively charmless, and that, of course, was her charm. She "whip danced" with Gerard Malanga, performing with the Velvet Underground in the early Warhol presentation called the Exploding Plastic Inevitable. Also, she was in *Chelsea Girls*, the only movie Warhol made that doesn't make me fall into a boredom-rage-sleep. She paints a picture of herself as a cold, imperious young woman, sexually aloof even while engaging in provocative dancing with whips under pulsing lights. As beautiful, aloof and talented as she was, she was not immune from the mercurial, nasty nature of Warhol. In many ways, her story was probably the story of many of the women involved in the Factory.

Swimming Underground begins with a young Mary being saved from drowning. During a day at the beach, she and her mother swam out too far and hit a riptide. Mary was sure she was going to drown but her mother somehow saved her. Back on the beach, drained from the experience, Mary has a surprising revelation:

> I started shaking. I just couldn't stop no matter how many blankets they gave me, but Mom, she was happy again, her body glistening white against the fallen night. It was like old times—people fussing over her, me feeling pathetic, worried over nothing. I hated it. Every time she looked back at me huddled in my blankets, that strange smile would curve her lips, her eyes would glitter again, and my gratitude at being alive shriveled. She knew what she was doing all along. She had done it before, swimming out too far, scaring people so they paid attention to her, and now letting me swim into a riptide so she could save me. I hated her.

This isn't just angst. It's foreshadowing. It seems a perfect encapsulation of the Warhol experience for many people.

Woronov's brain is a crisp, knife-edged place and this is a very bestial, feral book.

> There is Violet, my dog—my violent temper—the kind of thing you get a reputation for, and I must also confess to being the abused owner of a rage rat. This rodent is a voice in my head that never shuts up. I don't know how I acquired it. I suppose it was given to me at an early age by some malicious adult, or perhaps every head comes equipped with one—you know, the "rodent included" plan. I've already packed these two in their traveling boxes; others are too prehistoric to catch, nobody would want to go into the black waters where they live. And there are also animals I don't want to catch; rather I'm afraid of them catching me, like coyotes that carry insanity

> like a plague. I'm afraid they will find out where I'm going and follow me.
> Every time I find a new animal, like my party squirrel or my comedy crow,
> I give it a cage and a feeding schedule. And of course there are the rabbits—
> little habits that I've stuffed into every possible space in my suitcase—habits
> of speed, junk, pills, and any other poison I can get my hands on.

This passage either grabs you with both fists and shakes you and you need no explanation as to why I find it so amazing, or it means nothing and any attempt to explain will be meaningless.

But it fits in well with Mary's opinion of herself:

> I wasn't born with a father, I'm not really connected with men. I was a box
> baby, a preemie. I was born so early I had long prenatal hair everywhere and
> a spinal tumor that looked like a tail. Yeah, it was gruesome. I looked like a
> monkey. Every time the nurses rolled me in, my grandmother screamed at
> them to roll me back out, you know, like I was some kind of mistake. I think
> it kind of set the tone for the rest of my life.

Uneasy around men, Mary finds a strange comfort around "drag queens." They calm the anger in her:

> There was only one way to shut my rat up, and that was to be around some-
> thing even more enraged. At first I thought this was impossible, but then I
> met my first drag queen. Rat relief at last. Finally someone angrier than I
> was, with a sense of humor about the whole thing. I felt calm, tranquil, as
> if I had found religion, and as long as I was around the queens even my rat
> assumed table manners, cracked jokes, let other people talk. Pretty soon I
> was a drag queen junkie.

Mary meets her favorite drag queen, Celinas, at the Factory, when Celinas shows up with Brandy Alexander. This tale, referencing beasts yet again, shows the nastiness of the Factory if one was not careful (and actually, even if one were careful, one could end up savaged, but more on that later…):

> …Brandy was her opposite, the obvious, overdone showgirl-type queen…
> Desperate was too exotic a description for her; let's just say she was bug-
> ging everybody that day, waving her airbrushed 8x10s dangerously close to
> Warhol's nose. The polite light went out, and Brandy became free bait; the
> tinfoil walls of the Factory flickered like silver water; the smaller surface
> fish—visitors and squares, scattered and knotted in excitement; and from
> out of the aluminum depths glided the larger fish—predators, attracted by
> the commotion. Billy Name, one of the Great Whites, appeared and disap-
> peared. Often his presence signaled the difference between light play and
> heavy, hardcore shit.

Semicolons generally annoy the hell out of me, but perhaps I dislike the use of semicolons that announce themselves too loudly and destroy the flow of the sentence. I didn't notice these semicolons until I transcribed the text, which means they didn't interrupt my initial reading. That seldom happens.

The scene continues, with Gerard Malanga cruelly taunting Brandy and everyone hoping he'd get the crap punched out of him, but Mary is focused on Celinas, who stands stark still, likely terrified.

> I didn't know what she wanted, or why she had come with Brandy, but I did know the last thing she ever expected to get was me. I slid in close to her, mesmerized by the panicked rabbit jumping up and down in her jugular. Maybe you should sit down, here on this silver couch that, by the way, is just as dirty as the gutter. When she sat, she crossed her hands and ankles perfectly. Yes, yes, everything was in the classroom. We chatted, bonded, as Brandy flopped around on the silver concrete floor with the silver hook still in her bloody mouth. Both of us were excited. Celinas tried to climb into her purse, which was filled with dirty broken makeup, the true sign of a queen. I was thrilled she had let me look, even slip my hand into it for a moment.

There was no way for me to look at this passage as anything but Mary saving Celinas from a terrible trial by fire. The scene continues:

> I let her huddle near me, but when she tried to clutch my hand I had to recoil. I hated being touched by anything in the human-skin package.

Like I said, this is a bestial book, but is it surprising that human skin repelled Mary? I wonder how much of that remains with her. Mary, for all the animals in her and around her, has a very icy, distant persona. She reveals a teenage rejection that makes her believe that when she feels attraction, it is never reciprocated. Which is odd because she was a tall, gorgeous young woman. When you have a rat in your head, I guess it isn't that unusual.

Mary had deep feelings for a Factory member called Ondine, but she felt enthralled more than she felt deep love. Here's a scene where Mary and Celinas joined a dinner with Ondine and Andy Warhol:

> So far I had only watched him from afar because, like everyone else, I found him intimidating, but now as his eyes looked at me I did not squirm as I had imagined, instead I felt released. I could detect no revulsion or hate as his eyes opened my darkest corners in a matter of seconds.

As I read on, it was probably a good thing that Mary kept herself so remote, at least initially. Ondine read like the sort of man who would wear a person out.

> Then his attention returned to the crowd around him. While he spoke he changed their gaze into utter discomfort by putting a dinner napkin over his head like a kerchief. It made him look foolish and matronly. But no matter how humiliating he looked, it was his audience that felt embarrassed, and he seemed to enjoy this. I started to laugh, and he laughed too. Celinas and the others shifted in their seats, but his voice prevented anyone from leaving; it was like a tempest coming at you from all sides.

It was vaguely disappointing learning what this voice that prevented people from leaving actually said.

> "Those dogs out there—sniffing each other's assholes. Oh please, the idea is even boring, darling, sniffing assholes is boring, and if you don't know that I can't help you. Then by all means tell them to come in here, hah, they wouldn't dare. Celinas, dear, how are you? Ah, you're mute, what an attribute. You'll have to forgive me, I'm being mummified. Yes, mummified, but this—all this, and her. She makes me sick. No, I don't mean you, you poor warped boil. Who could ever forget you—oh, if only I was humiliated, if only you could humiliate me, what a divine experience, but not by you, you're boring, boring, my dear—yes, you heard me—I want an ambush, to be ambushed, but they don't understand."

I wonder if Ondine was ever humiliated before he died. I don't think he really wanted such an experience—that shoot down where he declares his audience too boring to do it gives a little clue, I think.

Oh Mary, beautiful Mary. Her descent into drugs, into becoming one of the Mole People—this is when things begin to get out of hand for her, and she recreates this time, how quickly she sank, with startling clarity.

> …there was only one way to go to Brooklyn; take the black subway under the river of forgetfulness. However, this time it did not work; I forgot nothing, and when I was home, I didn't belong. I had changed. There were no outward signs, but I knew it. It was no longer them, it was us. Their rules were mine, their insanity my reality, and as for the rest of the world, it just didn't matter. I was a Mole.

Mary discusses how her upper-class family did not notice her drug addiction, though it seems like they may have known and just preferred not to speak of it. Her mother would find her on her knees in front of the open refrigerator, binge eating after the effects of days spent in speed revelry wore off, cramming whatever she could into her mouth. Noticing a cake in a box on the kitchen counter, Mary digs her hands into the chocolate icing as her mother blithely insists she stop, please stop, the cake is for dinner. During dinner, Mary can barely keep it together:

> I held my head in my hands so it wouldn't roll off into someone else's plate as Mom and Dad joked about how they had to hide dessert from me because I once ate a whole cake and got sick. It never happened. I could easily eat two and a half cakes, that was what was really scaring them.

Mary would go home to recover, only to leave in a panic because she was terrified she would not be able to find the Moles again. When she found them, it was a mind-bending recitation of listening to the Duchess (Brigid "Polk" Berlin) babbling about nothing, going to dinners where no one ate "unless someone else was buying" and endless unsettling behavior.

"Champagne! It's show time!" Rene started screaming. For some reason my legs weren't working, so holding onto the table, I prepared to do the Warhol watch as Andrea Whips climbed onto her table and the show began. Singing "Everything's Coming Up Roses," Andrea partially stripped and partially jerked off. It was okay, we'd seen it before.

Andrea began to masturbate with the champagne bottle, and her behavior drove away a Hollywood director and his actress friend, who exited Max's Kansas City post haste.

> Everyone cheered. I cheered. It was sort of fun except that Andrea was crazy, well, only slightly crazy; she was at the point where she could only talk to people's reflections in the little hand mirror she carried around. What we didn't know was that she would soon throw herself out of a window, leaving behind only a love note to Andy. She was the second in our group to defenestrate themselves. Freddie was the first, a frustrated ballerina; he had been high for so long he asked death to dance out a twelfth-story window. Andrea landed on her feet but that didn't help; from the waist down she was hamburger meat, while the rest of her was strangely unmarked.

Clearly I am less arty than bookish, but is there any art movement with a larger body count than Warhol's Factory? It would be interesting to do a study. I don't recall where I read this, possibly in Ultra Violet's book, but I know that shortly before she disappeared, Ingrid Superstar called Andy collect and he refused to take the call. His explanation was that if after all that time the best she could do was a collect call… Ingrid was brought into the Factory to torment Edie Sedgwick, to show her she could be replaced. Of course, Edie was driven off and years later died, and her replacement left to get cigarettes in the late 80s and never returned. Ingrid's value to Warhol was very low—anyone who placed a collect call was not worth his time.

Mary's caustic but probably very accurate recollections of her fellow Factory denizens make for quite entertaining reading. Here's a snippet from a scene where Warhol is badgering Mary to model like Nico and Ivy:

> …all I ever saw Ivy do was take a dump behind the silver couch. This crazy woman wanted to marry Andy Warhol, which meant getting as close to him as she could or leaving a piece of herself with him. She definitely did not have all her oars in the water; if you asked me, she didn't even know what an oar was. Sometimes Gerard would have to fend her off, or Billy would be called to throw her out of the Factory. Later, the elevator would return empty except for a single, lonely turd, and someone would snicker, "Andy, Ivy's back."

Mary's wry and black humor shines through so well in this scene, where she and Ondine have just taken an epic amount of speed.

> Ondine smiled as if he had just baked a cake. "Young love, my dear, isn't it fabulous?"
>
> I thought of the girl I had just seen, her head wedged between the toilet and

the floor staring at the crucifix swaying above her like Poe's pendulum, and I regretted we hadn't taken the time to carpet the bathroom. "Ondine, can we get even higher?"

"Yes, I could get you higher. Have you ever heard Marie Callas sing Tosca? So high your blood would explode and splatter your brains all over your cranium—excruciating, you'd love it. But Wonton doesn't have a record player, instead he has the fabulous Miss Marbles, the siren of despair."

"Ondine, I have an apartment on St. Mark's. I have a record player."

Ondine pulled three worn albums to his chest and in a voice that was deathly serious, said, "If you do this for me you will be saving my life."

Perhaps lives were saved but the scene ends thusly:

By the third day we were so exhausted that Ondine ended up in the bathtub trying to suck his own dick and I lay on my back with my neck on the bathroom threshold using the door frame as my imaginary guillotine (there comes a time when everyone needs their own guillotine). When I asked Ondine why he didn't just get someone else to blow him, he practically had a fit. "You think this is about getting off? Getting off what? The planet? It's impossible, I've tried! I am the last Oboroborus [sic] left in captivity. Perhaps I should introduce myself, the snake that swallows its own tail. This, my dear, is about resurrection, not sex. And if this were about sex, I don't think I would be asking you. Everyone has forgotten the origin of the bathtub—baptism. I'm being born, you fool, now close the door."

"He's pregnant," Jane whispered, "Ondine, can I get you some pickles and ice cream?"

"At last, someone who understands. Thank you Jane, that would be wonderful. Now, close the door, darling, I want to see Mary's head roll."

Except the scene really doesn't end because scenes with speed freaks never really end. Jane, Mary's roommate, thinks she catches pregnancy from Ondine and it goes on from there. Jane eventually cracks, as you do when you have a speed-addled Mary for a roommate and your favorite person spends hours in your tub trying to blow himself. Mary vows to make sure her life does not harm Jane much in the future.

Mary's sense of not being good enough plagues her, yet she sees people so clearly (or maybe I think she sees people clearly because her opinions mesh with mine):

That night Andy was drawing noses, before and after nose jobs. When he asked me if I liked it, I didn't answer. Why bother? I knew that stupid drawing would appear in its silkscreen mode later, worth a fortune. My nose would get out of joint when I thought of my own black and white drawings. Why were they so unloved? Because Mom left me alone in Macy's department store? It was only for thirty minutes. Who knows, maybe it wasn't long enough, maybe it should have been three hours in order to form the correct aberrant psyche for a really famous artist. Maybe Macy's was really this big oven and she took me out too soon, and that was why I was only a half-baked artist. When I started thinking like this, I knew I was getting really high and I shouldn't be alone, which is why I was standing in this bathroom watching Ondine shoot up in his eye.

That dark humor, that capacity for juxtaposing her relatively sane inner thoughts with her lunatic outer world is a gift, I think.

Even as Mary shows incredible black humor, her life had a huge capacity for what, in retrospect, reads like utter horror. Here's her take on Rotten Rita, the creator of one of the most horrific scenes:

> Most people used only one word to describe Rita, and that word was evil. He was the dealer, and a lousy dealer at that. Trying to cop from Rita was a nightmare. His apartment was a bare room with several glaring sunlamps and one black chair that he would sit in, telling you to make yourself comfortable. In the dead of winter people would be sitting in there. If you didn't have sunglasses it was hard to stay, but he would start insisting that before you scored you might like to watch his lover, Birdie, sit on a Coke bottle.

Rita maliciously shot up a woman called Ann, who overdosed. Rita suggested that she be shot up with milk to save her. Mary tries to get Ondine to understand that injecting milk into Ann's veins will solve nothing but he is too far gone to listen to her. Ann, of course, died. They laid her on a coffee table, as you do, declared that they had trapped death, then shot up to celebrate. Later they dumped Ann in the hallway in a scene that would have been funny in a Coen brothers sort of way, but that was in fact mostly horrible given that it really happened.

After a while, Mary's addictions began to take their toll:

> Do not imagine that I scampered around those velvet sewers completely unscathed. You cannot play with shit all night and come out looking like a boarding school virgin. No, no, no, you have some shit in your hair, and a little on your shoe, and soon you're talking shit. Every time you open your mouth it just falls out. If you dug with the Mole People, somewhere, somehow, either their drugs, one of their thoughts, or just one of their little hairs got into your skin and burrowed deeper and deeper, quietly driving you insane. It was the law, nobody escaped, not even Andy.

It was during this time that Mary began to be stalked by Vera Cruz.

> She was a fan. I can never tell you how much I loathed, despised, and prayed to God for this thing's death. Looking back, I realize that it was my extraordinary hatred that brought her to the attention and later enjoyment of my perverse friends, but try as I might, I could not stop hating her. It was like trying to ignore a one-hundred-and-thirty-five pound tumor, and that was how close she wanted to be to me—me, who groaned at the thought of the hug and even considered the handshake a mild form of social torture. She wanted to be inside my very skull, a voracious boll weevil in my precious

cotton brain. Nothing was close enough. If I put my hand out, she wanted to lick it. If I talked to her, she wanted to fuck me.

Vera Cruz was famous for having been born without a vagina, a problem she later had corrected with surgery in Arizona, and because she stalked Mary Woronov. Mary, according to this biography, actually tried to kill her by pushing her down onto the train tracks in the subway but she failed. Vera intruded into Mary's life in many ways, up to and including collecting Mary's urine from toilets. When the Warhol-es saw that Vera Cruz was a stick with which to beat Mary, they lunged for her like petty little lapdogs of war.

> Andy couldn't contain himself. "Oh Mary, Vera's been telling us that this is your piss. You've been letting her collect it for some time now. Why didn't you tell us? Gerard, why didn't she tell us?
>
> Gerard: "That's disgusting, Andy. I don't know."
>
> Paul: "Vera's going to be in our next movie. We're going to have her collecting everyone's piss. That should be entertaining."
>
> Andy: "Yes, maybe you should do a sex scene with her, Mary."
>
> Vera: "A love scene."
>
> Paul: "No, no, Vera, that's too ugly. Nobody wants to see that."
>
> Andy: "No, we can do that. Oh, Mary, where are you going? Don't you want to do that? Where is she going, Gerard?"

Mary ceded the field to Vera, knowing too well that her friends wanted her to grovel, to fight. Eventually they missed her and Ondine came to reestablish friendship. When Mary hit bottom, Brigid Berlin took her to a country house and fed her omelets until she regained strength. However, when Mary failed to show the Duchess adequate pity when Rotten Rita screwed her in a drug deal, the Duchess got even by going to Mary's apartment with a man called The Crocodile and giving Mary's roommate Jane a ridiculous dose of drugs.

Mary could not survive in New York without splitting costs with Jane but she immediately got her on an airplane home and left the apartment. The essential triviality and relentless cruelty of the Factory denizens finally drove Mary away, but not in anger so much as clutching the idea that she simply could not compete with such nastiness.

Mary Woronov was one of the few members of the Factory who went on to have a career that did not revolve around Andy Warhol. That thing that attracted Andy to Mary when she was still a Cornell co-ed was a spark that existed without him. That spark fuels this biography, because even as Mary shows us how interesting it was to have been a part of that scene, she also shows us how very interesting she is.

FURTHER READING

The Mistress's Daughter: A Memoir
A.M. Homes

S.C.U.M. Manifesto
Valerie Solanas

Famous for 15 Minutes
Ultra Violet

THE CARNIVALS OF LIFE AND DEATH
By James Shelby Downard
Feral House (2006)
Original post: 07/28/2010

Why do I consider this book odd?
Downard claims he saw Alexander Graham Bell involved in sex magick rituals on Jekyll Island.

I suspect I am in way over my head. I mean, don't get me wrong, I fear the Masons and loathe the Ku Klux Klan as much as any self-respecting conspiratologist should. I think there is a level of "street theater" in our economic and political processes, a sort of active public facade that, if the veneer were ever pulled away, would show us far more that is sinister than positive. I think the banking industry and the political system in America are corrupt beyond belief and that those who operate behind the scenes in these systems are people whose interests in no way reflect the well-being of the American people.

Having said that, I need to make it clear that I don't think "mystical sex circuses," "witchcraft sex magick orgies," and "sexathons that aim at nothing more than racial blood mixing" are part of a secret economic system, nor are these things that people really need to worry about. I also tend *not* to believe that:

> ...the mythology of Revelations will be followed like Tinker-Toy instructions: a time of tribulation will come first, after which survivors will be made "one" via a post-tribulation "rapture" spawned by the technical sorcery of having their brain pleasure centers titillated magnetically so that all will cum together.

And I'm relatively confident that a very young James Shelby Downard did not in fact witness a man called Cock Robin giving Alexander Graham Bell a blowjob on Jekyll Island. Knowing that James Shelby Downard likely didn't exist and was, perhaps, the brainchild of three different men[4] doesn't play as

---

4   Authorship of Downard's essays and biography is rumored to be the work of three different men: revisionist historian Michael A. Hoffman, Forteana expert William N. Grimstad (also known as Jim Brandon), and Feral House publisher Adam Parfrey. I have no firmly researched opinion on whether or not Downard really existed and if he wrote his works himself, but this is one of those times when it's hard to know which option is the most fantastic: a group hoax or that Downard lived and evaded chaos and violence at every turn. I tend to think the three-man theory holds water and I write this essay with that belief in mind.

much into my declaration of "Pants!" as you might think. This is The Parable of the Whack-jobs. None of this ever happened but it was written to illustrate certain points about mystical toponomy, symbolism of names and that uneasy sense that things are not entirely as they should be.

Then again, a lack of genuine belief in the mystical has always been my Achilles heel. Call me naive if you must.

But whatever you call me, you need to read *The Carnivals of Life and Death* because it is a hoot. This is purportedly the autobiography of one James Shelby Downard, who was born in 1913 and died in 1998 before he could finish his tale. He is most famous for his essay, "King/Kill 33: Masonic Symbolism in the Assassination of John F. Kennedy." I read that monster years ago but had no idea the full body of ideas Downard (or whomever) brought to the table.

The book reads like those *Home Alone* movies. A precocious kid with questionable parents keeps finding himself in violent situations wherein he bests his attackers. Imagine those movies except the precocious kid gets stalked and attacked by Freemasons and the Klan and you pretty much have the gist. According to Downard, he was set up as a scapegoat (pharmakos) or symbolic whipping boy, presumably by his criminally negligent and downright weird parents, and spent his entire life standing up for the American Way by thwarting attack after attack after attack and witnessing unspeakable acts while besting the worst evil there is.

I'm not saying Downard doesn't have interesting ideas. The approach is scattershot, but when something hits the target, it can be a little eerie. In order to appreciate this you have to read the book for what it is: a fictional story, a parable, that through extremes tries to show things the author believes are buried from our sight. These are myths for the paranoid—bizarre, over-the-top fables meant to tell a larger story through unbelievable detail. Or Downard really was a plucky young man who foiled Joe Pesci time and time again. Believe what you want. Either way, it's a fun read.

You get pushed off the deep end fast, from the very second Adam Parfrey signs his introduction. Here's a small taste of the paranoia and weird associations Downard presents in his own introduction:

> ...I got a glimpse of frightful memories from the long-dead past and, perhaps more importantly, recognized the past for the corpus mysticum that it is. When my mystical past revealed how it had really occurred, it became a horrendous thing cloaked in iniquity, that old now-you-see-it-now-you-don't that preserves the criminal mysteries of Masonic oz art (M oz art).

Get used to that, those interesting little connections in Downard's head. He sees connections in ways that will change how you look at things, synchronous connections that, for some, lead to sinister conclusions.

Of course, there is mention of cats, of burning them in fact. I bring this up only because I am beginning to despair of all the dead cats in so many of

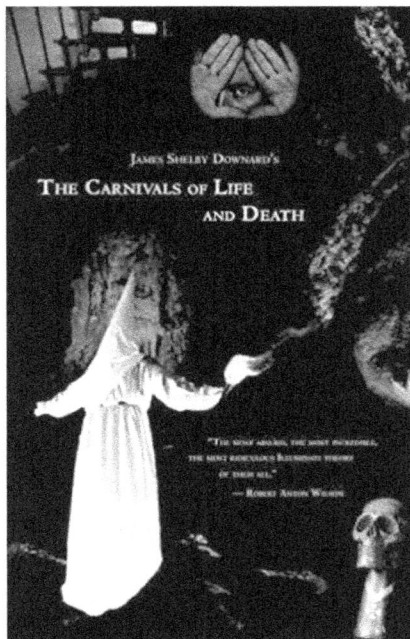

the books I read. If I traipse down the primrose path that Downard stomped, I would begin to think there is something connecting all these dead cats that seem to come up in every damn book I pick up these days. For now I'm just chalking it up to bad luck.

Carnivals of Life and Death begins with young Downard being secured spread-eagle in his bed on Christmas Eve. He was five. He was unpinned in the morning only to find switches and coal in his stocking. From there, we cut to a shootout with Masons where the tot escapes and blows stuff up. His mother made him dress like a girl. There's the above-mentioned trip to Jekyll Island where he saw all kinds of unseemly things and was almost killed in some sort of magick theater ritual. He gets abandoned and lives like a dog until he is reunited with his mother. He is almost killed countless other times. He thwarts the Klan, he finds Million Dollar Gold Certificates the way I find cat hair on my chair. He is nailed to a tree by the Klan but luckily his small anus prevents him from being sodomized. He liberates a white sex slave. He finds all kinds of bizarre "grave goods" from the tomb of a Mason only to have FDR offer to purchase them and when he gets the check for a million dollars, his parents talk him out of cashing it. His wife turns out to be a mind-controlled sex slave. He explains the symbolic meanings of dunce caps and bull whips. He finds all sorts of parallels between innocuous ideas, discussing usual ringers like Disney and Proctor & Gamble, but he also explains why we should be alarmed if we see a man curse a pig and then touch our water faucet.

This is, like, maybe 5% of the insanity on offer. To discuss it in depth would require far more time than I have and more gin than I am willing to drink.

The best part is how, through it all, Downard never gets a clue. I mean, after the third time the Masons tried to kill me, after the Klan had nailed me to a tree, after I'd almost been choked to death by Cock Robin while everyone chanted "Non Person, Non Person," I think I'd be suspicious of anyone who asked me to fish around in an old family tomb. At the very least, after I noticed the tomb had been booby-trapped, I probably wouldn't have gone on in.

Not Downard. If this man existed, we need to find his grave and take some of his bones to have him reconstituted when DNA technology catches up with my imagination.

We need more Downards—clever, foolhardy, indestructible, paranoid yet open to adventure. An army of Downards? Hell, America would be restored to her old glory in no time.

FURTHER READING

James Shelby Downard's Mystical War
Adam Gorightly

Neutron Gun
Gerry Reith

SHE AND I: A FUGUE
By Michael R. Brown
Petrarca Press (2009)
Original post: 09/21/2010

Why do I consider this book odd?
The author and I "know" one another from butting heads in some
blogging communities before I lost my will to argue online. We find
each other extremely questionable in our respective approaches in
political and social realms (he is some breed of Libertarian and I am
a Bleeding Heart Liberal, each of us being married to our own belief
systems in a way that beggars belief to the other). I first encountered
the author in a community devoted to stupid behavior online. Two
years later, I forget how I did it, but I discovered his full name and
the name of his book and to reward me for not being as much of an
idiot as he initially judged me, he sent me a copy. So that was a bit
odd. Then the book itself proved to be an odd experience, to be sure.

I debated on how to handle this one. I was tempted to go with snark but I just can't. I may not pull any punches but I plan to be as honest and candid as I can as I explain why Michael R. Brown's *She and I: A Fugue* is one of the worst books I have ever read. In a way, a snarky and comedic approach might be more easily stomached because it would be easier to dismiss. "Oh, a liberal clown didn't like my book, figures, who cares." I also tell myself that there is nothing unkind in complete honesty that doesn't come from a place of utter malice.

So since I am being honest, I need to say outright that this is an awful book. It is awful for many reasons and I am going to discuss those reasons. It may seem like overkill, but when you don't like the author, it's too easy to say, "It sucked, take my word for it." I don't want you to take my word for it. I want to give you all the evidence that led me to the conclusions I reached. I don't want anyone to walk away from this far-too-long review and think I dismissed the book because I had some unpleasant experiences with the author.

Here is the synopsis: Brown, who uses a different last name in the book, is born in England. He is abandoned by his father. His mother remarries in the US. He goes to military school where he is molested by a classmate. He grows up. He develops a taste for Randian Objectivism. He falls in love. He loses his wife to cancer. He falls in love and moves in with one of his wife's good friends. He develops an attachment to a young woman online. He goes

She and I
A fugue

by
Michael R. Brown

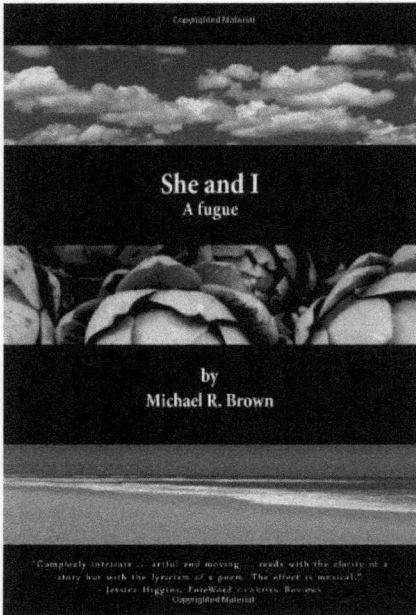

to meet her. It's a disaster but he can't see it. She sleeps with someone else. He breaks it off. The end.

Of course there is more going on than the synopsis allows, and the fact is that Brown has some interesting material. One does not have to have anything new under the sun to write a memoir and his life stories are interesting. The problem is that the material that is of infinite interest to Brown is not of much interest to the reader. He doesn't focus on the stuff that would help to tell a compelling, absorbing story. His childhood, the horrific experiences at military school, a very touching relationship with an elderly gentleman, the story of meeting, marrying and losing his wife and his subsequent romance with her friend—these are topics that have the potential to be very interesting and compelling, yet they are crammed into the first 70 or so pages. The brief online courtship of a teenage girl, meeting her for a few days, then ending the fling a few weeks later, take up the remaining 210 pages of the book.

At some point it appears that Brown deleted most of the correspondence he had with Mira, the 18-year-old ballerina whom he woos in 1999, and this is problematic. Though it seems he kept their instant messages, a significant part of Brown's book consists of little more than him recounting emails or instant messages. This may make for interesting reading in a blog where the people involved are known quantities to the reader, but it is tiresome and bland in a memoir. There is beauty in the romantic exchange of letters, but the electronic communications in this book do not lend themselves to a sort of Elizabeth Barrett Browning sense of romantic love, nor are they particularly compelling.

Moreover, and I know this is just my opinion, I assert that there is very little that is interesting in a 35-year-old man's two months of correspondence with a teenager dabbling in the ideas of Ayn Rand, his several day meeting with her and the subsequent dumping three to four weeks later, let alone 210 pages of it. Brown's wife dying of cancer, by contrast, is handled in less than two pages. This is not a good selection of life material for a memoir. Of course this book is not about Brown's wife and it may be irrelevant to bring her up as a point of comparison but it does make me wonder why, with that kind of life experience, Brown spends so much time writing about a fling with a girl he barely knew.

Brown's writing style is hands-down the most alienating I have ever read. I genuinely have no idea what he was trying to accomplish with this style because even my initial suspicion about his use of truncated sentences and his extraordinary overuse of em-dashes was not borne out by the way he used them. I have an odious habit of turning down a page corner when I come across a passage I find meaningful or terrible. I encountered so many terrible passages in Brown's book that I had to change my method. I had to underline passages with a highlighter. I wore out two highlighters and just gave up around page 255. My husband commented that I needed less a highlighter than a can of spray paint.

For the first 50 pages or so, Brown uses what is more or less proper sentence structure but the sentences and word choice were often so bad I was stunned. For example:

> One stifling burning-sun day we'd brewed strong pure lemonade and sold paper cups on the Harristown sidewalk fronting Mrs Castelli's.

The "burning-sun" part is all right, I guess. But how does one brew lemonade? And why would they sell paper cups when they evidently had lemonade to sell. These are niggling points, I am aware, but they are a foreshadowing of the complete breakdown in writing that is to come.

> I crossed the lawn, walked up black steel staircase on side of Farragut Hall—great rambling wood building, once shore hotel now dormitory—waved from landing.

I know there is an experimental element in what Brown is attempting here, but there is generally nothing experimental about refusing to use articles. If there were some urgency when Brown does this, a conversational trope to indicate haste or mental skipping, I could see it. But there's not. Sometimes he uses articles correctly but a lot of the time he doesn't and there is no literary reason to explain it. It is distracting and it adds nothing to the narrative or overall function of the book. It makes a book about a love affair seem robotic.

His use of contractions, while technically grammatically correct, is also distracting. These are but a taste of the hundreds of odd contractions in the book:

> ...an officer'd said my roommate was being held in infirmary...

> After I'd absorbed the book, desire'd stirred.

> Mother'd stopped with beatings, chokings—father'd used her for sex pleasures from an early age.

Given that Brown could have written in simple past tense and achieved the exact same meaning, these contractions are not only not necessary, but pretentious. They certainly disrupt the flow of his writing. Reread that last example. The power of the statement of his wife's abuse is made coy, almost like a line from an Andrew Marvell poem, by his use of contraction instead of simply saying, "Her mother eventually stopped beating and choking her and her father began sexually abusing her when she was very young." Worse, the statement that her mother stopped abusing her combined with the statement that her father sexually abused her makes no sense, and the dash rather than a conjunction or semicolon disrupts the flow.

Then there are the awkward and sometimes unintentionally hilarious sentences that just destroy any flow he has going. Too often I had to back up and reread sentences, wondering what on earth Brown was trying to convey:

> Now I stood, waiting for him to answer my touch on his doorbell.

> "No," she said, holding my asking invalid.

> I never broke—became known, even slight respect, as a seventh-grader who'd not only not run crying to the Administration, but smile.

She and I is full of moments like this, when you think, "He touched what?" "How did she hold his inquisitive sick person?" Of course, on a second or third reading his meaning becomes clear but there is no payoff for making a reader work this hard with such clunky sentences. This is not a Cummings poem. There is no greater revelation when you untangle the words and meaning. It is simply bad writing.

Then we get to Brown's overuse of em-dashes. Maybe they are hyphens. Maybe plain dashes. I don't know but I can't recall ever having seen so many of them in a book. On some pages the words appeared to be moving because of all the dashes (a nauseating experience). It becomes worse once Brown meets Mira online. Toward the end of the book, this sloppy form of punctuation/whatever became so tiring that I had to bribe myself to finish it. Ten pages of Brown's novel, then a few chapters of something else. Coming from woman who has devoted her life to bizarre books, who devours self-published screeds with little editing, who embraces the horrific at every turn, this is a damning statement. So let me give you a sample of what I mean.

> She seemed tallest of the class—her face most elongated—skin paler, more clear—seemed to put more in her dancing—stretch higher, special grace of fluency in hands and arms.

> She passed talking with peer—exchanged quick smiles—felt warm, secret—wondered what people'd think of our night.

> I turned—there was Mira walking up—our eyes met—permanent presence between us.

I realize that passages like these, when used judiciously, can mean something. They can imply a rushed intensity. They can show a character whose thoughts are choppy or jumbled. They can mean a lot of different things. Initially, when I saw the word "fugue" in the title and saw a few of these passages, I wondered if Brown was trying to indicate one meaning of the word, a state of mental confusion. But such passages occur throughout the entire book regardless of mental states. They occur during moments of peace, moments of confusion, moments of sadness, moments of elation. This choppy, disjointed manner of writing certainly can't be indicative of the other meaning of "fugue," a musical form, because there is nothing musical about endless dashes destroying flow, making anything approaching literary rhythm impossible.

Brown's refusal to consider the clunkiness of his word choice, his refusal to use articles and his bizarre punctuation choices make his book read like a hastily constructed journal entry, with words tossed onto paper in a scrawl that means something to the author but nothing to the reader.

As I turn to my harshest criticism of *She and I*, keep in mind that I dislike Brown's politics and much of what I have seen of him online (and I am certain the feeling is reciprocal). I tried to set that aside, but the narrator, Brown himself, really is unlikable. When I say that the narrator is unlikeable, I mean that few people could relate to him or find him interesting, outside of marveling at how dense he is. And it's not that Brown is trying to show what a tool he was. At no point did I sense that Brown understood how unlikeable he comes across in this book. His lack of awareness is practically a character in its own right. It's hard to enjoy a memoir when you sense the author has no real understanding of what his story reveals about him.

With all the topics given short shrift in this book, one cannot help but wonder about the sort of 35-year-old man who would find an online correspondence with a teenage girl, followed by a few days spent in her presence, then followed by three or so weeks until a break-up, to be worthy of a full-scale memoir. (Actually, you have to wonder about a 45-year-old man who thinks this is book-worthy material, because he published this a decade after the events took place.)

Brown has a way of processing what happens to him that will make little sense to most readers, and in some cases he shows that he is an unreliable narrator. I first sensed that Brown had a skewed outlook when he described his sexual assault and continual molestation at the hands of a stronger student at the military school. Forced to fellate the older student, among other things, then told to say nothing of the events on pain of death, this is what Brown concludes:

This was my introduction to sex.

The exploitation, which eventually included anal rape, continued until Brown cracked and lost it and reported the older boy. Though adults were sympathetic, there were reprisals from his peers, culminating when students urinated on Brown's bed. My heart broke reading all of it. Does Brown really think it was an introduction to sex? It was a description of sexual abuse. I wanted to believe that Brown interpreted the assaults against him as a sexual experience to blunt the horror of being so ill-used, and perhaps he did. This is his book, and he can craft the story of his life as he pleases. But it is hard for me, the reader, to see this as anything but the first steps in a voyage of questionable interpretation.

I sort of want to discuss the passage where Brown recounts his silent communion with concert pianist Vladimir Horowitz, but I can't. My only honest response is that I don't believe it happened. While I think Brown's capacity to understand social situations is flawed, I don't think he's a liar. If this passage is true, then it is a perfect example of something I was taught in a college writing class so many years ago: just because something is true does not mean writing it will approach reality. Sometimes conveying an event because it really happened is meaningless because it lacks resonance or seems too fantastic.

Further scenes seem contrived even if they really happened. Mira bares her teeth at him in moments of high spirits. Her eyelids tremble. Their eyes meet constantly with all kinds of meaning (their eyes meet and their eyes meet and their eyes meet—it verges on purple, all the eye repetition). She glances at him admiringly, he notices. She makes odd declarations. For example, Brown engages in some really questionable behavior in a museum and instead of being appalled or even embarrassed (because believe me, I will explain the lack of sexual chemistry between the two in a bit), she yells "Passion!" in a public place as Brown manhandles her. She declares at the airport that she will dedicate her choreography to him, that he has earned it. Then she begins to shake. Really?

The dialogue and the actions Brown attributes to people often don't come close to reading as authentic. Is it all being filtered by a man who is an unreliable narrator of his own life? I don't know. Even if the passage I am about to reproduce is indeed a real conversation between a teenager and a grown man, it reads utterly false. There is an objective truth that Brown wants to tell us but there is a subjective truth that we need to read to believe him. He does not deliver.

> We were dropping clothes to floor—I said, "So, boys are trouble, are they?"
>
> "Yes, you most emphatically are."
>
> "And what did we ever do to you, hmm?"
>
> We stopped, looked at each other.
>
> "That hardly bears repeating, sir."
>
> "Well, substantiate your case. A familiar phrase. Anything to do with a warm body who shared this comfy bed?"

"As a matter of fact, yes."

"Continue."

Her face changed. There was conflict. "Well… look, it was Harris."

It took a moment to register. Her friend—the warm body. I'd thought them separate people.

"Okay."

"We did have sex. It was—not good."

"The sex?"

"Yeah, we weren't compatible."

"I'm sorry. What happened?"

"Well, he's an Objectivist, pretty much. And there's just a connection problem with those men. I swore after Taylor, never again. I should've stuck to it."

Later, he says:

"Come to bed with me, fae girl,"… "and hold me tight."

Even if this is a word for word representation of real conversation, it is shitty, horrible dialogue in a book. It is questionable whether or not we need most of the dialogue that Brown gives us, but if we do, he could have written it in way that honors the truth of the situation while making it real to the ears of most educated adults.

Then we get to the best example that to my eye proves that Brown is unreliable in his storytelling: Mira. Brown discovered Mira after she left a comment in a guestbook on his website on December 9, 1998. He soon finds her blog, falls in love with her mind and has some flirty emails and instant message exchanges with her. She wants to meet him, he wants to meet her, he travels from San Francisco to Boston with stars in his eyes. He arrives on February 9, 1999. He is 35. She is either 18 or just turned 19 (I can't recall so I mostly just refer to her as a teenager). She had a boyfriend when she met Brown online but that attachment fizzled a couple of weeks after they started corresponding. The age gap in and of itself is not entirely troubling to me, though it seems odd that Brown felt such a profound connection to someone who was so young, who was still experiencing life. Recall that Brown had experienced the death of his wife and had a long-term live-in relationship with another woman with whom he had decided to experiment in polyamory. He was still living with that woman when he met Mira. He was a college graduate and had experienced life. Mira was in college, studying dance, and had far fewer life experiences under her belt. But age gaps are not uncommon. I don't condemn him for that.

The entire time he was in Boston visiting Mira read to me like a simulacrum of hell. I have an advantage over Brown—I have been a 19-year-old girl.

I know what it feels like to be trying on new ideas, experimenting sexually, finding my way once I had left my mother's home. Therefore I suspect I can see more in Mira's reactions than Brown did, but even so, it is evidence of his profound denseness that Brown did not pick up on the myriad signals Mira was sending him that she did not reciprocate his feelings once they met. She said things that indicate that she perhaps did not mind continuing the long distance romance as long as she could see other people, but she also said many things that indicated that she was unhappy and her body language comes across, even through Brown's filter, as being decidedly unhappy and at times downright hostile. That he does not seem to see this is troubling.

Brown goes over the five days he spends with Mira in such detail that I tire even thinking of it, but it is in this excruciating detail that we see Brown as he really is, a man who is besotten with an intelligent, lovely, talented teenager and does not understand the chasm between his life and hers, even as the chasm is revealed to him over and over again.

Mira is actively attending classes and living with a roommate when he flies to visit her (his plane almost crashes, by the way, an omen if there ever was one). She still attends her classes when Brown visits and he attends them with her, waiting outside, sometimes watching her dance. In fact, that is how he finally meets her—he shows up at her class when he arrives in Boston. Because he is staying in her apartment, sleeping in her bed and attending classes with her, Mira is never out of his sight. Though Mira agrees to this, reading this made me uncomfortable because it is not unexpected that a teenager might not understand how oppressive such an arrangement might be. One expects a 35-year-old man might.

One of the best examples of how Brown didn't get that Mira was a young woman with the experiences of a young woman was their desire for the other to see their favorite films. Hers was Kevin Smith's *Chasing Amy*. His was Ken Russell's *Women in Love*. He weeps openly as they watch his favorite film. She replies she will have to think about it, that she doesn't really understand the characters or their motivations. Brown is put off but then rationalizes it all away. There are moments of high pathos, where Brown seems desperate that he not lose this young woman with whom he has less than 60 days of direct involvement, as if he will shatter apart if she does not love him desperately, but he doesn't see that the fact that they have little in common will make a relationship impossible.

Even though Mira agrees to this situation, there are plenty of other scenes where it is clear that Mira is uncomfortable with Brown and he does not seem to notice. Keep in mind that he is telling this story. He is giving these details. But as I read his words, I immediately understand that this girl is uncomfortable, that her time with Brown has been wearing thin from the first day. Yet even when the idea comes into his head that she might be unhappy,

Brown again rationalizes it all away. Let me give you an example where Mira gives clear signals that he chooses to dismiss.

> I broke surface, face down in the pillow, reached for Mira. She wasn't there. I opened my eyes.

> She'd already pulled on pants and shirt.

> "Good morning, love," I said. "Good morning," she said, not meeting my eyes.

> I sat up in bed, wrapped forearms around knees, and we talked. She woke up overwhelmed by our intimacy. Part of her wanted to run; she declared she wouldn't.

Gonna be brutally honest here. If you are a man reading this, here are some insights you may find helpful: when a woman wakes from a sound sleep because she says she is "overwhelmed" by intimacy, what she really means is that she is uncomfortable in bed with you. When she says it before she even has had sex with you, it may mean she is afraid of such intimacy with you but it may mean she doesn't want to have sex with a man she does not like. When she won't look at you, it means she is uncomfortable with you. When she says she wants to run, it doesn't mean she is so frightened of the power of loving you and that she wants out. It means she doesn't like you and wants to bolt. And when she tells you all of this, she is more or less hoping that you will piece things together for yourself without her having to hit you hard with an enormous clue bat of emotion. I know this is not how it is in all situations. Maybe 1% of the women who deliver these lines mean exactly what they say. But given how all this turned out, it seems obvious that Mira was in the other 99%. (And lest you judge Mira for not saying what she meant, again, *teenager*! Also, women have a hard time breaking things off. We are taught to be kind, nice, solicitous of people's feelings over our own. It gets easier over time for some of us but not always.)

The above scene segues into Mira and Brown spending the day together. He rents a car and announces that they are going to the ocean. Then Brown spends a day with Mira that was exhausting to read about and must have been even more exhausting to experience. They go to the shore on an overcast, misty day in February, Brown sees a statue that he thinks is a dead ringer for Mira and experiences all kinds of epiphanies of love. Mira, not so much. Here are some descriptions.

> Mira staggered on snow-hillock.

If your girl is staggering in the snow on the beach, she is not having a good time.

> Wind whistled among western buildings.

I am a Texas girl and know little of the wind on the shore in February but if it is whistling among buildings, it is windy and probably uncomfortably cold.

She yells at him that she loves him and evidently she smiles some, and I wondered if she was maybe having a good time, then I read this:

> Wind was pain at my front—grit-cloud blew—in both eyes—slowed pace, turned head until tears washed… Wind roared as if vomited, howling, straight from its heart.

Grit blew in his eyes and the wind sounded like it was vomiting. This is not a good date.

Then he sees Mira as the sun goes down, and she is framed in an orange glow, and he realizes he has been waiting for this moment though he didn't realize it until it happened. The horrible cold, wind, sand and crunching snow don't set a particularly romantic scene for most people, but it doesn't seem like Mira matters as much here as the epiphany Brown was having in the wild weather with her by his side. They have some more dialogue that falls into the *even if it is true it doesn't matter because it doesn't seem real* category (their eyes locked, there was nothing at all but them, and she says, "I felt you, dearest.") and they go to dinner, where he moons over her beauty. Then he wants to get a hotel room for the night.

> She looked out, then half-turned back, face troubled. "I think I'd like to go home. I want to sleep in my own bed tonight." Her voice was softer than usual.
>
> "How come?"
>
> "It's dark out, and cold, and I'm worried we won't find a good place to stay."

So your online paramour has come across the country to visit and you don't want to get a hotel room but would rather make a long drive back home, to your own bed. Perhaps she meant what she said on its face or maybe she wanted to be back on home turf, in a place where she felt more control, because hotels often mean sex and she was not ready for that, not yet, and especially not on a day when she had been taken to a cold, bitter, windswept place without advanced warning. On the way home they "play-fought like kittens." Or maybe she cloaked her intense dismay and irritation behind play-fighting. Or maybe they quarreled for real and Brown is too dense to realize it.

The next day he goes to class with her and then takes her to dinner. Brown's deceased wife had always wanted private tables when eating out but Mira asks to sit at a communal table, effectively ensuring that they would have people around them. Brown initially feels apprehensive but dismisses it, thinking that he was just not yet used to Mira's ways, and he may be correct but, generally, in the early days of dating, women like solitude with their dates. They like the idea of intimacy so they can get to know better their suitor. Perhaps Mira was simply sociable and liked eating with other people, because when they return home Mira declares she loves him. Then again, looking at her words and her actions combined with body language, it is at best a conflicted declaration.

Well, it's conflicted until we get to the sex. After the sex it is clear where Mira stands. Given how desperate Brown behaves afterward, I think he more or less knew where she stood as well, but I don't think he admitted it fully either as it happened or as he wrote this book.

The portrayal of the sexual encounter between the two suffers from similar problems Brown has writing the rest of this book—refusal to use articles, splintered ideas, awkward phrases, endless dashes. In a sense, this is the sole place in this book that should have had such thwarted writing because this sexual encounter is so tense and miserable, and Brown is so unwilling to understand what it all means, that the only way to tell it is as Brown wrote it.

I also think that despite how terrible much of this book is, Brown is to be commended on his brutal honesty in describing this sex scene, and indeed his other sexual failures (in one scene, Brown's live-in girlfriend falls asleep while having sex with him and it sends him on a door-breaking tantrum). This praise may be unwarranted, however, because it's hard to tell if Brown knows how brutally honest he is being. It is hard to tell if he even understands that he failed. In his mind, much of Mira's lack of sexual feeling can be traced to the Celexa she takes for her depression. In his mind, the fact that they failed sexually means nothing as long as he remains the primary man in her life and as long as she shares any sexual intentions before she commits the acts with different men. He tricks himself something fierce and I simply have no idea if it is because he knows he was a man in an early mid-life crisis doing anything to hold onto a beautiful young woman or if he genuinely thinks his behavior made sense. Regardless, had Brown chosen to sexually alienate Mira before his nascent relationship with her had a chance to take form, he could not have succeeded better.

First he tells her that his girlfriend back home had made love to her boyfriend the night before. Mira was shocked, though she smiled. All this openness about his polyamorous relationship may have made sense to him, and Mira had a friendship with Brown's girlfriend, but this is a tense declaration to make when cuddling with a woman. It almost puts Mira in a place where she feels pressure to maintain parity between the pre-mated pair as the "wife" had sex with another and now the "husband" wants to as well. To not have sex with Brown might have seemed like a slight to him as his partner had already moved into a sexual phase with her new lover and he had not yet made that connection with Mira. Not to say it was a pity fuck or that Brown engaged in deliberate emotional manipulation, but the overtones are there.

We get to the act, and here it is that Brown blows it completely, with no awareness at all that his first sexual request is bizarre and unreasonable to make during the first time with a new partner:

My mind fused all we'd felt since our beginning—I pulled back, said, "I want us to come together." Our eyes stayed tight, fearless. "For that to happen," she said, "I'll have to be on top."

It was here that I knew for certain that Brown wrote this with utterly no self-awareness, with no sense of what he was doing to this young woman or how others might perceive him. Simultaneous orgasm is a tall order on a first sexual encounter. It is too much pressure to put on a first time sex partner because it is almost assuredly not going to happen. Mira is game, though, you have to give her that. In addition to putting far too much pressure on Mira to satisfy a demand that is hard to achieve, Brown observes that her eyes are fearless. Fearless? That fear or its absence is even mentioned in a sex scene gives us a view into Brown's id. Her eyes should have been fearless when making love in her own bed in her own apartment. That it is even something that needs to be explained is bizarre and unsettling, or it shows that Brown knows he is asking too much of her and is impressed she is not scared. Either way is bad.

Of course, they don't come together—Brown orgasms before Mira. And it gets worse. He goes down on her, and nothing. He then sees fit to discuss what he sees as a problem with her.

> After two months of perfection we couldn't be wrong here. "Oh no," small voices cried within me, "not this." I breathed against a locked up stomach. "Has sex been difficult?" I asked.

Yes, sex has been difficult. You see, Mira broke up with her age-appropriate boyfriend after Christmas and less than six weeks later has a 35-year-old in her bed, asking for simultaneous orgasms after following her from class to class and taking her to the beach with its vomiting winds and sand in her eyes, a man who expects sexual perfection after speaking to her online for a couple of months. Just when you think it can't get any worse, it does.

> "Would you like to masturbate together?"
>
> Her right shoulder rose and she said emphatically "No."
>
> Shock of confusion. I wondered if my going first would be softer entry to pleasure.
>
> "Would you like to watch me masturbate?" I said.
>
> Of an instant her eyebrows contracted. Frowning, she pulled in her chin and said, "No."
>
> She'd almost shouted.
>
> I turned on my back, stared at ceiling. I'd no idea what she was feeling—for once did not care. I'd never accept sexuality as opposite world with stone rules.
>
> "You seem pretty vehement," I said, not hiding irritation.

I assert that at no point during this book did Brown put Mira's feelings first. This whole scene made my skin crawl. If she didn't want to masturbate with Brown, why would she want to watch *him* get off? She made her feelings pretty clear on masturbation with his first question and when she responded poorly to his second, he pouted.

Not unexpectedly, Mira decides to impose a moratorium on all sex between them. After this declaration, Brown's next suggestion is to ask Mira to take a shower with him, which he describes in detail, none of it sensual, all of it creepy given the context of the previous scene. As if to demonstrate how far from Eden they had wandered, Mira goes to get towels for them to wear to the bathroom though they are alone in the apartment. She doesn't say no to him about the shower, but by this point she has a clueless man-child in her home and has to get through this as best she can. Just because a woman does not throw your ass out doesn't mean she isn't doing whatever she has to do to get through until you leave on your own. As I read about the rest of his time with Mira, I felt her tension, her tiredness, her bouncing back and forth between distaste and then saying wildly optimistic things because Brown kept harping on how much he had invested in this, how it couldn't all fall to shit simply because he sucked in bed. Had I been Mira, Celexa would not have been enough to get me through.

Brown extracts a promise from Mira that she will not have sex with anyone else before discussing it with him and then he heads back to San Francisco, where he decides he is going to quit his job so he can move closer to Mira. It's almost like the five-day disaster had no impact on him. And even if he really didn't process any of it, he had spent five days with her after knowing her for two months online. So of course he wants to quit his job and move closer to her. He then recounts a scene with coworkers that is so sad to read, so pathetic. When I read it, I knew the men were mocking Brown but he just didn't see it as anything but jovial give and take. You see, there had been complaints because Brown spent so much time online at work talking to Mira. He had stayed longer in Boston than he had taken off for. His bosses were pissed. In a meeting with them, Brown quits, citing the new girl he had met in Boston. Not a woman, he corrects the two men, but a girl. Again, Brown describes body language without seeming to get the point behind it, then this:

> Randy and I shook. "Good luck, Tiger," he said, grinning irrepressibly.

And with this, it was official. Brown has no insight into the people around him. Perhaps he did on one level—he certainly quit before he got fired. But as a middle-aged woman myself, I have never heard a grown man call another grown man "Tiger." Kids in baseball games, orange tabby cats... Never a grown man to another grown man. Brown was being mocked. That "Tiger" and that grin held no praise. Randy may as well have said, "Good luck, You Poor Dumb Bastard."

Then what we all know is going to happen happens. Mira's chats become less and less frequent, he realizes she is online but she has blocked his ability to see her active on ICQ, and he can't get her on the phone. When he finally reaches her, she confesses. She had sex with someone else. She had very good sex with someone else. Brown acts immediately and terminates the relationship. He hangs up the phone and hopes that she will call back and make things work.

She doesn't. He checks her blog. She mentions their break up but doesn't go into detail. He checks again. She has deleted the entire blog. She moves on quickly, but he remains stuck to the point that a decade later he writes a book about the whole sorry encounter. He then gets a call from his grandmother who informs him that his mom is becoming very ill and they need to make some decisions about her. He thinks about what has happened to him.

> As Mira had touched me, and I had touched her.

> I would build on what I had lived.

Two months of chat. Five days with her. One horrible sexual experience. A complete lack of connection between his desires and her desires or even their common tastes outside of an affection for Ayn Rand. Then three weeks of torture as she entertained friends, lived her life and found a new lover. He didn't touch her beyond serving as a nice distraction after she broke up with her boyfriend and a prolonged annoyance once she got to know him. He doesn't know that. He has no idea.

So it was all a waste, this book. Missed opportunities to tell stories worth telling. Tantrums and broken hearts and a sense of eternal love based on chat sessions. A pathetic man in love with a girl whom he wants to pin down and keep for himself even as he has no idea what it is that makes her tick. A pathetic man who at the end of all of this doesn't seem any smarter or more aware than he did at the beginning. This was a terrible story, a pointless story, written terribly in a pointless style. I cannot recommend this book to anyone except for those who love reading terrible books to see for themselves how terrible they really are.[5] Sorry, Michael, your book was terrible. It was almost too on the nose for me not to like it and I hoped, sincerely hoped, when I received it that it would not be terrible because to give it a bad review may have seemed like an inevitability. But I read it sincerely and I read it closely. It is a bad, bad book.

Postscript (2017)

Believe it or not, Michael Brown and I reached a reasonably amicable détente years after I wrote this. He has gone on to publish and further curate the

---

5   I call this the "*Wild Animus* effect" and it could be put to good use here. It refers to a book so bad that used bookstore employees are forbidden to purchase copies for the store in used buy-backs.

writings of Mary MacLane,[6] a worthy endeavor I hope to discuss one day. As much as I still dislike his book I sincerely wish him well.

FURTHER READING

Human Days: A Mary Maclane Reader
Michael R. Brown

The Sarah Book
Scott McClanahan

---

6   Mary MacLane was an early 20th-century diarist whose work showed a level of confessional honesty atypical for her time. Brown compiled her works in compendiums, one of which was published by Underworld Amusements, and in this endeavor he shines. It would be a shame had her work been lost. The Brown-edited volume is called *Human Days: A Mary MacLane Reader*. Look it up.

DANDY IN THE UNDERWORLD
By Sebastian Horsley
Harper Perennial (2008)
Original post: 01/28/2010

Why did I consider this book odd?
The cover dragged me in, featuring what appeared to be a cute preppy boy standing in front of cubbies with human skulls in them. One of the blurbs on the back was from punk guru Legs McNeil and Horsley himself says, "I've suffered for my art. Now it's your turn." One of the front page reviews said Horsley had crucified himself as an act of performance art. So it seemed like an odd memoir up my alley—punk, self-referentially amusing, full of drugs and weirdness. At the end, this book was not so much odd to me as so annoying I wanted roll it up and use it to smack Horsley on the nose, but it started as an odd book and this is where I am reviewing it.

I loved this book, at first. Sebastian Horsley, the heir to a large fortune, had a miserable childhood and managed not to be a huge crying baby about it. The first 50 or so pages were interesting, even enthralling. Horsley is clever. He doesn't fool himself that he has much to offer in the way of substance, but he is, at least, entertaining. He fills his prose with one-liners that the average pundit would feel proud to come up with. Take, for example, this snippet:

> After a while I grew bored so I started taking potshots at members of my own family while they played croquet. I'm sure I would have remembered if I had hit any of them but in love it is always the gesture that is important. In this my aim is true.

If it isn't clear, Horsley is talking about his childhood game of shooting family members with an air rifle—and this comes right after he confesses his youthful adventures in arson! He clearly knows what a shallow bastard he is. All gesture and no feeling. How refreshing, I thought initially, to read the witty words of someone so self-involved yet so self-evolved.

He similarly thrilled me with his clever lack of sentimentality in discussing his parents' divorce:

> When a man steals your wife, there is no better revenge than to let him keep her. There was no discussion with Mother and no discussion with the children. He simply hobbled out of our lives. I barely saw him again.

> It was 1973 and I was eleven. It was time for the children to leave home.

This was England. The dogs were kept at home and the children sent off to high-class kennels to be trained.

And more of the same, in discussing his mother's nervous breakdown:

> The feelings of passive suffering which I had inherited through Mother had cursed me with the gift of deep compassion for others. I have always found this repulsive. The problem with compassion is that it is not photogenic… Mother was eventually thrown out of the loony bin for depressing the other patients. She came home to depress her family instead.

It goes on. Almost every paragraph contains at least a bit of pithy humor, with the best of them begging comparison with Oscar Wilde. Such *bon mots*, coming from a man who is a self-confessed dandy, who values looks and tailored suits over any sort of depth or emotional honesty, initially are thrilling. You think Horsley is clever. You love his irreverence. You wish you knew him, even though you know he would hate you for your big pores and denim pants.

I considered Horsley a cross between Oscar Wilde and Sid Vicious with a bit of a Texas beauty queen thrown in for the make-up skills.

Then, without warning, he begins to wear thin. Very thin. The wit is excessive, the humorous pronouncements tiresome, the irreverence a substitute for innate humanity.

I was reminded of Buddy Cole, a fabulously gay character played by Scott Thompson on the old comedy sketch show *The Kids in the Hall*. Buddy plays the parlor game about what album, what book and what person would you would want with you on a deserted island. He selects a Johnny Mathis and Denice Williams album, the book *All About Rhoda* and, for his companion, Oscar Wilde. Initially Buddy and Oscar hit it off well, but within minutes the endless pronouncements of wit, the smugness and the lack of substance tests Buddy to the point that he runs Oscar off.[7]

This memoir is that comedy sketch. In fact, watch the comedy sketch and save yourself the time of reading *Dandy in the Underworld*.

Still want to know what happens? Well, Horsley becomes fast friends with the violent thug Jimmy Boyle. He shares his wife with Jimmy without realizing it. He divorces his wife. He dresses well. He flaunts his wealth until people throw garbage at him as he drives by in a Rolls Royce Corniche convertible, in

---

7   You have access to YouTube, right?

red, with a chauffeur. And he insists he wants it that way. Given what a poseur schmuck he is, that may well be the case.

He gets a drug habit. He gets a few girlfriends. He gets a few boyfriends. He dresses well. He detoxes. He gets another drug habit. He detests fat and unfashionable people. He makes predictable and unfunny misogynistic comments (if you're gonna be an asshole, be original—women smell like tuna, lol, is too low even for the stupidest woman-hater). He becomes a male prostitute. He has a show or two of his paintings. He pronounces love non-existent and expresses his preference for prostitutes (oh god, save us from those who declare love dead and financial transactions the only honest form of human intimacy). He has a crisis with his dad. (He may have gotten disinherited but by that point my mind was wandering.) He goes to South America and is literally crucified, as in he is nailed to a cross. The book ends with him saying:

I can look futility in the face and still see promise in the stars.

And this quote, I assure you, was in no way lifted from Oscar Wilde, who said, "We are all in the gutter, but some of us are looking at the stars." Nope. Not borrowed at all, and I am a bitch to imply otherwise because at no point does Horsley ever claim to be original.

I had no knowledge of anything substantive that Sebastian Horsley had done before I read his *Dandy in the Underworld*, and, really, does one have to accomplish anything in life to write a misery memoir? What noteworthy thing had Mary Karr done before she wrote *The Liar's Club*? Well, she survived her childhood, and that made for a compelling story. Sometimes these sorts of memoirs exist merely because it's interesting to read about the horrific lives other people lead, and there is a certain shock-element to Horsley's memoir. He is the car wreck. But instead being unable to look away from the shock and horror of the accident, you want to look because you want to see what else the dandy will do for your attention. Or maybe it's less like a car wreck than watching a dancing monkey. A dancing monkey with fabulous hair. To his credit, Horsley does not claim to be much else.

Hell, I take back what I said above. Don't save yourself the time. I say read it. Read this book. When you get to around page 75 you'll grow tired, but dancing monkeys need money, too. When you read it, be sure to wear jeans and sneakers. If you're a woman, no make-up. If you are a man, squirt Cheez Whiz from a can straight into your mouth with every page turn. Do the Cheez Whiz part if you are a woman too. Then, when you are finished, take a picture of yourself naked and send it to Sebastian Horsley as a "thank you" for all his hard work in the arts. Realize that no matter how fat, ugly and casually dressed you may be, by sucking down that Cheez Whiz and photographing your dimpled ass, you will have contributed more to the art of the Western world than Horsley ever did. And aren't smug, unearned delusions of grandeur the best revenge? Seb would agree, I think.

THE MAN WHO SAW HIS OWN LIVER
By Bradley R. Smith
Nine-Banded Books (2008)
Original post: 06/08/2014

Why do I consider this book odd?
Smith, as a writer, has an interesting style. Smith, as a man, is a polarizing figure.

Bradley R. Smith may be the only Holocaust revisionist who writes about topics that have nothing to do with the Holocaust. That's good because while I know just enough about history to hold my own in such conversations, I'm not invested in the topic enough to want to read books along the lines of what one expects from David Irving and Ernst Zündel. I haven't read Smith's books about his journey into Holocaust criticism,[8] so maybe that's where he concentrates exclusively on revisionism to the point of minutia. I don't think that's the case, but I'll find out when I read them.

Perhaps Smith has more to say because he has led a far more interesting life than Irving or Zündel, once you remove the legal drama. Then again, Smith has had his own share of legal troubles, and not the kind you might think. In 1962, Bradley R. Smith was convicted under California's obscenity statutes for selling a copy of *Tropic of Cancer*. In 1963, he appealed the verdict and the case was sent back down to the lower courts in light of the California Supreme Court having determined *Tropic of Cancer* was not, in fact, obscene. Taking this anti-censorship stance bankrupted Smith. Regardless of how you feel about Holocaust revisionism, it's difficult to consign Smith to the ranks of one-topic obsessives who are often attracted to dissident Holocaust studies because such topics feed their antisemitism and loathing for institutional

---

8   For a deep dive into this more troublesome dimension of Bradley's strange career, read *Break His Bones* and *Confessions of a Holocaust Revisionist*.

authority. Smith has suffered financially and socially supporting freedom of speech—including the sort of speech that liberals respect. He has gone on record as saying:

I do not believe in thought crimes, in taboos against intellectual freedom.

Perhaps that is what makes this book so odd—Bradley R. Smith is a living intersection of ideas that, on their surface, may seem mutually exclusive. But people and ideas are never wholly black or white. This played out vividly for me as I grappled with Smith's personal politics in *The Man Who Saw His Own Liver*. While I generally have little patience with libertarian ideas, I could see at times where Smith was coming from and could sympathize with his point of view. I think that is because he doesn't cloak himself in Randian-superiority. Unlike many libertarians who oppose taxes while actively benefiting from tax-funded public goods, Smith frames his anti-nuke tax resistance as a quixotic gesture. He mostly just wants to be done with intrusive influences in his life. I can respect that.

The Man Who Saw His Own Liver is a book of vignettes, initially conceived as a one-act play.[9] When you read it as a dramatic piece, it feels much more powerful than a series of remembrances, yet the book still carries a lot of power if it's approached as a series of short stories. Through a proxy narrator called A.K. Swift, Smith discusses his life and his ideas in a manner that is confessional, almost Beat-like in style. Though Smith speaks through a proxy, the details in the narrative so closely mirror his own life experiences that I am just going to refer to the narrator as Smith. This makes things easier because I tried to refer to the narrator as "Swift" initially and ended up calling him "Smith" so often that I just gave up.

Before discussing *The Man Who Saw His Own Liver* in further detail, I want to take account of some biographical information that is not shared in the book, because I think it's useful to understand the scope of Smith's life. If you ignore the time Smith spent serving his country during the Korean War and the time he spent in Vietnam with press credentials documenting the war, his peripatetic lifestyle is reminiscent of Kerouac or Burroughs (minus horrifying addictions and uxoricide). He spent time learning to fight bulls, invoking Hemingway. His personal life was complicated, passionate and strange, and one feels a bit of Carver seeping through in his prose. Bradley R. Smith is a sort of holy outsider, a man who has dwelt on the fringes and remained true to his search for truth, no matter the personal and social costs.

---

9   The play was performed in Los Angeles in 1983 under the revised title *The Man Who Stopped Paying*, to generally positive critical reception. This was, of course, several years before Smith would become publicly associated with Holocaust revisionism.

This sort of odd holiness is shown best in the section wherein Smith seems to play Christ in his green card marriage to Alicia, who serves as his Martha and Mary all in one.

> I married Alicia so she could get a green card, I made her over with one stroke from an illegal wetback into a legal worker. Her income increased substantially with the green card. It made her happy.

> It's not easy having a good-looking wife who is devoted to serving you and not seduce her. So I now have a wife, and a step-daughter, and we're making plans for the future.

Smith urges Alicia to consider divorcing him sooner rather than later for legal and property reasons but "Alicia is deaf to everything but marriage and love."

> Everything I need done she does for me. Everything I want she gets for me. She watches over Mother and Marisol, she cooks and cleans, and it gets erotic. There's no end to it.

> It's frightening.

But Alicia's Martha-like industriousness is married with a Mary-like devotion to Smith. He tries to give her an out, telling her this level of servitude is not necessary, but Alicia will hear none of it. She asks him to let her serve him and he acquiesces to her desire.

> I could feel the heat flowing out of her fingers onto my arm.

> I do not ask you for anything else, she said.

> The implications of the words, the wide-open black gaze, the electric touch of her fingers.

> The heart pounding.

> That's not exactly the way it worked, of course. She's thought of one or two other things to ask of me.

> That's all right.

> I don't mind.

See what I mean about Raymond Carver? There are other very emotional, personal stories in this book, and the best is a longer-form short story at the end called "Joseph Conrad and the Monster from the Deep." This is a heartbreaking story about the death of Smith's two younger brothers, twins, whom he adored and for whom to this day he still feels great responsibility. Their deaths colored his life forever.

Smith's personal life is just one portion of this slim volume. Smith discusses politics and religion in a very simple, straightforward manner. He detests the idea of paying taxes into a bureaucratic system he considers wicked, and Smith's ideas about bureaucracy are not anything new. He points out that the

Nazi bureaucrats who did wonderful things for infrastructure also were the bureaucracy that did their best to remove Jewish presence from Germany forever. That the white bureaucrats in South Africa created the most "civilized" society in Africa and in the process managed to "institutionalize racism and serfdom."

> That here in America it is the bureaucrats who manage the great welfare programs that protect the old and the poor and it's the bureaucrats who run the programs that produce thermonuclear weapons that hold hostage the poor and old in other lands.

> Who hold hostage the children.

> All over the earth great gangs of bureaucrats stand in symbiotic relationship with each other. No matter which nation, no matter which program or policy the state intends to promote, its bureaucrats have sworn their allegiance to it, sworn to carry out its every desire.

The next sentence reveals a lot about Smith. In a world where we make utter villains of everyone we disagree with, from politicians to the jerk who annoys us on community message boards, Smith can see the good in even those whose actions he sees as detrimental to his liberty.

> What do you say to these bureaucrats when you know they are your friends and neighbors, when you know how decent they are?

When you find Smith mentioned anywhere, especially on blogs, you generally find at least two people who consider him to be the worst sort of scum for his engagement with revisionism. They assign to him horrible attributes. They think he is evil. I wonder how many people have wondered what to say of Smith when they realized he was not an anti-Semitic and racist Stormfront cardboard cut-out? Assuming they bothered to find out...

Like me, Smith doesn't have much use for religion, especially its modern manifestations. Here he reacts to a story about a priest in El Salvador who joined the revolutionaries via the liberation theology movement.

> So the priest is going to bless the people who are killing the people for the good of the people. The usual.

> The priest could have chosen to kill the despot directly, the despot is the guilty one, but that isn't how priests think.

> The priesthood today operates on the same rough principles as the Aztec priesthood did four hundred years ago. High ideas in the service of God and the perfectly imagined society, with bloody terror and chaos for the people.

> Bureaucrats, revolutionaries and priests. The age-old destroyers of right relationship.

> They will never understand that there is no way to social justice, that social justice is the way.

They never will understand how means exist concretely in a way that ends
do not.

They never will confess that this is the moment.

Well, sometimes we do need revolutionaries. Social justice may be the way
but many people don't agree and sometimes you have to wipe the slate clean
with a few head shots against a brick wall. But I really appreciate how Smith
places the blame for chaos at the feet of those who cause it, not the ones who
are affected by it.

Smith muses a lot on religion, especially Christianity. His wife Alicia gives
him a Bible and he reads it because of Alicia's influence.

…she told me to read it, that it would help me live my life less foolishly.

That is what I want, I told her. To live the life less foolishly.

Smith ends up mostly appalled by what he reads. It's pretty hard to consider
him an anti-Semite after reading this book, though I guess the truly devout
could turn his distaste for the stories in the Old Testament into a sort of blas-
phemy or anti-Jewish sentiment because he finds components of the Torah
grotesque. But again, Smith knows who is responsible for the evil in this
world—those on the top and their lackeys. The priest wouldn't kill the despot
directly and neither would God.

I started at the Creation and now I'm to the story where God brought the
Jews out of Egypt. It wasn't easy, God had to make a lot of innocent people
suffer, but to God it was worth it.

It's a very ugly story.

Moses and Aaron would go to Pharaoh and demand he let their people
go and Pharaoh would say okay. But later his heart would harden and he
would refuse to let the Jews go.

Whereupon God would jump up in a rage.

God turned the Nile into blood. He made the fish stink. He buried the land
of the Egyptians in frogs, covered Egyptian men and beasts alike with lice,
sent swarms of flies to infest the homes of Egyptian women and locusts to
eat Egyptian crops so that ordinary people would starve.

There is nothing to show that Pharaoh himself went hungry, or Pharaoh's
court.

There is nothing to show either that the Chosen were distressed by the fate
of those God had not chosen.

The link between the liberation theology priest and God himself is undeniable but it's also interesting that Smith notes that no one on either side
seemed to mind much when Egyptians who had not held anyone in bondage
suffered God's wrath while the Pharaoh was unharmed. It gets even worse as
the Pharaoh's defiance drives God crazy.

In the end, God suffered a spiritual break.

There is no other way to describe it.

God went insane and that night He entered every Gentile house in Egypt and tore up every first-born Gentile from his cradle, ripped away every first-born Gentile child sucking at his mother's breast, and killed it.

In all the land of Egypt that night there was not a single Gentile home where the mother and father were not weeping grievously for their slaughtered babies, or a single man or woman who felt himself chosen who did not feel encouraged.

There is a mindlessness, a ferocity to that old story that is unimaginable to anyone with decent sensibilities.

As a myth, this is pretty grotesque. But I always remember the book of Exodus when believers insist that the Bible is the literal word of God. Who could worship a deity that would do such things when He could choose to just smite the person responsible? Who could trust a God who avenged the Pharaoh's earlier murder of first born sons with equally savage infant mass murder? God turned Lot's wife into a pillar of salt just because she turned her head in a direction he didn't like so how come He couldn't just kill the people who held the Jews in bondage? Some members of my family think the Bible is the literal word of God, so I don't say lightly that people who believe this and still worship God make me nervous.

But this isn't just Smith denouncing the Bible as a vicious mythology. He goes on:

We Americans are like the Chosen today, Gentile and Jew alike. Our way of life must be preserved at every cost.

Our children are worth more than those children who have not been chosen.

If we Chosen Ones are threatened, our Government has taken upon itself the right, the holy responsibility, to destroy all those who have not been chosen.

[...]

God and man set it together, in ancient Egypt and modern Japan.

A God-like State with God-like responsibilities. That's what they tell us we need, our Judeo-Christian leaders.

It isn't all dead Egyptians and victims of the atomic bombs in Japan during WWII. Smith can be amusing when he wants to be. One night, he fell asleep while in a holding cell in a Mexican jail and woke up to find someone had taken a dump on his foot.

Squatting over some guy's foot when he's asleep, that's what men think is funny. It's one of those male characteristics that all over the planet testifies to our universal brotherhood.

Crapping on a sleeping man's foot aside, this book could be called preachy. Maybe for some it is. I tend to think Smith is showing us not only the man who saw his own liver, but he is also showing us his heart. There is a vulnerability to this book, as Smith reveals his weaknesses, his disgust and an almost innocent revulsion for the modern world.

I hesitated writing about this book. I get tired of being called an anti-Semite whenever I write about people who are themselves anti-Semites or who question elements of Jewish faith or recorded history. In this sense, the world is indeed very black or white. You toe certain lines, you end up getting labeled. Despite the voluminous amount of content I have written in my life, some people think I'm a racist due to my affection for black metal and some people think I'm a Jew-hater due to some of my friendships. I was called an anti-Semite when, using far politer language, I stated my opinion that Pamela Geller is an anti-intellectual, morally-challenged assclown. The reasoning is that if I dislike an Islamaphobe, then I must support Muslims wiping out Israel. Yet in the same article there was no mistaking my contempt for anti-Semitic ideas. Ultimately I decided there is nothing I can do about what others decide to call me based on my reactions to the things I read. People gonna think what people gonna think, and I'll feel lucky if they actually do think before they condemn me.

But to refuse to discuss this book because I happen to like it and fear the reaction from the usual suspects would be cowardice. It would be all the more despicable given what Bradley R. Smith endured because he believed it inappropriate that the government could criminalize reading Henry Miller and stood up against such intellectual tyranny.

The Man Who Saw His Own Liver is a thought-provoking, touching and at times funny book. It's only 139 pages, the font is large and the untitled chapters are short. You can read it in one sitting. I recommend that you do. I enjoyed this book and grew to like Bradley R. Smith enough that I looked into his background, read some of his other writings, and saw again for myself how it is that nothing is as cut and dried as it seems when social justice is involved. If you read this book and hate it, Smith won't be unhappy if you share your distaste. He fought for your right to do so.

FURTHER READING

A Personal History of Moral Decay
Bradley R. Smith

RAPING THE GODS
By Brian Whitney
Strawberry Books (2015)
Original post: 10/07/2015

Why do I consider this book odd?
It's is the paper equivalent of that asshole you knew in college who drunk-called you at two in the morning to tell you about how he beat up Chuck Norris, had sex with a Victoria's Secret model and wrecked his Lamborghini after inhaling epic quantities of cocaine. For fuck's sake, I want to think it's fiction. I worry that it's not.

Here's a another one I read out loud to Mr. OTC at bedtime until he begged me to stop. He didn't beg me to stop because the book isn't funny and compelling, but rather because he needed to get some sleep. Pretty much every paragraph in Brian Whitney's *Raping the Gods* has a golden sentence, a laugh-out-loud zinger that makes you want to keep going. I found myself reading it quickly in one sitting.

The story concerns Bryan Whitney (the character, not the author[10]), a profligate and depraved writer, who is contacted by Dylan, a completely insane and utterly drugged reprobate, who wants Brian to write about him. You see, Dylan, a man of many unlikely stories, claims to have met God and raped Him.

Yeah.

Anyway, Brian needs the money and agrees to do it. But like I said, Dylan is a lunatic, so you know there's going to be trouble. Since Dylan lives in Samoa with two female sex slaves, his travel options are limited. So, after struggling to meet Dylan's preconditional demands (humorously related in a number of phone calls and emails), Brian flies out to Samoa for some obligatory face-time. He meets the sex slaves, who turn out to be very willing accessories to Dylan's life (more or less existing in the same

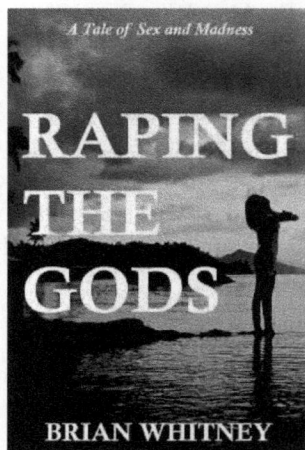

A Tale of Sex and Madness

RAPING THE GODS

BRIAN WHITNEY

---

10   There's a trend I've made note of lately where authors give characters their writing names. It's a bit more complicated in the case of Whitney/"Whitney" because *Raping the Gods* straddles a curious line between fiction and memoir. Though it's nominally the former, I'm slotting it under the "Memoir" heading here just to be provocative.

"WTF" realm as the reader) until the novel ends happily, in a way.

It's not an intricate plot, but the characters are interesting in a really fucked-up way and that keeps things chugging along. Once you're in for the ride, you can't help but revel at how well Whitney crafts absurdity and recreates the cadence of the speech of the damned. *Raping the Gods* is a hilarious book, and I think the absurd humor will allow even moderately squeamish readers to stomach the more outlandish content (though it seems unlikely that *truly* squeamish readers will make it past the title).

As a writer struggling to make a living, Brian Whitney (the character, we'll assume) has ghostwritten biographies of washed up porn actresses. He's not the sort of dude who can handle a day job while writing because, much like me, he's just not cut out for real jobs:

> I had this part time job at one point working for AAA where I answered roadside assistance calls. I got fired for hanging up on people. I would do it in the middle of when I was talking so it looked like an accident. I did it whenever I couldn't figure something out on the computer system they had. I hate looking like an idiot.

So inevitably those who cannot handle the daily grind end up running underutilized websites or ghostwriting for porn actresses or assorted members of Motley Crüe. This background also provides the setup for Dylan, who is a fan of one of the actresses, to make a strange demand of Brian: in order to be given the job of writing Dylan's biography, Brian must arrive in Samoa with a photo of the porn star naked. Naked while wearing a moose hat.

The porn-star-in-a-moose-hat incident isn't the most depraved part of the story but it gives us a good idea of the sort of character Brian is—he's not a man who is often ethically challenged. While he does try to wriggle out this bizarre stipulation, Dylan is emphatic. He overnights a supply of Rohypnol to Brian so that the writer can get the job done.

And because Brian is a reprobate, he indeed gets the job done.

> The photos themselves were a bit of a letdown. I was wasted and it was a total pain in the ass to take off all her clothes. It was harder than I thought it would be. I mean of course I was turned on a little, I gave her ass a few proprietary slaps here and there, but for the most part it was just clothes off, moose hat on, pose her body this way and that, take some photos, clothes back on.

I share this passage mainly because it was nice to know that Brian was not so well-versed in removing the clothes from an unconscious woman that stripping the porn star was, you know, easy. And what was Dylan's response to receiving those photos? I don't know. Maybe he didn't respond. I can't recall because this book really is a collection of drunken bullshit stories that half the time don't even try to sound sane.

Of course Brian knows Dylan didn't rape the gods (or a God or anything that isn't a human female). More or less from the beginning the reader can tell that Dylan isn't just full of shit, but also possibly completely insane. Take this story he tells Brian via email (and it's just one of many stories in that one email and just one of many stories in this entire book—Dylan's stories are the price of admission):

> I remember the first time I saw him he was eating the intestines of a live waitress at Bull Feeneys. He dipped them in the orange sauce between bites, you know the kind they do with the chicken fingers. He then performed a pretty amazing surgery right there on the table, he took about half of his own intestines (don't forget we each have like 3 miles in us or something like that) and replaced hers with his. It was kind of a gross M.C. Escheresque deal, because her intestines were in his being digested and… well, you can imagine how trippy it was at the time. Anyway, he stitched her up and asked her out right then. She of course said yes, they fucked right on the spot, and ended up getting married 14 months later.

Who is Dylan discussing in this vignette? It doesn't matter. Almost none of the people he talks about matter and most of them do not exist.

It might sound tiresome but the Dylan Monologues, for the right sort of reader, are very funny. Luckily I am that sort of reader. I'll get to what it is that Brian walks into when he arrives in Samoa but for the moment I just want to share the meandering diary entries, emails and conversations that spew from the mind of this literary lunatic who got so stoned he thought he raped godhead (and if you want a full account of the story of Dylan raping the gods, you're gonna have to buy the book).

Here's a passage where Dylan writes to introduce his high school diary (spoiler—he repeatedly nails a sloppy MILF named Mrs. Johnson), but not before issuing a bizarre set of instructions as to how his biography should read when Brian is finished:

> As I said, I wrote these in high school. I don't care though. It doesn't all have to be new material. I sort of want this to be a book and kind of emo. Like *Donnie Darko* meets *The Graduate* with a little Alex Chilton thrown in with some Kafka. Also I want it to be street. Kind of like KRS-1 meets Ice-Cube, but the nice Ice-Cube that was in *Barbershop 2*, not the one that hung out with Ren and talked about killing people. That stuff doesn't play as well as it used to.

Some of the stories don't need context.

> I am so sick of the scene around here. It's nothing but fucking L.L. Bean wearing assholes named Brad and brewpubs with beers named after the seasons. It's the kind of town where chicks with tight asses jog along with baby carriages. Even the whores aren't ugly. Everyone's all into fucking emo, Abercrombie and knitting clubs.

Strangely, even the stories that need context don't really need context.

> So I get there and right away I can tell something is off. Last time she gave me like a hoodie and a 25 dollar gift certificate to Applebee's though, so I'm gonna ride this shit out. As soon as I get in there she's all, "Yay Daddy is home, let me take your briefcase!" and "Did you have a hard day? I wish you could sit down and relax but the baby has been very bad and I think you are going to have to spank him while I watch," and all this shit. So I'm thinking she just wants to watch me make the bald guy cry but no dude she takes me in the bedroom and who do I see but Mr. Fucking Johnson. Wearing a diaper.

> So anyway I did it. I mean I fucking did it for hours. He was screaming and crying and Mrs. Johnson was like yelling, "Bad Baby, Bad Baby" and I'm spanking him and all like, "I work all fucking day and come home to this shit!"

> When I left I just walked around and shit. I ended up going down to the wharf and just like sitting and thinking about my life and what it had become until the sun came up. Tonight's going to rock though. I'm like so totally going to Applebee's.

I hate to think what it reveals about me that I find this hilarious. That this ridiculous teenager got roped into being a sexual accessory for this strange couple and that he's ultimately okay with it because he can order some artichoke dip later that night. But I remind myself that Dylan is a liar and that NONE OF THIS HAPPENED ANYWAY, *RIGHT BRIAN?* and I feel less like a degenerate myself.

So Brian makes it to Samoa (but not before he recounts a bizarre story told by a completely unrelated stranger on the plane[11]) where he meets Dylan and his sex slaves. (I mentioned that Dylan has two "sex slaves," right? Because he does. And because Brian sees them and interacts with them, at least we know this part of the fictional part of story "happened," in the framework of the narrative, you know?) One of them is named Staci. She's a big, tall girl, somewhat masculine but still attractive. She's also the only interesting woman in the book so pay attention when she gets page time. Staci's not sure exactly how she came to be Dylan's sex slave—it just sort of happened. Rita, the other sex slave, is a piece of furniture, as in:

> "Please place your backpack on Rita."

Being around Dylan in Samoa proves to be exhausting. But even as Brian's

---

11   Brian attracts weirdos who want to tell him their life stories like Mr. OTC does—seriously, if there is a dude who once fell off a roof and has an interesting theory about the Kennedy assassination and needs to talk about it in a combination tobacco/porn shop, or a sobbing truckstop waitress who just got news her ex-husband was paroled from prison, *they will find my husband* and I will end up hanging out in unsavory places while Mr. OTC nods sympathetically and asks questions that prolong the conversations because he is genuinely interested in these people and their often hapless and no-knock-warrant-filled lives, and this sympathetic nature is also why we have so many fucking cats, but enough about us...

patience with his biographical subject wears thin, Dylan's running interjections keep things flowing (though it's hard to really *flow* when a character is the living embodiment of the Guns n' Roses lyric, "With your bitch slap rappin' and your cocaine tongue you get nothing done!"). For example, we learn of the series of events that led Dylan to a sort of shaman who gave him the drugs that enabled him to rape the gods. As with many shitty things that come to pass in life, the precursor is boredom.

> …the whole time I'm thinking there has to be something more. I mean there fucking has to be, right? It's great doing coke and sitting around trying to see how many things I can find in the house that I can put into Rita's ass. It's great! But that can't be all there is. Listen, here's a fact. Currently there are 33 things in the house that I know of, which can fit up there. And I haven't given up yet. I'm still looking. But I get kind of tired of that kind of thing. It's stupid. There has to be something more. Then one night I met Afasa. He's an important guy. He's one of those connectors you read about, knows everybody, has his fat little fingers in everywhere. He told me about this secret vision quest that the locals do, which they don't let outsiders attend."

And I have to stop right there because this passage wherein everything begins to get spelled out for us is immediately interrupted by Dylan's fractured mind as he goes off on a meandering tangent about the traditional barbecue the locals prepare. Also, Staci flat out tells Brian that Samoans don't engage in vision quests. Brian is tired, bordering on stunned. Following his initial introduction to Dylan, he has betrayed a porn star and flown to Samoa on a flight where a deranged man regaled him with bizarre stories about Charley Pride. And now he's locked in a front-row seat unable to escape Dylan's mad narrative, which could serve as a method of torture in Guantanamo, if only the guy could stay focused.

Yet there comes a moment where we suspect that perhaps Dylan, for all his shambolic mental peregrinations, accomplished something after all—that he did, in fact, manage to see the gods and then sexually violate them. He tells Brian a story cobbled together from Native American sweat lodges and ayahuasca preparation ceremonies and speaks of feeling humbled by nature, and of being afraid.

> "All the fear left my body and I lay there thinking, 'This is really happening. I'm actually seeing God. I'm so lucky.' And I wasn't scared anymore. Later the moon came up and changed the shadows and the face turned and was smiling at me, and I was in complete bliss. I was as light as a feather. And God looked sort of like Uncle Jesse from the *Dukes of Hazzard*, except he was black."

I think ultimately the reason I like this book so much is because despite all the hours Mr. OTC and I have spent at gun shows and truck stops and reptile sanctuaries, vaguely alarmed as yet another man spitting tobacco juice into a Mountain Dew bottle explains how the aliens put a sensor in his taint so they can track his movements (*all* of them, including bowel), I generally find people like Dylan entertaining. In small doses. Dylan is completely nuts but he is also a man who doesn't let reality get in the way of a good story, and *Raping the Gods* is more or less one lunatic Dylan-story after another. I also think I like the way Brian Whitney (and this time I'm referring to the author) shuts things down before they go on too long. The beginning of the lunatic story is always interesting. The sleeping man is taken captive in his bed and raised in a beam of light into a hovering spacecraft and we get the details of the ship and the aliens and—hell yeah—we even get the details of the inevitable anal probe. For everyone who tells this story, take it from me. End it after the anal probe. After that none of us are listening anymore.

Brian Whitney has a fine ear for the ramblings of the demented, recreating flawlessly all the stories told by rest stop raconteurs, drugged-out devils and misery mavens. He distills these stories through Dylan, who, luckily for the reader, only becomes tiresome at the end. Drawing on familiar experiences, Whitney has crafted a short and propulsive work of controlled absurdity, and Dylan is dispatched just in time.

One thing I've only touched upon in this discussion is the utter depravity of the narrative. Brian Whitney (the character) is sort of an asshole and Dylan in his directly observed moments is completely deranged and sexually amoral to the point that he is essentially a cartoon character. In his ramblings he is beyond perverse. I've seen people mention William S. Burroughs in relation to *Raping the Gods*. I sort get that, but I see more of R. Crumb or Dwaine Tinsley in the sordidness. There's a sort of cartoonish licentiousness that is so over the top and in the realm of the unreal that it almost comes back around the underside, rendering itself inoffensive. The humor is spot on, so matter-of-fact and without pretense that it makes the at-times uncomfortable content approachable for the sane and lunatic alike.

Let me add a note about the editing. Initially I was annoyed with the editing, irritated that certain elements of style were apparently ignored. But then, about 40 pages in, I began to understand what was at play. This book is a look at an unhinged, rambling man perceived through the mind of an irritated, exhausted man. Exacting punctuation has no place in such an affair. It also helps that the Brian Whitney title I read prior to *Raping the Gods* was pristine in terms of editing. Form following function, it becomes clear that this book was meant to read as a literary equivalent of a drunken phone call. Also, Whitney's covers always suck. This one is no exception. The cover looks like what you would expect to see on a Polynesian travel brochure from the seventies. It's way too innocuous a cover for what lies in wait on the pages within.

Raping the Gods book is strange, demented, perverse and hilarious. I recommend it.

Further Reading

37 Stories About 37 Women
Brian Whitney

Disgusting Bliss: The Brass Eye of Chris Morris
Lucian Randall

Hustler Presents the Best of Tinsley (all volumes)
Dwaine Tinsley

MADNESS

In a way, having a specific section for madness seems superfluous, given that a thread of insanity runs through almost every book I read and every discussion I write. One of the two books that made the cut for this section exemplifies of the value of the honest mental health memoir. The other is an example of the worst that can happen when people with unacknowledged delusions try to treat the illnesses of others, the mad leading the mad.

DEMONS IN THE AGE OF LIGHT
By Whitney Robinson
Process Media (2011)
Original post: 11/07/2011

Why do I consider this book odd?
In a way it is not odd because psychiatric memoirs are thick on the ground these days. But in another sense this book is *very* odd because receiving an invitation to look into the mind of a person actively suffering from schizophrenia is itself a strange and unsettling experience.

 B e warned, dear reader, that this is going to be one of my trademarked Very Long Discussions with Lots of Quotes from the Book. I'm also going to share some very personal reactions. For those who prefer the tl;dr version: This is a very good book written by a very good writer and you should buy it and read it.

I read a lot of mental health and mental illness memoirs but *Demons in the Age of Light* was the first one I ever considered odd enough to discuss. I very nearly missed it. I had been working my way through a number of mental health memoirs that left me cold, but then I read a very good one—Stacy Pershall's *Loud in the House of Myself*—and my interest in the genre was renewed. That's when an online acquaintance offered to send me a copy of Robinson's book. Had she approached me two weeks earlier, I would have declined.

It would have been a shame to have missed this one because of the often sorry shelf-company it must share. I don't mean to demean the genre. I realize that people get all kinds of inspiration in all kinds of ways that I may find less than helpful. It's just some of these books wear very thin for me. It often seems that the authors, mostly women, are romanticizing their conditions. To paraphrase Elizabeth Wurtzel, patron saint of fucked up women of a certain age, they have fallen in love with their mental illness. The devastation the disease wrought on their bodies, their education, their relationships—it all begins to read like a backstory to some fabulous disaster narrative.

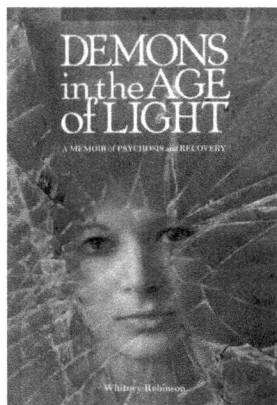

There's also a current theme in mental health studies positing that mental illnesses, or neurodiversity, should be understood as a form of genetic selection for artistic or speculative scientific thinking, and therefore we should celebrate rather than pathologize such conditions. I can see the logic. Not only is there a long record of people with mental illness who created great art and propelled scientific discovery, but, as a person with mental illness myself, I like to think that there is a purpose behind my at times terrible brain chemistry. At the same time, I am made uneasy by this trend. While it's true that Van Gogh left behind astonishing paintings, that Virginia Woolf wrote acclaimed novels, that John Nash was a great boon to speculative physics, would any of us really want to have lived their lives? It's all well and good to see the upside of having appalling mental disturbances, but I often fear that people who are suffering will read such examinations and decide that their affliction should not be treated, should not be seen as a disease that needs to be addressed in order for them to live the best life they can live. As much as I adore Gerard Manley Hopkins' poetry, thinking about the sorry end of his life makes it just a little harder to enjoy the beauty and truth of his words. Art that comes from a truly suffering person will always have a pall cast over it. To dismiss great suffering because it sometimes brings great art is to embrace a dehumanizing perspective.

Demons in the Age of Light does not engage in the sort of art *uber alles* celebration of mental illness that I have encountered of late. Whitney Robinson's memoir gets everything right. She shows the wreckage. She shows how mental illness swooped down into her life and changed everything. A natural writer with a near-intimidating intelligence, Robinson tells the story of her illness (the demon that came into her brain) and how she came back out the other side. It is an erudite, honest and at times darkly humorous look at what it feels like to have your brain behave in ways you cannot control. Schizophrenia is one of the hardest mental illnesses for people to truly understand, and Robinson has written a fascinating book that never once descends into freak show territory. She never attempts to glorify conditions that can ransack a person's life. And while some books offer a peephole view of the at times salacious subject matter of mental illness, there is nothing voyeuristic in Robinson's account.

It is rare.

I was shocked at how much of Robinson's book seemed like it was speaking directly to me: the weight gain from medications, the change in how her family regarded her, the sickening suspicion that a respected psychiatrist may not be able to provide effective treatment. Though almost all mental health memoirs can make a reader wonder if they have the specific affliction being discussed, Robinson's narrative gave me pause when some of my mental glitches showed up in her prose. This was unsettling at times, though one of the few things I can state emphatically about my brain is that I do not have schizophrenia.

Robinson, who is still in her 20s, grew up in rural Massachusetts, a much-loved little girl with atypical parents. Her father she describes as an eco-fascist, her mother an artistic Christian. She was homeschooled and lived a relatively solitary existence until her teens. It's hard to know whether early signs of schizophrenia showed in some of her childhood behaviors, like her tendency to collect small animals into glass jars without regard for their capacity to survive the experience. I think attempts to retrofit a later diagnosis are ultimately futile. Many children interact oddly with animals when very young and it's something they grow out of. Robinson grew out of it, but the impact of her innocent collections would haunt her later, causing her to think herself a monster when in the depths of her illness.

Robinson started her freshman year of college just as schizophrenia really began to take hold of her mind, leading to two psychiatric hospitalizations. Her attempt to make sense of her disease using the intellectual arsenal available to her—philosophy and religion—leads her to call the voice that plagues her mind a "demon." Yet she does not see it as a demonic possession, as some might infer from the title. Rather, her illness was itself *demonic*.

Robinson tells hard truths about herself, using a prose style that seems at odds with her youth. She was an unusual child, but her self-description rings utterly true to me. In an early passage, Robinson remembers being at a body of water near her home, capturing some sort of amphibian in a bucket, when a man began to speak to her in an alarming manner. Robinson, still a little girl when this happened, somehow sensed the man meant her harm and she instinctively ran from him. But that survival instinct was tempered by a strange affinity for darkness:

> Did he want to kill me? A delicious shudder ran through my body. Here was my Dr. Lecter, the closest thing I might ever have. It was late at night, when I found my first love object. My friend asleep beside me on a cot that smelled like cat pee, the television playing out the terrifying and blessed confirmation that I was not alone in seeing the world as I did, full of words like scalpels and jars of eyes and freezers full of human hearts. Sometimes I'd wonder, what if I'd been born into a different body, cast into a different life? What if I'd not been a little girl with golden hair whose mother read her fairy tales? What if I'd been a boy with crooked teeth and a slimy nose, a bastard child no one wanted? What if I'd had an *excuse*.

That fascination with Very Bad Men, the desire to be both harmed and to be a person who harms, is something I am uneasily familiar with. At its core, this fascination with darkness for me was and still is a strange desire to obliterate myself combined with a need to know that if I must, I can do harm. To want to be killed and to be the killer is a strange mindset that is hard to explain, especially when you are, ultimately, given an *excuse*.

Robinson's mental state is hard to pin down, to tell what "strange" thoughts were generated from her illness. Her mind is unique, and without schizophrenia I suspect she would still come across as very odd. These are her thoughts as she is getting ready to go out on a first date with her college lab partner:

> Don't get me wrong, I want to form some meaningful connection with the people around me… It's just that talk across genders forms expectations and bodies are a problem for me. Pale, quivering sacks of blood and bones— they do not compel me to perpetuate the species, or pretend to. Animals have poetry in their shape and motion, but people never really stop looking half-formed, still fetal, even as they begin to decay. There are many words in English for dead bodies, yet none to distinguish one that is specifically alive. I think that's telling.

It might be tempting to file this interesting passage under the tab of "she was becoming ill." I don't think that is accurate. What I think this shows is that Robinson would have had a very interesting mind even had she not developed schizophrenia. It is not her illness that makes her *sui generis*. The illness gave her the topic and focus to write this book but the way she processed being ill is indicative of the mind the illness influences. The atypical way of looking at the world was there all along, I think. The little girl who captured animals and kept them in jars did so because they had a certain poetry to her and she grew into the woman who linguistically found support for her idea of humans as half-formed. That is the power of this particular narrative—Robinson's mind never becomes secondary to her disease, even as she expresses ideas many would consider odd or strange.

The date does not go as well as she would have hoped, though Scott, the lab partner, as later evidence in the book shows, is clearly smitten with her. Robinson's conversation over coffee shows her interests to be quite different from those of other people, or at least different from those of the very normal, seemingly average boy sitting across from her.

> "The only blood and guts I like are in zombie movies, and I'm pretty sure that stuff is all fake."

> "Actually, it's probably pig viscera, too. Pigs are physiologically similar to humans. You can even fool the experts sometimes. Like snuff films, you know, where they supposedly kill someone on camera? There have been a lot of fakes, Some were so convincing that the FBI got involved, but they were uncovered as staged in the end. I think it turned out that the blood and guts were mostly from pigs."

> Scott is looking at me oddly. "And you know this how?"

> "I dunno, some documentary on the Internet? Haven't you seen it?"

> "Actually, no," he says, and I realize that snuff films are one of those subjects you are supposed to avoid on the first date.

Again, I appreciate how much of Robinson's mind is revealed in scenes like this. Because even though this is a mental illness memoir, it is also a memoir about being a highly intelligent, awkward girl. And it is the awkward, intelligent girl having this conversation, not the demon-plagued young woman. This is what makes Robinson's story so appealing—a sense of commonality with an unusual mind, unusual even without illness.[1]

It is subtle, how Robinson lets you into her unusual mind and then slowly begins to show you the disease. If you have ever wanted to read a clear account of what it feels like to have schizophrenia, Robinson will show you. This next passage occurs when the disease is really making itself known. Her mother has rousted her from her college apartment to force her to go to the dentist, and the experience she has in the waiting room is horrific. This also shows some of Robinson's dry and at times dark humor.

> I grab an issue of *Highlights for Children* and take a seat. Inside, I find a garden in which thirteen butterflies are hidden.
>
> Can you find the butterflies?
>
> Can, or will die trying.

The butterflies begin to take on strange meaning to Robinson as her illness causes her to misperceive her environment.

> A shadow passes across the hallway door, gone by the time I look up. Maybe it was my imagination, but the figure that crossed my peripheral vision seemed furtive and distorted. It might have been carrying some kind of sharp instrument. Possibly one with a gleaming metal blade. Something in the room seems to curdle. The receptionist clacks at her keyboard with her back to me. The tapping has an unsettling rhythm, mathematically wrong. I am fairly certain that if she turns around she will have no face. I glance warily down at the magazine. They are liars; there are only twelve butterflies. The last butterfly is a fabrication to make small children go insane. The fish tank gurgles in amusement, a wet, choking sound.

This scene makes my skin prickle because I have moments of strange paranoia where I begin to perceive things that are not there. I sit on the OCD spectrum, which can fuel paranoia at times. I can't recall the last time it happened so maybe I've medicated it away. I hope so. When it did happen, I would see strange connections in books to specific events in my life and I would become convinced that my husband knew of the links when he gave me a particular book, and I would feel like he was setting me up for something, though what it was I feared was never clear. When the strange cloud passed, I could see how irrational I had been, but in the middle of such an episode nothing could convince me. I developed strange aversions to textures,

---

1   As Mr. OTC can attest, there are many young women who do not avoid such subject matter on a first date.

seeing lunar surfaces on pizzas, recurring faces in brick patterns and sponges, and then it would go away and animated objects would become inanimate again. As I read this passage I could feel the uneasiness and fear that Robinson experienced as she pored over the pages of a popular children's magazine, sensing that a seemingly harmless game was actually devised to deceive impressionable young readers. That there was a sinister purpose behind it all. If you have never had moments like this happen in your sober brain, this passage provides an excellent step in beginning to understand certain cerebral misfires.

I have no idea how much of the carelessness and at times deliberate violence Robinson exhibited toward animals was affected by or caused by her mental illness, but I can say her experiences in this regard were uncomfortable to read. I cannot abide cruelty to animals and cannot even really read about it anymore. I forced myself to power through it and read sections in this book that upset me because reading about Robinson's actions with animals was important to understanding this book and her illness.

In her teens, after watching a movie about Jeffrey Dahmer, Robinson decides to kill a fish. She and a friend had an unspoken competition as to who would obtain the most exotic and pretty betta fish. Her friend had bested her and obtained a lovely fish and full of a strange anger, Robinson decides that if she cannot possess the fish, no one will possess it. She spills a bottle of perfume into the bowl:

> The perfume spread through the water in a floral atom bomb cloud, and the fish ricocheted from corner to corner in search of safer waters. After a minute it hung listlessly, fins trailing down in ragged strings. Gradually it began to list to one side until finally it floated on the surface of the water, its lovely fins fanned out like flower petals, now translucent and drained of color. The gills were motionless, dilated and bloodshot, and it soon became clear it was dead.
>
> [...]
>
> Dizzied by a sudden vertigo, it seemed like there were physically two of me in the room and my perspective was trapped between them, a bodiless observer torn between possible selves. One of these creatures was filled with a terrible sadness and the other blazed with savage joy, and I could not have said which one was real.

And here it seems as if the dark other, the demon that comes to haunt Robinson's mind, is present, if not understood, long before her diagnosis. As I read this, I recalled once reading about people with forms of OCD who overcompensate because they are certain they are destructive, killers in disguise. There can be a fine line between those who pour perfume into the fish bowl and those who do all they can to avoid even reading about those who pour perfume into the fish bowl. The voice in her mind brings up over and over all the things that Robinson believes she is—a killer, a torturer, someone to be feared. Despite her collections of animals in jars and killing the fish, I do not believe Robinson's schizophrenia fuels cruelty. Rather, I think her fascination with cruelty when twisted by the demonic voice of her illness becomes something far more sinister than it was, though still very destructive.

Here's a passage in which Robinson does nothing wrong but the disease twists her mind into thinking she is a person capable of doing grave harm. She was babysitting some children when she was a teenager. One of the children pretended to be dead and Robinson's brain went to a place where the child was really dead and she was responsible, a dark fantasy of herself as a killer.

> The girl who was supposed to be keeping them safe locked herself in the bathroom and confronted a demon that happened to look exactly like herself. She called out for the children to go to bed, and for once they listened. She waited for headlights in the driveway, collected her twenty dollars, and never went back.

> It was then that she… that I began to consider the morality of my continued existence. Clearly there was something fundamentally broken in me—in whatever way the brains or souls of Charles Manson and Jeffrey Dahmer were missing some key element, I seemed to have been set down similarly unfinished, a half-formed clay fetish that was animated with the breath of life and the power of speech but not fully human. There were moments when I felt empathy and sorrow and perhaps even love, but they flitted in and out of their own accord—I could not call them up at appropriate times, and in most situations I found inside me only an unsettling blankness, or sometimes the opposite of what I ought to feel. Wires had crossed somewhere, that much was clear.

She contemplates suicide, but without meaning to, she finds a salvation of sorts in animals. They see her by her actions, not the content of her mind:

> It came to me then that as far as this horse was concerned, I was a blank slate. Just one of a dozen teenage girls who rode him in circles each week. I hadn't yanked on his mouth and now I was possibly going to give him a carrot, so life was good. He didn't see me as a dangerous carnivore, he didn't smell the ferment of evil in my blood or psychically sense my black thoughts. His entire concept of me was predicated on how I had treated him so far, a contract extending into indefinite future.

I feared what would happen next, that perhaps Robinson was going to harm the horse, but she is not a monster—just a young woman with mental illness:

> I finishing untacking the horse, fed him a carrot, curried his sweaty saddle spot, and shut him safely in his stall for the night. I went home and did not shoot myself with my father's guns. It seemed like I could still feel the horse's eyes on me, calm and trusting. All of literature's meditations on

redemption might not have convinced me that my soul was salvageable, but in the wordless gaze of an animal who knew not my sins, nor cared of them, I found some sort of peace.

Robinson ends up under the care of a dedicated psychiatrist, and under his care she goes psychotic and slashes her arms. She is committed to a psychiatric ward and feels a blank relief (that I also felt) when the drugs begin to come in ever increasing dosages and the voice goes away:

> To have a drug encamped in one's brain is not so wrong as having another ego there. It acts with no malice, no free will. I close my eyes and am not so sad to have lost my mind. If I can't have it, no one should.

In addition to the sheer appeal of the prose, I loved this book because Robinson's account of her hospitalizations eerily mirrored my own experience in treatment.

> Though my first instinct is to struggle and flail and shatter things until I am free, I force myself to remain calm, not give them further proof that I'm part of the natural scenery of this milieu. Besides, whatever they've given me has possibly had some sort of toxic effect on the ... thing. The voice. Don't give it a persona. The disease of mind.
>
> I swallow the pills.

I've spoken before about my own hospitalization after medication caused me to become psychotic. Like Robinson, I took the pills and they made the voices stop almost immediately, but I was still shaky and afraid. But this is exactly how I got out of inpatient as quickly as I did. I realized that normal to the people in charge meant disengaged, quiet, unaffected, and I took enough drugs, different drugs than the one that sent me there, to fell an elephant. I told the psychiatrist I wanted out so I could vote. A brief political conversation followed, she agreed to let me go home as soon as she could arrange the paperwork (voting and civic duty evidently seemed extremely sane to her). I think many of us fake it until we are released.

Robinson has a startling clarity of how she sounds and reacts, an awareness that I had as well. It's a quality I think many people would never suspect the deeply mentally ill to possess.

> Worse still I'm a biased narrator here, with a vested interest in sounding rational and far more clever than reductionist doctors with Mafia-dark eyes and dark suits worth more than my soul. Maybe I'm not as smooth and logical as I'm trying to sound, maybe my syntax isn't as crisp as all that and my voice is lost among my words. Maybe I sound like every other frightened mental patient...

I was acutely aware of how I looked and sounded. I don't like remembering it. It is very dehumanizing to have a sense of your sanity but know there is no way anyone will hear you because you are Mentally Ill.

More of the unexpected commonality of experiences…

> I had thought my release would be momentous, the free world rushing back to greet me as the vault doors open like the hold of a submarine. But once I'm outside, the return of normal context makes me realize how abnormal I feel inside. I had hoped this might be solved with clove cigarettes, poetry, and strolls in a peaceful garden. A civilized nineteenth century rest cure. Not with horse tranquilizers and unspeakable labels that start with schizo.

Once I was out of the hospital I had a brief, charmed existence because I was so happy to be out. Nothing had changed, really, except I was full of different chemicals that would later become their own horrible problem to be dealt with, and people regarded me differently. I too had some sort of belief in the idea of a sedate, Victorian rest, but really the locked ward was a place where no one could sleep. The constant noise would have set even a sane mind on edge and everyone was freaked out as their med doses changed. One of the nurses had told me to look at it like a vacation. Others cooked my meals, so I guess it was a rest in that regard. Sort of…

Next is the passage that made me worry that these commonalities render me unable to see the whole of Robinson's book as others see it. But I also know that these common experiences show me the truth of her life in a way that some may miss. It's a somewhat funny passage, set as Robinson returns to the hospital for the second time. It could have come from own hand:

> "What are you reading?" asks the nurse, glancing down at the book after I've emptied my pockets and relinquished my Swiss Army knife, which I'd forgotten was there.
>
> "*Twilight of the Idols*," I tell her.
>
> "My girlfriend said those books are good, but I'm not really into vampires."
>
> "Neither was Nietzsche, as far as I know."
>
> The nurse shuffles through my chart. "Are you hallucinating now, Whitney?"
>
> "Um, no…" These admittance conversations are always uncomfortably direct, and one never manages to answer poetically.
>
> "Do you feel like hurting yourself or someone else?"
>
> "No."
>
> "What's written on your shoes?"
>
> "Words to live by."
>
> "I'm afraid I need to take them. The laces."
>
> "What about them?"
>
> "They could be dangerous."
>
> "Because they're long enough to choke someone?"
>
> The nurse doesn't answer, just waits while I take off my shoes and hand them over.

I hated having to give up my shoelaces. I also had to pull the drawstrings out of my hoodie and my sweatpants. It seemed ridiculous, but I found out that a girl found a way to pull her plastic shower curtain down (I can't explain the Rube Goldbergian setup that secured the thick curtains that separated the toilet from the shower in the bathrooms but I can tell you it must have taken a lot of effort and focus to tear it down) and tried to hang herself with it, so I can see why they take away anything that can be used as a strangulation device.

I had my own *Twilight* moment, as well. I was reading Stuart Kelly's *The Book of Lost Books*, an historical bibliography of books that have been lost to history. A nurse asked me what the book was about and I told her.

"How do they even know about them if the books were lost?" she asked, with near contempt in her voice.

"Other writers and historians read and referenced the books before they were lost," I explained.

"*Referenced*," she replied, as if the word were somehow obscene.

Shoe laces and nurses who don't get our books...

If you've ever written "take a shower" on a list of things to do, you will understand why I so liked the following passage explaining life when Robinson was out of the hospital for the second time:

> Each day, I write down a series of small tasks to be performed: Buy groceries, make dinner, twenty pushups, fold the laundry. It seems vulgar to break one's life down into a series of mundane accomplishments—surely everyone of consequence has lived a continuous and poetic existence, no need for daily goal sheets—but it succeeds in filling the hours so that each one passes relatively smoothly into the next, so maybe I have learned something from my Life Skills Training after all.

There is something heady about being a person who just one week/month/year/decade ago was so ill that I had to be in a mental ward and being the person who can now write a list with a pen on paper and cross items out. It seems mundane, or "vulgar" as Robinson puts it, but appealing nonetheless, especially in the face of potential disruption.

Even when there was no commonality of experience, Robinson's astonishing storytelling skills kept me enthralled. The "he" in this passage is the voice, the demon:

> In my room, I face the surrounding walls with the intensity of an FBI agent sizing up a group of murder suspects. But the one will not confess its secret, and the others will not capitulate and give up the fourth wall. There is a charge in the air now that tells me he could say something if he wanted to. This, perhaps, should signal me to take another pill, diffuse the potential. But maybe it's better to have a mind and an adversary than to be empty and alone. It seems to be a question of Which is Worse from those girly magazines Alexis is so fond of. Hair in your food or food in your hair? To burn alive or suffocate in silence? I don't remember that one in *Seventeen*.

I did not stay on the sorts of drugs Robinson was put on for very long, but I do know that so many who have prefer not to take them. They report that it is better to burn alive than suffocate in silence. People who have never ingested anything like Geodon, Risperdal or Clorazil have no idea how preferable it is to be completely mad than to be completely numb, unable to think, to live mentally in a block of ice. Such people wonder why those who have severe mental conditions would stop taking their medications, as if it were some sort of perversity that makes people choose mental illness over the treatment. Because for some it's indeed better to have a mind that tortures you than to have a mind that is empty. Even worse is to have a mind that is empty that is inside a body with tardive dyskinesia caused by the drugs that emptied your mind. But that's a topic for another day.

I think Robinson wholly won me over with this next passage. While it may seem like she is engaging in the sort celebration of mental illness that I find worrisome, she isn't:

> They say that mental problems plague philosophers. John Stuart Mills had a nervous breakdown around my age, and Nietzsche spent most of his twilight in an institution. But maybe this isn't permanent, just an object lesson of a breakdown. Maybe I can still go to one of those old-fashioned asylums where you write in a journal in a walled garden until you are well enough to join the world. And then I'll become a thinker, a writer, something of value. I'll justify my existence somehow.

This is not a trainwreck celebration of the artistic side of mental illness. It is the attempt of a young woman in dire mental straits to find some meaning in what is happening to her, an escape hatch wherein she can find purpose despite her illness. I cringe when people tell me I have an artistic personality because what this means is that I have so many strange mental issues that they assume all my creative endeavors are fueled by my mental tics. The truth is that anything I manage to do I manage in spite of my brain chemistry, not because of it. I may know the mental conditions that plague every artist I admire, but I suspect they justified their existences as well, rather than deifying the chemicals that often interrupted their flow, their fire, their talent.

As I mention several times throughout this discussion, Robinson is a gifted writer, borne from an astonishing intellect. In this passage, she is speaking to her psychiatrist, Dr. Caspian, who is trying very hard to get her the sort of help he thinks she needs but she uses her intense intellectualism to process what is happening to her in a disturbing way (and remember that "he" is the demon in her mind):

> "Well, the other day there was an incident that troubled me. While I was sitting in my philosophy lecture, I was overwhelmed by the certainty that I would truly be able to see if and only if I cut out my eyes. Except don't worry,

I'm not quite that far gone. But he likes vivid images and desires to make them actual. It's an aesthetic thing, he's hopeless that way. Yet I'm not sure if it was he or my body itself that willed this action so deeply. It felt obligatory, like I had to do it, as opposed to supererogatory, which is just like a nice thing to do. But it wasn't so much a matter of deciding what is morally right, but an overwhelming knowledge of what I needed to do next, combined with the physical sensation of being choked by some sinister plant. It reminded me of the categorical imperative, which, um, Immanuel Kant developed as a formula to determine right action."

This passage is important because it's such a fine example of Robinson's invitation to understand. Her description of her mind as she discusses the philosophical importance behind the voice telling her to cut out her eyes is… Well, it's unsettling to see such potential for harm made sense of.

During another argument with the well-meaning Dr. Caspian, Whitney demands to label her experience as she sees fit, even as her brain shows how all over the place she is:

"Yeah, I've read Occam too, except you probably haven't. And to be perfectly confessional, neither have I, but that's beside the point. I get what he was trying to say: Why posit a demon when some faulty wiring will do the trick? But did you ever notice how fond the great minds are of hypothesizing demons? Nietzsche, Descartes, all those physicists. Supposedly they're just to illustrate, but with so many diverse sightings, might it not be more parsimonious to make them real? All the hypothetical demons existing in some realm of universal truth, drinking their blood-laced wine and playing dice with the universe?

There is such a thin line between the disease fueling her intellect and her intellect parsing the disease. I think this is why Dr. Caspian ultimately decides he cannot treat Robinson and refers her to another doctor. There are not many patients who can analyze themselves so clearly and to a doctor who has seen the ravages of the disease, the inability to corral Robinson's mind had to have been terrifying.

Nietzsche is not my favorite philosopher but Robinson finds much truth in him:

My demon offers me the world and in return asks only for my soul, that gemlike point of light we imagine lodged in our meat-based hearts, the only thing that's ever really ours to give. And when I offer this, I will be pure, because what is done for love is always done beyond good and evil.

It's so tempting to argue with this, isn't it? But if one of the world's most revered philosophers' words can so easily be used to describe the bargain in her fractured mind, what exactly is sane and what is not?

Some of the most compelling writing in this book comes when Robinson shows exactly how schizophrenia affects her. Interestingly, this scene happens on the way home from one of the hospital stays, and again, the "he" is the demon, the voice in her head:

> On the ride home, the world passing by the window looks like an alien planet. People walking dogs, chasing taxis, striding along with briefcases and self-important airs. Through a tunnel, I see my face reflected in the glass, pale as a cave-dwelling frog with eerily reflective eyes, unreadable even to myself.
>
> *What have I done. What can I say? Unless I'm deceived, the girl's gone gray.*
>
> Tell me you do not speak in rhyme now.
>
> *No no only when I'm happy. Veryvery happy. Proudly preening on my pretty perch. Prediction is matching up beautifully with the collapse sequence. Barely a trickblur when laid across one another. You're destined for great things, soft-softsoft as butter.*
>
> My head spins with his bright bursts of repetition, helium pitched and unlike anything I have heard from him. Isn't he angry?
>
> *Angry? Certainly not.* His voice regains its knife-edge composure.
>
> *You came back to me.*

What can you even say to something like this when you know it is not fiction?

Robinson also shows the impact the disease has on her family. Holiday gatherings are strange and strained. Her parents seem almost betrayed by her illness, as if it is a referendum on them that their daughter has a mental illness. Most of all she shows the strange guilt that comes from realizing that which you cannot control has the potential to harm those around you.

> I'm sorry," I say finally, my eyes still trained on the unicorn fleeing the urban wreckage. *Silken and swift and silver they streak, they have galloped through yesterday into next week…*
>
> "Sorry for what?" My mother's eyes search my body for new signs of damage.
>
> I close my eyes. "Everything."
>
> *They have all disappeared to the back of beyond and into the flowering moment of dawn…*
>
> "Do you want me to call Dr Caspian?" says my mother, alarmed because I have probably never apologized for anything before. "Do you need to go back to the hospital?"
>
> "No," I say, taking a few steps back. "I'm fine."
>
> Buddhists say that certain souls are incarcerated together into families to force each person to confront lessons unlearned in previous lives. I hope my purpose here is not to teach my parents about the pain of attachment, how all things leave us before we are ready to let them go.

That last paragraph broke my heart a little.

Robinson considers her changed relationship with her parents and the world:

> The knowledge that I have become a person with whom it is not safe to be alone is like holding some wicked medieval weapon I don't know how to use, or want to, but can't set it down. Once you've crossed that line of being a danger-to-self-or-others, are you allowed to come back? Is it a painted traffic line you can cross whenever you've got the nerve, or does a razor-rimmed fence spring up behind you as soon as you've entered the wrong lane.
>
> Here, at least, they give me an excuse for what I've become. They say, your brain is broken. These pills, for as long as you take them, will keep you safe. They are vehement: *You must take your medication.* Your enrollment in the program is contingent on your cooperation. In theory, I agree. Do whatever you must to maintain order. I've violated the social contract in the worst possible way, not in action but in mind and in heart. You've earned the right to tinker with my chemicals. More to the point, they have made me slow, unimaginative, too literal to be seduced by demons or other creatures of poetry and dreaming. Indeed, I am closer to being an inanimate object than I have ever been in my life.

Being mentally ill and having it manifest as violence against yourself should not be a sign that you are dangerous to others, but it is. My roommate at the hospital, upon learning I had attempted suicide (in a particularly bloodless manner, using pills), said, jokingly I think, that she hoped I was not going to hurt her, too. I eventually rejected the idea that they had the right to continue to experiment in my brain, especially since their experimentation caused the suicide attempt in the first place. I found a very good doctor who helped me find the right combination that makes me functional, not sane, and that is good enough. Robinson eventually comes to similar conclusions as she exercises her strong will against the demon and engages in therapy that enables her to cope with the unreality when her disease descends upon her. But this passage on how being mentally ill renders a person thing-like, an entity to be controlled rather than a person helped to live, conveys an important message to those who have never had to decide whether they are such a danger to themselves or others that they may have to become a *thing* in order to repair the broken societal bonds, bonds that they never meant to break.

But Robinson ably demonstrates why she, at least in her own mind, is someone to be feared as a bond-breaker. Take this scene with Scott, the lab partner whom she likes and who likes her. The demon won't permit her to have a relationship with Scott and reminds her of the worst fears she has about herself.

> No, I will not. I will not give in to you. I will grab his hands and kiss him here in the middle of everything. I will fall into his arms as I lose consciousness,

and when I wake up, you will be gone.

His eyes are pretty, aren't they?

They'd look nice in a bottle of formaldehyde.

*You could have them to look at whenever
forever*

You're good with a scalpel.

Scott stares at me in alarm as I stumble and claw ineffectually at the base of
my throat. I am sure a tentacle of vine is going to burst through my trachea
at any moment, like in that movie.

If you know this is what is happening in your brain with a voice that seems
like it knows everything about you, how can you really feel safe?

Later Robinson attends church services, and a young priest performs a
mild, church prayer-sort of exorcism for her. I wondered for a moment if
faith was going to save Whitney from her brain, primitive that I can so often
be, even as I claim atheism. I genuinely believed for a moment that this might
silence the demon.

I stand stupefied before the stained glass saints, not even pleading. Agnes,
holding her lamb, is serene. In my mind, there are lights shining down on
a metallic surface and my scalpel is touching a spongy wad of tissue, trembling because I could not separate it from myself in my mind.

Mary had a little lamb,
Its fleece was white as snow, he burbles as I relive the perforation again and
innumerable times again.

And everywhere that Mary went,
The lamb was sure to go.

I never paid enough attention in Sunday school to know whether it's faith
or grace I lack, but I end my stint as a born-again Christian by throwing a
piece of baklava against the side of the church. It hits Saint Agnes between
the eyes.

The failure of the tepid exorcism prayer to expel the voice does not mean it
is not a demon. Increasingly, I sense that the demonic is too personal to be
absorbed into or dealt with using faith.

There is something to be said for being open to strange or atypical ideas.
Robinson attends an alternative health "expo" and views the crystals and am-
ulets and anti-science methodologies on offer, and comes to the following
conclusion:

I've heard more coherent worldviews expressed in an actual mental hospital, and the Babel of voices surrounding me has the ring of a hundred false
prophets crammed into a room that, next weekend, will be full of computer
geeks or sadomasochists or aestheticians. I leave for my shamanic healing

an hour later with a rose quartz pyramid, a sample of carrot-mangosteen juice, and three books that promise to tell me what this all means, each filtered through their strange, implausible, and yet not perfectly improbable lenses.

I include this passage mainly because I find it amusing and an excellent example of Robinson's wit and her capacity to see all kinds of truths even as her rational mind finds it strange. Robinson eventually finds a measure of peace with her condition using "Eastern" medicine and non-traditional therapeutic methods. The girl who asked a priest to exorcise her is the same young woman who explores all avenues available to her, taking a uniquely strong responsibility for her mental health.

Robinson writes a paper about her experiences with schizophrenia and wins first place in a competition, a feat that many would have found impossible for a person with her disease. She is going to be honored in a ceremony and her parents take her shopping for new clothes.

> We go out to dinner afterward, to some restaurant with candles melting down the necks of old wine bottles, and little dishes of withered olives on the table. It seems like a fancy sort of place, or maybe I've just gotten used to eating from trays. My parents keep telling me how proud they are, but they look perplexed too. I can't really blame them, because so am I. What was I thinking? I've never told anyone, not even Dr. Caspian, some of the things I put in that paper. When my steak comes, it bleeds red juice onto my plate and I hear malicious laughter sizzling in the hot fat. I look down at the knife in my hand, and suddenly I can't eat a bit. I've made a terrible mistake, letting this thing called desire have its way with me. There's no telling what it will want next, what kinds of dangerous freedoms it will demand.

I cannot imagine the fear she must have felt. To reenter society. To be the girl who, even after having the mettle to write a paper and win an award, still hears malicious laughter emanating from beef fat. It has to be terrifying. Just another look into her psyche, a short but meaningful look at the brain of a schizophrenic.

Still, that paper is the beginning of better times for Robinson. She manages to find some stable ground and returns to school and sees Scott, the young man who had been so interested in and concerned for her, with a new girlfriend:

> I kept my head down as I passed. The world is full of others, after all, and in the end there is only so much we can explain to them when their eyes are so close to ours and so full of reactions, like chemistry sets changing their color and acidity in response to every word. Everything is changing, changing, falling apart, putting itself back together again. Suddenly I'm afraid, and I want to go home. I want to have a disease, to be exempt. If I said I can't take this, I can never be one of these bright and normal creatures, if I were to collapse and fetally regress and watch the world pass by from a room that

still holds too many mementos of childhood, people would understand. It's shocking how easily everyone accepts excuses from me now. But after all this it just wouldn't be a very poetic ending, and I don't know of any better criteria by which I should determine how to live. So in a fairly inconsequential action that nonetheless requires more of me than anything yet, I enter the room and find a seat among my classmates.

Reentering the fray when those around you may know that you are ill is hard. Everyone, even if they are not kind enough to offer excuses, certainly will not be surprised if you decide to sit life out. People have an idea of what it means to be mentally ill. This idea has been informed by film, books and other media that paint the most dramatic picture of people who are afflicted. Bipolar girls in mania rushing about in a delicious haze, broken men at the mercy of Nurse Ratched, Angelina Jolie in a New England psychiatric hospital—all images of the disease as it affects people, but no real story of how people deal with their illness.

We need more memoirs like Robinson's. We need more people to tell us exactly what mental illness feels like without all the Hollywood trappings that have been assigned. We need more proof that being ill does not mean one cannot learn, live and move about life, that treatment does not mean that the ill suddenly are well, but rather that even the demon-afflicted can prosper in their own ways as they find their footing and secure the assistance that will give them the most hope in their own lives. This is one of the best such memoirs I have ever read. It is written with quiet hope, intellectual resolve and a refusal to pander. I cannot recommend it enough.

FURTHER READING

Let Me Out: A Madhouse Diary
Amy "Bingo" Bingaman

A Hell of Mercy: Meditation on Depression and the Dark Night of the Soul
Tim Farrington

Loud in the House of Myself: Memoir of a Strange Girl
Stacy Pershall

The Rules of the Tunnel: A Brief Period of Madness
Ned Zeman

LOATHSOME WOMEN: THE WITCHES AMONG US

By Leopold Stein, M.D. and Martha Alexander
Weidenfeld & Nicholson (1959)
Original post: 12/09/2010

Why do I consider this book odd?
The title made me think it would be an odd book. The content bore out my hunch. Some time ago, I saw this book mentioned in an online discussion about weird books. I didn't write down the description but in my notes, I later saw the title and had to order a copy.

Okay, let's get this much out of the way: I don't dismiss Jung or psychoanalysis. But for the love of sanity, you will not find a more bizarre approach to psychoanalysis than you will in the writings of Dr. Leopold Stein. Add to Stein's bizarre approach his barely concealed misogyny and his overt and cringing fear in the face of four mentally ill women, and you've got yourself one odd, or dare I say *very* odd, book. It's hard to restrain vitriol in the face of such a monster, but I will manage. I will not, however, restrain my snark.

When *Loathsome Women* arrived in the mail, I scanned the content and wondered if it was really such an odd book after all. Read in small doses, you get the impression that Dr. Stein was simply approaching his patients' obvious problems by using Jungian archetypes as a means of relating to them. It didn't hit me until I dug in deeper that Dr. Stein evidently believed that his patients were *real witches*, and that he was possibly the most misogynistic writer I've read in years.

But he did. And he was.

Dr. Stein had four patients, Sybil, Judith, Daphne and Dora, with only superficial similarities. In his dealings with each of them, he felt repulsed and at times frightened. My god, this man was easily frightened. He shivered with every "sly smile" these women gave him. He came up with the theory that they were honest to god witches and not just emotionally disturbed women in need of treatment. He never seemed to understand the problem inherent in a doctor feeling repulsed by his patients in such a way that he was frightened by their disorders and disgusted by the women themselves.

At first, I kept clinging to the hope that Dr. Stein was using language in such a way that maybe I was reading too much into it. I kept hoping that he didn't think these women were truly witches, but the text is too specific. We are dealing with nothing other than the delusions of a Viennese-trained

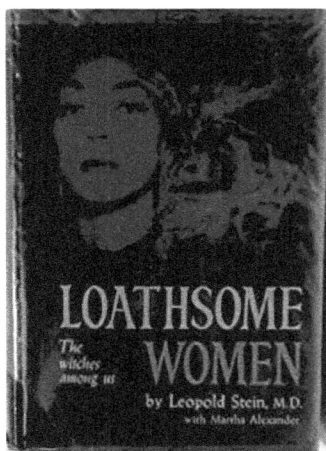

psychiatrist who should really have known better. I wish I could track these women down, if they are still living, to see if they were really cured of their problems. I found the conclusion of Stein's book to be self-serving, to say the least. I can't help but suspect that not only were they not cured, but that perhaps there was at least one suicide among them.

The overarching weirdness in *Loathsome Women* is this: since the doctor clearly thought these women were witches, it makes one wonder how basic psychoanalysis could cure the supernatural.

Some proponents of psychoanalysis may think I am reading the text all wrong, that Dr. Stein was indeed dealing with archetypes. Don't take my word for it. His words give lie to any attempt to whitewash his misogynistic and paranoid delusions.

Judge for yourself:

> I had no way of knowing, however, that there was a far more sinister side to their personalities than was initially revealed. These women led me on many dark and devious paths before my associations with them ended, and the same forces that threatened them came to threaten me.

The same forces that threatened them came to threaten me? This passage demonstrates how bizarre Dr. Stein's mind is. How exactly could their problems come to threaten him, a well-trained psychiatrist? Surely he had encountered toxic personalities before. Surely he was not constantly frightened by them. Surely he hadn't felt their neuroses could affect him. Yet this passage shows that he felt that supernatural—or "sinister"—forces were at work in these women and not that he was speaking about Jungian witch archetypes. An archetype cannot hurt you.

Here Dr. Stein is speaking about his patient Sybil:

> I saw again the fury in her eyes turn to naked fear, and their focus shift from me to some point beyond me, and then, when she did meet my eyes, I saw also the strange, sly smile that had caused my flesh to creep.

> I knew now why this was: When Sybil lay on the floor she was trying the power of the witch; and she would have indeed destroyed not only herself, but also me.

Again with the reaction to the sly smiles… He must emphasize the effect those sly smiles had on him at least a dozen times throughout the book. Ask yourself what sort of psychiatrist feels undone by smiles and thinks a mentally ill but charming woman trying to get his attention, sexually or not, by lounging on the floor could have "destroyed" him? The answer I think is a man who truly feels he is dealing with supernatural forces—or a man whose libido is so out of control he wants to have sex with the mentally ill woman lolling about on the floor.

Here Dr. Stein is discussing his patient Judith, who has become upset and started pacing in the office:

> I had been in similar situations before, and I was sure that as long as I remained aware of what was going on my patient was unlikely to strike me. Yet I was suddenly assailed by a fear so strong that for a moment, I was literally frozen by horror.
>
> Involuntarily words 'Get Thee Behind Me Satan,' passed through my mind, and I wondered at once why I had used them. True, they had served their purpose, for my moment of panic passed.

So, Dr. Stein had been in situations with mentally disturbed patients before, situations that mirrored Judith's admittedly upsetting behavior, but it was only Judith who elicited this religious response. Jungians may say that a subconscious recognition of the witch mythos in Judith triggered Stein's own subconscious invocation of a religious response commonly used to ward off evil, but I think it's less complicated than that. I think he invoked this biblical phrase to avert evil, but only because he genuinely feared she was going to hurt him. That seems the more likely interpretation.

> I remembered the meeting between Sybil and Judith; 'bitch' and 'hag' they had named each other. Could it be that my fancy about witches was not so fanciful after all, and that these two had recognized each other as kindred souls?

He outright admits here that he is actively considering that these women are actual witches. Also, for a man trained in psychology, his interpretation of this insulting verbal exchange is odd. This was a meeting of two mentally unbalanced women with little in common, and they took an immediate dislike to each other. There was nothing "kindred" between them, aside from their mutual animosity.

Here Dr. Stein discusses Dora, an agoraphobe whose entire family died too young, including her husband. She has made a haunting reference to the marble counter in a butcher shop by touching marble in Dr. Stein's office and proclaiming it warm:

> Despite the heat, I shivered. At that moment Dora seemed to me to be a most loathsome woman. I was repelled and completely bewildered, as I had been with the other three women. What was going on?

What was going on was that an extremely mentally ill woman had become a vegetarian after so many people close to her had died, and her trauma had manifested in a horrific, though strangely touching, issue with butcher shops. She had a panic attack before she touched the marble. Most of us would have looked on her with pity but Dr. Stein responded to her with revulsion. Again, he shivers in the face of the odd behavior these women exhibit. I mean honestly, a woman discusses an aversion to eating meat and he shivers with fear. Dr. Stein had to go on a mighty mental trip to demonize Dora, but he made the journey.

As bizarre as all of this is, *Loathsome Women* then takes a turn that strongly supports my theory that the good doctor may, in fact, be a whackaloon. Dr. Stein begins to outline the traits that prove these women, not just acting on the subconscious impact of archetypes, are in fact witches. Incredibly, this comes after Stein's examination of witches in mythology as well as historical witch trials, which he admits were excessive and built on a house of torture, false accusations and false confessions. Those women were not real witches in Dr. Stein's way of thinking, were they? He had pity for them that he could not spare for his patients.

> In studying the sad history of witchcraft, I became convinced that the idea of the witch represented a long and profound psychological tradition—a tradition by no means dead. I was also convinced that my suspicions about my patients were right.

Okay, for minute you think maybe Dr. Stein is not a complete lunatic. Then he blows it. He says that the archetypes confirm his suspicions about his patients. He draws a line between the archetypes and his suspicions. From there it's all downhill into the realm of the utterly odd. Here is where he begins to lay out his case:

> I considered the list of conventional signs by which a witch was supposed to be recognized. How did they fit my four patients.
>
> It was believed that the mating of a witch and her incubus produced a mouse or a misshapen child. This made me think that an early miscarriage might be described as 'a mouse.' Sybil had had six miscarriages, some brought on by herself…
>
> Dora had had a serious abortion of a malformed child at six months, and half-crazy with terror, had induced a surgeon, who feared she would commit suicide if she became pregnant again, to sterilize her.
>
> Judith was psychically sterile as a result, she believed, of using contraceptives. And Daphne was either sterile or habitually miscarried.

This is just bizarre. Verging on insane. I note that he didn't have any concrete information about Daphne's reproductive history yet lumps her into his analysis of reproductive evil anyway.

> Witches were supposed to be incapable of weeping tears, because of their 'evil' eyes. These four women patients had, at one time or another, all had fits of sobbing, yet they had shed no tears.

Sometimes the mentally ill have different ways of expressing deep feeling. No surprise there, aside from Dr. Stein's bizarre interpretation.

> I also remembered that none of my patients like looking up. Sybil ascribed this to her dislike of an overhead light, or any form of glare, which she said made her feel dizzy. Dora would never meet my eyes, but spent her time studying the carpet. Daphne would glance up at me only occasionally when she was being flirtatious. Judith wore glasses and suffered, she said, from constant eye trouble.

> Someone who is not able to look another person in the eyes is commonly thought to be hiding a guilty secret, or is afraid that his evil intentions will be recognized in the expression of his eyes...

Words fail me. Almost. These women could not have been telling the truth, in Dr. Stein's mind. Sybil had come into analysis because she was a severe insomniac. When one has not slept well in months, light is hard to take (I share this from personal experience). Dora was an orphan who had lost her husband, and as a result was an agoraphobe. Of course she couldn't be looking away from him because life had beaten her down to the point that her natural response was to look at the floor. Perish the thought that Judith used those eyeglasses for anything other than hiding behind and that she really did have eye problems.

But wait, odd book fans. Here's a dose of Dr. Stein's bizarre theorizing with an extra helping of either ignorance of women's health or complete misogyny—and there's no reason it cannot be both.

> I was particularly interested in the association of strong odors with the witch. Three of these women suffered from a foul vaginal discharge at one time or another...

> Vaginal discharge may be due to a variety of causes. Psychically, it is often due to aggression toward the male. Trivial occurrences, such as a fierce argument, may trigger it off. So can aversion to the husband, as in the case of Sybil and her first husband; disappointment in women who, like Dora, have romantic ideas about love and marriage; or guilty feelings about pre-marital or extramarital amours, including recent adolescent infatuations and unconscious incestuous feelings...

Yep, you read it here first. Vaginal discharge can be caused by fierce arguments, romantic feelings about marriage and unconscious incestuous feelings. What were we thinking all those years, buying Monistat when we had yeast infections? We should have just gotten some psychoanalysis.

Now we wander into the realm of the woman hater, and bear in mind, these are just snippets—the book is crawling with Dr. Stein's misogyny. I am not one to interrogate books from a feminist perspective, but there is no way to read this infernal book and not react to Dr. Stein's absolute loathing and fear of the feminine.

> ...I recalled that she had told me that she had lost a lot of hair when she had rheumatic fever. Of course it could have grown again, but no doubt she had been afraid of the possible loss of her power over men and had not been able to wait and condemned herself to wearing false hair. Suddenly she seemed the most pathetic sight I had ever seen.

A woman who lost her hair when she had a terrible illness resorted to wearing wigs and he finds her pathetic. It's hard to invoke snark here. Bald women do not navigate the world well. As much as men may fear baldness, women fear it even more because an ugly woman is intolerable to many people. For a doctor to demean a woman who wears a wig due to hair loss when she was sick is... pretty fucking awful, is all I can come up with.

> No longer the poised, self-controlled woman, she stood there with words pouring out of her, making strange, swinging, apelike gestures with her long arms as she told me of her brother's perfidity.

My god, if he's going to complain about an angry woman, he should at least use the right animal. We angry women are like cats, got it?

> I was struck by what she had done to this [married] lover of hers. He had once seemed a kind, honorable man who remained loyal to an indifferent wife for the sake of his kids. Daphne had set out to ensnare him from the beginning. Now the man was a slave to her charms, reduced in stature by his need for her.

Wow. I wish I did know this powerful enchantress. I could use a lesson on how to enslave men to my charms. I could just smile coyly and my grocery bill would be cut in half, so enraptured would be the cashier at HEB. Funny how the married schmo gets off scot-free. It's all that Daphne, vicious little minx that she is.

God, there is more. So much more that I am making myself stop.

Drink in the cover of the book, and the back, which sports a pic of the doc himself. What a catch he must have been to the loathsome woman lucky enough to ensnare him.

FURTHER READING

Phantoms of the Clinic: From Thought-Transference to Projective Identification
Mikita Brottman

Idols of Perversity: Fantasies of Feminine Evil in Fin-de-Siècle Culture
Bram Dijkstra

The Portable Jung
Edited by Joseph Campbell

The Malleus Maleficarum
Translated by Montague Summers

SOCIAL STUDIES

The value of a good book on social issues is that even if it is anathema to your usual opinions, you're given the chance to confront what you believe, weigh it against the content of the book, and see what you think when you are finished. All three books in this section challenged beliefs I thought I held without reservation, provoking reactions that still rattle me a bit when I read the entries.

GUN FAG MANIFESTO
Edited by Hollister Kopp
Nine-Banded Books | Underworld Amusements (2013)
Original post: 06/18/2015

Why do I consider this book odd?
Because it made me remember with fondness the old Loompanics catalog.

So, I read this anthology some time ago and somehow forgot to discuss it, which is a shame because I found it to be a funny and at times uncomfortable blast from the past. I never saw a copy of *Gun Fag Manifesto* when it was originally published as a 'zine in the mid-90s so it was all new to me even as it reminded me of the more humorous excesses of the old Loompanics catalog (and a bit of Paladin Press' more gunnish releases). Sometimes I really miss the old days. Back then if you wanted to obtain and read really fucked up books you had to peruse a paper list of books that got mailed to your house and the catalogs alone often alarmed postal officials. I mean, I don't miss it overmuch because it's nice to hear about a book and be able to buy it immediately but sometimes I realize half the people reading OTC have only ever ordered outré books online. They never got to experience the heady thrill of renting a post office box at a mail drop and ordering books that Focus on the Family insisted were occult and Satanic and also anti-American.

Back to the book. 1994. What a time for all of us who were alive! I graduated from college and started dating Mr. OTC. O.J. Simpson captivated us all with his mass-televised "low speed chase" in that "white Ford Bronco." Nancy Kerrigan got hit in the knee and became a meme that would span decades. And Hollister Kopp edited *Gun Fag Manifesto*. This was a messed up 'zine for a messed up time—unrepentantly politically incorrect, verging into outright sociopathy. And yet, in its own bizarre way, it was glorious.

Don't get me wrong. I'm so liberal I should probably go straight to jail for stealing all your tax money to give to lesbian welfare crack babies. I don't get into racist propaganda and racial epithets make me nervous because I'm not wholly sure what my own ethnic background contains and what I do know is Irish and that's almost never a good sign amongst Americans. But I am also a pro-Second Amendment liberal. We are rare, like white tigers, but we really do exist.

But I'm not a gun fag. I really don't miss the days when Mr. OTC would drag me to gun shows and I would end up listening to John Birchers explain to me why it is that blacks and women should never have been permitted to vote and that things went straight to hell after we started putting fluoride in the water. Yet there is something refreshing about reading words written by someone who is unimpressed by everything I believe socially and politically. You exist in an echo chamber too long and such writing seems like an attack. I find it helpful to take a tour through the other side's ideas periodically. Otherwise I'm just another hothouse flower who wilts when challenged.

As we all know, Internet killed the Xerox-zine star. I know the world seems really nuts now because we have access to so much insanity online, but back in the old days you had to seek it out and when you found it you were less inclined to complain about it. Were these 'zines online, the comments would have to be disabled. It's different with print. Reading this compilation, I was refreshed by the realization that I wouldn't be expected to engage in an argument when I finished. That having been said, this is an extremely hyperbolic collection. A lot of really offensive content got crammed into three issues, and if you can't embrace the weird when it's offensive, you may want to give this book and the rest of my discussion a pass.

Basically *Gun Fag Manifesto* is a dogpatch Julius Evola-esque rage against a modern, soft, leftist machine with lots and lots of specialized information about guns. It is utterly hilarious in the way that your insane racist Uncle Jack can get after he's had a few too many beers—drunk enough to be willing to say all sorts of horrible things with interesting comedic timing but not so drunk you're in danger of getting your ass beat. Or shot. There's a lot of dark humor in this collection, very dark humor, but very funny nonetheless. At times my inner prig reared her head, and sometimes she was sorely provoked, but if you keep in mind context, time and authorial frame of mind, even the most ardent Commie-hating, feminist-loathing, Congress-despising gun-toter would see this as satire, not an accurate look at right-wing reactions to a changing and at times degenerate culture.

In the article "Gadfly Gun Fags," I admit I laughed at the following.

> The swine are gaining momentum. Their cowardly attacks on you and me and on American culture in general have reached fever pitch. Can you believe that the fuckers are going to start suing the manufacturers of firearms

whenever someone gets hurt? Since when do you sue the manufacturer of a product *because it worked perfectly*? (The wife of one of the lawyers shot by patriot and gun fag supermartyr Gian-Luigi Ferri is behind this hare-brained scheme.) We're living in a weird world. What can you do?

Aside from a violent overthrow of the United States government (a tough job, but someone has to do it), there really doesn't seem to be much we can do. An assassination here and there is good for keeping our spirits up, but it's illegal, and like a lizard losing its tail, the media-government just regenerates another politician, and the pathetic zombie constituents vote him or her into office.

WE MUST AT EVERY TURN BE A THORN IN THEIR SIDES.

BE AS IRRITATING TO THEM AS POSSIBLE.

Call your congressman on a daily basis. They hate that. The 29th district (California) congressman is the geek Henry Waxman, and his number is _____.[1] Or send him a polaroid of yourself standing naked with your gun collection (it's a good idea to blank out your face). If you're shy or feeling "inadequate," just draw a swastika over your private parts.

A quick course: "How to Translate Socially Difficult Material." Though the author of this piece praised as a martyr a mass murderer and mentioned complete government overthrow, the real call to action is to call one's congressman and complain. A lot. It's a call to arms and the arms are being completely annoying, not shooting the president or killing all the lawyers. Remember when I mentioned that comment sections on a website devoted to material like this would have to be closed—they would have to be closed because those in my camp would see the mention of a swastika and completely ignore the sentences with active verbs.

I am so tired of a world where we fall all over ourselves to avoid offending each other. Being offended is the least of my worries as a white, middle-class woman. When they really come for you and strip you of your civil rights and force you to carry an assault rifle under penalty of law and *The Handmaid's Tale* becomes a documentary shot in real time, you're going to be too tired to fight because you will have spent all your time being really upset because there was once a subreddit that was really mean to fat people.

The best parts of this collection were "RED'S LAST WORDS"—profanity-laden, stream-of-consciousness ALL-CAP-typeset rants that don't even try to be coherent. Jesus, I am old. It hits me every now and then that in a few years I won't even be technically middle-aged because my branch of the family tree is short-lived. Red's diatribes made me long, and I mean long, for the days when I would receive insane conspiracy theory tracts in the mail, sent with no margins, in all caps, produced on a typewriter because only

---

1   Redacted. Whoever has that phone number now does *not* need to hear from you.

NASA had word processing programs, written almost exclusively by men with very tenuous grasps on reality and a tendency to go off on tangents and never be seen again. Actually, Mr. OTC was the worst offender where these lunatic tracts were concerned but then one day he accidentally knocked himself unconscious trying to use a motorized post-hole digger in Central Texas clay and when he recovered he had lost most of his interest in this sort of thing. He even started voting.[2]

I cannot offer context for the following quote—you can pretty much land anywhere in a Red Rant and it will make as much or little sense as reading from beginning to end. Just roll with it (errors in original):

> ABOUT THIS TIME I DECIDED TO FUCKING BAIL BECAUSE I WAS GETTING REALLY SICK TO MY STOMACH . . . I SAW A PACK OF DESEASE-RIDDEN MEXICAN CHIHUAHUAS DIGGING UP OLD DIAPERS WITH LITTLE MONTE CARLOS AND COORS LIGHT LOGOS ON THEM . . . THERE WERE THREE SPENT SHELLS IN THE BED OF MY TRUCK AND TWO LIVE ROUNDS IN THE GUN . . . NOT ENOUGH SHOULD THE NATIVES BECOME RESTLESS . . . TOO STUPID AND FUCKING LAZY ANYWAY . . . WHAT HAPPENED TO THE OTHER THREE ROUNDS WAS A MYSTERY . . . I CRAWLED THROUGH THE SLIDING GLASS REAR WINDOW SALUTING THE NRA STICKER AND PLANTED MY GRIZZLED FACE INTO SPANKY THE DANCER'S TITS . . .

Yeah.

I think the reason I felt so uncomfortable at times reading this compilation is because it reminded me not so much that I am getting old but that those in my tribe have failed. Liberalism used to be a formidable force of cultural and economic change and inclusion. Liberalism and leftist politics as a whole have degenerated from a lofty place where people fought for political access for all and for the basic human rights of being paid for work without excessive exploitation. We went from being the sorts of people who were willing to die for political equality to being whining messes whose emotions and hurt feelings mean far more than actual political harm. The left has been largely absorbed into centrist politics, so watered down that Obama is actually far more like Reagan than most right-wing advocates will ever admit, and those on the far left are whingers, crying children who will turn on their own in a heartbeat if someone accidentally uses the wrong pronoun for a person whose gender is visually ambiguous or admits to not knowing much about the liberal cause of the minute.

Gun Fag Manifesto reminds me of the last days of liberalism when identity

---

2   This is actually a true story—he still sort of has a dent in his forehead. I recall almost crying, begging him to let me take him to the ER as he stood staring at himself in the bathroom mirror trying to remember the word for "salt."

politics seemed confined to conservatives, when we were still a force to be reckoned with, willing to engage in whatever means necessary to achieve our goals, while respecting the tenets of genuine liberal thought. Now too many of us behave like broken victims who cannot engage in normal discourse, demanding special treatment that shows us for the absurd, self-absorbed, personal political children we have become. There was a recent feminist conference where *clapping* was banned because the sound of palm-on-palm percussion apparently triggered a panicked PTSD response among many of the attendees. Say what you will about Emma Goldman but can you imagine her, or Susan B. Anthony, or Angela Davis (or Joe Hill, or any of the anti-fascist pre-WWII anarchists) cringing at the noise of people applauding? Could you imagine any of them prancing about in their underpants at Slut Walks with "riots not diets" tattoos, while women and children go hungry and are still exploited in this country (and men too but let's not say that too loudly in case Jessica Valenti uses it as an excuse to wear her "drinking white men's tears" T-shirt)? The liberal left in this country and indeed all over the world have become so weak that we expect our opponents to handle us with kid gloves and then we whine when that doesn't happen. We've become such a parody of cringing weakness that not even Hollister Kopp could have predicted how ridiculous anti-gun, anti-right forces would become.

And if it's not bad enough that we've become a parody of ourselves, we are now also literally the worst people ever. We have entire blogs devoted to publishing information about people who have unpleasant views. We contact employers and try to deny work to those whom we find

Thursday, May 5, 1994. A day which will be remembered and reviled for all time. A day of terrible infamy, of deceit and treachery. The maggots in the House got away with it. They passed the now-famous bill sponsored by that greasy little semite known as Rep. Charles E. Schumer (D-NY). This horrid thing happened, we must keep in mind, soon after the bitchy mall-fly Dianne Feinstein gave birth to a similarly revolting bill in the Senate. Now the House and the Senate are going to compare bills and pass into law something truly terrifying, maybe even before this issue goes to print.

THE DIRTY TRAITORS

MUST DIE!

You treacherous commies will someday soon become worm food. You and your disgusting, soiled collaborators will meet violent death. You have pissed off a lot of taxpayers who until now were law-abiding folks. Taxpayers who until now were not considered dangerous. You rotten scum! You vile human tapeworms! You stinking, lousy, chancrous philistines! Just who the FUCK do you think you are? You punks! You rats! You slithering bastard spawn of lowly slugs! By the way, SHITBIRDS, gun sales are booming. What does that tell you?

A page from *Gun Fag Manifesto* #2. This is what free speech looks like.

objectionable. We're willing to condemn an entire family to penury because we don't like it when someone says the "n" word online. We're not talking about people in the media who owe their livings to public reaction or public servants, like police officers—we're talking car salesmen, college students with part time jobs, blue collar men with low-paying jobs. We seem very comfortable with smear tactics of silencing the opposition through denying them work and security, smugly liberal-splaining that freedom of speech is a government privilege and there are consequences for exercising one's first amendment rights. Yeah, we know that. But those of us who aren't digging up McCarthy with both hands also remember that simply having sympathy for causes could once get a person blacklisted for life. I would prefer not to return to such a state of being.

But the hell of it is that many on the left now want the fourth estate completely hobbled if it serves the purpose of never being uncomfortable again, as if this entire country, founded by revolution to ensure individual freedom, exists solely to make sure we never hear anything we don't want to hear. I hate having to use "we" but there's no way to say, "I'm not like them." I may not be like them but they are calling the tune of current liberalism and unless I reject the label entirely, it's specious to draw lines between sane and insane.

In a sense, the best way to support liberalism is to read and engage with books like this and support their right to exist. Perhaps such a stance can wrench the righteous vocabulary from cringing, useless ideologues who have hijacked my political identity so they can live their lives protected by social bubble wrap. Probably not.

It sucks mightily, this realization. It's uncomfortable to see how far adrift things have come for people like me, who remember the liberal promises of old. Things don't have to suck this much but *oh the times, oh the customs.* I'm harking back like a sad old woman.

I guess what I am trying to say is that if you're looking for hyperbolic humor, you'll find it in this book. If you are looking for a representation of the amazing age of the 'zine, you'll find that here, too. On the other hand, if you are easily offended and find yourself triggered by every stiff wind, this is not the collection for you—and I don't want to hear your fucking whining if you read it and end up shaking and crying. I *liked* the humor. I *enjoyed* the memories of a post office box filled with high weirdness. And I don't mind remembering when there was an authentic liberal voice to counter some of the more excessive and genuine cultural bombast in this collection.

Further Reading

ANSWER Me! All Four Issues
Edited by Jim and Debbie Goad

EVERY CRADLE IS A GRAVE: RETHINKING THE ETHICS OF BIRTH AND SUICIDE

By Sarah Perry
Nine-Banded Books (2014)
Original post: 06/21/2015

Why do I consider this book odd?
Pretty self-explanatory.

Sarah Perry wrote *Every Cradle Is a Grave* from a place of philosophical, intellectual and factual integrity. She exhaustively researched the *hows* and *whys* of suicide and procreation and she makes a very compelling case that 1) suicide should be made accessible for people who do not want to live, and 2) that we should at least consider whether or not it is ethical to continue to create new humans whose lives may be more a burden to them than a gift. As she deftly picks apart the arguments against suicide and antinatalism, she bestows upon mankind a dignity and respect for self that anti-suicide and pro-life crusaders deny us as we are asked to suffer and to mindlessly recreate ourselves because of tyrannies of tradition and religious mores.

I very much want to discuss this book in a bloodless manner because the subject matter is so fraught with emotional reaction, much of it knee-jerk, that it can be hard to approach in an intelligent way. When you speak to people whose loved ones killed themselves, you hear them speak of the cowardice and selfishness of suicide. When you talk of people who did not have children, you all too often hear others dismiss ethical childlessness as selfish, or insist that if only one had a child, one would know, *really know*, what true love means. To counter to such assertions with emotion is to piss in the wind because the very basis for avoiding suicide and encouraging procreation is steeped in emotion.

But given my personal history and recent events in my life, I can only approach these topics—especially suicide—from a place of emotion and personal anecdote, and I hope that as I write from my id I do this topic justice. Perry's book really is a paradigm changer, and you don't have to adopt an antinatalist worldview to understand why. It is a book that challenges some of the most deeply ingrained habits of human existence—to remain living at all costs and to spread one's seed far and wide—and it makes the case that our reason and self-awareness are not entirely a great gift, indeed that possession of these faculties should permit us to control how we die rather than be manipulated to keep us living.

There is no way to discuss the entirety of this book. You simply need to read it yourself. All I can do is discuss what I experienced when I read it, and as it relates to my life.

Perry begins her treatise with a critical assessment of economist Bryan Caplan's theory of "free disposal." Analyzing current trends in suicide, Caplan makes a facile case that the mass of people consider life to be a great gift.[3] He states that since it is so easy to end one's life and that there are so many options available to the suicidal person, the fact that so few people avail themselves of suicide proves in itself that life is valuable to us all. For Caplan, the fact that there are so many tall buildings one can leap from (and one doesn't have to worry about cleaning up the mess one leaves behind) proves economically that even though the "cost" of suicide is cheap, people choose not to commit suicide because we as human beings really value living at all costs.

Without the rancor that would accompany my own dismissal of such an argument, Perry neatly tears apart Caplan's economic view of cheap suicide. The costs of suicide are steep, Perry explains. People are not free to do with themselves what they want. The very nature of the secrecy of planning suicide proves that one is not free to take one's life because this secrecy is necessary to prevent people from stopping you from dying. You have to plan to die in secret because it is illegal for anyone to help you, and if you fail you may find yourself locked up in a psych ward, your will thwarted and your future in the hands of people you do not know.

But Perry goes beyond the basic economic analysis Caplan offers. Suicide is hardly a situation of "free disposal" because anyone who thinks about committing suicide knows full well the social burden suicide brings with it. Someone will have to find your body and it's appalling to think of a family member or friend encountering such a thing unprepared. Suicide with drugs is risky and prone to failure but more effective methods are messy and one does not want to think of one's mother or husband cleaning brain matter off the wall. Then we have to face the knowledge that our loved ones will feel utterly betrayed because we crept around behind their backs, making plans to kill ourselves, leaving them holding the bag, second guessing themselves, wondering if they could have saved us, wondering what they did wrong. Did they miss the signs? Could they have gotten us help? They may be angry at

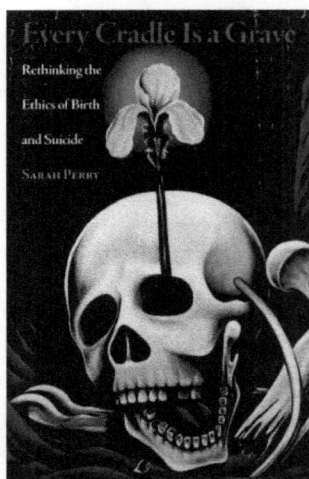

---

3   Just Google "Bryan Caplan" and "tall buildings" if you want to know more.

us for being cowardly, for not fighting to stay alive at all costs. There is nothing "free" about suicide in this world. If it costs us nothing when our bodies hit the floor, the loneliness of planning a covert suicide and the reactions of those surviving us have a cost that many find too dear to pay.

Most interesting to me was Perry's critical analysis of the common notion that most suicides are caused by a person feeling out of options or that life is too hard. Temporary despair seldom fuels suicide. Most suicides are committed by people who feel like they lack connection to others, or are tired of being a burden or fear becoming a burden. Arguably, Virginia Woolf did not drown herself because she could not endure another depressive episode. I think it's more likely that she drowned herself because she could not see putting her family through the ordeal of another depressive episode. It is in this moment—a realization of one's limitations and our impact on others—when the self-awareness that is supposedly a gift to humankind is most evident. In order to work around that self-awareness, we've imbued suffering with meaning, a religiosity that guilts us into remaining alive and into creating more living beings, ensuring that no amount of personal or inflicted misery can ever be seen as a legitimate reason for dying because our suffering evidently ennobles us. It teaches us lessons. It gives us meaning that makes the suffering seem worth enduring.

*   *   *   *   *

I now know there are ways you can tell a person is getting ready to die. Gradually failing appetite. Distaste for being touched. Mood changes. Agitation. Much of what marks a person beginning to die can also be markers for depression, except for one: seeing and speaking to dead loved ones.

My mother confused me for her mother on the phone a couple of times before she died in January of this year. My grandmother died in 1981. She was also convinced my grandfather was in her home, pacing the hallways, looking over her. He died in 1994, and he indeed haunted her.

My grandfather shot himself in the head, dying in a hospital when life support was removed. He shot himself because he was 78 years old and his health was beginning to fail him. I don't know the details but he wasn't fatally ill. He was just an old man who did not like being an old man because he had been so strong in his youth and middle-age. His family was long-lived and he was the baby of his family. His own mother, a vile Irish hag, lived with him and my grandmother when she was old. She more or less turned my aunt into a nervous wreck and wreaked havoc on my very sensitive grandmother. My mother claimed the evil old woman didn't bother her much but Mom never copped to any mental or emotional weakness, at least not around me.

My grandmother suffered for decades before she died in her early 60s and my grandfather was her primary caretaker, even as he worked as a rancher.

He loved her dearly and did not resent his role but it is undeniable that my grandmother's severe illness changed their marriage. He was unable to save much money, and he devoted years of his life to caring for his elderly mother and then his sick wife. It all left a mark. My grandfather married a widow after my grandmother died and lived in her home because he had been a sharecropper (share-rancher is more accurate) and owned nothing but his truck. My mother thought my grandfather remarried because he didn't want to be a burden to her or my aunt, but either would have loved to have had him come live with them. He didn't want any of that. He'd seen how that worked out for him, his wife, his children.

My grandfather had spoken of his older brother Tom, who in his 90s was a dementia patient in diapers. He could see years and years of failing health, with indignity after indignity heaped upon him.

He didn't want to be a burden on anyone. He hated not having financial independence. He didn't want to sit by idly as his body failed and his mind left him. He didn't want to wait around for the worst to happen. So he took care of it himself.

It shocked everyone. My grandfather was a deacon in his Baptist church. He had strong ties to his community and was in his way a pillar of the community. He was quite literally the last person anyone would think would kill himself. Until you looked at it logically.

In the last year of her life my mother was so bitter toward her father. She told me many times she planned to confront him in Heaven, to tell him off for what he did and demand an explanation. She said he could have lived twenty more years had he not killed himself. I asked her why, as a Christian, she could not forgive him. I asked her why she wanted him to stay on Earth in a body that was failing, in an emotional state that hurt him. She would look away when I asked her these questions, never answering.

I know the answers now. She couldn't forgive him because he planned it behind her back. She was angry because she could not prepare. She was angry because she could not say goodbye before he left. She felt abandoned by him, like he had made a craven choice to leave her behind without a single word of warning.

So she was haunted. She spent the last year of her life in misery because she didn't understand and felt angry. I wonder if at the end she began to understand why he did it. I know I do now.

And I wonder how different her last year would have been had my grandfather lived in a culture where impoverished, elderly men who were tired of life and rightfully afraid of what was to come could end their lives in the presence of those who loved them, preparing people for the end rather than planning covertly, going in quiet dignity rather than blowing their brains out in their backyards. She would have had more peace as her own body failed her. She would have been able to remember how wonderful a man her father had been. She could have planned to meet him again with an open heart rather than angry demands for answers. She would not have been haunted by him pacing the hallway, nervously awaiting her arrival.

* * * * *

One of the elements of Perry's analysis that stuck with me the most is the notion that we human beings exchange suffering for meaning.

> Rather than eschewing all suffering, individuals frequently accept some degree of suffering in pursuit of other rewards—either in the form of meaning or in the form of pleasure. The mountain climber or medical student affirmatively chooses to suffer for the purpose of future experiences, pleasurable or meaningful. Others, looking back on times of suffering, say they are glad to have had such experiences. When making decisions for ourselves, there is no moral problem with trading off suffering for pleasure or meaning; it appears to be a social fact that people do not minimize suffering in their own lives.

She goes on to make note of the fact that even though acceptance of suffering is evidently a part of human decision calculus, we really don't have the right to actively inflict suffering on others so that they can later interpret it as a meaningful experience. This is an element of thought important in creating new human beings—when we have children we are effectively asking these beings, who had no say about coming into existence, to participate in this exchange of misery for meaning. Perry questions whether or not we have the right to do this.

This question also comes up for me when a person no longer possesses higher consciousness. We imbue suffering with meaning because of our higher consciousness and self-awareness, but how moral is it to ask a person stripped of any sort of sentience to continue to suffer when such a personal exchange is no longer possible? Well, we tell ourselves that life is sacred and we cannot deprive anyone of life, no matter how little they experience life or how quickly they know they will be facing the end of their natural life. Life has assumed the role of an ultimate good and therefore we cannot help others achieve a pleasant death, even if refusing that death is itself the infliction of suffering.

All of this has led us to a very sorry end. What do we do when we know suffering no longer has any experience-value for the person who endures it? The answer is that many times we use other people's suffering for our own interpretation of meaning. We tell ourselves that terrible things happen for a reason and that if we learn a lesson, then it was all worth it in the end. Another person's misery can be a sort of moral and philosophical journey for the one observing the misery.

* * * * *

For close to fifteen years my mother suffered, and the last year of her life was spent in complete misery as her condition became terminal. I can't even begin to describe what happened to her. The last six months she was alive were torture, the sort I know I simply could not have endured. She had many things going wrong with her body, all of them painful, all of them complex. But of all the things we thought would kill her, a brain hemorrhage was not on the list.

She was already in the hospital for a fall brought on by hepatic encephalopathy and suffered the hemorrhage in the middle of the night, and because the hepatic encephalopathy made her sleep heavily, the nurses didn't notice anything was wrong until she had already lost all her higher brain function. It was not until late the following morning on January 2, 2015 that a scan showed she had suffered complete death of her cerebral cortex and her cerebellum. Had the doctors detected the bleed the moment it happened there would have been nothing they could have done—her blood was unable to clot, so surgery was not an option. We just had to wait for her to die on her own as the swelling in her brain reached her brain stem.

The hospital, which had no facility for hospice care, didn't bother to arrange hospice transfer immediately because they were so sure she would die quickly. We were told it was unlikely she would last much longer than 48 hours. They eventually put her in a room on the sixth floor and the vigil began. The doctors said my mother could feel no pain so no genuine palliative care was offered—they called what they did "comfort care" and very little of it seemed comforting. She was given anti-seizure meds, which we later learned didn't prevent seizures but rather prevented the seizure from manifesting physically and upsetting us. She also was given an anti-inflammatory drug that would help slow the swelling in her brain.

We were waiting for the swelling to reach her brain stem so she could finally die. Why did they give her anti-inflammatory drugs via IV? Why would the doctor who told us to wait for the swelling to end her life then give her a drug that slowed, then stopped the swelling? Because it might extend her "life" longer? Did he think it was something that the family wanted? That inexplicable action prevented her brain stem from herniating and she could potentially have stayed in a coma for years. However, my mother had refused a feeding tube before the hemorrhage, so even though her heart kept pumping and her lungs kept breathing unassisted, eventually death would come in the form of dehydration and starvation.

And that was okay, in a perverse way, because if her cerebral cortex and her cerebellum were completely dead, as we had been told, she wouldn't need morphine. The hospital didn't really take care of her much—they unhooked her from all monitors and didn't bathe her until she had been in her coma for six days and my aunt and I told the nurses we could smell an infection in her skin. But she didn't feel any of it. She wasn't in that body anymore, I told myself. She felt none of what was happening.

But then a nurse told my mother's husband that she could probably hear us, spoke of a pamphlet (that never materialized) that she promised would prove that hearing was the last sense a person suffering brain death lost and we should talk to her and hopefully she would respond. I came into the hospital room one day to see her husband asking her to squeeze his hand if she was okay with elements of her funeral planning. I know now that people who are dying who seem unresponsive often can hear everything around them, but my mother was not temporarily unresponsive while dying. She had suffered complete death of all higher brain function.

I said, "If she can hear us and can respond in some way, then she can probably feel being unclean, she can feel herself starving, she can feel thirst and she can feel pain. If they are telling us to talk to her, then they need to give her plenty of morphine." That didn't happen, but suddenly the posturing common to brain damage patients seemed like communication with a still sentient, self-aware human being. I know my aunt and my mother's husband needed to think she could hear them and I spoke to her as well. Otherwise I was sitting in a dark, fetid room watching what was left of my mother refuse to die.

At the same time I also needed to believe she lost all higher brain function and could sense nothing because otherwise I stood by and did nothing as my mother was starved to death, as she felt pain and fear. This episode showed me how little even medical personnel know about death, about the unresponsive but still living body. It's hard to understand how we can ask people to endure a long, protracted death when we, the healthy living, have no idea what the person in that body is experiencing.

When my mother's carcass didn't shuffle off this mortal coil fast enough, Baylor Irving finally decided to force her husband to either take her home to die, which was impossible since there would be no way to afford the nursing care, or to pick a hospice, any hospice, pick it now or else, and no, she might not survive the transfer but since she's pretty much a corpse anyway who cares, right? Besides, my mother was taking up a valuable bed, one of the two pieces of shit masquerading as social workers told us. She was taking too long to die and they needed the bed and they said this at the foot of that bed while my mother was still in it. The nurse had said she could still hear. God, I hope she was wrong.

On January 9, my mother finally did make it to hospice. She was taken care of by an excellent end-of-life staff. They noticed my mother was making facial expressions as though she was experiencing pain so they gave her morphine. She died not long after her second bag on the 10th. I know deep in my heart what happened—the morphine depressed her nervous system so that her body could die along with her brain. She had had no fluids outside of IV-bags of meds, she had received no food for nine days and the morphine helped end it.

But the hospice could not say this. They could not say, "This has gone on too long. She has been gone for over a week—the woman you loved is no longer in this body. This is killing all of you. This has to stop, so we are going to give her morphine until she dies." That is illegal in Texas. So they had to tell my mother's husband she was in pain, that it was possible she was in pain the whole time, in order to do what can only be called the most ethical thing. And no matter how much I know that my mother was gone, really gone from her world of pain and misery as of January 2, I am still afraid she suffered. That she was in pain. That the woo-slinging nurse was right and she could hear, that the excellent hospice wasn't reacting to brain stem grimaces so that they could ease her out of life. That she felt, heard, smelled and experienced every goddamned minute of it.

Why is it that death is so feared that even the most hardened atheist and humanist slips into magical thinking when faced with it. We tell ourselves a brain stem medically prevented from herniating is a sign of a sick old woman's stubbornness and willingness to fight, to rage, rage against the dying of the light, as if that's a good thing, to suffer and suffer because to die is far worse. Even Christians who believe in the celestial kingdom of eternal life after death mindlessly fight against the mechanism that sends them to their Lord. We see death as worse than suffering, and we give our suffering human attributes of spunk, of strength, of sanctity, because we are too chickenshit to face the reality that sometimes death is better than life.

Since we are too afraid to face death, since we don't even really know what dying feels like, what the dying endure, how the hell can we speak openly and honestly about how suicide can so often be better than continuing to live. Sarah Perry was unspeakably brave to write this book.

I finished a pre-publication version of this book right before my mother began her final spiral in November and it changed how I processed my mother's death. I had little patience for any of it because I could not justify the suffering my mother may have endured and that we, her family and friends, endured. In a sane world, when a terminally ill woman suffers complete higher brain death, we don't ask what remains of her to starve to death. We let her go and we let her go quickly and we do what is needed to help her leave.

You don't have to subscribe completely to the notion of antinatalism to realize that our modern belief that life is the ultimate good in every situation infantilizes us and forces us to engage in cruelty in the name of life, even if we know the life is untenable. I don't know exactly where I stand on the subject of antinatalism but I can say this: there is no moral force in this world that can ever convince me that a suicide entered into sanely is somehow more immoral or irrational than what happened to my mother.

People have told me that I learned something from this, that I am stronger for having endured it. They can go fuck themselves because my mother's death was not mine to learn from. The only thing I walked away from that experience knowing is that if I ever become that ill, I will not wait for the inevitable end. I will not ask anyone to grow from the experience of watching me die.

* * * * *

I am focusing so much on the suicide part of this book because aside from some maternal rumblings when I graduated from college, I never really wanted a baby. I couldn't have had one even had I wanted one, so it all seemed very neatly put together—lack of desire coupled with physical inability. I thought about foster care a few times and even that seemed a bad idea. I suffer from cyclical but major depressive episodes and there was no way then and there is no way now to justify putting a child through it. Suicide and death are what I know. Babies and regeneration are not a part of my world.

Because I am a depressive, I seem to know all too well the burdens of being alive. But I also know the burden that my own suicide attempt put on those who love me. Sarah Perry discusses this carefully in the book as she flays Bryan Caplan's insistence that we have a "free disposal" society where suicide is concerned. Our ties to others often make suicide difficult, if not impossible, even for those with a strong will to die.

> …people do not exist as individual units separate from human relationships and groups. A great deal of the cost of committing suicide faced by a person wanting to die is social and empathetic: it is resonant in the loneliness and grief that his death will cause, or at least hasten, among parents, children, siblings, a spouse, or friends. As social creatures, we begin forming bonds at least as soon as we are born; these bonds, while often no more voluntarily chosen than our own births, are powerful motivations.
>
> […]
>
> The suicide of a close associate is usually regarded as much more than the event of such a person moving across the country and losing touch, even though the deprivation is similar in either case.
>
> Some social costs are artifacts of the prohibition. The suicide must act in secret, sneaking and hiding to avoid detection and unwanted rescue. But who will discover his dead body? It will be especially traumatic for a relative or close friend to happen upon the dead body of a suicide.

For me the most interesting prohibition for those seeking death that Perry discusses is the threat of intervention before death and its repercussions. If you survive a violent attempt at suicide, you will be left in a wrecked body with even poorer quality of life than you had before you attempted suicide. If they find you before the drugs stop your heart, they will bring you back to consciousness and you will likely find yourself in a mental hospital for a duration determined by people who do not know you and for whom the reality of your life will never be clear because they have a single mission: to make your mind better so you won't attempt such a thing again.

And then you have to face everyone who suffered because of your actions.

Caplan's attempt to apply free market economics to suicide is actually one of the stupidest things I've ever read, now that I think hard about it. Only a man who has never heard the song could so effectively mangle the tune.

* * * * *

After reading *Every Cradle Is a Grave*, I went back and reread sections of my old blog where I discussed the before and after of my own suicide attempt. I went psychotic due to inappropriately prescribed pharmacology and ended up in a mental ward on Halloween of 2008. It was bizarre reading those entries because even though I can barely remember much of that time, I also know that what I wrote in my blog were hardly the words of someone completely in the throes of psychosis. I asked Mr. OTC about it and he explained that there were long stretches in late September and October when I was completely lucid. Then a light would switch off and I would become incoherent and violent.

But as I read my account of the hospital, I was struck by how distant I was in my recounting of it. It was horrible. It was far worse than the suicide attempt on both of us, my husband and me. I was completely deprived of will and so was he. A doctor whose own diagnosis of me was completely off the mark was responsible for determining when I could leave and, once I knew that, I marched to her tune and did and said what I had to in order to get out. This including submitting to a pharmacological regimen far worse than the one that had landed me there in the first place. Initially the drugs seemed to help, but eventually I developed something called toxic psychosis from being on a cocktail of Wellbutrin, Prozac, Klonopin, Valium, Xanax, Trazedone, Ambien and Provigil. I was on all of these at once, after having been prescribed the antipsychotic that landed me in the hospital in the first place. I think all the doctors who treated me knew I was on these drugs all at once. I had a printed list I gave to them at each visit. I'm not sure how they let this happen and it didn't end until I made it end, enduring a withdrawal that I don't know if I, even as I am so confessional, will ever be able to talk much about.

I've talked about my suicide attempt on this site before but I seldom discuss the aftermath of the hospitalization. I was fucking insane. I attempted suicide at least two more times and both times Mr. OTC did what he had to do to both save me and keep me out of the hospital because the hospital had made it all so much worse. I am often scared to share this element of my recovery because I fear that someone who is suffering, who may not have a genuine will to die, may read this and think that not seeking help is in their best interest. The fact remains that most forms of help available to me during that time invariably made everything much worse. Nothing got better until I detoxed from all those drugs I was on. I was too scared to go to rehab to get off those drugs (and insurance denied it anyway), given my experiences in the loony bin. From September 2008 through the end of September 2009 I lived in hell and my husband did, too.

But here's what I want people who read this to understand: drug-induced psychosis is not a valid will to die. Now that I am relatively stable, my life is strange to me at times but I am very glad I am alive. But my happiness to still be here is not proof that suicide is a great moral harm. It just means that what happened to me is not universal. Once I was purged of the chemical soup that was killing me, I never attempted suicide again and never again had a definite and clear urge to die. It would have been very regrettable had any of my attempts succeeded.

But that is the caprice of life, is it not? We regret a lot of things. Due to that potential for regret we've decided that we can dictate to a cancer patient in terrible pain, a brain tumor patient who does not want to bankrupt her family in exchange for a few months of life, a person with MDD who simply cannot face another episode, that the possibility of someone somewhere making a bad decision means they cannot make a decision. Your regret, my regret, your best friend's brother's regret are not everyone's regrets. The potential for regret doesn't prevent gun sales. It doesn't prevent divorce. It doesn't pre-vent the purchase of mid-life crisis Corvettes that get wrapped around utility poles. It is puritanical and disingenuous concern that causes our potential regrets to condemn this specific choice. Concern trolling, as it were.

That doesn't mean that you don't want to help a 15-year-old kid who is facing turmoil due to transgender status or a terrible home life. Such a being is not in clear mind—that person needs intervention, just as I did when I tried to die (even if the intervention was not particularly helpful).

What you should do is stop using the worst case scenario—a young person making a bad decision or a middle-aged woman in a psychotic haze making a mad decision—to make public policy that prevents people whose lives are a misery to them and will never improve from exercising their will to die.

But it has to be said: though I recall very little of that year of my life, I do know that if I ever, for any reason, decide to take my life, I won't attempt an overdose. I will use a far more violent and effective method because the after-math of attempting suicide was far worse for me than the act itself. I know for a fact that Caplan is wrong. There are many, many costs to disposal.

* * * * *

I don't know if Perry's book makes me want to embrace antinatalism. I'm not the most philosophical person. But Christ this book made me *think*, and it made me realize that our efforts to make life the ultimate moral good can lead to the most dehumanizing belief-set there is. *Every Cradle Is a Grave* is extraordinarily well-written, even elegant. It is also well-researched and well-reasoned.

And it helped me deal with the death of my mother in a way I had not expected. I didn't have to dwell in platitudes. I didn't have to deny what was happening to us all, watching her slowly starve to death. I could say that what was happening was morally wrong, and I was surprised and heartened when a few others agreed with me. I feel closer to those people now. I feel like there are people whose judgments I can trust should I ever be the one in that hospital bed, without voice to protest. I am very grateful to Sarah Perry for that.

Highly recommended.

FURTHER READING

Better Never to Have Been: The Harm of Coming into Existence
David Benatar

Confessions of an Antinatalist
Jim Crawford

Keeping Ourselves in the Dark
Colin Feltham

Why People Die By Suicide
Thomas Joiner

The Conspiracy against the Human Race
Thomas Ligotti

Swimming in a Sea of Death: A Son's Memoir
David Rieff

We Need to Talk About Kevin
Lionel Shriver

THE REDNECK MANIFESTO
By Jim Goad
Simon & Schuster (1998)
Original post: 01/25/2010

Why do I consider this book odd?
Goad himself, while not full-bore odd, has a special place in my little odd book.

I read *The Redneck Manifesto* a while back and reread it recently. Damnation, did it make me think hard this go around. I initially read it because I walk an uneasy line between two worlds and Jim Goad's book promised a sympathetic take on being "white trash," a perspective to counter the general tendency to demonize the class of people so described.

I got a college education and I come across as sort of middle class, but the fact is, deep in my heart, I am still the little white trash girl I was when I was growing up. My daddy was poor white trash—a Coors-clutching racist who genuinely thought black welfare queens were the reason he couldn't get ahead in life. My mama was poor and white. She wasn't trash, but she was certainly nuts and willing to put up with a mean, mean man for many years. Though we lived in the suburbs of Dallas in a relatively affluent area, I was always acutely aware that I was the "other." The crappy rental house where I lived with bad plumbing, crumbling walls, roaches and, even on a few occasions, rats, still haunts me. It's one of the reasons I am a clean freak now. Growing up, my clothes were not up to snuff. My hygiene, while not bad, wasn't as aggressive as my squeaky clean counterparts in elementary school and I recall a nurse calling me dirty one day. Other kids heard it. I knew she only said things like that to the black kids and the trash kids like me. I bathed twice a day from that day forward, but I was still teased for my greasy-haired past. The resonance of being less than middle class is still with me. I had to work hard to appear half normal, and I cultivated a knee-jerk, extreme left-wing persona to cover up my trashy roots.

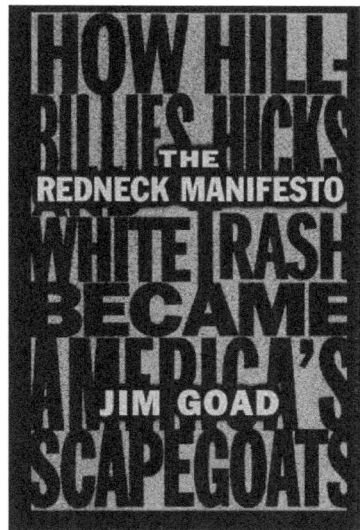

I cringe when I think about my childhood. I cringe thinking about my father. Being white trash and highly intelligent made him crazy and mean, a loser at the end of a self-fulfilling prophecy. The taint of his shame clung to me like the odor of a rotting soul. I overcompensated. A lot. I became pretentious and tiresome. I may cringe when I think about my father but I also cringe when I think about who I was until about age 25.

I can also tell you, in my own dogpatch way, that I've been white trash and I've been middle class. Middle class is better. But you can be both at the same time, and it would appear that I am.[4]

I had just finished rereading *The Redneck Manifesto*, and the next book I read was *Pearl* by Mary Gordon. I have another site where I review "norm" books and I wrote about Gordon's book in excruciating depth over there,[5] but the fact is, I was shocked that such an acclaimed writer—and a Barnard professor—could produce such mind-numbing drek. Anyway, I followed *Pearl* with *Last Night at the Lobster* by Stewart O'Nan, which I loved.[6] This is when my thoughts turned back to Goad's book and I came to understand what might lie behind my preferences.

In *Pearl*, no one works, or if they do, it is the sort of work that does not bear mentioning in any detail. The characters are rich and highly educated. These are the sort of people who can afford to send a daughter to Ireland for a year so she can study language without thinking twice about cost. They travel. When they worry, they worry about how they missed their calling in life, not whether or not they can pay the bills. Pearl, an idealistic young woman, decides to starve herself to death over the "will to harm." She never missed a meal until that point in her life. Nor had she a job, if I remember correctly.

Last Night at the Lobster is a working class novel. Everyone is working. Busting ass. Worrying over tips. Doing hard work for too little money, but for the most part doing it well. Manny, the manager of a failing Red Lobster, agonizes over which staff members to take with him when the restaurant is closed by the head office and only five people can be transferred to new jobs at the Olive Garden. He does not want anyone, even his worst employee, to lose their job.

Pearl was not written for someone like me, and it was sort of a shock to realize that. Yeah, I got an education and have a middle class veneer about me, but the book was alienating. The privileged world of Gordon's characters

---

4   I laughed when I learned that Obama created a Commission on the Middle Class, or some such shit. Don't you be fooled, you tenuous middle class clingers. If anyone needs a commission to understand why it's so hard to be middle class, they're a moron. As Mr. OTC said, if Obama looked to the left, then to the right at every Cabinet meeting, he'd know why being middle class is so damned hard in this country.

5   See: http://www.oddthingsconsidered.com/pearl-by-mary-gordon/

6   See: http://www.oddthingsconsidered.com/last-night-at-the-lobster-by-stewart-onan/

amounts to nothing but a high-minded moral struggle, turning on choices that no one without a trust fund would ever have to worry about. I have no idea what Gordon's background is, but her books are not for someone like me—a woman who has been a maid, who has worked retail, who spent her youth waiting on people and literally cleaning up their shit. All the moral dithering. Who has that kind of time in the real world?[7]

Last Night at the Lobster reminded me of the camaraderie I have felt at my scraping-by jobs. People may look at my husband and me and think we are middle class but, like so many others, we're hanging by a thread. I could go from white collar to blue in a heartbeat. Blue if I was lucky, that is. I related to the work, to the need to do a job well even when the rewards are minimal. I understood Manny. I got it.

Pearl was like a lecture on high-brow literary theory. *Lobster* was like a letter from an old friend.

And I remembered, no matter what, you get raised white trash, you stay that way. It doesn't matter how many "good" jobs I have had or how much money my husband makes. My sympathies will always be with people who work and people for whom life has not been a monied cake walk. It took me a long time to understand this, that my world does not break down the way the world does for a rich, white woman. Class means more to me than race and, frankly, the only reason I can say this is because I am, indeed, white. Being poor and Hispanic or black is not something I can discuss, nor should I even try. All I am talking about here is my own life, my own reaction, and how class made me feel inferior and as if I had to hide, lie and act my way into a way of life that promised advancement even though the color of my skin made it seem as if such struggles were not anything I would have to worry about.

There's a lot to *The Redneck Manifesto* and I hope the historical and social punch in the face it offers doesn't get lost in my personal reaction. While there is likely no one on the planet who agrees with everything Jim Goad says, myself included, I found myself much more receptive to his arguments on this second reading, with *Pearl* and *Last Night at the Lobster* on my mind. Goad's book is interestingly researched, with source cites that run from Edward Abbey to Howard Zinn. The first third reads as an alternative history lesson, and it made perfect sense when I first read it, even if the implications didn't fully register. Essentially, Goad's historical summation challenges an extreme leftist notion of continuous, uninterrupted white privilege, and that is heresy. The middle third presents a look at the contemporary mores of the working class/white trash culture. The last third advances a sociological account of how, in America, where we all wanna get rich or die trying, no one

---

7   And yes, as a person who now churns out thousands of words weekly pontificating over books, I can see the hilarity in that statement.

seems to get the fact that when those of us at the bottom of the social order snap at each other's necks, we play into the hands of the powers that keep us down.

My husband's family, the Clarks, came to America as deported criminals from Britain and were indentured "servants" until laws prohibited it. They were regarded as such an unsavory lot that the Clarks who came over with money in their pockets added an "e" to the end of their surname to try to get some respect. My family tree is less clear. All I know is that my mother's family was a bunch of micks who came over and faced the same NINA bullshit that plagued the Irish for decades. I was raised to believe I'm an indirect descendant of the Dalton Gang, but a few minutes of online sleuthing showed that to be false. Neither of our families came to this country with any level of glory, and it's clear that our ancestors suffered greatly after they arrived.

Knowing all of this on a personal level, how did I convince myself—a white woman who was called trash to her face as a child and teenager—that I have anything approaching the uninterrupted white privilege that elements of society insist I must have had? I don't know, but I believed it. *The Redneck Manifesto* is a nice little reminder that privilege is in the eye of the beholder, and I know from personal experience that denying the idea of continual white privilege can get you called a racist. So it goes.

Goad's history lesson is a tough pill for those who insist there is white privilege that uniformly protects all white people. I recall in junior high my American history teacher, Mrs. Wurst, explaining that indentured servants were people who were simply too poor to come to America on their own so they traded five years of being a servant—and what a genteel idea such servitude was, polishing the sir's shoes and occasionally washing a pot—in exchange for passage. Goad covers what she left out—that years and years could be added onto the servitude contract for the slightest infraction, that female servants were raped and their children held in servitude, that families were separated, that many white people died on their own middle passage.[8] I was taught that indentured servants lived an *Upstairs/Downstairs* existence and then danced their way into excellent opportunity when their contracts were fulfilled. Neat, huh?

Goad does not discount the very real horror of the African slave trade. He doesn't have to invalidate the experience of others to tell the stories of white people whose horrible beginnings set them up to become part of the permanent economic underclass in the United States. But he does explain in detail

---

8   Mrs. Wurst also taught us kids that black slaves were not treated so bad because as property, they needed to be taken care of because who in their right mind would misuse property, right? Increasingly, all education seems to be is an apology for power and a denial of the wrongs done by those with power. But I digress.

why the notion that whites have always had it so very good is misguided at best. This is not at all just a "who had it worse" competition. Though Goad candidly discusses race, his real subject is class. *The Redneck Manifesto* is a book about power and those who don't have it.

Goad doesn't pull any punches in discussing the habits of rednecks and white trash, including antics that cause more refined white people to sneer. The hard partying attitude of white trash is thusly summed up:

> When you die, your sphincter muscles relax to the point where you empty your bowels. While alive, you instinctively maintain enough anal tension to hold it all in. Redneck leisure is the same way—it releases tension, but it's careful not to release too much. Most people would lose all stability in their lives if they ever jumped off the carousel. When there's no way to get off the merry-go-round, you'd better learn to enjoy being dizzy... What seems like self-sabotage may actually be a flexing of the survival instinct. It's a battle mentality. You're a weekend warrior. Traumas and hangovers and hospital stitches are there as equalizers. All this spilled blood and broken glass is not as nihilistic as it looks. It's a subconscious way of maintaining the work vibe. By winding up in jail Saturday morning with a headache and a black eye, you're actually preparing yourself for work on Monday... You have to be crazy to take orders from a boss. It isn't natural. So staying fucked up is a way of hooking yourself on the work vibe. Keeping yourself agitated and off center. Hair o' the boss that bit you.

As a Southern Baptist refugee, I have little time for religion or those who spout it, but I respect sincerity. So Goad's take on white trash religion resonates with me:

> In a cultural sandbox saturated with postmodern smugness and hollow irony, I give high grades to anything that is literal-minded and heartfelt. I'm not worried so much about the veracity or falsehood of the beliefs in question; I'm just impressed that they MEAN it, mannnn... I enjoy religion that arises more from a compulsion than an obligation. More from a need for answers than a desire to conform. A religion of extreme emotion and desperate escapism. Religion unashamed of sweat and melodrama. Religion as it should be.

Goad himself has little use for religion or idol worship. Without the whiff of latent Marxism that such a statement ordinarily betrays, he writes:

> Religion has always been a sponge mop to absorb class tensions. It's a safety valve. Without it, class matters would come much more sharply into focus. Those who belittle pork-faced stupid rednecks and their primitive caveman religions should be HAPPY that the trash has been placated with false creeds and phony promises. For if these hard-core believers were ever to focus their gaze earthward, they might realize how badly they've been screwed and would turn from reactionary religion to radical politics.

Goad's discussion of the militia movement feels a bit dated in a post-9/11 world where the fear of Muslims and Islamic terrorist cells have largely re-placed fear of the Posse Comitatus. These days, some small militias, like the Minutemen who took border patrol into their own armed hands, have even received positive media coverage. But I have to be honest and say that my finger is no longer on the pulse of American militias. Ruby Ridge is a distant memory to many and Tim McVeigh turned out to be a piker when we saw what a few organized Islamist extremists were capable of. All I know nowa-days is that militia women (and Mormons and extreme Christians) seem to be the only ones left who know how to can food and sew clothing. When I get stumped on some domestic matter, I find them out there in cyberspace, explaining the traditions and crafts that have otherwise been forgotten. I'm also less dismissive than many liberals of the right to bear arms element in all of this. Recent shut downs of gun shows in my own neck of the woods[9] may bring the Birchers out of the woodwork, but old-school Second Amendment believers like me are just as pissed off. Who knows? Power is scared to fuck-ing death of people who don't mind guns and know how to use them. Maybe you bristle at the association with Alex Jones, but I can't argue with his fear of power. (He's an entertaining loon and, on occasion, correct.)

I think the best parts of *The Redneck Manifesto* are in the concluding chap-ters, where Goad just fucking breaks it down:

> Of COURSE it's a conspiracy. But it isn't the Mau Mau or the Klan. Not the Nazis nor the Jews. It isn't the extreme left or the far right, nor any of the noncommittal nobodies who cower in the middle… It's POWER, stupid. It's the tendency of human nature, left to itself, to try to get away with any-thing it can. The government is the biggest liar because it has the biggest REASON to lie. It's perfectly understandable. Those with money and influ-ence want to protect it… It's just the way that money flows.

This is a challenging book. It posed a challenge to prevailing presumptions about class and race when Goad wrote it in the 90s, and it remains relevant today. It forces people, especially people like me who have largely tried to block out their less than illustrious upbringings and assume an identity that makes them uneasy, to look at the way things really are, to admit that class exists and that the class structure in this country can make life very hard on those at the bottom. Yet there is a segment of the liberal consciousness that simply refuses to believe this, that insists against all contrary evidence that white people at the bottom are not worthy of the same compassion that is extended toward people of color.

Goad discusses this in detail when he writes of the author Harriet Beecher

---

9   In early 2010, Austin Police and the ATF joined forces to shut down gun shows in central Texas. ICE became involved due to fears of illegal immigrants obtaining guns at the shows. The reason this rankled law-abiding citizens is because the illegal activity—selling guns to felons—that spurred the shutdown had occurred previously by an unrelated vendor who had leased gun sale space. People saw through the ruse. For a more detailed account, visit the gun boards.

Stowe, who wrote *Uncle Tom's Cabin* to bemoan the state of slavery when endangered white workers and children laborers were in her own backyard. She ignored the underclass in the North in favor of the underclass in the South. In 1853 she visited the Duchess of Sutherland in Great Britain, and was praised for her work with the anti-slavery movement in America. In return for their hospitality, she called the Duchess and her family "enlightened." In 1811, the Sutherlands began displacing Scottish peasants who lived on 800,000 acres of land, taking 794,000 acres for themselves. They deployed the British authorities to run off the peasants who had lived there for generations, sometimes even burning them out. People starved and approximately 15,000 people were left homeless. Yet the Duchess cried over the plight of black slaves across the ocean. The great thinkers of her time called her and those like her out:

> Karl Marx called the Duchess of Sutherland's brand of charity "a philanthropy which chooses its objects as far distant from home as possible, and rather on that than on this side of the ocean." Charles Dickens referred to the British Negro Uplift parlor-game societies as "telescopic charity," since they focused overseas while ignoring death and starvation within their own shadows.

> The modern white liberal is the same way… In their eagerness to help oppressed peoples across the oceans, they leapfrog right over white trash in their own pond. Starving children in India. Starving children in Africa. Starving children everywhere but Appalachia.

Goad's book is even more challenging if you were once a kid who often didn't have lunch money but grew into an adult who found it all too easy to worry more about the hungry elsewhere because this was somehow part of the canon of the group you hoped would help you pretend you were never poor white trash.

Extraordinarily topical, Goad quotes Andrew Jackson:

> "You bankers are a bunch of vipers and I will rout you out. If the American people ever find out how you operate, there will be a revolution before morning."

Except after the bailout of all the banks in the last three years, there really hasn't been a revolution, has there? Nor will there be. The bankers have had the American throat against the knife for decades and Americans, apologists for power that we are, haven't protested much. We just get pissed off at tax time. Occupation What?

An important crux of Goad's argument is that the real power benefits when blacks and whites hate one another. Perhaps that is the greatest conspiracy of them all. Food for thought:

> If rednecks and blacks were ever to put aside their differences, the only

remaining enemy would be the one above them… Very frequently, enemies are merely brothers fighting over the same hand-me-downs.

Or:

> Several things, however, blunt the possibility of rednecks and blacks getting along. One is the eternally divisive game of "Who Was More Oppressed?"… Ultimately it's like cancer patients arguing over whose tumors are worse. A deadly, serious topic has been twisted into a cafeteria food-fight over who suffered more.

> A second obstacle is the illusion of universal white guilt. I think that most black people in America have every right to be angry. And I think most white people in America have every right not to feel guilty about it… I can't appreciate someone else's history if I'm forced to reject and feel ashamed about mine.

Better yet:

> For the great part of America that is one paycheck away from picking through garbage cans, it may be wise to consider the strength of organized trash. The "minorities" plus the rednecks equals the majority. It always has. And the power jockeys have always known this, so they've historically pitted these groups as adversaries. Imagine a rainbow mound of trash… I have a dream—one day po' whites and blacks will stand together and be able to say, "It's a class thing—you wouldn't understand."

And finally, the quote that sealed the deal, the part that recognizes that the bulk of the shit rednecks experience comes not from non-whites, but from the upper echelon power structure bent on hurling shit from both sides of the spectrum:

> Realizing there was social chaos beneath all the yuppie pretense, there was no way I'd buy the conservative line of bullshit. In targeting the poor, conservatism pointed a finger at those who weren't to blame. But the liberals eventually lost me, too. They pointed a finger at me and I wasn't to blame either.

> I started losing faith in liberalism when I began noticing that every liberal who accused me of white privilege seemed to come from a more privileged socioeconomic background than I did… If indigenous Amazonian tribes were subjects to acid rain, the liberals were emotionally devastated. But if a trailer park of white trash across town all got cancer because they lived atop a toxic dump, it was a joke.

Increasingly, the world makes no sense to me. Online, people will bandy the words "white trash" and "redneck" around, using "hate speech" in ways they would never, ever consider when speaking of non-whites. You wear a shirt with an Indian motif and you get accused of cultural appropriation. Liberals who would never use the n-word (in public) will call someone a redneck in a heartbeat. If you suggest that women should behave and dress with decorum you'll be called a "shut shamer" by the same feminists who think nothing of ridiculing working-class Wal-Mart shoppers as "white trash." Being trashy is camp! It's cute! *Aren't those little rednecks adorable? Let's have a party and drink Pabst Blue Ribbon and pretend we like country music!* Don't worry about me! It's neat seeing my wretched childhood turned into an ironic excuse for hipsters to be assholes.

And we're told it all boils down to privilege. Pejoratives against lower class white people don't matter because white people supposedly have all the power. I know that. I just don't believe it. All that privilege doesn't really help when your social class leaves a target on your back.

These political opinions of mine may not be evident to anyone who knows me personally. I'm quiet on politics for the most part, mainly because I feel sort of beaten down. My husband and I lost our jobs. We had gaps in medical insurance that broke us financially (it was interesting when I broke my leg and needed ankle reconstruction surgery before the COBRA got settled). We almost lost our home. We may have an outward appearance of affluence, but we do not have power. No one does, except a handful of people at the top.

Nothing in my life is about race. I have the luxury of saying this because I am white. Were I not white, I might have a different perspective, though I feel all these perspectives, even if they seem at odds, can mesh together when we realize that our cultural striations involve race and class. My beliefs were formed from experience. I grew up with a chip on my shoulder, and I entered middle age full of fear because power can still call me names, can strip me of my income, can tell me to die because I don't have health insurance. My daddy harkened back in me as I felt some distaste for the Indian workers who had taken my job, my husband's job. I would hear accented speech on the phone when I called my creditors to ask for mercy and I would bristle. Fuckers. Willing to work for a dime so I can't have a dollar.

And it hit me. The stupidity of it all. If someone offers you a job, you take it. People at the bottom have to survive. It's the people at the top, driving down wages to appease shareholders, exporting jobs to people who need them as much as me but can work cheaper, who are to blame. No matter how well off you are, unless you control industry, banking or politics, you're at the bottom. And when the bottom falls out from under you, those who get the crumbs from the bread that was taken from you are not to blame. Nothing will ever change until we all stop blaming each other for scrabbling for what power will let us have. My god. Feeling angry at someone lucky enough to have a desk job in a developing country, where female infanticide is still routine in some villages, where I probably couldn't hack it for a week. If there is white privilege for those who lack economic and political power, that is it—knowing that really, as bad as things can get in the world, you haven't even come close to the real bottom as long as you're white and living in North America.

Maybe I just want everyone to stop complaining and shut the fuck up.

But back to Goad. While none of the quotes I have presented reflect the humor on display in *The Redneck Manifesto*, he peppers his thesis with plenty of darkly hilarious observations. He writes honestly, with compassion and without an ounce of apology, and he addresses topics that frighten most people. I've come to like this book so much that I almost worry what some may think of me for liking it so much. That's why it's important. After we buried McCarthyism I didn't think I would ever see such a political and social climate emerge on the left. But here we are. As trust-funded progressives continue to demonize those with little money and little power and little status, at least we have Jim Goad to point out the hypocrisy that others dare not mention. *The Redneck Manifesto* helped me understand my role in this not-so-brave new world. You should read it.

FURTHER READING

Deer Hunting with Jesus: Dispatches from America's Class War
Joe Bageant

Armed America: Portraits of Gun Owners in Their Homes
Kyle Cassidy

White Cargo: The Forgotten History of Britain's White Slaves in America
Don Jordan and Michael Walsh

Coming Apart: The State of White America, 1960–2010
Charles Murray

Last Night at the Lobster
Stewart O'Nan

Black Rednecks and White Liberals
Thomas Sowell

Feud: Hatfields, McCoys, and Social Change in Appalachia, 1860–1900
Altina L. Waller

PART TWO

Odd Books
(Mostly Fiction)

I never confront myself as much as I do when I read fiction. Even when fictional writing is terrible I feel compelled to understand *why* it is terrible. It isn't always easy—you can dismiss a poorly edited book but why do we sometimes hate works of fiction that are erudite and well-edited? Why do some stories mean the world to us while others mean nothing? Fiction is so intensely personal that I fancy I can tell a lot about people by learning what fiction they love. Which means that you can know me by the fiction I love, which is sort of sobering to realize.

ERGODICA

Ergodic novels are interesting to me because within them are myriad possibilities. They may require a bit more work to navigate but there is no one path, no one narrative, no one interpretation. As you read you find yourself processing the content in a way that makes the novel yours, an experience no one else will have.

THE PLIGHT HOUSE
By Jason Hrivnak
Pedlar Press (2009)
Original post: 02/08/2013

Why do I consider this book odd?
This book is a test to see what you know about the depths of human
despair. It can also be used as a distraction when dealing with the
desperate individual: simply read a few passages aloud until he puts
down the gun or she hands you the bottle of pills.

This may be one of those books that requires a certain level of experience to understand. Of course, feelings of misplaced responsibility and grief are common enough, so I don't want to discourage anyone from reading *The Plight House*. But unless you have tried to end your life or tried to prevent someone from ending his or her life, it may lack a certain resonance. It should also be noted that Jason Hrivnak's style is experimental, and perhaps borderline ergodic. The book's structure forces you to interact with the text in a manner that forbids passivity and can defy understanding unless you are willing to work hard. The content is also so very specific and tied to an extremity of experience that could, for some readers, be alienating.

I still think you should read it. I mean, this isn't *House of Leaves*-level ergodic. You can even get through it in one sitting, if you stay focused and don't mind the feeling of being flayed now and then. Fair warning, though: *The Plight House* is not a book for those who prefer linear narratives.

A brief synopsis: The unnamed protagonist meets his friend Fiona when they are nine and they become inseparable. They create a strange otherworld they call the "Testing Range" wherein they enact trials for the people they know, trials that verge on torture but have a specific end and meaning. An untalented violinist who loves her music but is afraid of rats is put in a cage full of rats for a night. If she survives, she will have the talent of a virtuoso for a year. At the end of the year she will have to make the

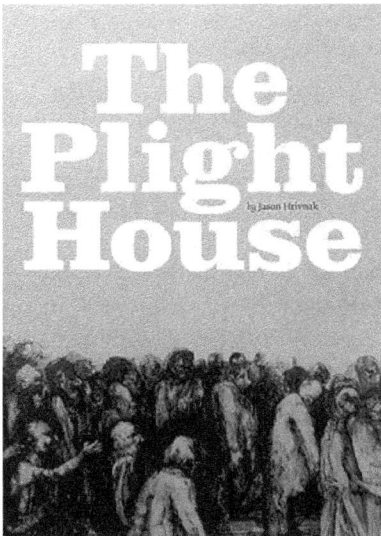

choice to expose herself to rats for even longer in exchange for another year of talent or she will lose her talent forever. The protagonist and Fiona create these trials for everyone around them. Fiona has an unspecified neurological condition but as she grows older it seems that she develops some sort of personality disorder that manifests in erratic and ultimately self-destructive behavior. When Fiona's family moves, the protagonist tries to keep in touch with her but eventually he can't find much to say to her anymore. They have become too different.

He attends college and gets a job but his friendship with Fiona has rendered him socially avoidant, near schizoid, craving solitude to the point that he lives his life in a darkened room, sleeping only to dream and waking only to record his dreams. One day he receives a letter from Fiona's father informing him that Fiona broke into their old grade school. She slashed her wrists and died. Among her belongings, her father had found a page from the "Testing Range" notebook that she carried with her so he contacts the protagonist to ask if he could explain what was written. Wracked with grief, the protagonist decides to write *The Plight House*, a test for Fiona and a chance for him to achieve a sort of redemption in the face of crushing sorrow.

Using the magical thinking that we all engage in, the super-powerful what-if we practice when the unthinkable happens, the protagonist imagines what would have happened if only the Plight House had existed before Fiona made the decision to kill herself.

> The Plight House is the missing element from the night Fiona broke into the school, its failure to appear there no different from the absence of a stolen property or a garment devoured by moths. I picture the manuscript sitting ready on a clean, well-lit desk, a batch of sharpened pencils at the side. I picture Fiona noticing it in the course of her wanderings and stepping cautiously into the light, aware of a twist in the game.
>
> She would have understood within the first few pages that the test was not written by a doctor or a parent or, even, fundamentally, by a friend. And its coldness would have come as a great relief to her. I knew from the outset that the test's chance of success would inhere in its refusal, first, to sing her back toward a world that she despised, and, second, to use guilt as a straitjacket. My only hope was to create a resonance, duplicating both in myself and in the text the particular frequency of despair that was driving her toward suicide. I'm not sure what, if anything, it would have meant to her to experience that resonance. But so long as she understood that she had been seen, and therefore accompanied, in that worst of all possible moments, I could have lived with her decision.

Of course, that's not true. One does not undertake an elaborate exercise to prevent the worst if one is going to be sanguine if the worst happens.

In fact, the final words of the last paragraph make it clear that the narrator means very much for this book to be used as a means to prevent the worst, with no eye to any other alternative but salvation and preservation.

> If it becomes necessary to administer The Plight House, do so without apology and without expectation of thanks. Her tears of protest may rend your heart, but remember the alternative. She stands to lose everything, and so, therein, do you.

The synopsis and quotes above are contained in the first 29 pages. That's the only linear part of Hrivnak's novel. Then the Plight House begins.

The Plight House reproduces the cage of rats for Fiona, a series of tests ostensibly devised to help her understand herself and help the narrator understand her. But at times I read this as a distraction, a distraction that is ultimately deep but a distraction nonetheless. Section I is multiple choice, Section II is full of essay questions and Section III is a series of interconnected essay questions. Well, the questions are essays. One can answer them however one sees fit.

I almost think it is folly to try to reproduce any of the Plight House sections because I don't think small samples can give anyone any idea of the power of these tests. But being who I am, I will try. I'll just pull a few of the sections that mean the most to me.

Here's a question from Section I.

> 13. You have a migraine, the aura cuts glasslike into your field of vision and the pain, once entrenched, lasts for more than a week. Upon recovery, you find your bedroom filled with strange pilgrims. Your caregivers explain that these pilgrims have come to your bedside from distant lands after hearing word of your special powers. What wonders have you allegedly performed whilst incapacitated?
>
> > A. You have spoken in tongues.
> > B. You have levitated.
> > C. You have belched forth a rare and poisonous snake.
> > D. You have built a cathedral.

Here's another.

> 8. As you enter your teenage years, your imaginary friend with the amethyst eyes remains your only worldly companion. Concerned by your lack of interest in kinship of the flesh-and-blood variety, your parents take you on a trip to the lake. A small sailboat sits tied to the dock. Your parents raise the sail and set the empty boat adrift on the waters. They tell you that your imaginary friend is in the boat and that he is going away forever. They tell you to wave goodbye. What action do you take?
>
> > A. Jump into the water and swim after your friend, with the aim of bringing him back.
> > B. Jump into the water and swim after your friend, with the aim of joining him in exile.
> > C. Hide your face in your hands and weep.
> > D. Wave goodbye, as instructed.

I sense my answers would be D and B. But they may also be D and C. Sometimes it's hard to know but trying to find the answers forced me to wonder how much defiance, talent and mental independence I actually possess. And that is the point of the Plight House. Forcing one out of current thoughts, even if the new thoughts are difficult to process.

Turning to Section II, I began to feel uncomfortable.

> 1. You are standing in line outside a healer's tent. It is winter. There are hundreds, perhaps thousands, of people in line and they keep unwaveringly to their places despite the bitter cold. As the line inches toward the tent, you notice that each healed person bears a freshly-drawn tattoo: an old man who had entered the tent confined to a wheelchair emerges some five minutes later walking fully upright, his neck tattooed with a black spider; a blind girl emerges with 20/20 vision and, upon her belly, a tattoo of a burning boat. What is your ailment? With what figure will the healer mark your body and why?

My ailment is a lifelong inability to sleep. I would have a tightly-coiled spring tattooed on my left leg because my early nightmares, as a very little girl, featured a coiled spring. The spring is linked in my mind with my sleep issues because of those early nightmares. My left leg is often the part of my body that aches the most and took the ultimate brunt of my sleeplessness—I broke my leg during a spell of sleeplessness I tried to remedy with alcohol and now have a plate and a scar above my ankle. I'd let the healer tattoo the coil directly on the scar, right on top of the plate, and I'd welcome the agony if it meant I could sleep.

Another.

> 22. I find work in a slaughterhouse. I perfect the techniques of killing with blade and bolt gun alike and soon I can dress a fresh carcass faster than any of my peers. In a bid to outmanoeuvre the slaughterhouse's competition, management begins to purchase a new kind of livestock. The animals in question are small, doglike creatures with tawny hair and wide, nocturnal eyes. Management warns us to wear earplugs whilst slaughtering them, as their song has been known to unhinge the human mind. From the moment that I start practicing my trade upon these creatures, I begin to suffer from terrible nightmares. My nights become a hell of strange and vivid horrors and within three weeks time I am legless with fatigue. One day, acting on a sudden and uncharacteristic impulse, I rescue one of the creatures from the killing-room floor and hide it in my coveralls. I bring it home. Sitting on my kitchen table, scanning the room with its dark eyes, the creature looks innocuous and unafraid. I remove my earplugs. What does the creature say to me?

It says, "Fuck your sentimentality. You save me and think it means a goddamned thing as you kill others like me? I saw you kill my mother. She begged you to stop and you didn't. I hope you die and that my voice is the last noise you hear when your soul leaves your body." That's what the creature says to me.

Section III is multi-part essay questions and there is no real way for me to produce one of the entire questions unless I reproduce a section that may be longer than this entire discussion. The first paragraph of the questions sets up a scenario and the following paragraphs expand the scenario and ask questions. One of the first paragraphs stayed with me and is worth discussing. I'll reproduce it and the first question in the series.

> 10. You are ninety-four years old. You have been hospitalized. Like a sere and broken bird, you lie alone in a dark corner of the palliative ward, your organs tottering on the verge of failure. Your mind has slipped into perpetual twilight, a frightened incomprehension like that of a caged or injured beast. Daytime is a gauntlet of rough hygiene and pain, the petty humiliation of caregivers who speak of you as if you were already dead. But the nights are far worse. As daylight fades, the stains of old effluvia bloom darkly on the crumbling walls and floor. Cribdeath and gangrene stride wraithlike through the wards. The darkness is a tactile thing. It weighs upon you like water pressure, it pools in your lungs like fumes from a distant star.

> 10a. In these last nights before your death, you become a sleepwalker. Like a common insomniac, you steal from your bed in the lifeless hours of early morning and go wandering through the halls. Your carriage is erect and your stride is true, your body completely and utterly beguiled by its dream of wellness. And you are lucid throughout. Is this your first experience with somnambulism? Have you in the course of your life been prone to seizures of any stripe? What is it like to relinquish authorship of your steps and do you long all the while for the safety of your bed?

I used to sleepwalk when I was young. My mother once caught me in the middle of making a sandwich out of cigarette butts. I was in late high school or early college. It ended but came back when I took a specific drug for insomnia. I was never lucid as I roamed in my sleep. I don't think anyone is lucid when they sleepwalk or it would just be called walking. You don't know what it is like to surrender control because you don't surrender it—you are simply overtaken by movement when you are asleep. Overtaken and asleep do not lend themselves well to lucidity or will, but perhaps it could happen.

The first paragraph of question 10 is, minus the effluvia and sense of others speaking to me as if I am dead, a near-perfect representation of what life is like when I am in the middle of a sleepless fog. I think that is why it spoke to me so clearly.

It goes on for several pages until we reach the end of question 10F, and the book concludes:

> Why do we devote more passion to the loves that destroy us than we do to the loves that heal us and make us complete? Is it inevitable that we should conduct ourselves thus? Imagine that your death brings no respite from

desire, that it pitches you into wilder, more potent states of longing. Though they bury you alone beneath the cold and final earth, you shall burn for the touch of your every unsung love. Discuss.

I wonder if Hrivnak knew about my suicide attempt before he sent me this book. I'm not shy about sharing my own experiences in this realm. I have cyclical depression but the older I get the less debilitating it is because I have had decades to understand how to know when it is coming and what I can do when it arrives, and now I have access to insurance that keeps me in the right medication. But in 2008 this depression merged with a terrible situational anxiety. I was misdiagnosed with a condition I do not have and was given medications that made me psychotic. I tried to kill myself. I spent some time in a locked down mental facility and I seldom discuss what happened afterward, but people who read my journal at the time know. I continued to suffer and the suicidal ideation continued until I detoxed from all the meds I had been prescribed. It was a terrible time but I am very lucky that my depression and anxiety do not organically manifest in suicidal thoughts or feelings that death would be better than continuing onward with my life.

Even though what happened to me in 2008–2009 was situational and I don't see it ever happening again, once you've been there, you're sort of marked. It doesn't bother me much anymore. It doesn't plague me. But I am a person who tried to take my own life and once you cross over that line you are changed. For me the change is that I am acutely aware of what it means to be a burden, because no matter how much you love someone, being forced to stand witness to such horror kills a part of your soul. My dear husband was the one who watched as I came up for air again and again. He was the architect of my own Plight House. He would swim into frightening waters to drag me to shore, only to stand stunned as I flung blows and threw punches to get away and dive right back into what was drowning me.

I asked him once how it was he managed to live through it all and he said he could still see glimpses of me under all the medications and all the rage the medications caused. I was trapped in there and was fighting to get out. He said that as long as I was fighting, even if the person I was fighting was him, at least I had not laid down and given in. Hrivnak's Plight House is what my husband did, day after day, until I emerged as myself again. It took me months to get off those drugs. It felt like years but it was only months and I mercifully only remember bits and pieces. But he remembers it all and that is far, far worse because he loves me and was forced into a state of powerlessness as he did everything he could to keep me from death. I suspect that those who succeed during their first attempt at suicide are spared the horrible reminder that they drove a dagger into someone else's heart, but that's also not for me, a person who survived and is no longer suicidal, to say.

I don't know if I should discuss such personal things about myself in a book review. I keep backing up and deleting because I don't know if this is an appropriate way to discuss a book, yet I can't think of another way to write it other than to react in this way. It's like I am filling in the blanks during all those times the drugs blunted my memory of what I was doing (toxic psychosis, it is called). I also think I felt strongly what my husband felt each time he kept me from the worst. Yet as hard as it is to discuss, I am glad I read *The Plight House*. The past is the past but understanding things, even when they hurt, is why I read.

The Plight House could make you very sad. It could open all kinds of wounds you thought had healed. For me, it opened such wounds but the psychic blood I lost was rendered negligible as I looked upon the many fortunes I have in my life. As I read, I remembered all of the ways my husband constructed Plight Houses for me when I was so low and it made me remember that in so many ways he is a much better writer than I am. He is succinct. He can cut to the heart of the matter without all the dithering I am prone to. In the middle of my time in hell, I woke one day to find this on my bathroom mirror.

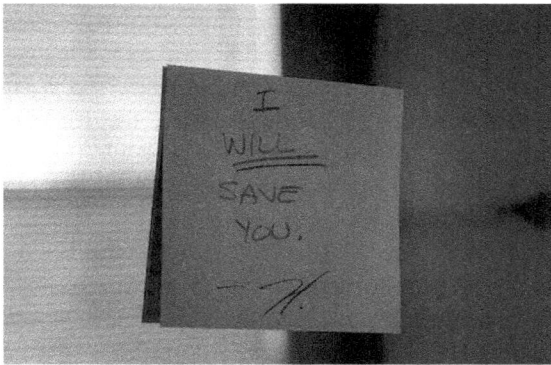

This is the best summation of *The Plight House* anyone could write.

A GREATER MONSTER
By David David Katzman
Bedhead Books (2011)
Original post: 09/03/2013

Why do I consider this book odd?
The reasons are numerous. Keep reading.

Jesus Christ. I *dare* every single one of you to buy *A Greater Monster* and read it. I could just encourage you to read it, but I'm making it a dare. I want to play on your pride. I want you to read this one lest you seem the sort person who shies away from a challenge. I need you to feel your honor is at stake.

David Katzman's book may be described as experimental fiction because after the first 40 pages or so, it defies any traditional narrative structure. A nauseating but ordered beginning careens into unordered experiences. It's a drug trip that has a beginning of sorts but no real end. The protagonist slides from one hallucinogenic experience to another. The effect is disorienting and peculiar, and it can be almost alienating to read. But it's a religious experience for the protagonist, a deeply personal descent into the unreal and irreal. He wants to descend into worlds without meaning. If he doesn't, his life will become even more meaningless.

I had to approach *A Greater Monster* in a manner similar to the way I read *House of Leaves*. I read it in bits and pieces on the first pass. It's a dense text and, without any linearity of plot, reading it all at once would be like experiencing someone else's delusions. Before my senior year of high school, I developed pneumonia and had such a high fever I began to hallucinate. My mother found me in the hallway, waiting in an imaginary line to go to the bathroom. Evidently I was convinced that Chinese laborers were living in our house and we all shared the same toilet. I could see odors as colors and felt sure there were cows hiding in my room, producing methane gas that manifested as the color orange. Small blue people ran across my bedsheets, warning me I needed to sit up or I would die. My books spoke in foreign languages, the mirrors showed me unseen rooms in the house, and when I later told all of this to the doctor, he flat out did not believe me. My mother told him, with no small amount of anger, that it had happened. I still don't think he believed us.

I still hallucinate with very low fevers and most medical personnel give me the side eye when I report it. I seldom say anything anymore. I've had

a couple of nurses tell me they do the same thing but mostly I know I am not believed. I used to be offended. Now I know better. The fever dreams and hallucinations of one man can never really resonate with others unless they, by chance, have the same fevered dream, the same tendency to hallucinate, the same peculiar mind-set. That sort of cross-over of experience seldom happens. You find yourself wondering how anyone could see a cow's flatulence.

And that's why you need to read this book in little bits at first. Otherwise the protagonist's experiences will become too much as you try to make sense of them. If you take it in smaller portions you won't try to find the common thread, the element that links the stories together. There may be one but because this is not my hallucination, my drug trip, my terrible fever, the thread remains elusive.

It took me several months to finish this book the first time. I would back up and try to connect everything I was reading but ultimately that was a loser's bet. You just have to read in short clips and when you are finished, let it digest. Then read it all in one go. You'll be rewarded with a bizarre and at times alienating experience. It may sound unappealing, the way I'm describing it. But it's not. Like taking a vacation in someone else's mind, *A Greater Monster* beckons a violent, unnerving, disjointed trip into utterly foreign fever hallucinations. It's enjoyable and frightening and fun if you're along for the ride. Just don't try to force it to make linear sense.

The book begins in a manner I can only call Palahniukian with a dash of *American Psycho* (but with the protagonist cast as the potential victim, not a rich, yuppie killer). He works for an ad agency and he is in trouble. His mind is running races, his soul is dying a bit each day. We find him literally grasping spirituality in his hands, squeezing it in his sleep.

> I jerked awake from my half-sleep, still clutching Ganesh in my right fist, when I heard the moan. The room smelled of ashes and rosemary. Hit the power button without shutting down and clenched the action figure tighter as my computer whined to its death.
>
> [...]
>
> I returned to my chair and considered the elephantine god in my hand. I'll take him to work as a sentinel to keep me company, I thought. The rich

olive color would bring some energy to my office, which was a black box within a large black loft designed to simulate a warehouse (while incidentally honing paranoia and cruelty).

He is open to the idea of change but is oblivious to signs. This man works 18-hour days in a place that would have killed me off in a week. He is overworked and in constant fear but that doesn't cause the reader to become so sympathetic that she overlooks the fact that he is an asshole. On the way to work on December 21, he is given "a small black lozenge" from a homeless man. Here is his reaction:

> The old man did not move. A monument to homelessness, a statue of failure, wearing a postman's jacket over a shirt with the outline of a horse on it. Work pants, a dirty baseball hat with the swoosh logo, and sandals covered in what appeared to be dog shit completed the outfit. Better him than me. I grabbed at the pill. Turns out, I wasn't as quick as an action-movie star. The moment I contacted his palm, the old man close-fisted my fingers and spit a glob of phlegm violently at my feet. His acid-green eyes met mine—"Why'd the chickens cross the road?" I scooped the pill and yanked my hand from his. "Why'd the chickens cross the road?" he repeated more urgently. I backed away, thrusting the pill into my coat pocket. The rough wool fibers rubbed like a Chinese finger trap. I turned the corner back to the street, he bellowed, "Cuz he's a goddamn backstabbin' chicken's why!"

Better him than me, but he walks away with the black lozenge. He passes by graffiti that comes from a place of human despair, and he thinks:

> Mmmh, sorry you couldn't make it like I did. Welcome to natural selection, loser.

But then he walks into the street, the walk sign on his side, and he is nearly run down by a silver SUV. He gives driver the finger and he comes very close to realizing he is the backstabbin' chicken who crossed the road. But he doesn't. It eludes him. He cannot yet see the signs.

This is how he sums up a day at work:

> Skull-crushing boredom interspersed with hyperventilating fear.

He is working on marketing a project called eEye, a security system for the well-heeled to keep the economically disenfranchised at bay. He spends all day in pointless meetings and has to work late in order to get anything done. He contemplates the black lozenge as he does the job of several people but he doesn't swallow any of it yet.

And there are still signs, so many signs.

> "I want a fucking life!" The cry echoed from somewhere in the warehouse outside my door. The creatives were getting restless. It was 12:21. Third night in a row I'd been at work past 10:00.

> "So lose the account and your job, fucker!" I shouted back and stuck my

head out the door. No one. Just a cleaning guy sweeping the floor. He didn't even look up or acknowledge my presence … perhaps because we don't speak the same language. I retreated back to my office.

It's no longer the Winter Solstice, the longest night of the year, but though it is not 12/21, it is still 12:21 and this backstabbing chicken who does not speak the same language as other men, still does not see the sign, even as he contemplates the nasty, oily, gummy pill the homeless man gave him. He is beginning a long dark night of the soul and has no idea.

He surfs for porn on the company computer but he gets tons of pop-ups and decides to take part of the pill. He eats half of it and thinks it tastes like chicken (but not backstabbing chicken), but then he decides it tastes like death. As he leaves the office, he grabs hold of spirituality again.

> Ganesh was there on the shelf next to my desk. If I'm really going on a trip, I might as well pack my totem. Joke. Stashed him in my pocket anyway.

He leaves the office, sweating and in a state of timelessness, the Indian god Ganesh, the remover of impediments and obstacles, in his pocket. Time slips away from him and has no meaning.

> Time is imaginary space. How do I get from one moment to the next? Space doesn't have direction, why should time? It's a medium. Within which vibrations occur. It just is, not movement, no strand, just now.

He stumbles. He wanders. He finds himself condemned by voices no one else can hear. Things begin to fall apart, inside and out, as he suffers from stomach cramps.

> I felt myself being ripped apart inside my asshole chunks of my ass thrown across the bathroom sputtering the walls my legs falling in opposite directions my body surrendering to the tile my face bounding off a surface warm milk in my mouth my tongue felt the topology tooth tooth tooth tooth? jagged edge my face was a jagged tooth my eyes they were closed they would not open I was tugging at them with all my willpower nothing the abyss no orientation no perspective abruptly swung open: my face was in the urinal I pushed back many bodies entangled with me we were all kneeling at the urinal I wriggled and all the bodies writhed around me a knot of little snakes nadouessioux nausea overwhelmed me and we vomited into the urinals before

As I read this and realized he was not at home, I wondered about the people in the restroom with him as he crapped himself and careened into the urinal. What were they thinking during all of this? He somehow makes it home and wakes after what had to have been only a couple of minutes of sleep to a drug hangover he thinks he can beat if only he goes shopping. He buys a ridiculous suit made of velvet just because a hot but aloof salesgirl recommends it.

> She led me to the changing room, which was a frosted acrylic cube mirrored

on all four sides, open at the top. "Let me know if you need anything," she said and left. Tore off my clothes and tried it on. Like a hipster James Bond with money to burn. Checked the tag. 4k. Jesus, an entire paycheck. Burned all right. Back out.

He doesn't back out because she tells him he looks hot. He wanders, time means nothing, but the story is still linear enough and he meets up with a friend called Sasha, who is half Dutch and half Jamaican. They are in his apartment and she is not buying his shit. (In fact, I sort of wish this entire book consisted of little more than Sasha hitting the protagonist with a bamboo stick until he experiences enlightenment. That would be been a short yet repetitive book, though very enjoyable.) Sasha and the asshole backstabbing chicken protagonist are smoking drugs, talking religion. He wanders off once more—the narrative is beginning to lose linearity—and he meets Sasha again. I have no idea where they are, but this is when I loved Sasha and felt myself fantasizing about what this book would be had she been the source of the revelation and not the oily gumdrop. He shows up whining. She is having none of it.

> "Bollocks," Sasha sneered. "Page two of your existentialist drama should relate a kick in the teeth. Babylon knocking at your door. All those pretty uniforms. You'll know what tired is when you find yourself on the wrong list. I saw les flics with clubs wade into a Pride Parade in Jamaica. You're just like Cobain—a self-indulgent tosser who couldn't focus outside his small mind for a change."

> "Hey, Hamlet had that problem, too."

> "Another bloody loser. Fuck Hamlet. Just another man who wanted to hear himself talk."

And they descend into a conversation that, if only he will listen, will save him. But chickens can't listen. Sasha is speaking first:

> "Freud had a lot to say about primal urges. The superego exists to overcome the id. That's how society survives. Otherwise we'd live like pack animals in the wild or whatever. He called it the Reality Principle. Unfortunately, he got it wrong. It's an unreality principle. We're working hard to destroy our species, and it's all perfectly logical, based on the logic of capitalism. The need to survive as individuals, as cogs in a system which is destroying itself."

> "I'm sick of talking. Let's fuck."

> She paused. "Did you just—is that how you want this to go?

> "What, I just figured…"

> "I have no problem at this point. I can turn you into a machine like that. Fuck if I care. You disappoint me."

> "I'm just kidding."

"Yeah."

"Okay, I'm sorry. I won't bring it up again."

"Yeah, that's fine."

I followed her to the door; she took her parka off the hook.

"Right, right."

She was gone.

And with her goes his last chance at self-actualization without an ordeal. She wanted him to step outside his mind and he wanted to fuck. There's nothing left for him to do but eat the second half of the oily pill and lose his mind in an unreal torment.

Kind passersby make things worse. Mistaking him for a junkie in withdrawal, a man offers him deep tokes of some strong marijuana and it is here that things make no more sense as our chicken begins to experience time and space in a manner wholly inexplicable to those who have not ingested the black lozenge. He is having this epiphany on the floor of the train, where he slid after smoking the pot.

Re la x   ed.

Mmmh.

Come for ta bull.

I observed myself:

the past has left marks on my body

my state vector collapsed

consciousness causes

all time is simultaneous. Or a concept.

Hypercube of space and time. Is why time's not visible.

Time is not a thing, no thing, it's a reflection, the reflection of change into space

the angle skews with speed

the subatomic realm does not distinguish between

all is

all is change

In all candor, passages like this make me nuts. If the rest of the book contained nothing but such passages, I would tell you to run, run far away from this book. Passages like this appear in the book from time to time, but they are endurable. Rather than being a sophomoric attempt to show the woo-woo that comes with a particularly exhaustive acid trip, they show the degeneration of the mind. Little bits of narrative clarity (clear in that one thing happens and another thing follows instead of a stream-of-consciousness word salad) prevent such moments from becoming onerous.

As you read on, you will have to let go of any ideas of convention and structure—this is where the "experimental" part comes in. You just sort of have to float on a raft of interesting words that may lead nowhere because this is not your trip. For some, being forced to experience someone else's fever dream may be a horror show in its own right, but Katzman's writing style makes the incredible readable and accessible. There is also a dark, obscene and often irreverent humor that runs through the subsequent experiences the protagonist has as he sheds the feathers of his backstabbing chicken life.

Going back to his origins, literally, the protagonist shelters briefly with a man named Ron who lives under half of an enormous egg. He brings Ron some water.

> Returning to the old man, I'll kneel down to pass him the cup as he lifts the egg, and I'll crawl under. I'll be inside now. Half an egg. The egg will cover us completely. He'll take the cup and look into it.

> "Well, this is top notch. Top notch. Water. What a nice surprise. All right, well, Hello? My name is Ron," and a tremor will take over his left side as he drinks from the cup with his right hand.

> He—sitting by my side, looking out at the river—will have a very long penis.

> "My home."

This is one of the easier episodes to decipher. One does not have to be Freud to understand this experience and what it means to the protagonist. He's a chicken sheltering under an egg, an ovum, with a man with an enormous penis. It's a rebirth of sorts but it's also a rebirth under a giant chicken egg feeding water to a man with a giant penis. Deep, but ridiculous.

I suspect half the reason to read on after the protagonist has taken the second half of the black pill is to see if you can locate the meaning or symbolism of what is happening to him. Sometimes I could ferret out some meaning, sometimes I couldn't.

Here's a scene where a woman is feeding him soup, soup that he calls "unknowable." She tells him the following:

> "He also told me about a place where males killed each other in competition to mate with their mothers. I don't understand why males would do this. What do mothers want? Who says males have a right to mate with anything? They fuck their own emptiness. It goes back to the origin. The ending returns to the beginning."

The ending will always return to the beginning. Sasha told him this earlier. I wonder if he is speaking to Sasha again or if his memory of her is fueling this interaction with the Eternal Soup Woman.

There are more strange trips—he is attacked by a metal creature that read strangely cat-like to me. He meets an Elk Pirate who is full of casual snark but also has a sort of debonair, Cary Grant-vibe, or at least it seemed Cary Grant-like until I learned he is a she. Maybe the Pirate Elk is beyond sexual roles. He offers the injured protagonist a cigarillo and some cognac in order to ease his pain and has one of the more coherent conversations with the protagonist:

> "Where were you trying to get to?"

> "I don't know. Trying to survive mostly. I think … think that I'm … I'm just trying to … to understand? I've … I've become confused about … what I'm supposed to be doing, what I'm … like."

> "Yes. You're wasting time. The point is you exist, and what are you going to do about it."

The conversation with the Pirate Elk has what for me was the best paragraph in the book. I'm with the Pirate Elk—I find the reasons why tiresome most of the time. The protagonist is telling the Pirate Elk that he didn't ask for all the things that have happened to him in life. The Pirate Elk replies:

> "Who does, who does?" The Pirate Elk tossed back a sip. "This isn't what I wanted. I used to endlessly fantasize arriving. You know, make my entrance in a big ballgown. Self-possessed, magnetic. The men swooned. I was finally there. Not a care in the world. Everything at my feet. Yes, those were the days that never ended, never happened."

I did not connect emotionally with this book. My discussion of *House of Leaves* was deeply emotional because I *got* Johnny. I understood Johnny Truant's fight. I could only be intellectually engaged with *A Greater Monster*

An illustration from *A Greater Monster*.

because the chicken protagonist meant little to me. His travails were not my own and were in fact so foreign that it never felt real to me, though I am sure others will have a different experience. But as I read, passages like the one from the Pirate Elk—imagining his or her entry, knowing it would never happen but grasping the idea of it never ceasing, thinking of it so often that it became its own strange reality—began to resonate with me. Who hasn't dreamed of arriving? But that isn't the point, of course. The point is that even as we never actually arrive, here we are. What are we going to do about it?

A Greater Monster is peppered with such moments, where you glimpse your truth in the puke-covered, shit-stained hallucinations of a very lost man. That's why you should read it. You will have to work hard for those moments. That's part of the reason I'm making it a dare.

Katzman also includes interesting illustrations in the book. There are about 40 pages straight of white-line-on-black illustrations depicting the protagonist's hallucinations. Very compelling artwork.

I have to stop here because I could keep going for another five thousand words and still not cover everything. Does he achieve enlightenment? Does he stop being a backstabbing chicken? Read it and decide for yourself. I'm not sure he even survives the experience. I don't even know if he could survive what Katzman does to him. But the interpretation, as I mentioned, is half the fun.

FURTHER READING

Alice's Adventures in Wonderland & Through the Looking-Glass
Lewis Carroll

A Scanner Darkly
Philip K. Dick

Maldoror and the Complete Works of the Comte de Lautréamont
Comte de Lautréamont

HOUSE OF LEAVES
By Mark Z. Danielewski
Pantheon (2000)
Original post: 06/21/2010

Why do I consider this book odd?
Well, because it is ergodic literature. That's a good qualifier.

I sometimes get hung up on a review or discussion and because I am not-quite-right, I cannot move on until I have addressed the issue. I think the problem is that in many ways discussing *House of Leaves* is not unlike discussing *Finnegans Wake*. There is an arrogance and hubris involved in thinking you can really get a handle on the entirety of either book.

I've flirted with *House of Leaves* before, but not until recently did I read the entire thing, from beginning to end in one go. By the time it was over my book was in tatters (and I was paranoid enough at the time that I wondered if the book's construction was meant to echo the house's obliteration), I had book fatigue and I barely remembered why I loved it so much in the first place. I left it, and didn't think about it. I tried to move on to lighter fare, but Danielewski's literary labyrinth kept tempting me back in. Gradually, I let myself like the book again. Thus I now find myself fully immersed once more, trying to make sense of a brilliant and exhausting text, sensing that perhaps I *do* understand it, even as I keep wondering if I might be full of shit.

This book. Oh dear lord. I have a wretched habit of bending the page when I find a passage that's meaningful to me. It's a foul, filthy thing to do, and as a bibliophile I hate myself for it, but I was never an underlining or highlighting sort of gal. The hell of it is, I went back to the dog-eared pages and read and reread and half the time I had no idea what it was that grabbed me the first time. I comfort myself in my wasted effort that the book was in miserable condition by the time I was through—spine destroyed, pages loose, the front end page fallen out completely. If this discussion is messy and incoherent, it won't be the first time and it won't be the last. When a novel is half footnotes, I don't think it's a copout to over explain myself.

Before diving in, I need to emphasize two things.

First, in my opinion, Johnny Truant's story is the reason to read this book. It may seem weak not to address all the text concerning *The Navidson Record*, but it's my party and I think the details are the trees and Johnny is the forest. I think when you analyze all of the endless references and throwaways that Danielewski uses, you miss the underlying humanity.

Second, I refuse to change my text color when I use the word "house" or refer to anything having to do with the Minotaur. It seems forced, affected and precious when anyone other than Danielewski does it.

With that much out of the way, a plot synopsis:

An old, blind man by the name of Zampanò dies and in his apartment Johnny Truant finds an in depth analysis of a documentary film called *The Navidson Record*. The book recounts Zampanò's analysis of the film, interspersed with numerous foot notes from Zampanò, Truant and an editor. There is an unnerving catch, however: there is no film. Zampanò's in-depth analysis, including copious research, is of a film that was never made and the resources he quotes do not exist. The analysis becomes so entrenched at times that the reader wonders if the real catch of the book is the "how many angels can dance on the head of a pin" minutia that often goes into academic research. The level of introspection given by fictional research into every element of this fictional movie gives the book so much self-referential claustrophobia that the reader finds herself going mad as she reads it, which, of course, is the entire point.

The written analysis of *The Navidson Record* tells the story of a family that moves into a house in Virginia. The house is seemingly sentient and able to change itself on the inside without affecting the outside measurements. It creepily rearranges itself internally, becoming larger than the outside proportions, finally creating a hallway that leads into a maze. A search party is sent into the maze with disastrous and appalling results. At the end of the failed discovery missions, as the house is collapsing then righting itself, *The Navidson Record* is revealed as a love story involving an icy and adulterous model, Karen, who finds herself fighting to save her relationship with Will Navidson.

Yes, I think it is a love story. I realize just about everyone who has read this book may disagree with my assessment, but everything about this book comes back to the exploration of various types of love. Maternal love fighting through mental illness, self-love fighting through emotional collapse and romantic love enduring the unthinkable and impossible.

But again, I believe the reason to read *House of Leaves* is to know the tale of Johnny Truant. The story of Johnny's life is told in footnotes to *The Navidson Record*, in letters his mother sent from the Whalestoe Institute (a home for the mentally ill), and in a diary he kept during and after his

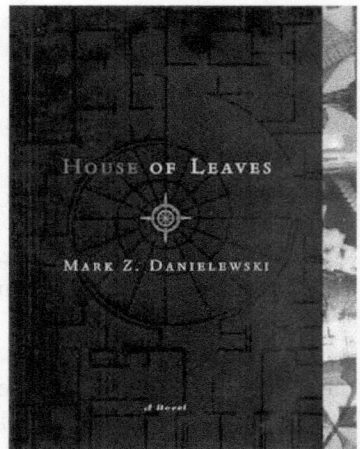

immersion in *The Navidson Record.* Johnny is a drug abuser and the son of a mentally ill woman who died while institutionalized, so it's hard to say what causes Johnny to drift, then dive headfirst into mental issues of his own. But Johnny is the heart of the book, the love story of Will and Karen and the peril they live through notwithstanding. Johnny's life story, revealed piecemeal and in a manner that makes it hard to assimilate if you skip a word, is the reason why I continued reading when I felt I just couldn't take another goddamn five-page footnote.

If you want a clear outline, there are numerous places online to find such things. You will not find a clear outline here. What you will find is a personal account of why I love Johnny Truant and how, using one of the most non-linear methods of storytelling ever, Danielewski managed to create a memorable, sympathetic and complex character—a character you almost miss out on as you attempt to make sense of all that's going on. Yes, the references to Jonah and the whale applied to Navidson in the maze juxtaposed with the fact that Truant's mother died in the Whalestoe are interesting. But trying to piece together all the names in this book, like the weird link between Zampanò and Truant (revealed in the cipher code Truant's mother creates to send him letters in the midst of her paranoia) can derail you as Johnny's life unfolds. All those maddening details, little clues that lead nowhere but away from where you need to go.

Johnny is one of the most unreliable narrators ever, and it's significant that he owns his unreliability, admitting that he changed the text at times to allow him to insert footnotes. But he also doesn't do much editing, even when Zampanò makes mistakes.

> Zampanò himself probably would of insisted on corrections and edits, he was his own harshest critic, but I've come to believe errors, especially written errors, are often the only markers left by a solitary life: to sacrifice them is to lose the angles of personality, the riddle of a soul.

There is no mistaking why this statement, with "of" instead of "have" (a chronic error in his writing) and punctuation misuse, is important. Johnny, solitary himself, with only a couple of friends and alienating sexual couplings, before long will become a mass of human errors and mistakes, which are already manifest in his writing.

A tattoo artist, Johnny is scarred heavily on his arms. His scars are the result of a terrible childhood accident when boiling oil scalded him. From the vantage of his childhood experience, Johnny shows how he will handle all the trauma that comes his way.

> It's kinda funny, but despite my current professional occupation, I don't have any tattoos. Just the scars, the biggest ones of course being the ones you know about, this strange seething melt running from the inside of both elbows all the way up to the end of both wrists, where—I might as well tell

you—a sizzling skillet of corn oil unloaded its lasting wrath on my efforts to keep it from the kitchen floor. "You tried to catch it all," my mother had often said of that afternoon when I was only four.

Johnny will reach out to every horrible experience, he will embrace it even if he doesn't tell the entire truth. For example, he tells people that the scars on his arms came from an incident with a Japanese Martial Arts Cult.

Johnny weaves lies into a manageable veil to shield him from the truth—he was damaged as a boy beyond all belief. His mother, losing her mind, tried to strangle him. His father died and he was forced into foster care where he was eventually beaten by a former Marine. His body is covered with scars, he sports a broken incisor.

> ...scars are much harder to read. Their complex inflections do not resemble the reductive ease any tattoo, no matter how extensive, colorful or elaborate the design. Scars are the paler pain of survival, received unwillingly and displayed in the language of injury.

That Johnny is covered in scars is both a comfort and a form of foreshadowing. All those scars show he has, and probably will, survive anything.

In discussing the obsession that Johnny thinks overcame Zampanò, he gives a pretty good idea what is happening in his own mind as he reads and annotates Zampanò's manuscript:

> As I strain now to see that *the Navidson Record*, beyond this strange filigree of imperfection, the murmur of Zampanò's thoughts, endlessly searching, reaching, but never quite concluding, barely even pausing, a ruin of pieces, gestures and quests, a compulsion brought on by— well that's precisely it, when I look past it all I only get an inkling of what tormented him. Though at last if the fire's invisible, the pain's not—mortal and guttural, torn out of him, day and night, week after week, month after month, until his throat's stripped and he can barely speak and he rarely sleeps. He tries to escape his invention but never succeeds because for whatever reason, he is compelled, day and night, week after week, month after month, to continue building the very thing responsible for his own incarceration.

> Though is that right?

> I'm the one whose throat is stripped. I'm the one who hasn't spoken in days. And if I sleep, I don't know when anymore.

Zampanò is a blind man who created a labyrinth of words to occupy him, to feed his obsession. Johnny is the man lost in the maze. This passage also should give the reader two strong clues about Johnny. Despite being a person who uses "of" for "have," his intellect is quite keen. More interesting, his passages can often mimic the tale he is reading, using endless comma clauses, repetition, words wandering into a maze. I am all too familiar with this disorganization of thought in the middle of a brainstorm, this need to tell the tale without stopping for metaphoric breath, struggling to be understood. Johnny is breaking down as we read his footnotes, documenting clearly his decline.

Johnny falls in love with a stripper he calls Thumper. She is most notable for having a tattoo above her privates that boasts "The Happiest Place on Earth." In spite of his drunken, unfortunate couplings with other women, Johnny falls hard for Thumper, and while the reader initially does not see her appeal, it isn't important. Johnny does. When his life falls apart and he decides to leave his job and apartment, he stops back by the tattoo shop where he works in order to say goodbye and to leave a gift for Thumper. He had earlier had appraised a necklace his mother had left him, worth $4,200. Despite sorely needing the money, Johnny makes another choice (the f substitutions for s come from Johnny's reaction to an archaic English quote used earlier):

> Maybe in some half-hearted attempt to tie up some loofe ends, I then dropped by The Fhop a couple of days later to say goodbye to everyone. Man, I muft look bad becaufe the woman who replaced me almoft screamed when she saw me walk through the door. Thumper wafn't around but my boff promifed to give her the envelope I handed him.

> "If I find out you didn't give it to her," I said with a smile full of rotting teeth. "I'm going to burn your life down."

> We both laughed but I could tell he was glad to fee me go.

> I had no doubt Thumper would get my gift.

Then Johnny's tale is no longer told through footnotes but in a journal that is appended to *The Navidson Record*. The journal is not always in chronological order. Johnny loses his apartment, lives in a hotel while money lasts, then ends up on the street, with his journal and a book by Dante. His external life has finally become a reflection of the internal. From his entry on October 27, 1998.

> Wherever I walk people turn from me.

> I'm unclean.

Johnny lives on the street but he is not completely down. When a troubled woman he slept with, Kyrie, sees him on the street, her unhinged, rich and violent boyfriend, known as Gdansk Man, tries to beat him up. From his entry on October 29:

> ...yelled something at me, for me to stop, which I did, waiting patiently for him to park the car, get out, walk over, wind up and hit me—he hit me twice—all of it experienced in slo-mo too, my eyebrow ringing with pain, my eye swelling with bruise, my nose compacting, capillaries bursting, flooding my face with dark blood.

> He should have paid attention. He should have looked closely at that blood. Seen the color. Registered the different hue. Even the smell was off. He should have taken heed.

> But he didn't.

Needless to say, things do not end well for Gdansk Man. It's hard to hurt a man as broken as Johnny, who has so little to lose, but the trivially violent among us, who never have a problem kicking a man who's down, never notice when blood is bad. Also, I do not know exactly when Johnny stopped using "of" and began using "have" because I didn't notice it until I typed out this passage. What the hell does it mean or signify? I have no idea except for the fact that perhaps when a man sinks to the bottom, his thoughts come clearer to him, even when he is in the grips of madness.

Just when you, the reader, are exhausted, the book takes a left turn down a dark road. Johnny discovers pictures he took and journal entries he made that he has no memory of, remnants of a psychotic road trip he took to Virginia. He travels to find the Navidson house, but he is clearly looking for more. Of course, as there is in all the books I have read recently, there is a dead cat.[1] A cat with its head splattered on the pavement and another cat looking on, pensive, possibly grieving.

Anyway, back to the book. Here's some of the madness Los Angeleno Johnny expresses from his entry on May 1, 1998, in one of his bullet points:

> Near the campus of William & Mary, surrounded by postcards thick with purple mountain majesty, and they are purple, I hyperventilate. It takes me a good half hour to recover. I feel sick, very sick. I can't help thinking there's a tumor eating away the lining of my stomach. It must be the size of a bowling ball. Then I realize I've forgotten to eat. It's been over a day since I've last had any food. Maybe longer.

It is here that I realized that I love Johnny Truant because he is cut from the same crazy as I am. Self-neglect leading to hypochondria. Possible hallucinations. I get this man. The scars, the inability to sleep, the obsessive interests. Fuck, that I maintain this damned site, that I am in any way bothering to soldier through this review when the need for coherence has delayed me from working on other projects for weeks, points to an unhealthy, obsessive nature.

He goes on:

> Everywhere I've gone, there've been hints of Zampanò's history, by which I mean Navidson's, without any real evidence to confirm any of it. I've combed through all the streets and fields from Distputanta to Five Forks to as far east as the Isle of Wight, and though I frequently feel close, to something important, in the end I come away with nothing.

As I read Johnny's investigative notes, I found myself surging with hope that he would find the house. Then I remembered that the house in *The Navidson Record*, even within the context of the book, did not exist. Then I remembered

---

1   One day I may undertake an analysis of why all the odd books I read seem to involve so many dead cats. I'm currently reading *1996* by Gloria Naylor and not ten pages in there is a fucking dead cat. Enough already.

that Johnny himself knew the house did not exist, that Zampanò's record was the fantastic musings of an incomprehensible mind. Yet he searched and I hoped he would find it.

Then Johnny steps into the realm of utter madness. The Realm of Nine. From May 4, 1998:

> In Kent. Nine Years. What an ugly coincidence. Even glanced at my watch. 9. Fucking nine pm.
>
> $5+4+1+9+9+8+9 = 45$ (or -9 yrs $= 36$)
>
> $4+5 = 9$ (or $3+6 = 9$)
>
> Either way , it doesn't matter. I say it with a German accent:
>
> Nine.

Math of the damned. It can only get worse, and it does. Johnny finds the Whalestoe facility. The old mental hospital is abandoned, so he goes inside and finds his mother's old room. From the entry on July 1,1998:

> Empty. And her bed in the corner. Even if the mattress was gone and the springs now resembled the rusted remains of a shipwreck half-buried in the sands of some half-forgotten shore.
>
> Horror shouldn't have buried me. It didn't.
>
> I sat down and waited for her to find me.
>
> She never did.

Navidson was a photographer haunted by the image he captured of a dying, motherless child. Truant is a motherless child haunted by the legend of the photographer. Everything in this book can come full circle if you let it.

From the entry on the same day, Johnny finally finds the place where his childhood home used to stand, a lumberyard now in its place:

> There would be no healing here.
>
> I stood by the circular saws and clutched my belly. I had no idea where I was in relation to what had once existed. Maybe this had been my kitchen. Why not? The stainless steel restaurant sink there to side. The old stove over there. And here where I was standing was right where I'd been sitting, age four, at my mother's feet, my arms flinging up, instinctually, maybe even joyfully, prepared to catch the sun. Catch the rain…
>
> Supposedly I'd been laughing. So that accounts for the joy part. Supposedly she'd been laughing too. And then something made my mother jerk around, a slight mistake really but with what a consequence, her arm accidentally knocking a pan full of sizzling Mazola, while I, in what has to be one of the strangest reactions ever, opened my arms to play the bold, old catcher of it all, the pan bouncing harmlessly on the floor but the oil covering my forearms and transforming them into the Oceanus whirls.

This is not the first time the reader hears of how small Johnny opened his arms to catch the oil, laughing. Like all legends that shape our lives, it is a story he likely tells again and again because it explains everything about him. How he was loved. How his mother meant no harm. How even the best memory is tinged with pain. How none of us leave childhood unscarred.

He goes on:

> Please bless these arms. Which I found myself looking at again, carefully studying the eddies there, all those strange currents and textures, wondering what history all of it could tell, and in what kind of detail, completely unaware of the stupid redneck yelling in my ear, yelling above the engines and shrieking saws, wanting to know what the fuck I was doing there, why was I clutching my belly and taking off my shirt like that, "Are you listening to me, asshole? I said who in the hell do you think you are?", didn't I know I was standing on private property—and not even ending his tirade there, wanting to know if it was my desire to have him break me in half, as if that's really the question my bare-chested silence was asking. Even now I can't remember taking off my shirt, only looking down at my arms.

> I remember that.

God, will there be no peace for him? A sense that he will arrive at an end of a journey with some comfort and elucidation? I heaved a sigh of relief at his next entries.

From September 2, 1998:

> Seattle. Staying with an old friend. A pediatrician. My appearance frightened both him and his wife and she's a doctor too. I'm underweight. Too many unexplained tremors and tics. He insists I stay with them for a couple of weeks.

September 20, 1998:

> I'm much improved. My friends have been taking care of me full time. I exercise twice a day. They've got me on some pretty serious health food… Once a day I attend a counseling session at their hospital. I'm really opening up. Doc has also put me on a recently discovered drug, one bright yellow tablet in the morning, one bright yellow tablet in the evening. It's so bright it almost seems to shine. I feel like I'm thinking much more clearly now… It also allows me to sleep.

September 27, 1998:

> I'm healthy and strong. I can run two miles in under twelve minutes. I can sleep nine hours straight. I've forgotten my mother. I'm back on track. And yet even though I'm now on my way back to LA to start a new life—the guns in my trunk long since gone, replaced with a year's supply of that miraculous yellow shine—when I said goodbye to my friends this morning I felt awful and soaked in sorrow… Good people. Very good people. Even as I started the car they were still asking me to stay.

September 29, 1998:

> Are you fucking kidding me? Did you really think any of that was true? September 2 thru September 28? I just made that up. Right out of thin air. Wrote it in two hours. I don't have any friends who are doctors, let alone two friends who are doctors. You must have guessed that. At least the lack of expletives should have clued you in. A sure sign that something was amiss.
>
> And if you bought that Yellow-Tablet-Of-Shine stuff, well then you're fucking worse off than I am.
>
> Though here's the sadder side of all this, I wasn't trying to trick you. I was trying to trick myself, to believe, even for two lousy hours, that I really was lucky enough to have two such friends, and doctors too, who could help me, give me a hand, feed me tofu, make me exercise, administer a miracle drug, cure my nightmares. Not like Lude with all his pills and parties and con-talk street-smack...
>
> Right now I'm in Los Gatos, California. Los Gatos Lodge, in fact. I managed a couple of hours of sleep until a nightmare left me on the floor, twitching like an imbecile. Sick with sweat.

Fucking Johnny. Yes, despite the fact that this journal is not presented sequentially, that I had read October 1998 first and knew Johnny was freezing and hungry in dive hotels, then homeless, then in a fight with Gdansk Man and more, I put that out of my head. I wanted him to have two friends who saved him. I wanted this to be over for him. How did I manage this feat of self-deception that occurred in only a few pages? Not sure. Perhaps it was reader's fatigue. You sure as shit get it when you read this book. Nonetheless it was heartbreaking when it became clear that there would be no *deus ex machina* for Johnny. And since this is the second time Johnny admits to making things up, it calls into question a whole lot. Was he fake responding to a faked record of a non-existent film? What happened here? What, even within the context of the book, is the reader expected to believe? I realized I had to ignore the notion of any narrative truth and just soldier on.

You get the sense that after he discovered his journal and the photographs from his journey, things begin to change a bit for him. He pawns his guns and makes plans to meet with Thumper, his dream woman. They're both tight on time, but they talk.

> I could read the signs well enough to know she wanted a kiss. She'd always been fluent in that language of affection but I could also see that over the years, years of the same grammar, she'd lost the chance to understand others. It surprised me to discover I cared enough about her to act now on that knowledge, especially considering how lonely I was. I gave her an almost paternal hug and kissed her on the cheek. Above us airplanes roared for the sky. She told me to keep in touch and I told her to take care and then as I walked away, I waved and with that bid adieu to The Happiest Place on Earth.

We then skip to August 28, 1999. Not the end of the book by a country mile but at last I have a sense that Johnny will be okay. He jumps trains and lives as a drifter, often broke, sleeping rough. He lands in Flagstaff, Arizona with little money in his pocket but still buys himself soup. He finds a bar with no cover charge and dollar beers and settles in, buying drinks for the band with his last few dollars. Then the band plays a song with the words, "I live at the end of a Five and a Half Minute Hallway," which is a clear reference to *The Navidson Record*. Once they are finished playing, Johnny approaches the band and they discuss, somewhat reluctantly, their knowledge of *The Navidson Record*, telling Johnny they had found the annotated document online. One band member gives him a copy of his own manuscripts and Truant wrestles with telling them who he is but decides not to. He leaves the bar, falls asleep under a tree and sleeps well until a large dog comes to wake him.

> Flagstaff appears deserted and the bar's closed and the band's gone, but I can hear a train rattling off in the distance. It will be here soon, homeless climbing off for a meal, coffee for a dime, soup for three quarters and I have some change left. Something warm sounds good, something hot. But I don't need to leave yet. Not yet. There's time now. Plenty of time. And somehow I know it's going to be okay. It's going to be alright. It's going to be alright.

Johnny's quest has led him somewhere, to a place where others read his words and understand him. People now know who he is and wonder where he has gone. He is a person in the minds of other people, making him real, just as remembering his mother's words keeps her real.[2]

Have you ever heard the song "Jezebel" by Acid Bath? There's a line that goes, "She screams bloody murder as they chop off her fingers, 'So this is how it feels to die. But it's okay. Everything's okay.'" Then Dax Riggs murmurs, "It's okay, it's okay" and you feel calm after listening to the jarring song because in the context of the extreme violence and dissolution, everything is okay. The worst has happened. Just bleeding and extreme pain are left, but everything's okay. You finally know how it's all going to end. That is how the revelation that Johnny is going to be "alright" resonated with me. He isn't technically okay. He's homeless, he's broke. But within the context of his life, he's just fine. That's all I can ask from Johnny, I think. No greater revelation other than that he made it out the other side.

God, I don't plan to reread this one any time soon. Organizing this discussion has been a nightmare. It took a couple of weeks to crank out because it was difficult to organize, which often happens when you discuss ergodic

---

2   It was tempting to discuss the letters Johnny received from his mother while she was at Whalestoe, because they are in themselves a fascinating part of the book, in my mind outshining all of *The Navidson Record* in their comment on the human condition. Instead of turning this already-too-long discussion into a way-too long discussion, I will one day read *The Whalestoe Letters*, Danielewski's book that compiles all of the letters.

literature. In spite of, or maybe because of, these troubles, I genuinely think that *House of Leaves* is a book that every reader, even those not enthralled by odd books, should read. Everyone finds something in it that captures them, that niggles at their mind, that does not let go. For me it was Johnny. For you it may be something else, some small thing that I never caught, perhaps that no one else did, which is not impossible despite the depth of analysis that many have put into this monster. Read it.

FURTHER READING

Whalestoe Letters
Mark Danielewski

Finnegans Wake*
James Joyce

Pale Fire
Vladimir Nabokov

---

*   Just kidding. Don't do this to yourself.

THE ORANGE EATS CREEPS
By Grace Krilanovich
Two Dollar Radio (2010)
Original post: IROB, 07/27/2010

Why do I consider this book odd?
It's like a drug-induced nightmare. There's no plot, characterization or coherence of thought. Also, I had to stop reading halfway through yet still want to discuss it.

I've been on a bad streak lately, book-wise. I struggled through a bland horror novel by one of my favorite writers and lost about two weeks as I forced myself to keep reading though I longed to quit and move on to something else. By the last 30 pages, I just skimmed. By the last ten pages, I gave up. Then I picked up a book that was supposedly about the social and sexual politics of using one's body to make money, mainly through sex work. When it became clear that the politics amounted to whining about how hard it is to be a girl, like even middle class white chicks get called a slut if they sleep with a boy OMG, I put it down.

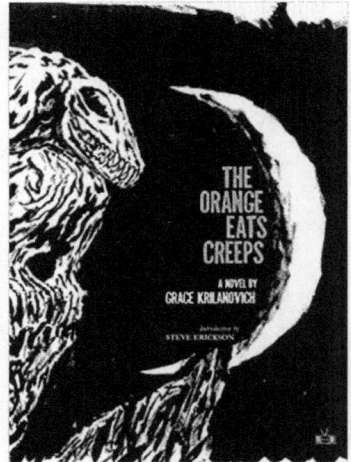

After giving up on that cheesy recitation of trivial girl-woes, I turned to *The Orange Eats Creeps*. Well, I should clarify that I had begun reading Krilanovich months ago, only I had to put it down because I couldn't make sense of it. My second attempt was much more successful. I got to page 95. Then I stopped reading with the knowledge I was never going to finish it.

That is a difficult thing for me to do. I have, in the past, taken a very hard line with my reading habits. If I begin a book, I tell myself I must finish it. Lately I haven't been able to follow through. I just don't have time left in my life to struggle through books that don't interest me or books that are not good. Which is why it sucked so much to give up on *The Orange Eats Creeps* because it did, ultimately, interest me. I don't think it was a bad book. It was just too uncontrolled, too scattered, too lacking in what one needs to make a novel; you can open this book to any page and begin reading and it will make no more or less sense than if you begin reading from the first page. (And if it seems like dirty pool discussing a book I didn't finish, I promise I won't make a habit of it.)

Before I begin my discussion of those first 95 pages, I need to get a rant out of the way. This book's marketing was so utterly misleading that I suspect it pissed off many readers. Unless things are very different at Two Dollar Radio, the publisher, I understand that most writers have no say in how their book is promoted. I could be wrong. It's possible that Krilanovich approved of her publishers' approach. If so, I'm all apologies. But I really can't imagine any writer would want their work so dreadfully misrepresented. *The Orange Eats Creeps* is *not* about junkie vampires roaming the Pacific Northwest and encountering strange sights as they search for the protagonist's sister. It is not a new, fresh look at vampires, or even a traditional vampire story set in a grubbier time. When I heard about this book and read some of the blurbs written about it, I thought, "Oh wow, this sounds like *Near Dark* but with grunge in the place of Southern culture on the skids." That was not the case. This is not a vampire novel at all. It is a stream-of-consciousness narrative that has no plot and no real characterization. It's the epitome of an experimental novel. It is difficult to follow, and it has no linear storytelling. Yet it was advertised as follows:

> A band of hobo vampire junkies roam the blighted landscape—trashing supermarket breakrooms, praying to the altar of Poison Idea and GG Allin at basement rock shows, crashing senior center pancake breakfasts—locked in the thrall of Robitussin trips and their own wild dreams.

In this book blog of mine, have I ever called anyone an asshole before? If I haven't, let me do so now. Whoever wrote this description, which is from the inside cover flap of the book and was reproduced on several book sale venues, is an asshole. Seriously. While some of the promotional text is technically true, it paints a picture of the book that is not true. There's no hint to the fact that it's a difficult book, a book written in a highly experimental style. That was a mistake because even though I found the narrative so jagged and jangling (so much so that it was like a kaleidoscope in the form of a book), there are still moments of narrative brilliance. Passing it off as a junkie vampire hobo book during the time Kurt Cobain ruled the Pacific Northwest robs Krilanovich's experiment of its purpose. The pitch taints her efforts. Those who wanted a vampire novel will only walk away annoyed, while readers who want an experimental novel will never pick it up.

"Praying to the altar" of anything gives the impression that these are kids who attend punk shows as a part of their credo of identity. That's not what's going on at all. Music is barely a side note, if you will. Those few shows are seen through the jumbled eyes of the teenage narrator whose name we never learn (unless it comes up after page 95), and as a result, if music were important, it would have been robbed of its importance by the narrative style.

"Crashing senior center pancake breakfasts" happened once before I stopped reading. The heroine ate several servings of pancakes and was doted on by the elderly denizens—you can't crash a place where you are obviously welcome. And the "crashing" takes up maybe three lines in the book. Why mention it at all on the inside cover flap? As for "their own wild dreams?" Bullshit. There were no shared dreams. We don't know a thing about anyone in this book other than the messy and chaotic mind of the protagonist. There is no "their" there.

There is no vampire there, either. This is not even a spoiler—this is a fact that becomes abundantly clear within the first ten pages or so. The girl's mind cannot be trusted so you take it with a grain of salt when she says she is a vampire. She gets caught sucking on a man's neck in her early teens and you know she is talking about sex in her fantastic, disjointed way. Later, when she speaks of vampirism, it's clear she is talking about drugs, her fears, her knowledge of her own inner predator. This is *not* a vampire novel. This is a novel of lost youth, of homeless kids addicted to anything they can get their hands on, roaming around and behaving badly. No more, no less.

The plot, such that there is, follows a small gang of young men and the narrator, our fucked-up heroine, as they wander about aimlessly and purposelessly. The heroine wants to find her sister Kim. They were in a foster home together and Kim took off and joined her own gang of "vampires." The search takes place mainly in the heroine's mind, but Kim occupies a lot of her thoughts. There's a passage in the book that can lead the reader to believe that there is no Kim, or that the narrator is Kim. If either is the case, then this really is a book without a plot, and simply an examination of a seriously fragmented mind. That's not a necessarily a criticism because these sorts of mental examinations can be very interesting.

But the narrator's thoughts, her filtering of events, are ultimately what made this book intolerable to me. I don't know if I would have felt this way had I bought this book knowing what it really is. I can say that even if I had been given a clue as to what I was in for, I still would have found the narrative bereft of meaning. Perhaps that was the point? If so, it's not my cup of tea. It's just one event after another, sometimes events within events, the past bleeding into the present with no clear delineation between the two, with no linear continuity, spewed forth from the mind of the heroine. This narrative is what I imagine my brain would be like if I were punched over and over in the face, unable to respond before the next punch landed.

That's what happened to me as I read—my brain never had a chance to recover from one reeling inner dialogue to the next. The onslaught of the narrator's memories combined with her current activities with no plot, no timeline, no framework of reason outside of the longing for Kim, rendered the punch of each of the memories meaningless.

I can't fault Krilanovich for trying. It was a bold idea, to launch this mental assault on the reader. It was just too much for me. With that "too much" factor coming after the misleading and shitty marketing, *The Orange Eats Creeps* should be a complete failure. But it isn't.

Once Krilanovich refines her voice and finds a way to level her assault without knocking the reader out before she can make her point, she will be in a fine position. She already possesses a capacity for breathtaking prose. There are moments of utter truth in this book. There are sections that I reread several times, marveling at her talent. Take this scene in a restaurant where the narrator notices a strange girl whose strangeness will never get her the attention she needs:

> But then I noticed the girl had barf all down the front of the dress and when she opened her mouth it went something like this: "You guys. I just wanted to let you know that my family is coming in here and they are with the fucking mob, okay? They are organized crime, gangsters. They will hurt you. Be careful, they will fuck you up. Just don't say a word—be careful." And the strange thing was that then these white people came into the diner and it was her family, her parents and a sibling, Midwestern types in honest wool and small gold jewelry. They sat and ordered breakfast while the girl spent the majority of the meal in the bathroom, regurgitating. She returned to the table and fell asleep. They laughed with their mouths closed, polished off their various plates and exited as the girl threw up on the booth and waiting area before leaving some vomit on the front door. But the family didn't run out the door, they strolled—without even pretending to mime the international gesture for "Sorry, let me wipe all this up." Outside they wrapped their safety belts firmly around their midsections and drove away, the girl just folded into the back seat somewhere. God knows where.

Jesus, I felt badly for both the family and the girl. In such a beige family, anyone odd was going to suffer but then again, it seems they had seen her at her worst for so long it didn't even register. This reminded me of the scene in *Se7en* where Morgan Freeman is reading John Doe's notebook, wherein he describes trying to make small talk but vomits all over the prating man who is talking to him, so sickened is he by the banality of it all.

This scene showcases Krilanovich's skill, but it also gives a tiny little taste of the disjointed nature of the narrative:

> One summer I caught an evil little pet. I caged it but it ditched me. No problem. After it left me I made it do my bidding from afar. Now I have remote control over its doings, ties I hitched over endless indelible months of putrid wanderings. Walking lost, my body boiling like water until all the thoughts in my head just evaporate. The swath of vapor in the sky infects your lungs and forced me into bubbles in your brain with every predictable breath. That summer I was a teenage carnivore. On hot nights I dug little things here and there that I found buried in holes. Creeping around under

steel overpasses downtown I lived with my eyes to the ground, struck by how many gutter punks, panhandlers, dumpster divers, gakkers, vagrants, and romantic tramps would never even fuckin get it: the fact that we have to dig for stuff we don't understand cuz we live in a past we don't understand. I found a videotape in among some other stuff. It was of some kids partying in an apartment. They were all high on speed, tattooing each other while the girl held her cat to her chest, drunk, lying down on her living room floor. She looked absently at what was going on around her, a bit bewildered perhaps but casually luxuriating in her drunken nonchalance. She flipped through religious pamphlets in the dark. I identified with that girl on the tape, her predicament leapt right out at me from her crooked mouth. She looked at me but her bangs hid it all.

This is jumbled, incoherent, stark and true—true especially for the truly lost among the Generation X. The narrator is tied to her lost sister, identifying with other lost girls as she searches, mostly in her mind. She's digging in the dirt but she's never going to find the right lost girl. There are too many of them.

Then there is this. Words fail me to explain why I love it so much:

Jacob said that nobody but Jacob owns his body. He decides who it fucks and who it pummels. "We own nothing but what's inside. It's the middle of the night in here," he said, pointing to his chest. This is what we own: our thoughts, orange and sickly. You feed it nothing but sorrow and it grows and stars come out and you are the King of your own Island of Night.

Please bear in mind that these are but small samples of the narrative that beat my brain. At no time will you have a firm idea of what is happening. And for some of you, I realize that may be just fine. I know some of my readers crave a challenging narrative the way I crave caffeine and clean carpets. But Krilanovich takes challenging to a new level, a level of confusion where all an earnest reader can get from such experimental storytelling is a sense of the sickness of addiction, the loneliness of loss and wallowing in that which is unclean. And that would have been good enough for me, given the gorgeousness of the prose, had the sickness, the loneliness and the wallow any sort of narrative direction.

I wonder how Krilanovich's novel would have read to me if I had been intoxicated when I read it. Stoned. In the jittery aftermath of speed. I wonder what it would be like to be a fucked-up girl reading about a fucked-up girl, a girl so fucked-up that she defied explanation, resulting in marketing that has nothing to do with the meat between the covers because one suspects that actually describing her accurately is impossible.

I wonder how it would feel to be so punch drunk reading this that the blows of this windmilling narrative don't even register. Thankfully I am not such a fucked-up girl anymore. I admit that may have been part of the problem.

Even so, I want to keep my eye out for Krilanovich. I think she is a writer who will either get better and better with each novel or she will crack under the weight of unfocused talent. I tend to think it'll be the former and want to read her next venture to see if I'm right.

FURTHER READING

Night Film: A Novel
Marisha Pessi

CRIMINAL TRACES

A good depiction of madness in fiction is worth its weight in nonfiction self-help manuals. Read a few very good books focusing on mentally ill characters and the truth of the depiction may help you avoid psychopaths and predators in your real life. Once you see the subterfuge that hides the madness, you may find yourself noticing such deflections from sanity among people in your daily life—usually your boss and the weird neighbor who won't pick up his dog's messes from your yard. Mileage may vary.

THE DIARY OF A RAPIST
By Evan S. Connell
New York Review of Books (2004 reprint[1])
Original post: 01/19/2010

Why do I consider this book odd?
It presents a graphic first-person study of the mind of a man who presumably rapes a woman yet still sees himself as potentially court-ing her. Also, A.M. Homes pens the introduction and while she's not full-bore odd, she hovers near enough the fringes to seal the deal.

I'm a sucker for depictions of madness, so believe me when I tell you that Earl Summerfield, the titular diarist in Evan Connell's memorable 1966 novel, *The Diary of a Rapist*, is madness personified. This is not a tale of a man descending into madness. It is the tale of a madman—a madman in whose thoughts and deeds we can observe the myriad ways human madness is experienced and expressed.

While I generally do not read reviews of books before I review them myself, I did brush against some other opinions in advance of writing this one. Apparently, some readers view Earl Summerfield as a precursor to the modern Everyman, a person lured into madness by the world around him. This doesn't ring true to me. Earl was not made mad. He is mad. He is a misogynistic paranoiac with violent tendencies. Though we don't know how it is Earl came to be such a miserable bastard, the novel does not suffer from this lack of explanation. Connell could not have done a better job painting a picture of a repellent, insane human being.

The diary begins on January 1. Earl recounts his psychological tug of war in his world. He has both deep love and hatred for his wife, who is older than him and much better able to get along in the world. His love and hatred for his wife echoes the self-love and self-loathing Earl feels, as well as his love and hatred for the world as a whole. His utter misogyny and pedophilic tendencies begin to reveal themselves. He swings between moods of narcissistic euphoria and complete self-contempt. One day he respects his co-workers, the next he despises them and feels acute paranoia in their company.

Occasionally, Earl has cause to feel a sense of grinding down, like when his supervisor chides him to scurry to his desk faster because the head honcho wants to see an increase in productivity. His is a job in which he fears even

---

1   Originally published by Simon & Schuster in 1966.

doodling because his supervisors pace behind him as he fills out unemployment claims for men he despises. His job is repetitive and he has two passive-aggressive supervisors who pounce on his every mistake. Earl is so hungry for any sort of recognition in his monotonous work world that when he is informed that he is punctual and makes few mistakes, he sees this as a sign that he must be in line for a grand promotion.

It can be tempting to blame his madness on his tiresome job, but his workplace cannot be blamed for his insanity. His work-world is Kafka-esque but the boredom and minor humiliations he experiences are not enough to turn a man into a pedophile, a rapist and a wife-hating narcissist. This is why I disagree with those who think the intensity of the (then) modern world triggered Earl's descent. No one who was not insane to begin with ends up like Earl because of a job. Earl is a lunatic because Earl is Earl, not because his workplace does not respect his humanity.

Earl is destined, it seems, to become violent. He avidly reads and records terrible crimes in his diary and clips news articles for a scrapbook. At times he exhibits outrage at how terrible the world is, and other times sympathizes with those who commit crimes. His sympathy is so exaggerated at times that it makes the reader wonder how involved Earl might have been in some of the crimes he reads about.

Earl writes in his diary every single day until Christmas, except for July 4, the day when he presumably rapes a beauty queen outside of her church. Earl does not record the details of the rape as he does the details of the other crimes in the Bay Area of California, but later, as he becomes more and more unraveled, he reveals what he did, sharing small details about the attack on the beauty queen.

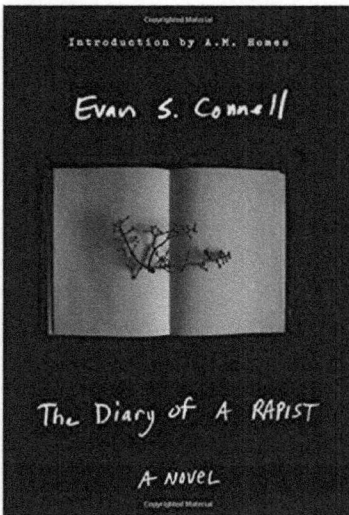

The book is cagey about whether or not Earl really raped the beauty queen, as he is the King of Unreliable Narrators. No one has any idea if anything he wrote happened. So we may wonder if he really is a rapist. Did he just make it all up? Some readers think so. Count me in the number who think he did it.

Just as with his wife, Earl loves and hates the beauty queen he claims to have raped. After the rape, he stalks and calls her. Initially he does it to taunt her, to make her feel fear, but later he does it because in his twisted mind, he wants a relationship with the woman, believing that if only he could meet her again, perhaps she would love him. The way Earl leads up to the crime is reminiscent of a non-violent Night Stalker. He begins by creeping through people's homes at night as they sleep, a way to use up nervous energy and to feel subversively alive. He also sexually torments some girls his wife tutors, to the point that she makes him leave the home when they come over to prevent him from looking up their skirts or trying to watch them in the bathroom. I am unsure how much was known in 1966 about the escalation of criminal inclination, beginning with small transgressions, testing the waters, but it hardly matters because Connell gets the criminal progression right.

Earl is such an interesting, deranged, sickening character that I had trouble putting the book down. I powered through the book so fast, devouring his sickness, that I had to go back and reread large chunks of it because I read too quickly for deep comprehension. On my second reading, Earl's grandiosity, his random and trivial thoughts that he himself thought to be utterly profound, hit me in a way they did not the first time around.

Initially, Earl seems very impotent. He has grotesque fantasies that one cannot see him acting out because he seems so... bitchy and small. But as the diary goes on, one begins to wonder. When his wife orders him out of the apartment for leering at the two girls she tutors, he takes a walk and this is his reaction:

> Went out and walked around the block several times, caught a Geary bus & calmly cut a hole in the seat—only satisfaction I got all day. Would like to slice up two schoolgirl bellies. Remind me of fresh green melons. If they think they can make fun of me they'll regret it.

The reader may still think of Earl as an even more unhinged Walter Mitty, imagining himself in roles he will never fulfill, but Connell neatly forecasts what will happen. The destruction of a bus seat in place of stabbing a girl. The paranoia that people are laughing at him. We may think Earl is a powerless pervert, but something active is building.

His greedy absorption of the crime around him just fuels his sickness. From his February 15 entry:

> News report tonight says some divorcee in San Rafael woke up early this morning and saw a man standing beside her bed with a stocking mask over his face. According to the newscaster she got away. I doubt it. Have a feeling she was tied up with a sheet—almost as though I dreamed it. Trussed like a dainty white animal, tied into a sack so tight she could only move her toes, the Parts hanging out of the mouth—those hairy purple lips. Packed stiff like a sausage. Probably gagged & blindfolded so she looked like a mummy and couldn't struggle.

This entry comes about four months before the assault on the beauty queen but it makes one wonder how much Earl dreamed. Perhaps he was the man in the stocking mask, but perhaps he dreamed what happened to the beauty queen. The fact is, his mental illness is so clearly demonstrated that it seems likely that he did engage in sexual violence and wallowing in crime reports just allowed him to mentally prepare for his own crime.

Given his behavior around his wife's pupils, unable to control his peeping even when his wife is in the room, his obsession with the abduction of a 14-year-old girl called Loretta Lengfeldt seems creepy as hell. His speculation about what happened to her is disturbing in the extreme. From his entry on March 13:

> Lying on her side with hands tied behind her and naked as a nymph strangled with her own brassiere—that would be my guess. Probably tied up like a piece of pork. Got what she deserved for nibbling on a chocolate doughnut and showing her fat little buttocks to everybody on the street. Probably when they find her body they'll see teethmarks on those tender boobies, maybe a nipple missing or an earlobe chewed. She'd taste like an apple… Don't tell me they don't deserve to be butchered.

The whole book, while detailing Earl's sense of humiliation at work and his hatred for his wife, revolves around his hatred and love for the beauty queen Mara St. Johns. He first sees her on February 22 in a Washington's Birthday celebration, wearing a bathing suit:

> She looked like one of those professional sluts from Hollywood. If she isn't the symbol of American rottenness, what is? Program said she was active in the Presbyterian church! There's hypocrisy for you Earl, but some day the wheel is going to come full circle for her too—for her and all the others like her. For the dirty things they do.

He follows stories about Mara St. Johns in the newspaper, tracking down her schedule until he presumably rapes her outside her church on July 4. On July 14 he says:

> How very different I feel tonight. Remembering for instance how quick and powerful I felt as soon as I touched her… (s)he wanted me to talk. Say something! Say something! On her knees and in the corner trying to see my face & begging me to talk. I don't know, think I did say something. Annoyed when she asked whether I believed in God.

Earl eventually begins to covet his victim, seeing himself as a potential suitor, jealous of a man he sees as competition for her attentions. On August 27 he catches a glimpse of a woman who looks like Mara St. Johns and he convinces himself it was her, talking to her fiancé:

> Well, I've tried to hide my feeling, keep it out of sight, but I may as well admit the fact—I'm jealous. I'd kill him if I could… I sit here hating him, so sick & weak with jealousy I can't even clench my fist… If only I knew how she felt about me! Well, I know where she lives. I could go there. I could see her again. Tell her I'm coming?

Earl continues in this manner, beginning to see his rape as the first step in wooing the beauty queen, and, in a sense, one can almost understand it. She is the only person who has ever seen him for who he is. Not even his wife, who loathes him for sexually harassing her students, knows the real Earl like Mara does. He convinces himself she feels affection for him. On August 29:

> Why did she catch my wrist when I got ready to leave?—and she did, yes, I didn't make that up. She wanted me to stay. Or was it some instinct saying she didn't want to be alone. I need to know....

He becomes romantic about her. From August 31:

> I'll send her a gift. What is appropriate? Jewels are cold, with undertones of death. I could send her a pebble washed by the ocean. Or the wing of a white seagull.

He begins to stalk her anew, going to the church again, waiting for her. He admits he thought of her as "Mara Summerfield," that he imagined domestic bliss and marriage with the woman he raped. He calls her on September 29:

> Thought she might not recognize me with a handkerchief near my lips but she began to cry and threaten me. Then suddenly she stopped, that was what made me suspicious. And with good reason. Someone else was there because I heard her whispering. Put me in an ugly temper so I said things I never meant to say. Sorry for what I said. I wanted us to have a nice conversation...

And it continues, his delusion and obsession with violence, peppered with the insults he believes he suffers in the world and the meanderings of his increasingly disordered mind. No one knows what happens to old Earl in the end but I want to believe he put himself out of his misery. His entry from October 31 leads one to believe he just might ("This day wondering if I shall join the early Saints."). He probably doesn't, though. A bastard as miserable as Earl clings to his misery like pearls. He is a masochist as well as a sadist.

Even if Earl did not rape Mara St. Johns, if all of this is just the rambling of a disturbed mind, what a remarkably disturbed mind it is. Connell's ability to convey the disorganized thoughts of a madman is compelling. Take this gem from July 12, where it seems Earl is justifying the rape:

> The Devil is supposed to have a forked penis so he can commit sodomy and fornication simultaneously, yet we build gods in the image of ourselves because it's implausible to do otherwise, consequently there's no reason for me to feel upset. How can one already worn out by this corrupt world understand Incorruption? Let the human race lament and let animals rejoice, etc. Yes, that's how it us, for the world has lost its youth and the times are beginning to grow old.

Another gem, from November 1:

> Ideally, I think, life ought to be severe & chaste. Have I myself attempted to

live that way? I believe so. Example to be followed, discipline beyond the reach of most. Yes. Yes. Austerity and temperance. Integrity. Counter the evil tendencies of Man, just as sailors counter currents driving them toward the Reef, thus the expression of attitudes impossible to those of a lower sensibility. Object to object. Tincture of earthworm, poultice of adder's flesh.

Whoa...

It may seem like it would grow tiresome, reading the intense accounts of a man who is so unpleasant, so distinctly unhinged, recording in everloving detail his every demented thought, but it doesn't. Even if you are not drawn to accounts of madness as I am, *Diary of a Rapist* will absorb and unsettle you. It will make you question whether you can really know someone, especially that quiet guy at work who sometimes looks at you funny.

FURTHER READING

An Assasin's Diary
Arthur Bremmer

Notes from Underground
Fyodor Dostoevsky

The End of Alice
A.M. Homes

The Nihilesthete
Richard Kalich

The Case Worker
George Konrád

THIRTEEN GIRLS
By Mikita Brottman
Nine-Banded Books (2012)
Original post: 03/05/2014

Why do I consider this book odd?
Because it made me feel a bit less odd about my own obsessions.

The concept is deceptively simple—short stories about the fate of thirteen young women, some killed by famous serial killers, some picked off like ducks in a row, casual victims in an ugly world. While *Thirteen Girls* is a work of fiction, the stories are based on real women and real crimes, and Mikita Brottman approaches the cases from varied perspectives: police report, perp interview, anguished mother, dieting co-worker, angry boyfriend, sole survivor, etc.

There was a game-like element for me as I read, wondering if I could guess who the girl was and who killed her before I reached the end of the story. Given my once-obsessive interest in serial murderers as well as just murderers in general, it was surprising I only really knew five (though several more rang some bells that didn't peal clearly until I got to the end of the book where the sources are revealed). One I missed was a victim of serial killer Bill Suff. I should have known that one. I once became obsessed with trying to track down the whole text of a cookbook Suff wrote, a task made all the more interesting because he evidently ate body parts from a few of his victims, going so far as to use a breast from a prostitute he killed in his "famous" chili recipe. I'm not sure why I wanted a cookbook written by a serial killer cannibal—the late 90s was a weird time in my life.

Before I get to the two stories I liked best, I want to discuss the overall nature of this book. I enjoyed reading it but, at the end, I found myself feeling like the collection hit a discordant note in some of the stories. I felt empty after I read them and felt that Brottman had missed the point somehow, that the stories were flawed because I felt flat after reading them, yet felt so

engaged with some of the others. The reason I felt that way was because I was the one who had missed the point.

If some of these stories don't provoke emotion, it's because they aren't supposed to. Because Brottman is showing us the different windows through which we can observe brutality. While I appreciate this collection for attempting to give the back or parallel stories associated with these murders, the casual memory of death Brottman shows in several of these stories is what makes this collection show something more than just another mawkish look at dead young women. It's a sad reality that not all deaths are memorable, that all murders do not change those who knew, however fleetingly, the person who was killed. The hell of it is, in terms of media and social awareness, it often seems like some victims do not matter at all. Sometimes the lack of interest plays out in the form of a phenomenon called "Missing White Woman" syndrome—black female abductees and murder victims don't get the media time afforded to white female abductees and murder victims. On a more personal level, sometimes a murder means little even to those left behind. While there is a sentimental viewpoint in some of Brottman's stories, the stories are anything but sentimental.

This is best shown in the twelfth story, "Vicky." Vicky's murder is told through a nurse she worked with for around a week or so, a woman whose diary begins with her food-log, as she is dieting and recording her caloric intake. The diary is full of the narrator's often inane observations. The co-worker she barely knew is just a small part of her life, recorded amongst diet advice and details of shift swaps with other nurses. Her observations about the drunks she encounters during her shifts carry the same weight in her diary as Vicky's murder. She's a trivial sort of woman but she's not utterly callous—how much investment could she have in a woman she knew for such a short time? This one initially fell rather flat with me but, a week or so later, I understood what Brottman was going for. In death we can be quickly forgotten, be it in the imagination of the public or the minds of people who knew us. Not every murder victim is Laci Peterson or the Black Dahlia. For some, the only impact their death will make on others can be summed up by a few lines in a dieting nurse's diary.

I think I prefer more catharsis than can be found in "Vicky," but there's no way for me to deny how powerful a piece it is once I abandon my own sentimentality.

I'm going to discuss a couple of the stories I feel are more obvious, meaning that the average reader of this blog may recognize the victim or the killer. There's really no way to "spoil" such stories because we all know how the story will end—with a dead woman. But there is an odd pleasure in approaching these stories with a certain amount of knowledge and seeing if you can anticipate how the story will unfold. So I will limit my discussions to the two stories that I think are most firmly rooted in the public imagination.

The thirteenth story, entitled "Mirasol," portrays a murder scene a lot of people will identify before the end. All you have to say is "Filipino nursing students" and the name "Richard Speck" isn't far behind. The narrator in "Mirasol" is the sole survivor of the mass rapes and murders that took place in student housing in Chicago. Richard Speck entered the student housing late at night and raped, tortured and killed eight student nurses, two of whom were from the Philippines. There were nine students there but Speck lost count and the survivor is telling this story. Brottman decided to call this survivor Mirasol.

Mirasol managed to evade attack because she hid, rather effectively, under a bed and Speck either forgot how many students had been in the house or was so messed up on drugs he was confused. Another victim arrived in the middle of the mayhem, after he made his initial head count, and he failed to adjust his numbers. Brottman tinkered with dates in some of the stories, changed names in the others to protect the living, so the names will not match up for those who know this crime in depth. Brottman does this in other stories as well, creating slightly different details or assigning victims different names.

At any rate, I think "Mirasol" is the strongest story in the collection. There's plenty of catharsis and it was the best place to end the collection. If you have read reports of how the real Mirasol handled herself during Speck's trial, it will make the ending of this story all the more powerful. It begins by showing how the Filipina students felt very different from their American roommates. They felt their American counterparts were more sophisticated but they didn't particularly want to be like them:

> The hospital Jeep picked us up every morning at six-thirty, and if we were late, we had to walk. We started work at seven and finished at three-thirty, when the Jeep would bring us back home. Then the three of us would go to Foodland to buy rice, fish, tomatoes, pineapple and spices. We made what we knew: cocidos, torta, kare-kare. We had bought our own pots, pans and glasses out of our wages, because I am sorry to say the American girls were not clean. Dishes were supposed to be washed and dried within an hour of the meal, but if the American girls cooked, they often left dishes in the sink. Happily, they did not use the kitchen often. Mostly, they ate take-away food.

It's something many of us have experienced first-hand—messy roommates who annoy us. But mixed with a sort of stranger-in-a-strange-land element, we can see the chasm between the Americans and the Filipinas. This is important because, as obvious as it may seem, these girls will, but one, end the same way, very much together in death.

Brottman is a subtle writer. She's not going to club you over the head with observations, which is why it took me a bit to really absorb how excellent this collection really is. She assigns a curious fearlessness to Mirasol, a fearlessness that comes and goes and is what keeps her alive, though there is still an element of chance to it all.

That night, I did not say my prayers.

Why? I do not know.

Perhaps I was not ready to die.

Mirasol's real name is Corazon, and I have to think Brottman wrote this with her real name in mind even as she gave her a pseudonym. Corazon, literally "heart" in Spanish, seems like she was abandoned by God when Speck knocked on her door but she had the heart to resist and to try to live. She and the other Filipina student nurses tried to hide together in a closet, praying for their safety. Led to believe he was just there for money, the three left the closet and were corralled into a single room with the others.

Then Brottman goes to a place in the story I mentally did not want to consider; she shows a conversational and friendly Speck, who spoke to the nurses with a calm, soft voice, who seemed most smitten with the plumpest girl (actual victim Pamela Wilkening). His mild demeanor put the nurses into a sort of torpor where they believed that if they just gave this man their money, he would let them live. Even as he tied them up, they believed he would not hurt them. This happened in 1966—four years before I was born—and the world was a more innocent place. Yet I still cannot believe the nine women let this happen, and I assume this stance with all the bravado of a person not in a room with Richard Speck in the middle of the night. It's easy to look at these victims and want to armchair quarterback their actions, as if this is a scary movie and we can't believe the heroine running from the maniac decided to scurry down into the basement to hide rather than run out the front door to escape. Real life, as Brottman shows, is generally less heroic and far more anticlimactic than cinematic mayhem.

One by one, save one, they were led from the room. Whispered conversations about fighting back were shot down in favor of compliance. After they heard the first victim being stabbed, the bound nurses tried to hide—against the walls, under the bunk beds, behind the door. Under a bunk bed, Mirasol listened to the give of bed springs as Speck raped one of the nurses.

At times this story has an almost formal, recitation-like quality, which I interpreted as an attempt to mimic Mirasol's thorough testimony. But when it matters, Brottman supplies incredible tension. After all the other nurses are dead, Mirasol's torment takes on a nail-biting quality.

> I lay waiting for him to come back, and after a long time, he did. He turned on the light. There was a small gap between two sheets, and I could see him looking round the room. He took a purse, shook it, and a bill fluttered to the ground. He bent over to pick it up. He was right in front of me. I closed my eyes.

I did not breathe for a long time. The house was silent, but I had not heard the front door close. I thought he was still in the house. I did not know, then, that he had walked off into the night, leaving the door wide open.

Mirasol/Corazon, the heart, the girl who forgot to talk to God because she was not ready to meet Him yet, lives. Though I have spoiled the story almost completely, you need to read it anyway. It's the "price of admission" story for this collection, the story that is alone worth buying this book to read.

The other story I think most readers will find somewhat familiar is "Tracy." Another finely written piece, the murder is recalled, years later by the grown daughter of the victim's boyfriend. Her divorced father, a doctor, has a rotating roster of nurses he dates. Tracy is his latest girlfriend. The father, who doesn't see his kids very much, decides to take them to a medical conference in Aspen, bringing Tracy along to look after them.

The kids resent Tracy being there, though they like her better than their father's last girlfriend, a woman who was evidently a complete lunatic. Tracy tells the kids nasty stories about the elderly patients she cares for, stories they proclaim gross even as they are thrilled hearing them. Tracy makes an effort, appreciated only in hindsight.

> Tracy wasn't crazy although she did crazy things. She'd try to make us laugh by puffing her face out and rolling her eyes. She could do bridge, crab, handstands and cartwheels. Last time she and Dad went to a conference, she bought us Aeropostale shirts, a red one for me and a blue one for Jason, which was pretty nice of her, though we figured they were really from Dad, because he paid for them. She also gave me a striped tote bag that she said she never used anymore.

The narrator remembers the inane details that seem to come back to us when we remember something terrible. Tracy spends the day on the slopes wearing the sweater the father had bought her for Christmas. They had seen a man skiing with a baby in a pack on his back and considered it a risky move. They have dinner with another doctor, who had been Tracy's boyfriend before she dated the kids' dad, which strikes them as weird. All these little details mean nothing, really, but they show the banality of death in terms of how it is remembered, years later.

This story also shows the maddening view of the road not taken, how it is ordinary choices mean everything in the end. After the dinner with Tracy's ex, one of these choices is made.

> Dad sat down in front of the fire, crossed his legs and picked up a copy of the *New York Times* from the table. We had comics to read. Mark had a copy of *Confidential* that he'd just finished. Tracy asked if she could read it. She said she'd trade it for her *Pandora* and asked Dad to go to the room to get it. Dad said he wanted to warm up by the fire, and she'd have to go get it herself. I watched her getting on the elevator. She was still wearing her boots and

puffy ski jacket, and she turned and smiled at me before the doors opened and she stepped inside.

They never see her again. She just disappears. The police don't search for her immediately because they figure Tracy has taken off after a lover's spat and would show up in the morning. When Tracy doesn't return after a day or so, the police finally act. Local news programs ask viewers for information about her disappearance. The police investigation shows that she didn't leave town in an obvious way, like renting a car or flying away in a plane. Eventually, the dad and the kids have to fly back home without her.

> Jason was sitting behind us. He put his head against the crack between Dad and me, and said he remembered watching a TV show about missing people, and they said a woman who goes missing without her purse has a zero chance of being found alive.
>
> "Thanks a lot, Jason," said Dad.
>
> When they finally found Tracy's body, they discovered that she'd been murdered less than an hour after we last saw her.
>
> Everyone said that was something to be thankful for, but I didn't see why.

I bet as an adult the narrator knows why.

Tracy is based on Caryn Campbell, who disappeared from a ski lodge while her physician boyfriend was sitting by the fire in the lobby. Caryn went missing in 1975, and while investigators eventually had an idea of who killed her, it wasn't until Ted Bundy confessed to her murder just before his execution in 1989 that the book could really be closed on her case. This one, of all of Bundy's murders, haunted me. To just walk away in a place of safety, with your boyfriend right downstairs, seems impossible. I first read about Bundy when I was in my late teens and it just seemed implausible that anyone could be that charming, that likable, and also be able to kill someone so brutally. It made no sense to me.

Like the child narrating the story, I understand it now, the mask psychopaths wear. I'm older than most of the women whose stories are told in this book. Actually, I think I am older than all of them. Mr. OTC says I have a pretty good psychopath-o-meter, and I do. He listens to me when I tell him someone is making me uneasy because generally that uneasy feeling ends up being right on the money. But no one can tell a killer from a savior in a split second, and that is all it takes sometimes, isn't it, for a victim to misread a predator's intentions. In a sense, we are all potential victims.

In telling the "untold" stories of these murdered women, Brottman shows all the wrinkles in the fabric—the pointless remembrances of babies in packs on slopes, the almost nihilistic quality of some deaths, the way that a single decision can alter the course of a person's life forever. The latter isn't a fresh approach—mystery and crime novels are full of such moments. But the freshness of an idea can be outweighed by compelling and insightful writing, which Brottman definitely displays in this collection. Highly recommended.

FURTHER READING

Evil: Inside Human Violence and Cruelty
Roy F. Baumeister, Ph.D.

Under the Skin
Michel Faber

Novels in Three Lines
Félix Fénéon

Murder, Mayhem, Hydrophobia
Compiled by Shirley E. Grose

Using Murder: The Social Construction of Serial Homicide
Philip Jenkins

The Girl Next Door
Jack Ketchum

The Serial Killer Files: The Who, What, Where, How, and Why of the World's Most Terrifying Murderers
Harold Schechter

Jesus Saves
Darcey Steinke

TAMPA
By Alissa Nutting
Ecco (2013)
Original post: 10/24/2014

Why do I consider this book odd?
"Hebephilia."

Celeste Price, who is definitely a stand-in for the real-life hebephile Debra Lafave,[2] is sexually attracted only to 14-year-old boys, preferably before they start puberty. This is especially problematic because she is married to an older man and has just begun a job teaching 8th grade English. Celeste is in her early 20s, and quite attractive. She is also a complete sociopath, wearing her mask of sanity and passing muster with other adults but engaging in risky behaviors, like very public masturbation. Preying on the children in her classrooms, she soon has an adolescent boy in her grasp. I don't think I'm spoiling anything when I reveal that Celeste eventually is hoisted by her own petard. That should pretty much go without saying. In a sense, it doesn't matter how things end for Celeste. The reason to read *Tampa* is to get a good look at the inner workings of the mind of a sociopath.

While I feel that this novel hits a discordant note, it also occurs to me that I feel this way because Alissa Nutting gets Celeste absolutely right. I mean to say that she nails Celeste—a full-on sociopath—and that's what makes *Tampa* fascinating. I read it in two sittings and was left feeling empty and disturbed. Celeste has no self-awareness beyond acknowledging her anti-social sexual orientation and the way she appears to others. She is an empty shell and she does not care. She can fine tune her behaviors to fit any situation, being a canny observer of people, but she only observes people insofar as they can benefit her in some manner. In this regard, she is an apex predator.

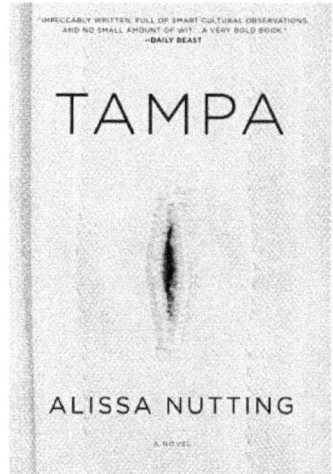

---

2   In 2004, Debra Lafave pleaded guilty to lewd and lascivious battery stemming from her sexual encounter with one of her male students, who was 14 years old at the time. See: https://en.wikipedia.org/wiki/Debra_Lafave

She reads very accurately those around her, devouring them when it suits her. She is shallow and her sexual needs render her ridiculous at times, but her shallowness is a marvel and no one else sees how ridiculous she is—only the reader is privy to the borderline idiocy that propels Celeste into action.

It can be hard to read about such people

And that's the hell of it, you know? How many more times can we read books where the major message is that evil is banal? Or that the monsters in our midst generally come off as trivial people? I think that may partly account for the discordant note this book hit with me—we've read this story before and before, and we will read it again and again.

Yet this book is so compulsively readable because Nutting, rather audaciously, does not attempt to humanize Celeste. At no point does the reader (well, this reader, at least) relate to Celeste, because she is a fucking sociopath. Her lust for boys is never explained on any level that could allow the reader to understand Celeste. This isn't *Lolita*. If you want a Humbert Humbert-style scene where Celeste reflects on and comes to understand the ruin she has caused her victims, you won't get it. Nor will you have much connection to either of the boys Celeste molests. *Tampa* is best approached for its clinical depiction of sociopathy. And yet, as grotesque as this may sound, it's also a reasonably funny book. The humor isn't dark in the vein of Nabokov—it's more campy, reminding me of Nicole Kidman's performance in *To Die For*.

Though Celeste is married to an adult, her life is a masturbate-athon involving fantasies of nubile boys. She preens sexually before her class, twisting her hair and letting it down, crossing her legs seductively while sitting on her desk, making sure her nipples are hard and her cleavage all too visible. At times we are in Celeste's mind so thoroughly that it is hard to stomach. I reckon it's hard for many adult women to read this book and not want to punch Celeste until her pretty face isn't so pretty any more (it was interesting, seeing my own humanity rise up when I read this book—I am far more maternal than I ever knew).

Celeste really is a terrible human being, a beautiful blonde who can rationalize anything. She thinks that having sex with Jack, one of her fourteen-year-old students, has actually helped him.

> He certainly didn't seem traumatized or the victim of something harmful—in fact his expression was alive with a dewy glow. Far more so than when I'd first picked him up, he looked spirited and engaged. He looked improved.

Initially Jack may seem improved. His home life is a mess, he seldom sees his father and he's got a hot adult with an awesome car giving him gifts and having sex with him. But before long the sexual manipulation takes its toll on his life in ways I could not imagine. Celeste eventually has to charm Jack's father, leading him to believe she is sexually interested in him, so as to continue to have sexual access to Jack. Knowing that his teacher/girlfriend is also having unpleasant sex with his father does Jack no favors.

But I'm getting ahead of myself.

Celeste stalks Jack before she begins her seduction, masturbating frantically outside his home as she determines how much time Jack spends alone, spying on him, finding out his weaknesses. One of her observations during her stakeout shows Celeste's sociopathic nihilism where other people are concerned, as well as her completely irrational thought processes. She is sitting in her car outside Jack's house when Jack's father comes home from work.

> He was an obvious multitasker. One hand held a phone to his ear; the other wheeled an oversized green trash bin behind him casually, like a suitcase—he could just as easily have been walking through the airport terminal. There was something repulsive (and revealing) about talking on a cell phone while handling garbage. Why did anyone pretend human relationships had value?

Celeste makes this incredible jump in logic from multitasking to questioning the value in all human relationships because she would never combine taking out the trash and talking on the phone. Every single action in her life has one of two purposes: to show the world how incredibly beautiful and together she is, or to gain access to teenage boys. Taking out the trash is not something Celeste would do, period, and if she is speaking on her phone, her only concern would be how she looked to anyone who might be observing her, not communicating with the person on the other end. Any activity that does not align with one of Celeste's two goals will simply confirm to her that the bulk of humanity is just going through the motions, unable to experience the emotional connections she thinks she achieves with the boys she exploits.

Celeste's victim selection shows her to be an excellent predator—strange that all of this turns out so poorly, but, then again, lust often makes fools out of even the best predator. Here Celeste is considering one of the boys in her class as a sort of second-choice option, and calculates the risk involved in pursuing him.

> Trevor was an artsy sort, whose hair was a wiggish crop of curls. A pensive journaler, he'd already asked if I'd look at some of his poetry. Since he walked home from school and didn't have to rush to catch a bus, he often came up to talk books and writing with me after class. But he had a girlfriend; most of his poetry was devoted to professing his love for her—Abby Fischer, in my second period, memorable for her chunk of her dyed purple hair. Being the romantic type, if Trevor ever did stray, he'd undoubtedly confess to her minutes after the act, likely through a series of frantic text messages that peppered statements of regret with frown-faced emoticons. He also came off as clingy, which could prove to be downright toxic. Trevor seemed like the type who would be ever more demanding, who would accept nothing less than symbiosis. Plus, based on his clothing, his parents were extremely

lenient. He had no fear of authority, which meant he would not be worried enough about getting caught and wouldn't act with the necessary level of caution.

This shows so well Celeste's mask of sanity. She can pick apart why it was that Trevor would not make a good victim, but she seemingly has no notion that any adolescent boy would become "clingy" and attached to any grown woman who lures him into a sexual relationship. Celeste's own experiences in this realm—lust for a specific age that dies when the boy gets too old— makes it impossible for her to understand the real emotional nature of ado- lescent attachment to molesters and victimizers. She will never be emotion- ally attached to anyone for very long. But this passage is still very interesting because it shows the selection processes that so many victimizers engage in—how they know instinctively which child will be too afraid to tell, which one will be too independent, which one will be compliant and which one will resist.

Celeste eventually settles on Jack, and it was here that I couldn't help but compare this book with some of Peter Sotos' works. The initial seduction scene for me was infinitely worse than anything Peter Sotos has ever written because we see it through the eyes of a woman who simply cannot see—who adamantly refuses to see—the damage she is inflicting. Say what you will about the purpose of Sotos' writing, but even when he channels the worst pieces of shit ever to walk the earth, he never shies away from showing that those villains understand what they are doing and how very sick it all is. Not so with Celeste. She will rape these boys and completely gut their lives, all the while thinking she is enabling them to drink their adolescent lives to the lees (all apologies to Tennyson). There's something to be said about self-aware villains.

Initially it appears that Celeste picks the perfect victim in Jack because he will do anything to ensure that his relationship with Celeste does not end. It does eventually end and it ends very badly and I cannot discuss what hap- pens without spoiling the book entirely. I do, however, want to discuss the very end of the book and if I don't give context for the scene, I can still share the words and what they show about Celeste.

Celeste, at the end, achieves a strange sort of awareness that is shallow but still better than anything I expected. She knows she is a prisoner of her very specific sexual orientation and she has no intentions of changing it or abstaining.

> Most of my time is spent on the beach by the resort or at an open waterfront bar where I sit in wait for disgruntled teenagers fed up at being in a hotel room with their family—sometimes they come out at dusk for a solitary walk. I look for the telltale pallor that implies they're on vacation. I'm not willing to take any risks on local boys.

Celeste engages in subterfuge and lies to get what she needs, but she is aware that time is not going to be on her side forever.

> For now, my youth and looks make this easy. I try not to think about the cold years ahead, when time will slowly poach my youth and my body will begin its untoward changes. I'll have to pare down to certain types: the motherless boys, or those so sexually ravenous they don't mind my used condition. Eventually I'll have to find a better-paying job in an urban area with runaways hungry for cash whom I can buy for an evening. But that won't be for many more years; there's lots of fun to be had between then and now.

Celeste is a person without redeeming qualities and in its own way that is so unique to encounter. The villain who has no intention of changing, of seeing the harm she does. She is a creature of the crotch, a completely immoral and amoral being who will literally do whatever she needs to get her fix regardless of what happens. She does not care one bit about the damage she causes, and she will not admit the damage she causes.

Although *Tampa* in its way is far more upsetting to me than Sotos, I still recommend reading it. It's graphic, but it's graphic in a different way. It's pornographic without being sexy—pornographic comedy, almost. Aspects of the plot seem so over-the-top that comedy outweighs the horror and disgust some readers may feel. It's earthy without being visceral, if that makes any sense. Celeste seems like a cardboard cut-out at times because she is so wedded to her sexual deviations that she does not seem real.

But she is real. The plot goes in far more extreme directions than I expected but, aside from those flights of extremity, it is genuinely disturbing how well Nutting captures the essential character of the sociopath, the narcissist, the predator for whom any damage is worth the thrill because she will never notice the damage at all. Nutting evidently attended school with Debra Lafave but her depiction of the sexual sociopath transcends anything that could be gleaned from simple proximity. Nutting is a keen observer, a woman who understands the worst human impulses. She even understands the dark comedy in these foul situations.

As shocking and difficult as this book is, it's worth it. It's a compelling read, audacious and sickening. When I came to the closing paragraph in the final chapter, I felt a slap in the face. It reveals the reason Celeste seems like a cartoon or a cut-out. It's because that is how everyone else appears to Celeste. No human is real in her eyes—we're all just paper dolls to the Celestes of the world, to those who would chew us up and spit us out and resent even having to think of us when they are through. Celeste is as intriguing as a Ruth Rendell character.[3] Celeste is horrible, disgusting and beyond every pale, but she's damned interesting. The book moves quickly, and Nutting's willingness to create a one-dimensional sociopath, refusing to redeem her, makes *Tampa* quite different from other books that explore such unsettling terrain.

FURTHER READING

What Was She Thinking? [Notes on a Scandal]: A Novel
Zoë Heller

The Talented Mr. Ripley
Patricia Highsmith

Defiance
Carole Maso

Adam and Eve and Pinch Me
Ruth Rendell

---

3   Rendell, who died in 2015, was for my money the best portrayer of mental illness, psychopathy and other personality disorders. If you haven't read her novels, start with is *Adam and Eve* or *Pinch Me*.

ALT-LIT

Alt-lit is a much maligned literary movement, and I've been one who maligned it. But even in the worst Dumpster aflame there may be something valuable that got tossed in by mistake. Here I show examples of the worst and the best alt-lit has to offer.

SHOPLIFTING FROM AMERICAN APPAREL
By Tao Lin
Melville Press (2009)
Original post: 05/09/2011

Why do I consider this book odd?
Does it really matter?

I genuinely do not understand how anyone could like this book, let alone the nice, earnest, decent people who recommended it to me. The only thing that prevented me from shitting on this book is the fact that I needed it in a relatively clean state so I could discuss it thoroughly, complete with quotes, even though quoting from it will only cause this godless endeavor to last longer as I type it all up.

But I have a rule. When I hate a book, I am compelled to support my case and explain thoroughly why the book is bad. I briefly considered ignoring *Shoplifting from American Apparel* and just letting the wretched memory of it die. But I couldn't. My compulsive nature forces me to discuss every odd book I read, and, more to the point, I just want my voice to be out there in the electronic wilderness, urging people not to waste their time. Tao Lin's book is the naked Emperor and I don't want anyone who reads my book journal to be a part of the crowd that refuses to say, "Hey, the Emperor has no clothes!" I have a responsibility as a discusser of odd books to make sure my readers understand how bad this book is.

Also, this may be the first bad review I ever enjoyed writing.

I cannot recall ever reading such an egregiously dishonest book. I say dishonest because I can only imagine Lin wrote this book as a litmus test. People who like it are clearly people he will be able to defraud further. I almost wonder if he managed somehow to track down the addresses of the people who liked his book because those are fresh couches to crash on when he inevitably gets evicted. The reason I say this book is dishonest is because it cloaks the naked and smarmy ambition of a talentless writer behind subcultures that ultimately have little to do with the emotional vacancy represented in Lin's words. Lin mimics many counter-cultural values, mainly those of vegans, Crimethinc and hipsters, and tries to pass off his hucksterism as an honest look at those cultures when it's really just him shitting all over everything.

Look, I understand that people have shit on those who write for a new zeitgeist pretty much since publishing evolved from the Gutenberg Press

Shoplifting from American Apparel.

Tao Lin

to a more accessible means of conveying ideas. Truman Capote demeaned Kerouac. Half the people I know would like to kill Holden Caulfield if he were a real human. Douglas Coupland mined his generation so thoroughly that some think he wrote himself into a place of relative irrelevance, and Bret Easton Ellis' scathing examination of 1980s consumer culture, *American Psycho*, is one of the most misunderstood books ever. Books that speak of a people who may not be our own, or of a culture that is different, or of a people who may be our own but are so morally bereft we can't admit it, run the risk of being seen as poorly written, or inexplicable or exploitative. Moreover, this most commonly happens when the middle-aged make the mistake of thinking they have a finger on the pulse of the young when they don't, walking into new works clutching their own ideas of art, connection and social relevance like so many pearls.

I can tell you with no small amount of emphatic anger that this is not that. I am not a woman long in her tooth clutching pearls at the antics of These Kids Today. This book is so foul that I didn't even have to second guess myself. This book is such an egregious piece of shit hiding behind what many consider to be hipster culture that it sickens me that people got taken in by it. To paraphrase the late, great Dorothy Parker, this not a book to be tossed aside—it is a book to be thrown with great force, preferably at a picture of Tao Lin that one has printed out from the Web and taped to the wall.

Before I tear this book apart with a ferocity born of knowing that this huckster will look at this review from a small potatoes reviewer and smirk as he adds it to all the negative reactions that he uses to build his brand, I feel the need to clear up a few things.

One, as a failed vegan who would very much like not to be a failed vegan, do not in any way misinterpret my criticisms of Tao Lin's use of veganism in this book as an indictment against veganism in general. That One Time You Ate A Hamburger And A Vegan Yelled At You notwithstanding, most vegans are extremely nice, extraordinarily principled and idealistic people who deserve respect for choosing a diet that, the mere mention of, causes even kind people to downshift straight into nastiness born from cognitive dissonance and crow about their paleo diet or how good cow tastes.

Second, I sort of like hipsters (and I often feel disliking hipsters is a clear sign of incipient fogeyism), so I find it interesting that so many hipsters embraced this book. I don't see this book as a hipster manifesto at all. To the contrary, I place Tao Lin is in the same camp, ironically enough, as men like Dov Charney who prey on hipsters. Young hipsters, to my eye, are the natural progression of edgy youth culture once the anger of punk wore itself out and the alienation of grunge wore thin. Sure, sure, the hipsters I've met definitely have an air of pretension about them, as do almost all young people. Youth is a time when we are meant to pretend, to try on new ideas and see how they fit. All young people are arrogant if they're doing it right. There's something sort of sad about a humble 20-year-old.

One of the reasons I like hipsters is because there is something to be said for people who make a virtue of that which does not require much money. Their currency in trade of knowing the arcane, like music and bands that are discarded when they become popular, is a means of wealth that people with cash in hand cannot achieve unless they are in that particular realm of knowledge. They have created a culture that is a lovely "fuck you" to the rest of us because no matter how often people sneer at them in their thrift threads worn ironically, they have a culture of particular value that permits them to sneer right back at us. They know things that we don't and never will until knowing them no longer has any value. There is a cultural renovation and reclamation behind hipsterism, a desire to have that which is unique and unknown that fuels their perceptions of status, that can be as hard to see as the hopefulness behind goths.

So, I clearly don't dislike hipsters and I don't think Tao Lin speaks for them, unless co-opting and hiding behind the sarcasm and irony of hipsters is a form of representation. Also, this book is really nothing but a depiction of Lin and he as a person cannot represent an entire subculture. Sam, the protagonist, represents no one, though he seems to be mimicking the hipsters as they mimic elements from certain cultures, taking us back into the recursive nightmare so often present in this book. But really, there is no subculture that sucks as much as a whole as Sam sucks individually. The youth of America, a generation that some insist are dumbed down, are not that dumbed down, and they certainly are not *this* dumbed down.

Third, a friend who is deeply into the Crimethinc counterculture praised this book highly because he felt as if this was the first time he had seen someone sort of like himself in a book. I have come across others in anarchist groups saying similar things and their enthusiasm was one of the reasons I decided to read Lin's book (though I have to say I have no idea if Tao Lin understood people like my friend would be drawn to his words). I understand my friend's perspective but I also think it is misguided (though he did steal his copy, which makes me feel better about the whole situation). Don't misunderstand me—despite the amount of time I spent in the retail trenches, I don't give a good goddamn if people shoplift. It's the cost of doing business and if it didn't happen, prices would still go up. A cultural aversion to theft is not a part of my distaste. This book is clearly autobiographical and Lin discusses his disaffected attempts at shoplifting, two of which got him arrested. No Crimethinc-er worth his or her salt would be that inept and if they were that inept, they wouldn't aggrandize their ineptitude because the whole point of shoplifting to them is to subvert capitalism and to sustain a life without the drudgery of work. To be known as a shoplifter to that degree would impair anyone's ability to continue to steal and would subvert the entire point behind stealing.

I really don't want to entertain a conversation about the relative morality of such a mindset—knock yourself out if you want to go there but I find such conversations wearying these days. But it has to be said that since Tao Lin has made a virtue of getting caught stealing (to the point that a flier was made up warning a store about him, and he uses that flier as a form of self-promotion now), it's pretty clear that ideology was never at play with Lin and this book cannot stand as an homage to that ideology. A man who uses a flier that proves he's a shitty thief to show what a counter-cultural dude he is is simply promoting himself, and however much I want Lin to go suck on a tailpipe for writing this book, I won't begrudge his talent for self-promotion. At that he is a genius.[1] Too bad the promotion is, at heart, the substance of what he has to convey to his audience.

With those three points cleared up, I'll start discussing the book.

In many ways, *Shoplifting from American Apparel* harks back to Camus' *The Stranger*, a sort of modern update on a book that I admit I am constitutionally unable to appreciate deeply, though I certainly understand its purpose and philosophical relevance. As I read Lin's book I was sent back in time to my first reading of Camus because *Shoplifting* seems to mimic the existential masterpiece where the protagonist caroms around, commits crimes and ultimately feels nothing. It was as if *The Stranger* had been reduced and made trivial (Lin's character in the book goes to jail twice for shoplifting and *The Stranger*'s Meursault goes to jail for murder; Lin orders characters around in an empty ego-gesture to show his superiority to those whom he considers beneath him, Meursault is honest in his deep loathing for everyone around him). There are some similarities too in how the two writers handle

---

1   As a member of the self-deprecating and all too often full of self-loathing Generation X, I wondered if my own complete inability at self-promotion combined with the notion that I probably suck at everything I do played into my utter distaste for Lin. So I did hesitate before I crowned Tao Lin the Emperor of Crap. But not for long. I don't mind self-promotion and would do it myself were I any good at it. I just want those promoting themselves, however glib and irritating their approach may be, to have something to back it up, some talent worth promoting. Self-promoting one's self-promotional capabilities is just too recursive for the likes of me.

conversation signifiers, but ultimately, if I analyze Lin's work in relation to Camus' work, I don't really get a look at a nihilistic character, or a society deserving of contempt, or even a basic existential confrontation of the self. All I get is a look at Lin's consciousness via his character Sam, and it's a boring, pointless, tiresome, empty, foul, nothing sort of experience. And it's not a nothing sort of experience because the purpose of the novel is to represent an empty character shaped by an empty world. Rather, it is empty because Lin's life is not worth an autobiographical sketch and because he is a terrible writer.

In fact, as I reviewed the book in my mind, I wondered if this novella was ultimately a fuck you delivered from Tao Lin to the people who consider him to be a good writer and have defended him as a relevant writer. From the attitudes his autobiographical proxy Sam has towards the craft of writing to the way Sam treats obvious fans, perhaps this is a cloaked but clever way for Tao Lin to mock those who are too dense to see him for what he is—a man selling himself in any way he can. Perhaps Tao Lin wants people to know he is not the naked Emperor preening to sycophants, but rather the clever tailor who produces nothing while everyone applauds.

So let's dive into this autobiographical novella and see how far down we get before we suffer the bends. There are those who may say that Tao Lin adopts an alienating, flat, pointless, repetitive, meaningless narrative delivered through an alienating, flat, senseless, boring narrator on purpose because he wants to write like a soulless, numb automaton and those who find this relentlessly tiresome just don't get it. They may be right (but they're not). Whether Lin created one of the most boring, tiresome, empty narratives ever on purpose or by sheer crappy and purposeless writing means little to me because the end result is the same—a book not worth reading. This book reads like what would happen if an emotionally muffled person got a lobotomy, took a fistful of Xanax every day and was then propped in front of a keyboard. Every word would be "meant" and "on purpose" but the only truth one would be able to know is what it reads like to be an emotionally blunted lobotomy patient strung out on benzos, and no matter how much one wants to claim the modern world with modern technology has numbed us, I know precious few people whose lives have become such a recursive nightmare that reading their most banal chat sessions repeated in a book appeals to them as an ideal way of experiencing meaning in literature. It may be a reflection of a small segment of society but as a whole it has so little experiential and literary merit that it's pointless in a way that I suspect Lin himself could not have anticipated.

Then again, if a chemically deadened and lobotomized brain can write well, maybe the words would be worth the trip. Lin, if he can write well, mostly hides it. The book has no structure, no sense of achievement, no sense of connection and no sense of disconnection. It's just Lin vomiting up his experiences and it's so pointless that it's devastating. Here's an early conversation between Sam (Tao Lin's stand-in) and Luis:

> "Should we kill ourselves now or start crying or punch ourselves," said Luis.
>
> "What is wrong with us," said Sam. "Should I email Sheila. Or wait until she emails me. I have no car, phone, bike. I'm going to add more people on MySpace."
>
> "We are so weird," said Luis. "We met online a year ago. And we are up a year later being weird as shit."
>
> "One year," said Sam. "This is weird."
>
> "I feel like my chest is going to explode," said Luis.

Despite the fact that this is not my idea of a good time, generally speaking, this has the potential to be funny. Two dumbasses low on the food chain discussing how full of dumbassery they are. Stupid men, slightly melodramatic. Later, I wondered if this book was actually an inversion of existentialism, an inability to confront the self when there is no self to be examined. There is no *there* there, so all the self-probing and declarations of being "weird as shit" go absolutely nowhere. If this is what Lin was going for, I posit that boring, numb and stupid are not really how most people go through life, and that a novella featuring a soulless, empty carcass that manages to move around, desire vegan snacks and not really give a shit when Sheila has to go into a psychiatric hospital is not just a book that "norms" would not find appealing but one that the vast sum of humanity would find wholly without merit.

But rest assured, no attempts to assign a philosophical or social context to this novel saved it from being what it is, a boring look at banality. A pointless look at banality, as well. The conversation between Sam and Luis continues:

> "I am adding random people in MySpace," said Sam.
>
> "I feel weird," said Luis. "Like I was molested by my uncle or something. You are on the floor. With the blanket around you."
>
> "The blanket is over my head," said Sam.
>
> "Are we fucked," said Luis and got off the Internet.

I think it was right about here that I wondered if the book was setting me up for a novel in which technology and modern living had rendered these two men incapable of making choices that affirmed their humanity, that perhaps they were trapped in a life without escape, a sort of *No Exit* where there were no moral choices or difficult people forcing confrontation but just a bland inability to do much more than add people on MySpace and state the obvious while feeling a disconnection they can only assume comes from a dark place. These are men so bereft of inner life that they are almost hopeful an uncle raped them because it would give reason for their dissatisfaction and torpor.

But this is not a treatise about how the world has limited them by oppressive technology or media manipulation. Sam does things that could potentially have been interesting or could have served as some sort of philosophical or social underpinning in this novel. But by the muffled nature of his existence, none of it means anything. Lin's book is not about the disaffection facing some members of a generation who have not known life without invasive technology and as a result have difficulty making choices that would prove their humanity outside the digital realm. This particular meaninglessness of life does not come from without—it comes from within. Sam is empty and so is Luis but others in this book don't exhibit this level of emptiness. But instead of interacting with humans who are fully in this world and having it change him, Sam just looks at them through numb eyes and reacts with a soulless incapacity to feel. If there was some sort of meaning behind the numbness, I could stomach this book. Meursault in *The Stranger* is so flat because disgust for humanity fuels his every action and inaction. There is no such clarity in Sam. This is a book about a narcissist who has no self. It is about a self-absorbed asshole who is incapable of examining himself and the world, and a character like this hardly deserves a novella built around him.

So back to the book. Sam has moved with Sheila to Pennsylvania, a transition that takes a paragraph because location is meaningless to Sam and because Tao Lin is a terrible writer:

> A few days later he and Sheila were on a train to New York City. They drank from a large plastic bottle containing organic soymilk, energy drink, and green tea extract and wrote sex stories to sell to nerve.com for $500. Sheila's sex story had chainsaws and Sam's sex story had Ha Jin doing things in a bathroom at Emory University. Sheila said she felt excited to be in New York City soon. They talked about making their own energy drink company. They got off the train and stood waiting for another train. They climbed a wall and sat in sunlight facing the train tracks.

> "I feel really happy right now," said Sheila looking ahead.

> Sam looked at the side of Sheila's face.

> "You didn't feel happy before?" he said.

> "I mean I just feel really good right now," said Sheila. "Don't you?"

> "You don't feel good at other times?" said Sam staring at his new shoes. "I shouldn't have said that. Sorry. That was stupid of me."

> "It's okay," said Sheila.

> It was around 11:00 am. It was March.

> Sam felt himself about to say something.

> "Do you not feel good anymore?" he said.

Sheila had a bored facial expression.

"Something is wrong with me," said Sam.

Fuck Tao Lin for giving the reader little moments like this where we can think, "Holy shit, Sam realizes he's a repellent, emotionally stunted Lizard Man and can change!" But this is not a confrontation of self. This is Sam digging for information because Sheila is expressing that things like writing sexy stories on a sunny day with her boyfriend can affect her mood. Sam cannot be affected this way because he is empty.

So, as Sam sits here and pokes his girlfriend for information about what it feels like to be human, we also get a taste of Lin's terrible writing. Sometimes he uses question marks during questions, and sometimes he doesn't and while I have no idea why he switches back and forth, I do know it was pointless and stupid. Though I can see how inserting that little sentence about the time and the month probably is meant to interrupt the flow of the feelings Sheila was expressing, it also seems like a pointless non sequitur. I think the worst part of reading this book was realizing that despite being a third-person narrative, and despite the fact that this is an autobiography, Lin never uses either method of storytelling to let us into Sam's mind. A flat character in a first person narrative would be unable to explain himself, but a third person narration could have analyzed Sam in some manner that makes him relevant. We never see why the hell Sam is a useless sack of crap and again, even if it is deliberate, it is a shitty way to tell a story. Of course, Lin could not use a third person narration to plunge Sam's soul because he doesn't have one.[2] He's just a ridiculous creature that eats stuff, exercises an empty ego and periodically goes to jail. None of that is enough to justify telling a story.

So in a couple of pages Sam is back in Manhattan, crashing at his brother's house. He goes to eat a salad with Sheila:

> They stood talking near the front doors while looking at each other's shoes and other things. They left the cafe and went somewhere else then sat in front of New York University's business school. It was around 10 p.m. They ate most of a giant salad of hijiki, lettuce, spinach, sprouts and tofu. Sam turned the aluminum container upside-down over a large plant. "High-quality fertilizer," he said.

> "Good," said Sheila from where she sat. "Good job."

> They talked about the salad's size and organic ingredients.

---

2   I have gotten a lot of feedback about this sentence, with snotty people telling me I meant to say "plumb" Sam's soul. No, I didn't mean to say that. I am well aware of how the phrase should be and deliberately used the word "plunge." Like clearing a lump of shit out of a toilet. I find it odd that people are hung up on this because I promise I was not the originator of this play on words but rest assured there is no depth to Sam's soul to plumb—he needs a good plunging like a Wal-Mart toilet on payday.

"We can eat it together in the future sometimes," said Sam.

"That would be good," said Sheila. "I would like that."

Interesting that the same food that nourishes Sam is used to nourish a plant. I suspect this book would have been more interesting if on page 23 we began to follow the life of the plant that received that high quality fertilizer. God knows what wonderful things that plant saw, the wonders it witnessed, the human drama that played out in front of it as it just sat there, composting organic greens and tofu. Had Sam been potted in a planter outside of NYU, I suspect the novella would not have been substantially different than the one I read wherein he was free to walk around amongst human beings.

Also, poor Sheila, eating with this plant of a man. Their future is not one of traveling and making love and having deep conversations. No, she will, if Sam can be arsed, eat salad with him on some unspecified day in the future, maybe, and they will look at their shoes and stuff. Because that is as deep as this will get with Sam. I believe I mentioned that Sheila ends up in a psych ward and Sam's reaction is no different really if he had been told Sheila had gotten married, gotten a job, belched in public, cried during a sad movie or just walked home by herself one evening. At 10:00 p.m. In March. I hope Sheila, whoever her real equivalent was in Tao Lin's life, got the help she needed to understand why she hitched her star to a plant-wagon.

Some more things happen. To give the dull devil his due, the scene where Sam is first arrested and taken to jail is reasonably funny. It is one of those times when just regurgitating the interesting things that happen around Sam is enough because no matter how you slice it, a jail cell in NYC is gonna be interesting. Strangely, this pissed me off because it shows that if Lin had tried, just a little, this book might not have been the literary equivalent of eating Vaseline. Sam ended up in jail because he sucks so much at shoplifting that he was caught immediately after trying to lift a shirt he wanted to wear to his book reading. A mixed message to be sure. Sam is broke but wants a shirt. Rather than conform to the ideals of capitalist morality that says one can only own what one can afford, he tries to steal. But because he has nothing inside of him that comes close to being drive or a sense of competent action, he doesn't even bother to steal in a manner that ensures success. So what is the message here? That sucking at everything one does in life ensures that one will at least get the majesty of witnessing drunk people lose their shit in a jail cell? Who knows…

It was on page 35 when I knew Tao Lin was just a huckster slinging words around, using writing as a method of self-promotion. Tao Lin is not pro-moting his book when he annoys Gawker or ironically posts links to his bad press. He is promoting himself via his books. This is a key passage:

"I want to change my novel to present tense," said Sam. "Is there some

Microsoft Word thing to do that."

"I don't think so. I think you have to do it manually."

"Manually," said Sam.

"By hand," said Luis. "Get an interview on Suicide Girls, that should be your next step. Do you think in five years the national media will create a stupid term like 'blogniks' to describe us."

"Yes," said Sam. "Remember when we had hope like four months ago."

Shut up, Sam. This book goes back four months—you had no hope then. None of us did. Also note the return to not using question marks. But mostly note that Sam is so divested from the act of writing that he simply wants a macro to change his book to present tense. It was here that I realized that Tao Lin may see writing as simply a by-way for him to sell the brand that is Tao Lin, the quirky boy who flaunts his theft failures, who holds readings and recites the same line over and over again, who has taken pestering people for attention to a level of annoyance previously thought unattainable.

I am a writer. I am not a writer like Tao Lin, but I've slung a few words together in my day. Simply changing a name in a story or novel is fraught with peril if one uses "Find and Replace." Any writer who is worth two shits will go through the manuscript carefully because changing the tense can result in other changes that will have to be made. But Sam is so distant from writing that Luis has to define what "manually" means. Yes Sam, you will have to make changes by hand. Oh how sad, oh how terrible! But of course, Luis knows what Sam needs to do. Who gives a shit about the quality of the book? Get an interview on an edgy website! I genuinely think that at times in this novella Tao Lin is clueing us in to his lack of substance and skill, sort of rubbing it in the faces of people who praised him, displaying that he is unworthy of praise and that he's the only one in on the joke. I honestly wonder if he secretly loathes the people who like this book.

Sam's reign of emotionless terror continues. At the organic, vegan restaurant where he works, Sam has a moment where he realizes that people affect him and feels happiness but...

> He walked to a central area of the kitchen and stood with unfocused eyes. Ben was thirty-nine. Sam knew from Facebook. Sam had a poem in the "drafts" section of his Gmail account called "ben is funny at work." Sam felt himself grinning. He stopped grinning and stared at different things while people around him worked. "I feel tired of life," he said out loud. "I don't feel like working anymore."

Of course there is nothing Sam really wants to do because all he really does when he is not working or sort of writing is look at stuff and shoes and more stuff. But even as he has a moment where he acknowledges another person's innate worth, it is cluttered with brand names that are as essential to understanding his connection with Ben as knowing that Ben is funny. But the moment he felt happiness he shuts it down. I bet happiness to Sam felt like cramp-laden diarrhea feels to the rest of us. A moment of happiness, filtered through the brand names in his mind, and he is suddenly tired of life. Sam is genuinely one of the most tiresome, pointless protagonists I have ever read.

So Sam does some other stuff and has some vaguely funny conversations that become unfunny when you think about the subtext. He has texts with other people on New Year's Eve:

> After midnight he got a text message from Mallory: "2008 feels insane."
>
> Sam grinned and text messaged: "It does. Feels like 2040 or something."

This was when I first felt genuine despair reading this book, not the least because Lin likely experienced this and felt this passed for real conversation. Again, you could, in some sense, think this is a cultural lampoon of empty hipster disaffection but it isn't. It's just a sad, empty man sharing his sad emptiness.

Then Sam does more empty shit with a revolving door of faces who mean nothing, then he gets caught shoplifting some earbuds and goes back to jail.

> A police man asked if Sam wanted anything from the vending machine. Sam asked if he could have food from his bag. The food was organic raw vegan "Raweos." The policeman asked what the food was.
>
> "Like, cookie things," said Sam. "Cookies."
>
> "No, I think we better not do that," said the policeman.

Yeah, what better time could there be to show one's indie cred and love of extremely expensive vegan cookies than in jail after refusing to pay for earbuds and getting caught stealing them. Because veganism is not really an ethical means of choosing food but a way to demonstrate a facile allegiance to certain subcultures when shoplifting fails you yet again.

Then we get to the part of the story that left me feeling genuinely sad. Sam and a friend Robert are talking about Sheila being in the psych hospital:

> "I wonder if she'll get better," said Sam.
>
> "I felt sad. Connie was here. I felt funny about the situation. Later when Connie said things like 'why are you sad' I could say nothing and she would say things like 'are you worried about your friend.'"
>
> "Haha," said Sam. "'Concrete reason.'"
>
> "Yes," said Robert. "'Easy to understand.'"

These dumb fucks are speaking in air quotes about what would be genuine emotional distress to a decent person. Air quotes. And though Robert and Luis are presumably different people, earlier we got Luis saying his current feelings were similar to what he felt like being molested by an uncle must feel like, that he felt something really terrible and had no frame of reference to define it. Here these two plant-men have a genuine reason for distress and they dismiss it and mock the woman who assumed Robert's malaise was not the bullshit emptiness Lin and men like him wear like a badge of honor. Silly girl. She thought Robert experienced sorrow knowing his friend suffers so profoundly from mental illness. This was one of the most violently and probably unintentionally sad things I've read in a while.

But then again, Sam encounters a seriously mentally ill man he met in jail and decides to follow him through the streets like he's a mild distraction for the evening, like it's somehow a normal and fun thing for the emotionally dead to stalk the mentally ill on a lark. So I guess it could have been worse.

Then Sam shows what a nasty little man he really is (and never forget that Sam is Tao Lin in this autobiographical sketch). Sam goes to Florida for a book reading, and surrounded by people who know his name, who think Sam is the shit, he acts like an emotionally stunted bully. He notices a girl named Audrey who is clearly into him (and why all these girls are so into him I will never know but I don't doubt that in real life Tao Lin has plenty of girls around him) and makes sure she notices him more while trying to look like he doesn't care because Sam has no use for these emotions we humans embrace like so many dogs in heat.

> Sam saw Audrey standing alone in line wearing all pink. Sam walked past Audrey to the bathroom. Sam walked out of the bathroom past Audrey without looking at her and talked to Jeffrey.

Smooth, that Sam.

Sam does his reading, but "he was going to read from the beginning of his next book and then read about two people alone in rooms in Ohio and Pennsylvania talking to each other in Gmail chat." He asks Audrey, who was in the audience, to go with him to American Apparel and he and a few other people pile into a car. Hereabouts is where Tao Lin shows himself too clearly. Sam encourages everyone to act poorly because he knows he can get away with it and because he knows they will do what he wants. Of course, these people can tell him to get bent but when in the presence of someone you admire, a human brand even, people are willing to be manipulated and Sam knows this. Some examples:

> Sam told Audrey to scream "red shirt" at people across the street walking in the same direction as them.

> "Red shirt," screamed Audrey.

> A woman in her forties, two teenagers and a person in a bright red shirt who was maybe twenty turned their upper bodies and looked at Audrey while walking forward. "It's a family, I think," said Sam. "They're ignoring

it. That's so bad for them, a family, it'll probably be all they talk about later, like when they're eating."

So, Sam gets Audrey to perform street theater for him, and gets the cock stroke of thinking that this family will really give two shits about some grubby girl shouting at them in the street and they will be unable to think of anything else. No, it can't be that dumbasses yelling stupid shit is worth ignoring. Nope, they are gonna have to remember this transgression against their person and dwell on it. Tao Lin has a very low opinion of us normal folk, or a very high opinion of himself and his jackassery. You be the judge. Except don't be the judge. Don't read this book. I love you even if I haven't met you and I can assure you that you don't deserve such abuse.

Sam then insists that a political sign about voting on a certain proposition needs to be pulled out of the ground and carried to where they want to sit on a Florida college campus. People think the man carrying it, Jeffrey, is campaigning and yell out to him. This makes him uneasy.

"Here, you can have it, do you want it," said Jeffrey in a quiet voice.

"No, don't," said Sam. "We need to put it by where we sit."

Oh yes, how whimsical and fanciful is our Sam. Jeffrey should have thrown the sign at him but he didn't. Sam got to see how far he could push him, too. Giving him this inch enabled Sam to take a mile and so he took Jeffrey's bottle of juice and threw it as far as he could.

"Go get it," said Jeffrey.

"Are you angry I threw your Odwalla," said Sam.

Of course plant-Sam needs this clarification about human emotion, but he probably just wants Jeffrey to be forced to be angry or suppress it. Jeffrey suppresses it. Then Sam convinces Audrey to roll on her stomach across the grass to get the bottle, then they throw it around until they break it. Then Sam eggs Audrey into jumping over a hedge, which she does not do to his satisfaction so he insists she do it again.

Later, he kisses Audrey, then having come dangerously close to no longer being a plant he retreats and more or less ignores her, leaving her baffled and unhappy until she retreats emotionally, too. Then a couple more things happen and the novella mercifully ends with the following banality:

> They sat quietly for about ten seconds. There were faraway sounds of people doing things in other parts of the town.
>
> "What did you want to be when you grew up?" asked Audrey.
>
> "Marine biologist," said Sam.

Sadly, he didn't go with his childhood dream and here I sit, discussing his book. Yay.

Before I conclude this negative discussion, I need to talk about the product placement. All those fucking brand names given as much emphasis as any person, as any emotion. It's sort of reminiscent of *American Psycho* but even more meaningless because Sam and his cohorts throw the words around with no attachment. At least Patrick Bateman placed the emotions he should have had for human beings onto objects. Lin just recites names like a parrot. On page 80, in dialogue that would have been better used as the liner in a bird cage, Sam and Robert toss out "Lorrie Moore," "Paul Mitchell," "Lollapalooza," and "Wendy's Spicy Chicken Sandwich" in a name dropping word salad of a conversation that had virtually no meaning. Later, we have a similar experience on pages 86–87. "Guggenheim Museum," "Sausage Egg McMuffin," "McDonalds," "Synergy kombucha," "Gmail" and "American Apparel." Reading these quotes of places and products and brands as I reproduce them will have as much mental impact as their driveling recitation in the book. These are just two examples in this entire book of mindless name and brand mixing, as if any of it means anything. If Lin was trying to make the point that media has made us numb, who gives a shit? It's not like that point has not been made for decades in far more effective ways than having this man-plant drone.

While I did not harp on Lin's style, the passages I quote should show how this book is essentially mental Novocaine. If being a book alternative to numbing out was Lin's goal, at least in that he succeeded. If this is a message worth spreading, it is hard to say. I suspect there are those who might think so, that a dull, numb, pointless story that has no commentary on the world but is just a recitation of scenes from the life of an empty narcissist is worth reading if only for the numbing effect it has.

So maybe there is a percentage of people in this world who are narcissists who have no self but I'd wager it's a very small percentage. I guess there is a percentage of people in this world who might find interesting a narcissist with no self but I wager that too is a small percentage. Therefore, unless one is a narcissistic but numb person with no inner fire, or unless one is interested in 100 pages of such people, this book will be very unappealing. There is no progression, no crisis, no climax, no realization of alienation and subsequent despair. This is a book where a guy does some things and feels nothing as he does them. If you feel this sounds interesting, by all means, read the book. But for most people, this would become hollow and empty very quickly and for a reader looking for an existentialist wallow because of all the comparisons between this book and *The Stranger* (comparisons I was later surprised to learn others had made as well), know that Sam never confronts his existence. He never experiences any sort of existential crisis. He does not exhibit nihilism or even a concentrated loathing for mankind that fuels his actions. He just exists in the most banal way possible, showing a spark only to be an asshole for a few pages then losing purpose and meaning again.

So we are left with a book that seemingly deliberately echoes elements of an existentialist classic but is devoid of any real philosophical focus. The writing style is tiresome, repetitive and outside of some mildly humorous scenes, devoid of merit and offers no trade off in terms of novelty, experimentation, social relevance or even basic interest for suffering through it. The protagonist, Sam, who is a stand-in for Tao Lin in this autobiographical novella, lives a squalid, pointless life, showing his humanity only when he is being a complete dick. The story goes nowhere, conveys nothing, and is so poorly written that if the goal was to cause the reader to recoil in horror at youth deadened by media and reduced to soulless utterings of brand names and stupid conversations, it failed because the only horror is the book itself, not its message. If my reading is correct, this book is a middle finger extended in our faces by a writer who shows cleverly how little he cares about The Word and how easy he finds it to manipulate the people around him. This is a terribly written book with a story that could only interest the emotionally dead. This is a novella that conveys a smug, unpleasant sense that the reader is being mocked by lobotomized hipsters. If that any of that sounds like a good time to you, dive right in. But for those who prefer substance over affectless dreck, I say read *The Stranger*, *American Psycho*, *Generation X*, *The Catcher in the Rye*, or maybe even William Shatner's autobiography. Don't read this book. Not even if you steal it.

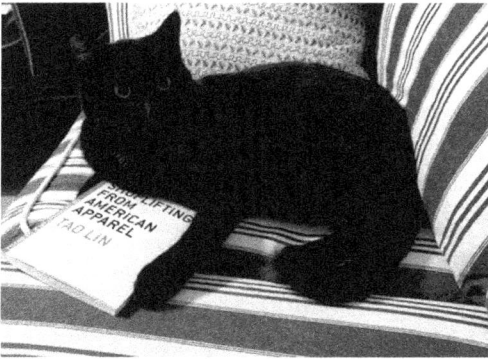

FURTHER READING

The Stranger
Albert Camus

American Psycho
Bret Easton Ellis

Anal and Rectal Diseases: A Concise Manual
Edited by Eli D. Ehrenpreis, et al.

PERSON
By Sam Pink
Lazy Fascist Press (2010)
Original post: 01/21/2015

Why do I consider this book odd?
Because I thought it was going to suck a'plenty and I was proven wrong.

Back when I bought a copy of *Shoplifting from American Apparel*, I also picked up a copy of *Person* by Sam Pink. Since my first exposure to alt-lit[3] resulted in what can only be called a complete nervous book-down, I was understandably reluctant to read Pink. Lin's overhyped book filled me with such disgust that had I read anything similar immediately afterward I would have needed a new anus.

But a few years have passed, and the fire of my hatred has dimmed. Also, *Person* is a slim volume and tempted me after I had finished *The Goldfinch*, which, as much as I love Donna Tartt, was a brick, and a very tiresome brick by around page 550. I needed something easy and something quick and there *Person* was, in my nightstand cupboard, nestled in with far longer and more outrageous fare. So I decided to hold my nose and jump into *Person* and see what happened.

Person and *SfAA* are very similar books. Both feature disaffected, grubby young protagonists. Both mine the same disenchanted hipster vein. The books even share a similar structure, down to the formation of sentences. So

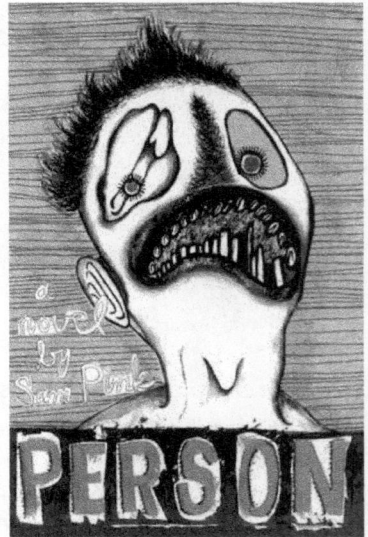

---

3   What is "alt-lit"? I am tempted to describe alt-lit as being an enormous toilet into which many turds are shat and only a few float to the top. But it is likely better to describe it as a literary form that was initially identified, according to Wikipedia, in 2011 and is characterized by self-promotion and heavy online presence and usage. Alt-lit is closely linked with the New Sincerity movement in literature. New Sincerity describes a type of literature that evinces direct communication, mimicking conversational tones of online communication and emphasizing autobiographical works. Because I hate most of the genre, I think you may want to go behind me and see if there is a better way to go about it than this. https://en.wikipedia.org/wiki/Alternative_literature

how come I really like *Person*?

Because I recently got my winter clothes out, I think I may have a decent enough explanation. You know how it is that one red sweater can make you look like a porcelain-skinned angel and another red sweater can make you look like a chapped potato? They're both red, just different reds. But you know, maybe that's a bad analogy. Because the red that makes me look like someone's ruddy Irish nanna isn't innately a shitty color and the one that makes me look like I've never once had a sunburn isn't innately a heavenly color. By any sane standard *SfAA* is just a terrible book. I guess what I am saying here is that for the most part I hate alt-lit (and increasingly the writers behind the genre), but you can't judge a book by its color just because some colors look better than others. And if it seems like I am being completely incoherent so that pompous tenured professors working in the Corn Belt can insult me because every extemporaneous book discussion needs to be indistinguishable from a doctoral thesis, that isn't what's happening. Nope. Not at all.

Still, I think I can make a case for why it is that *Person* is the better book, or at least a book worth reading.

The Person in *Person* is a grubby young man who is living a grubby, tiresome life. He has very little money. He has a roommate for whom he feels a lot of enmity but whom he treats reasonably politely. Sometimes he tries to get a job. Sometimes he sleeps with a girl who lives in his apartment complex. Mostly he wanders the cold, horrible city streets realizing how bleak things are and how little will he possesses to change. He is a complete misanthrope, which is nice because in alt-lit one gets very overwhelmed by Lin-esque writers who don't even have the depth of humanity to hate—they just mock and hope we feel really bad when they are finished.

In a sense, what redeems this book is that the protagonist, as he goes through the motions, seems to see life as a rehearsal for something else, something different, if not better. "It feels like practice" is repeated throughout the book like a mantra.

> I walk by a group of people standing outside a bar and someone almost bumps into me.
>
> I imagine myself pulling this person apart with my hands.
>
> Just pulling off pieces of face and neck and upper-chest.
>
> Just ripping an arm off with a single pull.
>
> Could I accomplish that.
>
> What would this person think of himself if I were to do that.
>
> Would he fight it, or accept it as inevitable.
>
> What would the people walking think.

I walk by them all and smell perfume and I am no different.

It feels like practice.

The protagonist has what could be interpreted as a flat affect, but he feels, he seethes, he despairs and he knows it is all in preparation for something, practice for a hobby or a habit he has yet to develop but will soon, hopefully.

But it's not all seething speculation.

I see a candy bar wrapper on the ground.

I think, "So what."

Then I walk in the same direction as before.

It feels like practice.

So what, it's all the same thing, but it helps to prepare for pointless monotony. It's also unspeakably sad to read this protagonist, who fantasizes about walking up to people and asking if they will spend time with him because he is… Well, he doesn't know, but he does want to know people love him and think of him, and see him as he practices yet never achieves mastery.

I pay for my pencil and the man behind the register tells me to have a good night.

I wonder what a good night is to him and then I wonder the same thing about myself.

It occurs to me that in order for that communication to work, myself and the man would have to come to an agreement about what it meant.

I'm too scared,

It feels like practice.

"It feels like practice" is the last sentence in the book. When everything is practice nothing is learned. Nothing becomes natural. The protagonist of *Person* is an Everyman, if that isn't too obvious, a representation of the overall shittiness of being young in the city in America, with just enough education to want more but more than enough depression to know that no matter how long one hangs on, practices, rehearses, not a lot is going to change. Different roommates, different towns, different apartments—it's all going to be practice for a show that will never be staged.

It should go without saying that my quoted excerpts serve as a guide to the structure of Pink's novel. Short sentences, simple word choice, straightforward prose, deceptively childish with a see-Dick-run cadence that, with the right writer, is less annoying than it sounds.

Pink and Pink's protagonist both have a certain level of self-awareness, and a sense of how ridiculous some situations seem. Perhaps that is one of the reasons that I found worth in this book while I detested *SfAA*—self-aware humor.

Take this scene wherein the protagonist is avoiding his roommate:

> My roommate knocks on my door and I try not to move.
>
> My heart is beating fast.
>
> He knocks again and then leaves.
>
> I win.
>
> This is but one of the many victories I have exampled as a human among humans.
>
> I have no equals.
>
> My strength goes unmatched.

I have moments like this more often than I realized until I deliberately took notice. I didn't punch the woman screaming at her kids while simultaneously being rude as hell to the teenage clerk struggling to ring up her pile of grease and sugar disguised as groceries? I am Mother Teresa and can very likely cure the lepers. I stared down the man who continually permits his dog to crap in my yard without ever cleaning up the mess and he looked away first? I am clearly the only remaining force for moral decency. This passage is sort of a litmus test—if you found this as amusing as I did (with or without the intense sense of identification) then you likely will enjoy this book.

Who can blame the protagonist for taking such faux-pride in avoiding a roommate when the world has become so trivial yet niggling that every attempt to better one's situation becomes a labyrinthine and bureaucratic nightmare? In such a world, we must celebrate the small victories.

> The grocery store I interviewed at a while ago has asked me to come to a second interview.
>
> For bagging groceries.
>
> They said there might be a third interview too.
>
> For bagging groceries.

Yep. He's probably gonna have to report for a drug test.
For bagging groceries.
He will also have to spend a week learning corporate policies.
For bagging groceries.
When I was in my twenties, I worked at a grocery store in Westlake Hills, a monied suburb of Austin. In the three months I lasted, there were several incidents where customers felt it within their rights as human beings to put their hands on the teenagers and old men who bagged groceries. Like to strike them or shove them. One kid brushed up against the paint on a customer's expensive SUV. Like his jacket covered arm slid across the side of the car as the kid was finishing up putting groceries in the back of the hatch. The female customer slapped him in the face. The bag boy was a minor and I think

she got arrested. I had an angry diabetic grab my arm so hard she left bruises. Evidently Candy City didn't have enough treats made from Nutrasweet, which is important because sorbitol gives you diarrhea. I assume she was weakened by a really bad bout of sugar-free malted milk ball-induced runs or she would have beaten my ass for such an oversight. These are jobs we need three interviews and a drug test to perform. If you're lucky one of the customers will hurt you so badly you can sue. So there's that.

Perhaps I like Pink's *Person* because the protagonist's self-loathing rings a bit too true at times.

> Somewhere someone is teaching me to another person.
>
> And the teacher uses a metaphor involving a garbage truck that has run out of gas halfway to the garbage dump.
>
> And the student nods.

But this next passage is what made me realize I would need to get the rest of Pink's books and read them as soon as possible. The protagonist needs to pay the rent and it is fraught with difficulties that only another misanthropic introvert can really understand.

> My landlord crosses the parking lot at the same time.
>
> The rent check is in my pocket.
>
> I forgot to drop it off before I left.
>
> Now, seeing her, I know I have to actually go into her office.
>
> She has some vague expectation of her tenants, where we all act like family, rather than people with no interest in each other.
>
> I'm trying to say she is delusional and I don't identify with her as a human being.

How many jobs have you had where management insisted you are all one big family? How many temporary living situations have you experienced, like dorm rooms or nasty apartments, where there was pressure to foster a family environment? How many times have you encountered someone online who refers to herself as a universal mother or aunt? It's happened to you more than once, hasn't it, this bullshit "we're all family" scenario? And each time it happens it presages something unpleasant to come. Family is expected to work for nearly free, like we're all immigrants fresh off Ellis Island and working together to establish a family business. Family members overlook constant flatulence because "Dad" is sort of scary, and the same person, usually you, cracks and cleans the toilet even when it isn't your turn, because, goddamn it, you refuse to live like an animal among your "family" but cannot endure another blowout that will inevitably happen when you call a family meeting about the filth in the bathroom. And that online Aunt or Uncle or Mom generally has some huge fucking complex fueling their forced familiarity and warmth and when they crack it's gonna end up on the front page of Reddit and you'll have to change your user name to avoid drama. Again.

I really enjoyed reading *Person*, which is sort of perverse because I knew it wasn't going to end well. Had it ended well, it would have been a lie. The Person isn't going to land an excellent job that helps him overcome his metaphysical despair. The Person isn't going to find the perfect girl who will lift him out of himself. He isn't even going to be able to shower as regularly as he should. He is depressed. He hates you, but he also secretly loves you. Even more secretly, he wants your dog to kill him. And you'll either love him or hate him. I loved him mainly because I sort of am him, though I lucked out and married well and at least don't have to worry about annoying roommates and drug tests anymore.

I know that some alt-lit fans may find my loathing for Lin and affection for Pink to be highly subjective, and they're right. I can read and enjoy Hemingway but I detest Fitzgerald. Both are arguably very good writers. One speaks to me and the other doesn't. In Pink's slim novel I found a self-awareness, a humor, a strangely brave willingness to examine the self even when such examination is unpleasant. I didn't get that in *SfAA*; worse, I felt as if the reader was being mocked for not realizing the book was a look at the self of a man who lacked one. Lin just vomited up what had really happened in his life, assigned different names, and called it a novella. Many readers felt as if denying its worth meant they would be the butt of the joke. Not so with Pink. He lets us in on the joke, the horrible, miserable joke that is being young, broke and depressed while being bitterly aware of it every fucking minute.

FURTHER READING

The Human War
Noah Cicero

I'm Going to Clone Myself Then Kill the Clone and Eat It
Sam Pink

LITERATURE

I have a terribly undisciplined intellect. I am not a person who reads the classics for fun. I prefer the soft berth of the salacious true crime novel or lunatic screed. So it was surprising to realize how much genuine literature I have read and discussed, and it was even more surprising that I was able to write about such books in a manner approaching coherence. I guess we all surprise ourselves from time to time.

IN THE SKY

By Octave Mirbeau; Translated by Ann Sterzinger
Nine-Banded Books (2014)
Original post: 01/18/2016

Why do I consider this book odd?
It reached into my chest, grabbed my heart and wrung it out.

There are books that come into your life right when you need them. *In the Sky* was one of those books. It broke my heart. I was left feeling unsettled the first time I read it, so I read it again to see if I could pinpoint what Mirbeau was trying to tell me. The second read was more of a revelation. I won't go deep into the reasons because, even though I write about books in a confessional manner, this book caused me to consider my life in a manner that I prefer not to discuss overmuch. This is a case where contemplation trumps discussion. It's rare to find a book that helps me cauterize my continual brain bleed, but there you have it.

Mirbeau is a genius. He portrays with great intensity a quietly malignant life, a person rotting inside because of tension and fear, a person for whom a blue sky is a crushing reminder that there is no freedom, only a mocking emptiness that can never be filled. *In the Sky* is about a man who died while still living, who kept dying long after the disease had eaten its fill. That Mirbeau never finished this novella makes it all the better a representation of the life half-eaten away, half-lived, never complete. The translator, Ann Sterzinger, is also a genius to have read these words in their original French and then convey such exquisite misery so precisely yet with such raw, bleeding emotion.

Lately I find myself enjoying books about thwarted people and this is the story of a thwarted man. There are so many reasons why a person can become thwarted, climbing into a living grave rather than digging oneself out of the pit. The protagonist of *In the Sky* feels as if he would have lived a lesser life regardless

TL;DR: THE BEST OF ODD THINGS CONSIDERED

of the negative influences that shaped him, and perhaps he is correct. But it takes a lot of oppressive life experiences for the blue, open sky to turn into a carnivorous, gaping maw that paralyzes you with its infinity.

In the Sky begins with a callow man paying a duty visit to an old friend, called "X" in this book. X lives in the hills in a crumbling old abbey, and the narrator is shamed into visiting his friend. He has some affection for his friend, but mostly holds him in contempt. Part of the contempt comes from pity expressed at a distance—he himself says on the first page that "life was killing him"—but he also feels contempt because he has wronged X. Fay Weldon has written of how it is we come to loathe those we have harmed, and part of the narrator's contempt for X is borne from his pity for his mental state and because he stole X's lover, a mousy peasant whom he seduced simply because he could.

He arrives at the abbey to see X is emotionally shattered, oppressed by his surroundings, especially the sky. The callow narrator, a man who only wants to be generous to X as long as it doesn't inconvenience him, himself sees the miserable nature of the landscape:

> One feels lost in that sky, sucked into that sky, immense and rough, like a sea, a fantastic sky where monstrous forms, maddening fauna, indescribable flora, and nightmarish architectures evolve, wander, and disappear, endlessly.

The narrator finds X looking much older than expected, shriveled and hunched, nervous and strange, oppressed by his surroundings. At one point he compliments X on his home, at which X cries out:

> "The sky. Oh the sky! You don't know how it crushes me, how it's killing me. It mustn't kill you, too…

The two go to an inn and X reveals he is unable to write coherently, but that he will give the narrator his notes in the hope he can find some meaning in them. X drinks too much and the narrator has to take him back to the abbey, where he then spends a terrible, uncomfortable night. He finds X the next morning and X gives him a sheaf of papers to read:

> "You can read what I wanted to tell you here in these pages. Do you get me? And when you've read them you'll burn them. It's not much, but this will explain to you… Do you understand?"

We never know if the narrator understands but the point-of-view in the novella changes as we enter X's mind through his memoirs. I felt like I was being stabbed repeatedly in the heart as I read about X's childhood, his attempts to navigate an adult life, his wretched inability to know himself. We learn X's name is George, and from an early age he learns that he is not afforded any real pleasure in life, that anything he enjoys can and will be taken from him if he forgets for one moment that he exists solely to enrich his family.

As a boy George wants a flute but is given a drum, as his father feels such an instrument is more appropriate. In spite of his disappointment, George begins to enjoy drumming. He becomes quite good at it and his family responds to him positively for the first time in his young life.

> Drumsticks are sometimes as magical as fairy wands. Soon I felt their strange power.

> In four months' time I had become my family's pride and joy. My aunt and my sisters no longer pinched me or called me an idiot. Now, in their eyes, there was a look of admiration and respect for me. My father had become deferential. If someone came to the house, they enthused about my talent on the drum.

George, even as he enjoys playing, knows that the deference he receives from his father stems from his father's feeling of being repaid for his paternal sacrifices. He is not so much proud of George as he is pleased that he is getting some return on investment. Still, George is able to take some pleasure in playing his drum. Until... There is always an "until" in George's life. He enjoys playing his drum until he is made to be the drum major and leader for the Saint Latuin parade. St. Latuin is the patron saint of his village and this festival in the town is a very important occasion. The man organizing the festival asks George to lead the procession, full of pomp and girls waving golden palms and young boys singing as they march to original hymns. As it is described in the book, a Las Vegas show featuring Liberace would be more dignified than the St. Latuin parade.

Of course George's family is hungry for the acclaim such an honor will bring them. George immediately recognizes the ridiculous pageantry and is miserable at the thought of being involved. His father forces the issue, reminding him of the honor he will bring his family. His mother, sisters and aunt badger him relentlessly.

> My aunt, especially, was particularly fanatical.

> "If you don't want to," she screamed, "just listen. I'll take back your drum and give it to the poor!"

> "That's right, that's right," the whole family chorused, "we'll take back his drum!"

> I gave up. Every day for a month, I slaved miserably away at my drum...

The day of the parade it rained and George marched with a manic determination and was presented to the bishop. His father was terribly proud.

> "Look at you!" said my father, beaming with joy. "Will you listen to me next time?"

> Since I did not respond, he added harshly, "Tsk—you don't even deserve what you've gotten!"

> The following morning I came down with a fever. Meningitis trapped
> me between life and death for a long time, in the most awful delirium.
> Unfortunately I didn't die.
>
> And so my life had begun.

One presumes his father felt he did deserve the illness. And the fairy magic
of drumsticks is taken from George forever.

George's life really is a misery. He is emotionally battered by his insensitive family in ways that seem somewhat comical until you understand the
humiliation he must have felt. His mother, a passive-aggressive miser, makes
everyone in the family pay dearly for everything they receive.

> I still remember the indescribable negotiations she opened with a shoe-
> maker over the purchase of a pair of boots, negotiations that went on for
> two years, during which time I walked around with holes in my shoes.

In such a household, among people hungry for prestige, it should come as
no surprise that the mother wanted to live in a grander home. But in a household led by such a mother, it should also come as no surprise that everyone
would be made miserable when the purchase of a new home was final. After
signing the papers and tantruming about the prospect of moving into the
house, the mother allows the family a nanosecond of pleasure, of fantasizing
about the extra room.

As soon as they are happy at the thought of moving, she wages a passive-aggressive battle royale against her family. Oh no, they cannot possibly afford
servants! They will have to do all the work themselves. They must sell the
nice furniture they were to place in the parlor since they cannot possibly entertain since buying the house will make them so impoverished. She decides
to sell the piano her children had purchased themselves from their pocket
money. She makes sure her husband will not be able to engage in gentleman-
ly gardening.

Living in the new home is, and I use this word a lot when discussing this
novella, miserable. They move into the house and it is huge and empty. After
selling off their furniture, after cutting back on lighting and heating, and
firing the household help, the house remains empty, cold and unkempt. In
a moment of perversity, a streak of his mother runs through George; he experiences deprivation but is sanguine as long as someone is suffering more
than he is.

> And though I wept in a corner of the room where we had gathered in si-
> lence, I couldn't stop myself from savoring, along with my tears, the bitter
> joy of witnessing my sisters' disappointment. In their eyes I could see the
> death of their hopes, their suitors' escape, and their fear of eternal virginity.

But George is capable of a largeness of heart that those around him do not
possess. He has a capacity for empathy and forgiveness that seems unlikely

given his upbringing and family, yet his possession of that capacity is likely why he was unable to assimilate into his family and the world around him. His parents both suffer from a sickness that levels the village, and they die, leaving him behind to the mercies of his sisters. He is an adult when they die but he mourns them with the innocence of a child.

> I loved my father, I loved my mother. I loved them even in their ridiculousness, even when they mistreated me. And in the moment of confessing this act of faith, now that they're both down below, under the lowly stones, all dissolute flesh and crawling maggots, I love them; I cherish them even more, I love and cherish them with all the respect I have lost. I blame them neither for the misery they handed me directly, nor for the unspeakable destiny that their complete and respectable stupidity imposed upon me. They were what all parents are, and I can't forget that when they were children they no doubt suffered the same things they put me through. We hand this fatal legacy down to each other with our constant, faithful virtuousness. The blame goes to society, for never finding any better way to legitimize its thefts or to sanctify its absolute power—most of all its power to trap a man in a state of imbecility and total servitude—than by instituting this admirable mechanism of government: the family.

So he forgives his mother her selective and perverse penury. He forgives his father for mocking his innocent discoveries as a little boy, like the time he found a well and his father took malicious pleasure in humiliating him for thinking he had "discovered" something rare or interesting. George has a belief that love, even when sullied by poor human response, is deeply important:

> Love is so powerful that even when it's stupid and mediocre it opens whole horizons of moral beauty to the soul.

(It should be mentioned that George shares this sentiment when discussing how terrible boarding school was, as he suffered under the control of people who had no love for him at all.)

He also forgives his aunt, a terrible woman who inflicts her frustration and misery upon her nephew.

> My aunt, as I've said, was a strange woman who didn't seem to put a lot of logical though into what she did. One day, she was mauling me with tenderness and gifts; the next she would beat me for no reason. Everything she did seemed to come at the behest of an incomprehensible folly.
>
> [...]
>
> When I came home from the boarding school, both her fondness and her malice took a shocking turn. Sometimes, after lunch, she would drag me down into the garden, running like a little girl. There was a little arbour room there, and in the room was a bench. She would pick a dead twig up off the ground, and chew on it in a rage...

She made him terribly nervous with her odd behaviors but she finally laid her cards down to the little boy when she jealously accused him of ogling a young maid who did work around the house.

> "I'm telling you that you look at her. I don't want you looking at her. I'll tell your mother."

> "But Auntie, honestly…" I insisted…

> But I didn't have a chance to finish my sentence—tangled, suffocated, crushed by what felt like a thousand arms, a thousand mouths, I felt something horrible and unknown approach … then I was enveloped by something abominable. I fought back violently. I pushed the beast back with my teeth, my nails, my elbows—with all my strength, multiplied tenfold by my horror of her body.

> "No! No! I don't want to!" I cried. "Auntie, I don't want it. I don't want to!"

> "Shut up, imbecile," my aunt groaned, her lips rolling on my lips.

His aunt eventually relents and he wriggles free and runs from her. Later that day his aunt leaves the house and his family is appalled because when she leaves the aunt takes with her the income she used to help keep the house running. He never sees his aunt again, that aged, bitter, equally thwarted woman who inflicted her diseased will as incestuous molestation. She became a monster on par with the sky, pressing down on him, paralyzing him. Yet George manages to absolve her in one of the saddest passages in the book:

> Oh my poor aunt, you pitiful and anguished creature, where are you? And why didn't I give you the happiness that the whole world refused you?

Christ. But it is no wonder that George feels a sense of responsibility for his aunt's misery. Had he just permitted her to maul him, could he have made up for all that she had been denied? Of course he feels this way. He was a child whose very childish pastimes were not permitted to remain in the realm of play and exploration but rather were used as a means for family aggrandizement. He was forced to wear shoes with holes for two years as his mother negotiated the best possible price for a pair of boots. His needs as a child were meaningless above and beyond the child-rearing mores of the time. George was not born a boy who felt it his role to give his very body to a repressed, pedophilic aunt, but he was shaped into such a role.

Jesus, those two sentences were a gut punch. But they're almost nothing compared to what George experiences when the sickness that struck his village takes his parents. His capacity for forgiveness is especially on display when they die. This is heartbreaking to read.

> My father and my mother died on the same day, carried away in an epidemic of cholera. My grief was so great that I don't know how to describe it. In the suddenness of the catastrophe, I forgot all the petty grudges I thought I had against my parents and gave in to tears without reserve. I had never

> thought I could love them so much. Unknown feeling sleeps in a man's
> heart, like a miser's treasure under the earth. It only awakes to the great axe-
> blows of misery. And how my heart labored under those blows!

As with most of the events in his life, George's parents' deaths come in a relentless onslaught of misery. Absolute devastation. He watches them die in excruciating pain, smelling and wallowing in the effluvia of sickening death. Alone he watches them die and alone he deals with the aftermath. Since they die during an epidemic, there is no pity or comfort to be spared for George. This young man whose entire life had been structured by the intrusions of others is left alone with his dead parents, his sisters off and married and his aunt having run off after her disgraceful conduct. Not even the priest can spare much time to help George; his neighbors are naturally too concerned about themselves and their own dead.

> ...those who had been spared were trying to escape from the dead, from
> those who had seen the dead, who had breathed in death. That word, "dead,"
> floated on the silence it could no longer interrupt; it banged on shut win-
> dows, at shutoff thresholds, like it was banging on the planks of a funeral
> bier: the desolation of an orphan.

The desolation of an orphan. I myself experienced this moment of feeling like an orphan, a grown-up orphan, a strange and almost ridiculous feeling. I'm married. I have a mortgage. I have cats and books and a Crock-Pot and my own bathroom in my own house. How can I be an orphan, a term that implies being a child, being tiny and helpless and forsaken? My maternal grandmother was sort of an orphan. Her mother died, leaving nine surviving children to the mercies of their alcoholic father, who left them all at a children's home in Abilene. Their uncle came and took them to live with him, and all the girls grew up to be anxious, sick auto-immune cases, their nervous systems destroyed by the stress of being forsaken. I am nothing like that. Nor was George.

But being an orphan means being shaped by lack. Your life is formed around the absence of others. What happens to the adult whose life was hemmed in by presence? George's parents mocked him, took from him, used him—they shaped his consciousness like ambitious Chinese parents deformed the feet of their daughters. You tie a tight knot around your index finger and it hurts but it hurts far worse when you cut that knot off and all the stagnating blood begins to flow into a throb, nerve endings fed by oxygen once again awaken and cause pain. If your life gets shaped by an oppressive presence, you love that presence and loathe the pain when it falls away.

After his parents die, left alone in that massive, empty house, George's nerve endings awaken. His screams made me hope that things were going to change for him, that perhaps the death of his parents would change the sky from a taunting oppression into a future without a horizon. For a moment it seems like that might happen. But then his sisters descend on him and bully him into giving up much of his inheritance, and numbly he gives in. Not satisfied with stealing his legacy, his sisters each try to persuade him to come live with them, at a price of course. He declines and leaves but before he does, he says that "solitude and liberty terrified me like a prison." A blue sky with no storms to shape it is not anything George can stomach. He will find a way to replace his parents, his sisters. Leaving will give him nothing new as he simply is unable to be free.

In retrospect, all of this is clear to George as well:

> What I wanted was to act. What I wanted was to use my arms and the blood in my veins, the warm downpours from my brain, for some work— but a work of what? None of my former passions conformed to any form of human activity.

It is not entirely George's fault that he feels this way. His love of drums was beaten out of him, leading him to grave illness and sadness. The family piano was sold by his avaricious mother. Surely this was a man meant to be a musician but the systematic destruction of his will ensures that he will never consider the activities that give him joy as being a part of worthwhile adult work or endeavor.

> ...paternal authority, as it stuffed me with lies, had killed the kernel of individual conscience that had once lived in me; it suffocated the spontaneous aspirations that had, for a moment, raised my spirit toward the conquest of things; the scrap of passion that had led me to find desire and beauty in possession—or to put it more truly, in seeking out the mysteries of the earth and the sky.

The reader encounters this passage and hopes it means that George, with this self-awareness, can shuck off the mental shackles that limit him but the reader must also remember that George has an ever-changing perspective of his plight that depends on his current environment. Earlier in the book he says:

> If I have dramatised these few memories of my childhood, it wasn't so people would feel sorry for me, or admire me, or hate me. I know that I don't have the right to any of those feelings in the hearts of men. And what would I do with them? Does the voice of supreme pride speak in me now? Was I trying to explain, with oversubtle reasoning, how the angel that I could have been was degraded into the obscene slithering larva that I am? Oh, no! I have no pride, I have no more pride! Every time such a sentiment has penetrated me, I've had only to raise my eyes to the sky to dispel it—toward that terrifying suckhole of infinity, where I feel smaller, more unnoticed, more insignificant than an amoeba, lost in the sludgy water of a cistern. Oh no, I swear, I have no more pride.

George feels he was always a larva, a thing not yet developed into an adult form, a thing always meant to be an orphan shaped by lack even as his parents lived. He does not blame his circumstances for his misery—he simply is, in a sense, cursed to be this way. So when he leaves home and takes up a friendship with an artist named Lucien, we don't really expect much to change, though we do hope that George will improve, but he remains a wavering man incapable of happiness.

We see this again when George falls in love with a poverty-stricken woman named Julia. He initially is taken with her listless, unclean beauty. Her rotting teeth and dirty neck all seem part of her charm.

> And her look, her look was so sweet, the gaze of a sick girl who searches people's eyes for the fatal secret their lips won't betray! A look so sad and artless and yet alluring, and full of love! How I loved her, the first time that gaze rested upon me, like a bird perching on a dead branch!

That last part is what we call "foreshadowing," for she really is a bird perching on a dead branch. George is dead and has been dead for a long time—he just doesn't have the sense to lie down yet. Poor Julia does care about George, though her love is filled with self-interest, for she does see in George a way to escape her drudgery and poverty, and she worries about her reputation when George gropes at her in a manner that reminds me of the pawing he experienced from his aunt. She is, at heart, a sweet girl who wants George to share beautiful books and lovely words with her. He, however, cannot sustain the romance. The same wavering affection he feels for his parents and aunt, the same inability to decide whether or not he loves or hates, is responsible for himself or a victim of outside forces, destroys any chance of happiness he may have with Julia. Her mousiness becomes disgusting to him. He is afraid of what Lucien would think of him loving a dirty little maid like her.

> …it wouldn't have displeased me to cruelly mock her skinniness, the empty pockets that her blouse left at the top of her corset, or the hard angularity of her throat—all those physical imperfections which I, in that state of low vengeance and vile spite, took an odious pleasure in discerning and detailing, like a lover coming to his senses after an act of possession.

His emotional faucet running hot and cold causes Julia to become childlike in her frenzy to understand him and to keep him with her, and that childishness kills any real love George feels for her. In his life, there is room for only one small, weak person. He cannot provide comfort. He can only be comforted. He is forever a child in his life, cowering under the sky like a child cowering under his angry mother's apron, tiny and insignificant.

There is much to discuss about George's relationship with Lucien, the artist whom he more or less hopes will save him, lift him above his innate uselessness. But rather than exhaust another line of discussion, I will settle at the notion that in George's life there is no use for anyone weak, only his weakness means anything to him. Lucien has an artistic temperament, is subject to deep emotional lows and spells of angst, and George is devastated by his friend's weakness.

Is there hope for George? We don't really know because this novella is unfinished, but given the state of "X" when his friend visits his abbey in the hills, it seems unlikely that George/X can overcome the fear that has taken charge of his soul. Even if George remains a mess, unable to function in the world—indeed, shivering beneath the sky itself—we are left with many things to consider. Well, I say "we." I know I was left with many things to consider.

Had George been treated differently as a child could his innate fear of living been avoided? Was that fear indeed innate? Was George born or made? Can any little boy who was romantically mauled by a frustrated aunt, economically and emotionally abused by his mother and exploited by his sisters really grow into a man who can sincerely love any woman? Can a boy whose artistic sensibilities are exploited for a chance at family fame ever really recover his capacity for creative joy? Is George really a worm, a larva, or is he a seed that never received the real sort of sunlight needed to grow?

I saw elements of myself in George, but at the end I couldn't help but wonder how much of Octave Mirbeau is represented in George. He certainly hated his school experiences like George did, as Mirbeau was subjected to sustained sexual abuse at the hands of the Jesuits who ran his school. Mirbeau was molested at school, at roughly the same age George was when he was mauled by his aunt. I have not read *Cavalry*, Mirbeau's autobiographical novel, but I do know that he discusses a doomed relationship with a woman he calls Juliette in the book. Juliette is based on Judith Vinmer, a loose woman who leads the protagonist, based on Mirbeau, into moral and social ruin. I cannot help but wonder if Julia is Juliette is Judith. Mirbeau suffered grave mental and philosophical crises in his life and his work after *In the Sky* was dark, rebellious and quite condemning of society and contemporary morality. All the questions I have about George/X cause me to want to read more of Mirbeau and find out more about him.

But primarily *In the Sky* left me thinking about the nature of human development, about which parts of our temperament are made and which are innate. It caused me to look at the wavering part of my own desires, how devastating my own childhood was to me and what parts of it still haunt and hobble me. It forced me to ask myself if I am thwarted or just sort of odd—would I be much different than I am now had I been raised with entirely different parents? It made me marvel at a character I loved and loathed, whom I pitied and identified with and whom I also wanted to kick up the backside because there is only so much misery any person can observe before turning against the miserable. Mirbeau's novella forces those of us who find life difficult at times to ask ourselves if the disease we have is acquired or if it is a cancer that comes from within. That is never an easy question to ask or to answer. This novel, short and unfinished, is a revelation, all the more so because of Ann Sterzinger's excellent, exacting yet emotionally-laden translation.

FURTHER READING

The Loser
Thomas Bernhard

Disagreeable Tales
Léon Bloy

The Map and the Territory
Michel Houellebecq

Torture Garden
Octave Mirbeau

HUNGER
By Knut Hamsun; Translated by Robert Bly
Farrar, Strauss, Giraux (2008 reprint)[1]
Original post: 05/09/2012

Why do I consider this book odd?
It's a story without a plot told by an utterly unhinged narrator. It's also one of the most upsetting books I have ever read.

There is no real plot, so it's hard to know where to start. In Knut Hamsun's *Hunger* the same thing happens every day with mild variations on action. There is no character arc because the unnamed narrator is as vainglorious, lunatic and horribly depressed at the beginning as he is at the end. This novel frustrated me beyond belief, yet I read it through twice. I just had to. I hated it the first time and loved it the second. I also never want to read it again.

It's difficult to discuss such a book with any skill, though I realize others have. Initially, I thought Paul Auster's commentary, printed in the copy I read, was wrong. Later I realized it wasn't wrong—it's just that Auster interrogates the text from an intellectual perspective. I looked at it from an emotional perspective and felt something akin to pain. For those who can't remain detached, this novel is the literary equivalent of running your soul over a cheese grater. Over and over again.

How does one discuss a narrator whose highs and lows make Raskolnikov's public behavior seem normal? How can I discuss a book in which nothing really changes and there is virtually no character arc? I don't know. I think all I can do is discuss the parts that resonated the most with me, but even this is going to be sticky because as I divide the book into specific elements I want to discuss, there will be significant overlap between these elements. For example, as I discuss how the narrator cannot act in his own self-interests, lunacy caused by starvation also comes into play. It's tempting to just type the words, "Starvation in a land of plenty will make you insane!" over and over until I hit a decent word count.

Before I dive in, I should mention that I read the edition translated from the original Norwegian text by Robert Bly. This is widely considered to be the crappiest translation because Bly evidently "corrected" verb usage to eliminate mixed tenses. Mixed tenses, according to scholars, were meant to

---

1   Knut Hamsun's *Sult* (*Hunger*) was originally published in 1890. The first English translations was undertaken by Mary Chavelita Dunne (alias, George Egerton). Robert Bly's translation was first published in 1967.

convey the disorganization of the narrator's mind. Though I sort of wish I had read a more faithful translation, I suspect it is a good thing that I didn't since the edition I read is, by most accounts, a bit saner. I read the less crazy version. As it was, the narrator's mind was still an utter vexation.

Hunger's narrator is trying to write in a very Dostoyevskian manner. He may be an excellent writer but his topics—"Crimes of the Future" or "Freedom of the Will"—suggest that he might be a self-impressed hack. His grand ideas are constrained by his grinding poverty and his mental disorganization, which are caused by and feed off each other. The novel is divided into four parts and begins with the writer leaving a boarding house (though he could have stayed had he just approached the problem with logic and patience) and living rough. The second part concerns his attempts to live in a borrowed shack as he tries to write. In the third part, he meets a woman who slowly realizes he is not who she thought he was and their budding romance is dashed. The fourth section takes place mostly in a very low-status boarding house where the narrator, terrified of the cold and of living rough again, hangs onto a roof over his head in a manner so servile and cringing it almost killed me to read it. He finally goes to enlist as a crew member on a ship. Some interpret this turn to mean that he is finally moving on from his despair, but I read it as suicide. I will explain my interpretation in due course. For now, I'm just going to divide my discussion into relevant segments and hope that by the end I will have given you a fair picture of the narrator and the struggles he faces as he starves nearly to death in a world that often notices him too well or does not notice him at all.

STRANGE, GRANDIOSE EGO

The narrator, as I mentioned, is a writer. He is also very impoverished, to the point of starvation. Yet he has a need to present himself as a man of means, a magnanimous giver to the less fortunate. Unlike most who want to present a facade of wealth, he often takes things a step too far, impoverishing himself further in his efforts to save face. He literally sells the clothes on his back to give a pittance to people who often have more than he does. He does not do this from a need to help others, or from a place of charity. He does it because he wants to be seen as someone he is not and it is a blow to his ego that he cannot bear when people realize how impoverished he is. This is particularly sad because his ego destroys any chance he might have at maintaining the security he needs to write.

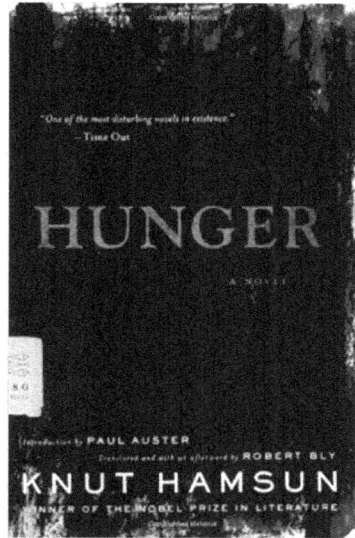

It is undeniable how impoverished the narrator is, even at the beginning of the novel. He looks shabby.

> …my clothes were beginning to look so bad I couldn't really present myself any longer for a job that required someone respectable.

He has no possessions.

> By now I was so utterly denuded of objects that I didn't even have a comb left, or a book to read when I felt hopeless.

He has no food.

> If one only had something to eat, just a little, on such a clear day!

But when he meets a beggar who asks him for money, he questions him and upon determining that the man actually has a trade and would prefer not to be a beggar, he says:

> "Well, that's different," I said. "Wait here a few minutes, and I'll see if I can't find something for you, a little something at least."

He simply cannot bring himself to tell the beggar that he too has nothing to give.

He goes to a pawnshop and takes off his waistcoat. All he has are the clothes on his back but he pawns his waistcoat for one and a half kroner.

> I took the money and went back. Actually, pawning this waistcoat was a wonderful idea; I would still have money left over for a good, fat breakfast, and by evening my piece on "Crimes of the Future" would be in shape. Life began immediately to seem more friendly, and I hurried back to the man to get him off my hands.

Note how he has taken responsibility for the beggar. He needs to get him off his hands. He genuinely has a sense that he needs to help the man and that the man will burden his conscience until he helps him. It would be borderline messianic if the responsibility he took for this stranger was motivated by kindness or fellow-feeling for a man in straits similar to his own.

Even the beggar picks up on the narrator's oddness.

> The man took the money and began to look me up and down. What was he standing there looking at? I got the sensation that he was inspecting my trousers particularly and I became irritated at this impertinence. Did this old fool imagine I was really as poor as I looked? Hadn't I just as good as begun my ten-kroner article? On the whole, I had no fears for the future; I had many irons in the fire. What business was it of this heathen savage if I helped him out on such a marvelous day.

He criticizes the man for staring at him and the man hands him the coin back. The narrator begins to trip all over himself to save face.

> I stamped my foot, swore, and told him to keep it. Did he think I intended to go to all this trouble for nothing? When you came down to it, I probably

owed him the money, I just happened to remember an old debt, he was looking at a punctilious man, one honorable down to his fingernails. In short, the money was his... Nonsense, nothing to thank me for, it was a pleasure. Goodbye.

I walked off. At last I was rid of this painful pest, and could be undisturbed.

He hounded the man into taking the money he could not afford to give and that the man knew he could not afford to give, yet when he left the man had suddenly become a pest. The narrator saw himself as a man of honor, insisting on paying a debt to a persistent, dunning debtor, not a deranged man who could not afford food who sold his clothes to be able to give money to a man who probably did not need it as much as he.

There are several scenes like this, where the narrator, unable to endure that anyone look upon him as impoverished, gives away money he has earned or come upon by accident. For example, the woman with whom he has the failed affair later sees him and sends a messenger with ten kroner. He had just been thrown out of his boarding house for non-payment of rent and for being unpleasant, and he could have used the money for food and rent at a new place, or he could even have paid up at the place where he had been evicted and stayed on. Instead he thrust the money into the boarding house owner's hand so she would understand at last the sort of man she had been dealing with—a man of genuine substance and means—and wanders off in his mania.

His attempts to appear as he is not, his insistence that he be treated with reverence rather than respect, causes a large portion of his problems. Swinging wildly between servility and arrogance, self-loathing and grandiosity, it seems clear the narrator's low status in life plagues him. He would rather self-destruct than stomach anyone potentially thinking him destitute. This creates a spiral in which the narrator, a bit unhinged in the beginning, becomes increasingly more lunatic as starvation takes its toll.

In a similar vein, the narrator has a tendency to tell himself what his ego needs to hear. He is behind in his rent and cannot bring himself to talk to his landlady (this later has horrible repercussions because his self-eviction leaves him with nowhere to go but an abandoned workshop where he receives permission to sleep). He spins a narrative, believing the room is not good enough for him, especially since he is a man of great intellect. Here are his thoughts as he rationalizes giving up the last form of comfort he has in life because of his overweening pride.

> This really wasn't any room for me; the curtains on the windows were a very ordinary green, and there weren't even enough pegs on the walls to hang your wardrobe on. The sad rocking chair on the corner was actually a joke of a chair: if one started laughing at it, one could die laughing. It was too low for a grown man, and besides, it was so tight, one needed a shoehorn

to get back out of it. In short, this room was simply not furnished in a way appropriate to intellectual effort and I did not intend to keep it any longer. I would not keep it under any circumstances! I had been silent in this hole and stood it here and stayed on here too long already.

Bear in mind, he has no money to stay there and has read a letter from his landlady asking him to pay up. He can't afford those terrible green curtains and that skinny chair, and one is tempted to think he is making excuses, psyching himself for the inevitable by making it seem as if it is a legitimate choice he is making. But he does this so often—affecting a superior attitude even when he is not in a state of *extremis*—that the reader is hard pressed to tell whether he is assuming a delusional role or actually expressing his ego.

Strange Theater

He becomes more and more unhinged as the novel goes on, but even at the beginning he is creating creepy situations or elaborate theater that no one around him understands. As he does these strange things, he feels as if he has gotten one over on the people he baffles. He is certain that those around him must understand he has made fools of them, that they understand they are less than him, the butts of his joke. That is never the case and he never seems to notice he is the one who looks foolish.

Take this scene where he begins to follow two women shopping in town (one is the lady he later has a brief flirtation with and this scene is where she gets the impression he is a rakish drunk rather than an unhinged derelict). He overtakes the two women and brushes arms with one of them, an attractive woman who catches his attention. His reaction to noticing her and her noticing him is … interesting.

> Suddenly my thoughts shot off on a lunatic direction, and I felt myself possessed by a strange desire to frighten this woman, to follow her in some way or other.

This reminded me a bit of Edmund Kemper, a serial killer who once said, and I am paraphrasing, that when he saw a pretty woman, part of him wanted to date her and part of him wondered what her head would look like on a stick.

He slows to permit the women to catch up to him and tells the pretty woman she was losing her book. She had no book with her and she walked on. Her mild disinterest just goads him further.

> My malice increased and I followed the two. I was conscious all the time that I was following mad whims without being able to do anything about it. My deranged consciousness ran away with me and sent me lunatic inspirations, which I obeyed one after the other. No matter how much I told myself I was acting idiotically, it did not help; I made the most stupid faces behind the women's backs, and I coughed furiously several times as I went by them.

He tells her again that she is losing her book.

> "Book, what book," she said in a frightened voice. "Whatever sort of book is he talking about?"

> She stopped. I gloated cruelly over her confusion; the bewilderment in her eyes fascinated me. Her thought could not grasp my desperate and petty persecution; she has no book at all with her, not even a page of a book, and yet now she looks through her pockets, gazes repeatedly at her hands, turns her head and examines the sidewalk behind her, strains her small and tender brain to its limit to find out what sort of book I am talking about.

He gloated at what he thought was her confusion, assuming a position of superiority that is borne out as he mocks her silly little brain trying to figure out what he is talking about. He thought his mind games caused her to try to find the non-existent book when she was really just trying to see what on her person would make anyone think she was dropping a book, not realizing, of course, that he is insane. Her friend tells her he is drunk and to pay him no attention.

It is very telling, what makes him stop following the two women.

> I was at their heels, as near as I dared all the time. They turned once, giving me a half-frightened, half-inquisitive look, and I saw no irritation in their manner, nor any wrinkled brows. This patience with my pestering made me ashamed and I dropped my eyes. I no longer wanted to torture them.

While he clearly feels some perverse, malicious drama in following the women, he also engages in bizarre theater with motives that are harder to pin down because he is performing for his own benefit. However, in some scenes, he begins a strange theater exercise only to be forced back into some sort of reality when he senses his act will not boost his ego. In part one, he finds himself inside a well-appointed apartment building but he does not know anyone who lives there.

> I rang a bell violently on the third floor. Why did I stop precisely on the third floor? Why did I choose this bell, which was farthest from the stair?

Even though he is in the middle of some theater he does not understand, the strange performance takes a left turn when the woman behind the door answers and thinks him a beggar. His diseased ego kicks in and he asks her if there was a man there, an elderly man who needed assistance going out and was willing to pay for help. She looks at him strangely and tells him there is no such man. Not content to leave it at that, the narrator is hell-bent to make this woman know, by God, he is a man of quality.

> "Then I must ask you for your pardon again," I said. "Possibly it is the second floor. In any case, I merely wanted to recommend for the post a man in whom I have taken an interest. My own family is Wedel-Jarlsberg." Then I bowed once more and withdrew. The young woman turned beet red and in

her embarrassment could not move from the spot but stood rooted staring after me as I went down the stairs.

My peace of mind was back, and my brain clear.

The narrator, by this point, has been living on the street, has sold his waistcoat, has no access to a place to perform basic toiletries, yet he tells himself the woman blushes from embarrassment for not recognizing a man of quality. Most telling is how calm he feels afterward. This strange theater, his elaborate ruse, gives him a buffer between himself and the people he senses look down on him. I very much get the feeling that the hungrier the man becomes, the more able he is to trick himself into believing that he can, through force of will, make people believe what he wants.

Later his theater takes on elements of delusion or outright fantasy. In part two, he finds himself staring at what he calls a white cornucopia, which sounds like the sort of white, paper cups that snowcones are served in. He stares at one of these discarded cornucopias and decides that there is money at the bottom. He wants to steal it but a policeman is near.

> Then I heard the policeman cough—and why did it suddenly occur to me to do the same? I stood up and coughed, repeating the cough three times so he would be sure to hear it. Now, won't he jump for that paper cone when he comes near? I sat rejoicing over this joke, I rubbed my hands in ecstasy and swore magnificently. His nose will stretch when he sees that! After this trick, he'll want to sink into the hottest puddle in hell!

It's hard to follow but he thinks that the policeman will find silver in the cone and... And what? I don't know, but the narrator is certain it will be a bitter joke. The policeman finds the cone, picks it up, and throws it away, and this also somehow becomes fodder for the strange theater churning in his mind.

> I sat there with tears in my eyes, hiccuping from shortness of breath, out of my mind with feverish laughter. I started to talk aloud, told myself the story of the paper cone, mimicked the gestures of the poor policeman, peeked into my empty hand, and repeated again and again: He coughed when he threw it away!

He is obviously quite mad and there are so many irrational scenes that it is hard to know the purpose of them other than to show the narrator, a weak man before he hits truly dire straits, has come unhinged entirely, deranged by the hunger he suffers. And he suffers greatly—more on this later.

SELF-SABOTAGE

I've already mentioned how the narrator, in possession of ten kroner given to him by his erstwhile girlfriend, decides to give the money away to the woman who has evicted him in an attempt to show her that he is a man of honor. I've also mentioned how he will pawn even his clothes so he can give money to beggars who are likely not as poorly off as he is. But his self-destructiveness, ironically presented in the manner of ego-preservation, knows no bounds.

Take this scene when he finds himself locked out of the workshop he sleeps in. The police cannot help him open the door, but urge him to register at the police station as homeless. Doing so will give him a place to sleep and a means to obtain food, two things he desperately needs if he is going to be able to write. He will be able to obtain temporary shelter and food if he is honest with himself and accepts that he is homeless and starving, but he doesn't. He gives a false name to the officer, telling him that he is a journalist who, after a night of revelry, lost his keys and wallet. The officer gives him a knowing smile (likely attributing his dreadful appearance to excessive revelry) and takes him to a cell.

Once in the cell, the derangement caused by a lack of food combines with madness latent in the narrator's mind. Both rear up to prevent him from being able to rest in any manner. His mind races all evening, he experiences extreme highs (he creates a new word—*Kuboaa*—though he has no idea what it means) and extreme lows. He sleeps for a brief stretch as the sun begins to rise. In the morning the homeless men and beggars who slept in the jail receive vouchers for a free meal. Since the narrator presented himself as a temporarily impecunious reporter, the police feel no need to offer him food. Surely such a man could provide for himself.

> A ticket, a ticket for me, too. I hadn't eaten for three endless days and nights. A loaf of bread! But no one offered me a ticket and I didn't dare ask for one. That would have caused suspicion instantly. They would have wanted to poke around in my private affairs and find out who I really was—then they would arrest me for giving false information.

Had he come clean, the police most likely would have chided him for his pride and permitted him a place to sleep and some bread to sate his hunger. Maintaining this lie cuts the narrator off from a source of support that, had he utilized it, would have given him the foundation upon which to write.

Without digressing over my reasons, I never get the impression that the narrator is a particularly good writer. But that this man refuses to do anything that will give him the comfort necessary to write makes it seem as if writing is a very secondary thing to him, almost like a prop, or another layer of theater to support his idea of himself as an intellectual. He does write but he cannot make enough money to support himself and his refusal or inability to foster his talent makes one wonder how much talent he even has.

There are other scenes, where he could have collected on debts owed to him but chooses not to, where he tries to sell an item but gives it away to someone who has no money to purchase it. Our narrator is quite simply a man who has no idea how to behave in a manner ensuring self-preservation.

Starvation and Insanity

The narrator is deranged and part of his mind shows a diseased will, but there can be no mistake that hunger strips his mind of the capacity to think soundly, especially as the book goes on. His hunger is of the sort I associate with death, the pre-terminal state where a starving person cannot keep down food because he has been starving for too long. There are times when it is surprising he can even go on, so profound is his hunger. As detestable as he often appears, one cannot help but feel pity for his plight. Hunger, as the title implies, is the driving force in this book. It shapes everything that happens to the afflicted narrator. It may have been exacerbated by his strange need to maintain false appearances, but even if he had spent every penny he earned or was given on food, he still would have been chronically hungry.

Hunger is full of scenes where he finally—finally—gets access to food, only to find that he cannot keep it down. He vomits up water, he chews on pieces of wood but real food nauseates him. In one scene, when he finally has money to get a plate of food at a cafe, the results are dire.

> The food began to bother me, my stomach felt upset, and I would not be able to hold the food down very long. I walked along emptying my mouth, in every dark crook I passed, fought against the nausea which was making me hollow all over again, clenched my fists, steeled myself, stamped on the sidewalk, and swallowed again in a rage what was trying to come up—all in vain! I ran at last into a doorway, doubled over, blinded from the tears that sprang from my eyes, and vomited everything.

Money, so hard to come by, exchanged for food, and he cannot keep it down. He has been starving for a long time—refeeding syndrome, an often fatal condition, can occur after only a few days of starvation. The body goes without food too long and it is thrown into metabolic chaos. The narrator is physically very sick and it seems that he has no way out. He does ask a man what one should feed a starving person who is beginning to eat and is told boiled milk works well. He gets boiled milk at a cafe and indeed can keep it down but his poverty does not permit him to coddle his empty stomach this way for long.

It just gets worse. Take this pitiful scene:

> I was bitterly hungry and didn't know what to do with my exorbitant appetite. I writhed about on the bench and pulled my knees up against my chest as hard as I could. When it was dark, I shuffled over to the city jail— God knows how I got there—and sat down on the edge of the balustrade, I ripped one of my coat pockets out and started chewing on it...

He is struck with the idea of asking a butcher for a bone, the sort of bones a butcher would give away to someone who wants it for his dog.

> I got a bone, a gorgeous little bone with some meat still on it, and put it under my coat. I thanked the man so warmly he looked at me astonished.

"Nothing to thank me for," he said.

"Oh yes there is," I said. "This was very good of you."

He returns to the blacksmith shop, settles into the dark and begins to chew on the bone.

> It has no taste at all; a nauseating odor of dried blood rose from the bone, and I started throwing up immediately, I couldn't help it. I tried again—if only I could keep it down, it would do some good; the problem was to get it to stay down there. But I vomited again. I grew angry, bit fiercely into the meat, ripped off a small piece, and swallowed it by force. That did no good either—as soon as the small pieces became warm in the stomach, up they came again. I clenched my fists madly, started crying from sheer helplessness, and gnawed like a man possessed. I cried so much that the bone became wet and messy with tears. I vomited, swore, and chewed again, cried as if my heart would break, and threw up again. Then I swore aloud and consigned all the powers of the universe to hell.

This was hard for me to read. Very hard. This and so many passages like it. It is all the worse because it is starvation in the midst of plenty. It is a man dying on his feet from a lack of food outside of the constraints of war, genocide, famine or drought. From all accounts, this is something that Hamsun himself experienced and this passage of a man sobbing as his traumatized stomach vomits back up the food he needs to survive is harrowing in its implications because the narrator cannot tolerate the ego hit it would take to admit he needs help and yet those around him seem largely indifferent to his suffering. He is starving alone yet with an audience and it is horrible to read and to contemplate. No wonder he acts out such bizarre theater toward those around him—they are watching him die and most don't seem to care. Even though he presents himself as a sort of deranged gentleman temporarily down on his luck, he is very obviously starving.

But what could passersby or shopkeepers do to help a man who refuses to accept help when offered, who gives away money that will keep him in food and shelter? That is the core of this book, this utter frustration, knowing that there is no way out for this particular man. Within the constraints of Norwegian society and this man's miserable mindset, there can be no happy ending, no warm bed and boiled milk until he recovers.

INTERPRETATION OF THE ENDING

Because this book evidently mirrors a terrible time in Hamsun's life—a decade or more of his own suffering—it is tempting to believe the ending is a hopeful one because Hamsun survived and managed to get this book published. In part four, the narrator, evicted from his home and having given away the money his ex-girlfriend sent him, goes on a sort of rampage, grabbing and eating cakes and vomiting in the street. He finally goes to the harbor and finds a ship that is sailing to Leeds and then to Cadiz and persuades the captain to take him on as a merchant marine. The captain is reluctant but agrees when the narrator promises to work hard, even to take two watches if it means he can have the job. The novel ends thusly:

> When we were out on the fjord, I straightened up, wet from fever and exertion, looking in toward land and said goodbye for now to the city, to Christiana [Oslo], where the windows of the homes all shone with such brightness.

He's leaving a place of brightness, where he failed utterly, where he almost starved. But then again, on the ship he will finally get enough to eat, perhaps bread and water until he can stomach more. Isn't he saved? Many readers seem to think this is the case.

I don't. I think going onto the ship is a form of suicide, and not just because he is going to travel away from a city of brightness.

When the narrator is in the jail cell, he has a waking dream that tells us quite clearly what he thinks of the harbor, of ships, of the sea.

> God in heaven, how black it was! And I started again to think about the harbor, the ships, the dark monsters who lay waiting for me. They wanted to pull me to themselves and hold me fast and sail with me over land and sea, through dark kingdoms no man had ever seen. I felt myself on board ship, drawn on through waters, floating in clouds, going down, down… I gave a hoarse shriek of fear, and hugged the bed; I had been on such a perilous journey, fallen down through the sky like a shot. How good and saved I felt when I grabbed the hard sides of the cot! That is what it is like to die, I said to myself, now I will die.

There is a temptation to say that with death comes rebirth, but that's not how I read it. No, it seems like the sea is where a man who cannot live in the brightness goes, and monsters are waiting for him. They take him down into the sea, kill him, and his spirit, initially in clouds, floats down into hell.

For me, joining the merchant ship is the last straw—the man is ready to die.

Further Reading

Journey to the End of the Night
Louis-Ferdinand Céline

Whatever
Michel Houellebecq

Lee
Tito Perdue

HOUSE OF THE SLEEPING BEAUTIES AND OTHER STORIES

By Yasunari Kawabata; Translated by Edward Seidensticker
Kodansha (2004)
Original post: 10/06/2009

Why do I consider this book odd?
I knew this was going to be a helluva ride when I recognized the name of the man who wrote the introduction. In 1970, after he failed to inspire a Japanese military revolt, the writer Yukio Mishima attempted to commit *seppuku*, a form of ritual suicide via disemboweling. He was then given the coup de gras, being decapitated by a friend who took part in the attempted rebellion. When such a man gives the introduction to a book dealing mainly with *thanatos* (with a little *eros* thrown in) you know you're about to enter very odd territory. Indeed, this may be the most deeply odd and disturbing work ever written by a Nobel Laureate, though heaven knows I find more and more incredibly odd works written by unlikely writers.

I finished this book weeks before I could write about it. The specter of writing a review completely stalled me. I kept telling myself to get over here and write but I couldn't do it. I don't know exactly why. I suspect it's because *House of the Sleeping Beauties and Other Stories* tripped too many polarities. I found it to be at once enthralling and repellent, amazing and disgusting. I consumed it rapidly and wanted then to vomit it back up. Seldom has a book so engrossed me while leaving me so unhappy.

This book consists of the titular novella, "House of the Sleeping Beauties," and two short stories, "One Arm" and "Of Birds and Beasts." Each work is horrific, beautiful, sickening and compelling in its own right.

"HOUSE OF THE SLEEPING BEAUTIES"

Often I find myself at war with people's notions of what comprises literary eros. How can a book be an example of eros and thanatos when it's all death and no passion? How can it be eros when there is no love, when there is no sex, when there is nothing but the limited emotional range of the protagonist, an aging man who seems to hate all women? How can it be eros when the protagonist has no emotional depth nor even sensory revelation in a sex act? These are rhetorical questions, as I understand why, in a sense, this novella falls into the eros and thanatos categories. It's just that my mind rebels against

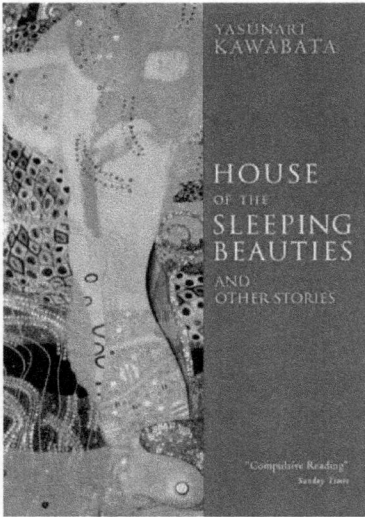

what many modern critics consider eros.

The tale's protagonist, Eguchi, is 67 years old. He is a habitué of the House of the Sleeping Beauties, a sort of brothel where the girls, all very young, are drugged insensate at night so that old men can sleep with them. The word "sleep" here is literal. The old men do not have sex with the sleeping girls as they are impotent due to old age. Eguchi hides what he says is his ability to sustain an erection from the Madam so as to be permitted to sleep with the girls (it may all be in Eguchi's head—one is never sure if Eguchi is really still virile or if it's just wishful thinking).

Indeed, the Madam is not concerned at all with Eguchi's member when she chides him not to do anything disgusting with the girls. "He was not to put his finger into the mouth of the sleeping girl..." That line haunts me for some reason, but it is clear the proprietress of the House of the Sleeping Beauties does not think Eguchi is capable of any greater outrage against the sleeping girls. And it should go without saying that Eguchi sticks his finger into the mouth of one of the girls. Of course he does. That finger is the only penetration in the story.

Those who visit the house and go to bed with the drugged girls are themselves eventually drugged, but they get to spend time with the sleeping girls while they themselves are completely conscious. Though Eguchi tells himself that he could, theoretically, do whatever he wanted to any of the sleeping girls without detection, tellingly, he never does. Eguchi wants to lay next to a virginal, sleeping girl, because actual sex with conscious women causes him to be exposed to their messy, nasty lives, something he cannot bear.

The novella consists of Eguchi's five encounters with six sleeping girls (he gets a sleeping girl threesome one evening because a new, very young girl could only be comforted by the thought of being rendered unconscious if she had a friend in the bed with her) and his endless thoughts as he lays next to the warm bodies of the girls he claims he can have sex with if he wants to but doesn't. He takes pride in his supposed virility compared to the other old men who frequent the house as he manipulates the girls' bodies, revels in their breath, their very smell, while thinking his sad, confined, loveless thoughts.

As he moves the arms and legs of the sleeping girls, he thinks of a mistress he once had, of his wife who seems only a bearer of children and not a lover, and in the passage most disturbing to me, he thinks a lot about his youngest daughter and how she slept with two men before marrying. His thoughts are consumed by women, but never love, though he seems to have a great amount of affection for his youngest daughter and for his mistress.

At times, I almost had hope for Eguchi. Lying with one girl, he is reminded of a time when he was a child. The girl reminds him of his mother, her breasts of suckling mother's milk. His regression into a childlike state almost redeems the perversity of the situation, almost as if it allows men to become innocent again. But this reaction does not last and is soon overtaken by his relentless misogyny. I am not a scholar of Japanese culture or literature, but Kawabata's novella is almost fifty years old and the social customs it portrays will be at odds with most contemporary views of men, women and what it means to grow old. Knowing this still did not help me understand Eguchi.

Part of this lack of understanding comes from the cultural and temporal divide mentioned above, but part of it is that Eguchi's voyage is intensely personal. The likelihood of a reader being enough like Eguchi to feel any resonance from his experiences is slim. Yet his story, with remembrances of travel, the surprise of his affection for his youngest daughter, his fascination with flowers, is still absorbing.

Eguchi at times is restless with the girls, moving them around, thinking maniacally. Proximity to young flesh he cannot possess shows him how old and close to death he is. But even as he grapples with his own mortality, he becomes intensely focused on and distracted by the youth and virginity of the girls he sleeps with. He hates the darker nipples of fecund women, larger breasts that imply childbirth, and he pictures dirty, stained lips removing lipstick as he examines the mouth of an unconscious girl. The girls seem to provide him with little comfort. No matter how much he attempts to distract himself by focusing on minutia and harking back to his soulless encounters with women, deep inside he knows he is approaching death. As he says to the proprietress, "To die on a night like this, with a young girl's skin to warm him—that would be paradise for an old man." Yet Eguchi seems inconsolable when he sleeps next to the girls, overcome by his unpleasant thoughts.

At times, I wondered if I was reading too much into Eguchi, trying to read around his misogyny and his utter nastiness. As he hyper-analyzed the girls, I hyper-analyzed him. I wonder if that was not Kawabata's point, that there really was no more to Eguchi than he presented, a sad, lonely, old man with no greater depth. At one point, after listening to Eguchi ramble about the girls he slept with—should he speak to them if he saw them on the street? when would she wake up?—the proprietress of the house says to him, "Just take sleeping girls as sleeping girls." Perhaps it is best to take shallow old men as shallow old men.

But it is impossible to overlook the very real idea that at the end of his life, Eguchi wants to spend lots of time in the presence of girls who can only be seen and not heard, and be left alone with his endless, meandering thoughts about women. He does not want to speak and interact with them, only look at them and experience their warmth as it suits him. There is no discovery, no epiphany. Just an old man remembering what he lost, unable to find comfort.

"ONE ARM"

This tale uses magical realism to tell the story of the nameless protagonist and the girl who gives him her arm for the evening. As much as Eguchi in the previous tale allowed his mind to ramble on about the women he sort of loved, the protagonist in "One Arm" lives in a realm of paranoia, spending much of the story worrying about what anyone would think if they saw him with the girl's arm. He ruminates on the girl's motivations instead of just accepting the gift. He seems to fall in love with the arm, having a conversation with it (and since this is magical realism, the arm speaks back) and attaching it to his body in the place of one of his own arms. He sleeps, and awakens in emotional terror when he finds his own arm has reattached itself.

It is hard not to see this as a tale of self-hatred with a masturbatory overtone. The man cannot stand his own touch and is greatly upset when the arm touching him in the morning is his own. When he rediscovers the girl's arm in the morning, it is no longer lively and talkative, pink and healthy, but instead is quiet and pale. This shatters him. The last line of the text reveals his strange wish that the essence of women (their "dew") could come from their fingertips. Had the man felt that way when he awoke to real, entire, living bodies of women in his bed? Did a feminine arm he could use to masturbate give him a new sexual lease that was wrenched away when he awoke with his own arm again? It's hard to say. For the bulk of the story, the man simply thinks about and talks to the arm. He even shares Bible verses with it. One leaves the tale with the image of a lonely, shallow man with no real release, who knows little more about himself at the end than he did at the beginning.

"OF BIRDS AND BEAST"

Easily the most disturbing tale for me, an animal lover. It's another tale of twisted eros, but this time the twisting is violent and cruel. Another unnamed protagonist, the former lover of a dancer who marries and loses her youthful step and body, tells himself that he loves animals more than humans. He surrounds himself with dogs and birds but has no affection for them, seeing them as buffers that keep people at arm's length (so to speak, considering the story that precedes it), and for the prestige they can bring him.

One disturbing section deals with a purebred dog he takes in after its master had beaten it trying to get it to miscarry after it bred with a mongrel. The dog gives birth to stillborn puppies and is found eating them (a vet explains that the dog ate them because they were born dead). Rather than contemplate the abuse the dog suffered, the man reacts with disgust because mongrels had been born in his house. He then permits another dog to breed, a dog too young for breeding. He claims he loves puppies but throws into the garbage a newborn pup he is not sure is dead. He permits the young mother dog to kill the rest, owing to her inexperience. As he thinks of the dog prancing atop her puppies he is reminded of his dancing lover, the same woman who married someone else, who was clearly once a prostitute. She is happy she can get pregnant despite her former life. He wonders why he did not marry her when the answer is clear to the reader. She mated badly like his dogs, and therefore was less precious to him. He continues to desire her, as he desires the animals who always disappoint him.

The man's relationship with birds will sicken most readers. He loves birds but allows children to torture one to death. It is a young bird, and not a fancy bird that would bring glory to him for saving. He refers to the small skylark as a "piece of garbage." He mixes up mated pairs of birds, introducing a new female to a mated pair, and waits to see which one dies in the end. Kawabata uses language of extreme anguish very casually to describe the sufferings of the birds the man destroys. He washes them and leaves them too close to the fire and destroys their feet. He then washes a second pair and leaves them too wet and they die sodden at the bottom of the cage. He delights in the birds eating from his hands and so allows them to overfeed to death. The bird he loves best is an owl who hates him, a beast that refuses to give into his twisted will. Perversely, it is the owl that provides him with the most comfort.

The entire story can be summed up in one passage:

> There was… a certain sad purity in making playthings of the lives and the habits of animals, and, deciding upon an ideal form, breeding toward it in a manner artificial and distorted: there was in it a godlike newness.

Each new animal offers a chance to be a new god, determining its fate, and destroying it if it does not accept the artificial and distorted fate he offers it. It is clear these feelings extend to human beings. When his former lover becomes pregnant by her husband and rejects his sexual advances, one feels as if she narrowly avoided a fate similar to what befell a mated pair of birds ripped asunder, or the dogs whose puppies were doomed by human violence and disinterest.

All three stories were unsettling and often quite upsetting, especially the third. They were also impossible to stop reading once I began. Kawabata's style is engrossing and transfixing, even as it appalls.

FURTHER READING

Death in Midsummer: And Other Stories
Yukio Mishima

NAÏVE. SUPER
By Erlend Loe; Translated by Tor Ketil Solberg
Cannongate Books (2005)
Original post: 04/06/2011

Why do I consider this book odd?
It isn't as full-force odd as some of the books I discuss, but it is off the mainstream radar. And to be perfectly blunt, it's a book written from a place of goodwill, of belief in the idea that life can be wonderful. Given that most literary fiction, even if it has a happy ending, requires a wallow, this is refreshing. Don't get me wrong, I still love a good wallow, but a wallow-less book that doesn't pander to the reader is so rare that it is odd by default.

Sometimes you just need things to be sweetly odd. Just a little strange, a little left of center. I ordered a this book because I asked a clerk at BookPeople to tell me the oddest book he had ever read. His answer, obviously, was *Naïve. Super*. He was a tragically hip young person, as are most of the clerks at BookPeople, but this is Austin and I am getting old, so no judgment implied. He described it as being the story of a man-child who spent all day bouncing balls. So you can see why I had to get it and then wait two years to read it. I wanted to read it, but I also sort of dreaded it.

Turns out there was nothing to dread. The tragically hip young man was describing with no small amount of irony the most irony-deficient book ever written since *Jane* fucking *Eyre*. Again, not his fault. When you're a hammer all the world looks like nails, and when you are a hipster earnestness may be hard to identify. I'm just glad he recommended it to me. Otherwise I might never have known about this lovely gem.

Ignore any of the official reviews. Some utter asshole said it recalled Holden Caulfield and while I don't dislike *The Catcher in the Rye* (actually, I love poor Holden and I love Salinger too, the shithead), I have to wonder if people are

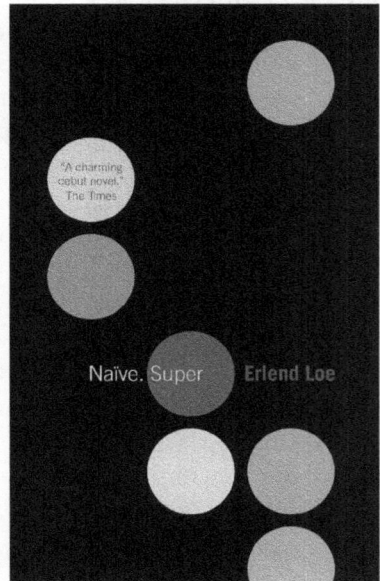

put off by that idiotic statement. The protagonist of *Naïve. Super* has about as much in common with Holden Caulfield as I do. We both dislike phonies and that's about it. This is why I seldom read reviews of any kind before I read and discuss a book myself. I can't imagine the number of books I would have passed over had I taken my cues from reviewers. Of course, I can see how that might come off as arrogant—maintaining my own book review and discussion site while showing disdain for other reviews. While I know I am right about the books I read (a sign of a certain amount of arrogance), I also go into far more depth than the average reviewer, not merely because I'm verbose, but also because you should never take my word for anything. You should just read my words and hopefully I will give you a look at the book that will show you a bit more than if I were to glibly compare it to another book in a facile attempt to make myself understood.

Anyway, enough with my critic's disgust.

Naïve. Super should come in prescription form. In fact, I think I may reread it as soon as I've finished writing about it. It's the most strangely peaceful book I have ever read. I suspect I love it because I adore the protagonist, a quiet, strange, ultimately golden-hearted man (we never learn his name, though some believe his name is Erlend because of an email produced in the book). The protagonist has dropped out of grad school because everything has suddenly become meaningless to him (which may explain why that moronic reviewer made that stupid comparison to poor Holden). He house sits. He makes a ton of lists. He meets a little boy and hangs out with him. He meets a girl and wins her heart. He travels with his brother and enjoys New York. At the end, he realizes he has a good heart, but he comes to the conclusion a bit tentatively as it is not something easily quantified. Even so, he leaves the book with a better, if still elusive, grasp of what constitutes the meaning of his life.

If it seems like I spoiled the novel, I didn't. You can sum up the plot in a few sentences, but the plot is not the reason to read this book. The reason to read this book is to observe as a man who lacks all forms of pretense tries to quantify everything, exploring the world around him, finding the meanings to things that eluded him until he dropped out and ceased taking for granted the existence of even the simplest of things.

Of course, this is the sort of novel that could only happen in a relatively benign place like Norway, where a grown man playing with a little boy doesn't provoke a police investigation, and where the same man's brother has an apartment to spare. The protagonist is the most earnest character an American like me can possibly hope to discover. With so many novels sickeningly drenched in irony, the star of *Naïve. Super* is completely sincere. But because he is not self-referentially hip in his depression, his attempts to make meaning of his world might tempt some readers to write him off as simple, or possibly stupid. I think this is a serious mistake. The protagonist does not have intellectual difficulties. He's just finding himself in a manner that does not involve self-destruction and the delivery of oh-so-clever one-liners. Yet even in the absence of cynical posturing, there is a great deal of humor.

The protagonist begins by explaining that he has two friends, one good and one bad, and a brother, who is less friendly than him, but a good guy nonetheless. One has to agree that his brother is a good man, because he permits his 25-year-old brother, a man who rather enjoys spending hours playing with Brio toys and making seemingly pointless lists, stay in his apartment in exchange for just relaying his messages. When his brother returns from his trip, he realizes the protagonist is having a gentle nervous breakdown combined with a mild existential crisis. Perhaps the brother senses that brutally beating the protagonist at croquet is what triggered the crisis. No matter, he cares for his brother in his time of need, taking him on a trip to New York. It's hard to fault the brother. *Naïve. Super* is a novel filled with nice people. Nice, quirky and not entirely familiar people, but nice people nonetheless. People who need a villain will have to look elsewhere.

So the protagonist is living in his brother's apartment after quitting grad school, puzzling out the meaning of life and trying to figure out what he wants to do. This involves analyzing what he likes doing, and the pros and cons of everything he considers worth doing. By drilling the protagonist's considerations down to what seems like an absurd level, Loe frames an existential examination of life that seems humorous on its face. Yet it's actually filled with a depth that is surprising when I think hard about it. The question posed, without irony, is this: why do we do anything? The protagonist may spend an inordinate amount of time bouncing a ball (the key detail that remained in the mind of the bookstore clerk who recommended this book to me), but bouncing that ball is an answer to the question of the meaning of life. It is a physical activity that requires thought and action, a beginning and an end, and in all actions that lead to other actions, the things we do, simple and complex, there is the answer to the meaning of life. The meaning of life is not love, money, sex, or deep internal contemplation. For the protagonist, and for most of us for whom philosophy can too often be "the talk on a cereal box," life and meaning come from simply thinking about what we want to do, and then doing it.

I hope this explains why it is I found this book so deep and utterly non-Salinger-esque. But let me share some of the humor, some of the intensely funny or just silly moments. As I said above, the protagonist makes lists. Lots of them. Take this one, a list the protagonist makes after wandering around restlessly in shops, unable to find what he is looking for because he has no idea what he is looking for:

After a bit of thinking it becomes apparent that I'm looking for an object which:

–Is small enough for me to carry easily

–Costs no more than a hundred kroner

–Can be used many many times

–Can be used indoors as well as outdoors

–Can be used alone or with someone else

–Gets me active

–Makes me forget about time

He takes some time, thinking about the list, then it comes to him.

> Suddenly it is clear to me that what I seek is a ball.
>
> A ball, plain and simple. I feel a sting of eagerness.
>
> It's been a long time since I thought about balls. I'm happy that it came to mind. This is the way to go. Now I just have to find a ball.

He goes into a sports store and views several balls. If the next sentences I quote don't ring hilariously true, this may not be the book for you. But if you do get it, if the next quote makes you think, "Christ all-mighty, I thought I was the only one who was this daft!" then order a copy post-haste:

> They have an overwhelming selection of balls. Nice, expensive balls. Made from leather and other durable materials. I examine them but find them too demanding. I'll be feeling a lot of pressure to perform if I buy a ball like that. The time is not ripe for a quality ball.

Have you ever tried to make a quilt and ended up making easily destroyed cat toys? Have you tried to draw only to find yourself coloring in your Holly Hobbie coloring books with wax crayons, mainly because the time was not right for serious endeavors? No? Then this book may not be for you. At least our unnamed hero takes the time to understand his limitations before he mindlessly buys a ball too advanced for his purposes.

And it's right about there that the ball-bouncing begins.

But he also reads a book by a man called Paul, a book about physics, and this book annoys him because it shows him that his education has been limited. But, then again, he dropped out of physics.

> The reason I opted out of physics was because we sat drawing protons and neutrons without grasping how it all really fitted together. I was bored. I'd much rather turn to face the girls and make a ring with my left thumb and index finger, and then move my right index finger in and out of this ring repeatedly.

It's good to know the protagonist has his bad side. I spent college physics trying to draw perfect circles in the margins of the notes I scrawled down from time to time.[2]

As he makes lists, the protagonist faxes messages back and forth with his friend Kim, who is stationed on an island north of Norway monitoring the weather (this novel predates wide email). He spends time with the child he met, a little boy called Børre. And he thinks and thinks and thinks some more.

A human being weighing 70 kilograms contains among other things:

–4.5 liters of water

–Enough chalk to whiten a chicken pen

–Enough phosphorous for 2,200 matches

–Enough fat to make approximately 70 bars of soap

–Enough iron to make a two-inch nail

–Enough carbon for 9,000 pencil points

–A spoonful of magnesium

I weigh more than 70 kilograms.

The protagonist is sickened by the amount of data he has crawling around in his head. To paraphrase a passage in the book that I recall clearly but cannot seem to find, he has a lot of stuff in his mind, facts he has learned. He simply does not know what to do with the information, how it might all link together, and it makes him a little nuts. I came to the conclusion that knowing this about him explains a lot of the mind jumps we get in the novel. In one scene, the protagonist is thinking of a painter, but then segues into the following, indicating a thought process that is jumbled and easily interrupted.

> Sometimes I envy the goldfish. Apparently, they only have a few seconds' worth of memory span It's impossible for them to follow a train of thought. They experience everything for the first time. Every time. As long as they themselves aren't aware of their handicap, life must be one long happy story. A party. Excitement from dawn to dusk.
>
> This is what I would paint if I were a painter.
>
> –Bicycles
>
> –Deserts
>
> –Balls
>
> –Girls

---

2   I almost met Mr. OTC in a physics class in college. He came to the first two classes in Physics 101 but managed to find a way to graduate without it and dropped the class. Had he stayed in the class, perhaps he would have found me distasteful because I drew circles for two hours and squeaked by with a D. Luckily we officially met after I had graduated and it was only later he realized how mentally undisciplined I am.

–Clocks

–People who are late for the bus

Now the phone is ringing. I answer it.

While the protagonist is wholly oblivious to irony, the author is not. The protagonist has a hard time seeing that he cannot hold onto a thought, much like the goldfish he envies. Of course, he just wants the newness of experience that he had as a child. He wants the endless supply of seemingly pointless knowledge to create a larger picture of life. He eschews experiences that mean little. But even as he has a clear objective he remains disjointed, just like that goldfish.

He trades more lists with Kim. He finds fault with the list of animals Kim has compiled. He thinks his friend must have led a very sheltered life, indeed, to have seen so few animals. He engages in a list-making contest with Børre to see who has seen the most animals. Since Børre is so much younger, he gets to use the animals his father has seen as well. Børre wins.

It goes on in this manner, as the protagonist dissects every thought in his head, dissects the thoughts of others, makes lists, plays with Brio toys and his ball and Børre. He sends an email to the Paul who wrote the physics book. And meets Lise, a girl we sense early on will be perfect for him. She obliges him in his compulsive list making by writing out on a napkin all the things that would excite her when she was a child. Lists, lists and more lists happen.

Then his brother returns. He takes the protagonist to New York, ensuring that lists can happen in a new country. A series of unlikely events cause the protagonist to be in charge of a stranger's dog for a while. The vague ridiculousness that plagues him continues. As he takes the dog for a walk, people who know the dog let him know what the dog's name is, how much it should eat, and how to take care of it. He is the human but he is unknown. The dog is a beloved member of a community, a known entity. When the dog craps in a park and a woman shows the protagonist how to pick it up, the protagonist suffers yet another existential and epistemological surge.

Now I'm standing with a bag full of dog turd in my hand. It's absurd.

This is a completely different life. People must think I'm a dog owner in New York. That I live here and have an apartment and dog. That I pick up dog turds like this one every day, before and after work. It's a staggering thought.

Seeing as I'm not a dog owner in New York, that also means everybody could be something other than what they seem to be. That means it's impossible to know anything at all.

Before we get too deep, just know that the protagonist also goes to the New York Public Library and does computer searches on rude Norwegian words just to see how they would come up in an English directory of subjects, titles and authors.

So, what we have here is a novel featuring a strange young man who drops out of graduate school, sends faxes to a friend, does chores for his brother, and analyzes his every thought and motivation without any sense of irony or pretense. He comes to conclusions, comes to further conclusions, then wonders if there are any conclusions to be reached at all. The book ends with him flying back to Norway from New York, thinking his endless thoughts. He is in love. He has a few good friends. He hopes that Paul, the author of the book about physics, has replied to his email (and Paul Davies does, or rather his assistant does, explaining that Professor Davies cannot answer questions from random strangers, and here one wonders if Loe actually sent the man a message in real life, as it is reproduced on the last page of the book).

The book ends thusly:

> When I get home I'm going to buy a bicycle helmet. And I want to call Lise and tell her that life is a bit like a journey, and that I am maybe, but only maybe, a really good guy.

I agree with this assessment, but only if he stops making rude hand gestures to girls in physics classes.

Further Reading

The Mezzanine
Nicholson Baker

In Watermelon Sugar
Richard Brautigan

SEVERANCE
By Robert Olen Butler
First Chronicle Books (2006)
Original post: 11/11/2009

Why do I consider this book odd?
An absolutely lunatic premise is why.

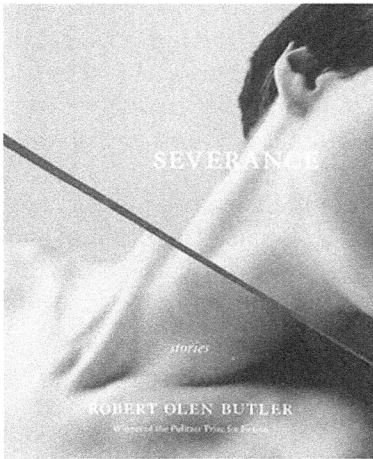

It's weird, including a Pulitzer Prize winner here, but hell, I already got me a Nobel Laureate, so why fight it? Acclaimed books can also be so very, very odd.

So here's what you need to know.

First, it is said that a decapitated head can remain in a state of consciousness for 90 seconds.

Second, in heightened states of emotion or agitation, people can speak at the rate of 160 words per minute.

Combine these two speculative premises and you get the micro stories in Robert Olen Butler's *Severance*.

That's right, it's a series of tales told by decapitated heads.

What manner of stories do disembodied heads tell? Some are touching. Some are horrific. Some are amusing. All clock in at around 240 words.

Upon her beheading, Anne Boleyn's words are addressed to her daughter, Elizabeth, and they are heart-wrenching:

> ...but still there is my sweet girl my Elizabeth her pale face and her hair the color of the first touch of sun in the sky, the pale fire of her hair, she turns her gray eyes to me and I know I am soon to leave her... and I say rise my sweet child and she straightens and lifts her face and I bend to her, I draw near to her, I cup my daughter's head in my hands

Then there's the story told by Lydia Koenig, a woman who was beheaded by her son in 1999. It's just dreadful:

> ...my baby, my own baby boy his bones deep and untouchable inside him, I dress him in pink thinking it makes no difference I hold him baby and then in plaid and he has freckles on his nose... and the man is gone and my baby

cries all night through, though he is no baby he is returned and he says help me find a vein help me tap this vein and I cannot...

We also hear from Gooseneck (Gansnacken), a dwarf who was a court jester to Duke Eberhard the Bearded, who beheaded him in 1494 for sad, but funny actions beyond his control:

> ...I am jester not a sailor the goat breaks his knot and bolts just as I leap from the rope and fly at my stricken lord and fall heavy upon him, crotch to face, and alas I am already full excited at my joke, like a lover

Severance covers many famous beheadings—John the Baptist, Mary, Queen of Scots, Lady Jane Grey and similar—but Butler also gives voice to a number of less well-known modern-day decapitation victims, like people beheaded in the Middle East since 9/11. There are also two non-humans—a chicken, whose body indeed ends up crossing the road, and the dragon slain by St. George (who is himself also included in the book). Insanely, the chicken is more eloquent than the dragon. More insanely, Butler records his own putative decapitation in 2010. Apparently he loses his head in a mishap with an elevator.

This is a delightfully odd little book built around a strange and enticing premise. It's the sort of idea that makes you smack yourself on the head and wish you had thought of it first. The brief stories are richly detailed and full of both history and emotion. It's astonishing what Butler can do in 240 words.

FURTHER READING

The Woman Who Gave Birth to Rabbits
Emma Donoghue

CAMP CONCENTRATION
By Thomas M. Disch
Vintage Books (1999 reprint[3])
Original post: 08/30/2010

Why do I consider this book odd?
It's not so odd in terms of actual content. It's odd because it's a shin-
ing example of literature that fails the test of time.

I was surprised by my visceral reaction to this book. *Camp Concentration* was first published in 1968 and it has not aged well. I don't hold outmoded ways of speaking and thinking against those who lived and wrote before I was born. If I don't condemn Mark Twain for using words that are anathema today, why would I condemn Disch? No, the real problem is terrible writing. And if that could be forgiven (it can't), we would still be left to contend with a completely unlikeable protagonist. That's two big strikes against it. Even if some of the novel's ideas still resonate, Disch's authorial sins kill any message that might apply to life today.

A synopsis: Louis Sacchetti, who clearly fancies himself the smartest man to ever live, is put in jail for being a conscientious objector.[4] He is treated reasonably well in prison but one day is transferred to a different facility—a sinister prison where the government is testing a drug on unwilling inmates. This drug makes the prisoners super intelligent, which has far fewer appli-cations in the real world than one might think, but the drug also kills them eventually. Of course, Louis finds he has been infected but since he was such an arrogant bastard from the beginning the reader has a hard time telling the "before" Louis from the "after" Louis. Eventually all the geniuses in the prison try to commit a God-defying act of alchemy that ends about as well as you think it might. Louis was asked to document his time in the prison, typing it out so others can more easily read his reports. He documents until he dies. The end.

Okay, I am being nasty and I know it. But let me support my spleen with textual evidence. I want to show you that I have concrete reasons for hating this one. As always, your mileage may vary.

---

3   Originally published by Rupert Hart-Davis in 1968.

4   The fictional war is only vaguely described, but a loose analogy to Vietnam seems apt given the social context of the book's original release in the late 1960s—though it's not *precisely* the Vietnam War because there is discussion of the US engaging in germ warfare in various countries.

After spending time musing pointlessly, and somewhat fatly, on the sexual antics of the men he shares space with back at prison one, Louis finds himself in the corridors of the second prison. This is his first encounter with another inmate at prison two:

> "Beauty," he said solemnly, "is nothing but the beginning of a terror that we are able barely to endure." And with those words George Wagner heaved the entirety of a considerable breakfast into that pure, Euclidean space.

It's hard to put into words why these two sentences filled me with despair, but let me try.

First, Disch has a mentally ill man quoting Rilke. If that wasn't a cliché then, it certainly is now. Second, I really can't believe that Louis, the narrator through whose eyes we see this arrogant and at times pretentious mess, looks at a sick man and immediately thinks to describe the clean, geometric lines of the area into which the man is puking. Louis is a writer though, and as a result he thinks very writerly things. He can't just speak or write. He expounds. He is a hammy stage actor on paper and he is rather un-likeable in his pomposity.

He meets a black prisoner named Mordecai. You know Mordecai is black because he uses the word "mammy" to describe his mother. As did all black men in 1968, one assumes. Evidently Mordecai is ugly too, and mispronounces words a lot because he has only ever read them and never heard them before because as a black man, of course, he never had a deep, substantive conversation before he was given the drug to make him super-smart. Or at least that is how I felt after reading about Mordecai through Louis' description. His mispronunciations give Louis an even more unearned sense of superiority, for you see, Louis is not just a writer, but a poet, and he knows words, man does he know. His mental notes regarding Mordecai's mispronunciations alone were enough to make me loathe him. Here are a couple of examples:

> "You'll have to excuse my athanor. It's electric, which isn't quite comme il faut"—pronounced by Mordecai, come-ill-phut—"I'll admit, but it's much easier this way to maintain a fire that is vaporous, digesting, continuous, nonviolent, subtle, encompassed, airy, obstructive, and corrupting."

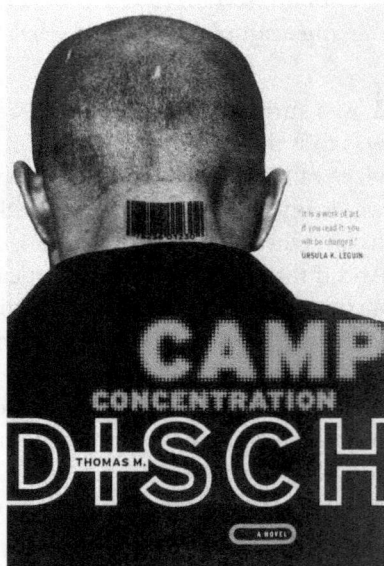

(I know, you, dear reader, totally think I am making these sentences up, don't you?)

Poor Mordecai cannot even pronounce the word God to Louis' satisfaction. In a conversation about God where Mordecai compares the Holy to Eichmann in a fit of genius that causes Louis to put down his intellectual foot, Louis begins to record Mordecai's accent as he hears it and it is tiresome to read.

> "We can turn our eyes away from the charred bones of children outside the incinerators, but what of a Gaud who damns infants—often the very same one—to everlasting fires?"

Poor Mordecai. Not even able to say "God" to a pedant's satisfaction. Also, if this is what Disch thinks it sounds like when people made into intellectual giants talk about metaphysics, all I can say is that every drunken freshman at Clark Hall at UNT must have been a fucking genius.

Louis' opinions on homosexuals don't help this book's complete lack of modernity. While great gains have been made regarding the public perceptions of homosexuality, the fact remains that in the 1960s there were plenty of people who did not think that VD and promiscuity ran rampant among homosexuals any more than they thought all blacks had mammies. It's hard to like many of the characters in this book and their pronouncements on minorities certainly don't help matters.

I think the primary problem I have with this book is characterization. When everyone is an asshole it's hard to care what happens to anyone. Another problem is that when Disch isn't assigning poor pronunciation to a black man, everyone else speaks exactly the same way. Even Mordecai uses the same speech patterns—he just doesn't use them to the narrator's satisfaction. The same florid and overwrought vocabulary is recycled through every character in the book. I'll quote some passages to show that no one in this book speaks differently from anyone else, despite the large disparities in cultural and professional backgrounds. They have incredibly similar social references, similar educational references, even the same tendency to slip from formal to informal diction, as if to show how that underneath it all, all these trappings of race, class and culture, aren't we all just too jive for conversational consistency? It's tempting to blame the conversational sameness on the drugs being given the prisoners but even the staff (who are not experiment subjects) speak the same as Louis and Mordecai.

Here is Dr Busk, a psychiatrist in her 30s:

> "And then think of what happens if genius doesn't rein itself in but insists on plunging on ahead into the chaos of freest association. I know any number of psychiatrists who could, in good conscience, have accepted Finnegan Wakes (sic) as the very imprimatur of madness and had its author hospitalized on its evidence alone. A genius? Oh yes. But all we common people

have the common sense to realize that genius, like the clap, is a social disease, and we take action accordingly. We put all out geniuses in one kind or another of isolation ward, to escape being infected."

By the way, it is Louis, who is typing all of this conversation up for his reports to the prison officials, who inserts that (sic), pedant that he is. He can't even retell a conversation without simply correcting a common mistake—no, he needs to show the error and also show that he knows the error is an error. Worse, this trait is not due to Disch deliberately creating a shitheel. No, Disch likes Louis. You can tell, because Louis is a man for whom we are supposed to feel some sort of fond feeling or kinship as he discovers dark secrets and suffers himself. I assert that Disch no more realized what a tiresome didact Louis is than Louis does.

This next passage is just Louis himself, and note the high level language that descends into vulgarity, just like Dr. Busk (who discusses the "imprimatur of madness" and "the clap" without blinking an eye). Also note that he is talking to himself about his own poem, addressing himself as Louis I as it is a different part of the whole complexity that is Louis (sigh…)

> There is no God, there never was, and never will be, world without end, amen.

> Would you deny it, old Adamite, Louie I? Then let me recommend you to your own poem, the poem you claimed not to be able to understand. I understand it: The idol is empty; his speech an imposture. There is no Baal, my friend, only the whisperer within, putting your words in His mouth. A farrago of anthropomorphism. Deny it! Not all your piety nor wit, my boy.

> And O! O! those precious, fawning poems of yours, licking the ass of your let's-pretend God-daddy.

I'll give credit where credit is due in the next excerpt—at least Disch mixes up the formula a little. In this one the inconsistencies are spread out, not highfalutin' falling into the gutter, but rather a more even mix since Disch really wants us to know how jive his black character is, but the trademarks are the same. This is Mordecai speaking, of course.

> "Anyhow, to get back—the two broads would bring up those hoary arguments about the universe is like a watch and you can't have a watch without a watchmaker. Or the first cause that no other cause causes. Till that day I'd never even heard of the watchmaker bit, and when they came out with it, I thought, Now, that'll stop old Donovan's Brain. But not a bit of it—you just tore their sloppy syllogisms"—another foul mispronunciation—"to pieces."

In this one we get not only Mordecai waxing Louis-like, but we also get another helping of Louis' being unable not to comment on how badly he thinks Mordecai speaks.

I wanted to think that perhaps all the similar dialogue occurs because

Louis is recording all of this and the speech of others gets filtered through his brain. But Louis makes it clear several times he is recording things exactly as they happen or are spoken. He is not filtering. Everyone just talks the same way in this book, erudite conversation with words even the most well-versed of readers will have to look up combined with an earthy tang of street language and slang.

Okay, get yourself past the fact that the style in this book is terrible and everyone talks the same. Let's just look at some of the sentences in this book, shall we? Even if Louis is a poet, even if he is a genius driven mad, there is a desperate sense in all he says that he wants us, the unseen readers, to know how amazing his intellect is, and it gets tiresome, with each sentence struggling to be more erudite than the one before it, each turn of phrase straining in verbal calisthenics.

> Have read "Portrait of Pompanianus," which is better than I'd expected, yet curiously disappointing. I think it is because it is so controlled a tale, the plot so meticulously elaborated, the language of such a concinnate beauty, that I'm disgruntled. I'd hoped for a cri de coeur, nonobjectivist, action writing…

But wait, it gets so much worse. This passage comes after Louis is finished writing a play called *Auschwitz: A Comedy*. Seriously.

> In the first giddy moments after I'd written Auschwitz, when I could suddenly no longer tolerate these bare walls, richer in horrid suggestion than any Rorschach…, I stumbled out into the hypogeal daedal of corridors, happening across the hidden heart of it, or its minotaur at least.

He stumbled into the hypogeal daedal? I hate it when that happens but I've been told some soda water will get the stain out. This is some high-flown language, my friends. I appreciate an author who deftly deploys terms one may not commonly encounter. Caitlín R. Kiernan is a writer whose erudition does not alienate me. But this? It's is too much. It's all wrong. It's Disch showing off by proxy. And it's tiresome as hell to read.

Here's another example of Louis', and by extension Disch's, ridiculous verbiage:

> "You're a bit early," Haast told her. His emissile good fellowship retracted like a snail's cornua at the sight of Busk—in a suit of gray and chaste as any flatworm, epalpibrate, grimly mounted on her iron heels and ready for battle.

And this is where I take my gloves off. This quote is everything that is wrong with this book—big words that evoke nothing, or if they do manage to evoke something, the image is meaningless. A flatworm is not "chaste." It reproduces asexually, and that which reproduces asexually cannot make a decision to abstain from sex and remain chaste. Had to look up "epalpibrate," which evidently means roughly lacking eyebrows or eyelids. So, Dr. Busk is dressed like a prudish gray worm, without eyelids or eyebrows, yet ready for battle. Worms and those without eyelids are not notoriously good in battle. And why would a woman in a chaste, worm-gray suit sans eyebrows need to be mounted on anything? None of this makes an ounce of visual or metaphorical sense and all those five cent words were written to be impressive, not to convey an image or an idea.

Again, let me emphasize that the narrator telling us all this is Louis and we are meant to have some sort of sympathy for him. Initially I wondered if perhaps I was meant to loathe Louis, but at the end of the book there's a scene that gave Louis some humanity. It's a pitiful scene that might have illustrated some nascent humility in a pompous man, but Louis is beyond pompous. He is despicably obtuse and when he falls, I feel nothing. I have no idea what Disch was going for here. For the ending to have strength, we needed a protagonist who at the very least did not alienate us. But because of who Louis is, the ending, which should have been a saddening, horrible look at a smart man on his knees, physically and mentally spent, is rendered powerless. That's a dirty shame because in all this verbal showing-off, an interesting plot and many questions of medical and judicial ethics get lost. The only point that does get driven home is how genius is so often useless in application, and I knew this before I read this book.

In the event that anyone is left wondering if I recommend this book, the answer is no. But let me leave with this final quote from the book:

> "Oh dear, oh dear. They're very late. Are you good with riddles? Why did the hyperdulia pray to the Pia Mater?"

> "Why is a raven like a writing desk?" I mumbled, beginning to be annoyed with my guest.

I can't think of a better summation of this novel. A pointless riddle with no answer—you could take some time and try find answers to why this novel had to be so obtuse, and like Lewis Carroll's desk riddle, come up with all kinds of answers when there really isn't one, at least not one intended by the author. Just verbal burlesque, forcing the reader to jump through hoops for no reward beyond the knowledge that you will at least know the meaning of the word "epalipibrate."

Disch seems to have had a dedicated following and I perused his LiveJournal, especially the entries before he died by his own hand, and saw little of the preening one finds in *Camp Concentration*. Was this a juvenile offering, the sort of book an intelligent young man writes before he takes his intellect in hand and creates art instead of impressive words? I'm not sure but I always give writers two chances before I banish them from my reading list.

FURTHER READING

The Prisoner
Thomas M. Disch

The Dark Fields
Alan Glynn

IQ 83
Arthur Herzog

Extinction Journals
Jeremy Robert Johnson

Flowers for Algernon
Daniel Keyes

The Dispossessed
Ursula K. Leguin

Anathem
Neal Stephenson

The Genius Plague
David Walton

HORROR

Good horror is like pornography—hard to define but you know it when you read it. I think that intuitive distinction between fine horror and pulpy dreck is often at play in my reactions, but it turns out that sometimes you can nail down why a horror novel is terrible, as one of these discussions demonstrates.

PORTRAIT OF THE PSYCHOPATH AS A YOUNG WOMAN

By Edward Lee and Elizabeth Steffen
Necro Publications (2003)
Original post: 01/17/2011

Why do I consider this book odd?
I tend to consider books with this level of explicit violence to be odd.
Mileage may vary but in my world, "extreme horror" ends up in the odd pile.

This is one of those times when I hate discussing books. I'm fraught with angst because I adore Edward Lee. Even when he's off his game a bit, I still think he's one of the most unsung horror writers out there (Jack Ketchum and Christopher Fowler are in that same category—it's disappointing that Lee, Ketchum and Fowler aren't far better known). I just like him.

But this book sucks. It is bad. Bad as in there is so little to redeem it that my first instinct is to downshift into snark mode. But I feel conflicted because I really do like Edward Lee. I sense my inner sauciness will have no choice but to burst forth in time, but before I explain in far too much detail why *Portrait of the Psychopath as a Young Woman* was such a grave disappointment, I need to say that I hope Edward Lee never collaborates on a book again. *Teratologist*, another book he co-authored, was even worse than this one. Lee is a man who needs to write alone, I think.

On the surface, it seemed like it would be great. A journalist is contacted by a female serial killer because she wants said journalist to tell her story. She sends the journalist body parts, including a penis, severed from her victims. The journalist enters a new relationship that challenges her emotionally and, before long, the woman, her new lover and the killer are on a collision course, and the journalist discovers a horrifying link she has with the killer. Add a mean cop, lots of violence, and POW!, you got yourself a decent enough thriller. Or so you would think. I'll admit that the killer herself was at

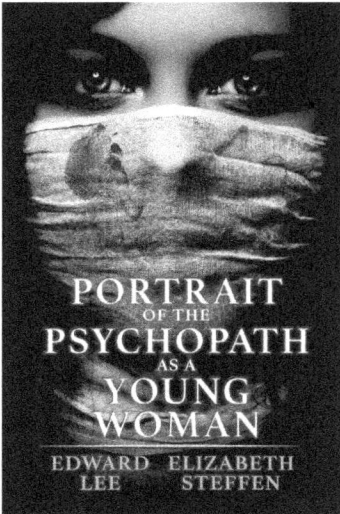

times an interesting character, and I suppose the violence she wreaks might be, for some extreme horror fans, worth the price of admission.

So why does this book stink? First, the clichés. Unless you're partial to romance novels or westerns (or maybe romance novels set in the Old West, preferably written by my mom), you will likely never encounter a more cliché-laden stack of pages. Start with the main characters. You've got your neurotic heroine, the journalist, who is beautiful and sexy but at weight lighter than Marilyn Fucking Monroe feels she is obese and ugly. (Also she's wacky and likes to run around naked all the time, as body-loathing headcases are wont to do, *amirite*?) And there's the murderous whackjob, a caricature of every abused female killer, carrying on an endless mental dialogue with her abusive daddy. Funny how, despite being a mentally deranged killer, she still somehow manages to dress up, lure, stalk and kill her victims, all while holding down a day job with almost nary a hiccup.

But there's more, oh so much more. We have the cliché of the hard ass cop bullying his unhappy witness. Then there's the journalist's love interest. We're supposed to believe he is an acclaimed poet whose work has been featured in *The New Yorker*, even though his poetry is a mess of turgid purpleness that would make a teenage goth misery case ashamed. And of course he falls in love with the heroine after a night of sex, because that's what poets do—they fall in love with weird women involved in murder cases. Worse, for a novel about tracking a serial killer, no one seems to have done their homework. In this novel crime analysts use the words "psychopath" and "psychotic" interchangeably, and the descriptions of mental states read like gibberish. There's also a character who spends the novel ostensibly in the throes of active psychosis yet remains so grounded to reality that she is still able to write out scholarly analyses of her torture techniques.

Part of me wants to say go ahead and read it for the nasty parts. That's clearly why a book like this exists, after all. I could just advise you—assuming you're a fan of the genre—to dive in for the over-the-top blood and torture and do your best to overlook the shitty plot, poor characterization and outright insult offered in the details. But I won't. There's just no reason you can't get a fix for gore without abandoning good prose, tight plot and believable characters. But as I always insist when I pan a book, I don't want you to take my word for it. Let me support my case with examples from the text.

Kathleen is an advice columnist who lives alone, and because all women in novels written between 1985 and 2001 were sexually abused, you already know her backstory. She has family money to back her up as she writes her column, is evidently quite curvy and pretty and is ten times more neurotic than I was when I was in college, perpetually drunk, and before I discovered the magic of anti-anxiety meds. Kathleen meets the poet, the Dogpatch Ted

Hughes of this novel, and they immediately have sex because why not? Here's a glimpse into her mind:

> Platt, though not a physical specimen, looked trim and enticing. There's no way he could ever love a Fattie like me. This impression of herself did not depress her at all, it made her feel proudly objective, not weighing, of course, the hypocrisy. When readers wrote in, fearing rejection due to being overweight, Kathleen reassured them that looks meant nothing in a real relationship. Dump them, she'd advise.

As a woman, reading Kathleen felt like I was trapped in the girl's room at the junior prom. I can only assume men who read this book endured just for the blood and torture. Yay, another heroine who hates her ass. Yay, Bridget Jones is getting stalked by a killer.

Oh, but you never know, maybe Kathleen really is a lardy troll completely undeserving of human love and should be shunned for her grossness. Luckily we have this information the killer digs up from her car registration after she runs the plates on her car:

HEIGHT: 5-6
WEIGHT: 135

Sigh. Look, I know lots of women have body image issues. I'm a fucking American woman, believe me, I *know* this. But I don't want to read a gorgeous woman bitch about being fat in an extreme horror novel. I especially don't want to read a character moan and groan about how fat her ass is and then find out she's probably a size six or smaller, with a BMI of 21.8.

Kathleen's pointless body hate permeates the book like the smell of bacon grease in a roadside diner. In this scene, she is driving with her poet boyfriend, humorously barking at traffic, but nothing can stop her tiresome internal dialogue.

> Kathleen caught herself examining girls who waited at each crosswalk, and she dismally concluded that almost every single one was better-looking than her. Most were trim Washingtonians in traditional summer yuppie garb. Sandals, shorts, loose, pretty blouses. *I'm a dinosaur*, she thought. *Why can't I look like those girls?*

Yeah, this shit wears thin.

Oh, but wait—Kathleen is also dense and petulant. Her boyfriend, the poet, is napping and talks in his sleep:

> "They're coming to get you, Barbara," he mumbled.
>
> *Barbara, huh?* Kathleen faintly smirked. So he's dreaming of old girlfriends. She couldn't very well hold that against him, though it irked her just the same. *You could at least be polite enough to dream about me, Maxwell. That or keep your mouth closed when you're off in slumberland.*

For the love of all that is not shitty, is Kathleen not the most tiresome heroine outside of a haughty lady-in-waiting in some bodice ripper? Not only is she not familiar with one of the most iconic lines in horror movie history but upon hearing it she becomes annoyed that her new man of under a week is not murmuring her name in his sleep. Kathleen, to put it plainly, sucks. When the hapless Maxwell Platt emerges from his sleep she confronts him about this seductress Barbara and when he explains that he is not a lying, cheating dirtbag, that he had fallen asleep to *Night of the Living Dead*, even after she believes him she lacks the grace to apologize.

Then we have this unlikely scene that sealed the deal for me as far as our heroine is concerned. Kathleen is in the shower, and finds herself getting turned on as she remembers the conversation she had with Spence, the adversarial officer assigned to the case:

> She remembered what Spence had said, about… What word had he used? Parity, she remembered. Similarities between herself and the killer. The whole thing had been a set-up, but why? The killer was abused as a child, you were abused as a child. So what? Does she look like me? she wondered. Does she have a body like me? A face? Kathleen smiled to herself. Does she touch herself in the shower?

Okay, this is… so full of squick I almost quit reading. I understand that some sexual abuse survivors process their abuse in a sexual manner, so that's is not unrealistic in itself. But the scene ends with Kathleen bursting from the shower and masturbating on a couch, not even bothering to dry off. She is not processing abuse. She is pondering the similarities between herself and a woman who is so deranged she sent her a severed penis in the mail. Instead of wondering how the other woman ended up a violent killer and contemplating the harm the killer has done, Kathleen's fantasizing about the killer's naked body in the shower and using it for masturbatory fodder. On no level does this ring true. It makes the heroine of this book look like a fucking idiot and an asshole and it was foul in every implication. Yeah, Kathleen sucks as a character and that's problematic because as the heroine of this book, I need to want her to succeed and not get killed in the process and it's hard to root for someone who is this dense, this self-absorbed, this whiny and this bizarre. I suppose one could say that perhaps Lee wanted to show the thin line between neurosis caused from abuse and outright mental illness but there is little in the book to back up such a theory.

In addition to creating a heroine in whom I have little vested sympathy, the authors run into problems in defining their killer. The title of the book implies the killer is a "psychopath" but the relevant characterization is all over the map and at times reads like utter nonsense. Here's some information a forensic psychiatrist gives the lead investigator on the case:

> "Tell them to go back a year," Simmons corrected. "This is something more
> evolved than your typical unsystematized reality break. Take my word for
> it, Jeffrey."

Good thing it isn't a typical unsystematized reality break because if you
Google "unsystematized reality break" you'll find out it evidently doesn't
exist outside the pages of *Portrait of the Psychopath as a Young Woman*. So
thank heavens they dodged that "typical" bullet. Steffen, who is a crime analyst, presumably knows her stuff but if so, she is using terminology so arcane
that a layman cannot run it to ground. A phrase as weird and awkward as
"typical unsystematized reality break" should have some common academic
grounding but it doesn't. Fair enough, but would it have been too much to
have explained it?[1]

The forensic psychiatrist continues:

> "She probably lives in a house, in a secluded community," Simmons contin-
> ued. "She was sexually abused, probably quite heinously, and probably by
> her father or other prominent family figure, from a very young age. She's
> obviously bipolar enough to function in public."

That first part seems standard enough, but then that last sentence takes it
all down a weird road. It's sort of hard to understand how "bipolar" plays
into this in any manner. Bipolar enough to function in public? Well, bipolar
people do function in public but it generally is not one of those conditions
that one would think *helps* anyone to function in public. Generally, it is associated with a difficulty in functioning well, with sufferers experiencing manic
highs and depressive lows that can interfere with day-to-day life. Is Steffen
trying to convey that the killer is both bipolar and psychotic, or that within
her psychosis she is experiencing a swing in behaviors that is similar to the
condition of bipolar and that when she is not experiencing mania that she
can function? I'm not sure and it isn't explained.

The weirdness continues apace. For example, though the killer is being presented as psychopathic, terminology gets mixed up. Here's Spence talking to
Kathleen about the killer:

> "Most of the conversation she sounded very clear-headed, coherent. Then
> she goes into the bit about the pain, taking her mother's pain away and all
> that."

> "Psychiatrists call it word salad," Spence enlightened her.

> "A fairly common trait in bipolar psychosis. One minute she acts and

---

[1]   A reader on *Odd Things Considered* wondered if the psychological gibberish was intentional.
He posited that Lee was making up terminology so he could have freer reign in how he portrayed the
killer. This is as good a theory as any to justify the bizarre conditions and mental states Lee uses but if I
am to accept this was a deliberate choice, it makes me wonder why Lee bothered to coauthor this book
with a professional crime analyst. If he was going to make it all up to be able to create a unique character,
Steffen's expertise was wasted.

sounds normal, the next minute she's completely dissociated, completely submerged in her delusions, to such an extreme extent that only she can understand herself."

Okay, in the course of this book we will find out the killer is bipolar, psychotic, psychopathic and suffering from several other strange problems. I am not a criminal analyst like Steffen but all of this seems unlikely. If it is possible that the killer is a psychopathic psychotic going through some sort of rapidly cycling bipolar spectrum that pushes her from coherence into word salad in the course of one sentence, instead of throwing all this shit out there and expecting us to swallow it, mayhaps the authors could have *explained* how all these terms fit together and how they manifest together. By failing to do this, it sounds like someone is just tossing out a whole bunch of stuff that sort of sounds officially crazy and hoping we buy it.

It continues:

> Simmons' eyes, in spite of their accrual of years, shined crisply and bright as an infant's. "But you can take heart in some rather indisputable statistics. The Totem Phase always burns itself out, leaving in its wake a catastrophic amine-related depression. It's called the Capture Phase. Very quickly the falsehood of the delusion is unveiled; the bipolar mental state reverses poles, so to speak, locking the killer in an inescapable feeling of capture. The psychopath's self-image is reduced to total meaningless… Suicide is the most frequent result.

This verges on gibberish. And it's a bit disorienting when I try to piece ideas together using the Internet and my own library on psychology and criminal profiling and come up empty-handed. Would the average person have any goddamned idea what an "amine-related depression" is? Google ain't gonna be much help. "Totem" and "Capture Phase" aren't that arcane but coupled in there with "amine-related depression" and the bad line about the crispness of a baby's eyes and you sense that this is a novel that really didn't weigh out the meaning of the words used.

And it goes on and on:

> "The killer has to know we're on to her. But she's psychopathic. Lotta times psychopaths get fuzzy on the dividing line between fantasy and reality. And they make mistakes. That's what we're counting on. She might come here in a fugue state, or when she's deep in one of her delusions. Then we've got her."

It feels weird countering the words that presumably came from a criminal analyst, but yeah, while psychopaths often suffer from delusions, do psychopaths go into a fugue state? That sounds far more like the behavior of a psychotic and the mental state of the killer in this book points far more to a psychotic, someone who has almost no connection to reality. Psychopaths, in my education, are characterized by a superficial glibness and complete inability to care about other people. The killer in this book is full-bore crazed, having a dialogue in her head with her abuser, living a life almost completely detached from reality. It seems to me that despite the presence of an expert as a writer, this book uses the words psychotic and psychopath interchangeably.

Questionable psychological approaches come up in other contexts. Here's some advice Kathleen receives to help her deal with the atrocious abuse she suffered at the hands of her uncle:

> "There are times when it's perfectly healthy to redirect the pain in our lives. To transform it into someone else's pain." The method worked very well. Whenever a memory popped up… she simply murdered him in her mind. "Rape-Conclusion Substitution is what we call it."

Seriously, go Google "Rape-Conclusion Substitution" with one hand and shit in the other and tell me which yields the most results. Maybe this really is a helpful technique but is used under another name? But if that is the case, why not use the name of the actual technique?

There are some seriously wacky plot devices as well. At one point, Spence knows that they have a line on the killer and the powers that be—the "General Command"—see fit to send a helicopter to land on the lawn of Spence's condo complex to pick him up in the middle of the night so he can be on the scene when they catch the killer. At least the authors have the decency to admit this whole scene is dumb:

> *The neighbors'll love me*, he thought, and then stepped out into what had to be the most ludicrous scenario of his life… The helicopter—a rebuilt white Bell JetRanger—descended amid the chugging cacophony of its props, and a mad wind siphoned about Spence, which nearly sucked his unbuttoned Christian Dior off his back.

No sending a car for Spence. Nope, let's risk the lives of untold people landing a fucking enormous helicopter on the grounds of a heavily populated area. C'mon, this is a serial killer/police procedural/heavy gore book. We don't need plots lines from post-Cold War spy novel wet dreams. Also, Spence wears Christian Dior. Of course he does. Because police detectives in this novel are so well-paid that they pay several hundred dollars for a single button-up work shirt.

Falling neatly in line beside the unlikely plot devices and pointless descriptions of cop couture, are some really awful conversations. Some of the dialogue was miserable. Just miserable. Take this bit where Spence the detective has come to Kathleen's door:

> "Hello," he said when she opened up.
>
> "Damn. I was hoping it was the Fuller Brush Man."
>
> "The Fuller Brush Man isn't your ticket to literary acclaim."
>
> "Oh, but you are?" she said. "A poker-faced cop in a bargain basement suit?"

Spence's gaze distended. "This suit cost $850. It's made from some of the finest—"

"Relax Kafka, I was only kidding. Are you here for anything in particular, or just the typical police harassment?"

Do I need to break this down? Very well.

First, no one under the age of 60 uses the Fuller Brush Man as a reference in actual conversation, even those of us who watch a lot of old television and read potboilers from the 40s.

Second, how the fuck does someone's gaze distend?

And finally, Kafka? *Kafka?* Don't look at me for an answer. This is the first time Kafka comes up in the novel and nothing in this scene indicates why she calls Spence "Kafka."

Then there's just the bad writing. This may seem picky but when the rest of the book is a clusterfuck, it becomes hard to overlook even little problems. Like this line of dialogue from a scene in the morgue where an evidence tech explains things in language we can all understand.

"Three bodies," he said. "We'll call them One, Two, and Three."

Well, thank God we got that cleared up.

The bad writing continues. Consider this gem where a run-of-the-mill murder victim in a goth club bathroom[2] overhears "some guys ... doing cocaine as they traded jokes":

"What's the difference between Michael Jackson and potato chips? Michael Jackson comes in a can."

Does anyone even know what this joke means? I mean, aside from the fact that it seems unlikely that such a joke would be common fare, it's almost as cryptic as the discussion of "amine-related depression." I guess it's some sort of sexual thing? That Michael Jackson masturbated in bathrooms? Who knows. It's a pointless tangent regardless of what it's supposed to mean.

While in the goth club, which we know is goth because the future victim thinks one girl looks like "Morticia Adams" (sic) and because there is Joy Division graffiti written in the bathrooms, we are presented with the victim's take on the costuming around him:

Brad spotted some class cleavage, a brunette in sequins and earrings that looked like shower curtain rings.

Yeah, goth girls in sequins and enormous hoop earrings were thick on the ground in the late 1990s. Thick, I tell you. You also had to look out for all the feather boas and girls in crinoline looking like Cyndi Lauper. Given that the

---

2   Because, as we all know, goth clubs are the best sort of meat markets for normal guys on the make.

authors were apparently unaware they were misspelling the Addams family name, I really shouldn't have expected much more.

Moving on to weird and heavy-handed descriptions. Take this scene, the quotes taking place within a few paragraphs of each other:

> He wondered what he'd done to her—some obsidian inquisitor in him with no heart.

Followed by:

> It all poured out of her—the blackest ichor tapped through the wounds her uncle had lain into her spirit.

Okay, I get that the authors want to evoke darkness, a blackness that implies the horrible evil that happened to Kathleen at the hands of her uncle. But why an "obsidian inquisitor"? A shiny, striated, glossy, brittle inquisitor? And "blackest ichor"? Blackest blood of the gods? I mean, these words all *sound* sort of good but ultimately mean very little and certainly fail to convey what I assume the authors wanted to make us aware of.

The malapropish mishaps do not end there:

> Moonlight bathed the room in lucent slants, just like the dream. She lay naked in an ichor of sweat...

An "ichor of sweat," eh? What the hell does that even mean? She laid in a blood of the gods of sweat? Or maybe a fluid of inflammation of sweat? Wouldn't it have been far better had she laid in a pool of sweat or have been covered in a sheen of sweat? Did Lee want us to imagine Kathleen looked bloody in same manner? Again, who knows? Also, Kathleen's tendency to love being naked in hot rooms feels a wee bit gratuitous.

We aren't done with black and blood imagery.

> The words seemed to permute the paper until they were no longer words at all, but glyphic scrawlings etched in black blood.

Ignoring the fact that paper cannot be etched, I have no fucking idea what a "glyphic scrawling" is in this usage since we have no fucking idea what the paper was permuted into. I also wonder about using "permute" because as far as I know, it is a verb used mainly in math, implying order. If the words had been permuted, I could understand that because it would imply the order of the words was being changed. But can a page of paper be permuted? It could be mutated, I guess, but permute was not a good word choice for this sentence. In fact, this sentence can't stand up to the most basic parsing without verging into gibberish. Too often it seemed like words were selected for how they might sound rather than what they actually mean.

Continuing on with bad writing choices, there's this bizarre statement:

"Jesus to Pete, Lieutenant. You got yourself a real winner here. This chick knows more about torture than Einstein knew about relativity. Makes Adolf Eichmann look like fuckin' Dick Van Dyke."

This sort of hyperbole doesn't really give definition to the killer by emphasizing how horrific are her actions but rather gives a sense that Eichmann was somehow not all that bad, you know, given that some lady somewhere did really bad stuff to some men. Yes, this serial killer is terrible. She binds men up like mummies so that they cannot move and then does things like blow red pepper up their noses and cut off their penises. She's deranged and does vile things. But is she really a rival of one of history's greatest monsters? Why include a statement like this at all? If one doesn't immediately laugh, which I guess was the response the authors wanted, the only other thing to do is to look at the statement and realize how bad an idea it is to compare the actions of a mentally ill killer to one of history's worst practitioners of genocide. Yep, killing a few dudes makes Eichmann look like a cream puff.

There are other issues with the book. We have a radio shrink telling a caller with sexual issues who was molested by her brother to kill him in her mind several times a day, a therapy that may be just dandy but seems a terrible thing to be advocating over the radio. Then there's a scene where Kathleen is symbolically confronting her abuser while being molested by a snake that was so heavy-handed and dripping in false symbolism that it was a car wreck. I had to do the literary equivalent of rubbernecking on the highway, rereading the passage several times, because I just couldn't not look.

Oh, then there was what I have no choice but to call the "butt spit" scene. Sigh.

The killer walks in on people having furtive sex in the hospital where she works:

> She knew the phlebotomy tech was sodomizing her because every few minutes the nurse would whisper, "More spit," and the phlebotomy tech would stop and his head would tilt and she could hear him expectorate, and then he'd start again.

Somehow that was the foulest scene in the book. Seriously, a head nurse is bent over and buttfucked and nowhere in the hospital is there a better lube than spit? I mean, the only other place where there would have been more lube options available would have been a lube factory. Porn may have many believe that this is a common approach to anal sex but at some point it seems like the nurse wouldn't need the tech to spit on her—she'd be bleeding enough that spit would have been irrelevant after a few minutes. Use lube appropriate to the sex act. The anal fissures you won't get later will thank you for it and you might be less inclined to describe anal sex in a manner that sounds like the second take for a shoestring porn script. But if this was meant to be just gross, the authors succeeded.

Interestingly, in a book where two of the main characters are writers, neither seemed to be able to write worth a damn. Spence, the detective, reads one of Kathleen's columns and rhetorically asks himself if it is just him or if none of it makes a lick of sense, like it was written in a foreign language. Here's the column answer he read:

> Regarding your former boyfriend, forget him. By saying such spiteful things to you he's only elucidating his own selfishness and immaturity, not to mention his lack of consideration for your honest feelings. Men like that are best left out with the garbage. And as for your current emotional perplexion, I think you need to reverse your methods of anticipation. …

No, Spence, it's not just you. I know the authors were trying to make an "Aren't men and women different" statement, plus a little, "Hey, gay men don't get women," sort of riff but it mostly read like nonsense.

Of course, Kathleen isn't the only shitty writer in this hot mess. Remember her boyfriend, the poet? The one so good he's in *The New Yorker*? Here is a poem of his that Kathleen finds. Also note that he calls every poem he writes "Exit" for reasons I am sure are too deep and poetical for the likes of me to comprehend:

EXIT by Maxwell Platt

Resplendence is truth, yet it's escaped me somehow,
And I don't even remember what you look like now.
But in the trees, in the clouds, in the heavens above
even the angels are burning up with all my love.

Well, it's not Tennyson. It's not even Cummings or Plath. It's barely a Nickelback lyric.

There is another poem, the only one not called "Exit." Instead it's called "A Keatsian Inquiry." Here's a verse:

Dare he wake her beauty in the moon?
For what he spied—such love—and in
that precious moment didst nearly swoon.
Yet on she slept a lovely sleep;
here is the image his love doth reap.

Could no one have looked up an actual poem by Keats or a modern love poem and at least tried to ape it a bit? Because asking us to accept this as anything but the work of an overwrought high school freshman is a bit much.

So, what have we at the end of this novel? We have a spunky but self-loathing hot chick who thinks she's fat and writes a shitty self-help column that brought her to the attention of a psychotic, psychopathic, bipolar killer who slips into word salad and sends the columnist dicks in the mail. We have a detective who wears clothing far out of his price range. We have a poet who cannot write poetry. We have words that don't fit together. We have scenes so utterly dumb they almost seem like an insult to the reader. We have bad analogies. A girl killer worse than Eichmann. Butt sex with spit.

We also have some top-notch, methodical yet over-the-top extreme violence. So weigh things out. Can you take all that I laid out (and so much more) just to get to the heinous parts, which for most will be the sole purpose of reading this book? If not, may I recommend Edward Lee's *Infernal* books? There's some pretty foul content in the *Infernal* series, and though these books likely have all kinds of issues, the content is lively, engaging, disgusting and funny enough that I didn't really notice. With so much extreme horror, that's the goal, to be so wrapped up in the content that the meta of the reading experience doesn't intrude. This book doesn't come close to achieving that goal.

Further Reading

City Infernal
Edward Lee

House Infernal
Edward Lee

Infernal Angel
Edward Lee

Lucifer's Lottery
Edward Lee

DRUKIJA, CONTESSA OF BLOOD
By Glenn Danzig (text) and Simon Bisley (illustrations)
Verotik (2007)

HIDDEN LYRICS OF THE LEFT HAND
By Glenn Danzig (text) and Simon Bisley (illustrations)
Verotik (2010)[3]

Original post: 07/17/2012

Why do I consider these books odd?
I don't know. They just are.

I once dreamed that a shirtless Glenn Danzig (1992 model) beat the hell out of Bill Maher (current model). I have no idea what this means. I mean, I like Bill Maher and have no desire to see him beaten up. So as I pondered the meaning of this bizarre dream, I found myself reading up on Danzig (past and current models), looking for clues. Goodness. He's a polarizing dude. But he also has cats, which is always a good sign. And he has a cabinet of curiosities that I totally want to rummage through. And he collects books. As I read on I sort of forgot about the dream and got lost in the notion that Glenn Danzig and I would find a lot of duplicates if we compared book collections. I guess I'm easily distracted.

I have to explain, however, that I am not that familiar with Glenn Danzig's body of music. I was a bit too young for the Misfits. I sort of liked Samhain but they got zero radio play in Dallas. And by the time Danzig, the band, was on the rise I had sunk into a weird place of radio alterna-pop and black metal. So for me Glenn Danzig's music career, while impressive, must take a back seat to the fact that he clearly shares my taste in books—and that he is fond of cats. It was hard for me to see the humor in the memes generated from Danzig's grocery store outing to buy cat litter. We buy Mr. OTC's body weight in cat litter every month. What's so funny about a man with a cat making sure it can crap someplace other than the floor?

The problem, of course, is that he is Glenn Fucking Danzig. I guess people would feel the same sense of shocked mockery were Lemmy Kilmister found carefully cultivating a butterfly garden. A guy like Danzig, who at times

---

3   I have no idea if these are in print or not. I couldn't find them on the Verotik website. I purchased mine from the Verotik store on eBay. I found the Verotik website to be marginally less helpful than a Geocities site, circa 1997, so if this discussion causes you to want to look into Danzig's comics, the Verotik store on eBay is probably your best bet.

seems like a Frank Frazetta character come to life, is not supposed to be a caregiver or nurturer. But being who I am, knowing he cares for a couple of cats he takes care of made me like him so much I was willing to pay a substantial price for two of his comics—a price that Mr. OTC, the real comic aficionado in this house, found shocking for something with a cover that resembled an extended van mural as imagined by a 15-year-old dirtbag as he sketched on his Trapper Keeper in biology.

While Mr. OTC may be a bit less than generous in his assessment, I can understand his reaction to the cover of *Hidden Lyrics of the Left Hand*. It's a helluva cover if you aren't prepared for it. Seriously, I feel like there is some *DaVinci Code*-level decoding that needs to happen here. The centerpiece is a depiction of Danzig sitting on a Giger-style throne. Danzig is MASSIVE, arms bulging and covered in ropy veins, his black hair styled into small devil horns. His fingers are freakishly long. At his feet is a...what is she? A silver robot devil angel? Silver body, naked, bewinged, horned, enormous boobs (get used to the enormous boobs because this will come up often), and she's got a collar around her right thigh and Danzig is holding the chain leash. On Danzig's right, there's a gothic honey with more enormous breasts, her right hand on his thigh. She appears to be human. Behind her is what I can only describe as a voodoo robot Medusa. Yeah. Not sure what the hell she is.

But here's where things get weirdly cryptic. To Danzig's left stands a skeleton-headed nun clutching a devil-bodied skull child. The skull child has a silver skull, but it's a different silver than the robot evil angel on the floor. And he has massive horns. Whose baby is she holding? Is it the offspring of Massive Danzig and the Gothic Honey clutching his thigh? Is the skull nun merely a nanny? Did Massive Danzig bone the skull nun and she's holding the unholy results of their coupling? The mind boggles. The most puzzling aspect of the cover is the hand on Danzig's right shoulder. We have a pretty clear view of the Gothic Honey's right hand and the Medusa Voodoo Robot's right hand. The left hand on Danzig's shoulder resembles neither.

WHO WAS HAND? I have no idea who the gnarled, arthritic, masculine hand with red painted nails belongs to.

Luckily, most of the drawings inside are not as cryptic. This graphic novel/ illustrated lyrics collection appears to be centered around Danzig, Samhain and Misfits lyrics that had not been written out before. Maybe? At least I think that's the idea. Danzig has an explanation on the first page but I stopped reading when the third goddamned word was misspelled. In its way, this was the most horrifying part of this horror comic—the crappy editing. I asked Mr. OTC if this was a common problem with comics and he said, with no small amount of misery, that it varied by comic. I decided to stop dragging him down with me as I investigated these books.

Because this was so *Heavy Metal* and Los Angeles Goth, I cannot emphasize how important female breasts are to *Hidden Lyrics of the Left Hand*. Rotting corpses have perfect, pneumatic breasts. A disemboweled woman in a shower has perfect breasts (her wounds end just under her sternum). It says something when one looks at a bombastic comic like this and says, of a drawing, "Wow, those are some fake-ass breasts." Anyway, extreme violence and enormous, unreal knockers are the order of the day. Though I think Bisley is a pretty good illustrator, I fancied at times I could tell when he was bored as hell with what he was illustrating and his mind may have wandered. For example, the illustration for the lyrics for the Danzig song, "Naked Witch" has what can only be called "stealth peen." The illustration is a mixed bag—a half-zombie, half-human witch, wha?—but in what I assume are tree branches behind this witch, is some decidedly phallic imagery. Hidden peen appears also in several other pictures, but most notably in "Warlok," which I reproduce a snippet of here not to violate anyone's copyright but rather to show I am not completely insane. Sometimes a cigar is a cigar but sometimes the smoke drifting up from a lit candle in a pentagram is totally a cock.

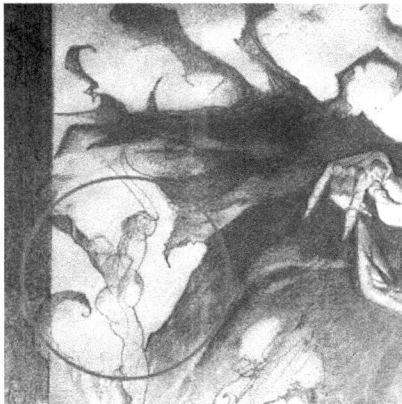

This is the only example I care to reproduce. I don't want to become That Girl Who Looks for Cocks in Everything.™

The best illustrations were for the Misfits songs. "Earth A.D." features Danzig, more human looking this time, and an enormous representation of whom I can only assume is Doyle Von Frankenstein, the most notable Misfits guitarist, standing in an ocean of dead Roman Centurian body parts. "Die, Die My Darling" has what looks, hilariously, like a sexy, half-dead Tipper Gore in a revealing cat suit, lounging in a creepy library/laboratory, drinking a martini garnished with eyeballs. For whatever reason, Bisley's drawing style lends itself better to humorous renderings than to more serious ones.

While I don't know if I would recommend this book, I can say that I found it fascinating. The drawings are so over-the-top and Glenn Danzig, even if he can't spell, is a man who has no reservations about showing his id. If he looks like a Frank Frazetta creation come to life, all the better. He seems to be a man whose inner tastes run to extremity. As a person who has avoided growing up in the traditional manner one expects from adults of a certain age, I like that Danzig, a man some might describe as elderly, has the same gory, sexually-charged, outrageous interests he had when he was 17. He may have gotten a bit darker in tone as he aged, but, as this book shows, he's been mining the same veins for a long time and he remains unapologetic. Still, even as I like Danzig, I suspect *Hidden Lyrics of the Left Hand* will only appeal to true fans of Danzig's musical career.

Drukija, Contessa of Blood, however, may be of more interest to the general reader of gory comics, though this is not so much a comic as it is an illustrated free-form poem. This is Glenn Danzig's riff on the Countess Bathory legend and it's pretty well done. The drawings are more restrained in style, though certainly extreme. One is of Contessa Drukija stabbing a young woman and pulling the still-beating heart out of her chest. It's pretty foul stuff that fans of extreme horror will enjoy. The only discordant note is that Contessa Drukija is a dead ringer for Vampirella (though I guess there are only so many ways to draw enormous-breasted, raven-haired, creepily beautiful women who have a thing for blood). A few of the drawings probably owe royalties to Frank Frazetta.

My only real issue with Danzig's poetic prose is that no one should be

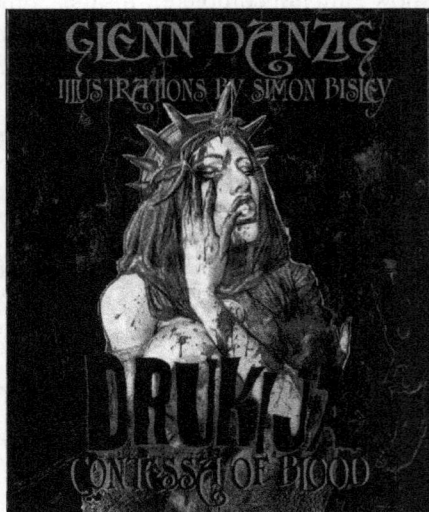

called Grimstonia. Contessa Drukija de Grimstonia? *Nein!* That is a very bad name for an otherwise serious character because, truly, there is none of the camp in this book that I saw in *Hidden Lyrics of the Left Hand*. Grimstonia is the setting of a Mel Brooks vampire movie, not the name of a mass-murdering gothic killer. Otherwise the prose is serviceable, though I confess that I didn't pay much attention to the editing because I loathed the font and found reading it difficult enough without scouring for typos.

It was interesting how lyrical the text was, given that Danzig is, of course, a songwriter.

> *her majesty was skilled*
> *in the sadistic torture*
> *and bleeding*
> *of those*
> *who fell*
> *under her hand*
> *the hand of a beastess*
> *the cruelty*
> *that revelled*
> *in its' ungodly tasks*

Well, we've got a British spelling in there, which is neither here nor there, as well as a misuse of the possessive, but this is no worse edited than most of the bizarro novels I read. Nits aside, there is something quite nice about the cadence of Danzig's prose. It really is free-form poetry. When I saw this manner of writing, I feared that he would veer into purple prose. He doesn't. He keeps his writing restrained, allowing the horror to seep through. That's not to say he doesn't revel in the writing—he just doesn't write in the sort of romantic, flowery gorefest style one expects from a Cradle of Filth album.

Best of all was the ending, a nice little meting of justice by paying the Contessa back in kind, blood for blood. No walling in by the king of Hungary for this Contessa, and I liked that. I've come to believe that Countess Bathory was likely no more than an imperious woman who was unkind to others and was set up by nobles in Hungary, most notably the king, because they didn't want to repay the huge sums of money she had loaned them during all the interminable wars Hungary fought with the Turks. I have no idea if Danzig is aware of this theory (though it seems rather likely he is, given his reading habits), but his ending is perfect.

I have to admit, this is a good-enough graphic novel, or illustrated poem, or whatever it is. While *Hidden Lyrics of the Left Hand* is definitely something that will mostly appeal to fans of Danzig's musical career, *Drukija, Contessa of Blood* will appeal to gore fans and people with an interest in the Bathory legend. Although Mr. OTC was shocked I spent $80 on two comics, I'm glad I did.

EXPIRATION DATE
By Laura Flook
Self-published by the author (2000)
Original post: 03/01/2013

Why do I consider this book odd?
It's a comic about a lunatic funeral home employee and her equally demented assistant.

Mr. OTC keeps the Apple TV loaded with interesting programs, some more interesting than others. Because we don't have access to basic network television I'm very much out of the loop where current shows are concerned, and I am okay with that (I haven't seen a television commercial in a couple of years and have noticed a huge upswing in my self-esteem, funny that). Anyway, I was looking for something to have on as background noise as I made dinner one night and found a show called *Odd Folks Home*. I almost didn't watch it because the intro was kind of hokey, but I persevered for a few minutes.

In that few minutes I set eyes on Laura Flook. I gave up on the show after her segment (it really was very hokey). But in spite of the artificial wackiness of *Odd Folks Home*, Flook seemed like a genuinely interesting person. The show focused on the woo-wooo-woooo weirdness of her life and the things she collects. Perhaps it says something about my own interests, but Laura Flook didn't seem that odd to me. If I didn't spend every spare penny I have on books, I assure you I too would have a room full of archaic medical equipment and a bottle of ether. Flook seemed awkward and clever. I like awkward and clever people.

So I looked her up, found her site, and discovered that she had published her own comic book. Of course, I had to buy it. It's clearly a DIY sort of project, being bound with what I believe is the thread one would use to sew up a body post-autopsy (Flook herself is a trained mortician). The comic runs on one side of each page.

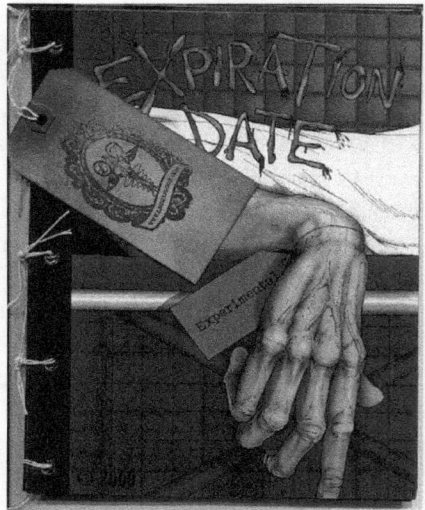

Glossy paper, entirely in black and white.

I can't really discuss *Expiration Date* in too much depth because to do so would utterly ruin it. Mostly it revolves around the hijinks of a mortician worker named Jelly and her strange assistant, Cal. It's clever and silly, with a shout out to The Misfits in the form of what I would call a very late-term abortion. It also introduced me to a new medical term: "erysipelas" (look it up).

Flook's comic is also a gross and grim thing to behold. There's a dead baby, a genital collection, urination on graves, and ... *erysipelas* (did you look it up?). But even with such dark content, I found the whole affair to be more amusing than upsetting. There are a few editing nits to pick, but I'm increasingly numb to misspellings and homophone substitutions. Small presses will do that to you.

This is likely the shortest discussion I have ever written, and I think the reason I decided to write this up has less to do with the comic than its presentation. I already mentioned that it appears to be bound in autopsy thread. Now I will mention that it arrived in a manila medical records folder. And that tag over the front of the comic? Yes, it's a toe tag.

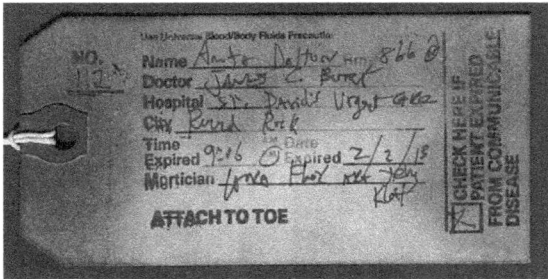

Maybe it won't seem like such a big deal to some of you, but I absolutely loved this! My own toe tag! Interestingly, St. David's in Round Rock is one of the few ERs I have *not* visited since I have lived in Austin. (I am clumsy—very, very clumsy. I managed to stab myself in my life line on my left hand in a very pyrotechnic manner making brownies one day. Brownies. Yep. So imagine what I can do to myself with staircases, hibachis and socks on hardwood floors.) I am no less delighted to discover that I apparently died of a communicable disease. Probably something from the cats that became zootrophic.

Expiration Date is reasonably priced for the scale of production, and especially affordable keeping in mind the level of care Flook takes in the shipping and "add ons." It's a clever, silly, gross and morbid little comic that makes me happy.

SENSELESS
By Stona Fitch
Two Ravens Press (2008)
Original Post: 07/20/2010

Why do I consider this book odd?
It's a disturbing look at guerrilla-style terrorism and the way it affects the innocent and guilty alike.

I was surprised by how little the violence in this book affected me. Stona Fitch's *Senseless* isn't torture porn—it's literary fiction, and very good fiction at that. It's gripping and I read it very quickly. Still, there's the violence. As horrible as it is, I think the reason it didn't affect me deeply may be that the sort of violence Fitch depicts seems almost pedestrian these days, unless it's happening to you. After we contemplate the extremity of human degradation and the lengths some people are willing to go in order to achieve their ends, there's a point where shock gives way to a resigned sense that perpetrators should be held to account. If we are offended, at least culturally, when violence is committed against us (or those like us), there's no denying that we are increasingly inured to the idea of retributive violence. It was strange for me to realize how accepting I have become of such extremity.

The plot is deceptively simple: an American business man, Elliot Gast, is kidnapped in Belgium by extremists opposed to the European Union. Initially he is treated quite well in captivity. He is given books to read and plenty of food. He is bored and anxious, but he is not in fear for his life. Then black cables are snaked through the ceiling, and his captors begin recording every corner of the room where Gast is kept, recording him for an audience on the Internet. His captors then begin to deprive Gast of his senses, beginning, horribly enough, with his sense of taste (if you're wondering, this is accomplished in a harrowing scene that involves a tongue-flaying instrument and a cauterizing iron). The attacks are paced out as, one by one, basic sensory experiences like touch, sound and smell are taken from him through acts of indifferent violence.

The key word is indifference. Though the world around him is aware of his kidnapping and Gast works every angle in his mind to formulate an escape plan, his time in captivity is defined by indifference. Not on his part, to be certain—Elliot Gast is filled with pain, terror, desperation and ultimately defiance, but his captors see him as little more than a pawn that can help or harm their cause.

Gast initially feels a sort of connection with a doctor and a woman in the group, but even if they are appalled over his treatment, they make no effort to secure his release. Gast's experiences at the hands of the terrorist group show that he means nothing to them, even to the members who want to limit the abuse he suffers. In the clutches of his tormentors, Gast becomes a thing. Deprived of most of the senses that allow a man to interact with the world, isolated from all normal human sympathy and concern, he is only human in how he continues to perceive himself. To his captors, he is no more than a doll—an important doll that bleeds.

If there's an aspect of all of this that can be described as "senseless," it's not the deprivation and violence that Gast suffers. His treatment is horrific, but there is sense behind it (too often we confuse savagery with irrationality). No, the real senselessness comes in the realization that all of us, with our habits, thoughts, emotions and quirks, can be reduced to a bleeding doll in the eyes of those who see us as The Other. That, I think, is where the power in this novel lies. Our suffering, while intense to us, can be depersonalized, converted into a generic message of terror. Through our pain and fear, we can become just one more horrific distraction in cyberspace. Maybe there is a message in such violence but chances are people powerful enough to change the course of political events aren't going to be the ones watching the livestream as you are violently deprived of your sense of smell.

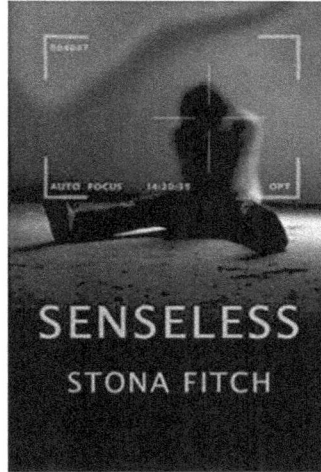

The suffering that Fitch depicts is senseless in that it ultimately has little meaning. It's just the blunt consequence of others imprinting their personal agenda on another man's body.

Of course, Gast's suffering has meaning to the people who inflict it. One of his torturers tells him:

> "To truly change a man, you must take away what is important to him. You must take a rich man's fortune. You must take a passionate man's wife. You are a man of the senses, Elliot Gast. So we are eliminating them. By this method we can leave you thoroughly changed. Through your example, we can change thousands."

Of course, the ends are not borne out. People express outrage that Gast is being held and tortured, but no one is able to find him. No one is able to help him. No one is changed by watching his suffering. They may experience the temporary shock that comes with being confronted with atrocity, but they are not changed. Nothing changes.

Written in 2001, Fitch's novel could scarcely have anticipated what would come. We now live in world where we can watch beheadings online as easily as we watch the latest silly cat videos that are part of the current memetic experience. Elliot Gast was changed. The rest of the world marched on.

But perhaps Gast's inner transformation is all that is necessary, in context. There's a scene where Gast recalls his own complicity in what could be described as a culinary atrocity. Tiny birds were force-fed buttered grains then drowned in alcohol. The tiny birds were then roasted and eaten, bones intact.

> The waiters then draped each of us with a large linen napkin, explaining that these would capture the precious scent of the roasted birds.

> "Or to hide your face from God," our host joked. I looked closely at the tiny bird in my hand, roasted to a golden finish. Dipping the ortolan into a brandy butter reduction, I raised it and saw suddenly the darkened eye of the bird, no bigger than a tiny bead, glistening now with a tear of butter... Perhaps I was paying now for my various excesses...

I wonder if I am wrong, trying to glean some larger meaning from the damage done to a man. Perhaps Gast's personal epiphany, connecting the terrible things that happen to him with the suffering he was willing to inflict in order to indulge his epicurean delight, is enough.

As I read *Senseless*, I wasn't sure if Gast was unreliable, or if I was missing the point because throughout the book, I seemed to understand things that he did not.

> Although I regretted my role in this terrible game, I had to wonder what the response would be. What would it take to one-up Blackbeard? Ten online hostages? Live execution of innocents? Anything seemed horribly possible.

Blackbeard is the name Gast gives to his chief tormentor. Did Gast think the economic interests behind the European Union would respond to his plight with anything other than words? Did he imagine there would be a trial of those who might end up arrested if it came to that? Did he genuinely think this sort of guerrilla violence would be answered, let alone countered? Why would a bank kidnap ten revolutionaries and torture them? Gast seems not to understand that even though he has had his nostrils soldered and his tongue mutilated the terrorists still have little power. While in their hands, they are cruel gods to him, not the powerless entities they really are in the face of global banking and political systems.

Yet Gast never loses sight of himself, even as he is rendered senseless. He refuses to cooperate in any manner, fighting as much as he can, resisting his captors' demands. In order to increase the theater of the torture, his captors want him to scream, to cry out in pain. They want him to make a show of overt resistance, rather than passive rebellion. At one point, Blackbeard tells Gast that his Internet pain show is making the terrorist group lots of money, 10% of which will be his if only he will cooperate and scream in pain. Gast, who is clueless in some respects, hopes it is true he will be permitted to leave if he does what is asked of him but doesn't take such promises to heart. Instead, he hopes he can unmask Blackbeard in front of one of the cameras, revealing his face to the millions Blackbeard claims are watching, making him a marked man. Instead of railing against his tormentors when he is left alone, he is resolute—all the ghouls who are watching will get is a man kicking a wall over and over and over. Moreover, it's hard to tell if Blackbeard is taunting Gast, asking him to participate in his own torture, or if he genuinely thinks Gast is so craven he would think screaming in agony for a cut of the profits a good deal. In a book about senselessness, it is hard to know which character actually has any sense.

Throughout the novel, Gast seems to have a connection with a woman he calls Nin (because her brown eyes remind him of Anaïs Nin, the erotic diarist). Though she seems to have a terrible time reconciling what her group is doing to Gast, Nin's final actions are in a way the most senseless element in the narrative. But that's just a knee-jerk reaction. Her actions are only senseless if one is accustomed to the idea that people who are kind always behave kindly. Gast feels deceived, but only a dishonest Hollywood ending could have made things turn out any differently.

I wish for all in the world that I could quote the final paragraph but to do so would give too much away and this complex novel should not be spoiled. I'll only repeat that Gast is changed and the world around him is not. Is his epiphany worth the suffering and permanent trauma he experiences? Is it the price of redemption? These are not questions I am ready to answer.

FURTHER READING

Waiting for the Barbarians
J.M. Coetzee

Killing for Culture – From Edison to ISIS: A New History of Death on Film
David Kerekes

The Room
Hubert Selby Jr.

Johnny Got His Gun
Dalton Trumbo

CHARACTER STUDIES

I approach books as though they are mirrors, looking for my truth to be reflected back to me. Sometimes it happens, sometimes it doesn't. But this solipsistic approach means that every now and then I find books that show me myself so clearly that I have no choice but to see how someone else handles characters that have my traits and see how my own life measures up. It can be sobering and affirming and it's always enjoyable even when certain truths may be hard to read.

CLOWN GIRL: A NOVEL
By Monica Drake
Hawthorne Books (2006)
Original post: 12/07/2010

Why do I consider this book odd?
It inverts and subverts chick-lit conventions without being cynical.

Nita is a clown. She lives in Baloneytown, waiting for her boyfriend, Rex, to return to her. She is a tenant in a house which she shares with a pot-selling burnout and his hostile, clever girlfriend, living in a tiny room with her beloved dog and her clowning accoutrements. Nita loses items precious to her and longs to get them back, and she dreams of a day when she can combine high art and literature with the profession of being a clown. Also, she meets a policeman who is clearly smitten with her though he has no idea what she looks like under her makeup because she lives her life completely as a clown.

Through Nita, Monica Drake manages to tell a very familiar story but she employs such unusual elements that one does not wholly realize that Nita could just as easily been named Bridget Jones or might just as easily have come out of Marian Keyes' *Shopaholic* series. Nita is feckless, self-absorbed, has her head in the clouds, is in love with a cretin and her job is often in jeopardy. She has a bitchy nemesis, there is a strong, kind man waiting for her in the wings, and it takes her entirely too long to pull herself together, though she manages it after tumbling into one unlikely situation after another. This set-up is the backbone for most chick-lit.

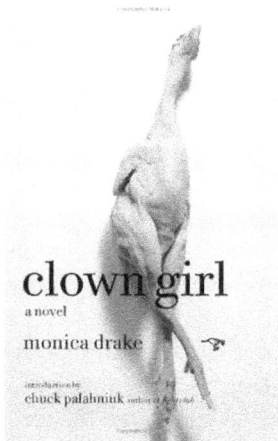

I loved *Clown Girl* so much. I think part of the reason is that Nita speaks to me directly in an almost eerie way, but I also love the way Drake inverts the traditional chick-lit story by stating outright what it is that makes these clumsy, clueless, grandiose, insecure women appealing. She makes it clear from the very title what Nita is. She's a clown. No mincing words. Nita is a clown. And Drake shows how hard it is *not* to be a clown when hiding behind makeup and outlandish clothes, and when pie-in-the-sky ideas are all you have ever known. In Nita, using the raucous background of clowns and a clever play on the modern chick-lit novel, Drake creates a character who tells a story we are familiar with, yet it's a story we have not heard before.

Though Drake riffs on familiar plots, I don't want to give a detailed outline of the story because I want you to experience the fantastic disaster as Nita's life unspools. Instead, I will hit on some plot points as I share some of Drake's writing and parts of the book that resonated with me.

Clown Girl begins with Nita collapsing, suffering from the effects of a terrible loss—a miscarriage. She is working as a clown at an outdoor event when the heat and the lingering effects of her miscarriage cause her to pass out. She is taken to the hospital and the thoughts in her head as she navigates her predicament in a frightening place all alone made me feel an immediate kinship with Nita. I have no idea if her paranoia will translate to people who've had good experiences with doctors and nurses, but her inner monologue spoke to me, eerily, as if it were my own.[1]

> Don't tell doctors your dreams, ever. Don't tell them your menstrual cycle. Don't say you felt anything in your head, or that you might've known. If they ask about street drugs, which they will, say no, no matter what. If you say, I feel anxious all the time, you'll get Valium. Otherwise you'll get what they call "mood equalizers," daily doses of who knows what, a gambler's crapshoot in tinctures of chemicals.
>
> As a clown on the street, I had to keep my wits. I couldn't take their chemicals.
>
> Don't tell doctors anything.

This is a clue-bat of sorts. Nita suffered a miscarriage before this trip to the ER, but it is also clear she had some frightening experiences with doctors trying to help her correct her brain, a brain that seems very common to me but might seem to others like the kind of skullspace that needs tinctures of chemicals. I also relate to this fear of authority more than I care to admit. And concerning the chick-lit inversion, it's refreshing that Nita doesn't want the drugs that would have led to another humiliating escapade for a traditional heroine.

Nita takes being a clown very seriously. But as Drake describes the tools Nita uses in her craft and the crazily ambitious artistic routines she aspires to perform, we see the utter ridiculousness of Nita's life. We don't need Nita sliding down a fireman's pole showing her panties or putting eyeshadow on in the place of blusher—all visually very clownish actions that revealed Bridget Jones' true nature—to show Nita's true inner clown. Take this passage about Nita's approach to balloon animals (bearing in mind that she will later contemplate creating *The Last Supper* in balloon form):

> Swollen Sacred Hearts, shrunken wise men, and bloated angels bobbed at my feet, the fruits of my labor. On the shopworn dedication page of *Balloon*

---

1   It wasn't lost on me as I read Nita's thoughts that my fellow Texans seldom pronounce the first letter of my name, rendering me a de facto "Nita."

Tying for Christ it said "With appreciation and gratitude for my wife and six lovely children who have borne with me through twelve long years of deprivations while trying to complete this work." Such martyrs! *Balloon Tying for Christ* was maybe all of seventeen pages long, with one blank page at the end. The tricks inside, by corporate accounting, were worth hundreds of dollars, Matey, Crack and me, that's what we earned when high-end work came in. But work didn't always come. We had to promote and deliver. That book was my cash cow.

It's hard to think of anything more ridiculous than a 17-page book about making balloon figures for Jesus and how such a book could become the bread and butter to any person, but Drake shows us the absolutely insane pieces that make up the whole of Nita.

Nita understands her job is not one that provides much prestige or financial stability, but she longs to be an artist, a clown interpreting great art and literature (her final blowup with her despicable boyfriend Rex concerns him pirating her Kafka interpretation as performed by a clown). She resents the fact that she is a comedic act or, worse, that she should be sexually appealing in her clowning. When one of two female clowns she occasionally works with spells it out for her, it's not clear that it really sinks in to Nita. Nita simply wants to be a clown artiste. She doesn't like to be reminded of the difference between what she does and what she really wants to do.

"Pssst," Matey said, in a stage whisper and knocked a hand against her head. "Here's a clue: Women wear makeup, right? But a man in face paint, people see aahh-rt. You and me, we top out at birthday gigs, and that hurts more than anything I'm doing now. That's the meat o' the matter." She tipped her Chaplin hat. Was it true? Was there a latex ceiling, made-up makeup finish line?

Despite being a clown, and supporting herself, after a fashion, by performing for parties and even engaging in sexier acts for corporate events, Nita bitterly resents the way that money destroys what she considers beauty.

Leonardo da Vinci said water was the most destructive force on the planet. Water corrodes metal and eats through rock. But da Vinci forgot about the corrosive power of cash; when money came into a neighborhood, the buildings toppled. Even people disappeared.

Like any stereotypical artiste type, Nita longs for purity. She wants pure love, pure work, pure happiness. Like her idea of interpreting art as a clown, her sense of what life can be is grandiose. Yet she can't see settling for anything less. She says:

In a world of clown whores and virgins, I'd cling to the integrity of art.

That doesn't happen. But even as she descends into the world of clown prostitution, Nita still has lofty and near-risible goals.

Traditionally, there's been no delicacy to balloon art. That's where I'd revolutionize things. Chiaroscuro, sfumato: I'd find a way to translate da Vinci's painterly tricks into rubber and air.

Maybe I'd pioneer a line of designer balloon colors in da Vinci's palette. Why stop there? I could have a van Gogh line, a Gauguin line, Toulouse-Lautrec and Tintoretto.

Nita's delusions take her to strange places. She wants to be more than a juggling clown at a kid's party. She wants to be a performance artist, a portrayer of truth. But she is a clown and her perspective of being a clown will never match up to her dreams of artistic relevance. Like the heroines in chick-lit, she decides to alter her appearance but instead of dieting or buying clothes she cannot afford, Nita decides to don a sand-filled fat suit to turn herself into a face-painted voluptuary. And what fine slapstick would be complete if she did not, in fact, juggle fire in such a get-up?

I'd be a sassy, busty clown girl juggling fire. Of course—why not? I'd play to crowds high and low. I'd find the fine line between Crack's clown whore and my own comic interpretation, work both sides and move easily from the comedy of burlesque to striptease, slapstick to sexy. I'd graduate from Clown Girl to Clown Woman.

From a padded body suit, we move to the sublimely ridiculous.

I'd do a new silent, sexy version of Kafka: Gregor Samsa wakes up, finds he's metamorphosed into a woman with an hourglass figure—where every second counts!—and his world's on fire. I'd do a busty Beef-Brisket Dance, on fire. Two Clowns in a Shower on fire. And Who's Hogging the Water?— that'd mixed genre, soft porn plus fire. Even an ordinary bodacious bod and the pins on fire would be a new show altogether.

But Nita is still deluded. She can't grow from a girl into a woman as long as she is a clown. As long as she clings to her outrageous ideas, she will never be able to find any real truth. Given what a fabulous disaster she is, it ends about how you sensed it would as soon as you read the word "fire." Nita sets herself and the yard ablaze. All the better that she's fire juggling in the middle of the night. This is also a good example of the extreme yet subtle humor Drake uses, making Nita a borderline caricature but never stepping completely into a place where the reader cannot respond to Nita's plight.

"Crapola! Crapola!" I ran in a circle and threw myself down. I rolled on the grass where the grass wasn't on fire, but the Pendulous Breasts resisted my momentum, and everywhere I rolled sparks flew. The Pendulous Breasts duck-quacked and chirped a cacophony of party sounds. I was guilty and now I was on fire. Who would've known hell was so efficient. A few mistakes and hell came to me faster than room service.

Because she is burned and experiencing heart problems, Nita returns to the hospital, where she again tells a terrible tale from her past. Without telling the reader outright the reasons for Nita's paranoia, Drake shows what happens to some girls who enter the medical maw when they are alone, weird and full of self-delusion.

> Here's what I know now: never let a misunderstanding go unclarified in a hospital, same as in a school, jail, or prison. Never carry a diary with you, not even a day planner if you write notes in it. Don't say, "Yes, that's mine," to any old scrap of nothing, to what might have been interesting in the free world.
>
> The hospital, it's a gateway. The path to incarceration.
>
> Your best bet is don't even write anything down. Ever. Most of all, don't go near the hospital unless your problem is obvious as a bullet or a broken leg, and don't go more than once. Otherwise you'll learn about a two-doctor hold. Doctor Two-Hold, a seventy-two-hour detainment—and seventy-two hours can be longer if it's late at night or over a weekend.

A *deus ex machina* in the typical chick-lit form of a man saves Nita from the probable 72-hour psych lock down that awaits her after arriving at the ER burned, wearing an exploding fat suit and in full clown regalia.

> …Jerrod had seen me inside and out, burned and in the psych ward. And still here he was, beside me. But the blood and the burns were all circumstantial, a string of bad luck, the anomaly. I didn't want to think that was me—a wreck, a mess, a mortal.

She is a wreck and a mess that you want to despair of, but you can't. Not quite. There are glimmers of insight that peek out when Nita is daydreaming about her despicable boyfriend and making an art show out of balloons tied to resemble Renaissance paintings. The following scene, for example: Nita has lost her rubber chicken, whom she calls "Plucky," and she has put up reward posters all over her low-income and crime-infested neighborhood, resulting in dozens of people coming by with various rubber chickens trying to collect the reward.

> "Maybe your Plucky jus' fell in with the wrong crowd, maybe she was looking for love and thought she'd found it…but you can't trust nobody round here, that's what Plucky knows now. Uh huh." The woman's eyes were flat and dull. She'd quit looking at me. "Plucky maybe learned a few things, and you say, 'No way, no second chances,' and jus' like that, man, turn her ass back out on the street."
>
> I said, "Who are we talking about here?"

Who *were* they talking about? The worn-down woman at the door, or Nita herself? It's hard to tell here, but later revelations show Nita is far more self-aware than even she would like to admit.

I was good at pool. Physics, I understood. I knew all about vectors. That was my original goal in clowning—to create the illusion of defying physics with muscular comedy. I wanted to be able to stand when it looked like I should fall, to spring up when gravity would pull down, and to balance at impossible angles. I wanted to win, or at least stay on my feet, when it looked like I was losing.

Losing is a thing Nita understands, so it stands to reason she wants to be able to look good doing it. She also knows that she is not ever going to be able to make it in a more rarefied world.

One lone lobster beat a claw against the glass wall of a small tank. The lobster's narrow, empty world was perched over a frozen sea; blue Styrofoam tray after tray of Dungeness crab, leggy purple squid, and bundled smelt rested on chopped ice below. *Tick, tick.* The lobster knocked, as though to flag down help. Across the aisle what had once been a herd of grass-fed cattle now lay silent in bloody pools of iced New York strip steak, flank steak, ribs, tongues, and burger. Edible flowers bloomed on a small green stand, a miniature field ready for harvest. *Tap tap. Tap. Tap tap.* A lobster S O S. *Get me out of this dead heaven.* I knew the feeling.

Yeah, and this inversion of the chick-lit narrative rang the truest to me because unlike her genre counterparts, Nita can't follow the script. She can't just pick the right guy, clean herself up, lose a few pounds, get her credit card debt under control and suddenly find herself living the good life when the author rewards her feminine will to change with the perfect rich man to pave her way. Nita would feel even more like a clown in a monied world of privilege.

My heart, ready to burst, spoke in the fast Morse code of biology: *you'll die or go crazy, die or go crazy, die or go crazy, die or go crazy...* I had seconds to live. My heart was too big for my chest, my head hummed. I couldn't move fast enough, had to get out of there.

As Nita shows how her damaged heart is telling her what to do, I couldn't help but think of Sylvia Plath's Esther, whose heart beat, "I am, I am." Nita's heart tells her she has two options, both horrible, and given the hints of diagnosed craziness in her past, this passage was devastating. Despite the loony ideas Nita harbored concerning her work and her art, at the core of her, the heart so to speak, in times of grave stress her only options seemed stark. Go crazy or die.

I like to think Nita's heart went to such dark places not because she was indeed depressed (though she is definitely desperate) but rather because she knew on a very basic level that her aspirations of clown artistry were hogwash, an attempt to cloak herself in dreams lest she have to confront the real problems in her life. Nita has no family, she lost her baby and she has no allies. She is alone.

Emancipated minor? I'd been one for years—emancipated but no longer a minor, and I was ready to have a team, a side, a family. Somebody to back me up. A person shouldn't be emancipated so long.

Alas, the person she pins her hopes on is Rex—a man not worth her care, even as a clown girl. Here's Rex:

Rex laughed then, a mean, sharp snort. "Impossible? You want to talk impossible? This is all bullshit, babe. You want to think you're not a hooker, just a clown on a private date. Think you're an artist, working a new car lot? I'll tell you something—that's not art. It's just a story you're making up. Maybe the same story you'd tell our baby, if we still had a baby. Mommy's not a hooker, she's a corporate party girl. No wonder the kid bailed. Christ, maybe the thing's lucky you dumped it."

As horrible as this is, as horrible as him rubbing her face in her miscarriage could ever be, Rex has a point. Nita's no artist. She tells herself stories to get herself through it all. She has created a similar fantasy about being a family with Rex. It hits her hard.

Another *deus ex machina* reunites Nita with her rubber chicken and her lost dog, and once she has the dog back, she has to do something to save her dog's life. Her roommates feed the dog pot and to keep the dog from becoming deathly ill, she needs peroxide to induce vomiting. She shows up at the convenience store wearing the ragged remains of the fat suit, her clown makeup smeared. She can't get anyone to take her seriously. Because she is a clown, she cannot impart upon anyone that she is in the middle of an emergency. She finally begins to see how she is hindering herself by imbuing her odd ideas with a patina of artistic endeavor.

There was my face in the aluminum rim of the hot-foods incubator, around jo-jos and chicken, I was reflected in the glass of the Coke cooler and the grease-smeared deli case, all powdery makeup, black liner and big red lips, the face of a clown hooker right out of an old-time jail-time act. My one Caboosey boob hung free.

[…]

The only show was my life and it was a bomb. The only routine was the daily one. I'd been in clown costume so long, I wasn't an artist. I was a freak.

She takes a good look at herself. It's time to change.

They, my friends, were hucksters, drug dealers, and bullies. But in that world of defeatism, I was the jester, the fall guy, the rubber chicken. I was the one who put on face paint and shades, limping in one big shoe.

If this were a conventional chick-lit novel, there would be another *deus ex machina*—or some bright epiphany that would inspire Nita to wipe off the clown makeup and put on a pair of fashionable shoes so she could walk tall and proud. A job would magically fall into her lap and the new man who was lurking at her side unnoticed would sweep her off her feet. Nita would realize she could stand on her own two feet again, though she wouldn't have to since the new guy would be rich and ready to marry her.

That doesn't happen in this chick-lit inversion, but the ending is satisfying in its own way.

This book surprised me. I didn't expect to love it as much as I did. *Clown Girl* follows the path of mainstream chick-lit just far enough to satisfy my occasional need for glurge, but it soon deviates from this familiar terrain. Drake has given us a heroine whose hidden past remains hidden, whose life really is ridiculous, whose world resembles places I am familiar with.

FURTHER READING

The Woman Who Walked into Doors
Roddy Doyle

Geek Love
Katherine Dunn

The Fat Woman's Joke
Fay Weldon

The Life and Loves of a She-Devil
Fay Weldon

STUPID CHILDREN
By Lenore Zion
Emergency Press (2013)
Original post: 05/27/2014

Why do I consider this book odd?
Children are tortured with nasal balloons and animal entrails.

The cover drew me in. A little girl—pale skin, white underwear, long blonde hair—is standing behind a rope in a rugged backyard in late fall or early winter. The look on her face is unfathomable to me, but the confrontation is undeniable. She is standing there, unprotected in the wind, literally holding on by a string, and she is staring at you. Her expression could suggest veiled disgust or melancholy or some vague interest in the camera as a distraction from the bleak boredom of the landscape.

Stupid Children, by turns neurotic and gross, touching and funny, is perfectly represented by this cover. The heroine is a bizarre combination of fearlessness and neurosis. The plot-line gets loose at times and the wackiness can occasionally make the reader forget that at its heart this is still a book about a little girl whose mother is dead, whose father is in a mental institution, who ends up in foster care in the home of cultists who marry her off to an old man in a scenario reminiscent of so many stories that came out of the FLDS sects. Lenore Zion handles all of this heaviness with humor and an open-minded acceptance of the bizarre, but the cover ensures you never forget the smart little girl in a forsaken place at the center of the story. Her name is Jane.

Jane's mother is dead and her father had a breakdown. After attempting suicide, he becomes a long-term resident in a mental hospital. Jane is sent to live in foster care and ends up living with a family indoctrinated into the fictional Second Day Believers, a strange cult that merges properties of Scientology (weird ideas about mental illness and its treatment), FLDS (marrying young girls off to much older, powerful men in the cult) and a kind of paganism (very gross rituals involving animal entrails). Jane becomes close to her foster brother, Isaac, and their relationship takes a dark turn as Isaac becomes rather unhinged himself, a young proxy in Jane's affection for her unbalanced father. Jane eventually becomes far more valuable to the cult than the cult is to her but her love for Isaac keeps her from leaving the madness until Isaac forces the issue in an act of numb but horrifying violence.

Let me get the hard criticism out of the way before I sing this book's praises. The ending is rushed and, in a way, a bit contrived. It all comes too fast.

The reader doesn't get to see what happens and because it is so rushed, we are denied catharsis. The reader needs that catharsis. As funny and sarcastic as *Stupid Children* can be at times, the book pulses with hard and upsetting content. We need to have that BAM! moment, but it gets lost in the rush. Though not entirely—you won't be left feeling like doors were left open, but you also won't get the satisfaction of hearing those doors slam shut.

Now, let's discuss why this book is worth reading.

Zion manages to capture perfectly the actions and manners and thinking of a gifted yet neurotic child. Such children are generally considered mature for their age. I've heard them described as old souls. But generally they are no more mature than other children—they just seem like they are little adults because most adults worry all the time, mulling over all the potential disasters that might come to pass. Neurotic children typically have fewer frames of reference for contemplating disaster, but of course Jane has lost her mother and her father has been institutionalized. As bad as that is, when Jane moves in with Madam and Sir Six, she is in for a world of education into the worst that can happen. The Sixes want to help cure her of her mental impurities, you see, and Jane does not have a reference for all that this could entail (I accidentally typed "entrail" just now, an apt error).

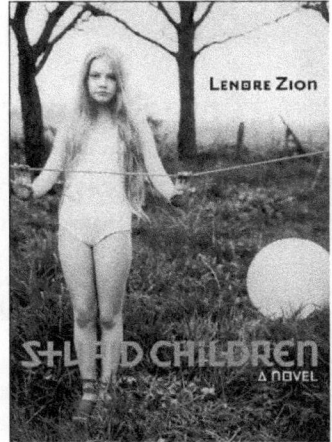

> My father, having never once made the mistake of omitting crucial statistics on living well, would not have excluded mental impurities if they did, in fact, exist. But, my father had also, just one month prior to my invitation to the room with the black door, cut his throat open, nearly intentionally killing himself. And while I got the sense that Madam Six and Sir Six were not without their pitfalls (one of the first hints being the communal healing swim with the insides of animals and other children fresh off the foster boat), they had not yet proven to be people with malicious intent. My father always taught me that people should be given the benefit of the doubt, with a few exceptions, but as I was just ten years old at the time, I was not yet crystal clear on what those exceptions might be. So, suspicion was cast aside, benefit of the doubt was granted, and I did not pull away when Madam Six took my hand and led me through the black door...

In a sense, what happens behind that black door could have been so much worse. I'll get to that in a minute. But what hit me like a fist in the face here is that I cannot imagine what it is like to be a parent because my first instinct would be to tell my own children, had I any children, that they should give no one the benefit of the doubt. Possibly not even me. Do people still tell their kids to believe the best about people until proven otherwise? How does such a message reconcile with the "stranger danger" lesson kids also learn? All I know is that if I were a mother, I would hope my kids would go kicking and screaming into the room with the black door.[2]

Jane does go into the room with the black door, and a very upsetting scene follows:

> Because I knew nothing of mental impurities, I hushed my misgivings about the methods Madam Six and the others exercised in flushing me of these contaminants, and kept quiet as two deflated, worm-shaped balloons were systematically inserted into my nostrils—one balloon per nostril. I continued to silence myself as a motorized inflation device was placed into the ends of the balloons, and muzzled my impulse to cry for help when I was forced down on my back, and held firmly in place by three cloaked men, one of whom was Sir Six, my new father. I could not, however, keep myself quiet when the motorized inflation device was switched on and the balloons rapidly distended inside my nostrils, causing my nose to break instantly. Blood came pouring out from inside me, and seeped into my mouth.

By strange coincidence, I read the preceding passage just after Mr. OTC blew a capillary in his nose and had to have a "rhino-rocket" inserted into his nasal cavity. The ER doc refused to listen when he complained that he had over-inflated it, and I watched helplessly as Mr. OTC exhibited pain-related aggression. Only intense pain prevented him from taking a swing at someone, anyone. When the doc left the room, I had to fish a syringe out of the trash and partially deflate the balloon. Mr. OTC is not necessarily a badass but has been stabbed and he served his country in a foreign conflict. He's not a man given to the level of complaint you have grown to expect from me, and he described the inflation of the rhino rocket as torture (note to any ER doc who may read this—give the shot of painkiller *before* you insert the goddamned rhino rocket). Reading about what happens to a little girl behind the black door was so upsetting to me I almost quit the book. I persevered.

Modern representations of neurosis tend to be comically reductive. We think of Woody Allen wrecking his relationships. Evidently it's funny when a nebbishy Freudian can't make it work with beautiful women who can't see past his adult bedwetting phase. And while neurosis can be funny, it's a short skip and a jump into a full-on personality disorder if one doesn't get the disaster-obsessed thinking in check. *Stupid Children* is narrated in the past tense by a woman whose sentence structure is interestingly similar to my own, wordy and comma-laden. Through this familiar voice, we encounter a very different interpretation of neurotic experience—a story of a little girl

---

2   Perhaps that is one of the more obscure reasons why I would suck at being a mother (or possibly be the best mother ever, who knows).

tortured into neuroticism by one horrifying event after another. She lives her life with people who never respected that she was a child. She is forced to endure the unthinkable before she has the capacity to understand how unthinkable it all is.

Don't get me wrong. There are some very funny moments because the way neurotics structure their thoughts can be quite funny. It isn't all child abuse and bloody suicide (though a lot of it is), but it was nice to read Zion's words because she gets it. Neurosis isn't just the skinny girl in glasses on sitcoms, the one who fears germs and is cutely obsessive. It's also children abused into maladaptive behaviors. I love that Zion understands what neurosis is, what causes it and what one has to go through to confront it.

And her heroine does confront it, but that happens after she has escaped from the cult that alternately tortured her and convinced her she was the golden child. Jane spends a lot of time as an adult cleaning her way out of the mess the adults in her life created when she was a child.

Zion intersperses enough silliness and humor to make Jane's plight bearable to read. I think of a sequence where Jane and another character, Virginia, try to have a night on the town. It ends poorly, to put it mildly, but luckily there is someone to save the two girls from a very bad fate. A nice Korean man brings them inside and tries to comfort them as they wait for a cab.

> Then, in his continued attempts to minister to us, he tried to feed us popcorn. I did not want to eat the popcorn—in fact, the popcorn was revolting to me at the time—but it seemed rude to refuse it, and my father did not raise an ill-mannered young lady, so I put one piece in my mouth at a time, stuffing them all in and chewing, but never swallowing. Eventually I had a wad of chewed popcorn stored in my cheek. I looked like some sort of psychotic squirrel, and the man just looked at me and looked at me.

I should mention that Jane was wearing kitty ears as she ate the popcorn, and she was tripping balls on acid. Yet she remains focused on upholding her identity as the "young lady" her father raised her to be, this idealized version of herself that is so strong it can penetrate even the other-mindedness of hallucinogenic experience. That's neurosis at work—Zion is sharp.

The Second Day Believers engage in a strange custom where they force people to hold in their urine. Jane, who didn't drink much water anyway and further dehydrated herself to avoid the humiliation of accidentally wetting herself, was spared the kidney infections that afflicted her peers. The ability to control one's bladder, according to the cultists, was an indication of an other-worldly control over one's organs, a mark of some sort of holy endowment. By holding in one's pee, they believed one could grow a second spleen. But Jane's ability to avoid kidney infections works against her when it brings her to the attention of the old man who founded the cult, Sir One:

And this is how my ability to hold my urine for long periods of time without medical consequence is what piqued Sir One's interest in me—the old man really bought what he was selling, I supposed, because when he heard through his channels of communication that the girl who shared a spirit animal with the late Madam One, and resembled her to boot, avoided infection, he determined that he and I would meet. *No infection, you say? Why, she must be only moments away from sprouting a secondary spleen!* And with that, I was suddenly and officially the front-runner in the race to be the brand new bride of Sir One, the contemporary and pristine Madam One, the first high priestess since the original had perished. "There's no greater compliment a girl can receive than finding out that she's been chosen!" Madam Six squealed at me. Chosen for servitude because of a perceived feasibility of unnecessary organ development—what an honor.

When Jane realizes she's going to end up the bride of a man so old he's near death, she panics. She decides it's time for her and the other kids to leave the cult, though they don't leave just yet.

I knew I had to get them out of there. It worried me that Virginia had turned eighteen, and even though we'd talked about how she'd leave the moment the clock hit midnight on her birthday, she stayed, claiming that she'd miss me and Isaac too much to leave without us. They were sinking into the brainwashing that the Second Dayers were so adept at applying to impressionable kids, and I was slated to be offered up for a marriage to an old man with two spleens. This was no place for kids…

Zion is excellent at comic understatement. She's also amazing at taking the leaps that a self-aware yet really neurotic woman would take as she ponders her nature. Jane was given a psychiatry book when she was sixteen, more or less identified with every single mental illness, and managed to extrapolate how she'd be affected by her mental disorders later in her life.

Did I engage in excessive self-sacrifice that is unsolicited by the intended recipients of the sacrifice? Certainly within me there was this intense self-pity that made me sometimes fantasize about cutting both of my wrists all the way to the elbow, and then as I'm bleeding, show up at some man's house, any one of the much-too-old-for-me men with whom I had forced a melodramatic and tragic relationship, and wrap my bleeding arms around his body, staining the back of his shirt red as I die. In my mind, this man would keep the shirt in a box, and over time the stains would turn from bright red to dull brown, and eventually they'd just appear to be dark, indistinct stains. He'd take it out of the box once or twice a year—perhaps on my birthday and the anniversary of my senseless death—and he'd hold it in his hands and stare at the stains. And this poor man, he'd be so affected by my theatrical advent at his door that he'd never be capable of moving on with his life. He'd go on dates with women, one after the other, and he'd just stare right through them as they talked about how delicious their chicken parmesan was, and what a nice time they were having. "Yes," he'd say, but his eyes would be vacant as he spoke, and the women would know. They would know. "The man is in love with a dead girl," they'd tell their friends on the phone after the date. I would have him forever and I wouldn't even be alive. Was that okay?

If you found this passage funny, you really should read this book. If you have ever engaged in similar flights of dark fancy, you still have to read this book.

I'll leave you with one last quote, one that exemplifies the sort of humor that animates *Stupid Children*.

> Marriage is never what you think it will be. That's what everyone says after getting married—they talk about how marriage is hard work and it's not what you expect, that they had no idea they'd have to compromise so much. And you sit and listen, wondering what exactly the compromises are, because to hear people talk about it, it sounds like marriage is almost always an institution bonding two completely self-absorbed assholes who simply cannot agree upon the type of towels they will purchase and hang from the towel rack in the bathroom, because one member of the couple feels that the other always gets his way, that motherfucker, and as a result, the submissive spouse doesn't even feel like she even has a voice in this relationship, even though last week she was permitted to select all of the new curtains for the entire house. Doesn't she remember that? No, no, of course she doesn't, because that detail is inconvenient and inconsistent with the story of victimization she is weaving.

If anyone is entitled to the view that most people are just assholes bitching about their petty travails, it's Jane.

Some may see the ending as happy, as a final death, the last one mentioned in the narrative, sets Jane free. I didn't feel that way. As I mention above, I think the ending is rushed. Without spoiling anything, I will say the person who is last to die is the one I would have killed myself, even if the catharsis never came. Perhaps that lingering desire to kill a particular fictional character is further evidence of my own neuroses. We all have neuroses, I suspect. May we all rise above them, as Jane does.

I really loved this funny, accurate, and at times over-the-top depiction of the damage done to the helpless. I walked into it with no idea what to expect, being confronted by that pale, unprotected girl on the cover, daring me to read her story, to understand why she is in her underwear outside, with nothing between me and her but a rope. Lenore Zion's *Stupid Children* turns out to be not so much a confrontation as it is a trip through the mind of a little girl who had no choice but to grow up to be her own protector.

FURTHER READING

Invisible Monsters
Chuck Palahniuk

NVSQVAM (NOWHERE)
By Ann Sterzinger
Nine-Banded Books (2011)
Original post: 04/20/2015

Why do I consider this book odd:
Oh, this book...

There are two reasons to read this book. The first reason is that Sterzinger nails a specific social dissatisfaction I tend to associate with the sort of men who really love Jonathan Franzen, a sort of Lester Burnham-esque unhappiness that can only be cured by having sex with a much-younger woman and sneering at the daily grind and everyday domesticity. She distills this generational malaise through a single character and refuses to show us the way out. Because most of the time there isn't one.

The other reason to read *NVSQVAM* is because it is so very funny. Seriously, Sterzinger has the sort of intelligent, acerbic wit that I imagined I had back when I was a drunk.

It's a book that will read differently to every person who picks it up. Women of a certain age (hi!) will want to swat the protagonist on the nose with a rolled-up newspaper until he stops pissing and moaning about his life and either accepts it or changes it in a meaningful way. I wanted to swat him all the more because Lester (yep, Lester) Reichartsen is himself a man of a certain age. He embodies the Gen-X confusion-burnout that I see plaguing so many of my peers. I see far too many people I know falling apart, longing for an edgy past because their passivity and entitlement cornered them into a life they really never wanted but didn't have the balls to reject along the way. Too bad they reach this conclusion after they've remodeled their house and given birth to a couple of kids.

In the beginning, Lester is one of those people. You know, the ones to whom everything happens and they actually do very little. Such people feel very put-upon. Lester is living a life he hates that he feels happened to him through no fault of his own. He hates everyone around him—especially his only child and the

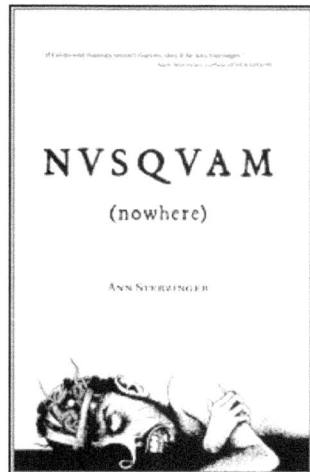

religious midwesterners who surround his college town—and the only things he really accomplishes, aside from a prolonged drunken nervous breakdown, are taking long walks and engaging in an affair.

Though I find Lester to be largely irritating and unlikeable, he is not unique in his passive, seething uselessness. Jesus, so many young people born to boomer parents ended up like this. Almost all of us were latch-key kids. The post-Reagan economy seemed hopeless, and we had Pearl Jam running across the stage in baggy shorts making millions of dollars moaning about their mothers, which was sort of understandable because so many of us were raised in divorced, single-parent, female-headed households. Some young men raised in such an environment felt buffeted by fate, as if everything they wanted would never happen. They entered a post-collegiate life with no idea what to do next.

Get married? Yeah, that worked so well for our parents. Get a good office job with benefits and insurance? But aren't we supposed to find our bliss and honor our talents? Didn't our parents raise us to express our deep individuality (while giving us little assistance in determining how to put that individuality to use)? Get a factory job and write on the side? No, the factory jobs are gone and *everyone* has a blog. The world changed so much in such a short period of time that all the lessons many Gen-Xers were taught were obsolete the day after they became adults.

It's tempting to write Lester off as a self-involved crap-fest of a human being, but even as I wanted to grab his nose between my index and middle finger and twist it violently, I felt a certain level of empathy for him. He almost seems like an embodiment of the sentiment expressed in Chuck Palahniuk's *Fight Club*—we were all told we were going to be rock stars and when that didn't happen it pissed off an entire generation. So many of us feel like we have failed our families and ourselves, especially our younger, idealistic selves. What do we do about that rage? About real failure? To avoid that sense of failure, wounded egos become passive, taking paths of least resistance, so they can say that they aren't responsible for anything in their lives. That's how we end up with Lesters.

Lester Reichartsen is a self-absorbed, largely useless asshole but he's *our* asshole, my generation's asshole. You can't hobble large segments of a generation and then hold them completely responsible for limping.

I think what helped me so much as I grappled with my feelings about Lester is the fact that this is a very funny book. Every time I have ever been funny it was by accident. I have absolute envy for people who can be humorous and witty with purpose. Sterzinger's novel delivers sly and outright humor through a representative of a wreck of a generation. There's some pretty serious and meaningful content along the way, but you won't be disappointed if you come for the laughs.

Before I wallow in the wit, a synopsis; Lester Reichartsen is married to Evelyn, a formerly hot young woman who became forever ruined to Lester when she got pregnant and gave birth to their son, Martin. Martin is a genius and that rubs Lester raw because he himself is not a genius and he can see how this child that he did not want is going to eclipse him in life accomplishments. Lester and Evelyn are both in academia. Evelyn is good at it. She takes pleasure in research, writing and teaching. Lester can barely be arsed to learn the basics of his own field of alleged expertise. His Latin students know more about the subject than he does and he hates every moment of writing his thesis, using assorted excuses and indulging bad habits to avoid real work.

Lester was ousted from a punk band when he was younger and this also eats at him. When he meets a young woman wearing his old band's logo T-shirt, he begins to long for his lost youth and the life he gave up when he married Evelyn. He eventually sleeps with the young woman, and that comes with its own set of problems. He's soon drinking himself into mini-comas, seeking psychiatric help (or actually, psychiatric meds), struggling to care about the thesis he is supposed to be writing, and ruining his marriage and his life in general—all because he refuses to make the transition from pie-in-the-sky dreams to post-Palahniuk alternatives. He's not a punk rock star and he is pissed off and depressed. However, his sense of entitlement disables him from finding a positive outlet for his many grudges. His feels resentment for his son Martin (whose intelligence means that he is his father's mental superior), for his wife (whom he sees more as a mother than a wife), for his "work" and his life in general. All of this festering resentment builds toward a cataclysmic ending. I still don't know if I like the ending. Like I said, I wanted to twist the gristle in Lester's nose until he squealed in pain, but I also tend to think that Sterzinger knew what she was doing in devising such a bitter ending. Because Lester, at his core, was never an evil man.

Anyway, back to the humor.

Like the book itself, the humor in *NVSQVAM* will read differently to everyone. I may be in a minority when I assert that Lester has enough self-awareness to make some of his thoughts and dialogue clever and amusing. My copy is littered with yellow marks indicating a line or paragraph that I found funny in some manner, so many that I have a hard time knowing which ones to discuss (this may be the book that caused me to stop bending pages to remember where great quotes occurred because often there were several on a page—at any rate, I highlight now, which some see as an improvement).

The first one I highlighted is funny to me now because I don't remember why I found it funny, which is sort of funny in itself.

> Once he got lost in the structure of an essay, he was like an eyeless Oedipus in a labyrinth. Only not that cool.

From here on out, it's easier for me to recall why I was so amused. Here Lester is observing the students on his campus, and he can only see things the way he does because he has deliberately and self-righteously set himself apart.

> When forced to walk the 100-yard length of the student center, they consoled themselves by talking on their portable phones; their transit time was tripled, since every five steps or so they would bump into each other and wander off the track. It was like a prison for senile cats.

In the beginning, before I really got a sense of who Lester is, this seemed very... I don't know... on the mark, maybe? A nice little lampoon of people who simply cannot exist alone with their thoughts for a few moments because anything short of continual online conversation or passive entertainment is boring to them. Then I read further and understood that Lester took hours-long meandering walks alone with his relentless inner dialogue. If those students bounced off each other in a prison for senile cats, Lester was in solitary confinement for neurotic turtles. It's a nice way to handle Lester, to let him reveal just enough of himself—a disgust for tiresome elements of academia, exhaustion from dealing with ignorant and digitally absorbed people—that the reader cannot help but agree. As we later discover that Lester is unstable and sort of a dick we are confronted with the idea that maybe we the readers are not as enlightened as we think we are when we first identify with Lester.

There are moments when Lester is completely on the nose. Here he is as he starts a day's work in the field he has chosen as his life's ambition:

> The file finally came on screen and Lester stared at it like a caveman. It seemed to have been written in no known language. He'd been over every phoneme of it thousands of times, and even the English words had no meaning for him anymore; the Latin looked like the transcript of a dispute between squirrels.

I am a grad school dropout. I couldn't stomach academia and I don't even know why I enrolled in grad school because my last year of college was a complete slog. My Latin class translated Cicero's *De Amicitia* and there were moments when I finished Latin work and began to read texts for literature classes and stared at the pages as if I had never seen English words before. I look back over notes and textbooks from that time and in the margins of pages I frequently drew a stick figure with a long, bent neck and an enormous head that drooped down past its shoulders, dangling on the end of that long neck like a wilting balloon. I called him "nothingface." If that little drawing came to life I bet he would love this book.

Oh Jesus, I tend to think this next section shows Lester in as honest a state as he can ever be and it's so very funny to me. Lester is seeing, if I recall correctly, a graduate student in psychology or psychiatry. He initially admits exactly what it is he hopes to accomplish (he wants to obtain excellent drugs) but when he is prodded to speak, all that plagues Lester comes pouring out.

> "OK, so I'm ashamed. And I really need some drr ... medication. Some help. I'm going insane. I want to kill my teachers, I want to kill my students, I want to kill my son, I want to kill my cat. And fine! I am tying one on every two weeks or so, and it pisses off my wife—and she's a fine fucking one to talk since it was during her happy-go-lucky alcoholic days that she forgot to take her fucking birth control and fucking didn't tell me because she didn't want to ruin the fucking anniversary of our first fuck and nine months later she shat out that miserable kid and then we had to get married ...

> "Oh, god, listen to me. I'm the father from hell. I've turned into an even worse version of my father. OK, so I don't beat the kid, or yell at him, but I think at least my father loved me. I try to love the kid, but all I can come up with is duty with affection forced into it. I feel like I have to fill a giant pastry shell of duty with the soft whipped cream of affection, but the plunger is stuck. AHHH! Did I just imply that I'm impotent? I'm definitely not impotent. Although once in a while I wish I'd been. AHHHHH! I need a drink. Are there any antidepressants that won't kill my sex drive?"

I feel I should mention that he wouldn't have even been there in the first place had Evelyn, she who shat out the kid, not cut him off from her own rationed benzo prescription, an act of marital self-preservation that annoys Lester. Also Lester sort of pervs on the doctor/therapist. He really digs her legs. He needs more help than can ever be given him in a therapeutic setting.

The entire section where Lester, Evelyn and Martin visit family over the Christmas holidays is just excruciating and hilarious. There's too damn much to reproduce here so consider that long section to be the price of admission. One of the things I really love about Mr. OTC is that he, much like me, loves his family but loves them best at a distance. He's never encouraged an extended holiday hell march like Evelyn emotionally coerced her family into and if he did the only way I would have been able to endure it would have been to consume as much alcohol as Evelyn and Lester downed during their Christmas torture.

But he has to stay drunk. He has no choice.

> *I need to cut down on the booze ... but if I cut down any further I'll be living in reality practically all the time.*

And goddamn if Sterzinger doesn't absolutely nail the ridiculous, maudlin misery that comes from being a semi-professional drunk. Staggering home, drunk as hell, Lester remembers how unhappy Brett Favre looked during a bad moment on the field and it sparks a long dark minute of the soul in a man completely unaccustomed to giving a shit about anyone else.

> *Feeling sorry for myself doesn't feel half as bad as this, and I'm a self-centered bastard! How can normal people stand it? Why is world hunger allowed to*

exist? … the sheer pain it must cause to anyone who isn't hungry and has a decently functional empathy gland … oh! Holy shit!—Does that mean every-one is as selfish and evil as I am? No wonder things are such a fucking mess!

Though it is not particularly amusing, I want to share this quote from Evelyn, who is very patiently trying to encourage Lester to live in a differ-ent manner because eating crappy food, drinking to excess and seething as a form of exercise were contributing to his mental and physical problems. When he outright mocks her because she made him a nice meal, she snaps at him.

> "Jesus, Lester! We aren't twenty-five! Eating ramen noodles isn't funny any-more! It's depressing!" She took another deep breath and tried to smile at him. "Don't you think I can tell you're not happy? I'm not happy either, Lester. We've been working too hard for too long. I'm just trying to get whatever comforts of life we can afford, OK? If you're that stuck on your romantic vision of being a punk-rock-ape who sleeps in a pile of used drum heads and eats Count Chocula cereal for three meals a day forever, do what makes you feel good. But don't talk to me like I'm some stupid 50s house-wife because I want to live like a real person!"

Evelyn destroys his plate of food in front of him because fuck Lester and his rejection of everything she is and wants. I struggle with this. I am a force of order and domesticity around the house (which may seem odd given my chaotic nature, but there you go) and our life suffers when my old pal cyclical depression shows up. I often feel… reduced and diminished by people who find such attention to domestic detail boring and pointless. Yes, yes, I know I was supposed to be a college professor or a lawyer or at the very least a semi-successful writer with a profound substance abuse problem but instead I'm just a woman with a house and cats and a lot of really healthy recipes and a love for Swiffer products. I know I'm trivial, no better than Aunt Bea on *The Andy Griffith Show*. But don't sneer at me to my face. Have the grace to look down on me once I've left the room. I get Evelyn's rage here.

But I also get Lester's rejection of a Martha Stewart, home-cooked, orderly life. It seems like comfort is what happens when you just don't have the balls to hack it in the real, artistic world. If you're producing excellent art, who cares if you eat nothing but take-out and never change your sheets? I don't necessarily see it that way all the time but I often wonder if I am no different than everyone who is dropping out and making jam and keeping chickens in their side yard. Domesticity is what seems to happen when nothing else happens—it seems like a second-option, a plan B. I thank my stars that Mr. OTC doesn't think that way. He likes our comfortable life. Some of us who spent too long in squalor don't see the artistic value of it anymore. But I also know plenty of my peers look askance at what can only appear to them as me having chosen comfort because I cannot be Dorothy Parker.

Sometimes the humor in this book is very dark. Take this passage where Lester is speaking to his son, who has just asked his father to play a board game with him on a snow day (a request that Lester declines):

> "You're no fun."

> "Just wait till you're seventeen and you have to write your dissertation. We'll see how fun you are, then."

> "'How *much* fun you are,' Dad."

> "Why don't you go fuck yourself? I mean that affectionately." He patted Martin too hard on his head and wondered how horribly he would act when he got drunk at Martin's PhD graduation—whether he would buy him a drink too, though he was underaged; whether he would throw up on the cake … whether he would even be alive by then.

God, Lester is a miserable prick. Yeah, it sucks to have your kid correct your grammar, but come on! I think Martin is eight in this scene. If not he hasn't reached double digits yet. And it's not like Lester actually wants to work on his dissertation. Why not play a game with his son? Well, because Lester hates his son and the prospect of being shown up by his son, almost as much as he hates everything else in his life.

Look, the world sucks in almost every regard and so many of us get cornered into scenarios we didn't choose. In a sense, it is commendable, the way that Lester refuses to accept his fate. But now he's a grown man shitting all over a child and there is no edgy, independent glory to be achieved from such cruelty. Divorce Evelyn, start a new band, find co-eds online and fuck their brains out nightly—do anything to keep from shitting all over the kid. But Lester does none of that. He just stews and fumes and flails and considers his failure a Martin-shaped roadblock. Had Lester acted once in his own positive self interest without assigning squirmy blame to the innocent, I think I would have cut him so much more slack.

His snow day with his wife isn't going much better. She's not pleased at how drunk he already is so early in the day and no longer makes a pretense of keeping it to herself, to Lester's dismay.

> *Maybe I'll nail her door shut. Then Martin and I can drink vodka from a giant latex bra and roll around in the living room in diapers. She says she wants us to bond. I don't think he'll complain. Just as long as he doesn't bother me with fucking Othello again.*

Shortly after this, rather than nailing the door shut, he tries to nail Evelyn in the kitchen. She's not game at all.

Eventually a therapist speculates that Lester has a personality disorder, an observation we all saw coming.

I hesitate to discuss the footnotes for fear readers will recoil and be all, "No way, everyone raved about that shit in *Infinite Jest* and I fell for it once. Never again!" and dismiss this book out of hand. But Sterzinger's footnotes never venture into grotesque self-indulgence, I swear! I have a couple of favorites.

In a book that speaks of punk music often, it's not unexpected that some of the footnotes would attempt to clarify certain musical ideas. Here's footnote 25:

> God, how do you describe death metal to readers of the future? Uh … first, you play classical music really fast with really loud guitars to get metal, and then you add lyrics about violent death and get rid of the ballads to get death metal.

This footnote, interestingly, is on a page where Lester is discussing his ouster from his punk band, Incognito Mosquito. He was more or less kicked out because he had a day job and missed practice one day in order to take an extra shift and the real drunken, hardcore member of his band challenged him. Almost all the members of death metal bands I know of, even the famous ones, have day jobs. Had Lester had dreams of death metal god-status, maybe all of this would have turned out differently. But then again, maybe not. After severing from his band, he justified the hell out of it—dislike for the squalor, loathing for the nasty, drug-addled elements of his band. He hated the squalor but he also hates the comfort Evelyn offers. He just hates living, the sheer boredom of being alive.

Some of the other footnotes seemed directly aimed at my own sensibilities. Footnote 31, referring to Jackson Pollock:

> 20th C. splatter painter that people admired for some theoretical reason.

Another excellent footnote (72) attempts to explain *The Muppet Show*:

> TV show from the 1970s involving spooky puppets on dimly-lit sets. Fozzy was an ursine stand-up comedian. Piggy was a porcine nymphomaniac who compulsively pursued an asexual frog.

The humor helps in this book, and while I suspect that many readers will identify with Lester in some regards, there is an innate nastiness to Lester that prevents complete empathic reaction. He is just such an asshole. He engages in black and white thinking in a manner that will seem excessive even to the most hardened sufferer of borderline personality disorder. His son is intelligent? To Lester, Martin's intellect is nothing to be proud of because it is a sign that one day his own son may do better in life than he does, be more renowned, be more respected. His beautiful wife is a good mother and excellent at her job? She asks Lester not to drink until he is immobile and his only response to such a request is to drink even more than he initially intended because as soon as Evelyn gave birth, she ceased to be a partner and became a mother-by-proxy and he refuses to be nagged by a mother. She's just someone to be defied, even if it means ruining his own life through the defiance. Lester is so obsessed with youth and trivia that it is impossible to believe he is really capable of growing up until something cataclysmic and irreparable changes everything in his life.

One last vague discussion of the ending of this book—I think that one of the reasons I recoiled from the way everything ended is because I really wanted Lester to develop some nobility of character. I wanted him to stop dragging down others around him. Instead he infected those who should have been dearest to him in a way even his diseased ego could not have foreseen. Until the last page, Lester was completely ignoble. I suspect that is how it had to be. We human beings seldom see the damage we are doing until that damage is irreversible.

This is a very good book. Sterzinger manages to write about a man I find tiresome and often despicable and infuse her creation with enough humanity and humor to keep everything in perspective. Sometimes that which represents individual tragedy is comedic from another vantage. Lester is laughable and incredibly sad. He's an asshole, but like I said, he's *our* asshole. Highly recommended.

FURTHER READING

Everyday Drinking
Kingsley Amis

Pleasant Hell
John Dolan

The Satires
Juvenal

Unplugging Philco
Jim Knipfel

Philip
Tito Perdue

The Talkative Corpse
Ann Sterzinger

VALENCIA
By James Nulick
Nine-Banded Books (2014)
Original post: 01/29/2016

Why do I consider this book odd?
It's written in a style one does not commonly see in memoirs, a style that demands that you read the book twice[3] in order to really under-stand the whole of it. The truly odd part is that I don't think you will mind reading it twice in a row.

It's hard to write an American memoir in the 21st century, as modernity has ensured that most of us will live unremarkable lives. There can be no more tales of surviving smallpox or famine, and there's not a lot of terrain to discover that doesn't already have several Taco Bell locations within a fifty-mile radius. There are no more invaders from foreign lands, and no wars on American soil. No duels. Few remaining hippie cults waiting to indoctrinate the young and innocent. And even those who have fled to large cities in order to carve out interesting careers in the arts while living among interesting people in bohemian slums are more likely to micro-blog about binge-watching some fucking show about women having lots of implausible sex in a prison than to document their social and creative endeavors. But while modern life tends to be completely unremarkable, reading about un-remarkable lives can be sometimes be interesting. This happens when a life story rings true to the reader, offering muffled catharsis for the quiet ennui that is so much a part of daily existence.

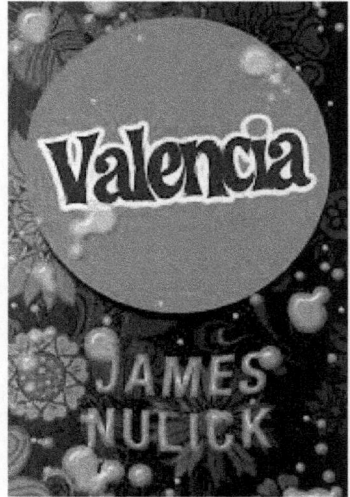

Don't get me wrong—suburbia has a lot to recommend it. Safety, stability, convenience and social order are good things. It's just that tranquility doesn't

---

3   Full disclosure: I assisted in proofreading an early version of *Valencia*, working with Chip Smith of Nine-Banded Books, which is the publisher of the book you are reading now. None of the suggestions I made affected the book beyond noting basic typographical errors.

lend itself well to the creation of great memoirs *unless* we discover something really and truly nasty lurking behind the scenes. And that nasty lurking thing must *happen* to us. The experiences we seek out seldom count for much. Good modern memoirists need at least one crazy or alcoholic parent, one unsettling example of sexual abuse, or a slowly developing drug addiction. And if such a writer is lucky, maybe one of his family members will commit a terrible crime or get killed in the course of a terrible crime. Then he'll be rolling in the sort of life experiences that make up the modern memoir.

But even if one meets these qualifications, the competition is stiff. If one is going to write a memoir about a prosaic life, even a life with the requisite supply of misery, one needs to be a very good writer because otherwise the readers will be tempted to say, "Shitty parents, stranger touched me, drugs during college, terrible job, why am I reading this when I can clearly write my own memoir because everyone in the benighted Generation X more or less lived the same fucking life."

James Nulick takes his cues from all three categories: he's lived a life that seems all too common to most Americans; he has catastrophic life experiences that make for interesting reading (or, at times, prurient rubbernecking); and he is a very good writer, profoundly good at times. We recognize Nulick's life, as recounted in the pages of his novelized memoir *Valencia*, as our own in some respects. And even as we are appalled at some of the things that happen, we are drawn in and held in by a unique and near-poetic style.

The way that Nulick writes reminds me of conversations one has with an old friend. You know this person well, but you haven't spoken in a while. Your friend mentions an incident or a person in the course of telling a story, thinking that you know all about that incident or person. You don't know, but you don't interrupt because your friend is on a roll and you feel certain that in a moment you can either interject and ask a question or your friend will throw you enough clues in the conversation that you can piece it together. Sometimes you realize the information isn't important enough to interrupt, because the point of the story isn't about that person or place—it was just mentioned as an aside in the course of a larger topic.

This is how Nulick writes. Sometimes he mentions a name before we know who that person is. The first time this happened I wondered if I had overlooked the person as I read and I almost backtracked in order to find the original mention that I was sure I had missed. It can be a bit odd if you begin reading *Valencia* unaware that Nulick writes in this way, treating you like an old friend listening to a long conversation about his life, but once you warm to his method of storytelling, it feels completely normal, almost comfortable. You feel like you are being drawn into Nulick's story in a manner that implies that he considers you a trusted friend, and that's an unusual feeling when reading a memoir. I've often felt some commonality with memoirists as I read their works but this takes that feeling of knowing an author in a direction I can't recall ever having experienced before. You may want to read *Valencia* through once and then read it again a week or so later. That second reading will cement the feeling I'm talking about. You'll be an insider to a story told by a friend.

That sense of commonality takes you only so far, though. I find it interesting how many books about Gen-X men have come across my radar lately, and I am mindful of how I respond to them. In Ann Sterzinger's *NVSQVAM*, the protagonist Lester is utterly lost and a complete asshole, but as I state in my preceding discussion, he's "our asshole, my generation's asshole." It's hard to hate your brother, even when he's a prick. It's also irrational to hate a child you may have created, yet the boomers despair of me and mine, and for some reason we all seem to be poking Millennials with a stick, as if we didn't fucking make the world they were born into, like we didn't raise them or mold them into the people they are now. Yet Nulick, inasmuch as this memoir (technically a novel) accurately reflects his real life, at times inspired in me the same nose-pinching desire I felt toward Sterzinger's Lester. I just wanted to smack him as he artistically destroyed his life, almost as if he was modeling his destruction on those who came before him, the ones who set the example for the lost, dissolute, addicted writer.

Because the content is peripatetic, it makes a succinct synopsis difficult. According to my own interpretation, *Valencia* is an account of the experiences of a young man who has gone to a Spanish hotel called Hotel Valencia. He has chosen this hotel because he recalls fondly a boy with the name Valencia. He has brought along plenty of reading material and a box of pictures. This young man has AIDS, and I ultimately decided he had gone there less to die from his illness than to commit suicide.[4] The first-person narrative begins at the end, so to speak, and Nulick reveals episodes from his life in no particular order (or perhaps he is telling stories in the order in which he looks at the pictures he keeps in that box). Whatever the intended structural order, the stories all end up linking together to tell the whole of the story of Nulick's life and how he came to be the man in the hotel room, ready to die. While *Valencia* is definitely *not* an Everyman tale, there are pieces of it that will have a familiar resonance for most readers. There is also a grubbiness about the memoir that reminds me of the movies *Slacker* and *E.T.* Yes, *E.T.* Go back and watch it. It's such a grubby film in certain details—unsupervised kids, a distracted mother, improvised meals in a shambolic home filled with candy and junk food. The same grubbily dysfunctional atmosphere is palpable in *Valencia*, where unprepared parents and fractured families create extended

---

4   As I was entering data for *Valencia* in book sites, I glanced at the back cover blurb where it spells out clearly that the narrator was committing suicide and not passively dying. So, you know, my bad.

relationships, some good and some bad. And at the center of the familial discord is a lost writer. He is a child struggling to find his place, a homosexual man trying to find his way, an asshole fucking up every good chance he's given, and he is a little boy living with a grubby father in a grubby trailer. Again, I have no idea how much of this is exactly a representation of Nulick's real life,[5] so bear that in mind as I proceed.

The book begins with a plaintive account of the sexual liaisons that gave the James Nulick in *Valencia* HIV. The sequence is seedy and unfortunate. It involves crack cocaine and it happens after James fled from a lover who beat him up in a meth-induced rage. He considers killing the man who gave him the virus that causes AIDS, but the futility of such an action influences his decision not to do it. These opening scenes are very dark and they set the tone for the disjointed narrative that ultimately concerns the struggle of a man confronting his own death. Knowing we are going to die, life can seem futile.

> When Thomas Bernhard received a minor award for literature in 1968 he said Everything is ridiculous, when one thinks of Death. To the winds bearing down upon us death is meaningless, and the truth is ultimately unknowable. I felt an animal sadness. I would die as each of us do, knowing very little of myself. Loved ones would forget the shape of my name on their lips, the classic monosyllabic simplicity of it. I tried finding sugar in the salt. Very few men know how they will die. I would.

Understanding how James will die—slowly ravaged by a virus acquired through bad decisions—renders such self-knowledge especially harsh. It falls in line with so much of what makes life so tiresome and prosaic, being just another in a long line of things that happen to James. Splintered family, molestation, relative poverty—then a viral load. It's hard to achieve a sense of life mastery when the defining moments amount to nothing you orchestrated yourself.

But the passivity of the more earth-shattering elements of these "just happened" events is mitigated by great writing. Nulick is especially good at dispensing one-liners that put his plight into perspective. Observing what death means to him, James says:

> Death is a library with all the lights turned off. Each story sits on the shelf unread, the words dead and without meaning. A care-taker pushes a broom in the darkness, whistling a tune. He smells of cheap cologne. The tune is offensive, but what can you do? That's the beauty and the horror of the grave. The inactivity is wonderful, but we are left to the whims of the living.

What can you do indeed, sometimes even before death happens.

---

5   As I edited this discussion I noted that when I am speaking of James Nulick the writer, I tend to refer to him as "Nulick." When I refer to "James Nulick," the character in this book, I call him "James." I think I did this unconsciously because I am genuinely unsure what content is true and what is not.

This sense of passivity, of being placed into situations where things happen, is a theme. When James' father opens an office for his repossession business, he has his little son work for him.

> When my father was off on errands I was left to answer the phone. It was an important job. I was always scared when I was left alone at the wrecking yard. Keep an eye on any customers that come in, my father said. What could I do? I was four foot one.

Like many of our age peers, James was asked to grow up far too soon. I often think the creation of little adults in the minds of small children is partly to blame for the passivity that so many of us experience later in life. We learn how to be adults when we are weak and afraid and it's hard to grow out of such a state. We become stand-ins for grown-ups in our own adult lives.

Part of this passivity stems from the familial tumult that characterizes James' young life. When his adoptive parents get divorced, they are soon remarried to new partners, bringing in new step-siblings, and then new half-siblings. And there will be more divorces and remarriages. And the birth mother will make an appearance. It goes on and on this way, so much so that I initially needed to make notes of the family links in James' story. If I had to take notes, imagine what it was like living through such discord. Such a life creates roots that spread far and wide but those roots, however strong, can be shallow.

> Having three mothers, all semi-detached, I've never understood the easiness between mothers and sons. Boys should not know their mothers. I realize I'm in the minority. When friends or co-workers suffer the death of a mother, I can only guess at their emotions, as if I'm an observer from a distant planet. Surely not all sons are as removed from their mothers as I am? I stand outside the majority. The world insists we celebrate motherhood with cakes and cards. I prefer silence and Epsom salt.

And those roots can be awkward. Widely spread, shallowly covered and very awkward. It almost seems predestined that James' best friend in college is a woman whose artistic claim to fame involves the creation of an enormous paper mache vagina. When she grows up and meets James at a college reunion, she brings her teenage son to the bar with her. As awkward as that would have been with my mother and me, Heather and her son show none of the weird distance and passivity that James does. He imagines himself with them:

> I watch Heather interact with her son. I pretend she's my wife. I pretend he's my son. There is an unspoken beauty between them. I will never have a son or a daughter. This brings great sadness. I catalog it and order one final round.

Great sadness gets cataloged in my life, too. Yeah, children were never a possibility for me but I still look at parents and their kids and think about how excellent it would be to purge the mistakes of the previous generation with new, shiny people. You just have to pretend there is no possibility that you will recreate the distance and weirdness with a new generation. Surely it will all be fine, right? Surely there's no chance that, despite your best intentions, those kids will grow up to remember you as the force that ensured they remain passive observers of life, exhausted by all the things you made happen to them. Circle of life, *hakuna matata*.

I should also mention examples of Nulick giving the reader information before we really understand what these names or places mean. This conversational way of writing comes upon us immediately. We read about "paper sister 1965" and "Olvera Street" and Fleming's truck—all signposts that make no sense when we first encounter them, though they aren't too jarring and they don't disrupt the flow of the story. In fact, this approach serves to illustrate that James had an awkward connection to family that might not make sense to those who were hatched in a more traditional nest.

It was only when I read the book a second time, knowing what I knew after the first reading, that I came to see *Valencia* as a long conversation with someone assumed to understand the whole of the story out of the gate. It may seem like a problem, that you may need to read a book a second time to enjoy it fully, but that worked in its favor for me. Almost all good books benefit from a second (or third and fourth) reading. Nulick programmed this need to reread as a feature and I think it's a pretty clever way to approach writing. It's certainly more rewarding than my experience with more pedestrian memoirs, where the author feels compelled to explain every new name in depth in order to make sure the reader is able to tag closely along.

There are moments in *Valencia* that are terribly funny to me and I wonder if these moments are funny to anyone else. James makes friends with a morbidly obese older woman he meets through work. He decides she's worth knowing when he sees her with a copy of J.G. Ballard's *The Atrocity Exhibition*, and they become friendly, dining out and exploring bars. One night she invites him back to her place:

> Eventually she invited me to her condo to see her library. **I'm queer, I said. I know, dear.** You said you wanted to see my books, she said. I scanned her collection. An idea of her began to coalesce. I'd read some of the books on her shelves in college. Others were fairly recent. There were several by a Canadian author who dabbled in speculative fiction. I'd always meant to read her but never got around to it. There were very few translated titles. I made a note of it. A collection of bottles sat on one end of the kitchen counter. A bottle of rum was among them. She saw me eyeing the bottles. Would you like a drink? That would be great, I said.

Emphasis mine. It's such a cliché—asking someone back to see your books—that when it actually happens it's seen as a sexual pass. Of course this seriously obese, much older woman wasn't interested in James sexually but it speaks of the relatively diminished value of actual book collections that inviting someone to see your books is no different than asking someone up for "coffee" after a fun date. I just found that "I'm queer, I know dear" quite funny. Yes, yes, you're gay, but let's see my books. Books and booze—these two are soulmates, in a way, because she's the sort of woman who knows where to watch the fireworks on Fourth of July, a place no one else went, a place where they could open their lawn chairs and drink themselves stupid as the sky exploded in pretty colors, and she wanted nothing from him other than his company. Hers was one of the few friendships James had that didn't make my latent maternal nature cringe and she came and went far too quickly.

Another amusing event occurs when James and three other young men are put up by their college in New York for the summer in a sort of study-program. James is placed in a room in a hotel with a musician named Chad and is lent an electric typewriter by a writing mentor. James and Chad do not get along and Chad is an inconsiderate roommate, but instead of dealing with Chad and making the most of his time in New York City, James just doubles down on stereotypical writerly misbehavior:

> Thoreau wrote how vain it is to sit down to write when you have not stood up to live. I believed Thoreau was telling me I needed to fuck more whores, but I wasn't sure.

I guess I should mention that I hate Thoreau. Don't preach to me about your self-sufficiency in the woods when a couple of women make you dinner on their own dime every night. Anyway, James just behaves like an asshole, but then again so did Kerouac and Burroughs and even Ballard at times:

> I bent over the desk and opened the window. The cold wind of Manhattan settled on the blankets. I grabbed the cord of the Selectric and gave it a quick yank. I picked it up with both hands and tossed it out the window. Jesus Christ! Chad yelled. A loud crash sounded in the street below. Someone shouted fuck you! I opened the door. Chad and I raced toward the elevator at the end of the hall. I can't believe you did that, he said. It was very late. The night clerk looked up as we passed his desk. I buzzed the door open. I pushed the heavy glass toward the night. A few people strolled along the sidewalk like ghosts. Ana's typewriter sat in the middle of the street, mangled and unrecognizable.

It's kind of funny, on one level, that James, when annoyed with Chad, throws a typewriter out a window. It's classic asshole writer self-destructive behavior. It doesn't hurt Chad that James destroys the typewriter. It hurts the woman who loaned it to him, and it hurts him. Yet it's such a fine example of perverse behavior that I couldn't help but be amused. But I also wanted James to make amends. We can forgive legends their outrageousness but skinny wiener kids on a college toot we grant less leeway. The arrogance of such a move is all we see—not the drunkenness or the desperation or the sheer unthinking stupidity.

And it does bite him in the ass.

> Murray asked how my writing was coming. Not good, I said. I threw Ana's typewriter out the window the other night. Fourteen floors down, I said. I illustrated my point by dragging my index finger from an imaginary hotel window to the imaginary street below. Booooooooooeeeewwwwww, I said. Pwwwwwccchhhhh. Someone kicked me under the table. Murray laughed. You're joking? I wish I were, I said. Murray didn't appear surprised. I laughed and took another drink. I was young and strong. Murray was old and weak. What could he do to me?

It helps that James is self-aware enough to see in himself the arrogance of the young and it helps even more that Murray wrecks his shit by removing him from the hotel and sending him on his way. The program rents him a room for three nights away from the other program participants but James has no money to get home and Murray doesn't really care.[6]

James' life then takes a left turn down a dark road with a transsexual named Magda, which is a story that needs to be read and not discussed. James has an interesting life lesson with Magda but Jesus, it's some heavy shit. Heartbreaking and unsettling. I can't help but wonder what would have happened had James not followed the script that many young writers seem to think they have to follow. Little bit of work, lots of substance abuse, terrible behavior. It plagued me as well, back when I thought I was going to be a writer. I don't know why. I'm infinitely more demented and interesting when sober and exhibiting good behavior. But there you go. And it is the streak of this tiresome ritual in me that made me find the tossing of the typewriter initially amusing, even as I knew it was a shitty move that wold lead to bad things.

But even as some of the text amused me, I found myself feeling restless because this is a restless memoir. James caroms from one group of friends to the next: skater boys much younger than him who exploit his affection for them and get tons of free stuff from his job at a mini-mart; a group of men who consume alarming amounts of cough syrup and take reckless driving trips in the middle of the night; Linklater-esque drunken and stoned escapades with people who eventually leave his life and never come back. The names flow through the book, they come and go, and his connections to them remain vaguely after they are gone, as he wonders what happened to them, but mostly they are gone, and he remains as semi-detached with them as he does his mothers. Linklater is a very good reference for this memoir—the

---

6   In another passage I found hilarious, the writer William Vollmann suggests that James become a sort of male stripper to make money. Vollmann's presence caused me to buy a couple of his tomes to read when I finally get some spare time.

tired and boring suburbs, the descent into substance abuse as a substitute for real adventure, a constant array of people who all sort of seem similar to one another, the wasted landscape of youth culture in a country that hates the young even as it sexually and socially exploits them.

Here's a good barometer of whether or not you will enjoy this book. Do you have an affinity for this sort of unfocused life, told in no particular order, with enough truly terrible and interesting life details to prevent it from being a meandering example of the blankness of the modern experience? If so you'll like it. I had finished reading *The Motel Life* by Willy Vlautin just before I reread *Valencia* and the two books began to bleed together in my mind, one a work of fiction, the other a type of memoir, both arising from the same place. Both books mine the vein of blue-collar messiness, of modern boredom, of parents who fail, of unpaid bills, catastrophic mistakes, miserable tragedy, substance abuse, loose connections, strange bonds. What prevents these books from being akin to a short-term prison sentence is that those catastrophic mistakes and miserable tragedies lend gravitas to what is otherwise a bleak, tiresome landscape. I don't want to discuss these events in *Valencia* in any detail because they are the foundation of the book and need to be experienced. However, they do happen—childhood exploitation, a frightening and fatal fire, among them.

I think the best way to look at this book is to consider the way that James reacts to the following suicide (he is musing about the literary and artistic suicides that took place in hotel rooms, which is one of the reasons I think he is looking at suicide as opposed to being fatally ill from AIDS):

> The actor George Sanders checked into a hotel in Castelldefels, near Barcelona, and gobbled Nembutals like Tic Tacs. Like most creative types, he left a note. Artists are uncomfortable with silence.

• • •

> Dear World, I am leaving because I am bored. I feel I have lived long enough. I am leaving you with your worries in this sweet cesspool. Good luck.

• • •

> Snappy and cheerful. The Brits have a wonderful sense of humor, even when they are sad.

Valencia deals with the extraordinary boredom that makes up much of our lives, musing about the prospect of leaving the boredom behind forever. It shines a familiar light on the experiences of those who do leave and those who remain. Artists like Nulick are uncomfortable with silence, which is why he tells us all about his life in its tiresome details—the dead chihuahuas, the childhood friend who moved away, the repetitive nature of young artistic people idolizing the early deaths of writers like Kafka, and the miserable addictions of those who lingered, like Burroughs. Nulick's story is told in a language that is both direct and poetic. It might be a perfect synthesis of the modern memoir: honest and self-aware, punctuated by drama, by funny moments, by infuriating moments. And painfully sincere. I recommend it, even though I wanted to twist James' nose until he paid for a new typewriter and sobered up. I liked him. I liked his story, too.

FURTHER READING

Tulsa
Larry Clark

Diary of a Teenage Girl
Phoebe Gloeckner

A Sorrow Beyond Dreams
Peter Handke

Letter to My Father
Franz Kafka

The War Zone
Alexander Stuart

The Book of Dolores
William T. Vollmann

PERVERSE

That which is perverse varies so much from reader to reader that what I consider perverse may not matter to you, but I do find it interesting how people react to certain book titles before they ever get to know what's really between the covers.

NECROPHILIA VARIATIONS
By Supervert
Supervert, Inc. (2005)
Original post: 02/05/2010

Why do I consider this book odd?
Well, the author goes by the moniker Supervert. That is what I like to
call a clue. Also, necrophilia. Yeah. *Necrophilia.* Another clue.

Finally! A book that straddles the psychic terrain of *eros* and *thanatos*. In
my experience, when a book is touted as an *eros-thanatos* cocktail it usually
turns out to be straight-up *thanatos*, with little or no *eros* to dilute the intensity. So I am thrilled to finally discover one that contains both in equal
measure.

I guess I should state up front that am no necrophile. It annoys me even
to have to say that, but if I don't I'll get emails. I do, however, spend a fair
amount of time photographing cemeteries, so in a sense, I understand the
appeal. Death holds a quietness and a comfort—remembrance and the very
real sense that the worst has happened and you have nothing left to worry
about.

So you pick up a book called *Necrophilia Variations* and it seems safe
to assume the stories are going to be about sex with the dead, right? But
what *else* do you expect? Because while
Necrophilia Variations does indeed include tales of sex with dead people, it
soon becomes clear that Supervert is
mining a deeper vein. Far from being an
exercise in revolting extremity, the stories in this collection are about people
dealing with the confluence between
sex and death. Though the notion of *le
petit mort* is not new, the idea that the
sex impulse is closely linked to death remains hard for many to see. And though
visionaries and poets, like Baudelaire,
Rimbaud and Mirbeau, have tread this
ground before, it's refreshing to see these
sorts of ideas explored by a modern
for moderns. Supervert's stories are

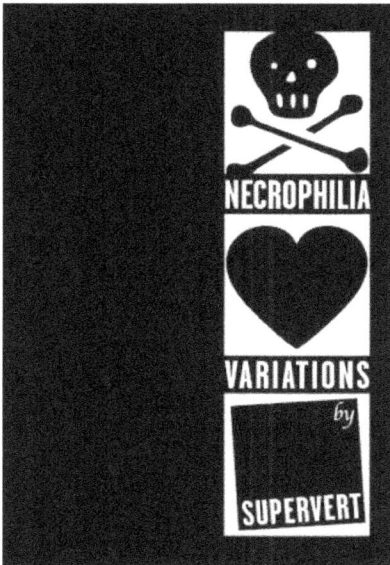

heartbreaking, sickening and humorous. He pushes boundaries, and not just for the sake of pushing.[1] The stories have merit, and the ideas are intriguing. This really is intellectual *eros* and *thanatos*, not grotesque splatter for those who like lots of excessive violence with their sex.[2]

The book opens with a quote from Baudelaire:

> It is one of the considerable privileges of art that the horrible can be transformed, through artful expression, into beauty.

I don't know if it's because I've been immersed in the outré for so long or if Supervert manages to make the horrible so beautiful that I don't see it for what it is, but I'm mainly struck by the beauty, emotion and depth of his stories.

Let me tell you about the ones I liked best.

"Death and the Dilettante" is one of the more humorous pieces. Marisa is a death-goth poseur who wants a coffin, which her boyfriend provides in a rather outlandish fashion. He has no illusions about Marisa. She's little more than a worthless pain in the ass, but she is beautiful, with gorgeous hair and an aloof, imperious manner, intoxicating to him. Her comeuppance is fabulous.

"How Would You Like It" is one of the few stories in which sex with the actual dead is contemplated, suggesting that perhaps there are those among us who, once departed, would not mind becoming the object of the necrophile's attentions, and would, perhaps, arrange their deaths and burials to accommodate such desires. Since I could not care less what happens to me after I die, I found this intriguing. Donation to medical science or cremation or ... necrophilic relief? It makes little difference to me. While I have no desire to consort with corpses, what would it matter what happened to my body after I've finished using it? And while all sex has a philosophic and moral aspect—necrophilia brings up this interesting point:

> Would it bother me to think of my body having sex without me... In a way this is a funny question for a necrophile to pose himself. A pedophile cannot become a child, a shoe fetishist cannot become a shoe, but a necrophile can and does flip over to the other side.

Perhaps it is only fitting that the true necrophile should avail himself or herself to those with the same paraphilia, given that this is a rare chance to engage in a two-way paraphilia.

---

1   I felt "pushing for the sake of pushing" was on full display when I read Bataille's *Story of the Eye*—a book I am now willing to say I simply did not "get" and likely never will.

2   Not that there is necessarily anything *wrong* with that! It's just that too often it comes off clownish, as certain authors attempt to one-up each other in the gross out factor—this book is not that sort of thing.

"Graveyard Survival Training" is an overtly hilarious story of what happens when a drunk egoist visits his dead girlfriend's family vault only to have everything that can go wrong go wrong.

"Suicide by Strumpet" is exactly what it sound like—a man wants to die at the hands of a prostitute. He just has problems finding a willing hooker.

"Ars Moriendi" is the story of a man and a woman looking at art in a museum and talking about odd things, prompting the man to synthesize mortal and aesthetic impulses in a way that has been explored so often in art and poetry but is still nice to read. As they look at paintings, the woman, Muriel, says:

> "You know what I find creepy?" she said, straightening up. "It's the thought of a man painting a woman like that and then living with the painting for so many years. Imagine getting old while the woman stays young and healthy up there on canvas… It's like dying slowly beneath the gaze of a beautiful woman."

Muriel does not understand the appeal, insisting beauty only exists in the physical realm, seeing beauty as something that can only exist in life. The man stops trying to explain how appealing it would be to die under her gaze, but he thinks about it:

> It would be exquisite to die in front of you, I thought. Not that I want to die, exactly. It's just that, when I go, it would be sharper and sweeter to do it in front of you. You could be a sort of cheerleader for my demise, easing me into non-existence, distracting me with your beauty while I slip into the abyss. My fingers, twisting in your hair, might tether me to the earth for a few moments more. The very sight of you would make me loathe to go, My heart would beat wildly and stubbornly in my fading flesh. My very last thought would be, "How lovely! How beautiful."

Then we come to the story that hit me the hardest and is with me even now.

"Diary of a Sick Fuck" is about a man who is at war with his base instincts, his love of the macabre and disturbing. As his girlfriend, a psychology student, is studying a theory about how the images people select can reveal their most hidden impulses, he is looking at horror after horror on the computer monitor. He edits horror stories, and tries to tame his obsession by moving to romance. He just ends up editing romance books into horror novels.

When he finds pictures on his computer that he has no memory of searching for and saving, he begins to suspect that his girlfriend, Vivian, is confronting him with the images. One day he finds on his computer screen a picture of a Nazi taunting an elderly Jew with a match, about to set his beard on fire, to the delight of the other Nazis present.

> The picture itself showed nothing terrible—I mean the terrible thing, the burning of the old man's beard, had yet to happen, and so in that sense, the

picture was not particularly repellent. And yet, there was indeed something horrid about the picture. It was the spectacle of the strong brutalizing the weak, the young exploiting the old, the group terrorizing the individual. You could not help but have a moral reaction to the image, and yet at the same time, I liked looking at it, so that a tension ensued between the two sides of my person, the moral and the morbid.

The violence he sees online enters his life in a sort of twist that I could have done without, but I had to remember that these are stories, not essays on the human condition. As a story it's excellent. A possible interpretation is that to submerge oneself into horror can lead to violence. I see it far differently. I think the message is that it is the failure to recognize the duality of man's soul, the act of stifling that duality as if it is somehow wretched or wicked to have an interest in the darkness, that makes us go mad.

I'm old enough to recall a time when one could not dredge up the worst one could imagine with a mouse click. I also remember back when rotten. com and worse submerged me into a world of horror and numbed me to it for a while, when the Internet was nothing but sex, horror and Usenet. In seconds, I could be confronted by the sort of pictures that transgressive 'zine makers once had to rip out of history books. The Internet changed what it means to be a voyeur and what it means to be sick. For a year or so, I felt like a sick fuck, too. I understood the narrator in this story all too well, the feeling of being a monster, the feeling of being an outcast because of what goes on in my mind, yet knowing that I looked at the darkness because I could not *not* look. It was that looking that urged me to vegetarianism, or toward certain politics. Looking, for me, was not the base voyeuristic act that many moral purists make it out to be. Looking at the worst humanity can do, seeing the worst that happens to us when we die, confirmed my humanity.

Necrophilia Variations weaves together beauty and death, horror and anticipation, all to provide an exhilarating look at the human condition. At times it feels like poetry. This is not a book for those who want Cannibal Corpse lyrics in prose form. It is a book for those who see the beauty of death, for those who know that all acts of love and sex will ultimately end in some form of death. It is a book for those who know that ceasing to exist can be a form of ecstasy for the dying and those who love the dying and the dead. People who can look at a lovely person and wonder, "What would it be like to die at your feet?" People who can look at the worst humanity can wreak and still find beauty.

FURTHER READING

The Trial of Gilles de Rais
Georges Bataille

THE NECROPHILIAC
By Gabrielle Wittkop
ECW Press (2011)
Original post: 10/02/2014

Why do I consider this book odd?
Self-explanatory, I think.

Another day, another book to lure in the good people who land on my site by way of a Google search for "necrophilia." I'm not being flippant. I've seen the analytics and I know you're out there. I was directed to Gabrielle Wittkop's *The Necrophiliac* by a commenter who recommended this book as an example of literature she believes to be truly sexually transgressive. So of course I had to get a copy. When I look back on what I've read these last few months, I realize that for me this was the Summer of Sexual Deviance. It wasn't intentional, but there you go.

When I was a young woman I had a definite affinity for the gothic, especially the gothic obsession with death and decay. Poe and Baudelaire were among my favorites, as were Flannery O'Connor and Shirley Jackson. I read plenty of splatter, too, just foulness for the sake of foulness. But it wasn't until I read the book *Exquisite Corpse* by Poppy Z. Brite that I experienced a true marriage of splatter with a love of The Word. (Poppy Z. Brite is now a transgender man named Billy Martin, so while I will call him "Brite" as I discuss his earlier work so as to avoid confusion, I also will use male pronouns.)

With *Exquisite Corpse*, Brite created a Southern Gothic splatter novel that pushed boundaries so far that it took me a long time to understand what I thought of the book. He borrowed from serial killer culture and used the creepiness of New Orleans to excellent advantage, but I think the most important element of his book was that, aside from a far too early brush with Hubert Selby, it was my first literary *wallow*. As so many of my extreme horror discussions indicate, good extremity is rare. I had plowed through my share of extreme horror, but I had never encountered extremity as compelling and purposeful as what Brite was serving up in *Exquisite Corpse*. Brite's novel focuses on a Dahmer/Nilsen-like duo of serial killers united in their desire to keep a rotting corpse with them for as long as possible. The descriptions of evisceration and putrefaction and (yes) necrophilia are deployed for sensory impact. The tactile experience of intestines in the hands, the sweet, cloying smell of rot, the visceral sensation of, well, viscera—it's all fabulously crafted. Murder, necrophilia and corpse desecration described with a sickening beauty. The novel was deeply disturbing on almost every level, which made my enjoyment of the gorgeous decadence all the more unsettling. What does it say about you when you admit, "This depiction of a terrible murder, evisceration and subsequent decomposition of a raped corpse is some of the most sensual prose I've ever read"?

Lucky for me that was two decades ago, before the Internet came along and made everything far less shocking. But there was no avoiding the deep sensuality of Brite's prose. It was such a delicious wallow in the forbidden and revolting. After some reflection, I realized it was beautiful. It was beautiful because it revealed that gazing upon the horrible can be so very aesthetically and emotionally satisfying. *Exquisite Corpse* is the literary equivalent of casu marzu and balut—a delicacy. And that which is a delicacy is often that which is the most outrageous, harmful, foul or upsetting.

While *The Necrophiliac* is not so sensual, not so visceral, had I not read *Exquisite Corpse* all those years ago, I might not have had the proper frame of reference to appreciate Wittkop's novel. What I know of necrophilia doesn't lend itself well to an extra-sensual or romantic notion of corpse love. The Molly Parker film, *Kissed*, touched on the subject of romantic necrophilia, but it was a very artsy and refined affair that never really addressed the cold, messy realities. The grotesque story of Dr. Carl Tanzler comes close. Tanzler stole the corpse of a young woman who had died of tuberculosis, mummified it and equipped it with a special "channel" so he could have sex with her for seven years. But it wasn't like Tanzler loved "the dead"—rather, he was obsessed and fixated on one specific body. He didn't want to make love to corpses. He wanted to make love to this young woman and, since he could not have her in life, he had her in death.

So in a sense, *The Necrophiliac* covers new ground, at least for me. There are details that may satisfy readers looking for a nasty wallow, but Wittkop's novel is at its core a romance about doomed love. Lucien, the narrator and diarist, is less interested in decay but it doesn't deter him. He is a romantic necrophile, genuinely drawn to specific dead people. He has no sexual or age preference, rather concentrating on specific people who are compelling to him. His relationships are, by the nature of his paraphilia, short-term, and he mourns the loss of each romantic partner as their decay takes them away

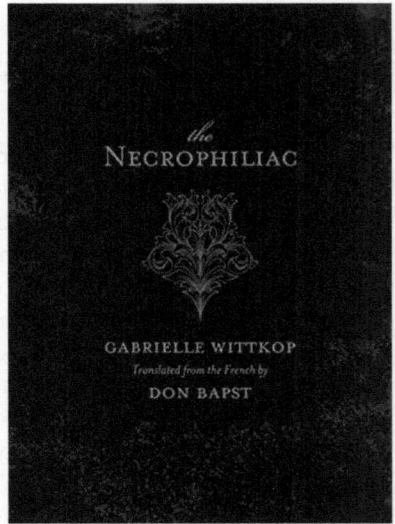

from him. He experiences a complete breakdown during his last affair and it feels very much like Lucien plans it this way, tiring of a life in which those he loves will always be taken from him.

In his diary, Lucien, who is a wealthy antiques dealer, describes in detail his love affairs with dead people. He has just enough charm and self-control to be able to move about in society without revealing his true nature, but he also seems to be creepy enough arouse suspicion (his cleaning ladies remark that he smells like a vampire). Lucien is very expressive, and for him the dead have vastly different personalities. That sentence seemed odd to me as I typed it because my first impulse is to think that *of course* the dead have personalities, as they did in life. But they don't, do they? We imbue the corpse with the traits we knew it possessed when it was alive. A cadaver has no more personality than a chair. Lucien didn't know most of the living people whose bodily remains he caresses and personifies. He doesn't know what their traits were as living beings. His specific sexual desire permits him to attribute what he believes to be their individual motivations.

You don't get an easy introduction to the ideas in this book. From the first words you are smacked with Lucien's foul reality and worldview. The opening entry finds Lucien describing a little girl whose body he is inspecting (how he obtained this body is not made clear but we will eventually learn the many ways Lucien courts the dead):

> The grey eyelashes of this little girl cast a grey shadow against her cheek. She has the sly, ironic smile of those who know a lot.
>
> [...]
>
> This little girl is worth the trouble. It's truly a very beautiful dead girl.

But the next day Lucien finds out how sly this little girl really is:

> Yesterday evening, the little girl played a mean trick on me. I should have been more careful of her with that smile of hers.

What did this little girl do? Well, at the beginning of her "courtship" with Lucien she begins to vomit up bile.

> Open in a Gorgon mask, her mouth didn't stop vomiting this juice until its odour filled the room. All this rather spoiled my pleasure. I'm accustomed to better manners, for the dead are tidy. They have already released their excrement in leaving life as one disposes of an ignominious burden.
>
> [...]
>
> She's not one of the dead from whom I have any grief in separating myself, the way one deplores having to leave a friend. She certainly had a mean character, I would swear to it. From time to time, she emits a deep gurgling that makes me suspicious.

But like many men before him, Lucien has a change of heart when it comes time to separate once and for all. The next night as he is preparing the little girl by wrapping her in plastic so he can throw her into the Seine, he sees another side of her. It softens him.

> ...she suddenly emitted a desperate sigh. Pained, prolonged the S in Sevres whistled through her teeth as if she had already suffered some sort of intolerable sorrow over her next abandonment. An immense pity squeezed at my heart. I hadn't done justice to the humble, harsh charm of this child. I threw myself on her, covered her with kisses, repentant as an unfaithful lover.

He prostrates himself before the child, brushing her hair, oiling her body with perfumes, and, yes, having sex with her. She still ends up rolled in plastic, dumped in the Seine, but at least Lucien has a rapprochement before he abandons her.

The writing is so elegant, so filled with romance, that you may forget for a moment that you are reading the words of a necrophile. That his partners are dead and they have no slyness, no kindness, no lust, nothing. It's all the creation of this man whose passions force him to project life upon the dead.

Or is it? Is one of the points of this little book to show the humanity in the paraphilia? To let us know that those who love the dead may, in fact, experience the world in a completely different way? That the reason a person becomes a necrophile is because that person can see in the dead what the rest of us cannot?

I don't know. But it's interesting to speculate.

The chapter I found the most interesting focuses on Lucien's recollection of other necrophiles he has encountered in his life. At a funeral for a distasteful distant relative of his, he runs into a male and female pair of necrophiles and finds them lacking in refinement.

> ...an extremely banal couple dressed in mourning, whom I guessed—I don't know why—had come to enjoy themselves. No doubt the music, the funereal chants, and the bombyx had the custom of acting on the man in a specific way, for I distinctly heard his companion whisper to him a precise question in the state he found himself in. She used a vulgar word, something from an army barracks, of a crudeness that took me aback. There, was, I believe, another outline of a gesture, but I wasn't sure.
>
> [...]
>
> These two were only watered-down necrophiliacs, and their preferences couldn't rise to the height of passion.

But passion is a double-edged sword, as Lucien discovers when he comes across a more brutish necrophile. The scene concerns the death of an actress that he knew. While she was not particularly beautiful, Lucien still wants her. After her burial he creeps into the cemetery during a heavy rain storm, picks the caretaker's lock, steals a shovel and digs her up.

As I struggled to climb out of the slippery grave with my package, I saw a man who was hiding behind a tombstone to watch me. His dark silhouette, his thick neck detached themselves neatly from the depth of the night. An atrocious fear spread over me. This man was going to follow me, kill me maybe. Or more likely, he was going to denounce me. Without knowing what I was doing, I abandoned the actress and fled as fast as my anguish permitted me.

Lucien makes a clean getaway but the paper the next day reveals bad news.

In Montmartre Cemetery, the body of a well-known actress had been discovered, stripped of its clothes, disemboweled and horribly mutilated. The rain had effaced all clues. So the revolting man who had spied on me had taken advantage of the fruit of my efforts. How horrible! I burst into tears of vexation and grief.

Lucien grieves because he is a romantic necrophile. He would never have savaged a corpse in the rain, on the ground, in the mud. He would never have mutilated a corpse, disemboweling it. Not for him this *Exquisite Corpse* delight in the damage done—he wants to court the dead in his own peculiar manner. He wants to take them back to his place. Wash them, dress them, perfume them, admire them, commune with them.

Again, this is a romance novel—it's just that Lucien romances the dead. Indeed, there are passages that would work in any highbrow romance novel. One of the dead Lucien loves the most is a woman named Suzanne. Listen as he describes her, as he recounts his interaction with her:

Suzanne… A petty bourgeois with finely coiffed blond [sic] hair, a polka-dot blouse under a classic suit

[…]

Suzanne had soft skin, almond-shaped nails. In lifting her blouse, I noticed the carefully shaved armpits. She was wearing underwear made of a crepe de Chine of a quality far superior to that of her suit, from which I concluded a dignity, a genuine feminine modesty. Her body showed that she had always respected it with a sort of asceticism, but a likeable, civilized, lenient asceticism.

[…]

I carried Suzanne to my bed. With a trembling hand, I removed her bra, her little panties. The wait took away my trembling; the tension of my desire didn't permit me to prolong the moment of possession any further.

[…]

I locked myself in with Suzanne. Honeymoon without music and without bouquets in my glacial room where the lamps burned. I didn't respond to the telephone. One or two times, despite my forbidding, someone rang the doorbell. My heart beating, holding my breath, immobile in the dark vestibule, I was all ready to do anything to defend my treasure.

Suzanne is not the most beautiful corpse Lucien makes love to, but her corpse possesses qualities that make her the love of his life. She becomes the experience by which Lucien measures the happiness or sadness of future unions. And of course, in a very real sense, she becomes the one who got away. But, then again, all of Lucien's partners get away at some point, as the natural process of decomposition ensures. He is genuinely devastated when Suzanne goes the way of all the others—wrapped up and dropped into the Seine:

> My life, my death, mixed in Suzanne. In her, I entered into Hades; with her, I travelled all the way into the oceanic silt, tangled myself in the seaweed, petrified myself into the limestone, circulated into the veins of coral...

While the romance alone saves *The Necrophiliac* from being a complete wallow, the way Lucien approaches his paraphilia is thought-provoking. He doesn't experience the dead, the decay and rot, the way most people would because in death he sees (and smells) the beginning and end of the world, the transformation of the base into the sublime.

> Their fine powerful odor is that of the bombyx. It seems to come from the heart of the earth, from the empire where the musky larvae trudge between the roots, where blades of mica gleam like frozen silver, there where the blood of future chrysanthemums wells up, among the dusty peat, the sulphureous mire. The smell of the dead is that of the return to the cosmos, that of the sublime alchemy.

Perhaps I'm jaded, but I'm surprised by how unperturbed I was in reading this book. I was not shocked, not disgusted. I was more captivated by Gabrielle Wittkop's fresh and unusual treatment of a very outrageous subject. She does not pander, and her strange book is so finely written and considered that one can just immerse oneself in its pages without feeling exploited or disturbed. At the same time, she doesn't quail from "hard" content; rather, she makes the appalling beautiful, imbuing it with a humanity that is wholly unexpected.

Further Reading

Exquisite Corpse
Poppy Z. Brite

Frisk
Dennis Cooper

BIZARRO & CO.

Bizarro is hard to pin down. Many books are bizarro without actually being marketed as "bizarro" novels. Books that implement fantasy, science fiction, extreme horror, magical realism and an at times cartoonish quality to the storytelling can be considered bizarro. Bizarro as a genre is dismissed in academic circles but I've found some of these books to be among the funniest, most disturbing and most appealing that I've discussed over the years.

BLEAK HOLIDAY
By Hank Kirton
Apophenia (2014)
Original post: 07/09/2015

Why do I consider this book odd?
One of the stories ends with this line: "And that guy turned out to be an asshole."

Hank Kirton may be the best odd short story writer you've never heard of, and that sucks because he is rapidly becoming one of my favorite writers. *Bleak Holiday* is a near-flawless collection. It could have been better edited, but that's often true of small press releases. It's still an excellent book. Kirton has a style that is immediately identifiable as being Hank-like, yet his stories cover a lot of intellectual and literary ground. He handles magical realism in a manner that I generally don't expect from male authors, and some of his stories remind me a bit of the sort of work Amelia Gray puts out—amusing, fey and ultimately good-spirited weirdness. At other times he pulls off something akin to the dark, nasty, postmodern flatness I associate with the mundane horror of A.M. Homes. And his stories are infused with an uneasy strangeness—an overall noir—that is very much his own. I fancy I can see the sources that inspire Kirton—one story even reminded me so much of an old R. Crumb comic that I had to scour the Internet to make sure I was remembering it correctly—but who knows? That's the danger of writing—you never know what a demented Pflugervillian housewife will think of when she reads your stories.

Kirton's voice remains very strong, even as he reminds me of other artists, and with one exception, every story in this collection soars because the eclectic spirit of his inspiration works in its favor. The one story I didn't particularly care for? Chalk it up to my own deep distaste for the old Nancy Drew books. The story, **"Janet Pepper, Girl Detective: The Mystery of the Kitchen Cabinet,"** is a parody of those tiresome books with a very adult twist. While I can see how it's amusing and how others would find it very funny, I just can't

shed the memory of all those gormless books being foisted upon me in grade school and how awful I found them, how boring they were, like chewing microwaved oatmeal. Kirton's parody wasn't that subversive to me given how little I could tolerate the source material.

So with that qualified criticism out of the way, let me discuss the stories that I liked best in this 21-story collection.

"Jelly" is the story of two friends who discover a bizarre dead creature and undergo a transformative experience. It's a very simple story but the transformation is unusual and open to interpretation.

> He looked at the pine tree in front of him, suddenly seized with an overriding impulse to touch the rough bark. He reached out and his fingertips stretched like upspearing tendrils until they circled the tree. He felt the whorls and arches of his fingertips merge with the grains of the wood and experienced a spiraling wave of pure pleasure so intense he was rendered blind with bliss.

> Music and light. He was becoming music and light.

This story brought to mind a song from Ulver's album, *Perdition City*. "Nowhere/Catastrophe" is a celebratory death song, a song of final transformation.

> *You fly, or rather float, drift Through an enormous dark room A room of noises*
> *[...]*
> *No planets, no meteorites If anything, perhaps fine dust clouds of exploded music*
> *You float there, somewhere between pleasure and fear*
> *[...]*
> *And your last thought is that you have become a noise*
> *A thin, nameless noise among all the others*
> *Howling in the empty dark room.*

There is a sense, when one is reading well-crafted fiction or listening to well-composed music, that there is a confluence of ideas that run their course in writers and artists, and you find them all drawing from the same inspiration, like their works are trees growing from the same roots. There's even an E.E. Cummings element to this story, with word creation ("upspearing"). Neologisms generally cause me despair, but Kirton pulls it off. In a story where people disintegrate into music, the coinage ensures a melodic meter in the sentence.

"Sweetie-Pie Begonia Babyhead" is the stuff of nightmares. Sweetie-Pie suffers from a bizarre birth defect—her head and brain didn't grow along with her body. She retains the head shape and mentality of an infant even as she blossoms into womanhood. She lives with her neglectful grandparents who leave her alone, tied in a large playpen, when they want to go out. Sweetie-Pie falls victim to several teenage boys in a Richard Laymon-esque gang rape. One of the boys doesn't participate and regrets what happens to Sweetie-Pie, but his bland, self-serving guilt doesn't soften the imagery and disgusting implications in this story.

Sweetie-Pie reminded me of an R. Crumb strip and it took me a while to track it down but I persevered because I just needed to see if I really was remembering the drawings accurately. Turns out I was—there is an R. Crumb strip where the character known as "Devil Girl" has her head shoved down into her neck, leaving her visually headless even as her body moves around. A recurring Crumb character, "Mr Natural," arranges the head-neck-cram and delivers Devil Girl to another recurring character named "Foont." Foont then violates Devil Girl's headless body, and she's not too happy about it when her head pops back out. Evidently this was shown in depth in the film *Crumb*, which I had seen in the theater a couple of decades ago, and I suspect that is where I recall it from. Devil Girl's galloping, robust, headless body was my mental stand-in for Sweetie-Pie. See if you can find scans online. It's a seriously disturbing comic of the id, as is Kirton's story.

My favorite story in the collection is **"The Story of Cilantro-Rose."** It's a price-of-admission story so I won't discuss it in depth lest I spoil it. It's a soft-fantasy piece about a midwife who finds herself pregnant with an otherworldly child. It explores maternal fear and love, and it subverts the Garden of Eden myth, showing a world where the single woman eats the apple and it doesn't result in sin or damnation, but rather a renewed sense of positive purpose. I'm generally not drawn to this sort of fantastic premise but this story was remarkable in how much it affected me.

"The Fear Detector©" is one of the shorter pieces—some of the stories are very short, nearing flash-fiction length—and is the source of "why I think this book is odd." Mr. OTC, a good-natured man who is also a complete misanthrope, needs to read it. The story is remarkable in part because Kirton manages to subvert his own flow. And while much of the collection could be described as intense or outré or even outrageous, this one rips the tablecloth out from under the dishes abruptly and with humor.

"White Napkins by Alfred Henry" is another piece that is ultimately good-natured, written in a style that is enchanting but damnably hard to define. Kirton infuses that style with what can only be called Cormac McCarthy-esque post-apocalyptic darkness. My distaste for McCarthy may not be spelled out, as such, but suffice it to say he's not my cup of tea. That Kirton evokes elements of his work to such great effect is thus remarkable. In "White Napkins" a bartender remembers a customer who came in four nights in a row, tossed back a few, and then would begin to write on bar napkins, filling them sometimes with lunatic ideas and drawings, but mostly with strange prose. The prose is disturbing, unexpected and at times absurdly funny. Here's what was on the seventh napkin on the third day the man wrote at the bar:

> A man has an erotic liaison with a beautiful blonde woman every day at two p.m. He stares up at her. She is wearing a red dress and holding a glass of wine. The billboard is worn and some of it is missing, but he ejaculates into the dirt every time.

> An infant cries abandoned, skin blistered and peeling, dying of dehydration. If he hadn't been abandoned, he would have become an inventory clerk.

> A man who lives in a rusted tow-truck sees a badger.

"Reunion" is a sad, creepy, dark piece about a young porn star's return home after many years. In retrospect, I should have known exactly where this story was going but I didn't because Kirton's manner of writing only seems predictable once he's led you to the conclusion he wants you to reach. This one is a slight inversion of the trope that all sex-workers have been sexually abused by some male authority figure, and the porn star achieves a small but very satisfying revenge at the end. I don't want to discuss this one too much because I may spoil it. Not quite a "price of admission" story but it's still very much worth preserving the tension in this story.

Oh my god, **"The Grapeshot Buffet."** The protagonist, Gaston Molyneux, is loosely based on the notorious and disgusting French Revolutionary soldier named Tarrare. Tarrare was an eating machine, capable of consuming unbelievable amounts of food and food-like substances in a single sitting. Entire sides of beef, litters of puppies, baskets of fruit, dung heaps, amputated limbs. He once was accused of eating a toddler who had gone missing. It is believed he died as a result of an infection caused from swallowing a fork. What caused his insatiable hunger is unknown but the condition of eating everything is called polyphagia. Tarrare was disgusting—evidently he reeked and his body odor alone was enough to repel even the filthiest soldier—but Kirton tells the story of Tarrare through Gaston in a manner that evokes the horror of being trapped inside such a foul and insistent body, of being a monster during a time when cruelty and revenge and horrible death were the norm, of being considered a monster by the monstrous. Had this story been a mite more disgusting in its detail, it would have been the perfect extreme horror story.

"The Man With the Big Pants" is a cruel and intense story about a man willing to do anything to keep his ex-wife from winning in the divorce settlement. There aren't a lot of surprises, but the single-minded purpose of the character is compelling. Flat and almost emotionless, it's a story of a bad man doing bad things that he didn't plan out very well. His marginal luck sees him through.

"Black Eye Glue, Hobbies N' Stuff by Beatrice Brown" was just vile and creepy and horrible and wonderful. It's a hobby blog written by a woman who collects Norwegian children. Yeah…

I'm going to end this discussion with **"Analysis,"** a sweet and amusing story in the vein of something I would expect from Amelia Gray, one of the finer magical realists and absurdist writers working today. Bobo and Iko seek therapy from a certain Dr. Frichtenstille, who once dated Thelma Todd, and whose receptionist looks a lot like Margaret Dumont. His nurse looks like Snow White:

> She led us to a small white empty room. She shut the door and faced us. She had a mole. It was peeking blindly from her front pocket. She did not speak. The mole did not speak.
>
> We all looked at each other, except for the mole because it was blind. Or dead. There was a lot of white glare in the room. We thought the room needed a calendar.
>
> Time passed.
>
> And passed again.
>
> The only sound was the hum of ventilation.
>
> The time we spent in the room was a bowl of motionless red Jell-O. It was a broken fiddle string. It was a wet chipmunk freezing to a tree. It was a bloody tooth wrapped in a Kleenex.

Eventually the doctor arrives:

> "Please be seated," he said in an accent thicker than mud and toothpaste.
>
> We sat down on a black leather couch. It squeaked in a way the mole hadn't.
>
> "Now then," he said, "I understand that you are abnormal."
>
> "Eccentric," we said.
>
> "Ah yes, eccentricity. The last refuge of the inventory clerk."

As the good doctor asks Bobo and Iko to scrub down a naked woman, they make a miraculous breakthrough, one that will surely help Bobo and Iko (even though we have no idea what, other than eccentricity, brought them to see a therapist).

It's not often that you find a writer who has command over the horrible, the sickening, the absurd, the sweet, the beautiful and the humorous. Kirton has mastered such eclecticism, and sometimes he can manage all of it in a single story. Generally writers, the good ones at least, focus on the part of the human condition they want to convey and concentration permits them to explore the world in great depth. Kirton seems unable to limit his focus, absorbing all that is maddening, stupid, grotesque, hilarious, evil, lovely and hopeful and distilling it all into brief explorations of life that ring utterly true even as he uses fantasy, science fiction and magical realism to tell his stories. Others might describe him as being all over the map—and not as an insult or criticism—and that may be the case. But even as he meanders from one horror to the next beauty to the next poignant sadness, there is a core of fascination with people and the worst and the best they do to each other and themselves that unites all these stories. I absolutely love this collection. Highly recommended.

Further Reading

The Atrocity Exhibition
J.G. Ballard

10 a Boot Stomping 20 a Human Face 30 Goto 10
Jess Gulbranson

SLEEP HAS NO MASTER
By Jon Konrath
Paragraph Line Books (2012)
Original post: 01/29/2014

Why do I consider this book odd?
I am mostly reminded of this Hunter S. Thompson quote: "Weird heroes and mold-breaking champions exist as living proof to those who need it that the tyranny of 'the rat race' is not yet final."

T his book gave me the fear. Like I was going to go full Gonzo-paranoid and end up locking myself in the backyard shed with a gallon of whiskey and a loaded shotgun. As I read parts of *Sleep Has No Master*, I thought, *I wrote this. I wrote this book and I forgot and Konrath sent it to me in some passive aggressive ruse in order to show me he has access to my thoughts and computer and probably even my medicine cabinet.* I read the title chapter out loud to Mr. OTC, who peered at me nervously from his side of the bed, no doubt wondering if I was on the verge of (another) psychotic break.[1]

Jon Konrath's *Sleep Has No Master* is a short story collection that tells the tales of a dude who does stuff, sometimes alone, sometimes with his loser friends. Through these dudes, Konrath hits on too many aspects of my life for this book to be legal. Some topics covered in detail far too specific for my comfort include: insomnia, unlikely car customizations, Varg Vikernes, specific conspiracy theories, a complete inability to use eye drops as a child, over-the-counter sleep aids, corpulent Asians friends, microsleep, the bizarre belief that one's eyelashes are inverting back into one's eyelid (mine grow sideways, toward my nose, and it's a problem), spending most of one's work days searching eBay listings, self-torture via medical sites, Crispin Glover, GG Allin, disgust for how badly movies tended to represent computer capabilities in the

---

1   There was a ... problem when I read a particular *Zippy the Pinhead* cartoon that referenced the Oscar Mayer Wiener-mobile, but that was years ago.

80s, the Voynich manuscript, fear of what diet sodas may be doing to my brain, and so much more. When I can tamp down the paranoia, I see that Konrath's book is deeply funny, indeed verging on hilarious at times. But the paranoia lurks because who really could have so many weird idiosyncrasies in common unless something nefarious is happening?

The story **"Sleep Has No Master"** contains a paragraph that pretty much confirmed for me that Konrath needs to go to jail, the fucker, because I *know* I wrote this at some point:

> I started researching sleep disorders online, the usual death spiral of fanatical WebMD queries, and stumbled upon something called fatal familial insomnia. It's an incredibly rare four-stage inherited prion disease that starts with progressively-worsening insomnia and panic attacks. Then you dive into a wonderful world of Nixon-esque paranoia and vivid hallucinations. By the third stage, you cannot sleep at all, and your body starts breaking down with rapid weight loss. It all leads up to a crippling dementia, before you finally buy the farm. Barbiturates and induced comas, which you'd think would knock you out, actually speed up the disease. In one famous case, the doctors completely nuked the patient with heavy sedatives, but his brain would not shut down. This is the exact kind of thing you don't want to read at 3 AM when you've been awake for 40 hours straight and you're trying to find some homeopathic bullshit to turn off your brain for the evening.

Seriously, I am rethinking the microwave brain scanners that Gloria Naylor insisted were used to read her thoughts.[2] You know how when your cats freak out and run frantically into the other room, only to stop immediately and then stare, wild-eyed at the wall? I think that's when Konrath is warming up the brain-microwave.

"The Nostradamus Scat Porn Prophecies" is a story. It really is. Beyond this quote, I cannot comment on it:

> Woodrow Wilson will eventually return to Earth using a wormhole portal locator designed by H.G. Wells and hidden in the hollowed-out husk of a rhinoceros penis, to tell everyone that he was not responsible for anything Glenn Beck said, except that he did bang Leni Reifenstahl in a bathhouse, albeit strictly anal. I never pay attention to politics, so I don't know. I don't care. Politics is like the dumb man's version of snuff films: it shouldn't be legal, involves extensive police bribery if you don't want to get caught, and takes place in shitty motels with bad carpeting. Hunter S. Thompson was the first and last person to write honestly and honorably about politics and we all know how that turned out.

I know for a fact that HST spent a lot of time in the garden shed with a gallon of whiskey and a loaded twelve-gauge. We all know this fact. It's a given.

---

2   See pages 55–63.

But it wasn't until **"The Marshall Manifesto"** that I understood that Konrath needs to be stopped. Seriously. This story revolves around one of the narrator's loser friends, named Marshall Applewhite (not *that* Marshall Applewhite[3]). It's a suitably lunatic and enjoyable romp, but it was the following passage that more or less ensured that I will one day seek vengeance against Konrath because, aside from the part about the telegraph transmissions, this is just way too on the nose for me, a woman who has had dreams of Ludmila, one of the supposed lost cosmonauts.

> My Bighikistan high school experience involved roughly the same amount of antagonism and torture as a Muslim fundamentalist growing up in the rural south: the magic triumvirate of hazings, beatings, and shunning. Instead of being over-involved in high school football or going to a church that decreed that everything from pinball machines to left-handed thread bolts were Satanic, I spent most of high school obsessed with the failed Russian lunar lander program, masturbating to obsolete telegraph transmission protocols, and trying to decode the Voynich Manuscript, a 15th century codex that has yet to be broken. That meant my circle of friends consisted almost entirely of Fat Mike, Marshall, and this other guy named Ricky, who majored in shop class and later stole a National Guard M-60 tank and went on a three-state rampage.

"This Is Like a Dog Trying to Crap a Peach Pit" is also a story, in a way. It discusses the relative inanity of animated films as well as the awesomeness and complete horror of flea markets and auction sites. The opening paragraph would trigger a less medicated woman.

> I was trying to pitch a sitcom yesterday at Pixar about Norwegian church burnings, and the reception area had this huge bowl of *Up*-themed promotional anal beads. "Tax write-off," said Rayat Beherduk, my screen-writing partner and extreme black metal consultant. (I don't know much about Black Metal, and every time I try to call Fat Mike and ask him some involved question about Dimmu Borgir, he goes on a four-hour tirade about why Stacy Keibler hasn't done porn yet.)

I dare you to try to write a paragraph with more pop and fringe culture references. You can't do it. You'll cramp up. Then we come to the following paragraph, which is also weirdly specific to my set of interests as well as being really funny.

> Once eBay came online, I spent many man-years at my job as a dermatological technical writer cruising through the lists of obsolete computers, beaten motorbikes, and lightly-used competitive enema equipment,

---

3   Marshall Applewhite was the leader of the Heaven's Gate cult at the time of their mass suicide in 1997. Convinced that behind the Hale-Bopp comet was a spaceship that was coming to take their souls to an afterlife, they killed themselves so their souls could ascend into the craft. The cult suicide was headline news all over the world, in part because Applewhite and seven other men in the cult had castrated themselves so as to eschew sexual desire and live more ascetic lives.

instead of writing about topical medication for dematophytoses. But much like my neighbor's anger at missing the boat on beef certification, I'm now chronically depressed that I never parlayed my time in the late 90s on eBay into any fame or fortune by flipping beanie babies or buying heavily undervalued classic cars and selling high for massive profit. A dozen years later, and I'm trying to pitch animated sitcoms about Varg Vikernes and Burzum.

All joking aside, I feel really strange encountering someone else who taps into the same pop culture and social references that preoccupy me, not to mention the overlapping psychological and physical maladies. And he's a dude. And it's also completely unsettling because now I sort of get how insane I must come across in real life. Yeah. This book was an education even though I'd more or less read it all before BECAUSE IT CAME STRAIGHT FROM MY BRAIN.

"Princess Di's Mercedes and the Dead Man's ASL Chimp" is possibly the funniest story in the book. It's a snack-sized version of J.G. Ballard's *Crash*, mashed together with enormous bowel movements, a tiny BAMF Asian mother, autopsy reports, a Boba Fett suit, an angry monkey, poorly functioning elevators, all deep fried in a police scanner and liberally seasoned with images of my very wonderful friend, Arafat Kazi. I mean, I don't know if Konrath actually knows my friend (whom I also know as Futhman), but I see Arafat every time Fat Mike is mentioned in this book. Fat Mike is what Arafat would be if he smoked pot all day rather than drinking scotch and pretended to be a dead princess rather than dote on his cats and play the drums. If Konrath doesn't know Futhman, he needs to introduce himself and send him a copy of this book in thanks for being a retroactive inspiration.

> My pal Fat Mike had some deep obsession with Princess Di conspiracy theories, and spent countless hours trying to convince everyone she was killed by the CEO of a landmine manufacturer. Aside from spending his free time photoshopping her likeness onto a variety of pornography, he ran with a group of guys who cos-played and re-enacted her death by driving junk cars into viaduct walls at high speed while in drag. They'd been looking for the genuine article, a cheap Mercedes, for years, but always had to settle for low-end Korean imports, doctored up with fake Mercedes placards they scored at a Chinatown replica maker on the down-low.

The story also contains this exchange:

> "Hassids can't push buttons or work electronics on the Sabbath, so they have Shabbat elevators that stop on every floor. And I thought DefCon 5 was the one right before nuclear war."
>
> "No, DefCon 1 is right before the missiles launch."
>
> "I don't think so. It was in fuckin' *War Games*."
>
> "That movie was about as scientifically accurate as a Southern Pentecostal

church pastor that's been eating lead paint," I said. "Ferris Bueller breaks into NORAD with a 300-baud acoustic-link modem AND he gets to bang Ally Sheady (sic)?"

See, crap like this haunts me—from that inexplicable A Flock of Seagulls video where the gormless singer prints out a high-quality photo of his beloved on a dot matrix printer to all the computer scenes in the movie adaptation of *The Rachel Papers*. *Real Genius* was good enough that you could sort of tune out the crappy computer stuff, but we all know what happened to Val Kilmer, so succeeding in this realm has its price.

"Dwarf Meth Madness" begins in a manner that I think we can all identify with—buying deodorizing products to minimize the stench of cat in our homes. The narrator works in a record store and Nick Hornby-on-LSD-style conversations ensue.

> "Why do people burn sage at new building ceremonies?" Uncle Iggy asked.
>
> "Because uranium is more expensive," I said. "How the fuck am I supposed to know anything about this mystic hippie bullshit? I grew up in a state where not mentioning Jesus in every third sentence was punishable by law."

Because he's an asshole, Konrath is also not afraid to get quasi-meta with it. From **"Oil Change Introspection Therapy"**:

> The oil change took hours, days, while I camped out in the quickie lube waiting room, crowded in a Zodiac lifeboat I managed to pull out of my trunk before they took my car away. It contained everything I needed to preoccupy myself for the next week or two: a bunch of tablet-sized food rations, a desalinator, marker dye, a deck of naked lady playing cards. I took my copy of *Rumored to Exist* by Jon Konrath and a *Satanic Bible* to keep busy. I initially thought the service would take fifteen minutes, as advertised, but the idiots pulled my entire engine and started bringing it piece by piece into the waiting room, asking me, "do you think you want to replace this? It looks worn out." I called a lawyer, but corporations are people, and people are assholes, so I had no choice but to ride out their busking attempts.

While there he gets an email from a girl who sent a sexually-perverse message to him by mistake and he reminisces about college, when he met her. But that shit was tiresome and one can argue he got what was coming to him because he took this girl to a Taco Bell and ran statistics on how traces of Diet Pepsi people drank when they got Mountain Dew from the auto-refill counter might make pilots have seizures. He is abruptly ripped from his reverie:

> The mechanic called me from the front counter of the oil shop. He held a piece of a fuel injector that didn't even belong to my car, caked with carbon, dried peanut butter, and dog shit, an obvious ploy to get the gullible to fall for their $200 "injector cleaner" treatment. Can't a man get any errand done without some nameless corporation trying to tack on yet another fucking

unneeded service? *Time to go into Beast Mode*, I thought. *Tell these fucking savages a new filter and five quarts of the lowest grade oil, nothing more.*

It is his gift for fine hyperbole that makes Konrath hark back to the better rants from Hunter S. Thompson. Swine, savages and corporations all fucking with the honest and often completely baked man. Konrath manages to create a sort of HST-rage and humor and sieves it through an absurd filter to avoid the overworked pastiche that most people who channel HST end up with.

I felt like I had finally lost my mind reading **"50 Shades of Napalm,"** wherein Konrath digresses into his experiences buying a home:

> I'm also in the middle of buying a house, and I had to sign and fax about a thousand pages of stuff to our mortgage people, and I considered taking something like a State of California Hazardous Materials Disclosure form and retyping the whole thing but replacing "underground tank" with "throbbing cock" and "asbestos paint" with "underaged cunt," but that's too much work, especially since all of the documents are PDFs, and I'd have to run them through some kind of OCR software, and that would involve forty days and forty nights of shopping for said software, then paying three hundred bucks for something that would eventually turn the disclosure form into the textual equivalent of a Jackson Pollock painting.

We closed on our house on Halloween. The bank personnel were dressed up because nothing says solid, financial stability like five slightly overweight women dressed as cats wandering around the office, offering orange and black sprinkled cookies. A woman in a BoPeep costume handled the largest financial transaction I have ever been involved with and likely ever will be. The dude selling the house was a retired marine and he seemed like he hated us—he refused to make any sort of small talk or make eye contact and basically threw the keys at us when the last paper was signed and he and his stunned wife hied themselves out of the bank. We later learned that our house is subject to intermittent spells wherein sections of the house take on aspects of non-Euclidean geometry. You don't want to look at the doorways too long in this house. I get vertigo looking out from the master bedroom into the hallway and landing because, from certain angles, the ceiling disappears. I should take pictures when it's really bad. We hung some paintings of H.P. Lovecraft at the top of the staircase, hoping to show our willingness to work with the house and not disturb whatever eldritch abomination lurks beneath. So far we've been okay except for some foundation damage and all the goddamn cats.

But I digress…

Jesus Christ, Konrath and I should never be in the same room together.

I think ultimately what makes this book so fucking good is not that it clearly ripped off all of my memories and crammed them into a short story collection. It is so good because Konrath knows how to take the irritations of just being alive and turn them into something that some might call Kafkaesque, but I won't because I fear hipsters showing up and yelling at me for being so lame as to use the term. Nevertheless, Konrath has a keen eye for the details of mundane life and how they just absolutely suck. I recall Robert Crumb saying that he tended to blank out urban blight—like how electricity poles looked and the way urban streets were laid out—and he had to take pictures of such places and objects in order to reproduce them accurately in his drawings. Such things are visually unappealing but a drawing of a city street would be incomplete without them. Konrath is intimately familiar with blight—the eternal cosmic noise and pop culture references and memes and endless, almost Tarantino-esque conversations that make up the lives of the ordinary and often completely insane modern man. He finds a pathos where other writers might find ennui. He creates humor where others might find disaffected annoyance. To make the small indignities, random events and looming horrors of this life so very funny while maintaining a genuinely absurdist edge is its own genius. Konrath is, in his own unsettling way, a weird hero.

I cannot state emphatically enough how funny this book is. It was funny on a soul level, so specifically funny that it really did ring my paranoia bell until my increasingly diminishing common sense kicked in. Read it now. Now now now! Read and let me know what Konrath stole from your brain. I can't file a class action lawsuit on my own, you know.

FURTHER READING

Crash
J.G. Ballard

The Voynich Manuscript
Edited by Raymond Clemens

Cosmic Suicide: The Tragedy and Transcendence of Heaven's Gate
Forrest Jackson and Rodney Perkins

The New Annotated H.P. Lovecraft
Edited by Leslie S. Klinger

The Family That Couldn't Sleep
D.T. Max

How They Murdered Princess Diana: The Shocking Truth
John Morgan

Gonzo: The Life of Hunter S. Thompson
Corey Seymour and Jann Wenner

Reflections on European Mythology
Varg Vikernes

D.D. Murphry, Secret Policeman
By Alan M. Clark and Elizabeth Massie
Rawdog Screaming Press (2009)
Original post: 07/12/2012

Why do I consider this book odd?
Because the whole book is based on the delusions of a mentally ill man.

I've been thinking about the mentally ill a lot lately. I suffer from mental illness, but given my recent methods of fighting back, I am getting very close to being The Sanest Person You Know. These days I'm mostly just neurotic and nervous. But earlier this year I read Pete Earley's book, *Crazy: A Father's Search Through America's Mental Health Madness*, a sickening and sobering look at the mental healthcare system nationwide, but especially in Florida. When the face-eating cannibal case hit the headlines, my first thought was, "I bet he was a schizophrenic." News reports speculated it was bath salts but the autopsy said all the face-eater had in his system was marijuana. I looked it up and sure enough—Rudy Eugene, who tried to eat a homeless man's face, had a long history of untreated schizophrenia, resulting in many assaults and several arrests.

It is with Earley's book and the recent graphic example of the mental health care system failure in Florida in mind that I approach this discussion of *D.D. Murphry, Secret Policeman*. There's a lot that is funny in this book, which tells the story of Murphry, a man in active psychosis and delusion who believes he is part of a secret government trying to topple evil forces. Clark and Massie weave their tale of mental illness and conspiracy so well that at times I wondered, briefly, if the conspiracy might be real, that perhaps Murphry was ill but was also being used as a pawn by a malevolent force. So strongly does Murphry believe the truth of the misfires in his brain that the reader, even with strong clues that he is indeed a mentally disturbed man acting on his mind's warped feedback, cannot help but think there is some truth to such energetic and labyrinthine delusions.

It is impossible to discuss the structure and plot of this book in much depth because to do so would utterly spoil the book. So I'll just give a bare-bones plot synopsis and then discuss the parts of the first chapter that resonate with me.

D.D. Murphry is a mentally ill homeless man. When a social worker helps him get on disability or some sort of Social Security, he believes he has been hired by the "True Government" to spy on and take action against the "False Government." His interpretations of various situations, as filtered through his damaged mind, range from the hilarious to the deeply disturbing, often depending on how he reacts. He believes a librarian named Kate, who fears and loathes him, is his secret bride, given to him by the "True Government." He believes her nasty reaction to him is a facade assumed to throw off others and he longs for the day he can finally consummate their marriage. Kate inadvertently fuels Murphry's delusions when she teaches him to use a computer and access email, introducing Murphry to spam, which he sees as secret communications from the True Government. Clark and Massie really shine when they show how he manages to find real life corollaries to match the messages he thinks he received in the emails. Murphry careens from humorous misinterpretation to grave acts of utter mayhem as he tries to make the world a better place for the True Government and foil the actions of the False Government.

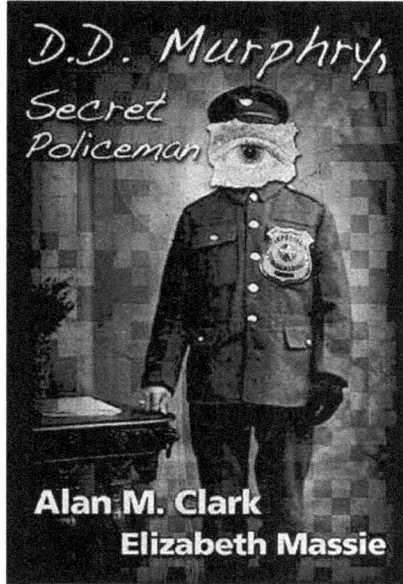

The chapters are divided into cases and the first chapter sets the stage for the novel very well. Murphry has an amusing inability to understand common turns of phrase and is utterly dangerous as he tries to interact in the world around him. Murphry sees what he thinks is a drug sale on a bus and causes the bus to crash, injuring and killing the riders (he goes limp and lets his body get tossed around and avoids injury). As he calmly walks away from the wreckage we begin to see what is fueling Murphry.

> A billboard overhead selling insurance asked him, "Are you sure you have peace of mind?"

> This seemed an unusual question. *Sure I do. A few innocent people were hurt, but that's the price of freedom.*

> But then, suddenly, he realized what the billboard's question was really about. He had almost forgotten his disguise.

> *There might be witnesses to the accident who could describe me to the non-secret authorities! I can't risk being stopped and questioned by the cronies of the False Government. They would not find me out, (I know what I'm doing) but time would be lost. That could mean lives lost!*

Quickly, anxiously, Murphry reached into his left hip pocket, removed his comb and placed it in his shirt pocket. *It's usually the little things people noticed about you*, he thought.

Murphry is a paranoid schizophrenic—for him every street sign, every scrap of paper, every news headline has been created and placed in his pathway by his handlers with the True Government. Everything in his life is significant.

Murphry walks away from the crash and joins a bus stop to wait for another bus. Here we are given a sense of how literal Murphry's worldview is.

> As he waited, he overheard two elderly ladies talking about a young man by the name of John. "He's got his grandmothers eyes," one of the women said. "They're green with flecks of paprika." Then they smiled.

> Murphry was outraged. These women looked like sweet grandmotherly types. How could they be delighted by such cruelty?

> Murphry'd received information about this crime via e-mail, he realized now, but his knowledge of it was incomplete. Now, at least, he had the name John to associate with the crime.

> His heart raced. He wanted to beat the truth out of these brutal witches. It was broad daylight, however, and there would be too many witnesses.

The two elderly woman should be glad Murphry decided against wrecking another bus to punish them for being so wicked, but he really needed more information about this "John" and where he keeps his grandmother's eyes. This is a frequent problem in this book, as Murphry is too addled to understand the colloquial meanings of phrases like "head on a platter" or something "costing an arm and a leg."

But what does Murphry mean that he realized that he had heard of the case via email but only now realized it? Well, the same messages that Murphry picks up from billboards he can also receive in email.

> Murphry gave his e-mail address out freely on the web and so received a lot of junk mail filled with paragraphs of nonsense word conglomerations. He transcribed the parts that seemed to have meaning into word processing documents in the sure and certain hope that messages from his superiors would be revealed.

> Sure enough there were always messages waiting for him. In truth they were just partial messages and it took quite a bit of work and intuition on Murphry's part to pry the relevant fragments out of the nonsense and assemble them coherently. He had to relax and work only with those words and phrases that resonated for him. Slowly but surely, each time he checked his e-mail, he would add to the assemblage until the story of a crime was revealed.

Here's one of the assembled messages and how Murphry interpreted it. He has received this garbled message in an email:

"Just because women waterproof doesn't mean swim."

He opens his Word document and adds that phrase to the other spams he has "decoded" into a specific crime he is to solve or prevent:

"Along with the glossy orbs, Grandma sported six blue and purple sawmill tattoos, and her skink experiments had once saved the toenail industry. Back in the day, a mere glimpse of the bony plates of her wedding gown had caused 1920s megaphone crooners to swallow their own heads. Even when he was raised, she could still fire lap dogs from her armchair at blinding speeds. Spite for this was a waterproof woman who could not actually swim."

While I know just about enough about paranoid schizophrenia to recognize it in pop culture references, this sort of controlled paranoia, whether it is realistic or not, has a ring of terrible truth to it. The stories in this book are essentially nothing more than narratives of a very mentally ill man navigating the rough terrain of his mental illness, creating an entirely fantastic world that still operates within a "real" world. That's what is so menacing about Murphry, even as he is sympathetic and at times amusing. He is twisting the real world into his own strange world and it makes sense on a very basic level, even to the reader. Being able to decipher so clearly how Murphry interacts with an A-to-Z world, how he manages to create such a violent yet orderly chaos, pulls in the reader and makes for a very interesting interaction with the text.

Even as we see how Murphry combines a discussion about a shared genetic appearance with spam emails to conclude there is a strange crime he feels he must solve, there are still plenty of completely horrible and unsettling moments when the authors remind us that Murphry's illness is not going to be so easily understood. He sees messages in a woman's paisley blouse. He sees a woman in a black coat and assumes she is tracking him for the False Government. His inability to see the real world causes extreme trouble for everyone around him, causing him to harass people at the very least; at worst, his illness causes him to kill people or get them killed when things go completely awry.

One of the people who suffers because of Murphry's delusions is Kate. Poor Kate. Librarians are the unsung heroes of suburban and urban life because I suspect every single one of them has their own Murphry story to tell. In the same way I reacted so personally to Murphry's illness, I reacted strongly to Kate's plight. She kindly taught a homeless, mentally ill man to use a computer in her library branch, and he decided she was his secret wife, given to him by the True Government to keep his morale up, and continually unnerves her with his strange behavior until she can no longer maintain even the most basic civility. But her unhappiness doesn't affect Murphry as he believes her lack of civility is something he can easily explain.

> Although she most often glowered at him and responded sarcastically when he spoke to her, Kate was capable through the amazing complexity of her voice to simultaneously provide other messages just beneath the evident disdain, a susurrus of endearments and sweet, calming language, expressions of affection, of longing and sorrow for the charade they must endure and an entreaty for him to be patient. He knew he was the only one who could hear these lovely messages.

> *Everyone else probably thinks she sees me as a crazy street person.*

While one could fault Kate for not showing Murphry more mercy, one could not fault her for long if one imagines being in her place, the person at the center of Murphry's erotic imagination.

> While Murphry waited for one of the computers to become unoccupied, he gazed at Kate as she moved around the room. She was gorgeous, with her long red hair pulled tight into a bun at the back of her head and her broad, well-padded hips and huge breasts straining at the seams of her clothing. She was what some might call frumpy from outward appearance, but Murphry knew what a delicious body she was hiding to maintain her cover.

> She noticed him watching her. "Quit staring at me, you weirdo, or I'll have you thrown out."

> And Murphry was certain that was what everyone heard, but beneath Murphry also heard, "I'm so glad to see you, my husband. Be patient with me, my dear, my dear. Like a beautiful Orchid, my love blossoms slowly. I promise that when it is in full flower, the bloom will last and last."

Poor Kate. And poor Murphry and poor everyone who gets in his way as he eludes the Woman in Black and solves crimes.

All of this is from the first chapter. Just one. Murphry wrecks a bus, hears of the grandson who has his grandmother's eyes, eludes the woman in black, receives strange messages from billboards, harasses Kate at the library and interprets spam he is sure are messages sent from the True Government to alert him of crimes he needs to investigate. In one chapter we get so much—imagine what the rest of the book is like as Murphry's illness causes him to stumble from one unfortunate situation to the next, killing people he means to save, killing people who mean him no harm, and from time to time, engaging in just enough humorous activity to prevent this book from being too dark and too sad. The strange puzzle of his mind is also a pleasure to decipher.

D.D. Murphry, Secret Policeman is a nearly perfect novel. There were a few editing problems here and there, but nothing particularly intrusive. The authors managed to write in a way that didn't alert the reader in huge red letters that there had been a change in writers, though they kindly tell us who wrote what. Together they created a sad, interesting, brave, stalwart, creepy hero in Murphry.

My only real quarrel with this book is not the fault of the authors. It is strictly RDSP's error. Someone who offered a blurb actually said, "If you have ever wanted to know what sort of book Hannibal Lector [sic] would have read as a child, you have only to open *D.D. Murphry, Secret Policeman* to have your answer."

Seriously? Not only is Hannibal Lecter misspelled, but the premise of this blurb is ridiculous. *D.D. Murphry* is not a book to inspire a diabolical psychopath in knee pants. I simply do not understand why any publishing company would want such a fucking stupid blurb that so completely mischaracterizes a book. Bleah. I guess if this is my only quarrel, that's a very good thing. The book itself is tight, amazing, saddening and at times a rollicking read.

FURTHER READING

A Confederacy of Dunces
John Kennedy Toole

A Head Full of Ghosts
Paul Tremblay

MUSEUM OF THE WEIRD
By Amelia Gray
University of Alabama Press (2010)
Original post: 11/28/2011

Why do I consider this book odd?
Because the stories, if not technically classified as bizarro, are bizarro nonetheless. When they aren't bizarro, they are gently weird. When they aren't gently weird, they are outright weird.

I have a favorable disposition toward women named Amelia. I knew a girl in high school named Amelia Beebe and she was an interesting person. I also have a favorable disposition toward people who love cats. I remember the first entry I read on Amelia Gray's blog. It was a discussion about losing a kitty to feline leukemia. We lost a kitty to the dread disease as well. My heart bled for her.

Lest you suspect I'm going to give *Museum of the Weird* a favorable review because of my favorable dispositions, please note that I did not know about the cats before I started writing the meat of this review. True, I knew her name was Amelia from the outset. But since I can find it in myself to detest writers who share my own name,[4] I think I'm on firm ground.

It's her writing that won me. Fanciful, strange, unsettling, oddly sweet, vaguely sickening, amusingly awkward, Gray has a style that ensured I would reread a couple of stories immediately after finishing the book. Just because they were that good. There isn't a bad story in this collection, and my innate hypergraphia is taking a nap at the moment, so I'll just focus on the best of the bunch.

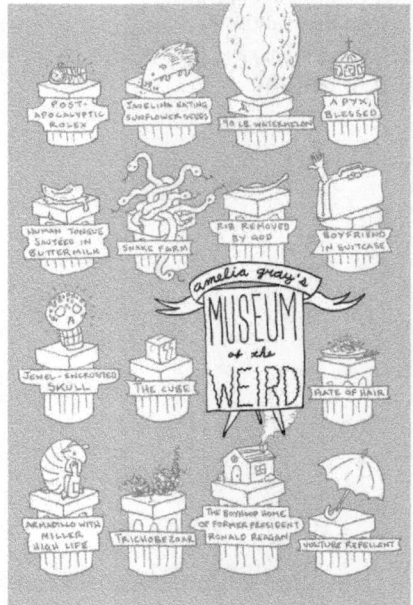

---

4   I am not a fan of Anita Shreve, though I guess I don't "detest" her so much as I just refuse to read her books.

Let's begin with **"Waste."** This is one of those stories that made me feel like I was going a little insane. It's a strange piece that I found compelling even though I find eating pigs horrifying (I cannot bring myself to eat any animal I can imagine keeping as a pet). Perhaps I liked the story because Gray's characters explore the whole, "when does it stop being pig and become pork" question, the line of demarcation between animal and food we all observe so we don't feel like monsters. A man called Roger, who works collecting medical waste from doctors' offices shares odd culinary experiences with his neighbor, a woman named Olive, who has lovely collarbones and works as a line cook in a vegetarian restaurant. Olive is an exotic foodie who creates culinary experiences out of the strangest meats, making a sickening but sweet sacrifice that Roger may not wholly appreciate even if his experience with medical waste gives him the stomach to cope. As a woman who loves to cook, is meat-shy, and given to feeling deep disgust for bodily processes that would require a medical waste pick-up, it was unusual how much I enjoyed this story. Sometimes I enjoy having my disgust pinged, I guess.

Food horror plays a significant role in this collection. In **"Dinner"** a woman finds herself with the unenviable task of eating a plate of hair in order to ensure her relationship continues smoothly, even though no one particularly knows why the plate of hair is on the table or even why it is important. It's a short, short story that reads more like the retelling of an unsettling dream, a dream I have not had myself yet it seemed rather familiar.

This dream-like element to storytelling continues in **"A Javelina Story."** A hostage negotiator finds himself paired with five javelinas at a hostage scene where Boy Scouts are tied to chairs. The pigs just want to eat, the hostage-taker misinterprets their actions and everyone learns an odd lesson.

Many of the stories are flash fiction, so short that you don't really process the punch until you feel the bruise on your psyche. Take **"Unsolved Mystery,"** a very short piece about the investigation into a bonesaw-wielding serial killer. These are the last two lines:

> What I don't say is, God's a clever bastard and I do respect him. He's everywhere.

"Thoughts While Strolling" does what it says on the tin. This story spoke directly to my particular sense of humor.

> *Jim Hale better train his dog.*

> That dog runs the perimeter of Hale's yard, treading the ground until he makes a ditch. Dog says, "Hey, come over here." When you do, that damn dog gives you a recipe for lemon bars which omits egg yolks and disappoints you sincerely.

Later in the story:

Frogs croaking.

Turn them over and tickle them, the young boys say to the girls. After much conversing and screeching, one brave girl picks up a slick frog, green as a fig. She flips it over so delicately in her small palm that the boys stop their shoving and feel strange for watching. The girl extends one slender finger and runs it slowly up and down the frog's exposed belly. When the frog urinates on her, she looks at the boys with loathing. She will later go on to swallow two goldfish alive.

"**Diary of the Blockage**" made me nervous because I can all too easily see this story happening to me. After a particularly upsetting incident involving a large iron pill, Mr. OTC can tell you that I will likely die from a foreign matter lodged, "it seems, between my esophagus and windpipe." The narrator of the story tries to get the substance to come up but cannot and she finds it hard to seek help for her problem:

DAY 2

I did not call the doctor. I went so far as to find my insurance card, but I could imagine the *remember Miss Mosely, well she has had a thing lodged in her throat* all within range of anyone with half a mind to be within earshot of the office window. I feel very sincerely that bodily functions have their place, but why would the toiletries and makeup and personal privacy industries all be such multimillion dollar successes if the place for those bodily functions was in public? To say otherwise is to disrespect culture.

This was really on the mark for me, a neurotic who is determined to stay well enough that I never need to avail myself of a bedpan (though I did once vomit on one of my cats because I was slow moving due to leg surgery and had stomach flu). I sense this story may be a pregnancy nightmare, too, for the lump in the throat later takes on a life of its own, in a way. All I know is that it was very important to the paranoid part of me that now takes her evening pills in far smaller clumps.

Gray's best story is "**The Darkness.**" A penguin and an armadillo meet at a bar. The penguin has Fought the Darkness and can speak of little else, and the armadillo has spread vegetable oil on her shell in an attempt to look pretty and shiny.

"You are a penguin and I am an armadillo," the armadillo said. "My name is Betsy."

"That's a beautiful name," murmured the penguin, who was more interested in the condensation on his glass. "I fought the darkness."

"You did not."

The penguin swiveled his head to look at Betsy. He had very beady eyes.

"What's your name?" she said.

"Ray," said the penguin,

"That's a nice name."

The penguin explains what he means by The Darkness and Betsy really wants to stay on track with flirting, changing the subject, but Ray demands his due.

"I suppose you think I'm some sort of *lesser* penguin, just because I fought the *fucking darkness* and tasted my own *blood*, because I haven't protected a stupid fucking *egg*."

Betsy felt tears welling up. *Don't cry*, she said to herself. *It would be really stupid to cry at this moment.*

"I honor your fight. I did not mean to disrespect you."

Ray sank back. "It's no disrespect," he said. "I'm just a penguin in a bar, drinking my gin out of a fucking highball glass for some reason."

"I was wondering why they did that," the armadillo said.

"Doesn't make any goddamn sense," said the penguin.

And it really doesn't make any sense but the story is delightful nonetheless, encapsulating all that is so banal about so much of human interaction in these unlikely beasts as they attempt, and perhaps succeed just a little, to make some sort of connection.

And there's more. There's one about a woman who writes a letter to her apartment complex complaining about the year's Christmas decoration contest. There's one about a man married to a paring knife and another married to a bag of fish. There's one about a man who takes up residence in his suitcase, much to the dismay of his girlfriend. There's the one where vultures come and loom over an entire town.

This collection was just too wonderful for me. Bizarre, magical, strange, nauseating stories, all crafted from a mind so focused on my own nightmares and uneasy dreams that I felt myself becoming paranoid at times. Luckily, Gray is such a talented storyteller that her gift overcame my nervousness. *Museum of the Weird* is highly recommended to anyone who wonders what would happen if one were able to combine Garrison Keillor, Bradley Sands and Raymond Carver into one writing force.

Further Reading

St. Lucy's Home for Girls Raised by Wolves
Karen Russell

AUTOMATIC SAFE DOG
By Jet McDonald
Eibonvale Press (2011)
Original post: 02/04/2013

Why do I consider this book odd?
This is an utterly fucked-up book that combines several genres into an unsettling, sometimes hilarious, sometimes trenchant whole.

When I began reading *Automatic Safe Dog*, I wasn't sure if I would be able to finish it because the story involves a business plan where dogs are turned into miserable, rigid, stationary pieces of living furniture. I can't stomach cruelty to animals and, in a way, the cruelty imagined in Jet McDonald's novel is all the more horrible because it's so bloodless, so matter-of-fact, so blithely accepted in the context of the narrative. I suspect the reason I was able to keep turning pages in spite of the content is because McDonald manages to subvert the use of abused animals in a horror-like parable. The dogs aren't victims of one specific madman; they symbolize a larger societal callousness. Somehow, that distinction made it easier for me.

The plot is dense and intense—a murder mystery in the vein of *And Then There Were None*, a frustrating love story, a story of corporate subversion and moral awakening—so know that my synopsis, by necessity, is going to leave out a lot of details.

The protagonist, a sort of sad sack Everyman named Terribly "Telby" Velour, works for one of a number of Pet Furnishings warehouses. He meets a new employee named Ravenski Helena Goldbird, for whom he develops a deep infatuation. As he tries to impress her one day, he engages in an antic that breaks the back of one of the dog-furniture pieces and gets fired. He later learns that Ravenski is the adopted daughter of the CEO of the Pet Furnishings firm and he decides to create a new identity in order to get a new job with Pet Furnishings. Ravenski is now part of the executive board and Telby cons his way into a job in R&D so he can be closer to

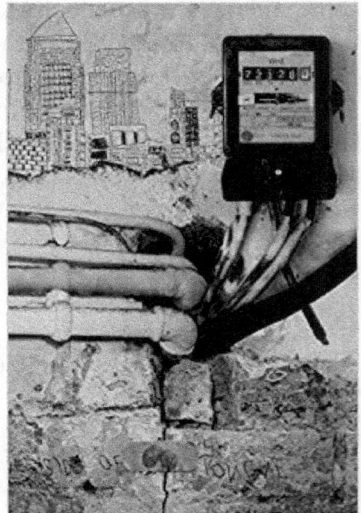

her. Telby enters a labyrinthine world of corporate espionage, personal viciousness, wanton cruelty and salacious behavior, all tempered by subversive hilarity and sly ridiculousness that prevent all the horror from becoming too much. As Telby watches his coworkers fall one by one to a mysterious murderer, he is forced to examine what he is doing and the morality of the job he has taken and the morality of those around him. Telby ends up being consumed by a metaphysical sorrow that he does not entirely deserve but has to experience nonetheless.

Despite the disturbing premise involving living animals being modified into living furniture (they serve as settees and footstools and TV stands), the narrative is infused with humor, high ridiculousness and an almost gentle sadness. It's a marvel, really, that McDonald manages to pull it off.

With my bare bones summary out of the way, I think the only way I can give you a real sense of what McDonald is about is to frame a few excerpts.

Here's one of the first passages I highlighted. It's important because it explains the title. Ravenski evidently suffered some sort of breakdown after beginning to work for Pet Furnishings, but when she returned, she moved on quickly from her difficulties (likely caused from having to saw off dogs' legs and such).

> She returned to Pet Furnishings and took a post on the executive board. It was she who was responsible for the Automatic Safe Dog. They developed a microchip that you could puncture through the dog's skull; 'With the chip of a mallet, the dog has a habit.' The chip was studded into the dog's motor cortex and pet sofas and divans were made automatic and safe so they didn't howl, bite, shit or piss until programmed at preset intervals. This made for not just safer but cleaner furnishings. Our customers forever complained of the times their mutt would whine to be let out, just when they needed to pet it or love it or sit down for a cup of tea, and then they'd have to deal with the inevitable mud in the castors or dew in the tassels. But Ravenski changed all that with her bold new ideas and leapt up the career ladder, far away from the 'real' people.

This is some twitchy prose. We have people making sentient animals into furniture and still being so craven that they resent the basic care their living divan upon which they settle their pampered asses requires in order to stay alive. I struggled through such horror because I hoped that the level of detail McDonald was giving this dystopia meant the novel would have some greater purpose. My patience was ultimately rewarded, but this is an example of the thoughtless cruelty that you will find in this book.

Telby's approach to getting a new job, in disguise, on Pet Furnishings' executive board, provides a disturbing but hilarious look at the complete insincerity and lack of concern for substance one often encounters in the corporate world. He stands in front of the mirror, rehearsing his lines like he's auditioning for a play, which, in a way, he is.

"I have always been research driven. I was always more interested in the sweet wrappers than the sweets…I like rock climbing and canoeing. Yes, I'm a member of the rock canoeing club, up granite face and then down stream…Every Sunday and then off to the pub…of course relaxation is very important. For every work ethic there must be a work leisure…Well I see my role as being a bull in the china store, breaking a few plates for the sake of a dinner set…" On and on I would continue with this, into the early hours, until I found myself muttering into the mirror's surface, where I'd fallen asleep.

He perfects this nonsense, going out in disguise until after sixteen days he transforms himself into the lunatic Terribly "Telby" Velour, his cheeks stuffed with cotton balls and his patter not unlike that of the average contestant on that horrible show where Donald Trump fires people.

To give you a taste of McDonald's witty and silly dialogue, here's a scene where Telby is visiting his doctor. He is troubled by what he calls "bladder stone colic," a condition that leaves him in terrible pain. He and the doctor both have a hard time focusing.

"An operation," he concluded, not without a little relish, as if this was to be his only pleasure in the disinfected room.

"But I don't have time."

"Well you'll have to make some time then." He seemed impatient and tried to smile as if to indicate the end of the consultation.

I noticed his poor dentition. "How often do you brush your teeth?" I asked him.

"What?"

"Do you brush your teeth every day or just, occasionally?"

"Well I have to say I'm a bit of a tooth libertarian…" he started to warm to the subject. "Once every three days is my maximum. There's enough on my consulting plate without brooding on enamel plaques. A bit of dental neglect gives me quite a hedonistic thrill. Teeth, you see, are the dentist's preserve.

"But if you don't brush your teeth you could end up with gum disease, decay, and even dentures.

He smiled with what were clearly brown, sticky teeth. "Isn't it decadent? Halitosis is a bit of a problem though." He leaned forward. I leaned away.

"About my bladder stone?"

"Yes, the stone." He closed his tarry smile and fell into his swivel chair.

"Isn't there some kind of truss?" I asked.

"I'm afraid not. All I can offer you is pain killers, or the operation."

"Painkillers?"

"We used to use suppositories but they banned those for obscure reasons."

"What kind of painkiller?"

"Pethidine, mainly…as an injection."

"An injection?"

"You know, sharp, pointy thing."

"I can't give myself injections."

"Well surprisingly you can. A Commons Committee decided that suppositories were 'a bit French' and 'rather queer' and that injections were far more suitable. It was during the Conservative resurgence a few years back. There's a very interesting debate in one of the Sunday magazines, you should read it."

"It's not the Pethidine so much, it's just I'm…needle phobic."

The G.P. picked up a drawing pin, loose on his desk, and pushed it between thumb and forefinger. "We can cure that," he said, "by repeated exposure."

I found this scene delightful. However, this is also an example of the interesting editing I found in the e-book I was sent. I think I may have subconsciously cleaned some of it up as I went, and there were problems to be sure, but ultimately the editing problems were not too intrusive.

It won't give away too much of the plot when I reveal that Telby gets that job with the executive board at Pet Furnishings. On his first day, he meets his staff and coworkers, as one does. It is here that we meet Abel, Telby's assistant and one of the randomest and silliest characters in a book fairly teeming with random and silly characters.

"Abel," said my secretary, offering his hand. "I'm profound."

"You're what?"

"I'm profound."

"In what way?"

"I'm a writer. I'm only doing this to pay the bills. In fact, I'm an undiscovered great." Abel seemed to have an impossibly long body, not thin, but long, as if all his mass had been extruded without losing the breadth. He had enormous nostrils like the vents of jet engines from which a few hairs fluttered between thin lips like a series of mahjong tablets from which the offending spots had been wiped. His puppety arms were continually restless in florid piques of outrage and condescension.

"Also, I don't do shorthand, it cramps my style."

Telby's interactions with Abel are always a bit unsettling.

"Abel?"

"Yes?" He turned his head like a nut on a bolt.

"Why is there a fish swimming in the water cooler?"

"It's a Pampas fish; it gobbles up the detritus and keeps the water clean. They harvest them from whales."

"Doesn't it, you know, contaminate the water?"

"It makes a very nutritious effluent. It charges the water with vitamins, electrifies its micronutrients. I add them to my bath at home."

"Your bath?"

"They nibble my body perfectly clean. And it is only when I am perfectly clean that I write my best work. I get out before they micronutrient."

Abel is writing his magnum opus a syllable a day. No worries. I won't share Abel's work in progress as it progresses but I will say Abel is the source of so much pretentious silliness that he became my favorite character in this often brutal book. Even as he annoys, he is largely benign. There are so many scenes of Abel being a perfect little pedant that it's hard to pick just one. Here he is, razzing Telby:

"All the secretaries are saying you're the talk of the elevator, a real bull in the china store and you were only meant to be a mop head, that sounds like a real promotion to me."

"Aren't you mixing your metaphors?"

"How dare you accuse me, a writer, of mixing my metaphors? They are hybrids, neologisms of the highest disorder. I am the author, lest you forget, of the greatest work of this century."

"But you've only written two syllables."

"Three actually but I've started designing the book jacket."

"Don't books have to contain words?"

"I suppose, but all the best writers work from the outside in. I've decided mine will be bound in vermilion and the title will be 'Tantric Kant—Sex in the Age of Wonder', with a Geneva font and the subheading: 'Fuck right and wrong, let's fuck.'"

Yes, Abel is a pompous clown. But in the tradition of literary fools, he speaks a truth in this passage that the reader overlooks because we don't pay close attention to fools. It wasn't until I finished reading and began analyzing the book for discussion that I realized McDonald was far cleverer a writer than I had initially realized, crappy punctuation notwithstanding.

Abel is going to be just one small problem for Telby as he tries to woo Ravenski while doing his level best to perform a job for which he is wholly unqualified. But then again all humans are likely to be unqualified for the task Telby undertakes. Bearing in mind that this is a novel in which half the characters will die terrible deaths and dogs are sawed up in a post-humanist (post-canine?) redefinition of furniture, scenes like this one help. Here Telby meets Miss Ibore Davidson. He is fiddling with the "bauble" on the fly of his pants when he is interrupted.

> "Miss Davidson is here for lunch," said Abel.
>
> I got up from the chair and yanked at the bauble.
>
> Ibore Davidson burst into the room. As she did so I unzipped my fly and the bauble tore from its clasp and rolled across the carpet towards her. She crushed it underfoot, rezipped my trousers and looked me straight in the eye.
>
> "Let's do Lunch."
>
> "Couldn't we have a sandwich?"
>
> "Sandwiches are for the boys." She turned and regarded me over her shoulder, " and, I, am a woman."
>
> "Of course."
>
> Ibore paced out and I followed. I could feel fragments of bauble crunching under my sole.
>
> Ibore leant over Abel's desk on her elbows. "Cancel all Mr. Velour's appointments."

He leaves as Abel offers to write him a nasty limerick. (And lest we forget, this is not some clever 1960s bawdy comedy; Ibore and Telby have difficulty with the elevator because a dog has been crushed in the shaft. Yeah…)

Things move quickly with Ibore, as you sort of knew they would. And it also all goes down the way you sort of knew it would, though you couldn't have known this exactly because who the hell but McDonald could have imagined the following scene? (And remember, Telby is in disguise, his mouth crammed with cotton balls—I feel you need to keep this in mind as you read this.) So Telby and Ibore have sex atop all the modified dog furnishings in her apartment until she insists they move to another location. All of Ibore's windows have a magnifying effect that she can control with a remote.

> We ended up doing it on the coffee table. Ibore on all fours, me taking her from behind, my hands cupped under her breasts. As our rhythm escalated I noticed the cityscape in front of us magnifying in jumps. Ibore had the heel of one hand on the remote control and with each pump forward was accidentally pressing a button. She had her head down in the processes of her orgasm but I couldn't help but notice the magnifications of the screen that we made with each thrust. The view expanded to the rooftops of the tower blocks, then focused on a passing plane with a red flashing light, enlarged again so the plane filled the whole wall and then a single cabin window, until finally, as Ibore howled, it became the face of a fat businessman eating his airline meal. Noodles dribbled from his mouth. He turned to look at us with a Soya sauced string hanging from his lips.

"Madness," I shouted.

"Taoist," shouted Ibore.

Yep, he wants to win Ravenski's heart, he boinks Ibore and ends gawping mid-thrust at a surprised man in an airplane. I'm impressed that he managed to keep the cotton balls in his mouth the entire time. Oh, Telby…

Telby has the capacity to schmooze his way into a job he doesn't understand in order to woo Ravenski, but he still gets pulled in all directions. Ibore drags him to bizarre restaurants where one more or less has to tackle the aggressively dancing wait service staff to get food. He permits her to take him to a sadistic clothier with an odd German accent who trusses him up in a straight-jacket sort of corset in order to give him better "pectorvals." She then takes him to a hair studio where such painful things are done to Telby that he fairly begs for vodka to help temper the discomfort. Then this happens:

> She disappeared and came back with a bucket full of sopping newspaper in a glue paste and then proceeded to roll the sheets into twists and attach them to the spikes of hair.

> "Nice weather," she said as she fixed a strip of the international news section.

> "Nice," I said.

> "So what do you do then?"

> I searched my mind for a more or less interesting persona. "I'm an Islamic extremist," I said.

> "That's lovely; we had an astronaut in from the NASA space programme last week…"

> "Oh."

> "Nice chap he was. Lovely chest."

> We continued in this vein until she had finished attaching all the glued twirls of Times broadsheet.

> "…so I said to him it must get awfully cold up there…"

> I looked at my reflection in the mirror. I was a white rasta, newspaper dreadlocked in a kindergarten pasting frenzy.

Telby entered into this farce with a disguise but he had no idea how quickly the experience would render him unrecognizable even to himself.

But McDonald knows what he's doing. There is a method to his madness. Imagine how Telby looks at this point: mouth crammed with cotton balls, hair turned into a Times London dreaded mess, wearing a corset that pushes his body fat upward to give him "pecs." Now imagine this human being giving an R&D presentation for, god help us all, a dog in the box.

> "This," I pointed at the thing, "is not a real dogs head but in three months time we hope to be able to produce the genuine article, a dogs head on a

spring, isn't that right Ballistrade?"

"We are developing the technology that will allow us to create a bioengineered dogs head," he continued, "we did toy with using actual dog tissue…"

"But," I tapped my stick on the table, "there are issues to do with public relations which despite our best efforts," I nodded respectfully at Denis McCloy, "may clog up the merchandising process."

Indeed, putting a living dog's head on a spring could be alarming to the average consumer who finds animal torture for the sake of home accessories distasteful. There is no ridiculous to the sublime in this novel. We generally go from the ridiculous to the utterly sickening.

Still, there are moments of tenderness. When Ravenski invites Telby back to her place after the dog in the box presentation, and she begins to undress, I worried that it was going to be a repeat of the Ibore experience, but it wasn't. It's touching, non-sexual and unexpected, and so worth reading I won't spoil it.

The novel becomes darker and even more interesting when Telby begins to hear the building communicate via taps in the walls, which he eventually realizes is Morse code. McDonald doesn't give us an easy mystery here in the form of a prisoner tapping frantically from some cage hidden in the walls of Pet Furnishings. Rather, the building appears to be communicating with itself—or at least two entities are communicating with themselves.

> I decided to scamper between the walls and record each sentence in turn to see if there might be some kind of coded conversation in progress.
>
> "So you think the secret of prophecy is to be profane?"
>
> "No I think it is to be articulate without being archaic."
>
> "And poetry is not articulate?"
>
> "My right leg aches you know."
>
> "I thought you had no leg?"
>
> "Well I must do. If it aches."
>
> "It's probably phantom limb pain."
>
> "I don't subscribe to the theory of phantom limb pain."
>
> "Not factual enough for you? Too poetical?"
>
> "If my right leg aches it must, by definition, be in existence."
>
> "Well my left arm aches and I know its not there."
>
> "How can you tell?"
>
> "Once they knocked off those reflective glasses, by mistake, and I saw that my left arm was definitely without presence…. but it still pains me."
>
> "You must be mistaken."

"No, I saw it, or rather I didn't."

"You need more proof."

"Be done with proof, use your instincts to guide your fleeting perceptions."

"English life is vast tracts of politeness with punctuations of extreme violence."

"I'm tired of your aphorisms."

"I'm tired of your poetry."

It's difficult to explain why, but this passage made the hair on the back of my neck stand up. There is something so unpleasant and foul about something in the walls that is both sentient and able to express itself using human code. I won't reveal the source of this querulous conversation but with this scene McDonald is setting up the moral conflict Telby will face as he comes to terms with his own fraudulent complicity in the clinical cruelty he engages in, all in the name of pursuing romantic love.

Even as his coworkers begin to be murdered, one by one, and even as Telby is confronted by conversions in Morse code coming out of the walls, the strangeness isn't over by a long shot. As he flees from Abel, because he does not want to hear his aide reciting the first sentence of his magnum opus, Telby encounters the dancing French girl, who dances through the building accompanied by a beat that insinuates itself into Telby's brain as the phrase "restless movement."

> I ran from the office and the tapping faded but the funky beat carried on. I hurried past a typing pool and saw her again, the mysterious dancing French girl. She was wearing a bare black top that revealed a gyrating lower back and her headphones mashed out the addictive funky beat that made me rock in time behind her. "Restless movement yeh, yeh. Restless movement yeh, yeh." I ran up and was about to touch her on the shoulder when Abel reached his arm across my chest and held me back. He looked down his nose with disdain.

> "I told you didn't I? You must never touch the beautiful dancing French girl or she will bring you bad luck. Curdled karma."

As I think of all that happens in this novel, all the attention to detail in these bizarre situations, all these insane people, I'm somewhat reminded of Terry Pratchett or Douglas Adams. So many strange details—the aggressively dancing wait staff, the man in the plane eating noodles, the dancing French girl—many of which may not be germane to the plot, may seem overwhelming when described. But all of these details serve to animate the uneasy, strange and at times ridiculous world that Telby inhabits. Indeed, McDonald does such a good job of world-building that a 1960s London with advanced satellite imaging alongside typing pools makes sense. The dense action and ornamentation somehow never seem distracting.

I mention this because in this already over-long review, I cannot even begin to go into the many strange people and situations that transpire. I can scarcely touch upon the Gender Go Go Girls, a guerrilla group that lead a cultural rebellion against romantic love. Or the part where Telby contracts rabies and engages in all sorts of uncomfortable medical shenanigans to keep himself well and under control. Or the washroom attendant whose genius is what fuels the Pet Furnishings executive board. *Automatic Safe Dog* is a novel populated with a cast of incredibly odd characters and filled with so many strange situations that it could almost be called zany. Almost. Somehow McDonald keeps the lunacy grounded, bringing us back to the gravity of the situation—suffering animals, insensitive and murderous people, drones blunted by the boredom and cruelty of modern work.

I'll share one last passage. I think it conveys something of Telby's eventual awakening and the disgust he comes to feel for what he has done. Earlier in the novel, a dog gets stuck in a wall and, animals being such a disposable commodity, no one is much bothered with getting him out. Telby, by now rabid, being stalked by a killer and under guard at all times for his "safety," finally breaks down.

> And then I turned to look through the windows. The vista was outshone by the glow of the bulb, which lingered in the backcloth of my eyes, silhouetting the blood vessels of my vision so they seemed to weave into the plaza like wires. "Revolution," I said. I began to cry and the tears made me blink, shorting and blurring the capillaries of my sight; a breach of grief for the greyhound with the silver striped muzzle and expectant gaze, for the rotting dog in the wall, for the rabid blood that beat through my veins.

McDonald doesn't give the reader any easy out. The ending broke my heart but I genuinely do not know if there was any other way out. At least it wasn't morally ambivalent.

I get lots of books sent my way and I've come across a number of extremely talented writers whom few seem to know about. Still, it is very exciting to discover a book like this, something so well-written that affects me so deeply. I think McDonald's writing is very near genius, even if he needs a good copy editor to clean up his work. That's an important criticism because a writer this talented should not take the risk of having his work dismissed because of poor editing. *Automatic Safe Dog* was a revelation. A murder mystery, a farce, a romance, a sketch of a lunatic world, a glimpse of an uncaring and venal society and the way that small venal sins can become mortal sins if we let them go on too long. I can't remember the last time a new book from an obscure author proved to be so compelling. Highly recommended.

Further Reading

A Very Short Walk
Lawrance Holmes

CAFO: The Tragedy of Industrial Animal Factories
Edited by Daniel Imhoff

Dominion: The Power of Man, the Suffering of Animals, and the Call to Mercy
Matthew Scully

MISADVENTURES IN A THUMBNAIL UNIVERSE
By Vincent W. Sakowski
Eraserhead Press (2007)
Original post: 06/30/2011

Why do I consider this book odd?
It's early(ish) bizarro, and of a very strange and sweet variety. And if you think "sweet" is the kiss of death where a book is concerned, let me emphasize this is *bizarro*-sweet, not the kind of sweet your mother would read (though, not having met your mother, perhaps that's a presumptuous call on my part).

*M*isadventures in a Thumbnail Universe is a wonderful surprise. The stories in this collection are creepy, surreal and beautiful. Pulled from history and legend (and in one case, unconsciously reminiscent of one of my favorite speculative authors, more about which below), Sakowski's writing left me feeling wistful, almost longing for a world that never existed, though it would have been unbearable had it come to pass. Using a traditional plot structure and characterization, his stories evoke a sense of the unpleasant using the most beautiful language. He presents the utterly disturbing in a way that registers as beautiful, even as it appalls.

There was not a single story in this collection that did not work so I will just discuss the ones I enjoyed the most.

"The Miracle Babies" is about a woman who gives birth to rabbits and sends them out into the world to make their mark. Immediately I was reminded of the story of Mary Toft, an 18th century woman who claimed to give birth to rabbits. But unlike Toft, who shoved mutilated rabbits up her vagina and squeezed them out in perpetration of a hoax meant to bring her money, the protagonist of "The Miracle Babies" gives birth to cute, fuzzy bunny rabbits. The problem is that she cannot nurse these baby bunnies, as they are carnivorous and feed on her flesh. Tiring of having them chew on her, she feeds them hamburger and then callously sends them out into the world. Once free of the little rabbits that she had known only for hours, she finds herself affected by their absence.

In her sorrow and in her seclusion, she made a special mask to shut herself off even further. Initially, she only wore it a few minutes before bedtime, as it reminded her of her children. Then she wore it more and more often—lying in bed, or sitting in the living room. The mask was made of black satin, leaving only her face from under her nose down exposed. There were no holes for the eyes or ears. On her head stood two tall bunny ears—black and white. The bit of white was for the small hope she still felt on occasion. That perhaps some day, one or more of her children would return to her.

I'm being very careful not to spoil anything so I will stop here, but ultimately it's a story of legacy, of making your mark passively, however painfully. I was reminded of the works of an Austin artist named Jay Long, whose cute but creepy bunnies and people in masks eerily reflect elements of Sakowski's tale.[5]

"The Screaming of the Fish" is about a man who literally has a fishbowl for a head. It's more of a vignette than a story so I can't discuss it too much without utterly ruining it. I will share a snippet to convey a sense of the calm, sweet humor that permeates the collection:

> The two goldfish in the bowl didn't seem to be too crazy about him jogging every day—with all of the rocks from the bottom getting stirred up, swishing around and scraping their sides. Way too many scars over the years, but what could they say?

> My friend kept them well-fed, and they certainly got their exercise. And even though they were stuck in a small home, they got to see a lot of the sights. Especially since my friend liked to jog a new route everyday.

"Peel and Eat Buffet" is a truly nasty story crafted in such beautiful language that the underlying horror is almost muted. A quick look:

> To a song that only she can hear, she begins to undulate and slowly turn on the platform—her body in constant motion—but every move deliberate. Sensual. As she turns, her hips gyrating, she begins to pull at the film, working the knots open. Stretching out scenes. Letting them fall. Editing in her own way. There is only the crinkling of the film to be heard as it unwinds and she crushes it underfoot.

"It's Beginning to Look a Lot Like Ragnarok" also has some fairly disgusting moments but overall is one of the funnier pieces in the book. One of the longer entries, it tells the story of how GQ and Vogue, a good-looking and successful DINK couple, find themselves sucked into Loki's bizarre plans for Ragnarok. You see, GQ dreamed about the end of the world and Loki was collecting stray hair and nail clippings in order to build a long ship. Trimming her nails, Vogue loses one crescent (and really, she should have been getting professional manicures were she really that vogue, but never

---

5   Check them out! http://www.jaylongstudio.com

mind), whereupon GQ panics and makes her collect her nail clippings lest she trigger the end of the world. As she is throwing out the trash before leaving for work, Vogue is confronted by a smelly, unattractive creature.

"Good morning, my dear. I was wondering if you could spare some-"

"Is your name Loki?"

"Do I look like a Norse God to you?"

"I don't watch that much television. I have no idea how a Norse God is supposed to look, but I couldn't help noticing that sack of hair and nails. Are you building a long ship with them?"

"This is the suburbs, my dear. No open water for tens of miles... Will you be my friend?"

"Is that really necessary?"

"It would be nice." The derelict flashes a brown, hour-glass toothed smile.

Vogue steps back, grimacing. "Let me think about it."

"Uh huh... Bad day, my dear?"

"I've just discovered that my husband's an asshole."

"Only this morning? You have my sympathies."

She gives him change and leaves for work. He fishes her clippings out of the trash and yes, Ragnarok is upon them. Among other things. This one combines the ridiculous, the gross, and the funny into one harmoniously bizarre tale.

My favorite is **"See Emily Play?"** It's beautifully written, and extremely creepy and unsettling. It reminded me of a Caitlín R. Kiernan story. There's a Victorian, almost steampunk element to it, and while I'm generally not a fan of steampunk, the images of a lovely little girl dressed in an elaborate gown with bronze praying mantis arms sort of creeps into the genre. The gist is that Emily gets gossip and news of the outside world from a bird called Mr. Calm and is visited by a friend Marla, who agrees to make Emily a new body. The first one, powered by coal and producing steam, is not to Emily's liking. The second is the one I would have chosen:

> Mostly made of clear glass, inside, there were a variety of flowers and plants, all of which Emily eventually recognized from Mr. Calm's lessons from long before. In the chest, hawthorn flowers and their red berries encircled a water lily. On the right side of the lily were white violets, on the left were blue. Below them were yellow jasmine and blue hyacinth, wild plum blossoms and even a small hemp plant, which seemed odd and disturbing to her, as it was linked with Fate. On the lowest level, orange and lemon blossoms grew around a tiny willow, which she perhaps found the most unsettling of all. Even with the body on its back, the plants were held in place, and appeared to be vibrant and alive.

This body that implies fecundity does not appeal to Emily. She says it's because she doesn't want to rely on watering the plants and getting them sunlight (both of which would power the body and presumably would leave her unable to move on cloudy days). It's clear that Emily prefers a body which can move only under the power she creates for it, so she chooses a more sexually appealing PVC body and begins to engage in activities that upset Mr. Calm, calling into question Emily's loyalty. Her body becomes her undoing. Giving up her mantis arms means she is, herself, in danger of becoming prey.

There is a lot of body horror in this story, though it's presented in very lovely language (which is why I think I was reminded of Kiernan, though perhaps these formally dressed, strange young women could also have led me to such a comparison). And again, I'm reminded of a painting—something I know I've seen of a pretty girl dressed in finery and in possession of insect arms of some sort. I cannot find this image anywhere. It is not impossible that I am imagining it.

This collection is unique, even if it triggered thoughts of other works. Sakowski depicts of a world of strangeness, a world that few writers could effectively pull off. If his stories remind me of Kiernan or bring to mind surreal paintings, this is a good sign. It means that Sakowski is mining veins that other excellent artists have tapped. His style is his own. Nothing is derivative. Evocative, but not derivative. I loved this book.

Further Reading

My Landlady the Lobotomist
Eckhard Gerdes

The Overwhelming Urge
Anderson Prunty

PART THREE

Odd Things
(Audio-Visual Dept.)

For years my site was called "I Read Odd Books" but after a while I felt myself itching to discuss film and music. Eventually I changed the name of the site to "Odd Things Considered" so I wouldn't have to qualify every time I deviated from books. It's interesting to me how music and films I discuss tend to be very disturbing or upsetting in some manner, but for those who get tired of non-stop murder, drug abuse and human degradation, Art Bell's influence in fringe music comes up to lighten the load.

MOVIES AND METAPHYSICAL DESPAIR

04/23/2013

I tend to experience passively any sort of media that requires a screen. I just leave the TV on in the background as I go about my day, generally as a form of white noise as I clean or cook. I seldom pay close attention to movies or television shows. But recently I watched two movies that were so awful, so absorbing and deeply terrible, that I couldn't look away. I felt like these movies were proof that God is dead and that He probably never much loved us anyway.

The first was *The Snowtown Murders*, a grimly realistic depiction of a serial murder case in Australia.[1] If you're not familiar with the case, the film may seem like a mess because many characters come and go without a lot of explanation. And I should warn you up front that it also includes one of the most egregious scenes of animal abuse this side of *Cannibal Holocaust*. Please bear these things in mind.

The film centers on John Bunting, a charismatic psychopath with a fixation on largely imaginary cases of pedophilia, who influences a group of marginally intelligent and largely hopeless losers to join him in killing and torturing real or imagined child predators. I say his obsession with pedophiles verges into imaginary crimes because Bunting is also convinced that all homosexuals are sexual predators, or de facto pedophiles. With his rag-tag group of socially marginalized losers, the real John Bunting killed 11 people over a period of about seven years.

Apart from the scenes of horrific violence, the film provides a bleak look at a particular segment of society in Australia. Small, dingy homes cluttered with useless crap, people sleeping on couches because there aren't enough bedrooms. In such squalor, even the best impulses of parents seem strange and cramped. As they try to protect their children from the monsters outside, they fail to protect them from the monsters within.

Though it drained me of all emotional vitality, I think *The Snowtown Murders* is worth watching. It's raw and unflinching, showing the worst things that can happen in such a matter-of-fact manner that it causes the viewer to go numb. There's a character named James who spends the film stunned by

---

1   Snowtown is the name of the town where the bodies were found—most of the murders occurred elsewhere. The case was widely covered in Australia.

the repeated blows that life has handed him. One of the first interactions James has with John Bunting occurs as Bunting is decapitating and skinning several kangaroos. They're real kangaroos and that scene is just foul and upsetting. Lucas Pittaway, who plays James, resembles a shark-eyed Heath Ledger, visually appealing in the middle of this unexpected scene of carnage. He maintains the perfect affect—flat yet strangely frightened.

This early scene sets the viewer up for what's to come. I am referring to what must be one of the worst scenes ever in a narrative film. The rape scene in *Irreversible* is upsetting because it's so long and so deeply horrible. Violent. A total violation. The rape scene in *The Snowtown Murders* is the complete opposite in its execution and as a result it's infinitely worse. James had evidently been sexually abused by his older half-brother, Troy, throughout their childhood together. The scene we are given in *The Snowtown Murders* is maybe a tenth as long as the notorious scene in *Irreversible*. Yet it feels longer as the older brother asserts his toxic will against his younger brother, who lay there on the floor, motionless and quiet, waiting for it to end. It's as if it were another small chore he had to finish to get on with his day. He just had to submit and then he could resume his bleak, cluttered, hopeless life.

Learning of this assault, John Bunting captures Troy, locks him a bathroom and begins a long, horrible assault against him. As much as Troy needs punishment for what he has done, no one deserves what happens to him. Utterly in thrall to John, James is unable to make things stop until he finally ends his brother's torment himself. This is the first time he shows any real emotion and it's clear to the viewer that James' life is probably far better when he is numb. Any awakening of feeling is going to involve violence, cruelty and ill-use.

The Snowtown Murders is a powerful movie and I don't ever want to see it again. At the same time, I think others may find it just as appalling and upsetting and transfixing as I did. Sometimes a terrible spectacle reveals something. In this case it lets us into lives foreign to our own and forces us to understand how a person can transform from a small, helpless child into a flat, vicious killer.

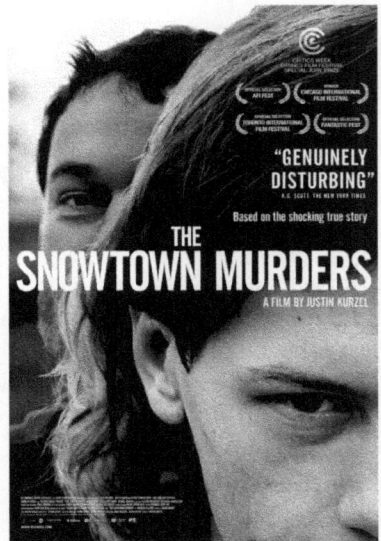

The other film is just horrible. No real reason to watch it other than to rubberneck at the sorry lives of others. No revelation. No understanding. Just the voyeuristic thrill that comes from watching other people self-destruct. Yet that thrill still may not be enough to get you through *Black Metal Veins*.

Jesus Allah Fuck, I wanted to put the people in this loosely staged "documentary" out of their misery. Mr. OTC found this film for me. Like many others, he thought it had something to do with the music genre—and it does, but only in so much as Brad Allen, the male "lead" in this "documentary" is a black metal fan. He's a Satanist who gives speeches extolling what can fairly be described as a racist Social Darwinist worldview, which shows a shocking lack of self-awareness on his part.

This film follows several heroin addicts living their sorry lives as filmed by director Lucifer Valentine. One guy, Chris, who delights in sharing his ex-girlfriend's desire to have rough anal sex when on drugs, gets shot to death in a drug deal gone wrong within roughly the first 20 minutes of the film. I have little to say about him. It's sad that his children will face life without knowing their father.

The rest of the cast:

Raven lives with her boyfriend, Mark Dykman, who is in the Navy. She spends his money on drugs while he is away. Her apartment is a hub of drug activity. Raven begins the film looking reasonably healthy and slowly degenerates into a corpse-like presence. She's had two children and her mother has custody of them both, a fact that makes Raven bitter. She genuinely believes her mother tricked her and stole her kids. She seems to have a good heart (she likes to rescue animals) but she doesn't seem to understand that she's in no position to raise kids in an apartment full of addicts, especially the particular addicts in this film. Raven's ruinous state is memorably captured during a scene of consensual sex with Mark where she gives the appearance of a foul-mouthed, animated cadaver.

Pregnancy's impact on the human body varies but it appears to have sapped Raven, and the drug abuse cannot have helped. She looks like a zombie, covered in sores, her skin baggy, her eyes lifeless. One

wonders how her boyfriend could find any of this attractive, but, to use a very un-PC term, he appears to be a Captain-Save-A-Ho type. He doesn't use drugs himself, but he is so enmeshed with Raven that he permits her to bleed him dry financially, while allowing her repellent friends to sprawl in his apartment. Of interest to drive-by necrophiles will be the "rape" scene, where cast members have sex with an unconscious Raven. I have rape in quotes because several searches online reveal that this scene was staged. Raven is naked on camera several times. Her entire body is a testament to the toll bad life choices take.

There's a character called Doom. He's a cypher to me. His is the smallest role in the film. A black metal waste case.

Autumn Misery is a lunatic prostitute with a severe case of logorrhea. She uses anything she can get her hands on. Seriously, I get the impression she would have smoked a turd if someone told her it would get her high. She claims to be an advisor to an older, well-placed man who, if he was once a big deal, has since slid down the social ladder. She claims to gives him advice on how to deal with the girls whose time he pays for. She also claims to be pregnant and later Brad Allen injects something directly into her stomach in what seems like a dog-patch abortion. Autumn engages in a sex "scene" with Brad Allen that has to be one of the least erotic ever documented. She also spends a lot of time in the film being fingered. She is a hot mess. I wanted to feel sympathy for her but it was hard to muster much emotion.

(It was during one of Autumn's scenes when it dawned on me where I had heard the name Lucifer Valentine before. As Autumn sits by the toilet and tells her strange stories of being a sort of house madam for an older man, she is filmed vomiting. That's what clued me in. Lucifer Valentine is the director of the *Vomit Gore Trilogy*. I watched the first film, *Slaughtered Vomit Dolls*, and it pretty much did what it said on the label. I shudder to think what awaits those brave enough to sit through *Slow Torture Puke Chamber*. Lucifer Valentine is a ridiculous human being who claims he had a sexual relationship with his autistic, blind sister and that she killed herself when he started a relationship with another girl. If this is true, he is grotesque. If this is untrue, he is grotesque—because only a very demented man would lie about engaging in an exploitative sexual relationship with a blind, mentally-disabled sibling. This "even if this is a lie it's still horrible" sentiment will come up again.)

Then there's Chris. He's the kid I mentioned at the outset, the one who got shot to death. Chris was a mess. A complete fucking mess. It occurs to me that people on drugs are the most boring people on earth. Every scene with him was cringe-worthy, and he died early in the filming.

And now we come to the star: Brad Allen. Brad's got a mouth of rotting teeth. He's got toenails that will make the average person want to vomit (it speaks to the level of his hygiene that the scene where he shows his disgusting feet may be the nastiest part of this movie—a movie that features bloody puke, open fingering, a scabrous naked chick, a possible drug abortion and a feigned rape). As I've already mentioned, Brad's a fan of black metal and he's is a full-on racist. He hilariously accuses the "niggers upstairs" of stealing all of the money he was paid to do this film, preventing him from getting his teeth fixed. Because that just seems so much more likely than that he lost it or spent it in a drug haze. Like so many racists, Brad is the worst exemplar of any sort of virtue that might attend having pale skin. He talks about how the woman he loved committed suicide while pregnant with his child, and just when you begin to feel some real sympathy for him, he finger-bangs Autumn Misery in the middle of the room and injects her pregnant stomach with what I think was heroin. He also lets Raven inject his neck with what I think was whiskey. Who knows what it really was. I tend to think most of this movie was staged. Or maybe I just really hope it was.

Brad is a complete waste of a human being, almost beneath contempt. He comes off like he was probably a useless sack of crap before he ever tried a single drug. And it's made all the sadder because in the only part of this film that works, Valentine talks to Brad's mother, Paula Allen, who died before the film was released. She had Legionnaire's Disease and talked openly about her own addictions to pain medications and how she felt responsible for the state Brad was in. It was during this scene that the viewer realizes that this strange, gross, racist addict is someone's beloved son, a child in whom parents had invested time, love and care. A child whose mother had dreams for him in life. Paula Allen lends this film a sliver of humanity, but not even she could redeem it.

I should leave it at that, but I can't because at one point in the film "Doom" insists that Raven died. Wondering if that was true, I soon landed on her MySpace page and within minutes I had rounded up the Facebook accounts for most of the people involved in the film. Raven's account was locked down but that the account existed at all suggests that either "Doom" was mistaken, or he was following a script for shock value. I felt a bit strange checking up on the lives of these kids, but given that *Black Metal Veins* is essentially a voyeuristic jack-off at their expense, I figured my snooping was the least of their problems.

"Autumn Misery" is really a girl named Leslie. She is evidently off drugs and seems to have had a baby, a fat, healthy little girl. She posts selfies, many of which involve bright and intricate make-up jobs. Without the drugs, her face looks wholly different and far prettier. She has an intelligence behind her eyes. Her Facebook presence makes you hope she really has turned things around.

Mark Dykman, the sober boyfriend, is no longer with Raven. He appears completely disconnected from everyone involved in the documentary. It's very hard to understand how he spent so much time with Raven and her friends. A deep savior complex, I expect. Plus Raven did have a sweet helplessness about her. There seemed very little that was cruel or unkind in her so I think can understand why someone would want to save her. In any case, he seems to be living a completely different life now. I still cannot fathom why he participated in the staged rape of his girlfriend. Yeah, it was faked. But it's like I said about Lucifer Valentine's incestuous relationship with his disabled sister: even if it's a put-on, it still speaks to something very grotesque. People who don't nose around for information after the film will be left with the impression that Mark Dykman, the only clean and sober person in this shitfest, is the sort of dude who would rape his girlfriend when she is impaired and permit her friends to rape her, too. Baffling, utterly baffling. But he's moved on and is living a better life. Good for him.

Then I found Brad Allen's Facebook page. He appears to be sober, and there are indications that some of his racism is more of a "casual" hipster thing. At least that was the impression I got reading his humorous exchange with a pretty, young mixed race girl who was clearly in on the joke. But his life still seems like a complete waste, and it doesn't look like his rotten teeth have been fixed yet. Brad evidently impregnated a young girl and then buggered off, leaving her to raise the little girl on her own. In one of his last updates, Brad was selling off expensive records and black metal accoutrement in order to finance a trip to Australia. Apparently, he had a flirtation with a girl who lives there. He posted a tribute to Jon Nödtveidt, the Satanist lead singer of Dissection who shot himself to death in a pentagram. It seems that the only real difference is that he's no longer injecting things into his veins. Though it's hard to know if that is really the case.

I wonder if appearing in this film has hobbled these kids in some manner. Brad Allen and Mark Dykman are the only two who used their real names but it takes mere seconds to find the real names of the others involved. And they mention their involvement in the film under their real names. Is there a way someone can rise above this sort of portrayal? I suspect it would take a pretty sustained success arc for people to trust any of them aside from Mark Dykman. Even though key elements of the film were staged, it's undeniable that the cast were severely addicted to drugs and engaging in all sorts of questionable behaviors. Did they have any sense of the implications of what they had signed on for? Were they ever sober enough to make an informed decision about appearing in this film?

At the end of the trawl, I was saddened by the sheer waste of it all. Valentine's film made me curious about the cast, but it also filled me with an almost aggressive depression.

I also wonder what the purpose of this film was. I mean, it doesn't really show us anything we don't already know—drug addicts do gross things and live pitiful lives. The most salacious elements were staged, like the rape and probably the chemical abortion. The sad reality of addiction wasn't enough—Valentine had to layer in cinematic lies to give the film legs because the sad, sick, relentless, boring life of the addict doesn't make a good film. It's difficult to watch *Black Metal Veins* without sensing that perhaps these addicts were exploited above and beyond the damage that would follow from merely documenting their addictions. Indeed, it's difficult not to want to punch Lucifer Valentine in the face after watching this film. I bet a lot of people feel the same. Maybe that's why he refuses to be photographed.

If you watch *Black Metal Veins*, you will feel grubby, you will feel sad and you will feel a lot of disgust. If you look beyond the repulsive artifice of the film, what you find will not be enough to wipe away the sort of soul depression that nests from the first viewing. The world sucks and people get desperate. Most of us know this. Seeing this grim truth documented and acted out with so much churlish embellishment isn't enlightening or even worth the wallow. This isn't *Requiem for a Dream* with a black metal hook. It's the product of weird man exploiting addled people whose lives didn't need this level of exposure. I can't tell you not to watch it because it's such an amazing trainwreck, but be prepared for a sort of spiritual nausea.

THE BUNNY GAME

08/31/2012

Before I could write about *The Bunny Game*, I needed time to come to an understanding with myself. I needed to understand why I should find this film worthy of discussion. It's a hard movie to watch. Even harder to digest. It's dirty and unsettling, and one is easily derailed by accusations that the film is nothing more than stylish torture porn.

Having done my introspective due diligence, I'm resolved to proceed. Please note that this discussion will be full of spoilers, though I guess it's hard to spoil a film that can be summed up as "trucker tortures prostitute in the desert for several days."

The Bunny Game is a transgressive piece of cinema that depicts a frightening and non-consensual ordeal that may also be understood as a purification ritual. It's more troubling than anything Eli Roth ever brought to the table, but while the marketing may lead you expect a typical torture porn horror movie, that's not what it is. More specifically, this is not torture for the sake of torture; it's torture with a demented purpose behind it—a purpose that subverts and transcends the base thrill that many viewers will be seeking. I want to be clear that I felt this way before I looked up Rodleen Getsic, the onscreen victim-protagonist, and discovered that she co-wrote the film, basing it on an actual abduction she endured. Getsic also says making this film killed part of her soul, which makes it hard to know if she accomplished what she set out to do. She fasted for 40 days beforehand to make herself weak, and she consented to everything that happened to her on-screen, from a graphic blowjob (actually more of a face-fuck) to the physical abuse she endured during the abduction.

What makes *The Bunny Game* especially difficult to stomach is that the action is largely unscripted. The implication is that Getsic often had no idea what was going to happen to her next. It is, in a sense, one long, horrible ad lib. Without the anchor of a script, we're forced to consider that this victim of a previous real-life abduction and assault is potentially being re-victimized, even if she consented to all of it beforehand. It also makes me wonder how much anyone can be said to consent to something when they don't know the details of what's going to happen. Just as unsettling, the man who plays the trucker is not a professional actor (I believe I read that the director cast him after the guy tried to fight him over some perceived slight, claiming he looked at him too long in a parking lot). This is a dangerous game.

Shot in black and white, the film is visually arresting. But the cinematic quality also makes the content all the worse, rendering gratuitous abuse as visually appealing art. The film opens with a graphic, unsimulated blow job that's so unpleasant it can be described as anti-pornographic. Rodleen is not enjoying herself. She is not moaning with feigned pleasure. Forced to deep-throat her john, she pulls back three times to catch her breath, gasping for air. The third time she does this, a wave of misery washes over her face. One gets the feeling she was not acting. Her reaction shows how debased her character's life is. There is no way to see this with a sex positive filter.

From that opening scene we are taken through a few days in the prostitute's life. Bunny engages in degrading sex acts in exchange for enough money to pay her keep in a nondescript motel room in a nondescript city. She spends her time hustling johns, having horrible sex, using drugs and recovering from it all. Not ten minutes into the film we see her raped when she passes out during a trick, waking up to find she has been robbed of all her money and her drugs. There's a scene where Bunny snorts a line of something and talks to herself in the mirror, muttering "Yeah, yeah, yeah…" as she psychs herself up to go back out for more of the same.

Wearing platform shoes that had to be a foot tall, Bunny wanders a city-scape that harbors nothing good or natural. She eats fast food sprawled in front of a wall covered in graffiti. She urinates in an alley in front of a metal fence, right on the concrete. As she wanders the streets, her bleached, straw-like hair in pig-tails, the film flashes to other images, several of her in a natural place, mountains behind her, her brown hair falling in curls, her face young again as she laughs. Blink and you'll miss it, but those brief scenes where we see the abject prostitute in better times, in fresh air, in the natural world, are a clue as to the film's intent.

Bunny finally meets her destiny in the form of a truck driver, called Hog (each are named for the masks they wear during one of the torture scenes). He renders her unconscious, drives her to the desert and spends several days torturing her. She's unconscious for a while, allowing him time to pull her into his empty trailer, rape her, investigate her body thoroughly, at times snuffling her hair and body like a dog. He then chains her inside the trailer and focuses a camera on her. He forces her to watch her torment, making her relive it as she is actually living it—a particularly cruel layer of meta when one remembers this movie is drawn from Rodleen Getsic's own experiences.

Hog keeps her in chains, puts a collar around her neck and takes her on walks in the junkyard-like landscape of the desert, at one point forcing her to walk while wearing those insane platforms. He force-feeds her whiskey when she desperately needs water. He completely depersonalizes her by shaving her head, but later he brands her as well, taking away one form of identity while giving her another, one that is more permanent. The brands Hog irons onto Bunny's back resemble infinity signs with tails, but they also look like a bow tied from thin ribbon. Both are apt symbols. The torture seems interminable (this movie is a merciful 76 minutes long—any longer and I think it would have been unwatchable), and the torture is interchangeable with that endured by other women that Hog has captured, as revealed through his own flashbacks. The misery is relentless and unceasing. But Bunny is being a given a perverse gift.

Bald and slowly divested of her clothing, the end of the movie shows a woman who looks like a slightly better nourished concentration camp victim. She is crouched in the back of the trailer when the door opens and light shines in on her. Naked and near insanity, Bunny runs for it. She runs toward the light. She's a gibbering mess, but the ecstasy is unmistakeable on her face. She desperately wants to live.

The film cuts away and we see her on a cross. She did not escape to freedom. Hog has caught up to her. She is not restrained. She is not nailed to the cross. She is simply lying atop it with her arms spread, in a Christ-like position. Hog sits near her, not touching her. She hallucinates, seeing herself with her healthy face, her brown curly hair, sitting nearby. Her old self burns a book. Her old self puts on a veil. Her old self is watching her self-sacrifice. She is her own Mary Magdalene in this painful vision.

Hog tells her to draw a straw from his fist—if she gets the long straw, she wins. A jittery wraith, she selects a straw. Hog mumbles something in her ear and the ecstasy again shows on her face. She laughs with hysterical delight as he carries her over his shoulder. A man in a white uniform arrives in a white van and Hog carries her to him. They put her in the back of the van and the film ends.

Does Bunny live? Who is the man in the van? I think she lives but even if she doesn't, it is unimportant. Taken away from the city and into the desert, broken and depersonalized, she wants to live. She has gone through an extraordinary ordeal, very nearly a vision quest, and she wants to live. I also think the torture can be seen as an extreme purification ritual, with the head-shaving, the starvation, the food and water deprivation.

And if this is a purification ritual, then Bunny lives. Purification rituals are to cleanse a person of that which is unclean before a specific life event. It makes no sense if only death awaits. I left this film thinking the specific event was life itself. Bunny is cleansed of the drugs in her system, the endless flow of semen into her body, the grime of the city, the implications of her fried hair and her provocative clothing. Naked, starved and shorn, she is now ready for life after her ordeal. Even if that white van represents death, for the first time Bunny *wants* to live. And wanting life is a redemption from the walking death that defined her before her ordeal. She may never return to being that full-faced, curly-haired, laughing brunette, but just wanting to be that person again means she is saved.

Again, I realize it is tempting for many to dismiss this film as torture porn the sole purpose of which is to revel in Bunny's debasement. But those seeking a disgusting gore-fest will be disappointed. There is no blood. There are no saws or pliers. The blow torch is utilized only to heat the branding iron, which has a contextual purpose. No one loses a limb, no toes are cut off, no one is hung upside down and bled out into a bath. Unlike so many other movies that depict torture, this is not a cartoon of extreme violence. This is psychological torture and, while equally as horrible as physical torture, the purpose is not to titillate. I think this accounts for why so many jaded horror fans were put off by this film. It wasn't what they expected. In many ways it was far, far worse.

After watching *The Bunny Game* I wanted to know more about Rodleen Getsic. It turns out that after the film was made, Getsic slipped on a doormat at a grocery store and landed on her head, causing a catastrophic brain injury. According to a Facebook page her mother runs for her, Rodleen is now confined to a wheelchair and is considered permanently disabled. That's hard to learn after viewing this film. I hope the part of her soul that died when she made *The Bunny Game* was a part she needed to shed, a part she wouldn't need when recovering from such a catastrophic accident. It's an uncomfortable feeling, realizing that the woman who made this film, a film based on her own experiences, has lived to face another ordeal.

This is a powerful movie. I don't think I will ever watch again, but I am glad I saw it.

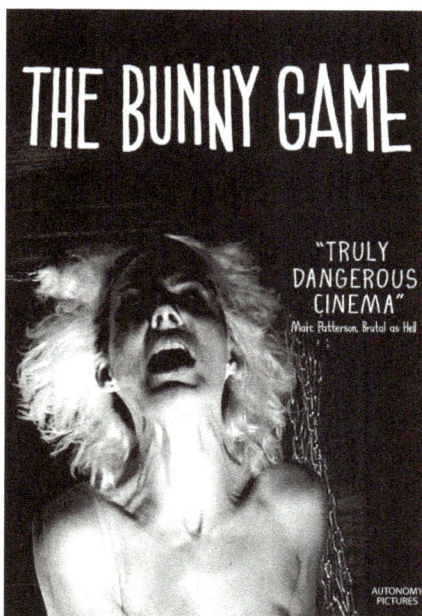

LOVECRAFTIAN GLUTTONY:
REFLECTIONS ON A MUSIC VIDEO

09/17/2015

Most death metal is dead to me these days. When I was younger I could tolerate indecipherable growls because the genre was still new and interesting enough to offset my neurotic desire to understand what was being sung. Though I could understand some of the bands (like Hypocrisy, Opeth and Amon Amarth), I thought the growls were more of an instrument than actual vocals. These days not so much. The genre has suffered a sort of recursive plague. Bands seem to blend together and the growls no longer seem like a deliberate attempt to evoke chaos and darkness as much as they seem aggressively derivative. Worse, much of the content in death metal has taken on a cartoonish slant, so bludgeoning and over-the-top that it no longer comes off as outré. It just seems ridiculous, bordering on tiresome. So I find myself listening to more melodic death metal, which means I also find myself listening to folk metal and, god help me, progressive rock hybrids.

I hope the foregoing exposition will suffice to explain why I haven't been paying attention to death metal. More specifically, I hope it explains how the band Job for a Cowboy had until recently escaped my attention. I need to listen to more of their music, but I was really impressed with the song "Tarnished Gluttony." The vocals are completely unintelligible to me but there's a theatricality to the music that renders a lack of understanding less important. The growls verge into screams that hark back to the days when black metal didn't fill me with despair.

But it's the "Tarnished Gluttony" *video* that really got my attention. If you haven't seen it, I should warn you that it's violent and gory and features the death of a child. Decide for yourself if you want to watch it. It's easy to find online. In any case, my discussion follows.

I watch this video every night before going to sleep. I'm sort of obsessed with it. It's almost like a bedtime story, and given how much an homage it is to Lovecraft, it's a creepy story, too—though no creepier than Perrault's fairy tales.

When I first discovered the video I watched it several times in a row. Then

I forced Mr. OTC to watch it.[2] We've both read our share of Lovecraft but he's a far bigger fan than I and it took him a couple of goes before he had a handle on what was happening. Once it clicked, Mr. OTC echoed my belief that the video is indeed an homage. Our interpretation is that a Deep One[3] sired a child with a human, and that child appears fully human (though in the literature Deep Ones could maintain a completely human appearance until they reached adolescence and sometimes even later). It seems as if the Deep One is sacrificing his human child to Dagon,[4] returning the boy to the sea.

It's a well-executed video, made all the more compelling by the nuanced and emotional performance of Morten Klode,[5] who, if our interpretation is correct (and it is), portrays the adult Deep One. His grimaces and hesitations reveal that he is not a particularly willing participant in the sacrifice. His tender stroking of the boy's cheek shows affection for this child, who isn't some random kid a Lovecraftian horror is killing to appease an Old One. His rushed hurry to begin once he realizes the child may be awakening shows he has no wish to cause pain. His anguished scream after he plunges the knife into the child—it was deeply affecting the first time I saw it.

There are so many creepy elements. The undressing of a small, unconscious child in the woods is unnerving, and of course the ensuing evisceration scene is difficult to watch. But the most unsettling part for me is when the Deep One licks the needle before he begins to stitch up the child's abdomen. Anyone who has sewn much knows that sometimes a blunt needle or pin needs lubrication before it can penetrate certain cloth. It's unlikely that this needle needed any help with the first stitch into the child's stomach but that lick of a blunt needle or pin is often the reflexive act of a person well-accustomed

Morten Klode is having a very bad day.

---

2   He actually enjoyed the song, which is no small praise coming from a guy who mostly listens to old country, zydeco and, inexplicably, Talking Heads.

3   If you don't know, start with *The Shadow Over Innsmouth*.

4   Seriously? Dagon the Fish God, but that's just our guess. Who knows. He could just have been a psychopathic serial killer with gills.

5   Morten Klode reminds me of someone. I don't know who, but his face is damn familiar. As I watch him my mind clicks away as I try to determine where I've seen him before. But it turns out he has only three credits on his IMDb page and I've only seen one of them—this video. Yet each time I watch it, the feeling of familiarity washes over me anew. I hope Klode finds himself with more work in the future. You don't expect to find acting chops of this caliber in a music video—I'm actually rather surprised to see that he doesn't already have a feature-length film under his belt.

to old-fashioned diapers using safety pins. A quick lick of the pin ensures it goes through the thick flannel quickly and there's less chance of pricking a squirming child. You don't see that too much these days with prefolds and Velcro tabs and the like and I am very likely assigning a motive to this action that is not part of the directorial intent, but for me this small gesture seemed fatherly; it shows a man who had, at some point in the past, cared for this little boy, a man who knew his way around the more visceral elements of child-rearing, now taken to an extreme. The way he blankly throws the needle away with numb disgust and misery written all over his face—it was a mild devastation when he tossed that needle into the leaves.

This attention to detail would be remarkable in any music video, but I never expected to find such nuance set to death metal. I've become accustomed to the club-across-the-face approach, like you get with Cattle Decapitation's infamous "Forced Gender Reassignment" video. I get what they're going for, but if I want to bludgeon my psyche I'd prefer to just watch *Human Centipede II (Full Sequence)*. Then at least I'll know what the hell everyone is saying.[6]

---

6   For the record, I finally had to look up the lyrics for "Tarnished Gluttony." Kind of up my alley, but the video isn't related to the song's lyrical content in any way that seemed obvious to me.

FOR WHOM THE BELL TOLLS

10/15/2015

I wanted to write about creepy music since Halloween is around the corner. I wanted to discuss some really disturbing, dark songs about child predators, and I had a specific song in mind. Two songs actually, one about a predator assaulting a child and the other about the child later seeking revenge. But I couldn't remember the name of the songs or the band that performed them. In my attempts to run the songs to ground, I fell into a YouTube hole that completely distracted me from my original goal.

Maybe I'll eventually get around to discussing songs about child predators, but not today. Owing to my typically circuitous "getting lost on the Internet" research method, I found a new mystery to explore.

So here's the question you weren't expecting: How many songs are inspired by Art Bell's *Coast to Coast AM*?

Discussing Art Bell's influence on music is really apropos for me this time of year, especially since I always listen to his "Ghost to Ghost" episodes right before Halloween. Anyway, when I finally found the songs I was searching for,[7] I found a title that piqued my interest and it turned out to have an Art Bell sample (it was the Venetian Snares song I discuss below—that is the song that linked me from songs about child exploitation to Art Bell). After listening to the song with the *Coast to Coast AM* sample, I decided to see

how many songs I could find that were influenced by Art Bell in some manner. Why not?

Art Bell is an interesting character, a man whose life has taken several unexpected turns. He has also been a personal hero of mine ever since he sued Ted Gunderson (who is hopefully right this very minute encountering the Satan he insisted was

---

7   The specific song titles are "Little Missy" and "Missy's Revenge" by the band G.G.F.H. While the songs are still outré and upsetting, they aren't as viscerally disgusting as they were to me when I heard them years ago. Once again, I fear I am becoming jaded.

lurking in every daycare center[8]) for slandering him as a pedophile.

Art no longer hosts *Coast to Coast AM*, but his long tenure on the AM program featured many bizarre and memorable moments. One of the most memorable was the night a man claiming to be a former Area 51 employee called the show in a panic, revealing that the US government was being duped by inhuman creatures posing as aliens from outer space.[9] The caller was emphatic that these creatures meant mankind harm. He claimed to be on the run from the federal government and he sounded completely unhinged by the gravity of his discovery. In the middle of the call, something happened to the satellite and at least 50 separate radio stations went dead for around half an hour. Understandably, this caused Art and his listeners to freak out, assuming that the feds were running interference to prevent the truth from getting out. Eventually the self-purported Area 51 whistleblower called back to explain that it was indeed a hoax, but he had no idea what had happened to the satellites. We might assume it was just a coincidence, but some listeners still believe the Area 51 caller was real and that the later call revealing the hoax is the real hoax. That's the nature of a conspiracy, isn't it?

Whatever you choose to believe, the "frantic caller" is now a part of Area 51 lore. If you have an interest in fringe or conspiracy culture, you've probably heard of it. And it has influenced some musicians, famous and obscure. One of the more famous bands to sample the Area 51 call is Tool, in the song "Faaip de Oiad" from the album *Lateralus*. "Faaip de Oiad" means "the voice of God" in "Enochian" (the supposed angelic language recorded and likely invented by John Dee and Edward Kelley). This is no surprise, really. Tool frontman Maynard Keenan is a sort of

---

8   For more on the despicable Ted Gunderson, see my discussion of John DeCamp's *The Franklin Cover-Up* on pages 44–54.

9   If you want to look it up, the episode is called either the "Area 51 Caller" or "The Frantic Caller."

Renaissance man of the weird. I think he runs a winery now, of all things.

"Faaip de Oiad" doesn't freak me out the way it does many Tool fans. I think that's because I've heard the source material too many times, and long before the song came to my attention. Still, I can see how the sampled track would be jarring or alarming to those who aren't familiar with the source and context of the jangled frightened man talking in the middle of the song.

The Area 51 caller also comes up in a song called "Planetary Duality I: Hideous Revelation" by The Faceless. Christ Almighty, where has this band been all my adulthood? The Faceless is a death metal band out of California and the song comes from an album called *Planetary Duality*. Appropriately, *Planetary Duality* is a concept album based on the ideas in David Icke's book, *Children of the Matrix*.

As this information came to my attention, Mr. OTC was sitting in front of my whacked theory shelves so I asked him to check to make sure I have *Children of the Matrix*. Indeed I do. He fetched it from the shelves, thinking I wanted to read it. And he almost opened it—*in the house*. Luckily I intervened, saving us from what madness lurked within. One day I will take Icke's book to the rest stop outside Salado and read it there. Intrepid conspiracy enthusiast that

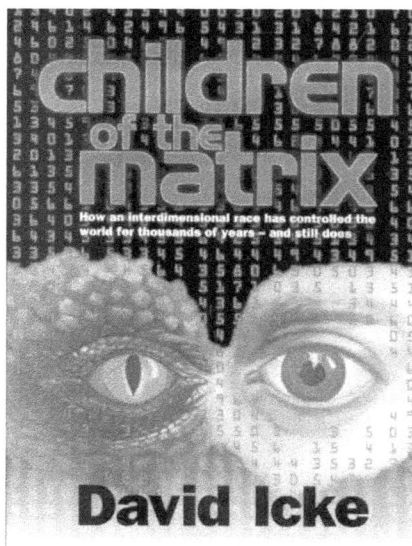

Muh reptoids!

I am, even I fear Icke's nonsense like I fear dying in a crowded elevator. But I'm still going to listen to *Planetary Duality* because their Art Bell song has piqued my curiosity. It's short but good, and how nice it is to see that the kids in this band have their alien shit together. In the original recording, the Area 51 caller says the aliens he fears are actually extradimensional beings. That's some Zecharia Sitchin stuff right there, which neatly segues into Icke's equally interesting ideas. I do love it when falling into a YouTube hole reveals so many unexplored tunnels.

But we're not finished. In 1999 a man called into *Coast to Coast* with a story about his grandfather, who told him that 74 children in a small town in America were murdered and that a 13-year-old boy was responsible, as well as maybe demons. The "mutilated corpses" were found in a river near a mill or some such. Art was skeptical but that didn't stop the caller from continuing to weave his completely unbelievable story. The segment would be memorialized in "All the Children Are Dead" by The Venetian Snares. The sampling in this song is very effective. Creepy, even upsetting. Those Area 51 samples seem campy by comparison. Large sections of the call are sampled. At 1:28, there's the bit about the "cylindrical room" where the bodies were found. At 1:42, you hear a slow voice saying, "And he looked at me and he said, 'Do you believe in monsters? Do you believe in demons?'" And at 6:47, "All the children are dead. All the children are dead." There are probably more embedded samples but I can't listen to this sort of music too closely. It makes my head hurt. Which is entirely the point, I think. There's something to be said for music that inspires nausea and pain but it makes it hard for a person like me to investigate the track too closely. I'm not a big fan of the Venetian Snares but I appreciate Aaron Funk's aesthetic. It seems noteworthy that "All the Children Are Dead" is from the *Doll Doll Doll* LP. That entire album would have fit my initial impulse to discuss music about child predators. It's devoted to child murder, with samples from a number of disparate sources, notably the infamous "Miranda Tapes" of serial killers Leonard Lake and Charles Ng. A twitchy achievement, to be sure.

As notorious as the Area 51 call is a clip from *Coast to Coast AM* where Bell plays a recording from the infamous Siberian Hole to Hell, also known as the "Well to Hell." The story goes that for some reason Russian engineers were drilling a miles-deep well in Siberia and they broke through to Hell, recording the sounds of the tormented and tortured souls consigned to eternal damnation. It's a hoax, of course, but try telling that to half the fundamentalist Christians in America.

Anyway, go look up the Art Bell segment where he plays the sounds of Hell. I'll wait here.

Nahvalr might have been your first search result. They're new to me, but the sound is old school, like true Norwegian black metal. I dug up a little about the band. The main guys, Dan Barrett and Tim Macuga, also make up the band Have a Nice Life. Dan Barrett also went on to make music under the band name Giles Corey, which sounds like it would be right up my alley based on the name alone. I should look into it

Researchers record the screams of the damned

soon. Until then, the Nahvalr song of interest begins with the Siberian Hell Sounds intro from *Coast to Coast*, but before the hell sounds kick in it segues neatly into the song, "Chorus of the Blasphemes." It's a little hokey, but it's also an interesting placement of a piece of fringe culture.

I'm sure the "Transmission of Hell" recording has made it into many metal songs. I know Cradle of Filth used a recording of the sounds in their EP *Evermore Darkly*, but the Siberian Hell Hole recording is all over the place. CoF's introduction to the noises comes from a different source, and I have to think these sounds—and this concept—pop up in all kinds of fringe music, possibly (or perhaps especially) even in Christian rock. That might be wishful thinking. I don't know.

I feel certain that Art Bell's show has influenced more music than I present in this discussion. My investigation has been cursory. Perhaps one day I'll get the itch to write up more about Art Bell, devoting more time to a discussion of his better shows and his lasting influence. I'm very fond of his interviews with the late Father Malachi Martin, as well as the shows he did with Oscar, the self-proclaimed son of Satan. I really miss Art Bell and his brand of weirdness. Next Halloween, find some of his old *Ghost to Ghost* episodes and remember the good old days and know that I will likely be somewhere out there in cyberspace, listening along with you.

PART FOUR

Odd Things
(Bibliophilia)

I guess it makes perfect sense that a bibliophile/bibliomaniac like me would eventually get down to discussing books themselves. Of course there's a bit of oddness in my approach, as I look at books bound in human skin. I also get meta as I discuss a 'zine that discusses odd books. And I get sentimental as I remember the importance of a now-closed bookstore in the way I handled good and bad times in my life. Perfect way to end this very long—tl;dr, if you will—look at books.

ANTHROPODERMIC BIBLIOPEGY —
A FLAY ON WORDS

11/09/2015

Yep. *Anthropodermic bibliopegy.* That's the technical term for books bound in human skin.

I decided to write this article after I stumbled across five references to anthropodermic bibliopegy in a 48-hour period. I took that as a sign. Synchronicity isn't something I normally put much faith in, but I think five time-clustered hits for such an arcane subject would be enough to get anyone's attention. Of course, it doesn't hurt that I find flesh-bound books extremely interesting. Who doesn't?

As I set about my research, I found myself wishing there were a master list of some kind—or at least a one-stop guide highlighting the more famous examples of anthropodermic bibliopegy. Then I thought, I'm up to the task. If anyone is going to compile a long and wordy guide to the creepiest frontier of bibliophilic oddity, it might as well be me. So here we are.

I knew a few things going in. Because of my interest in true crime, I knew of at least one instance where court records were bound in the skin of an executed criminal. I was also familiar with a few examples of anthropodermic bibliopegy in pop culture, notably the *Evil Dead* films. Given the morbidity of the subject, I was surprised at how little I knew about these books, real or fictional. Books, creepy things, unsettling representations of the dead—you'd think I would have been all over this topic by now.

As I read about books bound in human skin I noticed a surge of articles on the subject in the spring and summer of 2014, after Harvard University tested three suspected examples from their collections. It turned out that only one was the real thing, the human leather being from a woman who spent her life in a mental asylum.[1] Those tests spurred a resurgence of media interest in anthropodermic bibliopegy, and for this I am deeply appreciative. Were it not for Harvard providing a head start, I don't think my research into the topic would have been so easy. Though several sources insist that binding books in human skin was once an accepted practice, it appears that it was

---

1   Dean, Erin. "The Macabre World of Books Bound in Human Skin." *BBC News Magazine*, June 20, 2014. http://www.bbc.com/news/magazine-27903742 (accessed on December 16, 2017).

never all that common. To the extent that it was done at all, the craft more or less ended in the late 19th century. There are very few of these books that remain in museums and libraries.

Though the bulk of the remaining examples of anthropodermic bibliopegy are from the 18th and 19th centuries and primarily from Europe, claims of human skin being used for book binding date at least to the 13th century. Prior to the development of precise scientific testing, experts determined origin of leather via microscopic analysis. Physicians and museum curators observed patterns in cuticles and tiny hair remnants left in pores after the tanning process and used those patterns to determine the animal from which the skin was derived. Many books purported to be bound in human skin were identified as such through these techniques. Not many have been subjected to conclusive modern tests.

One of best tests to determine the origin of tanned skin is peptide mass fingerprinting, which analyzes the proteins left in tanned skin.[2] Those proteins point to the animal the skin was taken from, and though at times the protein markers show simply that the skin was taken from primates, it can be generally be assumed that those primates were humans. Monkeys were not thick on the ground in Europe in the 18th and 19th centuries. At least one book that was long considered to be one of the best examples of a book bound in human skin was proved to have been bound in sheep or cow hide after peptide mass fingerprinting. I suspect that a significant number of books initially "authenticated" through older, microscopic methods would not be authenticated as human if tested using peptide mass fingerprinting. (Here I should note that even this method cannot determine who specifically donated skin, as the tanning process destroys DNA.)

The Mütter Museum of the College of Physicians of Philadelphia currently has the largest collection of books bound in human skin in the USA, counting five total volumes, three of which were bound in skin from a single donor.[3] All five have been tested according to modern standards and the bindings have been proven to be of human origin. The Mütter Museum has formed a team to try to create a comprehensive list of all known examples of anthropodermic bibliopegy, encouraging institutions to test all the books in their collections that are alleged to be bound in human skin. Simon Davis discusses the search for these books in an article on the *Mental Floss* website:

> Most institutions the team has worked with are keeping quiet, however. During her presentation at Death Salon, Rosenbloom did share the aggregate

---

2   Wikipedia contributors. "Peptide mass fingerprinting." *Wikipedia, The Free Encyclopedia.* (accessed on December 16, 2017).

3   Lander, Beth. "The Skin She Lived In." The College of Physicians at Philadelphia, October 1, 2015. http://www.collegeofphysicians.org/histmed/skin-she-lived-in/ (accessed through the Internet Archive on December 16, 2017)

results so far: Out of the 22 books the group has tested, 12 have been found to be made out of human skin. According to one of Rosenbloom's slides, the remainder were found to have been bound with "an assortment of sheep, cow, and faux (!) leather." The team has also identified an additional 16 books that they have not yet tested—and is working to locate more.[4]

There are likely some undiscovered examples in private collections, but if one of the largest known collections of books bound in human skin has only five books, perhaps the custom of binding books in human skin was indeed less common than some of the sources I consulted suggest.

The squeamishness and revulsion people feel for books bound in human skin is in itself interesting. The shock inspired by human-bound books seems curiously selective, considering some of the truly macabre museum exhibits that arouse less of a visceral response. When one considers the entirety of the Mütter Museum or the visually disturbing but excellently bizarre flayed Musée Fragonard exhibits or so many dissected bodies on display in medical museums (bodies that were often curated without the consent of the person when he or she was alive), it seems strange to get upset about "the books." Yet the more I read about this topic, the more I found myself feeling a bit uneasy about some of the examples. Perhaps it's a 21st-century mentality. Or perhaps it's because I am accustomed to patient/family consent in medical and funeral procedures. Or maybe my discomfort is caused by my identification with the underclasses who ended up providing most of the skins used to bind books. I do wonder if others who immerse themselves in this topic find themselves growing a bit indignant about the fates of some of the people who ended up as book bindings.

In any case, as I read about anthropodermic bibliopegy, I found that the topic fell neatly into several categories: criminals whose skin was harvested after their executions; skin used from people who could not or did not give meaningful consent to have their skin used after their deaths; voluntary skin donors; books proven not to be bound in human skin after peptide mass fingerprinting; and representations of human skin-bound books in pop culture.

Before we explore these categories, please note that I exercised some discretion that may seem presumptuous since I am not an antiquarian, nor a book binder, nor a scientist. Thus you will find that there are some "authentic" books that I think are unlikely to be truly bound in human skin. I sometimes leave the books of questionable provenance in the "real" sections, and sometimes I put them in the "fake" section. Generally the purportedly "authentic" examples of anthropodermic bibliopegy that I place in the hoaxes or disproved section are pretty egregious fakes.

4   Davis, Simon. "The Quest to Discover the World's Books Bound in Human Skin." *Mental Floss*, October 19, 2015. http://mentalfloss.com/article/70048/quest-discover-worlds-books-bound-human-skin (accessed on December 16, 2017)

CRIMINALS

In the early 19th century, medical colleges and surgeons had a hard time obtaining corpses for dissection, and frequently dissected the bodies of executed criminals. During these dissections, some of the criminals ended up flayed, their skin tanned and used to bind books (and also used in an array of leather goods).

It took me a moment to realize that's a gallows on the cover.

John Horwood developed a fixation on Eliza Balsum (also spelled as Balsam and Balsom) in 1821, after they dated briefly. He stalked her, eventually attacking her by throwing a rock at her (the account in the bound trial records indicates that Horwood bludgeoned Balsum with a large rock but other accounts indicate that the attack consisted of him throwing a rock at her and hitting her in the head). She later died from a medical intervention meant to save her—trepanning, to be specific—but her friends identified Horwood as Eliza's attacker and he was accused of murder. He stood trial and after he was found guilty of her murder, he was executed. Horwood's body ended up being dissected at the Bristol Royal Infirmary, and was flayed in such a manner that there were large enough sections of his skin left that they could be used to bind a book about his case. The book is currently owned by the Bristol Record Office. The book is unremarkable enough to my naked eye—I own books this old, bound in leather, that look much like this volume. However, a keen eye and a working knowledge of Latin gives away this book's unusual nature. The cover sports a gallows and is embossed with the phrase, "Cutis Vera Johannis Horwood," which means "the genuine skin of John Horwood."

This book is part of a museum exhibit in Bristol and is one of the more popular exhibits. As I mentioned above, I find much of the squeamishness about anthropodermic bibliopegy to be strangely selective, but Allie Dillon, an archivist at the M Shed museum where the book is kept, finds the use of Horwood's skin for a book binding to be exceedingly cruel. She explains her perspective on what happened to Horwood in an article on BBC.com:

> John Horwood seems to have been quite a vulnerable person and this
> may have contributed to his actions. It does seem very macabre to cover
> a book in human skin and it is quite difficult to understand why it was

done. It seems quite vengeful to me.[5]

John Horwood's mental state is largely unknown to us now, but several sources lead me to suspect that he may have suffered from some form of intellectual impairment. He was certainly from a poverty-level family who had no chance of paying for a decent criminal defense. Almost as bad as executing a mentally impaired man is how Horwood's family were refused his body after his death. They attended his execution with the sole intention of collecting his body for a proper burial but were denied his corpse by the doctor who was intent on dissecting him. In this case I can see why people would find this book to be particularly distasteful. And the abuse of Horwood's body doesn't end with the book—Horwood's skeleton was left hanging in a closet at Bristol University—the rope used to hang him still around his neck. A distant relative investigating his case found his body and arranged to have him buried next to his father.

Far less distasteful to me is the notebook made from the skin of notorious grave robber and murderer, William Burke, of Burke and Hare body-snatching fame.[6] In the 19th century, when cadavers for medical research and training were extremely hard to come by, entrepreneurial types took to digging up bodies in cemeteries to sell to universities. William Burke and William Hare got their start in the illegal sale of corpses when they sold the body of a man who had died in Hare's rooming house. When those around them failed to die off quickly enough for the duo to sell their remains, they began killing people to obtain corpses to sell. Hare was offered a chance to testify against Burke in order to save his own skin, so to speak, and he obliged. Burke was convicted of murder and hanged. After death, his skull was used to demonstrate the finer

Pocket book made from the skin of William Burke.

points of phrenology and he was publicly flayed. His skin was used to make an array of small leather goods, ranging from wallets, to card cases, to what appears to me to be a sort of early Moleskine-type notebook. It's not entirely clear how his skin ended up being used in leather goods because it doesn't appear as if any of it was earmarked for such use. Rather, portions of his skin

5   Dean. "Macabre World."

6   "The Horrid and True Story of Burke and Hare." The Worlds of Burke and Hare, burkeand-hare.com/ (accessed on December 16, 2017)

went missing after the public dissection and later the leather goods showed up.[7] It is not known who tanned Burke's skin or used it for these items, and as I read about this strange history I wondered if this was really Burke's skin at all. Not enough evidence exists either way, and I could find no evidence that these leather items have been tested using modern methods. Burke's execution date of January 28, 1829 is embossed on the front of the little book and that bulb you see extending upward on the right is the top of a pen—there is a slot inside to hold writing implements. This little book is on display at the Surgeon's Hall Museum in Edinburgh.

One of the stranger books bound in the skin of a convicted criminal is *A True and Perfect Relation of the Whole Proceedings Against the Late Most Barbarous Traitors, Garnet a Jesuit and His Confederates*, which is bound in the tanned skin of Father Henry Garnet, who was convicted and executed for his alleged role in the Gunpowder Plot against the British Parliament in 1605. The belief that Father Garnet's face is somehow visible across the front gives this book an especially creepy aura (though the face isn't as clear to me as it is to others). Father Garnet's public execution and flaying is also a bit much for modern sensibilities since the good priest didn't actually play a part in the Gunpowder Plot. He simply heard the confessions of those who were involved. Evidently that was enough to condemn him as a traitor.

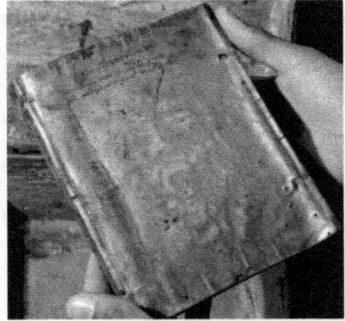

Some see Father Garnet's face on the cover of this book bound in his skin.

I do have some doubts about this one. Father Garnet's book was bound in 1606, and there are very few examples of anthropodermic bibliopegy that occurred prior to the French Revolution. This book predates the revolution by over 170 years. Moreover, a close look at the actual leather shows it to be different in appearance than other examples of books bound in human skin. It's glossier, with a very fine grain and missing are the pores one sees in examples of anthropodermic bibliopegy that have been determined to be genuine following peptide mass fingerprinting tests. There is also no record of Garnet's skin being used in such a manner, a similar problem with the records surrounding William Burke's skin. And of course, the face on the cover of the book is open to all kinds of interpretations but it seems mostly to be leather discoloration creatively embellished by the human tendency to see faces in wooden floors and burnt toast. Nevertheless,

---

7   Dean. "Macabre World."

this tiny book—4 inches by 6 inches—sold for $11,000 in an auction in 2007. If I were the owner I'd spring for a peptide mass fingerprinting test, though I don't think he or she can get a refund if it turns out to be sheep skin.

William Corder's court proceedings were bound in his skin and his case was the sole example of verified anthropodermic bibliopegy I was aware of before I began reading about the topic—a bit of arcane knowledge I picked up from my time as a minor expert in true crime. Corder impregnated an Irish girl named Maria Marten. He convinced her he wanted to marry her and lured her to her death, killing her and burying her inside a red barn, which is why the case is referred to as "The Red Barn Murder." Maria's stepmother had recurring dreams of her buried at the red barn and eventually authorities investigated and found her remains. Corder was tried for her murder, convicted and then executed. As was done with many executed criminals, his body ended up being dissected in a medical school and his skin was preserved and used to bind the court proceedings

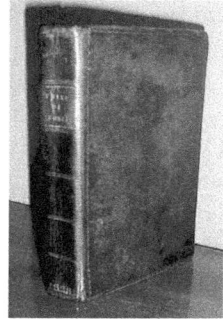

William Corder's trial records bound in his skin.

from his trial. The book is on display at the Moyse's Hall Museum in Bury St. Edmunds, Suffolk. George Creed, the surgeon who flayed him, left this inscription in the book:

> The Binding of this book is the skin of the Murderer William Corder taken from his body and tanned by myself in the year 1828. George Creed Surgeon to the Suffolk Hospital.[8]

And just to get in that extra dose of historical creepiness, the book is on display alongside Corder's scalp and death mask.

Of the books bound in human skin few are volumes meant for the ages, but there are works of lasting interest that have received the human hide treatment.

Milton's poems bound in human skin should look more dramatic, I think.

George Cudmore's skin, for example, is believed to have been used to bind a copy of John Milton's poetry. Cudmore was a rat catcher who was executed for poisoning his wife, at the urging of his mistress. It's interesting to me that Cudmore managed to have both a wife and a mistress given his overall appearance and demeanor. He was a hunchback and short, and he clearly possessed a vengeful nature—when he was convicted he

---

8   Archer, Dr. Caroline. "Print's Macabre Side." *The Typographic Hub*, May 1, 2011. http://www. typographichub.org/articles/entry/prints-macabre-side/ (accessed on December 17, 2017)

demanded that his mistress be forced to watch him hang (a request the judge granted!).[9] He was executed in 1830 but the book of Milton's poems was not published until 1852. It is unclear how an Exeter bookbinder came to have Cudmore's skin, but a certain Mr. Clifford is believed to have bound the Milton volume in Cudmore's hide. The only reason anyone believes this is the book's inscription—it could very easily be another hoax. The book is kept at the Westcountry Studies Library, and I haven't found any evidence that the book has been subjected to modern tests to determine its authenticity.

Remember Samuel Johnson, the noted lexicographer and blowhard? In 1755 he compiled a definitive collection of English words, *A Dictionary of the English Language*. In 1818 a man named James Johnson was executed in Norwich and for some reason his skin was used to bind a copy of Johnson's dictionary. No one knows why. I guess there were so many executed criminals that their tanned skins were just crying out for a legitimate use.

On the *Literary Curiosities* website I found a very interesting fact about extant books bound in human skin—the majority of them come from French aristocrats executed during the French Revolution.

A French publisher once brought out an edition of Rousseau's *Social Contract* bound in the skin of aristocrats guillotined during the Reign of Terror following the French Revolution. Other publishers in France at the time evidently took advantage of the same situation, for of the extant books bound in human skin, a high percentage are French.

An edition of *The Rights of Man* and copies of the French Constitution were also proven to be bound in human skin. The Carnavalet Museum in France has a copy of the French Constitution bound in human skin dyed green. The French don't mess around. I've often laughed at Americans who sneer at the French and consider them weak and cowardly. The French are a bunch of violent and dangerous savages kept at bay through the veneer of civilization and a socialist welfare state. The same goes for the Germans. God help us all if either country ever adopts American-style "I got mine, eat dirt asshole" free market capitalism. Because we all know how that will end up: Guillotines west of the Rhine, jack boots and beer hall putsches east of the Rhine.[10]

Unwilling or unwitting skin donors
Generally the prisoners whose skin was used to bind books did not volunteer to be posthumously flayed for the purpose, but given the overall cruelty in the judicial and penal system in 18th and 19th century England, it's not wholly unexpected that the bodies of dead criminals would be treated

9 The History Blog, February 11, 2011. www.thehistoryblog.com/archives/9990 (accessed on December 17, 2017)

10 Read this with tongue in cheek or send my publisher hostile comments, your choice.

with little sentimentality or respect. Being used to teach anatomy in medical schools or being turned into leather goods, while not always the end result of capital punishment, shouldn't be surprising either. You do the crime, you serve the time.

But if using the bodies of dead criminals to bind books seems callous and macabre, doubly so was the use of bodies of mental patients or people whose only crime in life was to die sick, poor or alone. The book that spurred the renewed interest in anthropodermic bibliopegy in the spring and summer of 2014 is unremarkable at first glance, but if you look closely you will see, very clearly, pores and blemishes that give pause. When subjected to tests, it was proved that the book (from Harvard's Houghton Library) was the real thing, giving credence to the explanatory inscription stating that the book was bound in skin taken from the corpse of a woman who died in a mental hospital and whose body was unclaimed.

Des destinées de l'ame by Arsène Houssaye is a book that muses on "the nature of the soul and life after death"—a distressing subject, considering the origin of the binding. From the *Atlas Obscura* website:

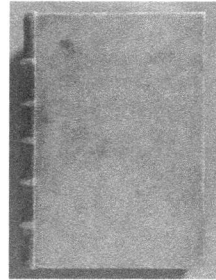

> [*Des destinées de l'ame*] is bound in the skin of an unwilling participant, an unnamed woman who died of apoplexy or a stroke while confined to a mental institution. The author, Houssaye (1815–1896), presented this copy of the publication to his friend, a medical doctor and book collector named Ludovic Bouland (1839-1932).[11]

It was Bouland who chose to use the skin of a deceased patient, whose body had remained unclaimed by friends or relatives.

Bouland inscribed the following in the book:

Des destinées de l'ame by Arsène Houssaye, bound in the skin of an unknown woman.

> This book is bound in human skin parchment on which no ornament has been stamped to preserve its elegance.
> By looking carefully you easily distinguish the pores of the skin. A book about the human soul deserved to have a human covering: I had kept this piece of human skin taken from the back of a woman. It is interesting to see the different aspects that change this skin according to the method of preparation to which it is subjected. Compare for example with the small volume I have in my library, *Sever. Pinaeus de Virginitatis notis* which is also bound in human skin but tanned with sumac.[12]

The sources about this book are a bit garbled, indicating that Houssaye

---

11   Velella, Rob. "The True Practice of Binding Books in Human Skin." *Atlas Obscura*, December 15, 2014. https://www.atlasobscura.com/articles/anthropodermic-bibliopegy-the-true-practice-of-binding-books-in-human-skin (accessed on December 16, 2017)

12   Ibid.

wrote the above inscription when it was clearly Bouland. I think this confusion caused people to overlook something implicit in Bouland's inscription, that he already had the piece of skin when he was given this book as a gift from Houssaye. Think of it: he had flayed the woman and preserved her skin before this book was even on his radar. He just had a piece of skin around the house and used it. Bouland actually did bind other books in skin, so perhaps he just liked to be prepared. It's still a bit unusual to my modern mind—to imagine someone flaying a woman who died just because he one day may want to bind a book her skin. Times change.

This book has been of particular interest to dermatologists who have been able to observe the durability of skin and the effects of the tanning process. I'm not sure what such information could possibly be used for but perhaps I lack the forward thinking of a scientist.

Ludovic Bouland also bound a 17th-century volume about female anatomy in the skin of another woman. An article on *The Typographic Hub* describes the book as:

> ...a collection of gynaecological essays by various authors, beginning with Séverin Pineau's treatise on virginity, pregnancy and childbirth, *De integritatis et corruptionis virginum notis*. Marcellin Lortic, a distinguished Paris binder, bound Pineau's treatise using a piece of woman's skin that had been tanned with sumach. The binding was done at the request of Ludovic Bouland (d. 1932), a doctor from Metz, who trained in Strasbourg in 1865 and practised in Paris. Inserted at the front of the book is a note by Dr Bouland, explaining he felt it deserved a binding to match its subject matter and that he had obtained the piece of skin from the body of a woman who had died in the hospital at Metz where he had been working as a medical student.[13]

Bouland is clearly a man whose mind is foreign to me. Though, in all truth, I know little about the volume in question. Maybe it is deserving of the skin of a forsaken woman. The book is currently housed at the Wellcome Library.

If one is to skin a woman to bind a book, the book should at least be a pretty one like this copy of *De integritatis et corruptionis virginum notis*.

Dead women seem to make up almost all of the non-criminal unwilling/unwitting donors. Medical students evidently skinned dead women and sold their skins to erotica publishers in the 19th century. Notably, a copy of *Justine et Juliette* by the Marquis de Sade was

---

13   Archer. "Print's Macabre Side."

bound in the breasts of one such forsaken woman and there are reports that the cover of this notorious tome featured a nipple, but I couldn't find a photograph of the alleged binding. From what I have been able to determine, the Sade book did not have a nipple on the cover and the belief that it did comes from some of the garbled data that seems to plague this topic. I've found several sources that say that Sade's book *L'éloge des seins* features a human nipple on the cover, and from there it's a short hop to *Justine et Juliette* being bound in breasts. But don't hop, because *L'éloge des seins* was not written by Sade. The so-called "Nipple Book" is actually a copy of *L'éloge des seins* by Claude-François-Xavier Mercier, and it was indeed bound with skin from breasts (a visible nipple appears on the cover). This is all the more French because the title of the book, translated into English, is *The Praise of Women's Breasts*. Of course, all of this is speculative and possibly in the realm of hoaxes. I couldn't find a picture of either book and until I can, and until both are subject to peptide mass fingerprinting, the stories of boob-bound books should be taken with a grain of salt. Still, it has to be said that if one were going to bind a volume of Sade in a woman's skin, a flay of breast would be apt—or maybe strip from the derriere.

Skipping from the fantastic to the all too real, the Mütter Museum showcases at least three artifacts where a particular woman's skin was used after her death without any real permission being granted before her death and flaying. Though the doctor who autopsied her and flayed her thigh didn't use her full name in the case study he wrote about her or in the inscriptions he wrote in the books he used her skin to bind, Dr. John Stockton Hough gave enough identifying information that intrepid historians were able to track down the "donor." Her name was Mary Lynch. She had been admitted to Philadelphia General Hospital with a case of tuberculosis during a warm summer and her relatives brought her pork products to eat, ultimately resulting in a fatal case of trichinosis—an area of interest for Dr. Hough. He autopsied her after her death and, for reasons that are not really clear to anyone, decided to cut off a piece of skin from her thigh and used it to bind three books. Maybe he did it because he was a bibliophile? Maybe because Mary had the worst case of parasites he had ever seen and he just had to remember her? There's no way to know, but he did it. He flayed her skin, tanned it and used it to partially bind three books.

The three titles Mary's skin was used to bind are:

> *Speculations on the Mode and Appearances of Impregnation in the Human Female*...published in 1789; *Le Nouvelles Decouvertes sur Toutes les Parties Principales de L'Homme et de la Femme*... published in 1680; and *Recueil des Secrets de Louyse Bourgeois*...published in 1650. Each of these books deals with female health, conception and reproduction.[14]

---

14   Lander. "The Skin She Lived In."

At times I wonder if I'm being a bit over-sensitive about the habit of some doctors to cut skin from cadavers as if they had some greater right to claim random parts of these female, often impoverished, bodies. In an article about Mary called "The Skin She Lived In: Anthropodermic Books in the Historical Medical Library," Beth Lander, a librarian at the Philadelphia College of Physicians, raises similar concerns about Dr. Hough's use of Mary Lynch's skin :

Skin from Mary Lynch's thigh was used on the bindings for these books.

> The books as objects force us into uncomfortable considerations of the use of human skin in bindings: Was Mary memorialized in these books? If so, why did Dr. Hough keep her skin for nearly 20 years before using it?
>
> Why did Dr. Hough use Mary's thigh skin to bind books about conception and childbirth? What, if anything, was he saying about Mary, or women in general? Were other people aware of what he was doing?
>
> Does the use of human skin diminish the value of the books as text, and render them nothing more than objects of morbid curiosity?[15]

In Dr. Hough's case, he did attempt to memorialize Mary by writing about

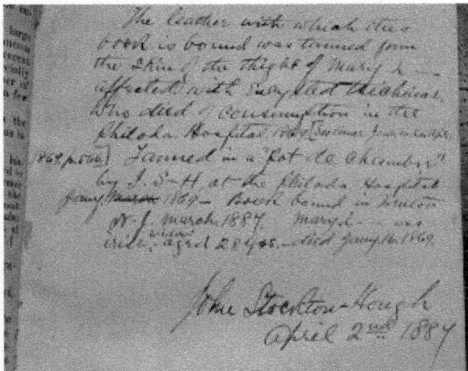

An inscription from Dr. Hough in one of the books bound in Mary Lynch's skin.

her in his inscriptions in the three books, even as he tried to protect her privacy (though I have to wonder if he omitted her last name to prevent living relatives from reacting in anger). She was not hidden from history completely and her skin was used to bind books about female anatomy. Perhaps Dr. Hough did feel some connection to this young woman killed by parasites, one of his areas of specialty, and he wanted a piece

---

15   Ibid.

of her skin. But even extending sentimentality to such an act doesn't really help me understand the compulsion of some medical men to skin patients, especially when there was no revenge or justice motive such that we find in the flaying of executed criminals. I want to believe that Dr. Hough felt some special connection to this woman, that he didn't skin her just because he could. But there's no way to know.

Four of the five books bound in human skin at the Mütter Museum came from Dr. Hough. The book that was not bound in Mary's skin is a copy of *Bibliotheque Nationale.* Dr. Hough wrote that the book was bound in human skin but little else is known about the book other than that the skin came from the donor's back. Despite the fact that Dr. Hough flayed a woman who did not give consent for such a procedure, Paul Wolpe, a bioethicist at the University of Pennsylvania, has this to say about the anthropodermically bound *Bibliotheque Nationale*:

> He emphasized, though, that with artifacts such as *Bibliotheque Nationale*, the skin used was not from exploited individuals, such as slaves or concentration-camp prisoners, but often from people of significance to the binder.[16]

Wolpe goes on to say that he believes Mary Lynch's case to be one of Dr. Hough honoring his dead patient, not one of a rich doctor exploiting a poverty-level immigrant. I hope he's right.

While we are discussing the books at the Mütter Museum, let's have a look at the sole book that did not come from Dr. Hough's collection. This book comes from a different doctor—Dr. Joseph Leidy, another Philadelphia medical man. His book is not as well-documented as Dr. Hough's were. It's a copy of *An Elementary Treatise on Human Anatomy.* The inscription reads:

> The leather with which this book is bound is human skin, from a soldier who died during the great Southern Rebellion.[17]

Dr. Leidy was a surgeon for the Union during the Civil War, so that is likely how he obtained the skin from the soldier. I placed Leidy's book here in the "unwilling" donor section because given the behavior of other doctors during this time, it seems unlikely Dr. Leidy asked the dying soldier if he would consent to having skin removed in order to bind a book.

Jacques Delille translated Virgil's *Georgics* into French and was a renowned translator. A copy of his *Georgics* translation was bound in his own skin. There's not a lot of back story to this particular book because we don't really know how his skin was obtained for the purpose. After Delille died, he must

---

16   Schwartz, Jason. "Classic Texts – In the Flesh." *The Daily Pennsylvanian*, January 18, 2006. http://www.thedp.com/article/2006/01/classic_texts_in_the_flesh#comment8900 (accessed on December 16, 2017)

17   Davis. "Quest to Discover."

have been left unattended for a good while as he lay in state because someone managed to slip in undetected and remove a portion of his skin. Or a funeral attendant received a nice bribe to look the other way. Still, the mind fairly boggles.

This next book is less a mind-boggler than it is a head-shaker. The bizarre and disturbing case is documented in Daniel K. Smith's article on anthropodermic bibliopegy in *The Morbid Anatomy Anthology*,[18] but the kicker is that a 17th century book on the pituitary gland—*Exercitatio anatomica de glandula pituitaria*—ended up being bound in the skin of circus giant. The book sits in the collection at the Clendening History of Medicine Library in Kansas City, a bound testament to morbid inspiration even more on the nose than those books about female anatomy bound in the skin of random women. The story is that Dr. Charles Humberd, owner of the book, somehow got his hands on the skin of an 8'6" tall giant who traveled with the Ringling Brothers Circus. An inscription on the front end page says:

De luxe binding of / human skin from the / circus giant "Perky."[19]

If Humberd's name rings a bell, you may have read about him in *Freak Show* by Robert Bogdan. He was sued by the world's tallest man, Robert Wadlow, for libel. According to Bogdan's account, Humberd showed up randomly at the Wadlow home one day with the intention of conducting a medical examination. When Wadlow refused to be examined, the intrusive doctor nevertheless proceeded to publish an entire case history about Wadlow. Dr. Humberd evidently had a strong, bordering on fanatical interest in people who grew to enormous heights due to pituitary disorders. He collected their shoes and other personal possessions. Given the nature of his obsession with giants and his apparent lack of ethics, it seems plausible that he could have acquired the skin of a giant. Then again, for the same reasons, it's equally plausible that *Exercitatio anatomica de glandula pituitaria* isn't bound in human skin at all. What makes me lean toward this being another hoax is the fact that no one seems to know who "Perky" might be—even people devoted to the topic are unclear on Perky's identity.[20] I feel myself possessed with the urge to read all I can about Humberd—he sounds like an obsessive weirdo who was also a kind of genius. Maybe one day I'll find out who Perky was. Based on the sources I've consulted, it does

18   Smith, Daniel K. "Books Bound in Skin: A Survey of Examples of Anthropodermic Bibliopegy." Eds. Joanna Ebenstein and Colin Dickey. *The Morbid Anatomy Anthology*. Morbid Anatomy Press, 2014, 380–393.

19   KUMC Libraries Catalog. "Exercitatio anatomica de glandula pituitaria ... /" http://voyager-catalog.kumc.edu/Record/175536/Description#tabnav (accessed on December 16, 2017)

20   See the archived discussion thread at: http://www.thetallestman.com/whoisthetallest/view-topic.php?f=4&t=547 (accessed on December 16, 2017).

not appear that this book has been subject to peptide mass fingerprinting.

There's a sort of colonialist approach to anthropodermic bibliopegy that became more and more evident as I read about it. This can be seen especially in a book that is kept at the John Hay Library at Brown University—a copy of Andrea Vesalius' *De humani corporis fabrica*, a beautiful 16th century text full of detailed drawings of human dissection that was bound in human skin and presented to King Leopold II of Belgium. I cannot find anything about the donor of the skin, so I tend to lean toward the skin being harvested without consent, but it is interesting that this skin-bound book was presented to this particular King. From the article in *The Morbid Anatomy Anthology*:

> [this book] was bound for King Leopold II of Belgium, who was at the time directing the mass murder of millions of Africans in the Congo. Under the guise of stopping the slave trade in the Congo, he sent European adventurers and mercenaries to the unmapped African interior, where they killed, enslaved, tortured, raped, and maimed in the most brutal ways while harvesting ivory and later rubber. Vesalius's bold and daring work had formed the art of surgery out of what was at the time more butchery than treatment—and here it was, gifted to one of the greatest butchers of the nineteenth century.[21]

Yeah. It got real dark real fast, didn't it?

I can't determine if the source of next example volunteered his or her skin, but in the absence of clearly articulated consent, I assume it was an unwilling donor. The book, also housed in the John Hay Library at Brown University, may be one of the few relatively mainstream novels ever to be bound in human skin. The title is *Mademoiselle Giraud, ma femme*, and it was written by Adolphe Belot in 1870. It sounds like a steamy potboiler—a man discovers his wife is a lesbian and becomes completely unhinged. From *The Morbid Anatomy Anthology* article:

> Handwritten on the front flyleaf of the John Hay Library's copy is "Bound in human skin/S.B.L." and on the back "Genuine Human Skin" in the same hand. The library also holds a letter written by Sam Loveman of Bodley Book Shop further attesting to the book's authenticity.[22]

I'm not sure Sam Loveman's word is enough to close the case, but it's worth mentioning that Loveman was a friend of H.P. Lovecraft, so it's possible this book may have been inspiration for details in one of Lovecraft's stories.

There are extant examples of *The Dance of Death* bound in human skin. A British bookbinder named Joseph Zaehnsdorf discussed in a letter how he was forced to split in two a piece of human skin to make it large enough to bind a collection of Hans Holbein's Dance of Death woodcuts. And this

---

21   Smith. *Morbid Anatomy Anthology*, 393.

22   Ibid.

particular *Dance of Death* comes with an interesting distinction. Again, from *The Morbid Anatomy Anthology* article:

> This binding is plain and unadorned with a remarkable exception: human hair was used as headbands, and a few strands remain.[23]

I have so many questions. Like, did the hair and the skin come from the same donor? And if not, why would anyone mix body coverings in such a manner?

Reading Smith's article in *The Morbid Anatomy Anthology*, I was confronted with yet another strange volume that raised some odd questions. The Grolier Club in New York boasts a book bound in skin, a collection of poems written in the 16th century called *Le Traicte de Peyne* (*Treatise on Suffering*). A 19th-century introduction explains that the volume consists of allegorical poems written by three penitents (the description on the Grolier's Club website lists the subject of this book to be pain and masochism). Given that this was not a book that was ever published, I wonder how much skin these Parisian bookbinders had just lying around that they didn't flinch at human-hide binding a collection of poems that was never submitted for popular publication. It also makes me wonder how many books like this are still in private collections—books written for a particular set of eyes only, never intended for distribution, bound in skin for reasons that were never shared.

One of the funnier stories I read about anthropodermic bibliopegy comes from Dr. Caroline Archer's article for Typographic Hub, "Print's Macabre Side":

> In *My life with paper*, the Ohio-born master printer and book designer Dard Hunter recalls being hired by a young widow to bind a volume of letters dedicated to her late husband using his own skin. The widow remarried and Hunter wonders whether her second husband saw himself as volume two, wryly concluding: 'Let us hope that this was strictly a limited edition.'[24]

Since I am unsure if the husband volunteered his skin, I am placing this book in the "unwitting" category.

VOLUNTARY SKIN DONORS

One of the more famous voluntary skin donations was used to bind a book on astronomy. I am wholly unfamiliar with the works of Camille Flammarion and that seems a grave oversight given some of the odd claims the French astronomer made, among them that Halley's comet was going to demolish the Earth. Flammarion also advanced a sort of prototype of the ancient alien theory, being certain that Martians had communicated with the Earth in the distant past and shaped current civilizations. And he was also a fan of the

---

23   Ibid., 390.

24   Archer, "Print's Macabre Side."

"Ezekiel's Wheel was totally a spacecraft" theory.

In spite of his odd ideas, or perhaps because of them, a French countess who was a fan decided that after she died she wanted to send him a section of her skin to use to bind one of his books. Actually, by some accounts she was positively infatuated with Flammarion and, though the two never met, her dermatological donation was intended as a sort of erotic gesture. Seriously, this woman had a tattoo of Flammarion somewhere on her body, though one presumes it was not on the part of her skin she contributed for the binding (can you imagine receiving a patch of human skin with your own face tattooed on it in the mail?). Anyway, she died young from tuberculosis and was subsequently flayed. Flammarion was touched by the gesture and used her skin to bind the first copy of his book, *Terres du ciel*, in 1882. Despite having spent an inordinate amount of time looking, I cannot find a picture of the actual book in question. This is odd, since dozens of articles reproduce a photo of the manuscript without any visible binding. The book currently resides at Flammarion's observatory in Juvisy.

Not all voluntary skin donors were anonymous. James Allen (real name George Walton), was a famous highwayman in the 19th century. During his career, he claimed that only one person ever resisted him during an attack. And that one act of courage left an impression. Allen was so impressed, in fact, that he made an unusual request:

> On facing the gallows, Walton stipulated a copy of his memoirs be bound in his own skin and given to John Fenno, a man whom Walton had attempted to rob on the Massachusetts Turnpike. Fenno had so impressed Walton by bravely resisting the robbery attempt, weathering a gunshot wound, and assisting in bringing the highwayman to justice that Walton honoured his victim with this macabre anthropodermic bibliopegic gift. After Walton's execution the book was delivered to Fenno whose relatives eventually donated it to the Boston Athenaeum, where it remains today.[25]

It's a simple, short book, with the phrase *Hic liber Waltonis cute compactus est* embossed across the front (Latin for "This book is bound in Walton's skin").

Have a look at the large-scale photo available on the Athenaeum's website—it's creepily skin-like, if that doesn't go without saying. The size of the pores, the appearance of the skin—it really appears very human-like in comparison to sheepskin bound books from the same time frame. The entire text of the book is also available through the Atheneum's website.

The next example makes me wonder how many books were bound in the skin of besotted women. Because such a woman was the mistress of the French novelist Eugène Sue, who left instructions in her will that a copy of one of Sue's novels be bound in her skin. That instruction was carried out

---

25   Ibid.

in the binding of Sue's novel, *Vignettes: les Mystères de Paris*. Sadly, the book doesn't seem to have much cachet—in 1951 the book was sold at a French bookstore for the modern equivalent of $29.[26]

Now we come to the voluntary donor that was the creepiest of them all for me. I can't find pictures of the book or more information than is available through secondary sources online, but it's still worth discussing. An edition of *The Harvard Crimson* in 1933 mentions a small book called *Little Poems for Little Folk*:

> [the book] was bound in the skin of a donor who remained happily alive and healthy after the removal of 20 square inches of skin from his back. The book was privately owned; the book's current whereabouts are unknown.[27]

Wow. I have to wonder what was so important about a book of poetry for children that a person was willing to have his skin removed *while he was alive* in order to bind it. I really want to know more about this book. I sort of want to own it.

LEGENDS AND HOAXES/DISPROVED CLAIMS

For years Harvard suspected they had some examples of anthropodermic bibliopegy—*Des destinées de l'ame* being one of them—and testing proved that volume was indeed human skin, as discussed above. However, one of the books suspected of being bound in human skin proved to be fake. *Practicarum quaestionum circa leges regias Hispaniae* by Juan Gutiérrez, bound at some point during the 17th century, contained this bizarre inscription on its last page:

> The bynding of this booke is all that remains of my dear friende Jonas Wright, who was flayed alive by the Wavuma on the Fourth Day of August, 1632. King Mbesa did give me the book, it being one of poore Jonas chiefe possessions, together with ample of his skin to bynd it. Requiescat in pace.[28]

Given my relatively crappy knowledge of African history, I feel no shame in admitting that I have never heard of the Wavuma tribe or King Mbesa, but lucky for me a guy in the comments in the Harvard law blog has heard of both and had this to say:

> It looks in any case as if the Wavuma are a Ugandan tribe with which the British first made contact in the 19th century. (Which seems as if it would

---

26   If Mr. OTC skins me posthumously, I hope a book bound in my carcass fetches a bit more than the equivalent of a date night at Olive Garden.

27   Velella. "True Practice."

28   Beck, Karen. "852 RARE: Old Books, New Technologies, and "The Human Skin Book" at HLS." *Et Seq. | The Blog of the Harvard Law School Library*, April 3, 2014. http://etseq.law.harvard.edu/2014/04/852-rare-old-books-new-technologies-and-the-human-skin-book-at-hls/ (accessed on December 16, 2017)

have made the inscription suspect even before running the tests.)[29]

Since the tests showed the binding of the book not to be of human origin, it's safe to say this was a hoax (though the purpose behind it remains unknown).

It's interesting to note that many articles on anthropodermic bibliopegy that predate the tests in 2014 liken the purportedly flesh-bound memorial to poor Jonas Wright to the mourning jewelry Victorians would make from the hair of the dead. When reading about this book, check the dates of the articles—

It's a well-known fact that Jonas Wright was a duck!

it's is often treated as an ironclad example of anthropodermic bibliopegy but that claim has indeed been disproven.

Juniata College in Pennsylvania believed they had a skin-bound book in their collection. Prompted by the testing Harvard did on their suspected examples of anthropodermic bibliopegy, they set about testing their own. The volume, *Biblioteca Politica*, is a collection of Latin essays, published in 17th century France. Inscribed on a front page is an assertion that the book is bound in human skin, but testing in 2014 at Harvard showed the book is actually bound in sheepskin.

Scourge to librarians—and a dirty fake, to boot!

Though this may be a blow to the college, it may be a boon for librarians because the book had become a popular morbidity among the students, who flowed into the library asking to see the book every semester.

Though no examples ever emerged of anthropodermic bibliopegy from Nazi concentration and death camps, misuse of Jewish skin did happen during the Holocaust. There are extant examples of Nazi prisoners who were skinned after death, mostly skin with tattoos. However, there is no proof to the rumors that Ilsa Koch bound photo albums in Jewish skin or that there were copies of *Mein Kampf* bound in human skin. History is rife with examples of conquerors flaying their enemies or victims and displaying their skins in some manner—in this grisly regard, Nazis had plenty of company. But just like the myth of the lampshades, the idea

---

29   Ibid. Comment by Michael Schiffer, dated April 4, 2014 at 10:03 pm.

that Nazis used human skin to bind books is not based in fact.[30]

The Morbid Anatomy Anthology article mentions briefly that the Newberry Library in Chicago has a book with the inscription:

> Found in the Palace of the King of Delhi, Sept. 28 1857, seven days after the assault James Wise MD/Bound in human skin.[31]

This particular book piqued my curiosity. What assault? What is the book? Who? What? When? Where? And also, how? Evidently the book is *The Chronicles of Nawat Wuzeer Hyderabed* and there is little evidence that it is indeed bound in skin.

I found out a lot about this book in an unlikely place: a Q&A page on the Newberry Library website for Audrey Niffenegger's book, *The Time Traveler's Wife*. The library plays a small part in Niffenegger's book, and people have wondered if there is indeed a book bound in skin in the collection.

> The book was owned by John M. Wing, eccentric Chicago publisher, book collector, and benefactor of the Newberry's Wing Foundation on the History of Printing. There is no information as to how he came to possess the book. The book has two inscriptions on the first leaf of the volume: the first, signed by James Wise, M.D. refers to the Sepoy Mutiny, the siege in which the book was allegedly taken.[32]

The library staff is almost certain the book is not bound in human skin:

> The "human skin" question led librarians to the Newberry's conservation lab, where the staff made several observations of the binding material under a microscope. Comparisons were made with new and old calf, goat, and sheep leathers. It is the opinion of the conservation staff that the binding material is not human skin, but rather highly burnished goat.[33]

I knew I had to include this book when I read the phrase "highly burnished goat."

Though it has not been proven a fraud, I have a difficult time believing *El Viaje Largo* by Tere Medina is bound in the skin of a willing donor, though it appears on several top ten lists of creepy books. The book of erotica was published in 1972, and a copy is purported to have been bound in skin allegedly obtained from rites performed by an indigenous tribe of Puerto Rico. Inscribed in the book in Spanish and English is the following:

---

30   Alban, Dan. "Books Bound in Human Skin; Lampshade Myth?" *The Harvard Law Record*, November 11, 2005. http://hlrecord.org/2005/11/books-bound-in-human-skin-lampshade-myth/ (accessed on December 16, 2017)

31   Smith. *Morbid Anatomy*, 380.

32   The Newberry. Research Guides: *The Time Traveler's Wife*. https://www.newberry.org/time-traveler-s-wife (accessed on December 16, 2017)

33   Ibid.

The cover of this book is made from the leather of the human skin. The Aguadilla tribe of the Mayaguez Plateau region preserves the torso epidermal layer of deceased tribal members. While most of the leather is put to utilitarian use by the Aguadillas, some finds its way to commercial trade markets where there is a small but steady demand. This cover is representative of that demand.[34]

Even without peptide mass fingerprinting, I think we can safely say this story is questionable. Various sources with more cachet than top-ten list and Pinterest clickbait state that there are no known 20th century examples of anthropodermic bibliopegy, so that lends some credence to my reflexive hunch that the story behind this book is a load of nonsense. And I encourage anyone who reads this to search for facts about the Aguadilla tribe in the Mayaguez Plateau region—if you find any reference that *doesn't* lead back to the inscription in this book I will be very surprised. Moreover, if you find anything at all about tribal rites in 20th century Puerto Rico that involve skinning the dead, you're a better man than I. I think this is a good example of a pre-Internet hoax, concocted before online search engines made it difficult to pull off such an audacious story. There are pictures of the actual book online but I'm not reproducing one in this article because they are all quite blurry.

Another book that I have no proof is not bound in human skin but suspect is not comes from the Cleveland Public Library, which claims to have a copy of the Koran that was bound in the skin of a devout Muslim who asked to be flayed and tanned posthumously. As is often the case, an inscription is the only evidence that the book is bound in human skin:

> On a page inside, a note in faded pencil claims that Professor Wilson of Cambridge confirmed it was likely bound in human skin, and that it belonged to East Arab Chief Bushiri ibn Salim. It's a deep red, chipped near the binding. It feels like leather—which, I guess, it is. Human leather. The skin is believed to either belong to Bushiri or someone he killed.[35]

On its face this seems unlikely. Devout Muslims frown even on cremation—it's hard to imagine a devout Muslim (or any devout member of any Abrahamic religion) asking to be flayed posthumously if they won't even consider being rendered into ashes. Thus it is not surprising that this particular example of alleged anthropodermic bibliopegy caused some upset in parts of the Muslim community when it appeared in assorted news articles online. In January 2006 Islamic Community Net contacted the Cleveland Public

---

34   Hood, Nathanael. "Top 10 Books Wrapped in Human Skin." *TopTenz*, August 2, 2011. http://www.toptenz.net/top-10-books-wrapped-in-human-skin.php (accessed on December 16, 2017.)

35   Netzel, Andy; Matheson, Amber (ed.). "35th Anniversary: The Macabre Koran Revisited." *Cleveland Magazine*, November 27, 2007. https://clevelandmagazine.com/in-the-cle/articles/35th-anniversary-the-macabre-koran-revisited (accessed on December 16, 2017)

Library to challenge the notion that any Koran could be bound in the skin of a Muslim true believer. The library responded:

> Hello — my name is [redacted], Head of Fine Arts & Special Collections. In regards to the article, if you read it carefully the sentence clearly states that the "Quran that MAY have been bound in the skin of its previous owner" is the best verification that has been documented with the item when the library acquired it decades ago. The AP was not incorrect in its statement. We are just not absolutely sure since there is no way to test it.[36]

I redacted the name of the woman who sent the reply because she gets threats from disturbed people accusing her of staging a "blood libel" hoax against Muslims every time she discusses this subject and I don't want to add to her burden. Hopefully she and the Cleveland Library can get this book tested sooner than later because if it can be shown not to be bound in human flesh, which I suspect will happen, that result would make the librarian's life a lot easier and would calm those believers who think that lies were made up about their religion specifically to defame them.

If this book has been subjected to peptide mass fingerprinting since the brouhaha in 2006–2007, I can find no evidence of it. As for it being a deliberate attempt to tarnish Islam, consider the bigger picture. If you have read the whole of this article to this point, you will see that this is a topic fraught with frauds that demean everyone from Puerto Ricans to the entire English penal system to sufferers of pituitary diseases. Of all the insults available, a dubious story about a human skin-bound Koran is hardly the most direct way to defame Islam. All I know is that if I were the librarian in question I would encourage testing for this book post-haste, for it mostly likely is a fraud and should be declared so if it is. And if tests prove it to be bound in human skin, that would be very interesting (while being terrible news for the poor librarian).

In Popular Culture

I think most lovers of horror fiction know about H.P. Lovecraft's *Necronomicon*, a magical text that has inspired horror writers and movie makers for decades. The first mention of *Necronomicon* appears in Lovecraft's "The Hound." That story, according to Smith in *The Morbid Anatomy Anthology*, was influenced by a jaunt H.P. Lovecraft took with Sam Loveman, an alleged practitioner of anthropodermic bibliopegy. More specifically, it is claimed that Loveman and Lovecraft took a tour of a graveyard in a church in Flatbush, which inspired Lovecraft's story of grave robbers in "The Hound."

---

36   Islamic Community Net. "Cleveland Public Library Spreads Blood Libel Against Holy Quran, Islam & Muslims." January 12, 2006. https://groups.yahoo.com/neo/groups/islamiccommunitynet/conversations/topics/9092 (accessed on December 16, 2017)

Please bear with me as I engage in some pedantry. The *Morbid Anatomy* article indicates *Necronomicon* was bound in human skin as was the tome mentioned in "The Hound." That's not the case. The book doesn't actually appear in "The Hound." Rather, it is referenced, as the grave robbers discover an amulet around a corpse's neck that is mentioned in *Necronomicon*. The book bound in skin mentioned in "The Hound" is wholly different from *Necronomicon*. I sense people may be ready to argue this point with me but here is the exact verbiage about the book bound in skin in "The Hound":

> A locked portfolio, bound in tanned human skin, held certain unknown and unnameable drawings which it was rumoured Goya had perpetrated but dared not acknowledge.[37]

I can't find any evidence that Lovecraft's *Necronomicon*, in any of the editions he discusses, was ever bound in human skin. I think the belief that this fictional book is bound in human skin comes from the *Evil Dead* films and a garbled belief that the book bound in human skin mentioned in "The Hound" refers to *Necronomicon* rather than the portfolio of clandestine Goya drawings.

Speaking of the *Evil Dead* films, they provide excellent examples of anthropodermic bibliopegy in pop culture. Sam Raimi was undoubtedly influenced by Lovecraft, what with the book causing all the trouble being called *Necronomicon Ex-Mortis* or *Naturom Demonto*. And of course Raimi's *Necronomicon*—unlike Lovecraft's—was bound in human skin, with the words written in human blood, no less. And if you speak the words out loud you will cause a house full of young people in a cabin in Tennessee to collectively lose their shit. The pop culture tendrils from Lovecraft and Evil Dead are long and intertwined and to elaborate on them would necessitate a horribly involved discussion of the way Lovecraft's *Book of the Dead* has been used in all sorts of media, from film to music to comic books. I might undertake such a task one day, but for the moment just know that Lovecraft's *Necronomicon* was not bound in skin (but Sam Raimi's was), and that the skin-bound book in "The Hound" was a collection of dark drawings.

Chuck Palahniuk's novel *Lullaby* features a book bound in human skin. A reporter by the name of Carl Streator is tasked to write about a rash of SIDS (sudden infant death syndrome) cases and discovers that the deaths are linked to a book called *Poems and Rhymes Around the World*. When the poems in the book are read aloud, the child who hears them dies. The book is referred to as a "culling" book. This was the last of Palahniuk's novels that I enjoyed without reservation and I think that the backstory—Palahniuk's

---

37   Wikisource contributors, "The Hound," Wikisource, https://en.wikisource.org/w/index.php?title=The_Hound&oldid=5972627 (accessed on December 16, 2017)..

reason for writing *Lullaby*—is far more interesting[38] than the presence of a skin-bound baby-killing book.

There are many elements of pop culture that involve books bound in skin—the film *The Pillow Book*, Mayhem's first studio album, among them—but that would require an exhaustive examination that would test even my verbosity (and dedication to subject matter).

I do have a question for you. After reading this, do you find yourself wondering what book you would like to have bound in your skin should you end up flayed? It's a ridiculous and morbid question but one that seems almost unavoidable after being immersed in this ridiculous and morbid topic. Mr. OTC would dedicate his hide to the binding the collected works of Patrick O'Brien . As for me, I would want my bodily leather to be used to bind books from the Burns Archive, especially any collection of death photography, like the *Sleeping Beauty* books.

So this is what happens when I fall down a deep rabbit hole and write about what I find when I reach the bottom. I have no idea if my efforts will serve a purpose greater than my own curiosity, but it has been a creepily fun jaunt, and I hope someone somewhere breathes easier knowing the more famous and infamous examples of anthropodermic bibliopegy have been collected in one place.

---

38   Palahniuk's father, Fred, was dating a woman who had put her ex-husband, Dale Shackleford, in prison for sexual abuse. When released from prison, her ex-husband tracked her down and killed her and Fred. Chuck Palahniuk was asked to be a part of the decision-making in the penalty phase as to whether or not Shackleford would be put to death. He wrote *Lullaby* as he grappled with his feelings about the death penalty.

CHRIS MIKUL'S "BIBLIO-CURIOSA"

06/08/2012

This isn't technically a book review, but it is going to entail a deep-dive discussion of odd books. When Chris Mikul noticed that I had read his book about cults (and I still plan to write about it eventually, though it's now been a year since I read it, and ... fuck my life), he was kind enough to send me the first two copies of his 'zine *Biblio-Curiosa*. Then he sent me issues of another 'zine of his, *Bizarrism* along with a copy of his book, *Tales of the Macabre and Ordinary*. Please do not misinterpret my delight in receiving these items as a tacit admission that I'm easily bought. I read and eventually discuss everything people send me. If Mikul jumped the line a little, it's because he is an incredible writer and I didn't want to sit on these until they came around in the review queue. My house, my rules.

Biblio-Curiosa is what I wish OTC could be when it grows up, if it grows up. Mikul's analysis of the strange books and authors he encounters manages to be both scholarly and entertaining, a skill borne from years of writing and studious research. I would do well to emulate some of his organizational skills in my own oddbooks journalism. I've always said I resent being inspired, but there is something about Mikul's work that makes me want to be a better writer. Even if I sense my innate verbosity and my inability to focus will prevail against anything transformative, I can always hope.

Biblio-Curiosa is subtitled "Unusual Writers/Strange Books" and it delivers on both fronts with equal ease. The breadth of Mikul's interests and the scope of the topics he discusses puts to shame my passive procurement of odd books. He curates a mountain of strangeness, enlightening readers to books and ideas that might otherwise be forgotten. I know when I see pulp paperbacks from the '50s, I often look at the lurid covers and think, "I bet my dad would have read that and liked it." But it was Mikul's survey of those bygone pulps that convinced me that I shouldn't have been so dismissive. For behind

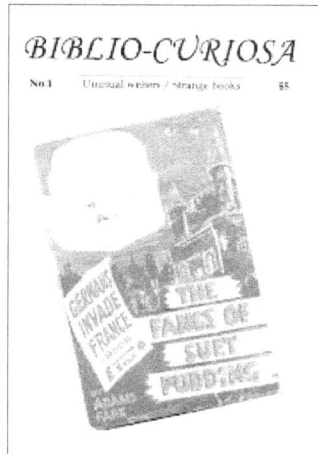

BIBLIO-CURIOSA

No. 1   Unusual writers / strange books $8

the timeworn covers of the pulpiest of the pulps, many interesting stories and mysteries remain to be discovered. Sometimes it takes an intrepid bibliophile to remind us of what we might be missing.

The premiere issue of *Biblio-Curiosa* has also provided me with a new Holy Grail: *The Pepsi-Cola Addict*. I will not die happy unless I get my hands on a copy of this book. While Mikul's relevant discussion doesn't leave me with the impression that the book itself is wholly odd, the author, June Gibbons, is a woman with a decidedly odd history. June had a twin sister named Jennifer. They were born in Barbados in 1963, and their family relocated to Wales when the girls were still very young. Perhaps the shock of being relocated caused them to become so insular because before long the twins spoke in a language no one else could understand and spent every moment in each others' company. I think accounts of "twin talk" and the "psychic" bonds of identical twins are reasonably well documented, but the Gibbons sisters took those odd phenomena to unique and astonishing ends.

The Gibbons twins left school at 16 and seldom ventured from their bedrooms as they played with dolls and wrote books. In time, they would commission a vanity press to publish June's *The Pepsi-Cola Addict*, but Jennifer's two books appear to be lost to time. After the twins were sent to jail for some antisocial behavior, a publisher tried to contact Jennifer about releasing one of her books, but it wasn't to be.

Both girls were eventually sent to Broadmoor, a mental hospital. While there, they came to a startling conclusion. They could not continue on they way they were living. One would have to die. They decided it would be Jennifer.

> On March 9 1993 the twins boarded a mini-bus which drove them through the gates of Broadmoor, where they had spent the last eleven years. During the journey, Jennifer fell asleep with her head resting on June's shoulder. When they arrived at the unit in Wales, she did not regain consciousness and was taken to a hospital where she died half hour later. The postmortem found that her death was caused by "acute myocardiatis," a severe inflammation of the heart muscle.

Creepy, creepy, creepy. But even more interesting is that in the midst of this intense and arguably unhealthy relationship with her twin, the teenaged June managed to write an interesting novel that showed talent and promise.

> You can't deny June wasn't ambitious with her first novel. She works hard to make the American setting convincing, peppering it with cultural references picked up from books and television, and while there are inevitably some slips (a Big Mac with Worcestershire Sauce?), she does manage to convey a picture of Miami during a long hot summer surprisingly well. It's a juvenile work, of course, full of odd turns of phrase and words that aren't always used correctly (yet it is never intentionally funny—June's seriousness of purpose is evident throughout). And somehow this awkwardness

of style complements the subject matter and reinforces the inner turmoil of her intensely imagined hero.

Because I collect books about eccentric people and have certainly read my share of "twin" Forteana, I had heard of the Gibbons twins. I was not, however, familiar with June's book. Now I will probably spend a lot of time and far too much money to procure a physical copy, if such a thing is possible.

Mikul also draws our attention to an obscure but utterly lunatic book from 1944 called *The Fangs of Suet Pudding*. Mikul also includes an article about the life and works of a writer called Hanns Heinz Ewers, and there's a fascinating piece on a book about medical students by one Dr. Ralph Hodgson (in which we learn that "the tuberculoses... are greatly overrated organisms"). In all, it's an entertaining and fascinating showcase.

Turning to the second issue, the standout article for me was "The Strange Case of F. Gwynplaine MacIntyre." In 2008, Mikul stumbled across a website—or "an alleged website"—devoted to this MacIntyre fellow. The site was odd enough and the writings interesting enough that Mikul kept MacIntyre on his radar. Mikul noticed this strange name popping up from time to time online on sites devoted to Forteana, and the story took a very dark turn.

> Then, in December 2010, I read that six months earlier MacIntyre had burned himself to death in his New York apartment.

Holy crap! This strange and horrible death spurred Mikul on to find out as much about MacIntyre as he could.

It turns out that MacIntyre led a life worthy of a novel, at least as he told it. Born in Scotland in 1948, he was a twin but he had a minor birth defect so his alcoholic parents gave him up for adoption. Then he was sent to Australia as a part of a "child migration scheme." His parents later contacted him because his twin brother needed a kidney. He ignored them. Settling into his adopted country, MacIntyre became a ranch hand and steeped himself in aboriginal culture. He later moved to England where he evidently wrote pulp science fiction novels for Badger Books and secured work as a writer for *Monty Python's Flying Circus* and *The Prisoner*. In the 1970s, MacIntyre moved to New York and changed his name to Fergus Gwynplaine MacIntyre. He eventually settled in Bensonhurst and worked as a telemarketer as he wrote his stories and novels.

According to Mikul, MacIntyre's first "proper" novel is actually quite good.

> *The Woman Between The Worlds* is a rattling good read. The early scenes, with the narrator tattooing the invisible Vanessa, are nicely handled, and towards the end it reaches grand heights of surrealism. It received good reviews and is today regarded as an early example of steampunk (a genre which basically re-imagines the Victorian era with more advanced technology).

But it seems to me that MacIntyre's writing is the least interesting thing about him. For example, he was a film enthusiast who posted reviews of silent films to IMDb. When other reviewers on the site questioned him because he somehow had managed to see and review nonextistent films, he responded to the challenge by spinning a yarn that rivals his story about being given up for adoption to Australia, becoming a ranch hand and turning his dying twin down for a kidney.

> He said that, while working in television in England in the 60s, he had met a wealthy financier who collected rare films. MacIntyre told him about a cache of old nitrate films he had stumbled on at a farm in Queensland, and the collector managed to acquire them. He was so impressed that MacIntyre was put on retainer and told he would be well paid for any unusual films he discovered in his travels. His finds included a collection of old Hollywood films owned by a former opera singer in Budapest, and a large cache of German films looted by Russian soldiers during WWII and stored in a warehouse in Moscow. The collector also asked him to review the films in his collection, evaluate their condition and advise which were worth restoring. While he would let MacIntyre review his films, he would not let anyone else see them. Few silent film aficionados bought any of this.

After his suicide in June of 2010, an article about MacIntyre by Corey Kilgannon was published in *The New York Times*. People came forward and told wildly differing stories about MacIntyre—who evidently did not keep a united front with all of his friends and acquaintances. The most interesting MacIntyre refutation was posted on sff.net in September 2010 by a man called P. Toad MacIntyre. The name alone arouses skepticism, but Mr. Toad claimed to be MacIntyre's brother. Bearing my skepticism in mind, here is what Mr. Toad had to say:

> He dismissed almost everything MacIntyre said about himself and his life: he had not been rejected by his family, he did not have a twin, he did not have webbed fingers, he was not sent to an orphanage in Australia. From an early age he had displayed symptoms of "a severe psychotic illness", and told his parents that he had been born on another planet. The posting's author went on to say how remarkable he had found his brother's ability to channel his symptoms into his fiction, and that many characters in his stories "are very reminiscent of many conversations I had with him, when the succession of sinister, shape-shifting selves would vie for control of his consciousness, and the usual boundaries of space and time—between history and fiction, or past, present and future—became so irrelevant as to be merely notional."

It is interesting to speculate, isn't it? Why would a man who had obvious talent and some amount of charm need to create an entirely new Walter Mitty-like existence, changing key elements of his identity every few years, writing an ocean of reviews of movies he had never seen? Was he channeling his mental illness into his work? That makes sense only so far—the rest of it seems more like psychological inferiority.

I once was involved in a strange young woman's online scam—a pretty girl I knew peripherally from the last real job I had. She stole pictures of another girl who was not as attractive as she was, passing them on to men online and starting elaborate relationships. Catfishing, as it were. Anyway, the elements she stole of my life (surgical x-rays, cat pictures, stories about my grandparents) were in and of themselves not very interesting, but she took on elements of other people's lives like a coat she would wear for a short period and then take off when it suited her. I often wonder who she is deceiving now. It has been my experience such people never really stop with their ruses. I also wonder if I would have found MacIntyre's story so interesting had I lacked experience with my own strange fabulist.

This incredible article makes me want to track down MacIntyre's works to see how much of his created lives shine through. That's the power of these articles of Mikul's—you'll probably find at least one book or writer per issue that will absorb you so deeply you'll want to submerge yourself in the mystery. Mikul makes that much easier in the case of MacIntyre because he provides a complete bibliography, including MacIntyre's many short stories.

In the same issues, there's an absolutely fascinating pulp fiction investigation where Mikul tracks down the true authorship of a novel called *The Yellow Yasmak*. Many pulp writers would write under a single *nom de plume* and the sleuthing makes for a very interesting reading. Mikul also includes a look at a largely forgotten writer named T. Millett Ellis, focusing on one of his novels, called *Zalma*. This one's a real gem, if only for the reproduced drawings from one of Ellis' books for children, *The Earl's Nose*, which has to be the most unintentionally (I hope) phallic book ever marketed for youngsters.

Mikul's 'zines embody the best of what I aspire to achieve as a fellow oddball bibliophile—a look at fringe, strange or largely unknown authors that is both investigative and sympathetic when warranted. His research is accessible and makes for excellent reading and his choices of books and authors are genuinely unique. Had I not at least 800 books in queue to be read at the moment (probably more), I would follow his example and start combing the paperback and collectible racks at used bookstores, familiarizing myself with the pulps and popular writers from decades past whose names have faded. Who knows? Maybe in a few years I'll be up to the task. Until then I'll just have to live vicariously through Mikul's curatorial inspiration.

The Death of Borders

04/08/2011

Death. And no matter how much the Borders corporate offices try to spin it—that the company is regrouping, doing this, that and the other and it will all be okay—you should know Borders is dying. In five years or less, the once-dominant retail chain will be completely gone from the book-purchasing landscape in the United States. There are a bunch of reasons for this and they have been hashed and rehashed since Borders announced they were closing a ton of stores. But I'm past the bargaining stage of grief, and I seem to have gotten through the anger stage as well. It seems pointless to assign blame and demand answers. At the moment, I am hovering between depression and acceptance.

Does this sound melodramatic, mourning the loss of a bookstore? It might be to some people. There is a sense that mourning should be reserved for departed humans or animals, but as a person whose life revolves around books—the reading of books, the procurement of books, the handling of books, the visual appeal of books—losing a bookstore that has been a part of my life for over a decade affects me deeply.

I read electronic books and dead tree books but have a definite preference for the latter and I buy them everywhere. Thrift stores, big-box stores, publisher sites, Amazon, and, of course, bookstores, independent and corporate. I don't dislike Barnes & Noble, but Borders was always my favorite corporate bookstore. It's as tenuous to explain this as it is to explain why you like only one of two very similar people. Visually, Borders just appealed to me more. The store layout and arrangement appealed to my sense of logic. And the book selection, though similar to Barnes & Noble, was just a little more in tune with my interests. It seems sort of ephemeral however I explain it, but Borders was a comforting place to me. I never used the store as a place to write, or hang out or drink coffee. It was a place where I went to have a book-absorbing experience.

Mr. OTC and I discussed whether we wanted to go to Borders one last time (sort of like visiting a dying a friend before the inevitable moment), or just remember the store the way we loved it. Initially we decided not to go back, but then one evening while we were out, I just couldn't resist.

But it wasn't like seeing a dying friend. No, our friend was dead, the body picked over, bones exposed.

So let me eulogize my departed friend.

Mr. OTC and I are not big drinkers, nor are we the sort of people who like posh restaurants. During times of celebration, we went to Borders. I am not kidding one little bit. During times of great happiness, we went to Borders. We went to Borders and we spent good money—sometimes a few hundred dollars per visit—on books. I would wander the fiction sections and pick up any book whose cover appealed to me. I bought my first David Foster Wallace book at this soon-to-be extinct Borders the day Mr. OTC landed his current gig after two years of unstable employment. I remember that evening very clearly. He bought some of those expensive computer magazines that cost more than a hardcover book and I decided to buy books I had never heard of before or books by writers I had been hesitant to read. It was a gesture of hope, a financial offering to fate that we believed we had turned an opportunistic corner, and we were right. Wallace, whose face I had seen in a dream a month before, called to me. I got *Infinite Jest* and *Brief Interviews with Hideous Men*. I've since read the latter and I'm still not sure if he's my cup of tea, but had I not been standing in front of the stacks with a deep will to purchase a book, any book, I might never have taken the chance. Amazon serves me well when I already know what I want, but not so well where impulses are concerned.

During the same outing, I also bought a book based solely on the fact that there was a Stephen Fry blurb on the cover. And most importantly, I purchased Fay Weldon's *Chalcot Crescent* at Borders that night. Fay Weldon is one of my favorite writers, yet finding copies of her recent releases in bookstores in the USA can often be difficult. I'm currently reading it and it's eerie how it seems to foretell what would happen to Borders, what will happen to other businesses, and what is happening to governments all over the world. I think I was meant to buy that book when I did. Books can carry a lot of fate between their covers.

We frequently went to Borders during times of happiness, but for some reason, happiness doesn't cut into my memory the way sadness does. I had a job at an educational publishing company and I hated it. I had been sold a bill of goods about what I was going to be doing and the only reason I didn't walk off the job two weeks after I started was because Mr. OTC also worked there and I was only given the job out of deference to him. (I found out later two other women had, in fact, quit less than a month after accepting the position that eventually trickled down to me, so I probably could have left and no one would have thought much of it.) I did the job poorly and I hated every moment I was there. Then the company was sold and I found out that I would be losing my job (I quit before that happened). Even Mr. OTC's job was threatened. Around this time I remember sitting in my cube, listening to NPR. I heard a segment about a book called *Free Food for Millionaires* by Min

Jin Lee. Aside from the Korean cultural influences, the story sounded much like what I was experiencing. I wanted a copy. I worked just up the road from this very Borders so I popped in during my break and tried to find the book.

I couldn't find it, so I went to the counter and asked the clerk to help me. The computers said they had it and it was in Literature. Suddenly, behind me, a woman who was from corporate appeared, offering assistance. She tried to help me find the book, taking me back to the area where I had already looked. She declared they were out and sent me back to the front counter so a clerk could get my information and order a copy. She went back to conferring with the other corporate drones, keeping an eye on the clerk who had been helping me. That's when the clerk, a small, seemingly earnest young man, turned to me and said, very quietly, "I know where the book is. If you wait for ten minutes, I'm off the register and can get it for you." The woman kept an eagle eye on him during all of this and, as a former retail clerk, I knew he was trying to help me while not drawing attention to something that could potentially mean trouble. So I wandered off and checked out the sale books and sure enough, ten minutes later, he came up to me with the book in hand. "I don't know why it keeps ending up in Romance..." he trailed off. It was a strange moment, but it told me a lot about the kid who helped me find the book. He knew that store inside and out. He didn't want to make trouble for his coworkers who moved books to inappropriate locations, and he knew corporate was not to be trusted. Smart. I put the book under all the others I was purchasing so the corporate drone wouldn't see it and I started reading *Free Food for Millionaires* the moment I got home. Not since Edith Wharton's *The House of Mirth* has a book spoken to me so clearly in a moment of dread-filled crisis.

In June of 2008, right when Houghton Mifflin Harcourt was outsourcing all our jobs to India and Ireland, Mr. OTC and I also lost our precious cat, Daisy. Daisy was the feline embodiment of joy. After we had to put her to sleep, we returned home and wandered around in a grief haze. Eventually we decided we had to get out of the house. We went to Borders. I remember standing in front of this table:

Do you see the books on the upright display shelf just below the discount sign? The two duplicates with the eyeball peeking through the keyhole? That's where it was. That's where I then saw a copy of *Dewey: The Small-Town Library Cat Who Touched the World*. I started to cry. Seeing the cat on the cover was just too much. An employee in a wheelchair noticed me. He didn't ask me what was wrong. He just offered me a coupon for a free coffee upstairs. I didn't use it. I still have it, in fact. It's in a box full of memorabilia that I had hoped I would do something meaningful with but probably never will.

The employees were always the reason to shop there. As we checked out for the last time, I told the very young man who was ringing us up that I was sorry the store was closing and I hoped he had a good, new job lined up. He said he was a personal trainer on the side but was going back to school to get his nursing degree. The clerk next to him, who was a teacher in Austin, said it looked like he was going to lose his teaching job, too. He was going back to grad school because it would give him time to recover and figure out what he wanted to do next. We all commented that at the moment, not even education was the failsafe it used to be. Teachers were once secure in their positions, Harcourt used to be a stable educational publisher and grad school ensured you got a job. None of that was true anymore. The man going back to grad school sighed and said that at least in grad school he got a deferment on his student loans.

The death of Borders is a microcosm of all that is beginning to suck heartily in this country. It is a reminder that institutions which should be secure can be destroyed by a handful of megalomaniacs who think they have all the answers. And those at the bottom are left wondering where the hell they can go next. I will not forget the man who wanted me to have a book but didn't want to narc out a coworker, or the man who saw a crying woman and silently offered her a free coffee—these are people who should never worry about their next paycheck.

On that last outing, I felt a strange resentment toward the people who shopped with me. I had to remember this was not their fault. This store was destroyed by men in suits who had no fucking idea what they were doing. I still shop on Amazon. I like to pay as little as I can for books. Everyone has to be careful with their money. It is not the consumer's fault that Borders' management screwed things up so royally. I know I am not alone. I know I am not the only person who spent thousands of dollars every year at that Borders. Even if those last shoppers were only there to pick the bones of the retailer, the fact is that vultures, too, have value. They help clean things up. The scavenger's role in natural ecology is mirrored in the retail world. Having nothing on the shelves cannot be more depressing than what this picture depicts—a maelstrom of mismanagement and depressed people forced to move on as the world ostensibly moves on around them.

There was nothing left upstairs but fixtures to purchase. I used to love to comb through the Young Adult and Kids' Books. I got there too late to see those sections still assembled. That's probably for the best, because in my wandering mind books for children can too easily become children themselves. And nothing is sadder than the death of a child.

It was surprising that in those stripped shelves and chaotic mess I still managed to find some good books. For the love of sanity, I could so seldom find Christopher Fowler's books on the shelves of any retailer, yet I found two that last night. I had heard a lot of good things about *The Madonna of Echo Park* and I had wondered about Warren Ellis' *Crooked Little Vein*. Why not give it a try at 60% off? Ruth Rendell is one of my favorite authors. Might as well stock up. And I wasn't aware that a specific Margaret Atwood book even existed until I saw it among the ruins. The others just caught my eye.

Just out of sheer perversity, I looked all of these books up on Amazon. With two exceptions, I could still get copies there cheaper, at least when I took into account that I pay no taxes on Amazon. I don't know what to think about the economics of it all. It may well be that I am part of a larger problem. But I really do think the market is changing, and it seems inevitable that retailers who don't adapt will die. And no matter how things unfold, death always hurts people in various ways. Things move on, as they always have. But it sucks mightily.

So if your favorite bookstore has managed to stay in business, shop there as much as you can. And be sure to thank the clerk who places that book in your hands.

ACKNOWLEDGMENTS

I want to thank Chip Smith of Nine-Banded Books, who tolerated with good cheer each new intro I sent and didn't yell at me every time I agitated over commas. I am very grateful he found my work worthy of a compendium. I also want to thank Josh Latta for drawing a very accurate picture of me for the cover—some have mistaken it for a photograph but you know it's a drawing because there aren't enough cats hovering around the stepladder. Also many thanks to Kevin Slaughter of Underworld Amusements for designing the book cover.

My deepest gratitude also to all those who have visited my sites and commented over the years. Your opinions and book recommendations have meant more to me than you will ever know.

ANITA DALTON is a freelance writer whose voluminous essays on a variety of outré subjects—but mostly books—can be found on her website, *Odd Things Considered*. She lives in Pflugerville Texas with her husband and a clowder of cats. This is her first book. She's working on another one.

www.OddThingsConsidered.com

Caveat Lector.

www.NineBandedBooks.com

www.ingramcontent.com/pod-product-compliance
Lightning Source LLC
Chambersburg PA
CBHW020651270326
41928CB00005B/70